A list of books in the series appears at the back of this book.

International Nietzsche Studies

Nietzsche has emerged as a thinker of extraordinary importance, not only in the history of philosophy but in many fields of contemporary inquiry. Nietzsche studies are maturing and flourishing in many parts of the world. This internationalization of inquiry with respect to Nietzsche's thought and significance may be expected to continue.

International Nietzsche Studies is conceived as a series of monographs and essay collections that will reflect and contribute to these developments. The series will present studies in which responsible scholarship is joined to the analysis, interpretation, and assessment of the many aspects of Nietzsche's thought that bear significantly upon matters of moment today. In many respects Nietzsche is our contemporary, with whom we do well to reckon, even when we find ourselves at odds with him. The series is intended to promote this reckoning, embracing diverse interpretive perspectives, philosophical orientations, and critical assessments.

The series is also intended to contribute to the ongoing reconsideration of the character, agenda, and prospects of philosophy itself. Nietzsche was much concerned with philosophy's past, present, and future. He sought to affect not only its understanding but also its practice. The future of philosophy is an open question today, thanks at least in part to Nietzsche's challenge to the philosophical traditions of which he was so critical. It remains to be seen—and determined—whether philosophy's future will turn out to resemble the "philosophy of the future" to which he proffered a prelude and of which he provided a preview, by both precept and practice. But this is a possibility we do well to take seriously. International Nietzsche Studies will attempt to do so, while contributing to the understanding of Nietzsche's philosophical thinking and its bearing upon contemporary inquiry.

—Richard Schacht

Nietzsche

NIETZSCHE

Attempt at a Mythology

Ernst Bertram

Translated and with an Introduction
by Robert E. Norton

University of Illinois Press

Urbana and Chicago

∞ This book is printed on acid-free paper.
Library of Congress Cataloging-in-Publication Data
Bertram, Ernst, 1884–1957.
[Nietzsche. English]
Nietzsche : attempt at a mythology / Ernst Bertram ;
translated and with an introduction by Robert E. Norton.
p. cm. — (International Nietzsche studies)
Includes bibliographical references (p.) and index.
ISBN 978-0-252-03295-0 (cloth : alk. paper)
ISBN 978-0-252-07601-5 (pbk. : alk. paper)
1. Nietzsche, Friedrich Wilhelm, 1844–1900.
I. Norton, Robert Edward, 1960– II. Title.
B3317.B4513 2009
193—dc22 2008035915

Everything that happens is symbol and, by perfectly representing itself, points toward the rest.

Everything is equal, everything is unequal, everything is useful and harmful, eloquent and mute, rational and irrational. And what one says about individual things is frequently contradictory.
—Goethe

Everything that is perfect does not express itself alone, it expresses an entire related world.
—Novalis

Contents

Translator's Introduction:
Attempt at a Demythologization xi

A Comment on the Notes xxxvii

Acknowledgments xxxix

Introduction: Legend 1

1. Ancestry 11
2. Knight, Death, and Devil 37
3. The German Becoming 56
4. Justice 79
5. Arion 88
6. Illness 107
7. Judas 121
8. Mask 134
9. Weimar 154
10. Napoleon 171
11. Jest, Cunning, and Vengeance 183
12. Anecdote 194
13. Indian Summer 203
14. Claude Lorrain 213
15. Venice 223
16. Portofino 231
17. Prophecy 239
18. Socrates 262
19. Eleusis 289

Notes 309
Chronology 365
Index 369

Translator's Introduction: Attempt at a Demythologization

In 1950, Walter Kaufmann did an extraordinary thing. Only five years after the collapse of the Third Reich, and as a German-born Jew who had fled Nazi Germany at the last possible moment in 1939, he published a book in vigorous defense of a thinker still widely viewed as an intellectual forefather of the same regime that surely would have tried to destroy Kaufmann had he stayed. It was a bold, not to say audacious, gesture. But whatever his motives, no one could question Kaufmann's credentials: having benefited from the broad humanistic education of the *Gymnasium* he had attended in Berlin, Kaufmann went to Williams College to study philosophy as an undergraduate and then earned his doctorate in the same subject at Harvard. Published by Princeton University Press, *Nietzsche: Philosopher, Psychologist, Antichrist* thus carried the weighty imprimatur of several major American academic institutions. And although it is, even palpably, the work of a young man—born in 1921, Kaufmann was only twenty-nine when it appeared—it was immediately recognized as a significant, and many thought momentous, work. Walter Watson, a professor of philosophy at the University of Chicago, declared in a review that "of the thousand or so books on Nietzsche, this is among the most important."[1] James Gutmann at Columbia University considered it equal in stature to Karl Jaspers's book on Nietzsche, then thought to be the best in any language.[2] And ever since, despite prompting occasional reservations about certain aspects of his views, Kaufmann's book has retained its status as a monument within Nietzsche criticism. Indeed, in 1996, the plausible claim was made that his "Nietzsche monograph is the most important American interpretation in the first half of this century (perhaps in the second as well)."[3] Principally on the strength of this book, then, enhanced by subsequent studies and especially his fluent translations of Nietzsche's works themselves, Kaufmann almost single-handedly laid the foundation on which the understanding of Nietzsche would rest for nearly two generations in the United States and beyond.[4]

In the preface to the fourth edition of his book in 1974 (itself testimony to its enduring impact), Kaufmann outlined his original reasons for undertaking what was then such a controversial subject: "When I began to work on Nietzsche, he was in eclipse both in his native Germany and in the English-speaking world, and it seemed needful to dissociate him from the Nazis and to show that he had been a great philosopher."[5] Today few people doubt Nietzsche was a great philosopher, and the majority would agree that Kaufmann succeeded in doing away with the notion that there was a necessary link between Nietzsche's thought and Nazism. It is a sign of how completely the critical consensus has changed that a recent book devoted to the subject of "Nietzsche and fascism" asks in the very first line: "Is it not almost a contradiction in terms?"[6] Ironically, however, Kaufmann's very achievement has made it difficult to appreciate the challenges he originally faced, with regard both to confronting the fifty years of Nietzsche interpretation preceding him and to persuading a contemporary audience made skeptical or even dismissive of Nietzsche by two world wars fought, as many then believed, at least partly under his banner.

Kaufmann clearly understood the enormity of his task. "The growth of the Nietzsche legend in Germany is so inextricably involved in, and so symptomatic of, the development of German thought," he explained, that any study of Nietzsche "might grow into a cultural history of twentieth-century Germany"[7] as a whole. Given that fact—and given the remarkable cultural efflorescence in Germany during the first part of the century, with no small part of it in constant dialogue and confrontation with Nietzsche—it is notable that Kaufmann concentrates his discussion of the "Nietzsche legend" almost exclusively on two figures whose names few people in the United States would have recognized in 1950 and are now almost entirely forgotten: Stefan George and Ernst Bertram. It was, Kaufmann claimed, primarily Stefan George—"beyond doubt the most influential poet since the turn of the century"[8]—and the people associated with him collectively known as the *George-Kreis,* or "Circle," who put the decisive stamp on the image of Nietzsche in Germany during the pivotal interwar years. And, Kaufmann continued, "the Circle's first and most successful contribution to the literature, Bertram's *Nietzsche: Versuch einer Mythologie,*"[9] originally published in 1918, had done more than any other work to shape that image for almost an entire generation. Indeed, as Kaufmann viewed it from his perspective at mid-century, "no other book on Nietzsche left so decisive a mark on the literature."[10] But in Kaufmann's eyes that "mark" was a black, disfiguring stain. "It would be idle to attach so much significance to Bertram's 'mythology,'" he insisted, "had it been less influential or representative."[11] Given the acknowledged, if in his eyes deplorable, prominence of Bertram's book, Kaufmann felt it necessary to submit it to a sustained and vehement critique. In doing so, he singled out for particular condemnation what he called "the cultivated incoherence of his chapters and a willful disregard for the sequence of Nietzsche's thought—even for the immediate context of his utterances."[12]

Conveyed here in somewhat telegraphic fashion are Kaufmann's three main objections to the book. First, that Bertram's account, both in its formal structure and its arguments, was willfully and deceptively equivocal, thereby suggesting that Nietzsche's thought, too, was fundamentally incoherent or contradictory, a position Kaufmann strenuously contested throughout his own work, and not only in relation to Bertram. Second, that Bertram similarly ignored, and thus distorted, the growth, development, and, Kaufmann felt, coherent progression of Nietzsche's thinking. And, finally, even more damningly, that Bertram violated the principles of intellectual and scholarly integrity, that he committed, as Kaufmann puts it, "an open break with previously accepted standards of scholarship."[13] The heat of Kaufmann's scorn is searing as he brushes aside "the alleged contradictions" Bertram saw in Nietzsche. They simply do not exist, Kaufmann writes, and are instead the product of Bertram's shoddy, even fraudulent scholarship: "The utterly superficial inconsistencies dissolve as soon as one checks the quotations and recognizes the meaning they had in their original context. Bertram makes this difficult by withholding exact references. His work abounds in phrases in quotation marks which are integrated into his own prose, though this sometimes involves an alteration of both text and meaning."[14] And it was here, in order to make explicit the fatal consequences of such an approach, that Kaufmann delivered the ultimate coup de grâce: "From such utter relativism," he concluded, "it was but one step to the Nazis' 'subjective' historiography; and one may note in passing that Bertram himself proceeded in this direction, and that, during World War II, he published a defense of the Nazis' suppression of free speech."[15]

Kaufmann did not say so, exactly, but he more than implied it: Bertram was, or would later become, a Nazi, and his *Nietzsche* was at the very least a "proto-Nazi" work, a rancid screed that was largely, if not wholly, the fabrication of a man who fashioned Nietzsche into an irrational, raging "schizophrenic,"[16] and thus half unwittingly, half complicitly turned Nietzsche into a precursor of Adolf Hitler. It was, as Kaufmann portrayed it, a natural progression: all that was needed was "to resign oneself to the complete relativity of historical truth, abandon the discipline of scholarship—and fall prey to the doctrines of totalitarian propagandists."[17] Not surprisingly, Bertram and his book subsequently sank into oblivion.[18]

But was Kaufmann right? Certainly, his assessment of the historical importance and impact of the book is accurate. In many ways, in fact, Bertram's *Nietzsche* uncannily mirrors the enormous success of Kaufmann's own work. Bertram's book was, by the standards of the day, a best seller: between its first appearance

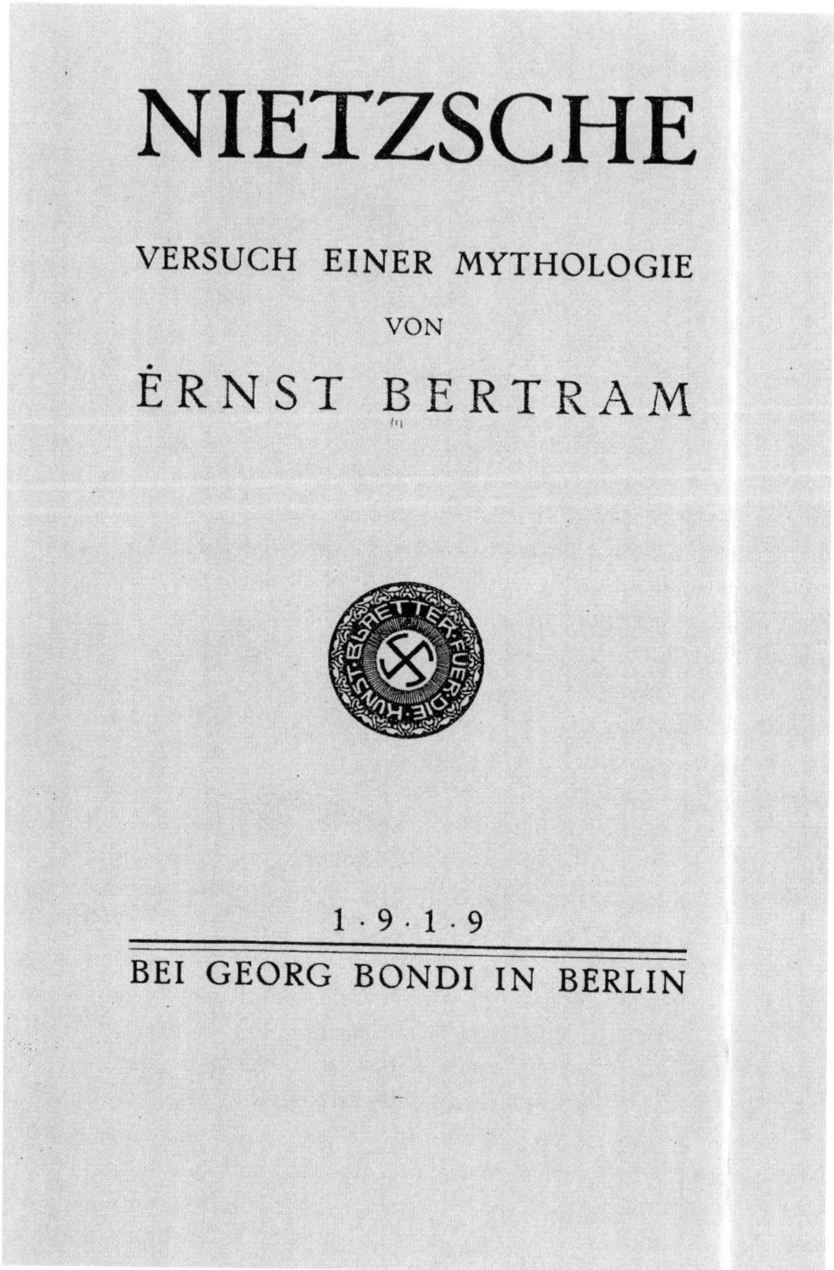

NIETZSCHE

VERSUCH EINER MYTHOLOGIE

VON

ERNST BERTRAM

1 · 9 · 1 · 9

BEI GEORG BONDI IN BERLIN

Title page of Bertram's 1919 edition

in 1918 and 1929, there were no fewer than seven editions, totaling twenty-one thousand copies in print. The year after its initial publication, it was awarded the newly instituted Nietzsche Prize, and the book was regarded as having sufficient academic merit to be accepted as Bertram's "habilitation," which allowed him to take up his first teaching post as a professor in Bonn.[19] It was thus by no means merely a popular success, and it quickly won the respect of a number of the best minds of the time. Writing within months of its appearance, the art historian Heinrich Wölfflin was struck by an "astonishing maturity in such a youthful author" and he marveled at the portrait he found "so magnificently broad and profound."[20] The following year, Hermann Hesse said he thought it was "the first profound and important German work on Nietzsche, certainly one of the most valuable books in Germany today."[21] Many readers, while also admiring what Hesse called Bertram's "psychological acumen,"[22] were perhaps even more impressed by the author's gifts as a writer. One reviewer wrote that it is "probably the most beautiful and significant Nietzsche book we have,"[23] while another predicted that "it will probably remain the most beautiful one of all about him."[24] Thomas Mann—a close friend of Bertram at the time—also referred to it in a speech he gave in 1925 on Nietzsche as "the most beautiful book about him."[25] Contemporary philosophers also acknowledged Bertram's work, including two of the most consequential interpreters of Nietzsche in Germany: Karl Jaspers and Martin Heidegger. In the lectures on Nietzsche that Heidegger held in Freiburg in the years just before the Second World War, he paid Bertram the rare compliment of merely mentioning his name and "his widely-read Nietzsche book."[26] And in Jaspers's *Nietzsche* of 1936—which, incidentally, Kaufmann deemed "one of the best books yet written about"[27] him—Jaspers counted Bertram's work among the three "most important" comprehensive studies then available.[28] On the fiftieth anniversary of Nietzsche's death—and the same year Kaufmann's book appeared—Gottfried Benn confessed that among the "abundance of brilliant, excellent books about Nietzsche, both from Germany and from other countries . . . I personally still find the book by Ernst Bertram the most marvelous."[29]

To have earned the admiration of so many discriminating readers, who were, moreover, of such varied temperaments, Bertram's *Nietzsche* must have seemed to offer more than merely the inchoate rantings of an incipient fascist. Indeed, as I hope this translation will reveal, it presents a powerful, often compelling, portrait of the thinker, one rich in subtle insight and conveyed in dazzling prose. This is not to suggest that it poses no problems: on the contrary, many readers will find it troublesome in any number of ways. But one can meaningfully respond only to what one knows. For those who do not read German, Bertram's work has remained literally a closed book. Such was Bertram's stylistic virtuosity—he understood himself primarily as a poet and, as evidenced by the many accolades of its "beauty," his *Nietzsche* puts his literary talents fully on display—that nonnative speakers are likely to have a rough time reading it and give up quickly in frustration. If it is true that Bertram's book was so central in forming the perception of Nietzsche from the time of its appearance up through the end of the Second World War, an influence Kaufmann himself acknowledged even as he deplored it, then it would seem necessary to engage with Bertram for an adequate appreciation of this crucial development in modern intellectual history. To make that possible, however, requires not just rendering Bertram's occasionally rhapsodic German into comprehensible English, but also placing him in the almost equally unfamiliar but vital context from which his book arose.

Bertram's *Nietzsche*

On the infrequent occasions that Bertram's work is now mentioned, it is usually linked, as it is in Kaufmann's account, with Stefan George and his Circle. Although that connection does exist, what it means is far from obvious, and simply referring to it may be more misleading than helpful.[30] Because the book was printed by George's "official" publisher, Georg Bondi—replete with the emblem of the Circle on the title page, featuring a swastika surrounded by the words "Blätter für die Kunst" (Pages for Art)—it is generally assumed that it conformed to George's own views, and by extension that it conveyed the doctrine of the Circle, and indeed that Bertram himself was in some meaningful sense a "member" of that select society. All of those assumptions, however, are false. Bertram never counted among George's intimates—"I am not suited to be a disciple,"[31] Bertram baldly told him on their first meeting in 1909—and his *Nietzsche* was very much his own work. Although it contains many elements that clearly appealed to George, and even though George did approve its publication—it would never have appeared with Bondi otherwise—there is also a great deal in it that stood in direct opposition to, or at least did not positively reflect, George's own values and outlook.[32]

By the time Bertram wrote his book, George had already transformed himself from a relatively obscure poet writing under the influence of French symbolism into someone who represented a major and growing cultural force in Germany. He had managed to perform this impressive feat through the mesmerizing quality of his poetry, the sheer force of his personality, and, increasingly, the work of his associates and disciples who had committed themselves to him as their personal master and to his vision of the world. Like many of his contemporaries in Germany, George intensely disliked and adamantly opposed many of the ideas we associate with liberal modernity, particularly its emphasis on individualism and personal equality, and he disdainfully rejected their political expressions—democracy and socialism—as self-serving delusions. But he also reviled the material excess he saw in the last monarchy Germany experienced, namely the second German empire ruled by a power-hungry Prussia, and he spent most of his life denouncing it as coarse, rude, and devoid of genuine culture. Many of George's poems, especially those written after the turn of the century, are filled with dark scenes of destruction and collapse, and indeed George believed that there was no solution to the perceived ills of society other than its total annihilation and rebuilding. Again, such notions were not unique to George—some of them, in fact, Nietzsche himself had articulated—but he conveyed them in a uniquely potent form. What would be put in place of the hated assemblage once it had been eliminated was not entirely clear. But the model George offered—a charismatic leader demanding the absolute devotion of followers who believed he possessed quasi-divine powers—resonated among Germans searching for guidance and meaning in a world that, most emphatically after the devastating defeat in the First World War, was short on both.

What is striking, however, is how absent all of these concerns are in Bertram's book. Nietzsche is presented as a great man, certainly, but not as a hero or leader of his people: any reader of Nietzsche would instantly recognize the absurdity of such a proposition. Rather, Bertram portrays him as deeply torn by the conflicting, perhaps irreconcilable, cultural, intellectual, and religious currents of his time. The image he gives of Nietzsche is not monolithic but multifaceted, as indeed Nietzsche was, and Bertram always strives to preserve, and to explain, the irreducible complexity of Nietzsche's thought and life. Above all, he does not make Nietzsche the mouthpiece of anyone else's ideology, but he tries to present him as the distinctive, captivating, and, ultimately, tragic figure that he was.

Bertram's *Nietzsche* contains nineteen individual chapters following a programmatic introduction, titled "Legend," in which Bertram outlines his method and general approach toward his subject. But nowhere does Bertram define the word that figures so prominently in the title: "mythology." Perhaps he felt he did not have to. As George S. Williamson has recently shown in his illuminating book, *The Longing for Myth in Germany,* which focuses primarily on the nineteenth century, the notions of "myth" and "mythology" figured so prominently in German historiographical, philosophical, and artistic thinking that they seemed practically ubiquitous.[33] Beginning with the Romantics, who rehabilitated myth after a century of Enlightenment skepticism, "mythology" became a predominant interest among German intellectuals, as evidenced by Friedrich Schlegel's *Rede über die Mythologie* (1800), Friedrich Creuzer's *Symbolik und Mythologie der alten*

Völker (1810–12), Jakob Grimm's *Deutsche Mythologie* (1835), and Friedrich Schelling's *Philosophie der Mythologie* (1857), to name only the most prominent.[34] And this preoccupation with myth and mythology continued well into the twentieth century, reaching its culmination—or perhaps better its nadir—in Alfred Rosenberg's *Der Mythus des zwanzigsten Jahrhunderts* (1930), which sought to establish the intellectual foundations of National Socialism.

As the last mentioned book forcefully reminds us, the idea of myth and its implications became closely intertwined with the most unsavory developments of modern German history, and that association alone would have served to make Bertram's own myth making unpalatable in the post-1945 era. But we should also remember that Nietzsche himself was profoundly interested in and influenced by the notion of myth, and he expressly saw his first major work, *The Birth of Tragedy*, as part of a larger effort to reestablish myth as a vital experience of present-day culture, which he hoped would fill the void left by the waning belief in Christian traditions. Indeed, as Nietzsche put it there, Wagner's music represented in his eyes nothing less than "the *rebirth of the German myth!*"[35] But, as George Williamson points out, even after Nietzsche became disillusioned with Wagner and repudiated his own religious convictions, he still grappled with the significance of myth in its various guises:

> Although he became the most vociferous of anti-Christians, Nietzsche identified closely with the traditions and culture of German Protestantism. Not only *The Birth of Tragedy* but later writings up through and including *Thus Spake Zarathustra* demonstrate a continuing engagement with the rhetoric and assumptions of contemporary Protestant theology, including its "secular" manifestations in art, scholarship, and politics. In the process, he would rework, extend, and ultimately dismantle the Romantic discourse on myth as it had developed from the eighteenth century onward.[36]

And it is precisely such apparent contradictions—the anti-Christian Protestant, the anti-Romantic poet of *Zarathustra*, the antipolitical revolutionary—that stand at the center of Bertram's own conception and portrait, in a word, his "mythology" of Nietzsche.

In his introduction, Bertram makes several interrelated arguments, and though he expresses his ideas in a jargon that will appear strange and perhaps slightly off-putting at first to those unaccustomed to the rhetoric of his time, the ideas themselves will undoubtedly seem familiar, even strikingly contemporary. First, Bertram insists that, contrary to a naïve understanding of history, there is no such thing as an absolute historical truth that, once revealed, would be valid and immutable for all time. Instead, what we have, he says, are narratives, stories, or "legends" from the past that must be read and reread to unlock their meaning, which itself becomes part of that incessantly evolving history. In other words, history, or the past, consists of texts that require interpretation, and as Bertram writes, citing Nietzsche: "The same text allows for innumerable interpretations—there is no 'correct' interpretation."[37] In the case of the "text" or "legend" called Nietzsche, however, the situation becomes exceedingly complex. For not only was he highly conscious of the instability of meaning and truth, and thus of the necessity for constantly questioning what we think we know, his mind ranged over a vast arena of concerns related to metaphysics, religion, ancient and modern history, art, ethics, and psychology. That is, Nietzsche did not just embody, he also thematized the very problems that confront anyone trying to come to terms with his thinking, and he did so on a scale and with a degree of sophistication that have few parallels.

But Bertram does see a continuous thread running through all of Nietzsche's life and works, a common element that consisted, paradoxically, in what Bertram regarded as the fundamentally equivocal or ambivalent nature of his thinking. It was, of course, this basic tenet of Bertram's view that Walter Kaufmann dismissed as being the merely "alleged ambiguity"[38] of Nietzsche's thought. But other interpreters of Nietzsche have also emphasized, in Georg Lukács's words, Nietzsche's "colorfully scintillating, mutually contradictory myths."[39] Karl Jaspers, too, pointed to "the contradictions and circularity in the movement of Nietzsche's thought."[40] And in 1971, Wolfgang Müller-Lauter raised this observation to the level of a governing precept in his *Nietzsche: His Philosophy of Contradictions and the Contradictions of His Philosophy,* where he writes that "his philosophy of contradictions leads to insurmountable contradictions in his philosophical thinking."[41] Even Nietzsche himself seems to have affirmed this aspect of his thought, as he wrote in a note (which is not quoted by Bertram) from the mid-1880s: "Deep aversion to come to rest once and for all at some comprehensive view of the world; enchantment with the opposite way of thinking; not forfeiting the appeal of the enigmatic character."[42] And for readers schooled in postmodern or post-structuralist modes of reading, the idea that a basic, irresolvable indeterminacy characterizes Nietzsche's texts—or any others, for that matter—will hardly seem a contestable notion.

What Bertram does is to make this insight, which was new at the time, productive in an original and highly suggestive way. In each of his chapters he addresses a specific topic or theme, which he then traces through an array of Nietzsche's works, including his letters and, above all, his unpublished notebooks. Bertram, again drawing on Nietzsche's own words, likens this procedure to drawing a composite picture of some immense phenomenon—the example he uses is that of a mountain—by adding successive dimensions, or "perspectives," to our perception of the overall image. What cannot be observed from a single vantage point, that is, must necessarily be seen from a variety of angles if one is to do justice to its scope and complexity. At the same time, however, Bertram does see a continuity linking the many facets of Nietzsche's life and thought, namely that same relentless urge to commingle opposites, to embrace conflicting ideas or traditions within a single, all-embracing conception. That this desire ultimately had to remain unfulfilled, that Nietzsche's efforts to unify the many discordant tendencies of his thought and inclinations, could end only in failure—albeit a magnificent, awe-inspiring failure—is one of the most affecting undercurrents of Bertram's book.

Thus, although Bertram's portrait is structured thematically, or "perspectivally," the book as a whole retains a remarkable consistency precisely through this emphasis on what he sees as the ultimately unresolved and unresolvable dualities in Nietzsche's thinking and experience. The first chapter, "Ancestry," is already exemplary of his strategy. There, Bertram works his way through an exhaustive number of contrasting terms—legitimate-illegitimate, tradition-revolution, old-new, beginning-end, fatalism-hope, past-future, and so forth—in his discussion of Nietzsche's indeed fraught relationship to his many and often conflicting cultural and intellectual inheritances. Similarly, in the subsequent chapters on Nietzsche's attitude toward Protestantism ("Knight, Death, and Devil"), music ("Arion"), illness, justice, Wagner ("Judas" and "Mask"), and Goethe ("Weimar"), Bertram always seeks to uncover the deeper tensions in Nietzsche's thought and life that point to an even greater unsettledness, an inherent inability ever to come to rest on one side of an equation, indeed a fundamental tendency toward self-negation or dissolution. (Although here, too, Bertram characteristically manages to turn even this trait into its opposite, writing: "self-critique is always in the end a self-affirmation through self-clarification: there is no absolute self-negation," p. 59). This may be a debatable reading, but Bertram takes great pains to show that these stresses reside within Nietzsche himself, and refuting Bertram's arguments requires more than simply asserting the opposite.

Adding to the perception that Bertram's account is willfully tendentious, arbitrary, or even spurious is the book's lack of a scholarly apparatus. Although Bertram liberally quotes Nietzsche (and many others) throughout his text, there are no footnotes or bibliography, and it contains only a rudimentary index. Kaufmann had noted and denounced this deficiency, more than implying that it was part of a deliberate attempt to distort Nietzsche's thinking by making it impossible, or at least very difficult, to track down the original sources and contexts of the citations. But in leaving out notes, Bertram was conforming not only to the standard practice of the George Circle—notes were considered ugly and pedantic and all-too bourgeois—but he was also following a convention observed by many other contemporary writers. Oswald Spengler's epoch-making *Decline of the West,* for instance, the first volume of which came out the same year as Bertram's *Nietzsche,* also dispenses with almost all such documentation. The absence of notes, however, does not necessarily mean the absence of scholarly rigor. Indeed, George himself was adamant that the books published under his aegis adhere to strict philological criteria, and he often castigated those of his followers who failed to appreciate their importance. It was therefore one of my principal concerns in preparing this translation to locate and provide references for the many quotations from Nietzsche's works, letters, and notebooks that Bertram incorporates into his narrative. That I was able to find the original sources in all but a very few cases—and that, again with few exceptions, they were accurately transcribed—is in itself an indication of Bertram's meticulousness.

But Kaufmann had also made the further, more serious charge that Bertram actually changed the wording and thus the meaning of the texts he cites. As evidence of this purported abuse, Kaufmann offered only one example, taken from the first chapter, "Ancestry," with the unspoken suggestion that it was representative of Bertram's technique overall. The first sentence, in quotation marks, is Kaufmann's translation of Bertram citing Nietzsche:

> "What a strange picture, this radical and revaluer of values for whom 'duration on earth' is a 'first-rate value'!" No reference is given. In fact, Nietzsche says (FW 356) that medieval society had at least "durability (and duration is a first-rate value on earth)." Surely, Nietzsche's view of the value of duration cannot be determined on the basis of an altered quotation from a parenthesis.[43]

But the only "alteration" Bertram made was to move the verb to the end of the clause, as is required by German syntax. Here a glance at the original German is perhaps unavoidable. Bertram wrote: "Welch seltsames Bild, dieser Unbedingte und Umwerter der Werte, dem 'Dauer auf Erden ein Wert ersten Ranges' ist!"[44] And the passage Bertram was quoting reads: "Dauer ist auf Erden ein Wert ersten Ranges!" Thus it is Kaufmann who, in his translation of the two passages, rearranges the order of the wording, making it appear that the difference between Bertram's quotation and Nietzsche's own words is greater than it actually is. Moreover, in the passage from *The Gay Science* that contains the contested phrase, Nietzsche does not speak of "medieval society," but of "the Middle Ages," and he does not say only, as Kaufmann's rather grudging rendition puts it, that the era had "at least 'durability.'" Rather, Nietzsche speaks admiringly of the period's ability "to erect those immense, broad social structures which distinguish the

Middle Ages and which one can at any rate still credit with: durability (—and duration on earth is a value of the first order!)"[45] Thus, not only does Kaufmann commit the very offense he accuses Bertram of perpetrating by changing the order of the words in the texts he quotes, it can also be argued that Bertram more accurately discerned in the cited passage something like a deeper intention, that he sensed Nietzsche was embedding a broader insight, perhaps even articulating a core belief or principle, within this seemingly offhand comment. But the greatest irony is that, on the basis of this one, brief sentence, Kaufmann not only ignores the thesis Bertram elaborates with considerable subtlety in the course of a thirty-page chapter, but he rejects by implication the entire book as well. Surely, Bertram's view of Nietzsche cannot be determined on the basis of an altered quotation from an isolated passage.

A related concern is Bertram's ostensible disregard of the growth and development of Nietzsche's thought as manifested by his taking quotations from texts separated from each other by many years, and sometimes a decade or more. But this objection is even less well grounded than the previous ones. As even a cursory glance at Bertram's text will reveal, he is acutely sensitive to the significance of chronology and, although he does freely draw upon the entire corpus of Nietzsche's writings, he is usually careful to indicate where a given quotation is found, or in what "time" or "period" in Nietzsche's life it was written. Bertram was interested in the deep infrastructure of Nietzsche's thought, so to speak, and though he does appreciate that Nietzsche's thinking obviously evolved over time, he is more concerned with its constants, with those abiding elements that could be said to be characteristically, indeed uniquely, Nietzschean. Bertram's method is idiosyncratic, that is true, but it was not unreasonable, and it had a point. For, looked at positively, one obvious advantage of Bertram's practice of bringing together passages taken from a wide variety of Nietzsche's texts is that it allows us to see patterns in Nietzsche's thinking that would otherwise remain hidden or unnoticed. Again, the reader may take issue with the conclusions Bertram reaches, but they deserve to be taken seriously, and may even contain unsuspected rewards.

All that having been said, however, Bertram does have his own personal predilections and tastes that inevitably color or shape his perception of Nietzsche. Many of these preoccupations he shared with Nietzsche himself: his love of music, his idolization of ancient Greek culture, his attachment to his Lutheran heritage, his fascination with Goethe, and, perhaps the most vexed issue of all, his incessant concern with the question: what is German? It is this question that drives the long chapter "The German Becoming," and it is obvious that it was close to Bertram's heart. But his answers are far from being simple or uncritical.

Only someone who has not actually read Bertram's book could make the claim, as Gary Shapiro does, that Bertram was "attempting to use Nietzsche in the cause of German nationalism."[46] Nothing could be further from the truth. In "The German Becoming," Bertram approvingly quotes a comment Nietzsche made in his notebooks from the summer and fall of 1884: "'Deutschland, Deutschland über alles'—that is perhaps the most idiotic slogan that has ever been uttered."[47] In his discussion of this passage, Bertram further elaborates that "nationalism seemed to Nietzsche both during his early faith in Germanness as well as in his later critique of it, the true original sin against the German character, the crime that is not forgiven; German chauvinism (even the language refuses to provide a German word for this inherent contradiction) remained for him the death of any German hope" (p. 72). Similarly, in a later chapter, "Weimar," Bertram cites an excerpt from one of Goethe's conversations with Eckermann that Nietzsche particularly prized. While speaking of the Napoleonic wars and their aftermath, Goethe said: "I did not hate the French, even though I thanked God when we were rid of them," and then continued:

> How could I, for whom the only things of importance are culture and barbarism, have been able to hate a nation that belongs among the most cultivated on earth and which I owe such a large part of my own formation! In general, national hatred is a peculiar thing. You will always find it strongest and most vehement at the lowest level of culture. But there is a level where it disappears entirely and where one stands, as it were, *above* nations and feels the happiness or sorrow of a neighboring people as if it were one's own (p. 159).[48]

Considering that Bertram's book was published after nearly four years of war against the French and their allies, after the devastating defeat at Verdun, and after the deaths and mutilation of millions of men, it seems remarkably, almost amazingly untainted by nationalistic bias. On the contrary: Bertram explicitly and repeatedly condemns nationalism as pernicious and dangerous.

Nevertheless, although Bertram's enduring preoccupation, even obsession with the "German question" is not in a narrow sense nationalistic, it does permeate the book and will probably strike the modern reader as one of its most alien, and alienating, features. But for Bertram, "German" meant above all the great, classical literary tradition of Lessing, Schiller, Goethe, Hölderlin, and Novalis, as well as the music of Bach, Beethoven, and, especially, Brahms. Music, in fact, was probably Bertram's greatest passion; he had originally wanted to give *Nietzsche* the subtitle: "The Music of Socrates." Indeed, the book's structure and tone reflect a musical sensibility: Bertram uses repetition as a formal device, repeating individual words and whole phrases as a means of holding together the larger composition. A contemporary reviewer by the name of Josef Hofmiller singled out this aspect of the book as providing one of its greatest attractions:

> The pleasure in reading this book is related to that in following a work of chamber music: the development of the themes is so artful and ingenious that the soaring mastery of the musician—for Bertram is that and nothing else to the core of his being—communicates itself to the reader and allows him to participate in the joy of creation that resonates in every line of this rich, deep work. It has in common with musical works of art that it is a completely self-enclosed world whose laws stand as high above those of all scholarly reasoning as does a good movement in a sonata above the best rules of harmonics. The much misused word "experience" is singularly appropriate with respect to this book, for what is valuable in it is just as much Bertram as it is Nietzsche. It has not only a congeniality of interpretation, but a geniality of free improvisation. Its twenty chapters are so many movements of a brilliant play of variations flowing from a font of inspiration, each one inwardly connected with all the others through their relation to a central theme that nevertheless remains fresh. I know of no other work of literature that is so crafted. It is, of its kind, not just new, but unique.[49]

Thomas Mann also recognized and applauded the musical structure of the book, and he told Bertram that "these repetitions act as links and leitmotifs, they refer backward, they give the whole an external unity, in addition to its internal one."[50] Typically, though, Bertram himself considered music not just as the supreme art form but as quintessentially German, asserting there existed an "identity of music and Germanness" (p. 93). Thus, "German" to Bertram represented primarily cultural, not political, values, and for him those values were, almost by definition, positive.

This almost devotional attachment to all things German placed Bertram in a rather complicated position given Nietzsche's often vociferous denunciations of his countrymen. Not surprisingly, Bertram's preferred method of dealing with this conflict was to turn it on its head: Nietzsche's professed hatred of Germans, he argued, was actually the expression of a frustrated love. "His fanaticism, his impassioned injustice toward everything that bore the name German," Bertram explains at one point, "can be compared only with the outbursts of his *Antichrist* and his *Case of Wagner:* like these, it is a love-hate, a hatred stemming from the most profound feeling of kinship, from the guilty conscience of an inner identity, which feeds his anti-Germanness" (pp. 71–72). In like manner, Bertram sees Nietzsche's continued adherence to the legacy of Protestantism as vital to an understanding of the avowed "Antichrist": "Everything positive, everything creative in Nietzsche is in fact *rooted* here, comes from his Lutheran, reformatory, northern and romantic heritage, no matter how much it is always intoxicatedly lavished on the Hellenistic, classically southern psychologistic element" (p. 48). Again, though one may disagree with Bertram's appraisal, it is not, as we saw in George Williamson's comments, one that is necessarily at odds with current scholarship on Nietzsche or, indeed, with Nietzsche himself.

Significantly, it was just these focal points of Bertram's book—his emphasis on Nietzsche's "Germanness," on his Protestantism, on the centrality of music in his life—that stood in greatest contrast to Stefan George and his world. When Bertram read the chapter, "The German Becoming," aloud to George, for instance, the master found it "not so exciting."[51] George spent most of his life vilifying everything officially "German," especially the German state, and Bertram's unapologetic Germanophilia no doubt grated. In addition, George had grown up as a Catholic during the height of Bismarck's *Kulturkampf*, which sought to eradicate Catholic influence from German public life in the newly formed and aggressively Protestant empire, and George forever detested Protestantism almost as much as he detested Bismarck and his reich. And George, who insisted that he "did not understand anything about" music, still did not refrain from labeling musicians "idiots."[52]

Nevertheless, in several other respects, the book does accord closely with George's views. Particularly in the final three chapters, "Prophecy," "Socrates," and "Eleusis," Bertram addresses concerns that were very much at the forefront of George's interests, and it is there that the presence of George is most clearly felt. George, who increasingly understood himself as the prophet of a new Greek ideal to be realized in a Platonic pedagogy through his followers, undeniably stands behind many of the arguments Bertram makes in these chapters. But, as is typical of the book in its entirety, nearly every positive assertion Bertram makes is almost immediately qualified or overturned by its opposite. Thus, in his discussion of Nietzsche's unfulfilled desire to have disciples of his own, Bertram writes:

> For, to be sure, these disciples, these Socratic pupils of his dreams, were forever denied to Nietzsche because they were necessarily denied to him, owing to an inner barrier that he was unable to transform into a threshold, owing to an ultimate individualism, that is, an ultimate indivisibility, an incommunicability of the individual, of which Nietzsche possessed a melancholy awareness. The personal mastery between two people was forever denied to him; for the same reasons, perhaps, for which his experience of his own discipleship to Wagner could not be completed: out of an innermost incapacity for fusion, a Protestant defiance of the individual, a Nordic pride and a will to the seventh solitude of the ego (p. 284).

It is in such passages, where Bertram's own ambivalence about George and everything he represented so patently informs his reading of Nietzsche, that we encounter the real limitations of Bertram's "mythological," thematic, and typological approach. When so much becomes symbolic, when the specific is lifted to ever higher levels of generality, the contours supposedly defining Nietzsche become ever more tenuous and threaten to disappear altogether.

Even a sympathetic reader will find much missing in the book. Many of the philosophical doctrines we now immediately associate with the name Nietzsche—his notion of "ressentiment," the idea of the Eternal Return, the revaluation of values—are either never mentioned or airily dismissed. In the chapter "Ancestry," for example, Bertram describes the Eternal Return as a "deceptively teasing delusional mystery imagined by the late Nietzsche" (p. 12) and in "Eleusis" as "a sublimely irrational and unfruitful private delusion" (p. 306). Nor was Bertram afraid to pass critical judgment on Nietzsche's works, calling *Zarathustra,* for instance, a "flickering mosaic," as well as "stiff" and "artificial" (p. 199). But, even though Bertram was not especially interested in Nietzsche as a philosopher—in fact, Bertram did not think of himself as having an aptitude for philosophy[53]—he was capable of making intriguingly philosophical observations, which are often concealed within apparently casual asides. In the chapter "Judas," for example, Bertram objects to the contention that Nietzsche "killed God" and says that the "murder of the old God" was "purely philosophically speaking much more Kant's deed than Nietzsche's" (p. 133). Not strictly philosophical, perhaps, but intriguing is another parenthetical remark Bertram makes in the chapter on music, "Arion," where he speculates that the late Nietzsche's preference for melody over harmony in music was very "aristocratic" "and perhaps psychologically not unrelated to Nietzsche's hero worship" (p. 99). Still, those with an exclusively or narrowly philosophical focus will no doubt be disappointed by Bertram, to whom Nietzsche was preeminently "a poet and psychologist" (p. 217), a supreme representative and incarnation of the profound, absorbing, but also deeply riven spectacle that is—or was—German culture.

After *Nietzsche*

When Bertram's *Nietzsche* appeared in the spring of 1918, his friend Thomas Mann greeted it with expansive enthusiasm. In a letter to Bertram, he wrote:

> The mixture of philology and music in the basic conception of the book, so appropriate to the subject, nevertheless seems new, surprisingly personal in this application. Never before has an essentially philological method been handled with such pulsating feeling. . . . Your mastery of the material is astounding, as is your overview of what was externally such a dissipated life's work, your ingeniousness in making associations. . . . If one compares "Nietzsche" with Gundolf's "Goethe," then one

> cannot help but think at what a stage of high culture, intuition and intelligence our literary history has arrived.[54]

As we have seen, Mann's reaction was widely shared by the book's many other admirers. But Mann also identified with its pronounced "Germanness" in an immediate and personal way, and his own *Reflections of an Unpolitical Man,* which appeared only a few months later, spoke a very similar idiom. As Mann described it in an autobiographical sketch he wrote in 1930:

> I shared the fateful emotions of a spiritual Germanness . . . and the "Reflections of an Unpolitical Man" were a form of intellectual service with a weapon to which I had been "drafted" not by the state and army, but by the time itself. . . . Ernst Bertram was the confidant of my boundless political-antipolitical musings, I read them aloud to him when he was in Munich, he respected them as a compulsive, passionate examination of my conscience and understood its Protestantism and conservatism.[55]

Yet soon after the war, Mann began to change his mind. No later than 1922, when he gave his speech "Of the German Republic," he had decided that this form of "Germanness" and "political-antipolitical" conservatism was positively dangerous, that it contained the seeds of reaction or worse, and he thus made a principled decision to embrace the cosmopolitan, internationalist, and, as many of his countrymen were convinced, "un-German" ideals of democracy.

It was a step Ernst Bertram would not, and perhaps never could, take. Although he and Mann remained on cordial terms throughout the 1920s, when the Nazis came to power in 1933, forcing Mann to seek refuge in Switzerland, Bertram accused him of abandoning Germany and implored him to return. Mann, whose house in Munich had been ransacked and ruined by the SA, replied: "I am not touched by the reproach that I left Germany. I was cast out of it. Reviled, denounced and plundered by the foreign conquerors of *my* country (for I am an older and better German than they), I have to create a new basis for my old years in a world that is more friendly to my being."[56] Indeed, as he wrote to Bertram a year later, "if I had followed your friendly advice and insistence, then I can say with as much probability that one can just as well speak of certainty that I would no longer be alive today."[57] All the while, however, Mann distinguished between what he called Bertram's "pious and perceptively brilliant Germanness" and the violent, murderous regime that viewed itself as the very apotheosis of Germanness, and it pained Mann that Bertram seemed to suffer from the same delusion: "That you are capable of confusing this Germanness with its coarsest travesty and the most disgusting bogeyman that world history has ever brought forth, of taking him to be the 'savior' your poet speaks of—that causes me persistent sorrow."[58]

Possibly Mann was being too generous. On May 3, 1933, Bertram had introduced his lecture series for the University of Cologne's summer semester with a formal speech. Titled "German Awakening," it celebrated what Bertram called the "Germanic miracle" of recent political developments. More than an exercise in academic phrase making, Bertram's speech exhorted his students to take active part in the transformations taking place in the name of German values. "In the enormous political-spiritual breakthrough battle, in the midst of which we now stand, our *Volk* requires all its spiritual powers and consciousness, and especially these." In urging his listeners to join the struggle, Bertram reminded them that the stakes were high: "if *this* battle fails," he warned, then it would mean "the end of the White World, chaos or a planet of termites." It was necessary, therefore, "always to remind oneself that we are in the middle of a war (perhaps in a battle of life and death for our highest Germanic-German values)." Bertram predicted that in future history books, "this war of liberation by the German *Volk* for its inner and external right to live will stand as an event without parallel: as a revolution." He also stated what this "revolution" sought to overturn: it was "against false Enlightenment, against the whole arrogance of Western civilization and civilized dogmatism." These were qualities, Bertram asserted, that had nothing to do with the true German spirit, with the inner character of the German *Volk*. And, he added, "what a *Volk* has truly experienced and recognized as its irreconcilably mortal enemy, it should be allowed to destroy."[59]

One week later, in Cologne and at many other universities throughout the Third Reich, books deemed to express an "un-German spirit" were duly destroyed in ceremonial bonfires. Although Bertram was able to prevent the planned burning of books by Thomas Mann and Friedrich Gundolf, as was done elsewhere, he nevertheless attended the event, apparently regretting only that it was not more spontaneous. "Young people should *improvise* something like that in a momentary impulse of enthusiasm," he wrote afterward to a friend, "but not as a theatrical performance 'with Dean and Faculty': to me that's not twenty-year-old enough."[60]

In the following years, as the full nature of the dictatorship revealed itself, Bertram seems to have gradually grown disillusioned, and he thereafter refrained from such open demonstrations of fealty to the regime and its ideology. But he retained his teaching position until the end, and in 1940 he was even awarded a distinguished prize named after the nineteenth-century political publicist, Joseph von Görres, which was conferred to him in a formal ceremony at the University of Bonn and presided over by party officials. When the war was over, Bertram was unsurprisingly classified as politically compromised; he lost his job and was prevented from publishing or speaking publicly. During the process of his "denazification," Bertram requested and received endorsements from several prominent figures. One was the physicist Max Planck, who in 1947 wrote vigorously on his behalf:

> Prof. Bertram was no National Socialist, even less a National Socialist activist. He was always a patriotically minded German and never made a secret of that. But the National Socialist ideology was absolutely contrary to his nature. He is a man of strictly lawful thought, who neither condoned nor promoted the discrimination, much less the persecution, of other people for any reason, be it racist or political or otherwise. Bertram has an upright character which contains nothing of the base, common and evil elements of National Socialism. His national attitude was completely free from any association with the thought of employing power or violence.
>
> He always felt he was a representative of the German spirit and unabashedly professed this notion in meritorious and productive activity. If his attitude is now in danger of being identified with the goals of the National Socialist regime, then that can be owing only to a disastrous confusion of two completely separate intellectual worlds.[61]

Although Bertram subsequently received the right to publish again, he never returned to the seminar room. He spent the remainder of his days writing poetry and entertaining the few guests that made their way to his apartment in Cologne-Marienburg. When he died in 1957, the once celebrated professor, whose name would forever be associated with the philosopher most people in Germany then wanted simply to forget, was quietly laid to rest. In one of the few obituaries that were published, it was noted with a mixture of relief and satisfaction that Bertram "will appear to many as the *last* German,"[62] or at any rate as the last of a particular German type. For his part, Thomas Mann, who followed his old friend's changing fortunes from afar, preferred to believe that Bertram had sadly deceived himself, and that his "Germanness" and Nazism were, as Max Planck had put it, "two completely separate intellectual worlds."[63]

In 1952, three years before his own death, Mann returned a final time to that world when he responded to a new publication on Nietzsche that had been sent to him by an American academic by the name of Walter Kaufmann. In a letter to the author, Mann generously praised his book as a "work of great scholarly superiority to probably everything that has been done so far within Nietzsche criticism and interpretation." Yet, despite his acknowledgment of Kaufmann's undeniable accomplishment, Mann did not hesitate to admonish the brash young scholar, nearly fifty years his junior, for so utterly, and he thought unfairly, condemning all prior scholarship on Nietzsche. "It is and remains unfortunate that you had to comport yourself, as you had warned me, so purely polemically toward everything earlier and could not allow for a little positive reference. That occasionally has the effect of being school-masterly and pedantically gainsaying, remediating, know-it-all-ish." Most of all, Mann missed in Kaufmann's account a feeling for the person, for the living human being who had played such an enormous role in his own intellectual life as well:

> As philosophically incontrovertible and penetrating as your admirable work is, it leaves a great deal of his humanity out, the tragedy, the immensely pitiful and miserable aspects, his horrible affectations (e.g., his praise of Heine), his wishful relationship to Goethe, from whom he had as much as I have from Hercules. Also the mythical element, his deliberate journey to the cross. It is too much the case, I find, that he is simply a great thinker in your book; one senses little of the artist-martyr.[64]

For that, for an intimation of the suffering, tormented soul, the sacrificial victim of a peculiarly German fate, a portrait Mann himself had so magnificently rendered in his *Doktor Faustus,* one had to turn elsewhere.[65] Here Mann loyally rose to the defense of his old friend, now disgraced and ostracized, and who had borne the brunt of Kaufmann's censure. "Bertram is criticized too harshly," Mann told Kaufmann. "His legend creation, which the subject truly invites, was not of the bad sort, and certain chapters of his book, such as 'Venice' and 'Judas,' are simply *beautiful.*"[66]

Perhaps that, in the end, is how Bertram's book should be understood, and its resurrection almost ninety years later justified: as nothing more, but also as nothing less, than a work of art. It was, after all, Nietzsche himself who famously declared in *The Birth of Tragedy* that "existence and the world are eternally *justified* only as an aesthetic phenomenon."[67] One of Bertram's favorite quotations, often repeated, comes from the preface Nietzsche added to the same work in 1886, when he was despairing of finding any readers, when he feared he might not ever be heard, and was wondering if he had chosen the wrong vehicle to convey his message, his vision, himself: "It should have *sung,* this new soul—and not spoken!"[68] In Bertram, Nietzsche finally found his bard.

A Note on the Translation

At the time Ernst Bertram wrote *Nietzsche,* the German language had arguably achieved its stylistic zenith. Well after French, English, Spanish, and Italian had been established as means of expression capable of the artistic refinement and grace previously accorded only to the Classical languages, German had become, finally, a literary medium of European stature. At long last, the language seemed to exude the self-confidence of a cultural entity that no longer had to make apologies for itself or regard its neighbors with a debilitating combination of envy and inferiority. And, as we have seen, Bertram enjoyed the reputation of wielding this newly burnished instrument with rare skill, so that much of the original appeal of *Nietzsche* resided in the language itself.

All that has changed. Bertram belonged to a generation of German intellectuals who memorized and could recite vast stretches of poetry by heart, and who loved the language of Goethe and Schiller with a passion, but also with an innocence, even a naïveté, that became impossible after 1945. Although the damage done to the German language by the twelve years of Nazi dictatorship is less visible or palpable than, say, the destruction of German cities, the loss—in terms of a living connection to the cultural inheritance of the past—is just as great. Bertram's German, like Bertram's Germany, is no more. As a result, even in linguistic terms Bertram's *Nietzsche* sounds almost as alien today in German as his translated idiom does in English.

The translator of *Nietzsche* is therefore confronted by a number of intractable difficulties, some endemic to the business of translation generally, but many inherent in Bertram alone. I certainly empathized on more than one occasion with Robert Pitrou, who translated the book into French in 1932 and wrote in his preface that "one could not present this book as easy to read even to those who read Proust and Valéry fluently."[69] My own goal was to be as accurate as possible, of course, and to preserve as much as I could of Bertram's distinctive rhythm and tone, while also making the book as readable and, ideally, as enjoyable, even exciting, as the original often is.

The following comments may give some impression of the challenges faced in fitting Bertram's lyrical prose in a more pedestrian, yet I hope serviceable, garb. Many of Bertram's central categories for understanding Nietzsche are, symptomatically, basically untranslatable, but of extraordinary significance not just for his book but also for the entire cultural and political context in which he wrote it and in which it was understood. Crucially, the all-important "Deutschtum," for which "Germanness" is but a pale approximation, suggests (or suggested) to a native speaker the whole spectrum of German qualities embodied by the culture and its people, of which the related term "das Deutsche" was a kind of essential distillation. No words, not even the grammatical forms, exist to render these terms adequately in English. Other words, not unique to Bertram, but the bane of any translator's life, are those such as "Wesen"—"essence," "being," "character," "nature"—or the notorious "Geist"—which signifies "spirit," "intellect," or "mind," as well as all three simultaneously—and its adjective "geistig": tellingly, and regrettably, there is no adjective in English for "mind" that corresponds. Or, more disheartening still, "bilden" and its various inflections, "Bildung," "gebildet," "Gebilde," "Bild," and so forth, all of which still contain for the German speaker the root meanings of "form" and "shape," but for which we have to use in each case a different word: "education," "cultivated," "structure," and "image." Sometimes, when a single word would not do, I used two English approximates to get closer to the original meaning. For example, Bertram writes of Nietzsche's psychology that it was "eine Form seiner Hingabe an das Böse," which I rendered as "a form of his surrender and devotion to evil" (p. 129), the sticking word being "Hingabe," which also contains the related senses of "sacrifice" or "dedication."

Compounding the problem is that Bertram invented many words, coining verbs, nouns, and adjectives with an almost delirious exuberance. Almost every page contains words and even entire phrases that had never existed before and that, strictly speaking, have no equivalent in any language. Thus, for example, drawing further on the resources inherent in "bilden," Bertram casually refers to Nietzsche as a "Sprachbildner," that is, a "former" or "sculptor" of language, for which the dull but I think accurate and unobtrusive "stylist" must probably suffice. But Bertram did this sort of thing on a grand scale, as evidenced by this (partial) list of his neologisms:

Ahnenverantwortung
augengemäß
beseelbar
Bildform
Bildwerdung
Brückenglück
Dankbedürfnis
dauerschenkend
Deutschdeutung
dunkelklar
eigenlebendig
entgötternd
Entleiblichung
entnorden
Entselbstung
Entwirklichung
Erkennertum
erlebtest (as superlative adjective)
erweckungssüchtig
Feuerhauch
fortzeugend
Gebildetheit
gedankenhaft
gewissensschwer
gleichnisfroh
Haßlust
heilkräftig
Herbstlichkeit
Hinaufwendung
hintergründlich
Hyperionverdammung
Jahrhundertaugenblick
mildreif
mischgeformt
Nachgroll
nächtlicher (as a comparative)
Nurdeutschtum
Rauschgegenwart
selbstbildhaft
Selbstentdeutschung
Selbstschau
Selbstverwechslung

sich entdeutschen
sinngebend
übernorden
überwirklich
Unauskämpfbarkeit
unerfahrungshaft
unterwölben
vergeheimnisen
vergessensdurstig
Verleiblichung
verschopenhauern
Versüdlichung
Verwandlungssüchtigste
vorbedeutsam
Vorspuk
Wahrdichtung
wahrträumend
wandelwillig
weltbindend
Werdegefühl
Zartgeist
zerdeuten
Zerrklang
zerspotten
zusammenschauend
Zweiseelenmann
Zwittergenie

Finding a solution to the conundrum presented by these, as well as his many other linguistic inventions, involved sifting, measuring, taking apart, putting back together various strands of meaning and allusion, and eventually, inevitably, bowing to some sort of compromise.

But even on the mundane level of ordinary language, Bertram employs metaphors—and Nietzsche taught us that all language (or, more precisely, truth) is nothing but a "moveable army of metaphors"[70]—with a poet's precision. This can be illustrated by an apparently trivial example. At one point in the chapter, "The German Becoming," Bertram precisely uses the common word "angehen" while exploiting its various attendant meanings, which he signals by putting the word in quotation marks. There Bertram writes: " . . . das Problem, welches ihn am meisten 'anging,' gegen dessen Angriff er sich am bittersten gewehrt hat . . ." "Angehen" used in this way commonly means "to concern, to regard, to interest" as in: "that doesn't concern me" or "that's none of my business," and here Bertram is leaning on this principal meaning of the word. But "angehen" also means "to tackle" or "to attack" a problem, an opponent, or a mountain. And, indeed, Bertram also intends this secondary meaning, as the next clause makes clear. In the end, the verb I chose to render "angehen," "to beset" (p. 57), contains something of both meanings, especially "attack," but it does not have the familiar, natural feel that the German does.

Throughout, Bertram is always fully awake to the literal sense of common metaphors, and he deploys them with consummate skill even in phrases that are seemingly no more than brief asides. For example, Bertram in another passage described an idea as being "so höchst deutsch, wie sie tief griechisch ist." In my version, I tried to maintain the play on the spatial metaphors of "high" and "low" while remaining within idiomatic English usage in the following way: it is "as supremely German as it is fundamentally Greek" (p. 59). It would work––just—to write: "as highly German as it is deeply Greek." But that, although literal, sounds to me inelegant and ungainly, which is something Bertram's German almost never is.

And then there is Nietzsche himself. For me, one of the many attractions of translating Bertram's book was the opportunity to try my hand on large amounts of Nietzsche as well, whom Bertram of course liberally quotes throughout his text. Given Nietzsche's own acknowledged stylistic brilliance and inventiveness, one of the challenges Bertram faced was to rise rhetorically to the level of Nietzsche's prose. The very structure of the book indicates that Bertram wanted to create the impression of seamlessness: the quotations are not set off, but woven into and among his own words, and his references to the sources are often pared down to a bare minimum (in the middle of one of his occasionally breathless elaborations, Bertram will simply write *Birth* to indicate the work he is parsing). I thus decided, or rather wanted, to translate all of the Nietzsche myself instead of using any of the existing translations so that the stylistic fusion, as it were, of Bertram and Nietzsche would be maintained. I did sometimes consult Hollingdale's and Kaufmann's renditions, as well as the helpful, but imperfect, online resource, the Nietzsche Channel.[71] But all of the existing translations are, necessarily, expressions of the translators' background, knowledge, and taste, and therefore contain both advantages as well as limitations.

Few philosophers—few writers—possessed anything like Nietzsche's sovereign control of German, and no one was more aware than he of the severe burden that transposing his voice into a foreign register would place on anyone who was daring, or foolhardy, enough to try. In December 1888, during those final, feverish days before his collapse, Nietzsche, at last hearing echoes from the wider world in the form of letters from foreign admirers, ecstatically envisioned being read in Paris, Copenhagen, St. Petersburg, and London. But he knew there was a vital stipulation. His voice, so distinctive and yet so imbued with the cadence, color, and texture of his native language, would require a translator of the first order if it were to be heard at all. To his delight, the French critic and historian Hippolyte Taine had discovered his work and had suggested that it be translated. Nietzsche immediately agreed, but added a condition that is as flagrantly immodest as it is apt: "To be sure, a perfect and even masterful command of German is the prerequisite for translating the book."[72] Georg Brandes, the Danish philosopher who first brought public attention to Nietzsche, also indicated in a letter that he would try to arrange for a translation, which elicited the same imploring demand: "Look for a master to be my first translator—I can use only masters of language."[73]

With stakes this high, something is bound to be lost. But, as anyone who has engaged in the exquisite torment of translation well knows, that is the price of entering the field. I certainly cannot claim to have met the criteria Nietzsche established for his translators in my treatment of either him or his remarkable interpreter. But I do hope that others will gain some profit from my efforts to lend Bertram's *Nietzsche* an English voice. The reward for me, at any rate, was immeasurable.

A Comment on the Notes

As I indicated in my introduction, there are no notes of any kind in Bertram's *Nietzsche.* To make this translation useful for scholarly purposes, I have thus identified as many of the sources as I could for the numerous references Bertram makes to Nietzsche's published works, letters, and *Nachlaß,* or "Notebooks." In addition, I have located many, although not all, of the sources for the quotations of Goethe, Hölderlin, Novalis, and others whom Bertram liberally cites throughout his text. Finally, there are some "hidden" quotations or allusions that, when they seemed significant enough (and I recognized them), I have also cited in the notes. Obviously, this effort would have been impossible without the digital and Internet resources now available, in particular the online version of the historical-critical edition of Nietzsche's works provided by Past Masters and the search engine Google. Where I was unable to pinpoint the source of a quotation, I indicated this with "Not found." Perhaps an enterprising person will fill these gaps; fortunately, there are relatively few of them.

For Nietzsche's works and letters, I used the standard *Kritische Studienausgabe,* edited by Giorgio Colli and Mazzino Montinari, and I employed the usual abbreviation for each: KSA for the edition of the works and notebooks, and KSB for the letters, which comprise fifteen and eight volumes respectively. To enable cross-referencing to English-language editions of Nietzsche's works (where they exist), in each note I have given the English version of the title of the work in question first, indicating wherever possible the section in which the quotation is to be found, followed by the reference to the original. For the notebooks, most of which have yet to be translated into English, I simply indicate where the original can be found.

For all other citations, I used the standard editions when I could, or I referred to the book Bertram consulted where this was necessary or possible. And, so as not to make this substantial book even longer, the explanatory notes have been kept to a minimum.

Acknowledgments

I am grateful to several institutions and individuals for helping me undertake and complete this project. The idea of translating this difficult but fascinating work came to me while teaching a course on Stefan George and his Circle as a visiting professor at the University of Chicago in the spring of 2003. As we worked through the text, it became clear that a great deal, probably too much, stood in the way of an appreciation of Bertram's view of Nietzsche. The libraries of both the University of Chicago and my home institution, the University of Notre Dame, were instrumental in providing materials along the way. I was fortunate to have been able to work at the Deutsches Literaturarchiv in Marbach am Neckar, which houses Ernst Bertram's *Nachlaß*, or literary estate, in the summer of 2005. This collection houses many treasures relating to Bertram's eventful life and career that would repay careful study. My thanks go to the director of the archive, Dr. Ulrich Raulff, who hosted my stay and invited me to give a lecture on the project, as well as to the Humboldt Foundation, which provided funds to support it. My research assistant at Notre Dame, Chris Blauwkamp, traced many of the quotations in the original text, and my colleague Catherine Schlegel helped with the Greek passages. And I am indebted to Richard Schacht, editor of the Nietzsche series at the University of Illinois Press, for taking an interest in a translation of a book now nine decades old. And, of course, I am very pleased that the press itself is willing to give Bertram's *Nietzsche* another chance to reach a wider audience. Both he and Nietzsche deserve it.

Introduction: Legend

For do we control the past?
We serve what is to come.

All of the past is but a parable.[1] No historical method can give us a window on lived reality "as it actually was,"[2] as nineteenth-century advocates of a naïve historical realism so often seem to have believed. History, which is after all the study and testimony of souls, is never synonymous with the reconstruction of some past phenomenon, or even with the closest possible approximation to a past reality. It is, rather, precisely the de-realization of that former reality, its transposition into an entirely different category of being; it is an establishment of values, not a production of reality. The form a historian creates (or the one he serves: for even while conducting his most sober and objective reasoning, the historian is still led by something that *wants* to assume form), that form is a reality of an absolutely new and higher degree, a replaying, so to speak, of the turbid past in a more crystalline element and according to more transparent laws. This becomes clear especially when we are speaking about history in its most concentrated manifestation, namely the history of an individual who has remained visible to us or who has become visible again. We do not make a past life present to us, we remove it from the present when we view it historically. We do not salvage it within our time; we make it timeless. In explaining a past life to ourselves, we are already interpreting it. What remains, no matter how much we try to elucidate, comprehend, reexperience it, is never the life itself, but rather always its legend. What all human activity leaves behind as history is always in the end—and the word is to be understood without any religious, romantic, or much less literary overtones—*legend.*

In this secular sense, legend is the most vital form of historical tradition, its most primitive as well as its ultimate embodiment, simultaneously its oldest and its deepest expression. Legend alone actually connects the primeval past with the present through a continuous dynamic bond; only it unites the saint and the people, the hero and the peasant; the prophet and posterity meet only here. And even the most sharply outlined personality, even the one most clearly delineated by historical knowledge, persists through time as an active and generative power only in the form of legend. (For a "work," too, is a personality and is subject to the laws of legend.) It thus lives only as image, as form, only as myth, not as knowledge or perception of a past phenomenon. No philological procedure, no analytical method is capable of shaping that image, or of hindering or accelerating its transformations, which are instead propelled by their own inner law.

The legend of a personality that is historical in the narrower sense is not defined by the categories, for instance, of the miraculous, of unsubstantiated anecdotal stories, or of traditional tales that are interesting, charming, or touching, yet unhistorical. Even less is it something like an unreliable biography that, at best, makes up for its lack of credibility through romantic colorfulness or didactic symbolic value. Rather, the legend of a life whose memory has survived up to our day on the strength of his deed, his work, his word, belongs from the outset to an entirely different sphere than everything that is biographical in a scholarly sense or merely interesting as anecdote. It has nothing to do with either knowledge or charm. The legend of a man is an image that is newly active and vital in every new present. It is not the product of the current state of exact research, nor is it a deliberately artistic narrative, nor a philosophical interpretation of a subject that is refractory but still capable of being animated. Instead, this image is a living, autonomous organism leading an independent existence. It is changeable, indeed desirous of change, and does in fact constantly change, exhibiting ever fewer and broader contours; it becomes at once more typical and more unique, at once parabolic and incomparable. It rises slowly in the starry sky of human memory; it seems to pause once under each of the mythic signs of the zodiac, the twelve great "houses of the heavens," as if it had been born under just that sign and felt truly at home there. And if the inner orbital power of the legend is strong enough to be called eternal among men, it gradually ascends so high toward the pole that, like a northern star, it never again descends below the horizon of our memory.

The psychologically visible process of this kind of legend formation is determined by laws that can be observed operating in the same manner in the most varied types of legend. No fundamental procedural difference exists, for example, between the formation of the heroic myths in antiquity and the legends of the saints in the Middle Ages. The process by which the form of a personality becomes legendary adheres to a typical pattern and, despite its varying external form determined by the character of a particular time, is always basically the same. Too, the intensity of legend formation in no way depends on primitive intellectual or cultural conditions. For even in very self-aware, analytically inclined times, in periods of so-called general culture, legend is not eliminated; in fact it is not even inhibited. Increasing self-consciousness, self-possession, philologically based knowledge about the actual conditions affecting the life of a great phenomenon: all of this has only a very minor influence on the emergence of legend. The power of that influence either to impede or to promote its rise is negligible. No less than in previous eras, if today a myth wants to assert itself, our watchful and vigilant intellect is still constrained by inescapable bonds. Any time, however, an individuality lives on, continuing beyond the threshold of a personal life, we are witnessing, as Jakob Burckhardt says, magic, a *religious* process, and as such one that is impervious to any mechanical or rational intervention. The most significant external characteristic of this process is that it is unscientific, unphilological in every respect. What begins to grow gradually as the legend of the great, twice-born man, whether it arises during his lifetime or after his death, lives, if not quite in complete opposition to, then certainly in perfect independence from any biographically anchored perception based only on knowable facts. Such facts, as respectable, even as indispensable (as raw material) as they may be, nevertheless represent merely the baser type of genuine tradition. Goethe once expressed the idea of this kind of independence in a conversation with Eckermann in 1825: "The lack of character in some individuals who engage in research and writing . . . gives us a paltry truth, thereby depriving us of something great, which would be better for us. But what are we supposed to do with such an impoverished truth! . . . If the Romans were great enough to invent such things, then we should at least be great enough to believe them."[3] (Within our context, only the term "invent" is too active, too conscious: legends in the sense we are talking about here are, of course, not invented.) This seems to be what Aristotle means when he says that poetry is more philosophical than history. "Poetry is always right; it extends far beyond history," a German skeptic asserts.[4] This poetry—not to be understood, however, as conscious artistic invention, much less as an anodyne rearrangement of the past—is the very myth-creating power that necessarily radiates from a truly great figure and that, without any design or intention, forms its own posthumous body, its legend.

For, like the process of geological sedimentation, the generational layers of an imperceptibly changing consciousness tend to settle very gradually over the earliest image of the Great Man. It is a process that is as inconspicuous as it is unstoppable. The individual periods of the continuing vitality of a legend cannot be kept artificially alive beyond their "geological" epoch. The unique earthly existence of someone of genuine greatness, which is enduringly fruitful and adaptable, fulfills its inherent and promised mission only in a predetermined temporal succession of profound and expandable multivalence. At no single present moment can one ever comprehend the full nature of a Great Man, or experience every possible influence of his spiritual power as a whole. Only by historical, intellectual means can something like a comprehensive estimate of his effect be made retrospectively apparent, but it cannot be individually experienced or calculated in advance. Even in the possession of every methodological resource, every psychological insight, every philological tool, one will never be able to discern at any given present moment the future stages and possibilities of a particular legend in that most impenetrable of all obscurities. Full insight into the timeless essence of its nature, a prophetic overview of the entire breadth of influence exerted by a creative power is, as it were, even perspectivally unthinkable. This is especially true for the people of his own generation. "Only after you leave the city do you see how high its towers rise above the houses." What contemporaries perceive are always perspectival illusions. For they are standing at the very base of a mountain whose height can be seen only from a distance. At best, a few may have an intimation, however fleeting or partial, of a timeless power, even though they remain in the dark about the nature and direction of its future agency, of the legend to come. But the following generations never perceive the definitively true image, either, an image of "how it actually was." They, too, see only what is commensurate with their own, albeit more favorable, perspectival distance, and all of their methodological instruments can artificially make this image appear to move closer, but they cannot change its constitution.

The history of every great human image that has wandered and changed across centuries teaches us this perspectival modesty. Despite all of our accumulated knowledge, our methods, and our objectivity, we know only what we see, and we see only what we are and because it is us we see. In the solitary singularity of every image, in the absolute uniqueness of every single perspective, we find both resignation and happiness. A great, which is to say a "significant," man is always inescapably our own creation, just as we are his. If we attempt to explain the image of a man to ourselves, then it occurs with the awareness that it "appears" that way only today, only to us, only as a single moment in time. But this awareness, far from tempting us to succumb to historical skepticism and agnosticism, teaches us rather the importance of increased conscientiousness in recording and bequeathing every single moment of a legend's growth, which will never repeat itself. For, even with regard to the most minute segment of a past, we are witnesses to a past that will never *appear* again in the same way. In that realization lies the ultimate rescue from all historical skepticism, from all relativism: every moment of a legend, like that of everything living, contains eternity. What is more: every one of these moments is indispensable to the entire legend; no subsequent form of the legend is produced, even if it is unwittingly, without the aid of all its previous incarnations. To work toward the completion of a great image, which each individual will see only in a mirror, in an obscure word, but never face to face: this quiet, resigned joy filled the souls, if not also the consciousness, of all those who dedicated themselves during the past two millennia to the remembrance of some great phenomenon, be they Christians, Platonists, and so on. The neophyte in Lenau's *The Albigenses* speaks of the happiness of actively working toward a great image coming into being,[5] and it is no accident that we find the following in a poem by Angelus Silesius:

> Come! let us awaken the sacred story from the dead,
> Which comes alive only in the mind and in its light;
> With this beacon shall mankind travel down into
> The miraculous, deep and holy shaft, the heart of the savior.
> Christ in His entirety did not appear on earth,
> His divinely human image has yet to be fulfilled.[6]

These lines—which basically reformulate once more the old Pauline opposition between Christ as *χατὰ σάρχα* and as *ἐν δυνάμει*—express as clearly as possible the essence of all genuine historical knowledge (which in the end pertains only to the image of a man who is somehow sacred to the memory of humanity): history is active image creation, not a chronicle, a reproduction, or a preservation of the past. Legend truly is what the word in its plainest meaning says: not something written, but something that is always to be *read* anew, that comes into existence only through a constantly renewed rereading.[7] In the introduction to his *Griechische Kulturgeschichte*[8] as well as in his *Weltgeschichtliche Betrachtungen* (Reflections on World History), Burckhardt writes about the nature of the historical source in the same vein, saying that Thucydides may have reported a fact of the first importance that will be noticed only a hundred years from now. And next to the historian Burckhardt there is Nietzsche the philologist: "One and the same text permits innumerable interpretations—there is no 'correct' interpretation."[9] What is true of everything that is written—its legendary character in the sense we have indicated—is even more so with regard to the entirety of the past. It has never "appeared on earth" anywhere in its full reality; its image, sacred or profane—even though every image becomes "divine" in the end, that is, it turns into the image of god, just like man himself did—is always "yet to be fulfilled." All of the past wants to become image, all that is living to become legend, all reality myth.

And thus everything we can express about the essential nature of the men whose memory has come down to the living is myth. Everyone who dies is already a myth—"all of the dead become gods" is how the Japanese express the idea in cultic language, in a strangely simultaneous intensification and negation of the ancient notion of the hero—and the power that emanates from this myth, the orbital period it is granted, its transformational capacity: all of this corresponds, according to inflexible laws, to the power that the essence of the living man amassed. The short path of the nameless is erased with the memory of the last grandchild. The stars of Socrates and Christ, Homer and Shakespeare, Caesar and Napoleon have orbital periods whose length seems to equal the life span of the entire human race. Their myth—that is, the pressing appeal always to complete their image anew—does not die. No one person can or ever will compose the final version of their legend, the completed myth of their essential being. All an individual or an individual generation is capable of giving are fragments of their great secular mythology.

The following pages are intended to provide studies toward a mythology, thus defined, of the last great German, to record some of what the historical moment of our present seems to see in and as Nietzsche. The myth that carries this turbulent name is still in its beginning phase. But its initial metamorphic forms are already behind it: the stages of unconditional idolization, fanatical hatred, faddishness, as well as contempt are all behind us. Certain traits that were entirely foreign to the image of Nietzsche in the 1890s are becoming increasingly more apparent to us. Other traits are rapidly fading. His countenance sometimes shimmers uncertainly in a transitional light. What we see today or believe we see is already something other than what that first generation, in ecstatic dismay, imagined it saw in the visionary of the overman and in the glorifier of the blond beast. We are probably still too close to measure the precise stature of such an exotic figure—a figure that at first seemed so exotic, particularly among the Germans—in comparison to his immediate predecessors. It may be that we see Nietzsche the same way St. Gotthard was viewed until the nineteenth century: it was always included among the highest elevations on the continent because it was believed that a summit in which the mightiest mountain ranges of the Alps meet and from which rivers run down into the four corners of the earth must also necessarily be one of its highest peaks. We may be making such a perspectival error today as well in our estimation of Nietzsche, whose name embraces the mightiest intellectual upheavals of his century—and of more than his century—and who sent down emanations of his being, which gravitated toward both the north and south, into all four corners of educated Europe. But the deep impression that the experience of Nietzsche left on an entire generation is also entirely independent of such a comparative estimate of his stature. Quite apart from any absolute evaluation one might make of it, the enormous impression Nietzsche made—in itself a singular phenomenon within recent intellectual history—seems to be so strong because this man embodied and exemplified the spiritual fate of his centenary moment with rare purity, because he simultaneously was and saw, fought against and suffered from the incurable affliction of his century. Like his century, Nietzsche was born under the sign of Libra, that balance of a "dangerous Perhaps" that constitutes the magic and the calamitous fate of his intellectual century, which was uneasily suspended between two worlds. That, too, is possibly a perspectival illusion, and perhaps every great image stands at some point once under each of the twelve constellations of the heavenly zodiac. The only certainty is that it is none other than Nietzsche, in the current moment of his myth, in whom we see the most authentic representative of that "dangerous Perhaps," whose new philosophers he already saw emerging: "Philosophers of the dangerous Perhaps in every meaning of the word,"[10] as *Beyond Good and Evil* refers to them. In this respect as well he resembles today the image of his Wagner, "about whom, as about an especially successful type of German opacity, one can say absolutely nothing without adding such a 'Perhaps.'"[11] We understand Nietzsche as he understood German philosophers: "Leibniz, Kant, Hegel, Schopenhauer, their German dual nature";[12] we experience him as he understood the romantics: as "typically ambiguous";[13] we see him as he saw the Platonic Socrates: as "a caricature in the literal sense, because he was overladen with qualities that can never coexist in a *single* man."[14] He is for us the great typical phenomenon of the boundary, the most recent historical incarnation of the Pauline *ἀνὴρ δίψυχος*,[15] the man with two souls; the most unforgettable demonstration of Lichtenberg's dictum that the strangest creatures always straddle a boundary. Kant says that we "perceive" an object when we have established unity in the manifold of its intuition. This unity of the manifold that Nietzsche's appearance presents is established and expressed, paradoxically enough, in the very *duality* that extends down into the very core of its existence. (Thus the confusion about the phenomenon of Nietzsche for the many who hold onto one side of its oppositions, and who, from the vantage point of that one side, cannot of course force his contradictions into a single human being, much less an image.) Indeed, it seems to us as if the entire development of Nietzsche's image were taking a course toward a myth of the believing doubter, toward a legend of the god-seeking blasphemer, toward the figure of a prophetic beginning of the end.

Despite its ceaseless metamorphosis, every legend nevertheless strives toward a single embodiment in its most extreme and purest form, a manifestation that would represent the highest possibility of humanity, the most concentrated transformation of a soul into a figure that, having finally shed all earthly remnants, would live on until the end of human days on the strength of its allegorical being alone. It is true that most legends, depending on the degree of their inherent intensity, provide only the rudiments of such ultimate epitomes and models, offering no more than mythic possibilities that flutter like tormented shadows around a great original image whose destiny it was, unlike theirs, to drink from the blood of the soul and perfection. In the end, these tragic, incomplete shades serve their greater likeness, and their brotherly traits are eventually all transferred onto one single, final portrait. The law of accumulation, which states that he who has shall receive so that he shall have in abundance, holds true for the legend of human greatness as well. *On ne prête qu'aux riches.*[16] The eternal store of great deeds and immortal words is gradually lavished on fewer and fewer. Humanity's memory is ungrateful, but where it does give thanks, it gives profusely, and robs all smaller altars of the past in order to decorate its greatest monuments. Plato and Alexander, St. Francis and Dante, Leonardo, Rembrandt, and Goethe have in this way been transformed from powerful individuals into independent worlds. All of the lesser kings achieved their victories only for the renown of the greatest ones; and it was only for the glory of the greatest poets that the minor ones toiled.

> Ten thousand die without a sound: the Founder
> Alone gives the name . . . for ten thousand Mouths
> Only one holds the measure. In every Age
> There is but one God and only one his Prophet.[17]

Nietzsche, too, seems magnetically to attract the fates and the memory of his predecessors by the pull of his equally revered and maligned name. He appears, today, to be the last and greatest heir of all the descendents of Lucifer's defiance—but of a defiance that is perplexingly mixed and almost identical with divine homesickness; the heir of all Promethean arrogance, of the Promethean will to a new, godlessly divine human being, and of all proud, Promethean endurance. He is the heir and partner in fate with all those whose nature does not only strive, like Goethe's, out of the dark into the light, but which a deep distress also forces out of the light, out of the all-too-lucid realm, back down into the dark, into uncertainty. He is a companion to those whose being, "uniform and twofold" like the poems of Goethe's *Westöstlicher Divan,* like Persephone, are fated to reside in two realms of the soul. And if Nietzsche, the murderer of God, is also in his own way the prophet of a god, then it is most certainly a god who carries, in addition to the bright name of a god, a very dark name as well—like Plato's Eros and the "twice born" Dionysus.

The individual chapters that follow thus seek to elucidate the intrinsic spiritual duality of this mind, the great balance in which his nature and his values indeterminately hover. Yet each chapter offers a particular perspective made possible by contemplating Nietzsche. In this way one takes in the image of a beloved mountain from the standpoint of several lower promontories that radiate down from its summit, and the views afforded by each one, which occasionally offer contradictory perspectives, still complement one another to form an image of the mountain that would never result from a single aspect. The aggregate image of Nietzsche that emerges from these chapters is the image of the moment in which his myth appears to us to be standing at present. As its orbit progresses, it will move into other houses of the heavens. It is enough that Nietzsche's figure will have once lived before our eyes in just this way. For it possesses in this moment of its slow development as image a truth that will not diminish the validity of any higher stage of his future legend, any deeper myth of his being.

1

Ancestry

Poets, however, establish what remains.[1]
—Hölderlin

Then the past enduring,
The future lives in advance—
The moment is eternity.[2]
—Goethe

Everything revolutionary both obeys and enforces the law that ensures that the best part of what is opposed actually continues to endure. Revolution, above all in the spiritual realm—and every revolution is ultimately spiritual—is the rejuvenating bath of all that endures. Catiline,[3] according to Nietzsche, is the preliminary form of existence of every Caesar: all legitimate greatness must first traverse the stage of disreputable and criminal illegality. Yet Caesar, as a type, also requires repeated baptism in the Catiline element. Caesar, as a rightful heir, always has to remember that he possesses an usurper's power within himself so as not to wither away in mere Augustan legitimacy; yet Catiline is also Caesar's forefather and thus even in revolt occupies a legitimate place in the order of things. Those who bring the most novel wickedness and outrage at the same time always preserve and restore what has been accepted all along. The truly revolutionary element of an epoch, that which is most genuinely novel and the most vital, is simultaneously always somehow the most deeply rooted in the ancestral past—*nemo contra regem nisi rex ipse.*[4] The Catilinian bearers of the new are usually never aware of this law within themselves or become conscious of it very late, just as they are on the threshold of their own legitimacy. For no one may guess where the wind of the spirit is coming from or where it is going if it is to embolden the setting of sails for new shores. No one may suspect that sailing around his world will only lead him back to his own harbor. And it is no doubt an integral part of Nietzsche's nature—that perplexing, very rare, and always fateful double refraction that unites, in hermaphroditic fashion, the thirst for understanding with a demonic blindness—that this Genovese spirit and seeker of the most distant seas, of the most hidden shores of knowledge and the soul, nevertheless seems to have known from early on that he was bound by the same ancestral law, that his being occupied a fixed and determined place, even that his circuit had a tragic limit. That he knew "from whence I came"[5]—and where he would end. Perhaps the pseudo-revelation of the Eternal Return, that deceptively teasing delusional mystery imagined by the late Nietzsche,[6] is only the symbolization of the shudder, of the vertigo one feels when faced by the inexorably closing ring, the return to the haven of oneself. The more one learns, the more one knows, the more one sees: round and round it all goes—thus the mystical warning contained in Goethe's dictum.[7] The eternal return of all things within himself, the intellectual circumnavigator's pedagogical secret, which constantly threatens to erupt in festively extravagant ecstasy, the triumphantly conscious curse of having to return to the eternally same port of origin, this seems to be only the metaphysical form, the demonic formula, of the deep ancestral feeling that from the beginning throbs in Nietzsche's blood and mind. This man who more than any other craved, who reveled in transformation, who was more aware of his own transformations than anyone else—"only he who changes will remain akin to me"[8]—is still bound like almost no other leader of souls and seducer of minds by the strongest inner obligation and attraction to conscious tradition, to the idea of inheritable enduring values, to the affirmation of being determined by one's ancestors. The man who called for the destruction of the Old Tablets and advocated love for the "land of your children"[9]—that same person expresses reverence for ancestry in everything he preaches, indeed even in the way he preaches it. The disciple of Wagner who is intoxicated with hope, for whom the art of his master is the true "music of the future"[10] heralding a completely new culture, that same man writes in the preliminary studies for "Richard Wagner in Bayreuth": "I could also imagine a *forward*-looking art that seeks its images in the future. Why does such a thing not exist? Art is connected to *piety*."[11] What an odd image: this radical and transvaluer of values for whom "duration on earth is a value of the first order!"[12] this glorifier of the delirious Dionysian present, of the Sacred Moment, who also declares that it is not the strength but the duration of an elevated feeling that constitutes elevated men! The same man who believed that in every respect he brought not peace but the sword, who took pride in exultation ("I swear to you that in two years we will have the earth in convulsions"),[13] also confided to his own heart: "I want to give back to people the tranquility without which no culture can develop and endure. Even my style [should be] a reflection of this effort, a result of the most concentrated power of my nature."[14]

This cultural revolutionary and transvaluer—who counted Stifter's *Nachsommer* (Indian summer), the most blissfully tranquil work in all of German literature, among his most beloved books—took the great, productively self-renewing *duration* of the highest human values as his guiding dream. The mother of all human duration, however, its wellspring and guarantee, is memory. Memory created humanity, just as it has created every kind of human community. "Whoever has memory ought never to envy anyone"[15]—Goethe confided that remark to his diary not in retrospective old age but in his pre-Weimar days. To be in the midst of the most vital moment of youth and to remain respectfully mindful of that power whose magic alone expands the moment into eternity—if that is Goethean (and Goethean too is the lack of envy both in and based on the feeling of ownership that arises from the ability to commemorate)—then it is preeminently Nietzschean as well. Even despite the *Untimely Meditation* on "The Use and Disadvantage of History for Life," a work that should be understood and interpreted as a bold cure and antidote for his own inner temptation to indulge in an exaggerated idolization of all great traditions, of all merely retrospective memorializing—a romantic temptation. (As always with Nietzsche, here too he means and opposes an adversary that is external to himself only in the superficial sphere—namely his own desiccated era, bled dry by the all-too-historical urge; at a deeper level the book, like every one of these books that arose out of greater suffering than any others during his century, was a battle with himself, a struggle with his most pressing and most cherished danger, an act of self-defense and a sacrifice.) A gratitude for memory, a deliberate, self-consciously heightened and productively interpreted dependence on the past in biological, intellectual, and spiritual terms: on this, as on a firm psychological fact, rests a significant part of Nietzsche's intellectual life. The only one of the Old Tablets that the laboriously and artificially hardened hammer of his will left unbroken during certain radical periods in his life was the genealogical one. Duration, continuity, reverence for tradition as the basis of all culture, spirituality, humanity—here we have the most powerful fundamental ideas that attracted the young student at Schulpforta[16] to ancient philology, that transformed the free spirit of the *Human, All Too Human* into the visionary of *Zarathustra.* "Preservation of tradition is the main task," he wrote shortly after arriving in Basel; "a magnificent, unobstructed view from the heights. Both are eminently compatible."[17] "In revolutions everything is forgotten,"[18] Napoleon once said, and *therefore* Nietzsche hates everything revolutionary as perhaps no other person has ever hated it. The "will, instinct, and imperative"[19] of tradition lives deep within him, which in the *Twilight of the Idols* he identifies as the prerequisite for every lasting institution, a will that is "antiliberal to the point of malevolence: the will to tradition, to authority, to responsibility over the course of centuries, to solidarity with generational ties stretching backward and forward ad infinitum."[20] Tradition—so often nothing more than a refuge and rhetorical cover for creative impotence and senility—is here passion, intoxication, even demonic possession. None of our other thinkers betrays such obsession with ancestry coupled with such individualistic isolation, virtually none shows such a strongly pronounced "thinking in terms of generations." The old saying "woe be to you that you are a grandson" seems to be turned into its exact opposite: "Everything good is an inheritance"—those are some of the most deeply experienced words Nietzsche ever uttered, the most deeply rooted in his nature. "The good things," he was still saying even in the *Twilight of the Idols,* "are immoderately costly: and the law always applies that whoever *has* them is someone other than the one who *acquires* them. Everything good is an inheritance: whatever is not inherited is imperfect, is a beginning."[21] It is true that Zarathustra, by contrast, knows that it is dangerous to be an heir. But, for him, danger ennobles, danger legitimizes, it proves, gives evidence of value, danger *is* value. The danger of inheritance: that is for Nietzsche nothing other than the happiness, the distinction of inheritance.

This double feeling for heredity—that to be an heir is a blessing and a danger, that every heir is privileged and marked—is combined in a completely unparalleled fashion with Nietzsche's peculiarly strong and willfully emphatic sense of family. Every reader of Nietzsche feels the strangely conscious adherence to blood, the proud fatalism of his fantastical and strict love of ancestry, which only increases all the more as the years go by ("only in the man do the typical family traits become completely visible; they are least apparent in easily excitable, suggestible adolescents. Calm must have settled over them first,"[22] we read in the Notebooks for the *Transvaluation;* and there, too, even: "One is the child of one's four grandparents much more than of one's two parents. . . . The seeds of our grandfather's type become ripe within us, the seeds of our parents in our children").[23] He thought he owed the singularity of his nature, which was in every sense so extreme, to the particular mixture in his blood of opposing elements (opposed with regard to nationality, temperament, innate ethos, the degree of vitality), a biological mixture that he even amplified and stylized into something legendary, super-German, and half-German. Inheritance from two conflicting components defines his life for him as a task, a distinction, a fate. For the person standing under the most acute tensions suffers from and experiences life as a task of reconciliation, of uniting what cannot be united. He is the storm-laden cloud born of an antagonistic polarity, which can discharge itself to bring both ruin and fruitful blessings. *Ecce homo,* above all, plays on this theme, whose basic motif betrays the romantic musician, as unromantic as he would like its exposition to appear. But two years earlier, in a letter to his sister, Nietzsche already drew on the same basic sentiment when he spoke of "our true family type, which excels in reconciling contrasts."[24] And his sister herself once offered the opinion that her brother had his ideality from his father, but his sense of reality and his skepticism toward human affairs from his maternal forebears; Nietzsche, she claimed, felt this too. In the very first words of his autobiography, Nietzsche gave voice to a fundamental feeling of dependence on the particular ancestral mixture within him: "Why I am so wise. The good fortune of my existence, its singularity perhaps, lies in its fate: to express it in the form of a puzzle, I am already dead as my father, as my mother I am still alive and growing old. This dual descent, as it were, from the highest and lowest rungs on the ladder of life, at once décadent and a beginning—this, if anything, explains that neutrality, that freedom from any partiality with respect to the entire problem of life, which perhaps distinguishes me."[25] What gratitude, a few pages later, for the paternal heritage of his so extraordinary life: "I consider it a great privilege to have had such a father: it even seems to me that that explains all of the other privileges I have—*not* including life, the great Yes to life. Above all that there is no need for me to intend to do so, but merely to bide my time in order to enter involuntarily into a world of elevated and tender things: I am at home there, my innermost passion becomes free only there. . . . To understand even a little of my *Zarathustra* one must perhaps need to have a constitution similar to mine—with one foot *beyond* life." For an extremely strange feeling of mystical dependence, even of a mysteriously supercausal connection, links him with the early departed existence of his father: "My father died at the age of thirty-six: he was delicate, kind, and frail, like a creature allotted only a temporary stay—more a benevolent memory of life than life itself. In the same year in which his life declined, my own also declined: in the thirty-sixth year of my life I landed at the lowest point of my vitality—I was still alive but unable to see three steps ahead of me."[26] This mysteriously intensified repetition of the father's life in the life of his son is also echoed in *Zarathustra:* "What the father left unsaid is expressed in the son; and I have often found the son to be the father's disclosed secret."[27] A letter to Gast written in Genoa just at the time he was composing *Zarathustra* sounds mystical: "It is pouring rain, from the distance I hear music playing. *That* I like this music and *how* I like it is something I cannot explain from my own experience, rather from that of my father. And why should not—?"[28]—here the letter mysteriously breaks off. And another letter from the same time admits to Overbeck: "From my childhood on, the sentence 'my greatest danger lies in feeling pity' has been confirmed again and again—perhaps the evil consequence of the extraordinary nature of my father, whom everyone who knew him counted more among the 'angels' than among human beings."[29] Nietzsche's friend Deussen relates in his memoirs that during a visit to Sils Maria in August 1887 Nietzsche showed him a requiem (apparently the *Hymn to Life*) he had composed for his own funeral, and said: "I think that I will not last much longer; I am now at the age at which my father died, and I feel that I will succumb to the same affliction he did."[30]

But if such curious individual confessions tend to emphasize the danger, even the curse of his paternal heritage, the overall evaluation of this heritage still comes entirely out of a proud gratitude, out of something like a feeling of nobility. The conscious adherence to the family pride in "the racial quality of those who are named Nietzsche" accompanies him to the end of his days: "To prefer to die rather than to abandon one's cause: now that is Nietzschean!" he writes about his sister in 1887, to whom a year later he admits: "How strongly I feel in everything you say and do that we belong to the same race: you understand more about me than do others because your body shares the same origin. That fits very well with my 'philosophy.'"[31] Similarly, to his brother-in-law: "in summa, a *courageous* future awaits my sister. In all of that she resembles me: it appears this belongs to our race."[32] Or to his friend Gersdorff: "Our Nietzschean way, which I have been delighted to discover even in all of my father's siblings, takes delight only in its independence, knows how to occupy itself and sooner *gives* to people than asks much from them."[33]

The pride in his paternal race becomes materially and symbolically condensed in the legend, so dear to Nietzsche, of the Polish descent of his family. As we know, this hypothesis, which rests on extremely questionable genealogical grounds, made him, with all of its interpretive possibilities, almost touchingly happy. It seemed to distinguish and trace out his entire destiny, his mission, and his end. Nietzsche read into what was for him the certain fact of his super-German descent, of his dangerously brilliant hereditary mixture, a genealogical prophecy of himself, a shadowy "it is written," a fate. And in *Ecce homo* he does so with the unmistakable accent of a supremely fatalistic satisfaction that "the scripture has been fulfilled." The *amor fati*—"there is no alternative but to go on"—is also valid precisely with respect to the ancestral roots of his existence. But even as a boy he was preoccupied and enthralled by the legendary family tradition, elevated and unconsciously educated by the governing notion of a lineage that placed exceptional obligations on him. His sister explicitly attests to there having been nothing in their childhood environment that would have given rise to that idea; no one in the family, she says, attached any significance whatsoever to their noble descent. And, symptomatically enough, the only thing the young boy draws from this imaginary and lovingly cultivated ancestral legend is a morally binding conclusion. As his sister reports: "Truth and lie were, incidentally, the only matters in regard to which we both (I being influenced by my brother) expressed a certain arrogant awareness of our rank: we did not lie because it was improper for us, the Counts Nietzky, to do so. Others may lie as much as they wished, what befitted the two of us was: truthfulness." It was probably an observation of her brother that his sister added on this occasion with characteristic poise: "Perhaps a Nietzschean family trait emerged in us as class consciousness. I remember that one of our aunts once said with cool pride: 'We Nietzsches despise lying.'"[34] Several notes Nietzsche made during the first year he was composing *Zarathustra* relate the formative impression the ancestral legend had on the boy:

> I was taught to trace back the origin of my blood and name to Polish nobility. . . . I do not wish to deny that as a boy I derived no small pride from this, my Polish extraction. It almost seemed to me as if I essentially still remained a Pole . . . abroad, in Switzerland as well as in Italy, I was often addressed as a Pole. . . . A small notebook of mazurkas that I had composed as a boy carried the inscription "In remembrance of our forebears!"—and I did remember them in many of my judgments and prejudices. . . . It did me good to think of the right of the Polish nobleman to overturn the resolution of an assembly with his simple veto. And the Pole Copernicus seemed to me only to have made the greatest and most worthy use of this right against the conviction and visual evidence of every other human being. . . . In Chopin I especially admired that he had liberated music from all German influence.[35]

One easily senses the peculiar satisfaction with which Nietzsche here, as in other places (in *Ecce homo* in particular), supports his status as a "good European," his harsh cultural criticism, and his romantic, Hyperion-like[36] condemnation of everything German and all-too-German with the biological legitimacy, so to speak, of his Polish descent (for which there was in truth such scant evidence and that at best had been almost absorbed by his German ancestral components), and how he attempts to lend the supreme un-Germanness of his last years the air of a venerable necessity. (In the same way, Nietzsche's great philosophical teacher also loved to explain his so genuinely German inner universality through genealogical derivation. Schopenhauer's biographer even says of him: "He enjoyed no greater freedom from any other weakness than from that of national pride . . . he was ashamed, like many other great Germans before him, of being a German and was fond of recalling that his ancestors came from the Netherlands."[37] One sees that the apparently individualistic trait formed by Nietzsche's cult of his foreign ancestors is simultaneously as German as it is "philosophical.") But just as Nietzsche is, on the other hand, still "perhaps more German than the Germans of today, than mere Imperial Germans, can ever be—he, the last *antipolitical* German"[38] (*Ecce homo*), his pride in his maternal "very German" ancestry is also extremely characteristic. And there is something moving, sometimes almost slightly comical, about the degree to which, in *Ecce homo* as well as in the biographical outlines to his letters, he is at pains to align his maternal ancestors with the most important German cultural center: Weimar. "It may appear," he says with reference to his supposed Polish descent, "that I belong only among those who have a tincture of Germanness, but my mother, Franziska Oehler, is in any case something very German; the same is true of my grandmother on my father's side, Erdmuthe Krause. The latter lived throughout her entire youth in good old Weimar, not without contacts to Goethe's circle." (In a letter to Brandes that same year, he is already writing off-handedly, and in more stylized fashion: my grandmother belonged to the Schiller-Goethe circle in Weimar.)[39] "Her brother . . . was called to Weimar as the general superintendent after Herder's death. It is not impossible that her mother, my great grandmother, appears in the young Goethe's diary under the name 'Muthgen.' She married superintendent Nietzsche in Eilenburg. On the day Napoleon entered Eilenburg with his general staff, October 10 in the great war year of 1813, she had her confinement." (One notes here another of the countless examples of the ancestral obsession with dates and with the mysteriously prophetic confluence of events in world history with personal or family history.) "She was, as a Saxon, a great admirer of Napoleon; it could be that I am, too."[40] Perhaps even more peculiar and characteristic of Nietzsche's piety before values and criteria handed down within his family is his adherence to respect for certain dynastic ranks. He tells of his father's activity as an educator of princesses with a satisfaction that seems almost naïve. He mentions the "deep piety" his father felt for Friedrich Wilhelm IV: "the events of 1848 greatly afflicted him."[41] Nietzsche himself, born on the birthday of the aforementioned king, October 15, received, "as was appropriate," the Hohenzollern name Friedrich Wilhelm. One reads as if it were a touching anachronism in Nietzsche's own history the little confession in *Ecce homo*—so strange in the mouth of the poet of *Zarathustra,* for "of what account are kings anymore?"[42]—that his heart was drawn even closer to the town of Portofino and the surrounding landscape because of the great love that Emperor Friedrich III[43] felt for it. "I was coincidentally on that coast in the fall of 1886 when he visited that little forgotten world of happiness for the last time."[44] And, confronted by these long-preserved emotional remnants of an inherited legitimizing piety, one recalls the orally transmitted admission of the intellectual revolutionary Nietzsche who said that basically he found "everything illegitimate, in fact, abominable."[45] Legitimacy—what a sound in the mouth of the transvaluer! And yet not surprising—for it is after all a validation, a guarantee of continuity and duration. Nietzsche is indeed an admirer and proponent of legitimacy in its strongest and most original sense: in the sense of family, of blood, of ancestral lineage, even of consciously narrow and restrictive tradition, where by virtue of its one-sidedness it has an intensifying, cultivating, and preparatory effect. It appears strange only on the surface to hear Nietzsche justify pride in ancestry, the very man who proclaimed the "new nobility." But is not pride in one's ancestry also responsibility toward one's ancestry? And what could sound more Nietzschean than the word "responsibility"? An early passage already emphasizes such a responsibility toward one's ancestry: "One may be justifiably proud of an unbroken line of *good* ancestors down to one's father. . . . The descent from good ancestors is what constitutes genuine hereditary nobility. A single break in that chain, *one* bad ancestor, cancels hereditary nobility"[46] (*Human, All Too Human*). That is already terribly Nietzschean: the preciousness, the relative rarity of a good heritage rests on just this stipulation that there be an unbroken chain, a steady accumulation of a heritage through generations. "*One* bad ancestor cancels hereditary nobility"—perhaps no one had ever previously dared to define the concept of hereditary nobility so narrowly. But duration—that is, wholly unbroken tradition—is here, too, a value of the first importance for Nietzsche. The *Will to Power* puts it even more uncompromisingly: "There is only hereditary nobility, only nobility of the blood. (I am not speaking of that little word 'von' in the Gotha Kalender:[47] a parenthetical remark for idiots.) When people speak of 'intellectual aristocrats,' it usually means there is no shortage of reasons to keep something secret. It is, as we know, a favorite word among ambitious Jews. For intellect alone does not ennoble; rather, something else is required to ennoble intellect. What, then, is required? Blood."[48] But that kind of intellectual blood develops only through unbroken, continuous breeding: "There is no doubt: if a race of people has lived for generations as teachers, doctors, pastors, and role models without constantly looking out for money or honors or positions: then there finally arises a higher, finer, and more spiritual type. In this way a priest—provided that he propagates himself through strong women—is a kind of preparation for the future development of higher men"[49] (Notebooks to *Transvaluation*). For, as *Beyond Good and Evil* puts it, one cannot wipe away from the soul of a person what his ancestors had done continuously and did with gusto: "The offspring of shopkeepers are unseemly"[50] (Notebooks to *Zarathustra*). "Go in the footsteps in which your fathers' virtue has already traveled," Zarathustra advises the higher men; "how do you propose to climb higher if the will of your fathers does not climb with you? Whoever wants to be the first should be careful that he is not also the last! And you should not wish to see saints where the vices of your fathers are!"[51]

An autobiographical element, an analysis and appraisal of his own type, of his own ancestral history, clearly shimmer through such passages. It is significant enough that the Antichrist, who felt himself to be "the issue of entire generations of Christian ministers," sees in teachers, pastors, priests as a *caste* a kind of preparation for Zarathustra's higher men of the future. Indeed, he owes himself, the higher man within himself, to this ancestral wealth accumulated over whole generations: "It occurred to me, dear friend," he was still writing to Gast in 1881, "that the constant inner struggle with Christianity in my book (*Daybreak*) has to be foreign to you, even embarrassing: but it is the best example of ideal life I have encountered. Ever since I was a child I have inquired into it, looking into its every nook and crevice, and I believe that in my heart I have never been mean toward it. After all, I am the issue of entire generations of Christian ministers—forgive me this limitation!"[52] An ancestral piety that Zarathustra also shares with him: "There are priests here: and even if they are my enemies, go quietly past them and with sleeping sword . . . my blood is related to theirs; and I wish for my blood to be honored even in theirs."[53] Zarathustra is also an heir, and more of an heir than Zarathustra himself knows: a bridge backward perhaps even more than a bridge into the land of children. In the same way, an ancient priestly heritage, collected and handed down through the Old Testament, is rekindled for the last time in the most extraordinary words of his prophetic language—and then spends itself in belated rapture. But all people who live by the word, all prophets and all artists, "including orators, preachers, writers," are for Nietzsche heirs; both heirs and accumulated inheritance at once: "they all are people," as *The Gay Science* says, "who always come at the end of a long chain, in every case people born late . . . and in their essence squanderers. . . ."[54] They squander the surplus of the power and art of expression that had slowly accumulated within entire races and generational chains, wasting "a fortune that had been gradually amassed and now awaits an heir who will lavishly spend it."[55] In *Twilight of the Idols* he takes up this idea once again: "Great men are like explosives in which an incredible force has been stored up. Their prerequisite, historically and physiologically speaking, is that there must always be a long period of collection, accumulation, saving, and conservation leading up to them—that no explosion occurs for a long time."[56] The ability to be profligate, or rather the necessity of being profligate, thus constitutes the heir's happiness, his "giving virtue."[57] And it also constitutes his danger, insofar as he may easily turn out to be, in every respect, the end of the line; he may approach an abyss over which there are no more bridges leading to the future, except those composed of desire and delusion. To be expelled out of the accumulated inner heritage, to be made infertile for any further line, so that the youngest and richest link in the intellectual chain is also the last one—that is always the one imminent "danger of the heir." "The danger that lies within great people and great times is extraordinary," we read in *Twilight of the Idols;* "exhaustion of every sort, infertility are one step behind them. The great man is an end. . . . The genius—in his work, in his deed—is of necessity a squanderer: that he spends himself is his greatness."[58]

Yet for Nietzsche the other hereditary danger, more modern and less tragic, but almost even more imminent, is the possibility, even the increasing probability, of being the point of intersection between two long hereditary lines that conflict and will never inwardly merge. He grew convinced that he was falling into a problematic whirl in which two components, equally strong in their own way, are suddenly mixed. That is the specifically modern danger of the heir, and here too Nietzsche's analysis is only superficially detached and rationally cool. Mixture—in other words, the lack of a guiding and determining heritage and procreative will, in the biological and of course in the intellectual sense as well—that is the fatal modern predicament. "Biologically, modern man represents a contradiction of values, he sits between two chairs. He says yes and no with the same breath. . . . All of us have within us, against our knowledge and against our will, values, words, phrases, morals of conflicting origins—we are, viewed physiologically, *false*"[59] (*The Case of Wagner*). The mixture of contradictory values, in this sense, is the reason "why everything becomes play-acting—modern man lacks: a sure instinct (the result of a long, homogeneous form of activity engaged in by the same type of human being). The incapacity to produce something perfect is merely the result of that."[60] (*Will to Power*). For "even the most talented person can do no better than to experiment incessantly once the thread of development has been severed"[61] (*Human*). But the telltale sign of such inwardly conflicting origins, of such a struggle among heterogeneous forms of activity (whether they be within an individual, a class, or a cultural generation), and thus the stigma of modernity—is skepticism. "Skepticism," Nietzsche announces in *Beyond*, "is the most intellectual expression of a certain polymorphous physiological condition . . . it always arises whenever races or social classes that have remained separate for a long time are crossed in a sudden and decisive way. Everything in this new lineage, which inherits in its blood, as it were, different standards and values, is in a state of disquiet, disruption, doubt, experimentation. The best powers have an inhibiting effect, even the virtues do not allow themselves to grow and become strong. Both body and soul lack equilibrium, gravity, perpendicular sureness. But what becomes most gravely ill and degenerate in such people of mixed-blood is the *will*."[62]

That, too, is deeply autobiographical: no doubt, Nietzsche is also speaking of himself here, of a danger he has overcome, overcome thanks to the triumph of having taught himself a long will. He senses his own inner and perilous complication caused by the convergence of a long ancestral line, the inheritance of entire generations of Christian ministers, into which a sudden mixture has somehow been introduced, even if that had not occurred, as he assumed, in the more dramatic sense of a sudden atavistic reemergence of the Polish heritage in his blood. (One thinks of what he said about "reconciling contrasts" and about the parental opposites in *Ecce homo;* and one also remembers the broad and still-active Slavic strain in the biological and intellectual constitution of the people in Upper Silesia and their particular character—a fact that makes the Polish hypothesis all the more unnecessary, even as an explanation of the family name, and still permits almost the same assumptions and conclusions that Nietzsche made based on his genealogical legend.) The "good" that came from the slowly accumulated inheritance, supplying the powers he gratefully received and *forcefully employed,* was fatefully mixed in him with skepticism, bathing all experience in twilight and delivering a heavy blow to instinctive will, which Nietzsche observed in himself and fought against. The unprecedented shift in his intellectual and spiritual stance toward what were always the same, unchanging problems, which pursued him almost like Furies (" . . . nothing around me except my old problems, the old pitch-black problems"[63] [1886]), is a simplified symbol of the conflicting nature of his being, extending down into his ancestral roots, with its constitutive mixture of rigid, unquestioning loyalty and irascibly distrustful skepticism. He is himself, and saw himself as, the typical hybrid and liminal figure, and those dangers are his own. It is not merely coincidental, but of deep symbolic significance, that Nietzsche not only perceives the forefather of his own Zarathustra—namely the early Hellenistic prophet-philosopher Empedocles (to whom he, like Hölderlin, considered dedicating a tragedy and who was, next to Heraclitus, Nietzsche's earliest intellectual ancestor)—as the great all-loving unifier, the way Hölderlin did, but also characterizes him (in his lecture on the pre-Platonic philosophers) as a typical liminal figure in a passage that has strikingly autobiographical overtones: "He hovers between doctor and magician, between poet and rhetorician, between God and man, between scientist and artist, between politician and priest, between Pythagoras and Democritus . . ."[64] Two epochs struggle within him: the epoch of myth, of tragedy, of orgiastic frenzy, and that of the democratic politician, orator, enlightener, allegorist, scientific man. He has, as Nietzsche says elsewhere, a dual nature—he combines the agonistic, belligerent element with the loving one. The conscious experience of this Empedoclean discord even becomes a method of Nietzsche's thought: Darwin's law of atavism, of the particularly intellectual regression to prior ancestral stages and the consequences of crossbreeding such atavisms, the interpretation of an individual being or fact on the basis of its ancestry, the analysis of the heir—all of this serves as the most precious heuristic principle in Nietzsche's physiological investigations. (And how characteristic the very title is for the *Genealogy of Morals*! How partial and willful the method of this book is, or, for example, that of the chapter "What is Noble?" in *Beyond Good and Evil*! What genealogical investigative zeal and combinatory skepticism go into the making of the family tree of virtues and value judgments!) Indeed, he sometimes employs this means of seeing through and of hunting down things so furiously, he becomes so consumed by interpretive passion, that one can only conclude that the method is also a form of experience. *The Gay Science* offers perhaps the most evidence of this methodological passion, this peering into the "hidden gardens within us." "Many epochs seem to be entirely lacking this or that element, as do many people: but just wait until the grandchildren or great grandchildren appear, if one has the time to wait. They bring to light what lay within their grandfathers, those inner qualities of which even the grandfathers themselves were still ignorant. Often it is already the son who betrays his father: the latter understands himself better once he has had a son. We all have hidden gardens and thickets within us; and . . . we are all growing volcanoes that will have their hour of eruption."[65]

We find a typical example of the implementation of this method in the section from the same book, "On the Origin of Scholars." Entirely in keeping with the positivistic manner of his middle period, before he is "beyond" such things, Nietzsche almost systematically elucidates here the genealogical strata of the modern European scholarly class. The scholar, he writes, grows in all sorts of classes and social conditions like a plant that needs no particular kind of soil: thus the scholar essentially and involuntarily belongs to the supporters of the democratic idea. But this origin betrays itself:

> One will almost always be able to observe behind a scholar's intellectual idiosyncrasy—every scholar has one—his prehistory, his family, and especially their occupation and trade. Where the feeling is expressed: "now that this is proven, my job is done," it is usually the ancestor in the scholar's blood and instinct pronouncing the work good from his perspective. The belief in proof is only a symptom of what the hard-working classes have seen as "good work" from time immemorial. One example: the sons of actuaries and office clerks of every variety, whose main task it has always been to organize various materials, distribute them into files, and in general to systematize, all demonstrate, if they become scholars, a predilection for considering a problem virtually solved once they have placed it within a system . . . the formal aspect of their fathers' trade has become the content of theirs. The talent for classifying, for creating tables of categories, betrays something; there is always a penalty for being the child of one's parents. The son of a lawyer will also necessarily be a lawyer even as a scholar: he will be principally concerned that he be proven right, and perhaps secondarily that he is right. One recognizes the sons of Protestant ministers and school teachers by the naïve certainty with which they,

> as scholars, regard their case as having already been proven if they have presented it with animation and warmth: for the simple reason that they are so thoroughly accustomed to being believed—that was part of their fathers' métier. A Jew, on the other hand, in accordance with the business circles and the entire past of his people, is the least accustomed to being believed. Just consider Jewish scholars—they all think extremely highly of logic, in other words of compelling agreement through reasons . . . even when racial and class-based aversion toward them is present, even when people unwillingly believe them.[66]

And he uses this biological interpretive method almost to the point of parody, as for instance in his analysis of Darwinian dogmatism:

> The fact that our modern natural sciences have become so entwined with Spinozistic dogma (with the so-called instinct of self-preservation, most recently and crudely in Darwinism, with its incomprehensibly one-sided doctrine of the struggle for survival—) is probably due to the origins of most natural scientists: they belong in this respect to "the people." Their ancestors were poor and humble people who knew all too well the difficulty of getting by. Something like the bad air of English overpopulation, the little-people smell of want and closeness, wafts about all of English Darwinism. But, as a natural scientist, one ought to get out of one's human cubbyhole: and scarcity does not prevail in nature, but rather abundance, even extravagance to the point of absurdity.[67]

He detects a similarly atavistic law in the type represented by German scholars: "The German scholars who invented the historical sense reveal, every last one of them, that they do not come from any ruling caste; they are, as inquirers, impertinent and lack a finer sense of shame"[68] (Notebooks to *Transvaluation*).

Yet Nietzsche does not of course see his law of heredity at work primarily in the petty and negative sphere: it is important to demonstrate that precisely what is rare and precious is an inheritance. And thus the most precious thing, the significant person, is for him in itself atavistic—as one can see, an almost romantic-reactionary train of ideas. He conceives of rare people of a period (in *The Gay Science*) "preferably as late offshoots of past cultures and their energies that suddenly spring up: as the atavism, so to speak, of a people and its customs. . . . Now they appear alien, exotic, extraordinary: and whoever feels these forces within himself has to nurture them, defend, honor, and cultivate them against another world that is resistant to them. And he will thus become either a great man or an insane and eccentric one, provided he does not simply die young. . . . The families and castes that conserve a people," Nietzsche continues, still characteristically and here, too, in latently autobiographical fashion, "are principally those in which such aftergrowths of old instincts appear, whereas there is no probability that such atavism will occur where races, habits, values change too rapidly."[69]

Nietzsche thus defines the mission of families and castes that conserve a people in an extremely aristocratic sense—an aristocracy once-removed, as it were: they should not merely steadily preserve a precious type, they should instead maintain the possibility of the rare person, of the person who does not take after his immediate predecessors, but instead embodies a very old cultural heritage and the most distant biological memory. They should continue to enable such reemergence and regrowths of ancient, precious instincts and drives within an increasingly rapid democratic mixture of races, habits, and values. Following his favorite idea to its logical conclusion, the atavistic person thus advances to the highest category in the biological scale of values. For, according to a Notebook fragment, a family, a caste, a race *can,* "like any other organic form, only grow or die; there is no stasis. A race that has not died out is a race that has constantly grown. Growing means becoming perfect. Duration in the existence of a race necessarily determines how high it will develop: the oldest race *must* be the highest."[70] For that reason the rarest people are always the people with the longest inner memory. He therefore regards Jews as "the strongest race in our uncertain Europe: for they are superior to the rest owing to the length of their development"; thus "Jew [is] practically a word for superiority."[71] That great men "come to rule over their time is solely due to the fact that they are stronger, that they are *older,*" *The Twilight of the Idols* tells us. "Between a genius and his time there exists a relationship as between . . . old and young: his time is always relatively speaking much younger, thinner, more immature, more uncertain and more childish."[72] For that reason, "because Napoleon was *different,* the heir of a stronger, longer, older civilization than the one that went up in smoke and flames in France, he became the ruler there, he *was* the ruler there alone."[73] The atavistic person is necessarily a ruler, is necessarily even a Caesar—that is the extreme consequence of this theory promoting the primacy of biological memory.

And it is just as logical that, within this highest caste of rare individuals, of the *papabili*[74] of their time, Nietzsche also elevates philosophers into the noblest rank, implicitly aligning them with the Caesars, as those with the most comprehensive memory (memory of blood and of mind), as the abbreviated chronicle and vital self-remembrance of humanity. On the basis of the knowledge he had gained through experience about the proud mercilessness of all inherited inner hierarchies, he categorically concluded in the section "We Scholars" in *Beyond:* "One must be born for every elevated world; expressed more clearly, one must be *bred* for it: one has a right to philosophy—taking the word in its larger sense—

only by virtue of one's descent; one's ancestors, one's 'blood,' are decisive here, too. Many generations must have preceded the emergence of a philosopher. Every one of his virtues must have been individually acquired, nurtured, passed on, internalized, and not merely the bold, light, delicate gait and course of his thoughts, but above all the readiness for great responsibilities, the majesty of a commanding gaze and overview . . . the joy and proficiency in administering grand justice . . ."[75]

Beyond the prerequisites of blood and breeding, Nietzsche goes on to refine the idea of ancestry as an increasingly intellectual and spiritual category, so that his proud gratitude for a distinguished parental inheritance ultimately finds a magnificent transformation into a consciousness of a mystical ancestral lineage of intellectual blood. "My pride is: I have an *origin*"—we read in some critical personal remarks made during the *Zarathustra* years—"for that reason I do not need fame. I already live in the same element that moved Zarathustra, Moses, Mohammed, Jesus, Plato, Brutus, Spinoza, Mirabeau, and many things are coming to fruition in me that slumbered embryonically for a few millennia. We are the first aristocrats in the history of the mind—the historical sense is beginning only now."[76] And farther on, in a variation of this idea of intellectual ancestry, he writes with the pride of a grandson: "When I speak of Plato, Pascal, Spinoza, and Goethe, I know that their blood courses through my own—I am proud when I speak the truth about them—the family is good enough not to have to invent or conceal anything: and I therefore stand by all that has happened, I am proud of humanity and proud precisely because of this absolute truthfulness."[77] Finally, in tightly compressed form, he sketched a last ancestral lineage during the time he was composing *Zarathustra:* "My ancestors Heraclitus, Empedocles, Spinoza, Goethe."[78]

It is the most genuine, the oldest, the most noble ancestral lineage in the world that points toward Zarathustra and advances beyond him toward the descendent constellation of the overman. Their connection is closer, older, more mysterious than that of any ancestral bloodline. For it is the creative mind, whose broad vision integrates the world into a philosophical and religious survey—which those last-named great four symbolize perhaps most purely—who is the most powerful form on earth in which the law of atavism, of the secret great-grandsondom, manifests itself; indeed he is the form of a Heraclitean return of the same in the intellectual sphere, of a Platonic recollection of a primeval vision. *Beyond* puts it this way: all philosophers "always follow anew the same orbital path as if under an invisible spell: they may feel as independent from each other as they wish with their critical or systematic will, something in them leads them, something pushes them along after each other in a particular order. . . . Their thinking is in fact not so much a process of discovery as it is one of recognition, remembering, a return and home-coming to a distant, ancient universal habitat of the soul. . . . In this respect, philosophizing is a kind of atavism of the first order."[79] And, in a less Platonic context, a similar law applies to the artist: in *Human, All Too Human* we read that people will soon "regard him as a magnificent relic and pay him the kind of respect that we do not readily show people such as ourselves, because we will view him as a wondrous stranger on whose strength and beauty the happiness of earlier times depended. The best thing about us is perhaps inherited from sentiments passed down from earlier times and to which we are now almost no longer able to gain immediate access."[80]

How strongly and, above all, how extensively the idea of atavism dominates Nietzsche is demonstrated even more clearly, perhaps, by the minor but revealing tendencies of his associative thinking. A strange need for symbols of his intellectual ancestral history, for mystical harbingers and omens of his own destiny, for a legitimizing integration into a great fate, for veiled divine signs and prophesies pointing to himself, is rooted deeply in his being, to a degree that reminds one of the ancients. Many passages in his works and letters speak almost euphorically of such fragments of a pre-individual biography, of oracular clues and of coincidences fulfilling the oracles. A humanistic as well as theological intellectual heritage is revealed in this predilection. Just as one observes typological juxtapositions of prophetic scenes from the Old Testament with scenes depicting their fulfillment in the New Testament on old stained-glass windows and altarpieces—a practice of erecting thematic parallels still used in sermons today—the grandson of entire generations of Christian ministers unconsciously applies this Christian, mythological technique of preaching and graphic description to the text of his own life until, in *Ecce homo,* he quite consciously treats it as a legend, while subtly lending it even deeper meaning. No amount of evangelistic zeal can match the passion in seeking out exegetical intellectual linkages of this sort that Nietzsche displays in looking for such minor, often miniscule associations and connections with dates that, occasionally in almost Strindbergian fashion, allow him to appear to be linked in a very special way with "forces," forces that govern his destiny. This desire to integrate himself into a mystical tradition is probably the most peculiar aspect of Nietzsche's ancestor cult. "I was born on the battlefield of Lützen. The first name I ever heard was Gustav Adolf"[81] (to Brandes, 1888). His father was born in 1813 on the same day Napoleon entered the small Saxon country town in which his grandfather worked as superintendent. Nietzsche does not fail to mention in his little résumé for Brandes that his pulse rate was as low as that of the first Napoleon: exactly sixty.[82] (In the same way, he even "sees an abundance of symbolism and significance" in the "physiological perfidy"[83] of his illnesses.) His great-grandmother appears in the adolescent Goethe's diary. In 1865, he coincidentally enters his name into the registry of the University of Leipzig on the very day Goethe had inscribed his own there one hundred years before.[84] And the twenty-three-year-old student writes two years later: "I cannot tell you what a refreshing effect this coincidental event had on me. It was definitely a good omen for my Leipzig years, and the future provided that it could rightly be called a good omen."[85] His first encounter with Schopenhauer's magnum opus, which was decisive in every sense, did not take place without a demonic shadow being cast over it. He finds the book, with which he was completely unfamiliar, in a secondhand bookshop in Leipzig. "I don't know which daemon whispered to me: take this book home with you. In any case, I did, despite my usual habit of not rushing into the purchase of a book." This he writes when he was still a student in Leipzig. During the same time, he says to Rhode: "How much we are both really traveling down the same path was again made clear to me by a truly amusing synchrony. That is, we were both steeped in romanticism at exactly the same time and were greedily inhaling familiar and congenial fragrances without either one of us knowing about the abnormal pursuits of the other" ("abnormal"—because the date was 1868). "To call something like that a coincidence would be a sin against the sacred spirit of Schopenhauer."[86] After the publication of *The Birth of Tragedy:* "The first notice of my book has also appeared and it is very positive—but where? In the Italian *Revista Europea!* That is nice and symbolic!"[87] In later years Nietzsche thought the experience of Wagner particularly rich in such prophetic acts of providence. When the Basel-based acolyte went to Tribschen for the first time and long stood in front of the villa before entering, he heard coming from inside a painful accord, repeated again and again.[88] It was, as Nietzsche later discovered, the passage from the third act of *Siegfried:* "Verwundet hat mich, der mich erweckt" ("He wounded me who awakened me").[89] "By a miracle of meaning in coincidence," on the same day he sent his Voltairean *Human, All Too Human* to Wagner, Nietzsche received a beautiful copy of the *Parsifal* score: "To his dear Friend Friedrich Nietzsche, Richard Wagner, Member of the Church Council." This crossing of the two books—to him it seemed to strike an ominous note. "Did it not sound as if swords were crossing? We both certainly thought so, for we both remained silent."[90] The final section of *Zarathustra* was "finished at exactly the same sacred hour that Richard Wagner died in Venice. . . ." The overtones of his fateful connection with Wagner are still clearly audible in the few lines he wrote to Gast just after receiving word of his death: "The news of his death has just arrived from Genoa. I came here today without any reason and have just bought, as is not my custom, the evening edition of the *Caffaro,* which had just appeared. My first glance fell on the telegram from Venice."[91] He was shaken by the massive earthquake in Ischia in a particularly "horrible way: this island has been so much on my mind: when you have read *Zarathustra* II to the end, it will be clear to you *where* I sought my blissful islands. 'Cupido dancing with the maidens' is immediately understandable only in Ischia. . . . I had only just completed my poem, and the island collapsed onto itself." And, entirely under the spell of these mystical connections, he then adds: "You know that in the hour that I completed the final manuscript of the first part of *Zarathustra,* Wagner died. This time I received at the same hour news that so offended me that there will probably be a duel with pistols this autumn"[92] (1883 to Gast). In the last letters from the euphoric period at the end of 1888, this mysticism intensifies: "There are no more coincidences: if I think of someone, a letter from him politely walks through the door. . . ."[93] "In my life now there are curious instances of meaning in coincidence that have no parallel. . . ."[94]

In the same way, Nietzsche also likes to view the places he chooses to live—his "residences"—as being overshadowed with ancestral significance. Indeed, he occasionally makes his choice based on the need for such significant and propitious reminiscences. In Rome, the most obscene place in the world for the poet of *Zarathustra,* he becomes exceedingly agitated: "I tried to get away—I wanted to go to Acquila, the antithesis of Rome, which was founded out of hostility toward Rome, just as I will found a place one day that will be a memorial to one of my closest relatives, the great Hohenstaufen emperor Frederick the Second, an atheist and enemy of the Church *comme il faut.* But the whole thing was a disaster: I had to go back. I finally settled for the Piazza Barberini after my efforts to find an anti-Christian area exhausted me."[95] "So now I am back in my good city of Turin, the city that Gobineau[96] also loved so well—it probably resembles us both."[97] "In the end, there must be some element here in Turin that imparts energy: if one feels at home here, one becomes the King of Italy. . . ."[98] Writing to Gast from Genoa about *Daybreak,* which he completed there, he says not many books were as substantial: "Am I now speaking as the father of the book? I don't think so. It seems to me that my three Genovese patron saints, Columbus, Mazzini, and Paganini, all had a slight hand in it."[99] When he was writing *Zarathustra,* he wished he could build a wooden cottage on the Chasté peninsula that juts into Lake Sils, "where a Roman camp once stood"[100]—in reality, there is evidence only of some sparse remains of a medieval stronghold—just as the young *mulus*[101] loved to visit Roman roads or the ruins of Roman forts during his first trip along the Rhine. In 1885, he wanted most of all to go to Corsica, "and in particular to Corte, my residence, or so it has seemed to me for the last four years that I have had this notion. It was there that Pasqualae Paoli, the most well-rounded man of the previous century, was lord of the island; it is the place for great conceptions (Napoleon was conceived there in 1768: he was only born in Ajaccio!)"[102] One year later, again: "Corte is the city of Napoleon's conception. . . . Does it not seem that a pilgrimage there would be an appropriate preparation for the 'Will to Power. Toward a Transvaluation of all Values'?"[103] And he even perceives the Engadine landscape, "with a pleasant shudder," as a double of himself, "inwardly familiar and related to me by blood, indeed even more than that."[104]

Finally, we may also recall here the many instances of *back-dating* that serve to stylize his own life. These efforts to push back certain impressions or intellectual experiences into the dawn of his existence are typical of Nietzsche, these attempts to make the child, in an especially intensive manifestation of Goethe's dictum, appear to be the father of the man. His own life is, so to speak, lengthened backward by deepening his perspective into its earliest nebulous period, plunged into the enchanted atmosphere of his own ancestry. "At an absurdly early age, at seven," he already knew that "a human word would never reach"[105] him. "I must be deeply related to Byron's Manfred: I found all of those chasms within myself—I was ready for this work at thirteen."[106] He once wrote to his sister that even as a child he had seen the figure of his Zarathustra in a dream. On another occasion: "At twelve I saw God in his glory"[107]—the expression of a strong, half-conscious drive toward self-stylization in the guise of legend, as the ideal type, as the founder of a religion. Similarly, when the printing of five hundred thousand Christian hymnals delayed the publication of *Zarathustra* in what he thought was an act of malicious symbolism, he actually writes to Gast, only half ironically: "These are entirely the experiences of a 'founder of religion'!"[108] Even as a thirteen-year-old boy, he is pursued by the problem of the origin of evil. At an age at which one is "half preoccupied with children's games, half with God,"[109] he dedicated his first literary child's game, his first philosophical exercise to it—"and, with regard to my 'solution' of the problem at the time, well, as is only fair, I gave God the honor and made him the *father* of evil. Was it my 'a priori' that wanted that from me?" Nietzsche adds in highly characteristic fashion, "that new, immoral, at least immoralistic a priori . . . to which I have since increasingly lent an ear and not only an ear?"[110] When he performs *Parsifal* for his sister in Naumburg in 1882, he is overcome by a strange sensation of encountering a double of himself. He suddenly knows that he made exactly the same kind of music as a boy, when he composed his *Oratorium*—"and just now I took out those old papers," he writes excitedly to Gast, "and played them again for the first time in a long while: the identity of mood and expression was magical! A few passages, such as the Death of the Kings, seemed even more moving to us both than everything we had played from *Parsifal,* yet still very Parsifalesque! I admit: it was a genuine shock to realize once again how closely I am related to Wagner."[111] "As a boy I was a pessimist, as ridiculous as that sounds," we read in a note from the introductory drafts written in his final years; "several lines of music from my twelfth or thirteenth year are, of all of the pitch-black music I know, fundamentally the blackest and most uncompromising. I have never found thoughts or words by any poet or philosopher that so clearly emanated from the abyss of absolute negation."[112] In a retrospective note written around the same time, he even detects an early indication of a kind of turning away from Wagner: "As a boy I loved Händel and Beethoven: but when I was seventeen *Tristan und Isolde* came along as a world I could understand, whereas I felt that *Tannhäuser* and *Lohengrin* were already 'beneath my taste'—boys are quite shamelessly proud in matters of taste."[113]

Finally, this need for such ennobling back-dating manifests itself even with regard to his relationship to his own books, about which he says in the second preface to *Human* in 1886: "All of my writings, with a single, albeit important, exception, should be back-dated: they always speak of a Behind-me. . . ."[114] That is the tendency of *Ecce homo,* in which Nietzsche deliberately creates an artificial perspective, a conscious distance from himself in order to win the right to his own legend, so that he may already see the "I" still bound by flesh as the progenitor of his future, more spiritualized form.

This peculiar inclination and ability to think and visualize in ancestral form, above all to visualize *himself,* reveals, even in the smallest details, that it is a matter of instinctive will and not a retrospective pastime of the trained historian. For it is obvious that Nietzsche's proud or reverential ancestor cult is completely different from either a merely historicizing inclination or a passively tinged determinism, a feeling of being oppressed by an ancestral fate, which during his productive years often determined fashions in public thinking under the influence of Darwinian ideas. Even less than for Goethe, the phrase, "You must be thus, you cannot flee yourself"[115] contained nothing fatalistically paralyzing for Nietzsche during any of his phases. True, he becomes an increasingly determined fatalist the closer he comes to the *fatum* that lurks behind *Ecce homo.* But that is an active fatalism, it is not the resigned but the joyfully convalescent *amor fati,* which also characterizes his attitude toward all "illness," all inadequacy within the course of his life. Two things decisively elevate his belief in ancestry above mere determinism. The first is the strong imperative of the will regarding a responsibility toward time, that will to authority, to accountability for centuries hence, to solidarity with linked generations running backward and forward in time ad infinitum; the responsibility that thinks in terms of generations and creates its image in the pedagogical idol, the edifying phantasm of Zarathustra, and finds its highest and most challenging formula in the word overman. "It was also there that I picked up the word overman, and that man . . . is a bridge,"[116] out of the affirmed past across into the greater Yes of his future. The second, however, is that every remnant of determinism in the passive, resigned sense is destroyed by the absolute attitude of the will not only to the future but also to the past, through a prophetically tinged will to redeem the past, a redemption in which everything that has been is not negated, but rather intensified. Confronted by this will, the past is not only a parable and a hesitant pre-dream of future possibilities; it is a creation of the poet-prophet himself, not merely an interpretation, but instead a true fiction. The romantic adage that the historian is a backward-looking prophet acquires here for the first time the true depth of its meaning. And Zarathustra, who asks himself if he is someone who makes promises or fulfills them, if he is a conqueror or an heir, an autumn or a plowshare—a poet or a truth-teller, answers himself: "I walk among men as among the fragments of the future: that future which I see. And in all of my poems and works I aim to unify and gather together what has remained as fragment and riddle and horrid coincidence . . . as poet, riddle solver and redeemer of coincidence, I taught them to work on the future and thereby to redeem everything that *was*. . . ."[117] To redeem the people in the past and to recast every "It was" into a "I willed it thus!"—this redemption and fulfillment of all ancestral reverence through an active fatalism, this memory that is not sentimental but volitional, makes the stance of Nietzsche the historian, of the backward-looking prophet, an entirely unique phenomenon in all of intellectual history. Hardly anywhere else in his work does that delirium of synthesis, the drunkenness in unifying what cannot be unified, which is his romantic heritage, appear to reach such a stirring ecstasy of will—except in relation to his own past, to illness and the deficiencies of his own self. The synthesis-loving sense of transport from being the interpretive middle between the past and the future, the happiness of being the bridge of the high noon between what was and what will be, is peculiar to Nietzsche not only after he wrote *Zarathustra,* even though it is augmented and transformed to the point of rapture then and during the last year of *Ecce homo.* As early as in the second *Untimely Meditation,* he applies with perfect clarity the "measure of the middle," that highest power of the present and of the divine moment, to the past, so that already at this point the true historian is described and proclaimed as a prophet facing backward and standing upright: "Whoever has not experienced some things more greatly and more exaltedly than everyone else will also not know how to interpret anything great and exalted from the past. The utterances of the past are always oracular: you will understand them only if you are architects of the future, initiates of the present."[118] "You may interpret the past only out of the greatest power of the present."[119] "One ought to know today that only he who builds the future has a right to judge the past."[120] And, again with full clarity, *The Gay Science* states not the demand but the law that every great man has a *retroactive* power: "All history is placed in the balance again for his sake, and a thousand secrets crawl out of their hiding places into *his* sun. There is no end to the things that might become history again"—that is the most decisive pronouncement Nietzsche made on the philosophy of history. "The past perhaps still remains essentially undiscovered! So many more retroactive forces are still needed!"[121] The historian does not describe history, he creates the past: history is creation, what has been is a becoming. "Zarathustra does not want to *lose* any of humanity's pasts, he wants to cast everything into the mold,"[122] reads a passage from the materials for *Zarathustra;* he wants "to make the old sacrifices to a new spirit, to transform the old soul through a new body."[123]

Yet Nietzsche's distrustful intellectual conscience does not allow him to overlook the dangers that unavoidably grow out of such a will to dissolve and transform, out of this intense desire to interpret and uncover the past. What if the knowledge of the magical ability of this retroactive power to awaken the dead should stir the desire to possess it, if its possession would tempt him to use it as a means to personal, solely personal ends? If it eventually became, even latently, half-consciously, a magic of the most villainous ambition, a black magic to lure a thousand secrets of the past from their hiding places into none other than his own sun? What if the orphic leader of souls and abductor of shades from the Hades of the past became a cunning Pied Piper who would force all of the souls craving resurrection into the magic mountain[124] of his own glorification? Nietzsche was not unaware of this diabolic temptation. The intellectual history of his century offered him more than one illustrative example of the magnificent perspectival violation of the past by a powerful will, a philosophical and artistic will to interpret and resurrect, a will that believes all roads from yesteryear perspectivally converge within itself, that imperiously forces the waters of all that has been to rush through the narrows of his own ego. In the intellectual atmosphere of early romanticism, which was still close to Goethe and to which Nietzsche's thinking is deeply indebted (without him ever realizing to what degree of inner identity), it was a fundamental tenet that, as Novalis has it, the world originally is the way I want it; that the world has an originary capacity to be animated through me. In Schopenhauer's proudly reverential establishment of his intellectual lineage in *The World as Will and Representation,* which brilliantly unites Goethe and Kant, Plato and India, and even more in Hegel's sovereign construction of a pyramid of the spiritual world from above leading up to his own standpoint at the summit—in all of these Nietzsche had the most powerful and dangerous examples imaginable of such a subjugation of the past by intellectual despots. And in his most immediate and painfully personal proximity, moreover, there was the spectacle of an artist with an insatiable desire for a legitimate intellectual ancestry, for an almost theological confirmation of his own Good News, which always needs some sort of Old Testament with prophetic figures and typological premonitions. More than anything else: Nietzsche senses and recognizes this tempter within himself. He knows the temptations of Zarathustra, the burning, jealous desire of Catiline to see himself as Caesar, the tragic envy all predecessors feel toward heirs, their own heir—"If I had been my own grandson!"[125] was Napoleon's revealing sigh at the end of his trajectory—and from the most human proximity, he knows the nearly superhuman sacrifice that the Bible has John the Baptist perform: "He must increase, but I must decrease."[126] He knows the inextinguishable, malevolent ambition of Macbeth, which wants to conquer and violate not merely the future but also the past. "Above all, one must take care to secure the spirit in which history is to be written"—that was the maxim of the Corsican Caesar, Catiline. That is the most devious wisdom of ambition, which *Human, All Too Human* sees through: "Because people actually respect only what was established long ago and has slowly come into being, whoever wants to live on after his death must therefore ensure not only that he has offspring, but even more that he has a *past,* which is why tyrants of every sort (including tyrannical artists and politicians) like to do violence to history, so that it appears to be a preparation and stepladder leading to themselves."[127] This magnificently purposeful will to the past, to an intellectual ancestry, is most clearly exemplified for Nietzsche, together with all of its dangers, in the figure of Wagner, that cultural Condottiere who was hungrier for the joys of legitimacy than any other artist before him. Aiming more precisely at Wagner, another passage of *Human* concentrates this idea further: "There are people who are so presumptuous that the only way they can think of praising a great man, whom they publicly admire, is to portray him as a preliminary stage and bridge *to themselves.*"[128] Finally, Wagner's obsession with ancestry—in response to which Nietzsche indirectly attacks the same tendency and danger inherent in himself, as is always the case when the timbre of his voice becomes ill-tempered, when his observations become vindictively sharp—is characterized with consummate pitilessness in the preliminary studies to *Richard Wagner in Bayreuth:* "It was a particular form of Wagner's ambition that he placed himself in relation to the great men of the past: to Schiller and Goethe, Beethoven, Luther, the Greek tragedians, Shakespeare, Bismarck. Only the Renaissance resisted his efforts to establish a connection with it. But he invented the German spirit in opposition to the Romanic one. Interesting characterization of the German spirit in his image."[129] Even in *Zarathustra,* we encounter the image of this Wagnerian thirst for power over everything great from the past, the desire to reinterpret everything that was as a bridge to oneself: "A great despot could come, a shrewd fiend, who would unconditionally force and compel the entirety of the past to submit until it became a bridge to him and portent and herald and cock's crow."[130] And thus, significantly, Zarathustra's first gesture of compassion is toward all of the past that he sees: "it is at the mercy of—the benevolence, the spirit, the madness of every generation that is to come and that reinterprets everything that was as its own bridge!"[131] But a lack of ancestry, a lack of reverence for the past, immediately becomes again the other impending danger and Zarathustra's other object of compassion: "whoever is of the rabble thinks back to his grandfather—but time ceases with his grandfather. Thus all of the past is imperiled: for it could happen one day that the rabble will be in control and all of time will drown in shallow waters."[132] The past can be redeemed from both dangers by one thing only: "For that reason . . . a new nobility is needed that is an adversary of both the rabble and all despots."[133]

This new nobility, equally distant from intellectual tyranny and spiritual ochlocracy,[134] is embodied for Nietzsche in none other than Zarathustra, the longed-for ideal and chimera of a thousand-year predecessor and heir of himself. He sees in Zarathustra the man composed of a historical and prophetic synthesis, the man of the longest will and the longest memory; the new initiate who intensifies his sorrowful knowledge about all that has passed into an affirmative view of the future, the poet who uses the integrative power of his intuition to bestow the gift on the past of simplifying its indistinct aspect by raising it up into the fertile realm where the future is anticipated. Such a poet-prophet would be the actual overman that Zarathustra teaches, that is, the man of that true future humanity that, prior to *Zarathustra,* appears as a vision as early as in *The Gay Science.* There, the first stage of that envisioned humanity is found in nothing other than the "peculiar virtue and illness called 'the historical sense'": the man

> who knows how to feel the history of mankind in its entirety as *his own history.* . . . The man with a horizon of millennia stretching in front of him and behind him, who is the heir, the legal heir, of the accumulated refinement from all past spiritual distinction, who is the most aristocratic of all the old noblemen and simultaneously the first-born of a new nobility, the likes of which no era has ever seen or dreamed of: to take all of this onto his soul, the most ancient and the most modern things, the losses, hopes, conquests, victories of humanity; and to have, finally, all of this in a single soul and compress it into a single feeling—that would have to result in a happiness that man has never known before—a god's happiness full of power

> and love, full of tears and full of laughter . . . this divine feeling would then be called—humanity![135]

With that, in a last bold ascendant turn, Nietzsche achieves an ultimate triumph of the "reconciliation of contrasts" that he had found characterized his family type; it stands as one of those exemplary syntheses that allow Nietzsche to experience his most profound intellectual joys. In the idea of highest humanity he sees the unification of history and prophecy, in the image of the new aristocracy both ancestry and childhood. That is the meaning of Nietzsche's self-characterization as the first aristocrat, it is the actual content of his paradoxical utterance that there would be a historical sense only after him (even though, in the beginning, he himself had protested against its suffocating excesses). Prophecy directed at the past, the yearning for ancestors projected into the future—that is Nietzsche's divine feeling of humanity. The mature individual who, conscious of his responsibility, shoulders the entire burden of human tradition, who is the highest point in the arch of the bridge spanning what was and what will be, the divine moment "on the high pass," like Zarathustra, "between two oceans, traveling between the past and the future like a heavy cloud,"[136]—that is Nietzsche's man of the true future humanity. The poet is, in his view, the creator of the past, the founder of all that remains;[137] the philosopher, however, and the sage are the preachers and the seekers of the future: "Whoever has become wise reflecting on old origins," Zarathustra says, "behold, he will eventually look for sources of the future and for new origins."[138] To redeem the past by interpreting it affirmatively as the cradle of the future; to work at constructing the future by building a vaulted crypt that will provide a permanent sanctuary for the powers of belief throughout centuries—with that, the grand fusion takes place that merges Nietzsche's early "philological" ideals with the Dionysian ecstatic dream of Zarathustra's demanding will. There occurs a marriage, not a compromise, of apparent opposites, in the final sense of that pure "humanistic" humanity in which Nietzsche's earliest education began and back into which the best aspects of his influence flowed and lived on. It is a humanity that is, in a Goethean sense, devoid of envy, devoid because this humanity alone is permitted to preserve the highest human good and simultaneously to raise it even higher: memory, that most noble, atavistic power that alone elevates us to the height of Platonic recollection, uniting us both backward and forward with the timelessly divine.

2

Knight, Death, and Devil

. . . You, sir, are the Knight!
. . . He feels the tremendous shift of time . . .
What *was* and what *will be* struggle in his soul,
like a pair of intertwined wrestlers gasping hard for breath.
His mind is the battlefield of two epochs—
I am not surprised that he sees demons!
—Conrad Ferdinand Meyer, *Hutten's Last Days*[1]

Ultimately, the romantic man of the north wants, as in Schopenhauer's metaphysics, to fathom the essence of the world by hearing it as music, not to comprehend it by grasping it as form. Nietzsche, who considered himself "too much of a musician not to be a romantic,"[2] was not as remote from the sensual sphere as many have thought. But he admits himself: I am very unphysical. "Representations of historical scenes, human beings in motion, always leave me cold."[3] Only landscape paintings can put him in a "calm and expectant" mood; they place him in that heightened state of vaguely hopeful euphoria that tends to precede his productive periods. All figurative arts remain remote to him; their joys in and of the present are denied to this questing, change-loving spirit, whose musician's gaze is trained inward. People have looked in vain for even the tiniest trace of an impression that might have been made on the boy by the immense space of the cathedral in Naumburg, for example, with its dual choirs and its noble and severe Romanic sculptures of donors; nowhere is there a hint of the Gothic cloister atmosphere of Schulpforta. In the exuberantly descriptive letters from the young student at Bonn, in the enthusiastic reports about his trips to Cologne that are laden with musical details—not a word about the interior of the cathedral or about the most beautiful Romanic architecture north of the Alps. Out of Basel we hear nothing about the peculiar architectural physiognomy of that ancient city, with its mix of imperial and bourgeois styles. We do not even hear the great name that, if Nietzsche were even slightly visually attuned, would have had to strike him as congenial no less in his guise as psychologist than in his role as super-German—namely that of the master Hans Holbein.[4] If Nietzsche ever does mention a particular painting, say by Raphael, as rare as that is, then he does so for the exclusive purpose of illustrating allegorically some psychological or philosophical idea and never, as is the case with musical examples, with an undertone of grateful delight. Even the sole pictorial love of his life, the landscapes of Claude Lorrain,[5] is strangely nonsensual and allegorically inclined; he never mentions a particular painting by the master by name (he saw a number of them in Dresden and then later in Rome), and it is always the type, the *idea* "Claude Lorrain" that preoccupies him: his paintings "make him think,"[6] as he writes from Rome. It is a "poetic Claude Lorrain" for whom "his heart makes him yearn"[7] (in *Human, All Too Human*). In all of this, Nietzsche is entirely the descendant of the Lutheran Reformation, which, even when it did not express itself in the symbol of iconoclasm, still robbed the German people of the cheerful pleasures of the eye they had during the Middle Ages and, in its place, endowed them with the homesickness of the ear, that unquenchable and metaphysical thirst for music.

We know of only a single pictorial representation to which Nietzsche remained attached over the course of many long years, only one that he viewed and admired as a better part of himself: Albrecht Dürer's[8] engraving *Ritter, Tod und Teufel* (Knight, Death and Devil), from 1513, the year that Luther, returning from the convulsions of his trip to Rome, was struggling with the slowly growing visions of his future prophecy. It is the only gift, concentrated within a specific form, that the visual arts were ever allowed to give to the half-blind, sound-obsessed romantic Socrates. And, in a kind of convulsion, he felt it to be autobiographical, a warning to himself, the way one only feels those things that appear to be spectral concretizations, as it were, of points where different curves in one's life intersect, where decisive lines in one's trajectory converge.

"A local patrician," he wrote from Basel to Malwida in 1875, "gave me a significant present in the form of a genuine Dürer print. I rarely derive pleasure from a pictorial representation, *but I identify with this image, 'Knight, Death, and Devil,' in a way I can hardly explain.* In *The Birth of Tragedy* I compared Schopenhauer to this image, and because of that comparison I received the picture."[9] Nietzsche's first inclinations toward the Dürer image in fact date from the time he was writing *The Birth,* and, indeed, it was Wagner who, as with so much else that was decisive for Nietzsche, provided the impetus here as well. In Tribschen,[10] Wagner studied the two engravings, *Knight* and *Melancholia,* through the lens of Schopenhauerian ideas and analogies. He received both pieces from his friend and disciple in Basel as a morning gift in their new musical and philosophical friendship.

On Christmas Eve 1870, Nietzsche traveled to Tribschen bearing as a gift for Wagner "a favorite print by Albrecht Dürer that he had long desired": this favorite print was "Knight, Death, and Devil," which a fortunate coincidence placed in his hands, as he reports to his mother and sister. From that point on, the print also accompanied Nietzsche's external life. He gave it to his friend Overbeck, a critical theologian, as a kind of emblem and memento of their mutual Christian-Unchristian knighthood of truth. And when, many years later, his sister emigrated to far-away Paraguay, where "a brave future" awaited her, Nietzsche again could think of nothing better, nothing more vividly symbolic to give her as a wedding present and good luck charm for the trip than the Dürer print with the armor-clad knight between death and the devil.[11]

What was it about this print in particular that so magically captivated the young Nietzsche (whereas there is, characteristically, no evidence whatsoever, apart from some allusions to it in two poems from July 1871, of a similar interest in *Melancholia,* despite Wagner's predilection for it), what magic bound him to it even as he outgrew Schopenhauer and Wagner? Nietzsche's earliest answer to that question is, at the same time, the most important one: it is the passage in *The Birth of Tragedy,* because of which he received the print from a grateful reader in Basel; it is also the passage that Cosima Wagner admired the most in his first book. Indeed, she indicates precisely that fruitful spiritual moment, metaphorically condensed, in which the connection between Schopenhauer's metaphysics and Wagner's musical will became possible in Nietzsche's mind. That connection arises out of the same inner disposition that a letter of Nietzsche's to Rohde from October 1868 identifies: "What appeals to me in Wagner is what appeals to me in Schopenhauer, the ethical atmosphere, the Faustian odor, cross, death and crypt . . ."[12]—an overall mood that Nietzsche gratefully puts into words a few months later in his letter to Wagner on his birthday: "I owe it to you and to Schopenhauer that, to this day, I have held onto the Germanic seriousness toward life, that I have a deepened view of this so puzzling and questionable existence."[13] The characteristic passage about Dürer in *The Birth of Tragedy* grew out of the "Germanic seriousness toward life" during these early years in Nietzsche's life, out of the shadow cast by Schopenhauer and by the Schopenhauerian Wagner. It was intended to bring home the feeling of the solitary man who, still without the "new belief" in an imminent rebirth of Hellenic antiquity, without hope for a renewal of the German spirit through the fervent magic of music, is searching in vain for "something with a future" in the middle of the wilderness of our exhausted culture:

"An inconsolably lonely man could choose no better symbol than the Knight with Death and Devil, as Dürer has drawn him for us, the armor-clad knight with the steely, hard glance who knows how to steer his terrible course, unperturbed by his dreadful companions, and yet without hope, alone with his horse and dog. Our Schopenhauer was such a Dürer knight: he lacked all hope, but he desired truth. He has no equal"[14] (*The Birth of Tragedy*). This symbolic image is complemented by notes for a later outline of *The Birth of Tragedy* (1871): " . . . Germanic pessimism—including rigid moralists, Schopenhauer and the categorical imperative! . . . We *need* a particular kind of art. . . . Dürer's picture of the knight, death, and devil as the symbol of our existence!"[15] Both passages together represent the entire ethical attitude of the young Nietzsche: "cross, death, and crypt," as well as the already latent will to life, the moralistically rigid defiance that seems to be contained in the concept of Germanic pessimism; the Schopenhauerian romanticism of death, as well as the courage for truth in general; the youthful delirium of painful and knowing "hopelessness" as well as the particular kind of art that emerges from it; the Kantian imperative and the Lutheran Nevertheless—and finally the two demons of that seventh loneliness, that fatefully "Protestant" isolation of the individual, to which Luther once lent the bravely resigned words: "Your life is a knighthood. . . . Everyone must be in his own person armed and prepared to do battle with the devil and death. . . . I will not be with you then, nor will you be with me. . . ."[16] Demons of that malevolent will to knowledge, which has to be a "will to death"—"comprehension is an end,"[17] knowledge *is* death. All of that Nietzsche senses in the print's sublime gloom, like a threatening storm, which is so thoroughly German and so Nietzschean in its super-Germanness, even with regard to the ambiguity of the print's half-artistic, half-philosophical, and humanistic origins, even with regard to its purely formal androgyny, which, on the one hand, arose out of Dürer's studies of Leonardo da Vinci and Mantegna and, on the other, his fantastical pleasure in the northern fixation with devils, a northern love of solitary woods and romantic castles, making it appear to anticipate the analogous compositional history of the greatest work of German literature.[18] But above all it is the image of the "courageous man" as such that enchants Nietzsche about the print, which arose out of the mood of the approaching Reformation, the quiet and imperturbable "Nevertheless" of a soul that gallantly chooses and pursues its demonically ordained path "between the epochs." It is the knight of truth (be it Christian or un-Christian), the truth of the brave man, the truth at any price, above all at the price of one's own happiness. An entirely unrevolutionary knight of truth: lacking all fanaticism, in other words, and devoid of hate, that is, a Reformation knight, in the mold of Hutten, of Luther in Worms, who stood there alone and could not do otherwise,[19] who has to go where he had to declare it, "even if there were as many devils there as there are tiles on the roofs."[20] As late as 1884 there is an aphorism about Schopenhauer, whom at that point Nietzsche claims to have "overcome" long ago, that contains a perhaps not entirely coincidental literal allusion to the Lutheran notion of the freedom enjoyed by a Christian who, as the lord over all things, is "subservient to no one":

> What he taught has been abandoned;
> What he lived will continue to stand
> Just look at him—
> He was subservient to no one![21]

And even in the *Genealogy of Morals* of 1887, he unmistakably returns to the Dürer comparison from *The Birth of Tragedy* in a passage that mentions a "truly independent spirit such as Schopenhauer," who was a "man and knight with a steely glance, who has the courage to stand by himself, who knows how to stand alone."[22]

A "symbol of existence" is speaking to him, he who always felt that he needed "a particular kind of art": the symbol of "Germanic pessimism," which is neither skeptical nor romantic but rather "Reformatory," moralistic, "Schopenhauer and the categorical imperative," Luther and Can-Do-No-Other. "There is a will to the tragic and to pessimism," the second preface to *Human, All Too Human* says, "which is a sign just as much of the severity as of the strength of one's intellect (of one's taste, sensitivity, conscience). With this will in one's breast, one does not fear all of the terrifying and questionable things that are inherent in existence; one goes out in search of them. Behind such a will stands the courage, the pride, the desire for a *great* opponent. That was *my* pessimistic perspective from the beginning—a new perspective, it seems to me? . . . I have maintained it up to this very moment."[23] That is how the late Nietzsche saw the dominating perspective of his life. From the beginning, there stands behind his knightly pessimism the *courage* not to avoid what is terrifying—death—or what is questionable—the devil—but rather to seek it out, to affirm it, to *will* it. A courage that intensifies and transforms the tragic into the Dionysian, pessimism into the will to recurrence, Schopenhauer into Zarathustra. Nietzsche perceived the image of such courage in Dürer: he perceived himself while thinking he saw Schopenhauer. Just as the print is the only one that stays with him, the idea of intellectual and spiritual courage also stays with him and dominates his thinking, the idea of a Knight Templar of truth—*that* truth which does not kill, but makes one live. "What is good? To be brave is good,"[24] Zarathustra asks and answers himself. He glorifies man as the most courageous animal: courage—with it, he overcame every animal (and even himself as animal): "But courage is the best killer, courage that attacks: It kills even death, for it says: Was that life? Very well! Once more!"[25] In *Ecce homo,* he elaborates and supports the same notion in a more personal vein: "I am warlike by nature. It belongs to my instincts to attack."[26] In a letter to his mother, just before writing *Zarathustra,* Nietzsche is already speaking of himself as someone who is, if not the happiest of men, then in any case the most courageous, and he calls *Daybreak* one of the most courageous books ever to have been born. "Three-quarters of all the evil done in the world happens out of timidity,"[27] the same book says, in whose paralipomena a "religion of bravery"[28] is postulated in an entirely Protestant manner, and where the demand is made that science become more dangerous, that it involve more sacrifice: "I want to bring things to the point where one needs a *heroic* temper to devote oneself to science."[29] Nietzsche knows like no other about the temptations, about the "death and the devil" of timidity, of every kind of timidity of the mind. The truth—that is, for him, a question of courage and an answer of courage. "In the sciences, too, everything is ethical," Goethe had already noted; "one cannot actually know anything in them, it is always a matter of doing."[30] "One has only belatedly the courage for what one actually *knows*"[31]—that is one of the most often repeated and modified sentences in late Nietzsche (it is in the *Will to Power*). The *Twilight of the Idols* puts it similarly: "Even the most courageous among us only rarely has the courage for what he actually *knows*. . . ."[32] At greater length to Brandes (December 1887): "It seems to me that what a person considers 'true' or not depends more on his courage, on the strength of his courage. (Only seldom do I have the courage for what I actually know)."[33] In the same year to Overbeck: "If I only had the courage to *think* everything I know. . . ."[34] Finally, most bluntly in *Ecce homo:* "How much truth can a mind *endure,* how much truth can it risk? That increasingly became the actual measure of value for me. Error is not blindness, error is cowardice. . . ."[35] And a mind has value only as a positive martyrdom, namely as a struggle: "The most intellectual people, provided that they are the most courageous, also experience by far the most painful tragedies: but for that very reason they honor life because it pits its greatest forces against them"[36] (*Twilight of the Idols*). For *everything* decisive comes about only "nevertheless," as Nietzsche, quoting himself, says in *Ecce homo.*

The most severe reproach the mature Nietzsche makes of Schopenhauer as a thinker is, symptomatically, that—of cowardice. Although he venerates him in 1870 in the image of the Dürer knight, celebrating him as the model of philosophical bravery, he later accuses him of having retreated from the greatest enemy of existence, of having withdrawn from the tragedy of his own life: of having not wanted to *suffer* for the sake of truth. "I find Schopenhauer somewhat superficial regarding matters of the soul. He enjoyed little and suffered little; a thinker should take care not to *become hard:* where is he supposed to get his material then? His passion for knowledge was not great enough to want to suffer on its account: he entrenched himself"[37] (Notebooks to *Daybreak*). To entrench oneself—that is most unknightly. Caution is the worst temptation for a thinker. Thinking is war, knowledge is a ride between death and the devil. But Schopenhauer flees, as he once fled from his philosophical post out of fear of death, which he so loudly preached; he *knows,* but he does not *do*—Nietzsche does not forgive him for that. His doctrine lacks the validation of Lutheran courage: that is what arouses Nietzsche's later displeasure; that is why he disowns the doctrine; because no "blood" certifies it, it cannot legitimately procreate. "Erasmus loves peace more than the cross"[38]—that was Luther's judgment. And one notices a certain Lutheran impatience, the impatience of a Hutten in the face of Erasmus-like natures—"*vale* Erasme! Dead and done with!"[39]—in the unconscious attitude Nietzsche takes toward his friends: toward Overbeck, the circumspect and prudently silent historian of the church and Christianity,[40] toward Rohde, the cautious interpreter of the Greek psyche,[41] who was enough of a guild member not to mention the name of his great friend, the "philologist of the future" and heretic, in his book even though no one would have belonged in it more; this impatience rumbles perceptibly even within the admiration he maintained until the end for Jakob Burckhardt—how revealing is an early passage in a letter from 1870 about the skeptic who wrote the *Weltgeschichtliche Betrachtungen:* "This older, extremely peculiar man is, to be sure, not inclined to misrepresent the truth, but certainly to conceal it; yet in private conversations during our walks he calls Schopenhauer 'our philosopher.' . . . I believe I am his only auditor who understands the deep trains of his thought with their strange refractions and reversals, to the point where the matter almost becomes dubious. . . ."[42] Or the note he made in the preparatory studies for "Richard Wagner in Bayreuth": "Those who hold themselves back, out of desperation like Jakob Burckhardt."[43] And to Overbeck, in a tone of indulgent but clearly condescending tolerance: "Your situation in Basel, truly not to be envied, but at least not to be lamented either, has something cautious and fine about it. . . ."[44] Cautious and fine—that is Erasmus, who loves peace more than the cross.

But where his teacher disappointed him, where his friends stayed behind, his ideal readers, the pupils he dreams of, should at least take the chance of following him on reformatory paths without sparing oneself themselves à la Erasmus: "In my view, all 'feminism' in a person, including in men, closes the door: such a person will never enter the labyrinth of audacious knowledge. One must never have gone easy on oneself, one must have acquired *hardness* in one's habits in order to be cheerful and serene amid nothing but hard truths. When I imagine the perfect reader, it always turns out to be a fiend of courage and curiosity . . . a born adventurer and explorer"[45] (*Ecce homo*).

Hardness, audacity, courage, and adventurousness—as time goes on these become Nietzsche's cardinal virtues; "dangerous" his favorite label of distinction, next to "evil" and "terrible." He wishes for everyone "who matters to him at all" to experience a Great Danger, for "the only thing that can prove today whether someone has value or not—*that he stands his ground.*"[46] Only a Great Danger proves the knight—indeed it is what creates him. It creates the individual as well as entire peoples: "The peoples that were worth something, *became* worth something, never did so under liberal institutions: a *Great Danger* made something out of them that deserves respect, a danger that first makes us acquainted with our own resources, our virtues, our defenses and weapons, our *mind*—that *forces* us to be strong. . . . First principle: there must be a necessity to be strong: otherwise it will never happen"[47] (*Twilight of the Idols*).

Nietzsche repeatedly makes this realization with regard to the fate of the German spirit. "Whenever a German has done something great," *Daybreak* says, "it happened in an hour of need, in a state of bravery, of clenched teeth, of the most tense calmness. . . ."[48] And it is deeply significant that the only German quality that Nietzsche positively values and affirms to the end, even at the height of his anti-German passion, is the quality out of which the German Reformation arose: the quiet boldness of the knightly individual, the bravery of "Here I stand, I can do no other." Inward boldness and outward modesty, no matter what the external circumstances, is for him "a German combination of virtues"[49] (which at that point, to be sure, he thought could be found best expressed in Swiss artists or scholars). In his penultimate year, he was still characterizing his own language as "bold and German."[50] In the Basel lecture of 1871/72 about the "Future of our Educational Institutions," Nietzsche writes that, in opposition to "Romanic civilization," he adheres "all the more to the German spirit, which revealed itself in the German Reformation and in German music and which in the enormous bravery and discipline of German philosophy and in the recently proven loyalty of the German soldier has displayed that enduring, genuine power from which we may expect a victory over the fashionable pseudo-culture of the 'Here-and-now'."[51] In *Beyond* he finds, to the honor of the German nature of Richard Wagner, that he had been stronger, more audacious, harder, higher, than any Frenchman of the nineteenth century could have been—"thanks to the circumstance that we Germans still stand closer to barbarism than the French";[52]—perhaps even the most remarkable thing that Wagner created would not just today but forever be inaccessible, impenetrable, inimitable to the entire, so advanced Latin race: the figure of Siegfried, that *very free* man who indeed is much too free, too hard, too cheerful, too healthy, too anti-Catholic for the taste of ancient and decrepit cultures. Likewise, *Beyond* characterizes a skepticism of audacious masculinity, which found its first entrance into Germany in the figure of Frederick the Great[53] as the *German* form of skepticism: "This skepticism despises and nevertheless usurps; it undermines and takes possession; it doesn't believe, but it doesn't lose itself in the process; it gives the mind a dangerous freedom, but it keeps the heart in check; it is the *German* form of skepticism, which, as a continuation of Frederickanism on the intellectual plane, brought benefit to Europe under the dominion of the German spirit and of its critical and historical distrust."[54] And that is the Dürer ideal of the Christian knight, of the severe and brave skepticism "despite death and the devil," transposed into a psychologically and historically younger sphere, transformed into the myth of Frederick, whose Luther-sized "Nevertheless" defied the entire world and held its ground. And the humanistic phrase is not missing here, either, the interpretation of the scholar as a "Christian knight" of knowledge, an anti-romantic Hutten-figure: "Thanks to the invincibly strong and tenacious masculine character of the great German philologists and critical historians . . . a *new* conception of the German spirit took hold despite all the romanticism in music and philosophy, a spirit in which the trait of masculine skepticism prominently emerged: be it, for example, in the form of investigative fearlessness, of analytical bravery and hardness, of a persevering will to dangerous journeys of exploration, to intellectual expeditions to a spiritual North Pole under desolate and dangerous skies. There may be good reasons why warm-blooded and superficial advocates of humanity cross themselves when confronted by this spirit: Michelet called it, not without a shudder, *cet esprit fataliste, ironique, méphistophélique.*"[55]

Here we already find the path cleared for the equation of "German" and "Mephistophelian"[56] that he expressly takes up later. It exemplifies in highly characteristic fashion Nietzsche's very "German" technique of *amalgamation* that he adopted from Wagner. With brilliantly audacious interpretive skill, he forces together all of the inconsistencies within himself into the synthesis of the identifying moment. Here, the one element of the German spirit he still affirmed, its "audacity," is supposed to be united with the super-German yearning of his adoration of the south, the fusion of the Reformation with paganism, Faust with Helen. For Nietzsche, the point where the two deep currents of his own being converge, as in every "super-German" nature, carries the name Mephistopheles, who is here again lent traits of Frederick the Great.

"What I like to see in a German," he says in a passage in the Notebooks to the *Revaluation,* "is his Mephistophelian nature: but, frankly, one has to have a higher notion of Mephistopheles than Goethe did, who found that, in order to magnify his 'inner Faust,' he needed to *diminish* his Mephistopheles. The true German Mephistopheles is much more dangerous, more audacious, more evil, more cunning and *therefore* more candid: one need only think of the inner life of Frederick the Great, or of that much greater Frederick, the Hohenstaufen Emperor Frederick II.[57]—The true German Mephistopheles"—here again there is the typical equation of "very German" with southern super-German—"climbs over the Alps, believes that everything there belongs *to him*."[58] An exemplary masterpiece of that sovereign exegesis of everything "written" that the late Nietzsche especially loved to perform. The "de-Germanization" of Goethe's devil into the *true* German Mephistopheles (Luther said that a German foreigner is a *diabolo incarnato*)[59] is both a model and a symbol for the transferal of Nietzsche's German ideal (for there is such a thing for Nietzsche even in his most de-Germanized period) into the dangerously southern realm, even beyond Goethe's alienation from the north, to the extreme polar opposite of the German character, to the outermost limit—the most remote from Luther—of all inner German possibilities as a whole.

And yet—*the* very German quality, thanks to which Nietzsche can construe his super-German ideal, namely the "dangerous audacity" of the German spirit, its inner, malevolent Frederickism, this very quality keeps him tied to the most northern opposite of the German character, to everything that the name of the Lutheran Reformation implies in terms of what is great and catastrophic, of the most German and all-too-German destiny and *fatum*. More: it points to the place, it *is* the place, where Nietzsche is most deeply rooted in the essence of his own people, in the essence of his language and of his being "beyond language." It is the place where Nietzsche most furiously attacks Germanness; the place where he engages in the most bitter struggle with himself, indeed hates himself; the place where he imagines he sees the death and the devil of the entire German character, believing that he had challenged and defeated them. That place is designated by the name that there is no getting around when confronted by the Dürer print, and that also signifies the oldest German name in Nietzsche's intellectual ancestry: the name of Martin Luther. One should not be led astray even for an instant by the extreme vehemence, even the unrestrained venom of Nietzsche's antagonism toward Luther after his Wagner period. It is, like the struggle with Wagner and Schopenhauer, or the struggle against romanticism and Christianity, only a symbol of a fraternal strife within his own breast, just as it can perhaps occur only in a German heart so fiercely, so brutally toward himself, a discord that is so Faustian and super-German, so disastrously unwinnable. Nietzsche's hatred of Luther—that is the place where our view of Nietzsche's worldly-intellectual landscape expands out onto the mountain range of the larger spiritual and religious problem in which only one, albeit tremendously arresting, summit carries the name Nietzsche. For, as much as the many different perspectives we have on Nietzsche are valid because they are both possible and productive, one is always reminded, from every thematic standpoint, of the enormous *theological* problem[60] that a figure such as Nietzsche represents. There is no question that the poet of the prophet Zarathustra, viewed from the proper height, is one of the most magnificent phenomena within the history of northern Christianity, indeed, understood with the requisite intellectual sensitivity, even within "church history." We have long been accustomed to viewing Nietzsche's half-brother Schopenhauer as a thoroughly *Christian* intellectual figure, not with respect to the superficially rationalistic and Latinate aspects of this thinking, but regarding the innermost direction of his philosophical drive and will, where one can recognize in him a legitimate heir of Gothic asceticism and metaphysics. Nietzsche himself was probably the first to express that fact in full clarity, unperturbed by Schopenhauer's pseudo-Voltairean hostility to the church and Christians. "The whole medieval Christian world-view and sense of humanity was able to celebrate a resurrection once again in Schopenhauer's doctrine, in spite of the annihilation of all Christian dogmas achieved long ago"[61]—he writes in *Human, All Too Human;* indeed: "I believe that it would now be very difficult for anyone to do justice to Christianity and its Asiatic relatives without Schopenhauer's assistance."[62] But only for someone with a very superficial point of view is there some ultimate boundary or threshold of Christianity between Schopenhauer and Nietzsche. The phenomenon of Schopenhauer, which in intellectual-historical terms is to be classified under the rubric "Christian romanticism," repeats itself only higher up in a thinner atmosphere, made more dangerous by the increased proximity to deadly self-knowledge. Just as Schopenhauer is not so much the heir of either Seneca or Montaigne as he is the inheritor of a Christianized Plato, of an India seen through a Christian lens, so too the primary impulse in Nietzsche's soul is more deeply related to Pascal and Angelus Silesius than to the "supra-Christian gaze"[63] of Leonardo or the Hohenstaufen Frederick II. He is, with the theocentric primacy of the idea of *life* before the concept of *knowledge,* still worlds closer to the soulfulness of St. Francis than to the "spider of skepticism,"[64] the Enlightenment of his revered Voltaire. To be sure, he is Socrates, and like him a dismantler of mysteries and a destroyer of the myths of gods. But he is also Paul, the man who overcame the law, the "Old Tablets," the prophet, servant, and exegete of a new lord over souls. Not the same Paul, it is true, whom the "Antichrist" savagely interprets as a decadent character out of the most vengeful self-hatred, using all of the instruments of a malignantly fanatical psychoanalysis. Not Paul the "dysangelist,"[65] the histrionic "genius of hate,"[66] the "chandala-type,"[67] the power-obsessed invalid, the "greatest of all the apostles of revenge"[68]—(it is only the morbid side of Nietzsche's nature that creates here a distorted fraternal phantom so that he can denounce, persecute, and furiously destroy it in a fit of passionate self-hatred, just as the same hatred of himself forced his all-too-intellectualistic Half-Ego to combat his *Doppelgänger,* Socrates). Rather, the affirmatively directed half of his being is more closely related to Dürer's Paul, who stares out of the apostle paintings in Munich holding both a book *and* a knight's sword, combining in his nobly searching vigilance an image of concentrated masculinity and slightly painful consciousness, composed half of Attic wisdom and half of Nordic brooding, an image that is simultaneously related to the "Saint Paul as robust as a knight"[69] that Goethe's Reformation dictum gives us. This reformatory Paul, the brave and earnest knight of Christian truth, to whom Luther lent his own defiant "Nevertheless!" in Worms, this Paul no longer has a single trait in common with the Asian, passively malicious apostle of revenge in the *Antichrist,* with that slave genius conceived out of overwrought French psychologism and the world of a Russian novel—as Nietzsche puts it—and in which he sees the prototype of all religious and moral decadence and the whole of European "nihilism." Nietzsche calls everything "Paul," forms everything into the shape of *his* Paul, that he hates and combats in himself, including "the blood of theologians, which gives anyone with it in his veins a skewed and dishonest stance toward everything from the outset,"[70] and including that deep morbidity and decadence of which he recognizes himself as an heir and type. But he could have also understood and respected that conqueror of decadence in himself ("allowing that I am a *décadent,* I am also its opposite"[71] he writes in *Ecce homo*), he could have understood and honored that great religious yea-sayer in himself under the image of Paul, of the Paul who is a poetic invention of Luther, a poetic work of the Reformation, the creation of northern man. Everything positive, everything creative in Nietzsche is in fact *rooted* here, comes from his Lutheran, reformatory, northern, and romantic heritage, no matter how much it is always intoxicatedly lavished on the Hellenistic, classically southern psychologistic element. In 1875 he was still able to speak, to Rohde, about "our good pure Protestant air" and all of its "liberating spirits," he can even admit: "I have never felt my innermost dependence on the spirit of Luther more strongly than I do now."[72] And even in the unpublished writings from the last years we find the testimony: "The two most refined forms of humanity I have personally encountered were the perfect Christian—I consider it a point of honor that I descend from people who were in every sense serious about their Christianity—and the perfect artist of the romantic ideal, whom I found to be far beneath the Christian niveau. . . ."[73] *Northern Christianity:* that is the native soil in which his ethical powers grew, no matter how many other branches of his being also strove toward more Hellenic heights. It is after all from this northern Christianity that he launches his attack against a Christianity, against the slave religion of *his* Paul, that he saw as a product of Asia Minor, an outgrowth of degenerating Hellenism. The Reformation did exactly the same thing, wherein the specifically northern form of Christianity merely sought its most powerful expression. From the time of the *Heliand*[74] and the first Lower-Saxon cathedrals onward—it is always the ideal of a more active, anti-pessimistic, of a yea-saying, yea-doing Christianity that the north would like to realize, an anti-Asian, anti-ascetic "Nevertheless" and "Yes" to life. And Nietzsche's self-misunderstanding as that of an Antichrist is just as valid an expression of this northern Christianity (if not of attachment to the church) as was Luther's provincial, anti-papist power to shatter the "Roman" Middle Ages. Even Goethe, whose Hellenism was still half of northern provenance, did not avoid making the energetic confession:

> It is to the credit of all German men
> That they hated Christianity
> Until the noble Saxons fell to
> Lord Charles's accursed sword.
> Yet they had fought long enough . . .
> Yet they groused only once.
> They were laying only in semi-slumber
> When Luther put the Bible into German.
> Saint Paul, in the guise of a sturdy knight,
> Seemed less austere to knights themselves.
> Freedom awakens in every breast,
> And, filled with joy, we all protest![75]

Goethe's notion of such a knightly, joyous, Protestant freedom, of an "anti-Christian," "Saxon" Christianity, is for Nietzsche as well the creation of *northern* man, whereas the Roman Church, and with it and through it the entire European south, had "become the inheritance of the deep Orient, of ancient, mysterious Asia and of its *contemplation*."[76] And this is precisely what Nietzsche attacks most bitterly in its various transformations: as "historical sense," as Schopenhauerian pessimism, as *Parsifal*'s music, as Jewish-Christian morality, as Paul. "The most significant thing that Luther accomplished," he writes in *Daybreak*, "lies in the mistrust he awakened toward the saints and the entire Christian *vita contemplativa*."[77] In searching for and demanding a "yea-saying, yea-doing" ideal for life, one that is truly vital, with all the intensity and all the unapologetically biased injustice of Luther, his Upper-Saxon compatriot, Nietzsche is drawing on the same Lutheran, northern Protestant heritage as Goethe does in the first part of *Faust*. His fury toward the stylized image of Paul, with its Oriental distortions and Asian contemplativeness, comes from the same forceful northern counter-ideal that the Lutheran Reformation had established in Paul, as Paul. It is no coincidence that Protestant Christianity erects itself on the very foundation of a new *Pauline* ideal, as Goethe himself had expressed it in the verses just cited. And it is no coincidence that Albrecht Dürer, the loyal adherent to Luther, creates the new, more masculine, courageous, northern image of Paul. "Whoever has stood under the power of this Apostle's eye," Wölfflin writes about the Paul portrayed in the Munich panels, "knows that not only has a new conception of holy men made its appearance here, but also a new conception of human greatness in general. The work of the Reformation was performed by such men. The era was a virile era, and Dürer was able to give his best only in masculine types."[78] Dürer thus merely fulfills and pictorially represents the northern Christian ideal. What began in the *Heliand,* Dürer brings to completion. What Wölfflin says in his book on Dürer about the art of the Reformation master is true of the entire Germanic north: "One can say that Dürer introduces a new idea of Christ, in so far as he infuses strength and manliness in the suffering and resignation which had previously been seen as the essential content of his figure."[79] (Wölfflin was speaking of the countenance of Christ in the "Veil of Veronica," which dates from the same year as the print "Knight, Death and Devil.")

With that we have identified the point at which Nietzsche's elective affinity with Dürer's art becomes completely intelligible. "Knight, Death and Devil," this most "Protestant" of Dürer's prints, full of Pauline courage and Pauline confidence—"O death, where is thy sting? O grave, where is thy victory?"[80]—*had* to form, like no other work by Dürer, an electric connection between these two Reformation masters, who as artists, to be sure, had *no* sensibility, *no* organ, hardly a single trait in common—except perhaps the deep longing for the south they both shared and because of which they stand out as so German, so fatefully German in the history of art and thought. "A new conception of holy men appeared, but also a new conception of human greatness in general"—if it is Dürer's accomplishment to have longed for that conception, to have fashioned it and given it to us afresh, then is it not a preeminently Nietzschean one as well? Is it not the most noble meaning of his existence to have given a new conception of great and "holy" men, to have lived out a new form of human greatness and, even if he did not achieve it, still to have demanded it? Nietzsche's ideal, too, was a reformatory, virile one: more masculine value judgments, more masculine virtues, more masculine role models—Nietzsche, like Dürer, could see and give his best only in masculine types. And was it not the noblest task of his entire life "to infuse strength and manliness" in the suffering and resignation of his own inner Passion? Was not "overcoming" the ultimate and most literal meaning of both their lives? "What Dürer accomplished is great," Wölfflin wrote, taking stock of this most German of artistic lives, "but perhaps the greater part lies in what he overcame in the process."[81] Is that not also a precise description of Nietzsche's life, achievement, and fate? What seems reminiscent of Dürer in Nietzsche's philosophy, what appears Nietzschean in Dürer's art, is embodied in the print depicting the Christian knight. And it must have caused the young disciple of Schopenhauer and the Wagner enthusiast to feel he was being addressed by a subliminal yet perceptible "tat twam asi"—"that is you"—to sense that a "vision" was gazing out at him, that a premonitory phantom and prophetic dream had approached him in the guise of art. ("Radiant and severe,"[82] is how Peter Cornelius described Dürer's art and style; "radiant and strong"[83] is how Zarathustra, when his time comes, is said to leave his cave in the last sentence of the book.) Something similar resonates in the words he sends to Wagner five years after giving him the Christmas present: "I identify with this image in a way I can hardly explain."[84]

The reason he seemed to identify with it so closely is expressed in that passage from *The Birth:* it was the analogy to Schopenhauer that fascinated him in the figure of the lonely rider between the demons. The fact that behind the idea of Schopenhauer it was the Christian connection that exerted its power in this attraction, and in particular the notion of Christianity in a moment of world transformation, of Reformation, an image of combat and a bridge between two worlds, just like himself—all of that Nietzsche would not have been able to admit at that point. Yet, beneath the mask of Schopenhauer, it *was* the Christianity of his pious childhood and of his ancestral blood that spoke to him in a strangely familiar accent, that "best example of ideal life"[85] that he, according to his own testimony, had ever really gotten to know, that from the time he was a child he had explored in its many nooks and crannies, and about which he claims even in his last anti-Christian decade that he "had in his heart never been base toward it." During Nietzsche's youth, Schopenhauer is the form in which his Christian, Protestant inheritance remains possible for him—that is evidenced and revealed by his predilection for the Dürer print. "Cross, Death, and Crypt": that is what he likes about Schopenhauer, about the Wagner of *Tristan* as interpreted through a Schopenhauerian lens, what attracts him to Dürer's melancholy bravery and also to the deeply devout, heroic Reformation art of Johann Sebastian Bach. His Schopenhauer-inspired interpretation of the St. Matthew Passion is a precise counterpart and example of his instinctive understanding of "Christian" events as experiential examples of the doctrine of his favorite philosopher. In the same year in which Wagner interprets Dürer's work of art for him, Schopenhauer interprets for him the most sublime Christian musical structure. During Holy

Week in 1870 he writes to Rohde: "This week I listened to the St. Matthew Passion by the divine Bach three times, each one with the same feeling of immeasurable astonishment. Whoever has completely forgotten the meaning of Christianity hears it here truly as the gospel. This is the music of the negation of the will without any reminder of asceticism."[86] Later, when both Schopenhauer and Wagner count among the things Nietzsche has overcome, he finds Dürer's print "sinister"[87] and "too gloomy,"[88] and in Bach, who (as in Dürer, who looks back toward the German Gothic period while standing on the threshold of the European Renaissance) "looks back toward the Middle Ages on the threshold of European music, still too much crude Christianity, crude Germanness."[89] Nevertheless, even late in life he can think of no more noble a gift than that print; nevertheless, during his last spring in Turin he is still excited and enchanted by a symbolic synthesis of his early and later life, that is by the news that Paris was wild with enthusiasm for—the St. Matthew Passion, and that even *Le Figaro*—"truly *Le Figaro!*—had devoted an entire page to reprinting part of the score: namely the melancholy aria "Erbarme dich, mein Gott . . ."[90] Nevertheless, Dürer as well as Bach are incorporated into the chromatic fantasy of *Zarathustra,* just as Schopenhauer and Wagner are part of its passionate solitude, its ecstatic tempos—as, above all, Luther is present in the powerful rhythm of his pious wrath. That the *style* of *Zarathustra* became a late, baroque intensification and dissolution of Luther's Old Testament is merely the expression and symbol of an even closer inner affinity and descendancy. In all of German literature we possess virtually no work of such high stature that owes so much of its rhythmic qualities to Luther as does *Zarathustra.* And just as the word "overman" has its forbear in Goethe's *Faust,* one could trace the ancestry of the overman himself to the divinely free Christian man whom Luther's Protestant individualism had first preached: "Every single Christian is such a man as Christ himself was on earth, and can govern the entire world in divine things. . . . Thus, Christians are the true helpers and saviors, *indeed the masters and gods of the world.*"[91] And despite all of his hostility toward Luther during the middle and late years when he was drawn more and more to the south, Nietzsche was always still dimly aware of this ancestry. Occasionally, in a flash, he will elucidate it himself. "Our last event still remains Luther."[92] "There was, after Luther and Goethe, a third step still to take,"[93] he writes to Rohde about the language of *Zarathustra.* And in the *Notebooks* to *The Case of Wagner*—in other words, very late: "Luther's language and the poetic form of the Bible as the basis of a new German poetry—that is *my* discovery! The imitation of classical antiquity, the complex rhyme schemes—that is all wrong and does not speak to us deeply enough[94] . . . playing with the most diverse meters and occasionally unmetered verse is the right thing: we are surely able to take the liberty that we have already achieved in music in our poetry as well! Finally: it is the only poetry that speaks powerfully to the heart!—thanks to Luther."[95] He even finds that his favorite music exhibits the German Düreresque Luther trait in spite of all southern stylization: "You know," he writes to Gast during his last summer in the Engadine, "that I regard your operatic music as very German—*old* German, good sixteenth-century German!"[96]

As early as in *The Birth of Tragedy* he celebrates Luther almost as his own Dionysian predecessor: "The German Reformation emerged out of the abyss of a tremendous, inwardly healthy primeval force (which, to be sure, bestirs itself violently only at extraordinary moments but once, and then falls back into dreaming of a future awakening), and the future melody of German music first resounded in its chorale. This, Luther's chorale, rang out as deeply, boldly and soulfully, as exuberantly good and tender as the first enticing call of Dionysus. . . . It was answered by the solemnly boisterous procession of Dionysian enthusiasts to whom we owe German music—and to whom we will owe the rebirth of German myth!"[97] And "Wagner in Bayreuth" praises Luther's German *cheerfulness,* in other words precisely that which Nietzsche to the end valued most highly in every new truth: laughter. But even his malignant hostility toward Luther's accomplishment (the restoration of Christianity by attacking Rome), like his enmity toward Paul, occasionally betrays the tone of a hatred between "hostile brother geniuses," who, in the words of *Beyond,* "tend toward the opposite poles of the German spirit and in the process do harm to each other, as only brothers can do harm to themselves."[98] Nietzsche had the dark premonition that a destiny could be in store for him that was similar to the one he saw having befallen Luther: namely, of restoring what he attacked, and in fact doing so *by* attacking it. In Luther's case: medieval Christianity already caught up in the most colorful disintegration in and through Rome. In Nietzsche's case—? But something like embitterment toward his own inner allegiances rumbles in the words of *The Antichrist:* "If people do not get over Christianity, it will be the *Germans'* fault. They have Protestantism on their conscience."[99] But within the German development, what would be more "Protestant" in this sense than the "always joyfully protesting" spirit of Nietzsche? Who would have ever inwardly "got over" Christianity less among the Germans than this most radical and fearless atheist, more radical and fearless even than Schopenhauer? "A Christian wants to *get away* from himself,"[100] we read in *The Case of Wagner*—who would have ever been a more passionate, a more heroically ascetic, more hopelessly Christian than Nietzsche? We can follow the traces of this unrelenting battle with his "inward Christian" into the last moments of mental transition. And as it sometimes happens to people, whose overall intellectual image is transformed by premature madness into an awe-inspiring torso, a fragment demanding interpretation, that just at the moment of their affliction and transformation they stammer a few slurred phrases that throw brief flashes of light on the landscape of future intellectual possibilities that will soon be lost forever, Nietzsche also made several utterances in the muddled writings he scribbled just after being overtaken by fate that hint at the synthesis that was still yearning to be fulfilled in this bipolar religious genius who misinterpreted himself as an atheist: a number of his final missives are signed "Dionysus," others bear the signature "the Crucified One."[101] Dionysus on the cross—was this more than a hybrid hallucination—was it the last, desperately condensed formula for his ultimate religious experience and insight? This delusional vision almost seems like a late birth and final fulfillment of that eternal northern longing for an affirmative Christianity, for a Christian spirit of the most heightened, intensified life, no longer in the mirror of an obscure word but face to face. Like a new premonition of the knightly freedom of a Nordic Christian who, after Luther, is master of all things, an entirely free man and subject to no one, of a reborn Hellenic-German "idealism of the living for life": "A cross enshrouded in roses, like Goethe in secrets"[102]—we can already find that in a fragment in the Notebooks for *The Birth of Tragedy.* Nietzsche's beginning and end meet here mysteriously; thus he completes life's circuit and returns whence he came.

But the Dürer engraving seems to be a presentiment and formula of this entire development, of this widely spanned arch of a problematic religious existence. An inkling that he was seeing something like an allegory of his own fate graphically prefigured here must have shocked the young Nietzsche's untrained eye when the print came within his purview. He thought he could interpret this shock as an artistic vision of the lives of his great teacher Schopenhauer and of his mighty friend and inspiration Richard Wagner. But just as the later Nietzsche regarded "Wagner in Bayreuth" as a vision of his own future, whereas his innermost history, his "becoming," was inscribed in "Schopenhauer as Educator," above all his pledge—"both speak only of me, anticipando!"[103]—so, too, would the print, had he seen it in the final years, have eerily appeared to have been, like his own earliest works, a "Self-portrait with Death and Devil." Nietzsche's last comment on the engraving was that it was "too gloomy,"[104] and indeed the mood of the Reformation print may have appeared more characteristic of the "Germanic seriousness of life" embodied in *The World as Will and Representation* than of the late halcyon cheer, the music of the south, that Nietzsche dreamed of in the end. Yet what Nietzsche says about the Schopenhauerian character of the print is true of his *total* outlook. Nietzsche's theological friend Franz Overbeck, with his Erasmus eye, had already perceived that early on, when he wrote to Nietzsche in 1871: "In your expressive portrait you remind me of the bold Dürer knight you once showed me."[105] A prophetic word from a friend: for Nietzsche is now "such a Dürer knight" for us as well; not, to be sure, "without any hope," and one who wanted *more,* more from himself than "the truth." But, akin to Schopenhauer's and Luther's free Christian man, "subservient to no one," he fearlessly goes his own way at the hour of a dangerous twilight, accompanied by his demons, between death, which is "knowledge," and the devil, who calls himself the "temptation of solitude." Above him gleams in the shades of an evening light the fortress of Gothic romanticism, from which his conscience bid him take a difficult farewell. But the path, the terrible path through the narrow pass between two eras, grows dark in the night of a future fate. Where does it lead, where does it end? But does it lead anywhere, does it ever end? "Nevertheless—"

3

The German Becoming

Until now the German has been the fool of the earth . . .
He is an Adam, though in chains, in the circle of animals . . . [1]
—Hebbel 1861

. . . Germany, resembling the Divine Image of Hellas . . . [2]
—Stifter 1859

Throughout all the changing epochs of his thought, Nietzsche, in his need to display gratitude, always honored Heraclitus[3] as the oldest ancestor of his philosophy. This great figure, who had discovered and justified Becoming, was for the poet of *Zarathustra* perhaps the most fruitful prototype and model of himself. Heraclitus's veiled and indirectly transmitted conception of the world gave Nietzsche an early experience of that austere, intoxicated joy that came from encountering a heightened version of himself, as he was later to experience only through his own conception of Zarathustra, in whom so many features of the Ephesian sage were incorporated. No other philosopher or philosophy elicited such tones of delighted *certainty* from Nietzsche during even the most varied periods of his thinking, which constantly moved within the intermediary realm of a "dangerous Perhaps."[4] And, not incidentally, his magnificent fragment on "Philosophy in the Tragic Age of the Greeks" culminates in a portrait of Heraclitus. "The world is eternally in need of truth, thus it is eternally in need of Heraclitus";[5] "what he saw must from now on be seen eternally";[6] "Heraclitus can never become obsolete"[7]—one encounters stylizations of such an unconditional nature almost nowhere else in Nietzsche. "When I am near Heraclitus," he still writes in *Ecce homo,* "I feel generally warmer, better than anywhere else. His affirmation of the passage of time *and of annihilation,* the decisive aspect of any Dionysian philosophy, his saying yes to opposition and war, *becoming,* together with a radical rejection of even the concept of 'being'—it is that which I absolutely have to recognize as being more closely related to me than anything that has been thought since."[8]

The powerful fundamental conception, the tragic Dionysian secret of Eternal Becoming (which subsequently, under the influence of Pythagorean and Empedoclean ideas, would be further intensified in Nietzsche's thinking to become the doctrine of Eternal Recurrence), was for Nietzsche, next to Schopenhauer's conception of the world as will, undoubtedly the strongest confirmation of his own fundamental philosophical direction, the most decisive encounter with himself in a great archetype. (And it was a matter of a true "encounter," not of mere dependence or discipleship, leaving aside the fact that the *choice* of a teacher already indicates an original spontaneity of the soul, the direction of one's will and instinct; we possess comments Nietzsche made during his school days that already show him brooding over the problem of eternal becoming.) Nietzsche himself, and not only in the passage about Heraclitus in *Ecce homo,* perceived and described his own philosophy preeminently as a philosophy of *becoming.* And if the name of Heraclitus is absent on such occasions, then some turn of phrase, some image from the Ephesian's marvelous metaphorical register will often recall the ancestry Nietzsche unconsciously or half-consciously maintained: "What separates us just as much from Kant as from Plato and Leibniz," we read in the late Notebooks: "we believe in becoming only in the intellectual sphere . . . that is the great shift. Lamarck and Hegel . . . Heraclitus's and Empedocles's way of thinking has risen again.[9] . . . The only philosophy I still recognize is as the most general form of history, as the attempt somehow to describe Heraclitean becoming and abbreviate it with signs (to translate and mummify it, as it were, into a sort of apparent being)."[10] At the time of *The Gay Science,* he writes, using a thoroughly Heraclitean image: "If you could see more keenly, you would see everything *moving:* the way paper curls when it burns, everything is continuously passing away and curling up[11] . . . we are not *sensitive* enough to see the presumed *absolute flow* of *occurrence:* what *remains* does so only by virtue of our coarse organs . . . a tree is something new at every moment: its *form* is *asserted* by us. . . ."[12] And in the essay in the *Genealogy* on "Becoming in Morality," we read: "There is no 'being' behind doing, acting, becoming: the 'doer' is merely a fabrication added to the doing—the doing is everything."[13]

Nietzsche applied the great idea of *transformation* to all of his problems with a passionate, unconditional determination that leaves his predecessors Goethe, the romantics, and Hegel far behind in their elaboration of this basic idea. Above all, he applied it to *that* problem which "beset" him the most, against the attacker he warded off most fiercely—against himself. Nietzsche always understood himself to be the eternal wanderer, a catalyst and transformer—this was *his* "justification of becoming": if there was a single part of himself that remained constant, to which he remained faithful, it was this. "Only he who changes will remain akin to me"[14] is one of his most profound self-interpretations. Nietzsche's existence seemed justified to him only in that it transformed itself, only in that it was always *becoming*—just as becoming, the "conflict of things," discord, is the justification of being in Heraclitus. And one can say that Nietzsche lent his problems an ever greater "justification through becoming"[15] the closer to his center he felt them to be: the measure of their involvement in the concept of transformation indicates precisely the degree to which they *beset* and mattered to him. Just as, for the same reason, Nietzsche's hostility toward something also indicates a high degree of inner kinship with it.

In his portrait of Heraclitus, Nietzsche quotes a passage from the first book of *The World as Will and Representation* to illustrate the "Heraclitean conclusion" "that the entire essence of actuality [*Wirklichkeit*] is in fact merely activity [*Wirken*] and that it there is no other mode of being for it."[16] The being of matter is its activity, Schopenhauer says; and it is thus particularly apt that in German the quintessence of all materiality is called *actuality* [*Wirklichkeit*], a much more descriptive word than *reality* [*Realität*]. If a special attunement to the active and evolving aspect of being is thereby attributed to the German language, as opposed to the existential realism of Latinate tongues, then this attunement undoubtedly possessed for Nietzsche the attraction and significance of a symbol pointing to a deeper connection. For his conception of Germanness belongs foremost among those problems that, owing to both the degree of animosity they arouse in Nietzsche and their connection to the idea of *becoming*, unambiguously reveal a "perilous" proximity to the vital center of Nietzsche's essence. The affinity for *becoming* that repeatedly emerges within the German character, indeed the identification of "becoming" with "being German" that appears in Nietzsche in an ever-changing variety of masks—all of that suggests the presence of a deep inner self-identification with the German character, which no one had opposed with such devastating "truths," such impassioned rejections as did Nietzsche himself. Every accentuation, every foregrounding of German becoming, and specifically of its *German* manifestation, takes on the significance of a self-analysis, a self-critique: within German "becoming," "even while radically rejecting the very concept of 'being,'"[17] he is always compelled to acknowledge something essentially related to him, forced to recognize himself. Just as he identifies himself most fully with Heraclitus, so too he rediscovers the German character in Heraclitean becoming—and thus *himself* in the German character.

"We Germans," *The Gay Science* announces, "are Hegelians, even if there had never been a Hegel, inasmuch as we (in contrast to all Latin peoples) instinctively attribute a deeper meaning and greater value to *becoming*, to development than to that which 'is'—we hardly believe in a justification for the concept 'being.'"[18] That is identical with Heraclitus's radical rejection of the concept of "being." But if German thought thus instinctively attributes a deeper meaning and greater value to becoming and to development than to everything that "is," then that is simultaneously a form of self-affirmation, if you will, as well as a self-critique of the German essence (self-critique is always in the end a self-affirmation through self-clarification: there is no absolute self-negation). The German essence perceives itself as becoming; to be German *means* to be in the state of becoming, German is the same as: becoming. For this reason the German word for all that exists, *Wirklichkeit*—actuality—expresses not a state of being but of acting, *becoming:* Germanness perceives itself, experiences itself as a puppet of the mind, as nonpresence and as growth, as vexing inadequacy and immense hope. "Just as every thing loves its own image," we read in *Beyond,* "Germans love clouds and everything that is indistinct, nascent, crepuscular, damp, and overcast: they feel that everything that is uncertain, unformed, displaced, growing is 'deep.' The German himself *is* nothing, he is *becoming,* he is 'developing.' 'Development' is therefore the one truly German discovery and achievement in the great realm of philosophical formulas."[19] One sees again and again that Nietzsche's delineation of the German character ends up in that inmost and innate Hegelianism that, in his own view, is a peculiar inheritance of all Germans. Fichte says the same thing when he finds that the belief in the "endless *improvability* of the German character"[20] is the most profound aspect of that German character itself. Friedrich Schlegel, too, when he says: "Germanness is not behind us, but rather ahead of us."[21] Or Novalis: "the people are an *idea:* we should *become* a people."[22] This entire conception of the German character as that of a postulate, as an endlessly unfulfilled, unfulfillable guiding idea, is as Kantian as it is Platonic, as supremely German as it is fundamentally Greek: born entirely out of a distinctly German Platonism to which Nietzsche himself owed so much, even though he also said the harshest things imaginable about it (just as he did about everything that was a part of himself); it was a German Platonism that nourished Goethe ("we must not want to *be* anything, but to *become* everything"),[23] just as it inspired Hölderlin ("we are nothing; what we seek is everything").[24] And Luther's declaration of faith in becoming is as German as anything this most intrinsically German man ever said, a statement in which for the first time the German people laboriously and conscientiously pondered over and sat in judgment of itself: "This life is not one in which we *are* pious, but rather *become* pious, not where we *are* healthy, but rather *become* healthy, in general it is not a *being,* but a *becoming,* not calm, but rather action. We are not yet there, but we will be, it is not yet done and passed, but it is on the way, it is not the end, but it is the path. . . ."[25]

All of this completely accords with the young Nietzsche's perception of all things German, as he searchingly sought to recall it in the Notebooks for the *Second Untimely:* "Is it true that part of the essence of being German is to lack style? Or is it a sign of being unfinished? That's probably it: what is German has not yet emerged with perfect clarity. . . . *The German character is not even here yet, it first has to become; it has to be born so that it will be visible to all and honest with itself. But every birth is painful and violent. . . .*"[26] Sentences that Nietzsche underlines in the manuscript for good reason. For the conviction that there *is* no German character, that it is *becoming* . . . that actually remains Nietzsche's most concentrated formula for all Germanness. But this becoming is also the reason why Nietzsche constantly raises the question about what constitutes the essence of the German character, why the question "what is German?" will never die out among Germans: it is *indicative* of the Germans, *Beyond* explicitly says, that this question will never die out. And it cannot die out precisely because the German becoming, as a multiplicity of possible developments, logically and even metaphysically excludes a definable being. A German is always only the *intention* toward a German, the mere intention of what we think we "actually" know or surmise about him. Germanness appears as a disposition, an embryo, but never, not even in purely intellectual terms, as a completion and entelechy the way the Greeks, the Italians or French, the English possess an identifiable character. These other peoples all find themselves to be somehow "embodied," see their image somehow given form; the Germans, however, find in the very absence of any such physical incarnation, of any form, they discover in the search and longing for such a concrete manifestation something like *their* characteristic, *their* "image." "What the German spirit *could* be: who has not already had melancholy thoughts about that,"[27] the *Twilight of the Idols* says.

Indeed, it is peculiar to the German character, in contrast to all other peoples, that it exhibits the strangely split self-consciousness of a humbly proud tendency to "Go above itself"—with the "above" always meant in the sense of "beyond," as both a *heightening* of its own essence as well as its *transformation.* "To become more German" is an entirely and uniquely German idea of improvement. (A corresponding notion of "becoming more French" as an ideal of the French spirit, or "to become more English" as a dictate of English character, would be absurd in and of itself. The French spirit *is* as French as it can possibly be, even if its possibilities over the course of history naturally take shape successively; the English character can never be or be imagined as "more English." The degree of comparison here cannot be expressed, even in purely linguistic terms: it is an impossibility to say: "Englisher.")[28] At the same time, however—and this is the strange, truly unprecedented development in the psychology of all peoples—to become more German also means: on a higher plane to rid oneself of Germanness, to overcome the German in oneself, in order to achieve German perfection, to attain German being all the more completely. That is precisely Nietzsche's decisive discovery: "To be a good German means to rid oneself of Germanness,"[29] is how *Human* formulates not so much Nietzsche's insight as his *experience.* He accuses the Germans in the new empire of betraying their Germanness by seeming not to follow him in this realization. "It seems that I am something like a vanishing breed of German," a late passage in the Notebooks resignedly puts it. "'To be a good German means to rid oneself of Germanness'—I once said: but no one will grant me that today. Goethe perhaps would have agreed with me."[30] For "Goethe's voice and example," he elaborates in *Human,* "indicate that a German has to be more than a German . . . and in *which direction* his efforts should be aimed, to go above and beyond himself."[31] To go above and beyond oneself—that is the German predestination; and even his conception of the overman is fed by this German fatefulness, this German metaphysics. "Everything that is perfect of its kind must go beyond its kind," Goethe says, "it must become something else, something incomparable. The nightingale is still a bird in many sounds it makes; but then it rises above its class and seems to want to demonstrate to every other feathered creature what singing really means. . . ."[32] And in another passage: "Who knows if all mankind is not merely an attempt to reach a higher goal?"[33] That clearly is already the seed of Zarathustra's doctrine of the overman: "All beings until now have created something beyond themselves . . . man is something that should be overcome. What have you done to overcome him?"[34] And if Zarathustra's overman, as Nietzsche portrays him, seems to be less a future reality, a prophesied actuality, than a guiding phantom that draws us up but remains inherently unattainable, then this deeply Platonic, deeply German notion of the forward-cast ideal that can no more be reached than the foot of a rainbow can also be found in Goethe, who despite his supreme adherence to the present moment and his unwaveringly confident possession of the greatest perfection a German has ever achieved, still gave voice to this "Above and beyond" in *Poetry and Truth:* "No one, no matter how much he may possess, can survive without longing; but true longing must be directed toward something *unattainable.*"[35]

Thus there has always been something of the Beyond, something auspiciously and alluringly unattainable associated with the concept of a German *being;* it is actuality [*Wirklichkeit*] only insofar as it is active [*wirkt*]; like God's realm it is always "coming," at most "near," never "here." Innate to the German essence is this Faustian, this Gothic "Beyond itself." The German language itself is an expression and symbol of it: there is no other language that is so "imperfect" in all of its immense and transcendental grandeur, no other that so easily succumbs to harmful formlessness or abstruse license. No other language is so powerless against debilitating foreign influence, no other so stubbornly resists mastery, perfection. But there is also no other language in the European sphere that harbors within it such possibilities beyond itself, none can express all that is becoming, in the future, that is dimly approaching, all that is truly Sibylline, as can ours. It repels like no other the merely logical; it is, as the French rightly conclude, *déraisonable.* But since Plato's day there has been no other that is as capable of exhaling the other side of the logical, the mystical, of so immediately foretelling what is eternally coming. It is never finished, never complete at any given stage, as for example French has been for centuries; it is, like the people that speak it, forever a language that is "expectant." That is meant by Goethe's comment to Schiller that it was certainly true that such a peculiar language as German will always leave something to be desired.[36] And the same is true of all German art: "Northern beauty," Wölfflin explained, "is not a beauty that is self-contained and delimited, but is rather boundless and endless. . . . The finished form means too little to the Germanic imagination, it always has to be enlivened with the stimulus of movement. . . . In all German architecture the rhythm of movement is the decisive element, not its 'beautiful proportion.'"[37]

Nietzsche's experience of the German language, of the German character—and lack of character—is anchored in the substratum of this peculiarly turbulent feeling of becoming. This is where his impassioned super-German critique is rooted, where we find the whole harshness of a disappointed lover of his people, his Hyperion severity and ultimately his "tremendous hope"[38] as well, which he expresses not just in *The Birth of Tragedy.* There is hardly a single comment by Nietzsche about Germanness, be it positive, skeptical, or negative, that did not have its innermost core within the immanent German *becoming.* Nietzsche worked toward the same goal that all leading German minds have worked toward: to concentrate a wave of that Heraclitean current of eternal German becoming—of which our language is the flowing reflection—into a crystalline drop, to rescue an image from the chaos, to wrench from the musical and multifarious frenzy a clear, uniquely defined *shape.* For until now there have been only rudiments, fragments, tragic torsos of such image formation. It is not accidental that "education," "formation," [*Bildung*], the creation and development of form, was Goethe's favorite word and task, indeed the real Goethean idea. And indeed, as a comment in Nietzsche's Notebooks has it, there had been "so far no German education: there have been hermits who knew how to keep themselves hidden with astonishing skill in the midst of the coarsest barbarism"[39]—for "barbarism" is Goethe's expression for the still-chaotic aggregate condition of a people, the same Goethe who in a famous conversation with Eckermann in 1827 said that a couple of centuries would still have to pass before people would be able to say of the Germans that it was a long time since they had been barbarians[40]—a passage that Nietzsche cited in the *First Untimely Mediation* with such special emphasis.

German education, Nietzsche says with Goethe, has not yet existed; as yet there has been no German form, no image of the German essence, no shape of the German person. The Germans are the only people who have lived for a thousand years within the brilliance of the European, Greek-Christian cultural sphere and who, to the profound and lasting unease of all their neighbors, to the helpless and shameful consternation of their own most noble minds, do not permit a plausible and lasting image of their character to form in the soul. There is about them something of the mystical "imagelessness of all images" that contains all images within it, but, so to speak, in an eternally prenatal condition. The Germans' own arduous process of becoming conscious of themselves (one cannot say that Germans possess self-consciousness, which is perhaps also the deepest reason why they have always been so desperately self-conscious in the everyday sense), this process of becoming conscious is always mysteriously intertwined with the mournful question Hölderlin posed: "When will you *fully* appear, soul of the fatherland?"[41] And there has been only *one* full response to it until now: German music.

Nietzsche's special relationship to music (which permeates *all* of his problems with a common musical heartbeat) also gains a central importance in connection with his German critique. He experienced the German character and German possibility most deeply, most hopefully, and most bitterly painfully as German music—*The Birth of Tragedy* is after all merely the classic testimony of that experience, but not the only one. He consciously juxtaposed the "civilization that grew out of the Romanic character"[42] to *the* German spirit that revealed itself in the German Reformation—the most powerful protest of German becoming against European being—and in German music. And even in *Beyond,* at the height of his super-German, anti-German period, he concluded his masterful analysis of the prologue to the *Meistersinger* by saying that this music best expressed what he thought of the Germans: "They are from the day before yesterday and the day after tomorrow—they do not yet have a today."[43] Nietzsche never acknowledged his own Germanness as profoundly as he did with regard to his relationship to music; the "fate of music"[44] was, by his own admission during his final year, the last thing that still "mattered"; life with music seemed to this soul to be an exile, an error; "only he who changes will remain akin to me,"[45] confessed this spirit who, above all others, craved becoming, reveled in transformation; from the earliest days of his boyhood up through his insanity ("Sing a new song for me: the world is transfigured . . ."),[46] nothing remained so inwardly congenial to him, so much an expression of his own self, as music. Therein, despite his pronounced anti-Germanness, despite his most severe and cutting words about none other than German music, Nietzsche is a living parable of the German essence: for it is here and here alone, in the fluid, incessant *becoming,* in the formless murmur of the "art of the infinite"—as the German romantics understood it—that Hölderlin's soul of the fatherland has so far "fully appeared." But to fathom its essence demands no less than a German soul born to music, which, as Nietzsche expressed it in a late wish, should always sing and not speak; in the sphere of the word, of image and form, this singular interpretation of the German character falls mute. It is not as if the German soul had not tried to give itself shape in this sphere as well. But there its greatest and most daring creations never entirely shed the tragic Beyond, which prevented them from achieving independent perfection, from attaining wholeness and self-sufficiency. What other architecture in the world brutalizes and tortures its own material with such ardent contempt as the great German edifices do, including the edifices of our philosophy? How telling that precisely the most significant works of German painting and sculpture always grapple with the problem of portraying what cannot be pictorially expressed, so that the more German an image is, the more it points beyond the image (one needs only to think of Dürer)! The inner compulsion to look for what is fundamental, most essential, for "being," in what is not present, in the "other"—that is the German fate, it is the true German "suffering from oneself." "Every incomplete creature *suffers,*"[47] writes Hebbel a year before his death. "It is reserved for the Germans," Wölfflin says in his Dürer book, "to portray the apostles not as magisterial, flawless beings, but as men who are consumed by painful inadequacy."[48] Formlessness in this sense, musical immateriality, the unrestricted—"unlimited"—but also uncontainable, effusiveness of the German mentality is what often makes Germanness seem so discordant, so deeply suspect to "educated"—that is, already defined, formed—peoples. Nietzsche, particularly the late Nietzsche in the year of *Ecce homo,* makes himself the exponent of this universal suspicion toward all things German, now preferring to see a great cultural crime in the Reformation, *warning* every "existence that believes in itself"[49] away from German music, now deliberately believing himself to be part of Romanic civilization, proud to write in a more French, a more Latin style than a German one; now he finds the Germans to be the "irresponsible race," who "had something 'else' on their mind at all the decisive moments of history."[50] It is true that in this, his late animosity toward Germans, Nietzsche is above all a symptom and phenomenon of the German "suffering from oneself," the typical German self-hatred; just as, conversely, Nietzsche's hatred of Germans is a symptom and phenomenon of his own self-hatred, that noble obsession of self-overcoming that Nietzsche himself saw as "basically his greatest strength."[51] (His hatred of Germans belongs psychologically on the same plane as his hatred of Christianity, of Wagner's music, Socrates, and Platonism:

it is a form of his "asceticism.") Yet objectively speaking, Nietzsche is the legitimate exponent of a general, true intellectual hostility toward the German character, to which Nietzsche merely lent more weapons than he took from it (and therein, once more, Nietzsche is thoroughly German). This general hostility has nothing to do with political matters (even Nietzsche's hatred of the German "empire" is unconsciously directed predominantly against the self-"de-Germanification" of a people whom he saw descending from a rich becoming and settling into a petty, premature being, into an offensive and very un-German self-contentment); we have examples of it from every century and every one of our great minds has felt it. "There is no nation held in greater contempt than the Germans," Luther says; "the Italians call us beasts, France and England, and all the other countries, ridicule us. Who knows what God wishes and intends to make of the Germans? Even though we probably do deserve a flogging before God."[52] And on another occasion, more resignedly: "in other lands, nothing is known about the Germans." At the end of the eighteenth century Hölderlin saw Germany as "all-abiding as the silent mother earth and everywhere misjudged."[53] In 1869 Hebbel wrote in his diary: "All nations hate the Germans. . . . But if they were ever to succeed in getting rid of them, a situation would arise in which they would want to dig the Germans back out of the grave with their bare nails."[54] Seen from the outside, an atmosphere of indescribable *foreignness* seems to envelop the German character—even Luther's words point to that. "Ce peuple est d'un autre âge,"[55] a French author said in 1871, sincerely trying to comprehend Germany's puzzling "actuality," only to give up with a shrug of the shoulders. These people belong to a different age—that, in the final analysis, is what is also meant by the word "barbarian," be it in the mouth of Goethe or in the imagination of nations that "know nothing about the Germans." And Nietzsche means the same thing—this belonging to a *different* age—by his embittered comment about the race that always had something else on its mind at all the decisive moments in European history, full of a deep foreignness and in an unreachable inner remoteness, lost in dark and confused preoccupation with its own "salvation." It is always something "other" that the Germans seek, something Beyond, something that is "not of this world," something that does not belong to the "fear of the mortal." Precisely because of this eternal belonging *d'un autre âge,* the Germans are the constant source of disquiet to the European sense of time, a continuous doubt about what they "actually" are because they do not seem to be anything "fully." A German is always *something else,* and usually his precise opposite. He combines what is strictly incompatible, indeed that is what is barbaric about him (for, in the Greek sense, only he is educated who resolutely rejects certain possibilities of chaos in order to embody others all the more clearly); for that reason he is the object of ridicule as well as the ineradicable source of fear for all others: fear of the incommensurable, which necessarily seemed offensive and inimical to "Greek" humanity and to its late-Roman heirs who depended on measure and boundaries. The *odium generis humani*[56] is at its metaphysical core the hatred of all that is formed for all that is unformed, of the educated for the chaotic, of what has become for all that is becoming, of the unequivocally clear for the ambiguously dark.

It is at this point that Nietzsche initiates his "vivisection of the German soul," interpreting this unformed diversity as its vagueness, its foreignness. "The German soul is above all multifarious," he says in *Beyond,* attempting to explain this phenomenon along racial biological lines, which is to say to simplify it conceptually; "it is of diverse origins, more assembled than actually constructed: that is owing to its provenance."[57] (Nietzsche's favorite notion of atavism, of predestination through the mixture of ancestors, comes into play here as well.) "A German who would have the impudence to maintain that 'two souls reside, alas! within my breast'[58] would be violating the truth, or rather would fall short of the truth by many souls. As a people resulting from a fantastic mixing and combining of races, perhaps even with a preponderance of the pre-Aryan element, as a 'people of the middle' in every sense, the Germans are more incomprehensible, more unwieldy, more contradictory, more unfamiliar, more unpredictable, more surprising, even more terrifying than other peoples are to themselves—they escape *definition* and with that already drive the French to despair."[59] Indefinable, illimitable, incapable of being contained and confined within any boundary (it is symbolic that no other people in the world has linguistic borders that are so ill-defined nationally): that is indeed always the final judgment of the German character by foreigners (the conscientious foreigners), for whom Nietzsche in his super-Germanness becomes a spokesman here, as in almost all of his late works. But it is the "despairing" judgment of Latin peoples in particular whose German perspective Nietzsche makes in a narrow sense his own. "Si je ne vois pas clair, tout mon monde est anéanti"[60]—Stendhal's comment holds true for the entire French-Latin viewpoint, and it is precisely by being measured against that standard that the contradictory unpredictability of the German character fails. "In contrast to all the Latin peoples," Nietzsche says, "we instinctively attribute a deeper and richer value to becoming than to what is—." Latin intellectualism feels that its world, a world of belief in being, is negated and destroyed by this Hegelian Protestantism of becoming, which, according to Nietzsche, hardly believes in the legitimacy of the concept of "being." ("Being" is a Roman reality, just as "becoming" is a German actuality.) No "clear," rationalistic approach is adequate to a people who, to the dismay of educated peoples and of those who emulate them, do *not* acknowledge *raison,* civilized and civilizing reason, either as the highest measure of culture or as the meaning of existence. The Germans are *déraisonnable* (Nietzsche himself borrows this term from French), they are profoundly eccentric, not capable of being reduced to any one intellectual category; their eternal self-contradiction seems utterly irresolvable. "It is characteristic of the Germans," the passage cited from *Beyond* continues, "that one is seldom entirely wrong about them. The German soul has corridors and passageways, it contains lairs, hideouts, secret dungeons; its disorder has much of the appeal of the mysterious; Germans know their way around the hidden paths to chaos."[61] (Here too one perceives the traces of a disguised self-description, as is always the case when Nietzsche characterizes the German essence; one is reminded of the passage in *Ecce homo* in which Nietzsche ascribes to himself the "pleasant depravity"[62] that in his view distinguishes the Thuringians: "We prefer the hidden paths even to arrive at the truth.")[63] "Foreigners are amazed and attracted by the riddles posed by the contradictory nature of the German soul (which Hegel put into a system and Richard Wagner even recently set to music). . . . How disorderly and rich the entire inner economy is! How the most noble and most base elements stand next to each other!"[64] Before Nietzsche, this most merciless judge and self-judge, it was especially Goethe who frequently and sternly mentioned this "baseness," which is to say chaos, as a danger and even a hallmark of the German soul: "The Germans, among whom baseness in general finds the opportunity to gain prevalence far more frequently than in other countries . . ."[65] we read in an example of genuinely German self-criticism in *Poetry and Truth.* Baseness—that is the unformed primordial ground common to all, the dangerous and fertile proximity to chaos, which forever thirsts for revenge against the will that forced it into form, but whose energy nevertheless unwillingly nourishes this form to its fruition. This inner nearness of the chaotic Earth Spirit, which the German spirit is fated to feel so keenly (Germans "sense that there is something voracious, insatiable, murderous in man. . . ."[66] [Notebooks 1873]), this nearness of "terrible visions," the danger of falling back into dissolution, determines the immanent inadequacy of the *individual* German, his fragmentariness, his inner conflicts, his vacillation between a weak need for support and an arrogant selfishness, his "excessiveness" in whatever may be the major productive trend of his individual nature—to use a clarifying analogy: the eternal Jean Paul in him.[67] Even the educated German does not appear as a diminutive yet faithful copy of the entirety of his people, a miniaturized national harmony, as does the individual French, English, Italian, for instance; the German is almost always like the lone voice that sounds slightly off-key, seemingly out of place in the grand, all-too-richly harmonized fugue of the German collective character, whereas in every Latin person, for example, a hint of the clear melody of his people seems to resonate with a conciliatory and clarifying tone.

The shortcomings inherent in the German self-contradiction, the incomprehensible, unpredictable aspect of the inner German otherworldliness and nearness to chaos, which Nietzsche everywhere emphasizes, particularly in *Beyond*, are what make "education"—*Bildung*—such a German ideal and almost an idol: education understood as the taking shape, the taking form of one's own material. For that reason, education has been an "idea of the middle" for all German leaders; none has held it so passionately as Nietzsche, who here too proves himself to be almost more German than German. This pedagogical educational passion of the German character (which created in Luther and Lessing, in Herder and Goethe, in Schiller and Jean Paul, in Novalis, Stifter, and Wagner only the most distinct types and mediators) is one with the genuine German homesickness for all *being*, for the final, late, and grateful rest in being and presence that has so tragically attracted Germans throughout their history to all *formed* creations, countries, and peoples. The unquenchable longing for the Roman and Romanic south, which is so closely wedded to the educational drive, this "yearning for the south" that is so peculiar to Germans, has its deepest roots precisely in this enchantment of conditionality, of what has already become, of being, which everything in the south possesses for the German wanderer (for those who "wander" in every sense). It is the joyous "present" that Goethe drank in with such enthralled delight in Italy and never tired of extolling: "How true, how *real!*"[68] seemed to him everything that lived there after the nebulous always-becoming of the lugubrious north. This super-German presence of a world that has taken shape in form and image attains its final, painfully delightful charm, which only Germans seem to know, precisely through its inner temptation toward chaos, through their seductive proclivity toward the abyss of that "baseness" from which they had only just arduously emerged. Thus the German spirit remains on the eternal threshold between the magical realm of what has become, which deludes Germans into believing that their own, very different, future has already been achieved, and the temptation of a regression into barbarism, confusion, the mystic past, and yet constant threat toward all that is human. That is how the anxious, doubtful glance of every super-German sees them; that is the way they see themselves at those moments when they become aware of themselves: they are from the day before yesterday and from the day after tomorrow—they do not yet have a *today.* The *transition,* the transformation from the day before yesterday to the day after tomorrow, is what constitutes the spell and curse and noble destiny of the German character and becoming.

But that is the intellectual stance of Nietzsche himself, his own conscious and unconscious crossing over from the day before yesterday to the day after tomorrow, his own singular fate to be a transitory moment forever frozen in time; it is *his* yearning for the south, his homesickness for being, his pedagogical educational ideal, nourished by his Lutheran inheritance and Goethean humanism, his loving hatred for the sweet seductions of musical chaos, which was what Richard Wagner's unending melody symbolized to him during his late will to form. Nietzsche is more than the classic symbol of German becoming that he himself exemplifies; his constant confrontation with Germanness is a grand, perhaps the grandest, confrontation of the German character with itself: the German spirit confronts itself in Nietzsche, *as* Nietzsche, it passionately seeks to explain itself to itself, to "get over" itself; Nietzsche is *one* form of German becoming, one unforgettable gesture of German "Above and beyond oneself," of German self-overcoming, of which his individual, personal overcomings, his passionate asceticisms, are only a reflection and allegory. "A people that becomes conscious of its dangers produces the genius"[69]—this early comment by Nietzsche, from the Notebooks, is valid for the relationship of the German people to Nietzsche himself. "Where there is danger, however, salvation also grows"[70]—there is perhaps an unconscious echo of this late line by his favorite Hölderlin. Nietzsche is such a "salvation" not only in the temporally definable moment of a particular danger—the danger and crisis in which Germanness found itself at the moment in which Nietzsche wrote his first book, in 1870–71—he is not only the becoming conscious of such temporal dangers, but rather a brilliant coming into self-consciousness of the German character itself when it hung most dangerously, most fatefully between the day before yesterday and the day after tomorrow, between chaos and form, in an eternal moment of *becoming:* Nietzsche is the dazzling minute in which a people gained self-knowledge at the moment (at the metaphysical moment) of its most pressing inner danger—and it is simultaneously an awakening and an expansion of the instinct of preservation and the will to salvation.[71]

For it would be a misappreciation and a misrepresentation of Nietzsche's stance toward the German character—a misappreciation that a superficial impression admittedly encourages—if one were to see in his description of German becoming only his perception and not his hope as well, only what was inadequate and not what was extraordinary too, only "danger" and not also "salvation." Both, after all, constitute the quintessence of becoming: the day before yesterday and the day after tomorrow. Thus, for Nietzsche as well, the eternally "Other" in the German character displays traits not only of chaos but also of a Platonic "image"—perhaps even of a Dionysian hope. We of course know how the "tremendous hope"[72] that by his own admission speaks out of *The Birth of Tragedy,* a hope for a rebirth out of the spirit of German music—that it did not survive the period of the *Un-*

timely Meditations: his skeptical mockery of Germans already begins in *Human* and grows in intensity up through the invective and indictments of *The Case of Wagner, The Antichrist,* and *Ecce homo.* But Nietzsche's "German hopes" merely changed: they are visible as masks in Nietzsche's middle and late works and reveal to the attentive reader their vitality at every turn. Just as Nietzsche himself hoped to become the principal heir of the best part of Wagner's influence, so too did he actually inherit those early German hopes from him, which he joined with youthful enthusiasm to Wagner's ambitions for a German cultural rejuvenation in the spirit of the Reformation. Nietzsche now controls his own realm, in which the name "German" remains taboo; but unbeknownst to him this realm itself has become a realm of German becoming and German hope, even if the greatest of those hopes carries the otherworldly name of Zarathustra: the very word that describes him, the *over*-man, bears the stigma of his deeply German essence, of German becoming. And Nietzsche himself occasionally suspects this, as when he says, for example, that today the German spirit can no longer be found in the "empire"—if anywhere, then in Sils-Maria.[73] The "empire" no longer seemed German to him; but his own realm was and became all the more German in its stead.

From the beginning, Nietzsche drew his will to critique German reality, but also his courage to hope for the unreal, unrealized, super-German future, from his experience of German becoming. As a disciple of Wagner, he is a thoroughly German cultural enthusiast, someone filled with hope in the sense Luther meant: "Who knows what God wishes and intends to make of the Germans?" or that Goethe intended in November 1813: "I hold fast to this belief: yes, the German people promise a future, they have a future. The fate of the Germans, to quote Napoleon, has yet to be fulfilled . . . it is my belief that there must be a great destiny in store for them."[74] "We can hope again!" Nietzsche wrote to a friend in 1871, "our *German* mission is not yet over! I am more courageous than ever: for not everything has succumbed to French-Jewish vapidity and 'elegance' and to the ravenous tumult of the 'here and now.' There is still such a thing as courage, and it's called German courage, which is something *inwardly different* from the élan of our pitiable neighbors. . . ."[75] Courage—that was for Nietzsche in his later years no less than in his earlier ones the test for inner *future* content, a proof of power for new possibilities of future being. "The German spirit is courageous"[76] he said in his lecture "On the Future of our Educational Institutions" during the same period in Basel; that means the German spirit can still be formed, that it is still material, it still dares to *become* (because "being" is a form of aging and of cowardice before old age). Thus, "Schopenhauer as Educator" speaks of "that old German type that is admittedly hard, rough, and obdurate, but also the most precious material, with which only the greatest sculptors are allowed to work because they alone are worthy of it."[77]

That is the appraisal Nietzsche makes of the German character in his earliest years—one that is still completely positive and faithful, but one that even then did not pertain to the German present for a single moment (as brilliantly gilded by external success as it may have seemed), referring instead to a phantom of hope. Yet the deepest disappointment of his life, the long-prepared renunciation of Wagner, also transforms Nietzsche's German dream: his faith in the German cause seeps more and more rapidly down into the subterranean recesses of his nature where, although unchanged in its essential character, it is forced to the surface in super-German, even anti-German eruptions, feeding his bold otherworldly conceptions, fueling the grandiose becoming of the idea of Zarathustra. Nietzsche's visible hopes for German becoming abruptly wither away in the first post-Wagner years: "A German is capable of great things, but it is unlikely he will do them,"[78] we already read in *Daybreak;* "if a German ever did something great, then it occurred during some crisis, as an act of courage. . . ."[79] We still see here that the cardinal German virtue upheld by the young Nietzsche, the courage of the German spirit, remains untouched. But, characteristically enough, it too is turned into its precise opposite by Nietzsche by the end: his conception of German non-presentness, which he regarded with such reverence, with so much hope before, now receives the evil eye: he calls it "cowardice before reality."[80] For that reason, Germans now seem to him to be "procrastinators par excellence,"[81] who "have all of the great crimes of culture on their conscience."[82] And the chapter of German hopes, which had made Nietzsche "more courageous than ever" in Basel, is apparently definitively closed by the case of Wagner with the brutal verdict: "The Germans themselves have no future."[83] For Nietzsche, this future had become crystallized in a single name: Zarathustra.

And yet we possess the psychological evidence that, although the externally visible connection between Nietzsche's *hopes* and his vision of German *becoming* had disappeared, deep down it had never been severed—just as little as Nietzsche himself, even in his most super-German period, had never ceased to be an entirely German figure, indeed a rare example of the type. This evidence is his incredibly irascible, passionately nurtured hatred toward the *nouveaux* Germans of the victorious young "empire," opposed to which he understood himself to be a German of a dying breed, as the "last German," as a German from "the day before yesterday," but secretly also as a kind of "first German," as a German from "the day after tomorrow." His fanaticism, his impassioned injustice toward everything that bore the name German, can be compared only with the outbursts of his *Antichrist* and his *The Case of Wagner:* like these, it is a love-hate, a hatred stemming from the most profound feeling of kinship, from the guilty conscience of an inner identity, which feeds his anti-Germanness. It is a hatred of his own dangers, of a threat to what is best in himself. The diminution, the caricature-like distortion of his own ideal, the premature self-restraint, and the humble realization of something destined for a higher entelechy—that is what Nietzsche cannot forgive the Germans of Bismarck's "empire" (that is the only way to explain his strange distortion and misunderstanding of Bismarck, whom he of all people, from a detached distance, would have doubtlessly placed in a row with his favorite Machiavellian power merchants). Fundamentally, the only thing he did not forgive Christianity was its diminution, falsification, and reinterpretation of the Greek inheritance; he did not forgive Wagner that he, the creator of Siegfried, Tristan, the "Lutheran" Meistersinger, "condescended" to their opposite ideals, that he had forever robbed the mighty pyramid of his existence of its ultimate crowning peak; that for the sake of an all-too-rapid success during his life, he had let his revolutionary becoming solidify prematurely into a pseudo-legitimate being: that, in a word, Nietzsche's own vision of himself (for that was what *The Birth of Tragedy* and "Richard Wagner in Bayreuth" in essence were) had been violated by a grotesque realization in the form of the real Bayreuth (the dream of Tribschen and the rich patronate hoi polloi of 1876, as Nietzsche puts it). Thus Nietzsche did not forgive Germans that, through their smug complacency with the "being" of the new empire that was acquired all too quickly, all too easily, they had robbed themselves of that noble self-dissatisfaction that alone could have forced the still-evolving German spirit to attain its preordained height. He did not forgive them the repulsive modesty with which they took an achieved state of security and civilization to be a culture; nor did he forgive an equally repulsive arrogance with which they dedicated themselves to a form of nationalism that necessarily made the German becoming into a parody of older peoples' being. That was the young Nietzsche's instinctive fear, just as it became the older recluse's fury. (The introductory pages of the first *Untimely* and the invective of the *Ecce homo* chapter "The Case of Wagner" arise out of the same depths and say basically the same thing.) But this nationalism seemed to Nietzsche both during his early faith in Germanness as well as in his later critique of it, the true original sin against the German character, the crime that is not forgiven; German chauvinism (even the language refuses to provide a German word for this inherent contradiction) remained for him the death of any German hope. Germanness is conceivable to him only *as* hope, as a tremendous possibility, as a demand (above all, of oneself), as a postulate, and as a spur to renewed effort. A Germanness that believes it has arrived at its goal, that thinks its embodiment (its "culture") has already been achieved, is for him nothing but a grotesque abomination. Is there really a more exalted view of the German character, a more discriminating estimation of its inner possibilities as, for example, the comment out of the Notebooks from the *Transvaluation* period demonstrates (which formally is already fairly unrestrained): "'Deutschland, Deutschland über alles'—that is perhaps the most idiotic slogan that has ever been uttered. *Why* Germany at all—I ask: if it doesn't *want, represent, exemplify* something that has more value than any other previous power represented! . . . Where is the new *idea?* Is it only a new combination of power? All the worse if it doesn't know what it wants. . . . To rule and to help the highest idea to victory—the only thing that could interest me about Germany. What do I care whether Hohenzollerns exist or not? England's small-mindedness is now the great danger in the world."[84] When had a German ever spoken more proudly about the German character as a German responsibility? "Deutschland über alles"—that could, that had to mean only one thing to him: Germans must retain an inner world expansiveness, that singular feeling of responsibility (which reveals itself in the most superficial sphere as "cosmopolitan"): to be a world, a genuine cosmos with all of its evolving possibilities; to bear the burden of a world, the future of a world—not "this" world, but rather "another" one, a new world of German actualization.

But what is the new dominant idea? What is the Goethean "direction in which every German should strive to go above and beyond himself"?[85] What is the tremendous imagined future of German becoming that Nietzsche felt was threatened by the new German contentedness with an illusory actualization and deceptive presence, by premature satisfaction with an "empire," with national narrowness and a supposedly attained culture? For the sake of which hopes is there this passionate, plaintive, and accusatory, almost desperate hostility toward the "imperial Germanness," instead of, for instance, a cool Schopenhauerian indifference toward political developments, instead of an ironic resignation that would after all be the only appropriate expression of a really genuine inner hopelessness? Nietzsche gives the answer early on, which remained the answer all his life: immediately after the war, he recognizes the highest culture "until now only as the *reawakening of Hellenism.* The struggle against civilization[86] . . . restoration of the true German spirit[87] . . ." as he puts it in the preliminary studies for the lecture "On the Future of our Educational Institutions." A profound predetermination of the German character for inner Hellenization, a peculiar affinity, and one that completely contradicts current appearances, between the "true German spirit" and Hellenism, guides the experience of the young Nietzsche who still drew upon Hölderlin's German Greekness. "It is very difficult to comprehend the equally mysterious bond that truly links the innermost German character with the Greek genius"[88] we read in that same lecture. And no actual formation or formal development of the German evolving character is possible or conceivable "until it is the noblest desire of the true German spirit to grasp for the hand of this Greek genius as if for a solid support in the current of barbarism, until a consuming longing for the Greeks bursts forth from this German spirit, until the laboriously acquired vision into the Greek *homeland* . . . has become a place of pilgrimage for the best and most talented people."[89] The path to that Greek homeland, to the Hölderlin-homeland of the German soul, is still all too long for the laborious self-liberation of the German spirit, for its long and problematic inner self-becoming. To this day, "this German spirit, bound to the Greeks by the noblest desire, has proven itself at difficult moments in the past to be persistent and brave, pure and lofty in its goals, qualified by its art to undertake the highest task of redeeming modern man from the curse of the modern"—to this day, this spirit is still "condemned to live in isolation, alienated from its heritage. . . ."[90] But its heritage *remains* this timeless Hellenism: "There is something in Germans that could be *Hellenistic,*" reads a passage in the Notebooks from the final years, "which awakens at contact with the *south*—Winckelmann, Goethe, Mozart."[91] The Greek character is simultaneously the inheritance and the uplifting augural phantom of German becoming: Hellas is the Platonic idea of a "more German" Germannness. Pindar's words, which Nietzsche chose as the prologue to his life, which guided and accompanied him from early on until the very end, and which also made its way into *Zarathustra,* are: γένοἰ οἶοζ ἐσσί "Become who you are!"[92]—this Pindaric summons is also valid for his Germans. Become what you already are: become Me!—that is the constantly renewed and mystically ambiguous summons of the Greeks across millennia; and the German conscience becomes restless when it hears this half-warning, half-promising voice that sounds like an inducement to love, to transformative love. "Man, what you love is what you will be transformed into"[93]—so warns the voice, and that "consuming longing for the Greeks,"[94] which bursts forth out of the Germans again and again, like a primeval flame, is only the expression of the will to transform oneself into one's own more authentic self, to become what one fundamentally is. The exaggerated German obsession with intellectual acquisition, the excessive gratitude in learning and assimilating the Hellenic inheritance in particular, is itself a form of this Greek homesickness. The greatest and most grateful of the German pupils of the Greeks recognized: "Someone who is becoming will always be grateful . . . in general we learn only from someone we love."[95] This noblest and oldest tradition of the German character: the will to transformation and the longing for perfection toward the Greeks—it was nothing less than this that Nietzsche saw being endangered by the pernicious self-satisfaction that after 1870 seemed to paralyze German becoming with the poisonous delusion of premature being. He saw the *meaning* of his intellectual existence being endangered, a typically *evolving* existence ("only he who changes will remain akin to me"), an exemplary German-Hellenic search and "pilgrimage" to the Greek homeland of the soul. Thus his "hatred of Germans" represents an act of intellectual self-defense, as does his anti-Socratism, a battle against a tendency that would negate him in his essential core.

But probably nothing demonstrates so immediately how deeply the positive valuation of Germanness (a self-valuation, in the final analysis) is rooted in Nietzsche as his unmistakable stylization of the Greek essence itself into the German character of becoming. Nietzsche is perhaps the first to have had the audacity to stylize historical Hellenism as the pinnacle of a kind of "German" development. His own predilection for the early *formative period* of the Hellenic spirit is not without significance in this connection as well—no one had so decisively, so consciously neglected, almost unjustly minimized the so-called classical epoch of the Greek character, its moment of "being," in favor of the epoch of Greek becoming as exemplified by the pre-Socratic philosophers. And just as he considers "the ideal of antiquity is perhaps only the most beautiful blossom of the Germanic longing for the south"[96] ("Homer and Classical Philology"), he then also lets it suffer a kindred fate; the "classical" height of perfection represented by Winckelmann's vision of antiquity is portrayed, as if in consolation to German becoming, as the final reward of a parallel, arduous self-becoming, an exemplary promise. If Nietzsche perceives the upward striving for Greek heights out of the inner twilight of an innate chaos as German, then he describes the Greek achievement as having grown out of such an innate twilight and proximity to chaos, and he thus also bends the fates of these two peoples and cultures across an immeasurable span toward each other in mystical identity. "A presentiment of *the height* from which alone beauty bestows its charms even on Germans drives German artists into the heights and beyond and into the excesses of passion: a truly deep desire, in other words, to go beyond ugliness and maladroitness, or at least to look beyond them—toward a better, lighter, more southern, sun-filled world"[97]—that is how *The Gay Science* explains the uplifting homesickness for Greece in the German character through the inner fate of its talented artists. But his lectures on the history of Greek literature indicate that this was also his view of the psychological condition of Greek artists; that he had attempted to see the all-too-lofty exemplarity of Hellenic art as more encouraging, more possible, *more exemplary,* by interpreting it into something "more German." "The striving toward light out of an in-born twilight, as it were, is *Greek,*" he writes there; "we still find this in Euripides, in Plato. Their fertility is to be measured by this struggle." And again: "We allow ourselves to be easily seduced by the famed Greek transparency and lightness into believing that it was all natural and given to the Hellenes: Lichtenberg thought that the Greeks were simply *unable* to write poorly. That is not true at all. The history of prose from Gorgias to Demosthenes shows a heroic struggle toward light, pure composition. . . . Generally I have the impression that the Greek masters worked *very hard and slowly* . . ."[98] (Similarly, in the second volume of *Human:* "On the Acquired Character of the Greeks.")[99]

German *learning* as well, that excessive gratitude of German becoming in the acquisition of foreign cultural values, its inner, productive cosmopolitanism—this Nietzsche also sees as a typically Hellenic capacity: he legitimizes German permeability with the primal example of Greek universal openness. Nothing is more foolish, he says in the "Philosophers' Book" written in Basel, than to claim that the Greeks have an autochthonous culture; "rather, they absorbed the living culture of all other peoples, they went so far precisely because they understood how to throw the spear farther from the spot where another people had left it. They are admirable in their ability to learn productively. . . ."[100] That is, quite obviously, the ideal image of a *German* possibility and aptitude; and the teacher of the Germans immediately adds to the Greek historian's words: " . . . and thus, like them, we *should* learn from our neighbors, for life, not for academic knowledge, using everything we learn as a pillar on which we can climb up and higher than our neighbor."[101]

The second *Untimely Meditation* develops this theme of a genuinely German productive danger as being a truly Hellenic fate:

> There were centuries in which the Greeks found themselves faced with a danger similar to the one we face, namely of being overwhelmed by foreign elements and by the past, of foundering on "history." Never did they live in proud, untouched purity: rather, their "culture" was for a long time a chaotic mix of foreign, Semitic, Babylonian, Lydian, Egyptian forms and concepts, and their religion a veritable battle of the gods from the entire Orient: similar to the way today "German culture" and religion, for example, is an internally conflicted chaos of the entire Occident, of the entire past. And nevertheless Hellenic culture did not become an aggregate. . . . The Greeks gradually learned *to organize chaos* by reflecting again, in accordance with the Delphic oracle, on themselves, in other words by being mindful of their true needs and letting the apparent needs wither away. In this way they took possession of themselves again: they did not long remain the overwhelmed heirs and epigones of the entire Orient: instead, after a difficult struggle with themselves, they succeeded in enriching and increasing their inherited wealth and became the original and example for all coming peoples. This is a parable for each one of us: we must organize the chaos within so that we can be mindful again of our true needs.[102]

Equally unmistakable is the parable expressing German hopes through the Greek past.

Indeed, as this passage demonstrates, Nietzsche was able to incorporate even the proximity and threat of chaos, that immanently barbarian and form-hating element and yet repulsively excessive openness to all more formed foreign elements that is peculiar to Germans, to integrate even this most anti-Greek of all the German characteristics into his image of Hellenism (his higher valuation of the Dionysian principle over the Apollonian is perhaps rooted here). The entire *The Birth of Tragedy* is in fact already such an inspired Germanized interpretation of Greekdom. And, strangely enough, in this bold Germanized interpretation even the latest Nietzsche can still be found in the Basel philologist. When he writes in *The Will to Power* that there is something fundamentally immoderate, dissolute, Asiatic in the Greek character: that the bravery of the Greeks consists in the battle with their own Asiaticism; that beauty was not given to them, nor was logic, nor the naturalness of manners, but these were conquered, wanted, fought for, they are the *victory* of the Greeks—then that is only a concentration, almost a repetition of the same stylization of the Hellenic character into German romanticism we already encountered in the Basel lectures on Greek literature. There he wrote, with the youthful lyricism of *The Birth* and almost to the word verbatim: "The danger of falling back into Asiaticism (that is: chaos) always hovered over the Greeks, they could not do without it from time to time, and a new current of dark, mystical impulses from that region occasionally had to come over them, not to submerge them completely, but from which the true *Hellenic* genius would emerge with renewed vigor. For that reason"—Nietzsche adds with one of his characteristically bold "thus's"—"for that reason poetry falls under σοφία and the poet is σοφός,[103] that is, someone of penetrating knowledge."[104]

What the last sentence unmistakably betrays: a secret, almost unconscious *equation* of the Greek poet, as someone of the most relentless *knowledge,* with Nietzsche's own ideal self-portrait—this process, so typical of Nietzsche's method of thinking, is repeated in the more general sphere of all these passages as an equation of the true Hellenic genius with the German one, as Nietzsche himself characterizes it. Exactly the same thing occurs in his portrayal of Germanness as happens in all the portraits Nietzsche loves and heightens as an expanded ego, as possibilities of *his* cosmos; there is no more certain proof for the positive valuation of Germanness at the heart of Nietzsche's hatred of Germans as the fact of this Hellenization of German becoming, which culminates in the interpretation of the Greek soul as a Nietzschean "German." He lets everything he most cherishes flow into whatever he wants to infuse with his own so un-Greek nature, which is so all-too-German in the deepest sense—he constantly transforms everything that is inadequate and kindred to himself into what he loves as perfection: into something Greek. In a display of brilliant exegesis and stylizing license, he reinterpreted German music, and specifically Wagner, as Greek tragedy; he forced his fundamentally Protestant Christian instincts into the figure of Dionysus, placed his innate Lutheran language, Lutheran pathos, and Lutheran wrath into the mouth of the "Dionysian fiend,"[105] Zarathustra; he shaped his experience of Schopenhauer into his poetic transfiguration of the pre-Socratic philosophers; finally, he wrested from his own illness, his asceticism, his inner "inadequacy," the formula for a Greek affirmation of life in which, to use his own expression, he even "over-Greeked" the Greeks. In the same fashion, Nietzsche's philosophy of Germanness, as that of a physical illustration of Heraclitean becoming, belongs in the series of problems that he recognized as a part of his innermost nature by virtue of their Hellenization: whether in devotion or passionate rejection, the individual phases of these problems are always no more than the breathing of his Greek-obsessed German soul.

4

Justice

Justice: Quality and phantom of the Germans.[1]
—Goethe

Bossuet writes: justice is a kind of martyrdom.[2] It is symbolic of Nietzsche's thought, which always finds ways to martyr itself anew, that he is compelled to take such self-tormenting, brooding, rigorous pains in making repeated attempts to solve the problem: "How justice (theoretical and moral) is possible—rather: how justice must be understood in order to be possible?—for it *has* to be possible."[3] And there is something moving, after his constantly renewed struggle with the problem of justice over the course of many years, in still encountering words such as we find in this very late passage in the Notebooks:

"It happened late that I figured out what was actually still entirely lacking in me: namely, *justice.* 'What is justice? And is it possible? And if it should not be possible, how then would life be tolerable?' I incessantly asked myself such questions. I was deeply alarmed to discover that wherever I dug down within myself I found only passions, only partiality, only the absence of scruples to be expected in someone who lacks even the preconditions for justice. . . ."[4] Justice becomes an ineluctable question and decision to this degree and in this tone of severity only when a danger is present; where life itself, where the will to self-preservation and self-overcoming enters, with its inherent injustice, into the ancient, tragic contradiction with the ingrained need for justice that is both inherited and acquired. Where the thinker's desire for justice, the scholar's circumspect conscience encounters the need to be unjust in the artist, in the prophetic person who wants the future because he is the future. But the future is always and inescapably somehow unjust and wrong with regard to the form of any present. This is, with symbolic precision, the case and fate of Nietzsche.

The question of conscience—"How is justice possible?"—is first articulated in the second *Untimely Meditation* (first at least in theoretically pronounced form; he had already thrown an anticipatory light on the problem of justice and of the theodicy of Great Crime in a passage about Aeschylus's *Prometheus* in *The Birth of Tragedy*). Here, in the essay "On the Use and Disadvantage of History for

Life," the two major tendencies of Nietzsche's approach meet for the first time: the will to justice of the historian, of the thinker trained to be conscientious in the exercise of theoretical judgment, who wants to see "what was and what is," and the already unstoppable will to vital injustice of the artist and prophet, who must see "what *shall* be." But even here, where the young Nietzsche acts with Schopenhauerian earnestness and Wagnerian willful passion as an advocate of *life* and of the necessity for "perspectival injustice" against the "purely objective" historical or historically packaged mere-justice of his all-too-historically aware century, even here he still makes great efforts to remove the concept of justice from the dangerous dilemma, and yet at the same time somehow to give it precedence over that seemingly inescapable antithesis: "life or justice." A basic sentiment, a basic need of Nietzsche is expressed in this glorification of justice, which still clearly betrays the influence of ancient moralists and the looming shadow of Schopenhauer:

"Truly, no one has a greater claim to our admiration than the person who possesses the instinct and energy for justice. For in justice the highest and rarest virtues are combined and concealed as if in an unfathomable sea that receives currents from all sides and assimilates them into itself. The hand of the just man who is entitled to sit in judgment no longer trembles when it holds the scale; merciless toward himself, he places one weight on top of another, his eye remains clear as the pans rise and fall and his voice sounds neither hard nor broken when he pronounces his judgment."[5] Whoever "rises up from the rare virtue of magnanimity to the rarest one of justice"[6] reaches a lonely height "as the most honorable example of the human species."[7] "Only insofar as the truthful man has the unconditional will to be just is there anything great about the pursuit of truth everyone so thoughtlessly glorifies."[8] "Although the world seems to be full of people who 'serve the truth,' the virtue of justice is still rarely present, even more rarely recognized and almost always hated to death."[9] (*Human* adds that justice is a quality of genius, and the genius of justice should in no way be deemed inferior to any other philosophical, political, or artistic expression of genius.)[10]

Immediately, however, he rejects the commingling, the contamination of this—very moralistic—ideal of justice with the "historical objectivity" of the nineteenth century that was so eminently conscious of its exalted impartiality, and he asks the searching question whether "the historical virtuoso of the present is the most just man of his time?"[11] Whether only the rapt observer, the passive recipient and great mirror—as Schopenhauer's pupil might have thought obvious—was the model of the wise and just judge, in line with the often-cited statement by Goethe that no one has a conscience except he who observes?[12] Here Nietzsche phrases it with the decisiveness of his final years: "Objectivity and justice have nothing to do with each other."[13] (Zarathustra later puts it this way: "I do not like your cold justice."[14] " . . . The greatest thing you can experience is the hour in which you say: 'What does my justice matter! I see that I am not fire and flame. But the just man is fire and flame.'"[15] And in the Notebooks to Zarathustra, in a related confession: "You all struggle not for the law, you just ones, but rather that your images of man shall prevail. And that all of your images of man shall be shattered by my image of the overman: behold, that is Zarathustra's will to the law.")[16] Justice, as Nietzsche already conceives of it here, is a thoroughly and supremely *active* virtue. It is a mark of strength, it *is* strength. Most historians, it is true, "manage to achieve only tolerance, a 'letting be' of what cannot be denied or wished away, a tailoring and a reasonable, benevolent glossing over of things in the shrewd assumption that the inexperienced will interpret it as a virtue of justice when the story of the past is told without harsh accents and without an expression of hate. But only a superior power can judge, the weak have to tolerate it if they do not want to feign strength and thus turn justice into an actress on the judge's bench."[17] "*You may interpret the past only out of the greatest power of the present*"[18]—Nietzsche emphasizes this sentence in his text, as the confession and the heart of his observation; and again: "Today one ought to know that only he who builds the future has a right to judge the past."[19] This thought, that only the person who establishes values may negate values, only the upright may pronounce on what is right, this Zarathustra sentiment is thus already present and fully formed in Nietzsche very early. In the same way, in the period after *Zarathustra,* in the *Genealogy of Morals,* Nietzsche unconditionally defends this conception of justice as proof of the strength "to search for the origin of justice, in contrast to recent attempts, in an entirely different arena—namely in that of ressentiment."[20] Against this derivation of justice from revenge, Nietzsche, with clear reference to the *Untimely,* observes the following: "To be just is always a *positive* way of acting . . . the active person, the person who attacks, charges ahead, is still a hundred steps closer to justice than the reactive person. . . . Indeed, for that reason the aggressive person, as the stronger, bolder, nobler one, has throughout history also had the *freer* eye, the *better* conscience on his side."[21] Here Nietzsche clearly approaches the biologically determined, dialectically refined conception of justice that the Greek sophist Thrasymachus advances in Plato's *Republic* when he defines what is just as that which benefits the stronger and what is unjust as something more powerful, noble, and mighty than justice. But *Human* already finds that socialistic justice is possible only as an active gesture, not as a principle or demand, "only within the ruling class, which in this case *performs* justice with sacrifice and renunciation. To *demand* justice, on the other hand, as the Socialists do, is never a product of justice, but of covetousness."[22]

The active, even "aggressive," character of justice that Nietzsche so strongly emphasizes and exaggerates thus contains and demands as its prerequisite the ability to embrace and absorb within itself the inherent injustice of all existence and becoming. That was already present in the *Untimely,* but with the undertone of a still genuinely Schopenhauerian *sorrow,* which is so entirely foreign to the *Genealogy of Morals,* over the unremitting injustice of "this world," but with the robust resolve of the affirmative "Nevertheless."

"One needs a great deal of strength to be able to live and to forget to what extent living and being unjust are identical. Luther himself once said that the world came about only through God's forgetfulness; if God had thought of 'heavy artillery,' he would never have created the world."[23] "Man has to have, and from time to time use, the strength to crush and dissolve a past in order to be able to live: he achieves this by putting it on trial, carefully examining it and finally condemning it; every past is worth being condemned—for that is how it is with human affairs: in them, human violence and weakness have always been powerful. It is not justice that sits in judgment here: but rather life itself, that dark, surging, insatiably self-desiring power. Its sentence is always unkind, always unjust, because it has never flowed out of a pure fountain of knowledge; but in most cases the sentence would turn out to be the same if justice itself were to pronounce it."[24]

If justice itself were to pronounce it—with that, the germ of his later concept of justice, still in modest form, is already adumbrated: namely, that life, even in its apparently most unjust guise, and the highest justice must in the end be somehow mysteriously identical. This idea gradually matures in Nietzsche into the *amor fati,* the yea-saying love for one's predetermined fate, that characterizes his final years.

At first, beginning with the predominantly skeptical period, from *Human, All Too Human* up through *The Gay Science,* the idea of justice as well is illuminated more from its negative, problematic side. It is the time when Nietzsche, now castigating his need for an artistic explanation of existence and morality after experiencing deep disappointment, can hardly get enough of rationalistic simplifications and clarifications of reality. One finds, for example, such a complacently positivistic, clearly "worldly" derivation of justice as the following:

"Justice originates among people of approximately *equal power,* as Thucydides correctly understood (in the terrible dialogue between the Athenian and Melian envoys): where there is no clearly recognizable superiority of power and a struggle would lead to fruitless mutual harm, the idea arises to communicate and to negotiate over the conflicting claims: the character of *exchange* is the originary character of justice. . . . It is thus reprisal and exchange with the precondition of an approximately equal balance of power . . . it naturally harks back to the perspective of prudent self-preservation, that is, to the egoism of the consideration: 'Why should I injure myself needlessly and perhaps still not achieve my goal?'"[25] Or Nietzsche sometimes seems merely to play the role of advocate for the anti-justice of life, against the "just eye": "You should learn to grasp the *necessary* injustice in every Pro and Contra, injustice as inextricable from life, life itself as *determined* by perspective and its injustice."[26] "For an artist or thinker to perfect his practice, he probably has to possess that belief which is an injustice and narrowness toward the belief of others. For he must see *more* in it and something greater than it is: otherwise he will not employ all of his energy."[27] He sees even the possibility of *knowledge,* the highest concept of value during this period, as fundamentally endangered by justice; the two great opponents "knowledge" and "life" from Nietzsche's last phase threaten here to ally themselves against justice: "As soon as we take justice too far," he writes in the Notebook sketches from the time of *Daybreak,* "and the bedrock of our individuality crumbles, causing us to give up our firm *unjust* point of departure, then we give up the possibility of knowledge: then that *thing* is missing to which everything stands in relation (including a just relation)."[28] Justice even becomes a disintegrating principle, it becomes a dangerous inclination toward chaos: "To give everyone his due would be to want justice and to achieve chaos,"[29] a passage in the paralipomena to *Zarathustra* warns, and Zarathustra says resignedly: "But how could I have wanted to be just from the outset! How can I give everyone his due! This shall be enough for me: I give everyone my due."[30] But in the antithesis of justice and love that frequently arises during this period and culminates in Zarathustra's painful question: "Tell me, where is that justice to be found which is love with seeing eyes?"[31]—in this "greatest and most indissoluble disharmony of existence"[32] a distinct glimmer shines through of the old moralistic homesickness for justice as something more difficult, more noble: "Justice is more difficult than devotion and love."[33] The modification of this idea into the theological realm is characteristic for the intellectual ancestry of the problem in Nietzsche's thought: "If God wanted to become an object of love, then he first would have had to give up judging and justice: a judge, and even a merciful judge, is not an object of love."[34] Even in this skeptical period, Nietzsche's thinking still cannot abide the unconditional equation and opposition of the two great opponents "love" and "justice." The office of the just man here, too, turns into an inflated authority that enables us to compromise and reconcile what has been antagonistically divided, to love with seeing eyes. The division, the tragic *mixture* of Nietzsche's own being combining mind and fire seeks and finds its ultimate unity solely in the hope for possible justice: "We whose beings are mixed and are now enflamed by fire, now chilled by mind, want to kneel before justice as before the sole Goddess we acknowledge above us."[35]

And this veneration, which grew entirely out of his most individual experience, this thoroughly personal sensibility was also decisive in determining (as is so often the case) Nietzsche's theoretical stance. His justice must be able to assimilate everything vital—everything vital *in him*—every origin and every future, all knowledge and all conscience; and because this justice is compelled to do so out of an innermost necessity, it is thus able to. This ability to do so is its touchstone and ultimate meaning. The seeker of justice, as Nietzsche sees it, travels through stages of individual injustices to attain finally a highest level that comprehends all previous ones within the achieved height and view. Thus the partial injustices during the ascent, for man and human history, become necessary conditions for a vital, living, highest justice. They are transformations and masks, preexisting forms, as it were, of justice itself.

"Do you want to become a universal just eye? Then you must do so as one who has gone through *many* individuals and whose last individual *requires* all the previous ones as functions."[36] "We occasionally demand the truth by way of a double injustice, namely when we see and portray both sides of something in succession that we are unable to see together, but in such a way that we always misunderstand or deny the other side in the delusion that what we see is the entire truth."[37] This is the same development in the theoretical sphere, namely toward a kind of theodicy of evil, within this "justice of the unjust," as in Nietzsche's stance toward his own personal suffering: an interpretively open, Hegelian affirmative enthusiasm, not so much for what has become as for what is becoming, for what should be, which, like all becoming, is a violation of boundaries, an injustice and profanation toward being. Injustice becomes a bridge to justice for this active fatalism; for, as a passage in the Notebooks to *Zarathustra* reads, the future is just as much a condition for the present as is the past: "What shall be and must be is the basis of what is."[38] And it looks like a strange premonition, like a Second Vision of his own fate, when Nietzsche's earliest work, *The Birth of Tragedy* from the winter of 1870–71, which is so oddly rich in self-prophetic pronouncements, interprets Aeschylus's *Prometheus* thus:

"Let me now contrast the glory of passivity (in Sophocles's *Oedipus*) to the glory of activity that illuminates Aeschylus's *Prometheus*. What the thinker Aeschylus had to say to us here, but what he as poet lets us only imagine through his symbolic image, the youthful Goethe was able to reveal to us in the daring words of his 'Prometheus': 'Here I sit, forming men in my image / A race that would be equal to me. . . . '[39] The most wonderful aspect of the Prometheus poem . . . however, is the deep Aeschylean pull toward *justice:* the immeasurable suffering of the bold 'individual' on the one hand and the divine predicament, even an intimation of a twilight of the gods on the other . . . all of that most strongly recalls the center and fundamental principle of the Aeschylean view of the world, which envisions Moira reigning over the gods and men as eternal justice. . . . The best and highest things that humanity can obtain are acquired through sacrilege and we must now accept its consequences, namely the entire flood of suffering and sorrows with which the offended gods must afflict the nobly aspiring human race. . . . This titanic drive is the element shared by the Promethean and the Dionysian. In this regard, Aeschylus's Prometheus is a Dionysian mask, whereas the aforementioned tug toward justice betrays to the discerning observer Aeschylus's paternal descent from Apollo, the god of individuation and of the boundaries of justice. And thus the dual character of Aeschylus's Prometheus, his simultaneously Dionysian and Apollonian nature, could be expressed in the following conceptual form: 'Everything that exists is just and unjust and in both cases equally justified.'"[40]

But this is where the ancient *tragic* interpretation of justice turns back into the *metaphysical* one, into that early Hellenic metaphysics of justice that unmistakably sustains Nietzsche's broadly conceived idea of justice, indeed is basically identical with it—the metaphysics of Heraclitus of Ephesus. "Aeschylus's heroes are related to Heraclitus,"[41] Nietzsche once remarked; thus the tragic justice of Aeschylus's Prometheus also shares a deep commonality with the Heraclitean justification of the world, out of the experience of which Nietzsche's *Zarathustra* emerged. As we know, Heraclitus was for Nietzsche the *most Greek* among all the Greek philosophers. And if Nietzsche (in his outlines for "Homer's Competition") finds that the entire notion of justice is taken much more seriously by the Greeks than by us (for "Christianity does not know any justice")[42] *because* the idea of competition, of *envy,* had been so much stronger in them, then Heraclitus's view of the world is also more Greek than the others because it grants the highest, world-forming, world-judging status and meaning to justice, Dike, the daughter of Zeus. "I perceive," Nietzsche has Heraclitus say, "the entire world as a spectacle of justice prevailing."[43] With a sense of delight in which aesthetic enjoyment is intertwined with the ethical, Nietzsche, in perhaps the most beautiful of all of his unpublished fragments (in the torso of "Philosophy in the Tragic Age of the Greeks," from 1872–73), fashions a poetic rendering of the imperious intuition of Heraclitean metaphysics, the most Greek of all conceptions of the world, as a mixing bowl that has to be constantly stirred so that it does not disaggregate, that great mixed beverage that, as honey combines bitter and sweet, consists of the most diametrically opposed elements, and exists precisely *through* this opposition:

> All becoming arises out of the war of opposites. . . . This struggle continues through all eternity. Everything happens in accordance with this conflict, and *this very conflict* reveals eternal justice. It is a wonderful notion, drawn from the purest founts of the Hellenic spirit, which views the conflict as a continuous prevailing justice that remains consistent, severe, and bound to eternal laws. Only a Greek was capable of seeing this idea as the foundation of a cosmodicy; it is the good Eris of Hesiod, transfigured into a world principle, it is the notion of competition shared by the individual Greek and the Greek state . . . translated into the most general terms so that now the gears of the cosmos turn within it. . . . Things themselves do not actually exist at all, they are the flash and spark of drawn swords, they are the glint of victory in the struggle of opposing qualities.[44]

And out of this imagining of the world as a site of joyful battle in which "the judges themselves seem to do battle, the fighters themselves seem to judge," out of this perception of a *single* prevailing justice Heraclitus *dares,* in Nietzsche's words, to formulate the "even higher intuition," the proposition of a first philosophy of identity: "The conflict of the many itself *is* the one justice!"[45]

What had to entrance the disciple of Heraclitus (which is what Nietzsche calls himself), to captivate the pupil of the Greeks about this metaphysics of justice, was the profound affinity with his own experience of necessity: that genuinely Greek mixture of aesthetic conception and vitalistic interpretation that characterizes the thought of the Greeks, those "artists of life," as Nietzsche calls them, and which found perhaps its purest form in the vividly simplified, passionately unequivocal interpretations of the world offered by the pre-Socratic philosophers. In Heraclitus's justification of the world, as Nietzsche understood and construed it, in the notion of justice as the eternal synthesis of individual injustices caught in animated conflict, as embattled harmony, there is in fact an original image and model of Nietzsche's own vitalistic philosophy as it took theoretical form in *The Will to Power* and artistic, "musical" form in *Zarathustra,* namely both aesthetic and voluntaristic, both perceptive and volitional, both "musical" and formative—and thus the very way in which Nietzsche is given the *problem* of justice is Greek, that is "artistic and vital," theoretical and passionate, tragic music and yea-saying will for power. He wrestled with the problem in both forms, experienced it in both. It is Hellenistic, it is Nietzschean, when he believes he *hears* the *idea* of justice, in Heraclitus's sense, truly as music, when the philosophical cosmodicy of his most venerated Greek master audibly flows together with the sensible art of the most beloved master of his youth, as the essay "Richard Wagner in Bayreuth" attests:

"Above all of the resounding individuals and the conflict of their passions, above the whole vortex of antagonisms there hovers, with utmost calm, an overwhelming, symphonic understanding that continuously produces unity out of the struggle: Wagner's music as a whole is a representation of the world as it was understood by the great Ephesian philosopher, as a harmony that conflict bore out of itself, as a union of justice and hostility."[46] That is poetically, musically the same fundamentally Greek experience Nietzsche had as a seeker of justice, which the later transvaluer would voluntaristically, imperiously formulate in a brief passage in the Notebooks in an image and command of austere nakedness:

"*Justice* as a constructive, expulsive, destructive way of thinking . . . : *the supreme representative of life itself.*"[47]

5
Arion

Before we were human, we heard music.[1]
—Hebbel

Music provides the innermost seed that precedes all formation.[2]
—Schopenhauer

Music is the element in Nietzsche's life one first perceives when approaching him, gratefully or polemically, as an observer: music is the most colorful flare radiating out from his existence into the outermost periphery of his influence; and music is perhaps the last echo that will be heard rising up nostalgically when his name is uttered after the completion of preordained centuries.

It was undoubtedly the musical element that first made Nietzsche's life and work visible and valuable to his own people. Not the "aristocratic radicalism"[3] first admired by Georg Brandes, who introduced the German philosopher to his European audience after he had been completely disowned and maliciously ignored in his fatherland; not the mercilessness of his psychology, which captivated the best minds in Europe from St. Petersburg to Paris; not the dangerous attractions of a linguistic and polemical refinement unprecedented in Germany, of a wickedness not displayed since Heine[4]—none of that, no matter how strongly they individually affected individual readers, made the entire phenomenon of Nietzsche as familiar to the German mind as did his life's tragic proximity to music. Not only the tragedy of his friendship with Wagner and of his betrayal of Wagner—both of which were, after all, merely a symptom and symbol—but rather the entire relationship to music and inner musicality that Nietzsche's soul has in common with the German soul; both souls are "intimately related to music, were born of it, so to speak, and are connected to things almost solely through unconscious musical relations"[5] (*The Birth of Tragedy*). Thus what Nietzsche writes in his penultimate year to his musician friend holds true not just for his own musical production, but for his entire life's work as well:

"The minor affiliation to music and, almost, to musicians, to which this hymn ("An das Leben"—"To Life") offers testimony, is of inestimable value with respect to an eventual understanding of the psychological problem that I am. . . . Finally:

it is something for Germans, a little bridge on which perhaps even this dull race will come to find one of its oddest monstrosities interesting."[6] That proved to be true: as the great, Jean Paul–like musician that he is (musician even as a passionate anti-musician), Nietzsche found the bridge to the innermost gratitude of his people, no matter how much the broader, more European influence of his life's work emanated from the anti-Romantic psychologist, the Socratic ironist, or even, on the outermost periphery, from the preacher of power in the intellectual-political sphere. One of the noblest German spokesmen of the generation that had been decisively affected by Nietzsche first characterized him as the German poet of knowledge; and the most important German poem that has thus far been offered to the name of Nietzsche concludes by taking up Nietzsche's own words about *The Birth of Tragedy,* concentrated into a sublime lament:

> And when the austere and tormented voice
> Echoes like a hymn through the blue night
> And the brilliant tide, it makes this lament:
> This new soul should have sung, not spoken![7]

It was as a musician that the awakening Nietzsche found himself, as a musician that the young man experienced the deepest enthusiasm of his life, and it was as a musician that the mature man, declining at the peak of his perfection, still understood and described himself. In the Notebooks from the final years, there is a note of almost Lutheran geniality: "From the time I was a child I have been a music lover and I have likewise always been a friend to good musicians: this . . . resulted in my having little cause to concern myself with the people of today—for good musicians are all hermits and 'outside of time'"[8] ("I have always liked *musicam;* singing has nothing to do with the world,"[9] Dr. Martin Luther confessed to his table companions). In truth it was Protestant church music in whose guise his beloved art first revealed itself to him and immediately enticed him with the compulsion to produce something in response. According to the schoolboy's résumé, when he left Schulpforta, Nietzsche, awakened to music by a singular coincidence, began to love it passionately in his ninth year, and did so by turning immediately to composing, "if one may call composing the efforts of an excited child to bring harmonious and successive tones to paper and to sing biblical texts with a fantastic accompaniment on the pianoforte."[10] An oratorio composed at the time stunned the older Nietzsche by the "almost magical identity"[11] of its mood and expression with the music of *Parsifal.* The pupil at Pforta, destined by his family to study theology, very seriously considered devoting himself wholly to *the* art that, according to Luther, is close to theology. There survives a host of compositions from his final school years and the first few at university in the German romantic style, primarily in that of Schumann, his earliest favorite. Even in their old age, his friends remember being delighted by his "wonderful improvising"[12] (Deussen); Freiherr von Gersdorff writes in his memoirs: "His improvisations [during the time at Pforta] remain unforgettable to me; I like to think that even Beethoven could not have improvised more movingly than Nietzsche, especially when a storm was threatening in the sky."[13] Nietzsche truly seemed to be submerged in the bath of his most proper nature while improvising: never did he seem to be so much himself. Gast still spoke of his good fortune at having heard Nietzsche play the piano in Basel; and in Basel itself there were people who spoke of the strange self-forgetfulness that could take hold of Nietzsche when he improvised: how, at a social gathering during one winter in Basel at which music was to be performed—the city's musical director was present—Nietzsche, in his reserved and elegantly shy manner, at first only unwillingly acquiesced to the guests' polite request for a little music, how his playing, growing warmer, soon turned into free improvisation of an ever bolder inventive élan. He seems to be someone entirely different from the unapproachable, deliberately formal, even ceremonious professor that one otherwise knows him to be, he even forgets the occasion, the place, the time, on and on he improvises, the guests are embarrassed, the music director, whom they actually did want to hear and who wants to be heard, becomes derisive, impatient, offended—Nietzsche notices nothing, he continues to improvise, he is *alone with himself*—and the disturbed party has no other choice but to leave him with himself.[14]

Such a return to himself in musical improvisation is even in fact the authorial ideal of the youthful Nietzsche; as a student in Leipzig he writes in the spring of 1867 to a friend: "I have to learn how to play on my style as on a keyboard, not just memorized pieces, but rather free improvisations, as free as possible, yet always logical and beautiful."[15] "But the book of a musician is simply not the book of an 'eye' person," he writes one year later about the book of a Leipzig music critic; "basically it is music that is coincidentally written not with notes but with words."[16] That is true of Nietzsche himself, above all of *The Birth of Tragedy*, but also for *Zarathustra* and his swan song, *Ecce homo*. "Under what rubric does this *Zarathustra* actually belong? I almost think under 'symphonies.' It is certain that in it I entered a different world"[17] (1883 to Gast). In *Ecce homo* he sees a sudden and profoundly decisive change in his taste, above all regarding music, as a portent announcing *Zarathustra:* "One may perhaps classify *Zarathustra* in its entirety under music; certainly a rebirth in the art of *listening* was a precondition for it."[18] Even a reawakening of musical production counts among these omens that advertise *Zarathustra:* "Yesterday I was assaulted by the demon of music," we hear him write to Gast in 1882; "my current condition in *media vita* wants to be expressed in sounds as well: I will not escape."[19] This passage in his letter refers to the composition, "Hymnus an das Leben," which Nietzsche sends to his friend a week later: " . . . This time 'music' is coming to you. I would hope that I have made a song that could be performed publicly—'in order to *seduce* people to my philosophy.'"[20] And an unquenchable thirst for music characterizes the creative period surrounding *Zarathustra:* " . . . Whether anyone has ever had such a thirst for music?"[21] (1884 to Malwida). "Music is by far the best thing; I would like to be a musician now more than ever"[22] (1884 to Gast). Indeed, something awakens in him like a late regret at not having been enough of a musician; like the German romantics, to whom he belongs even unwittingly, he also occasionally seems to have thought that he reached his goal only as "music," but that he remained a great promise as "literature." Not to have ventured song instead of the word is Nietzsche's final self-reproach, which was applicable perhaps not solely to *The Birth of Tragedy.*

The preface from 1886 says about the youthful poet philologist who wrote that book: "Here speaks a foreign voice . . . here spoke a mystical and almost maenadic soul . . . almost irresolute about whether it wanted to communicate or hide itself. . . . It should have *sung,* this new soul—and not spoken! What a pity that I did not dare say as a poet what I had to say at the time: I might have been able to do it!"[23] And he calls his first work "a book for the initiated, a music for those who were baptized in music. . . ."[24] For him, not just this first visionary book, but indeed his entire philosophy, turns into music, the philosopher into a musician, Socrates into Dionysus: "Has anyone noticed," *The Case of Wagner* asks, "that music makes the spirit *free?* that it lends wings to thought? that one becomes all the more a philosopher the more one becomes a musician?"[25] Like *Birth,* like *Zarathustra,* his best and most characteristic work always turns into "music" in his eyes: in one of his very last letters, from December 27, 1888, he calls a page of "music" about music in *Nietzsche contra Wagner* perhaps the most noteworthy thing he had written.[26]

From the beginning, music not only elevated Nietzsche as a thinker, it also gave direction to the flight of his thought. It leads him to his first decisive and constitutive intellectual experience, the philosophy of Schopenhauer: the "daemon" that, as Nietzsche relates it, whispered to him in a used bookstore in Leipzig, telling him to take home the completely unknown book on *The World as Will and Representation,* was surely none other than the daemon of music. For this *magnum opus* of romanticism is after all music, a carefully composed symphony in four movements, towering powerfully over the themes of madness and redemption; the entire metaphysics of this inwardly wretched spirit of homesickness nothing but a magnificent apology and glorification of music as the perceived foundation of the world. Schopenhauer was a presentiment fulfilled for Nietzsche, in the same way that Wagner's personality became for him the embodiment of Schopenhauer's genius, just as Wagner's art became a fulfilled predestination. "From the moment there was a piano score for *Tristan,* I was a Wagnerian,"[27] *Ecce homo* still says. And in a letter to Rohde from the Tribschen period: "I felt like someone whose premonition is finally fulfilled. For that is exactly what this music is and nothing else! And that is exactly what I mean by the word music when I describe the Dionysian and nothing else!"[28] Wagner fulfilled for him physically what Schopenhauer had prepared intellectually: he shattered the last thin partition that still stood between Nietzsche's consciousness and his musical ego—thus the overflowing, boundlessly devoted gratitude of the disciple, thus the sudden, joyfully extravagant production of "musical" works, in *The Birth of Tragedy* and in the works thematically and temporally related to it. Wagner, through the powerful impression left by the experience of his person and his art, gave Nietzsche the courage to experience himself as the musician he was, the courage "to come to himself"—even in his latest period Nietzsche never forgot the "great benefactor of his life."[29] The enormous violence of the Wagner experience, his life-changing and life-threatening importance for Nietzsche's character and work, a significance both fateful and disastrous, can be explained by this breach of his dammed-up inner musical will into the deeply furrowed riverbed of a great personal will. And by surrendering himself, seemingly abandoning himself entirely, Nietzsche fully came to himself for the first time. Here, for the first time, he experienced himself as his own fate, as a blood relation of music, whose soul "is connected to things only through unconscious musical relations."[30] And here for the first time Nietzsche became productive: his first work was a birth out of the spirit of music in every sense. But beyond that, the young Nietzsche's entire cultural enthusiasm, the intoxicated, tremendous hope for a rebirth of the German character through a baptism in the Greek essence, a rebirth of ancient Hellas through a baptism in the German future, is also an ultimately and supremely musical fantasy, possible only in the soulful moment when a musical predisposition gratefully and ecstatically merges with the goal-oriented energy of a powerful will that engages in a demonic seduction toward productive delusion. The cherished phantom of a new Hellenic culture arising out of Germanness and music—that is itself music, a music that is the furthest removed from the reality of every "day," entirely and utterly romantic, and profoundly German.

"If I consider," he wrote in 1871 to Rohde, "that only a few hundred people in the next generation will take from music what I have from it, then I expect a completely new culture! Everything else that refuses to allow itself to be comprehended through musical relations sometimes creates a feeling of disgust and aversion in me, and when I returned from a concert in Mannheim I actually had that strange intensified dread of the day which comes after a sleepless night: because that reality no longer seemed real to me at all, but rather otherwordly."[31] All of the elements of the young Nietzsche's musicality are combined in such a hope: the Schopenhauerian metaphysics, the Tristanesque hatred of the "dreary day," the Wagnerian tension of the will, and the cultural enthusiasm for a rebirth of Hellas—for Nietzsche culture is always synonymous with a conscious adherence to Greece—a rebirth out of the *German* spirit, out of the spirit of the German Reformation and German music, as Nietzsche envisaged and expected in his Basel lecture on "The Future of our Educational Institutions," as opposed to "Romanic civilization." Even the "disgust and aversion" occasioned by the reality of modern civilization is in fact basically a musical will, which as such is always directed toward what is beyond reality, toward chaos, perhaps. Music always means hostility toward civilization; from the beginning an unbridgeable chasm has yawned between the two; they cancel each other out. Thus we read in *Birth:* "Richard Wagner says of civilization that it is abrogated by music, as is the glow of a lamp by the light of day."[32] And in the preliminary studies for "Richard Wagner in Bayreuth": "*Meistersinger:* opposition to civilization, the German principle against the French one."[33] The identity of music and Germanness, which the young Nietzsche sees everywhere, causes him to view this Germanness as the most serious and eternal opponent of everything that is merely civilization—and thus as the vehicle of a "completely new culture" in the future born out of the spirit of music. (The idea of the polar opposition between civilization and culture is just as typically Nietzschean as it is typically German. We read as late as in *The Will to Power:* "Civilization wants something other than what culture wants: perhaps something opposite. . . .")[34] The instinctive hatred, the deep Lutheran antipathy toward civilization in the Romanic sense that has always burst forth in such elemental fashion in all German crises and in all great German individuals (but the great man is always the most decisive crisis) is, for Nietzsche (as it is for Wagner), one part music. It is music itself that rises up against its enemy, civilization, with profound disgust, as *Beyond* says *admiringly* of the German spirit that it "arose with profound disgust" against "modern ideas,"[35] the ideas of the French Revolution. The German character has always fulfilled itself only as music, its future culture—for "to this day, there has been no German culture"[36]—will thus fulfill itself only as a culture of music: that is the recognition that fills the young Nietzsche with enthusiastic hope (as it later fills the mature Nietzsche with deep disappointed sadness, which only too mercilessly recognizes that a culture, that is, a total form of life, can never be based on music, because music is a form of experience beyond all concepts of culture, simultaneously a condition prior to all form and a condition of the final dissolution of all form). German, as an adjective, was always synonymous with "musical": that is how Nietzsche understands it. "Beethoven did it better than Schiller, Bach better than Klopstock, Mozart better than Wieland, Wagner better than Kleist"[37] (Notebooks to *Human*). "How much Schiller . . . is in Beethoven! Schumann contains Eichendorff, Uhland, Heine, Hoffmann, Tieck. Richard Wagner has Freischütz, Hoffmann, Grimm, romantic legend . . ."[38] (*Will to Power*). There is a parallel in a passage from a letter to Brandes in his last year: "Your 'German romanticism' made me think about how this entire movement actually achieved its goal only as music. (Schumann, Mendelssohn, Weber, Wagner, Brahms); as literature it remained an enormous promise. The French were more fortunate."[39] And "just as the French reflect the courtesy and the ésprit of French society"—in other words, their Romanic civilization—"so too the Germans mirror something of the profound, dreamy solemnity of their mystics and musicians, but also something of their puerility,"[40] he writes in the Notebooks to the *Transvaluation*. In its mixture of mysticism, music, and sublime childishness, German romanticism always affords Nietzsche the most perfect expression of the German character: "Of all the German poets, Clemens Brentano has the most music in his being,"[41] the Notebooks to *The Gay Science* approvingly notes. Heinrich Heine gives him—in *Ecce homo*—the highest conception of the poet. And the truest image of the German character stares out at him from the mirror of romantic music:

> I heard, again for the first time—Richard Wagner's overture to the *Meistersinger*. This is magnificent, overwrought, heavy and late art, proud to presuppose for its understanding that two centuries of music still live on—it does honor to the Germans that such pride is not misplaced! What vitality and power, what seasons and latitudes are mixed together here! At one moment it seems old-fashioned, at another foreign, austere and immature, which is just as arbitrary as it is ostentatious and traditional, and is not infrequently roguish, more often crude and coarse—it has fire and courage and at the same time the loose, pallid skin of fruits that ripen too late. . . . All in all, no beauty, no south, nothing of the fine southern brightness of the sky, not a hint of grace, no dance, hardly a will to logic; even a certain awkwardness that is further emphasized as if the artist wanted to tell us: "that is part of my intention"; a clumsy vestment, something capriciously barbaric and ceremonious, a flurry of erudite and venerable finery and lace, something German, in the best and the worst senses of the word, something that is in a German fashion multifarious, shapeless and inexhaustible; a certain German powerfulness and superabundance of the soul, which has no fear of hiding itself under the refinements of decay—which perhaps feels most at home there; a real, genuine emblem of the German soul, which is both

> young and ancient, overripe and still over-rich with the future. This kind of music best expresses what I think of the Germans: they are from the day before yesterday and the day after tomorrow—*they do not yet have a today*[42] (*Beyond*).

This extraordinary passage—extraordinary as "music about music," as psychology, as a masterpiece of exegesis and as a mask—this piece of mastersong precisely indicates the moment of an inner balance in Nietzsche's stance toward music, as well as toward Germanness, both of which serve here, and not only here, as symbols of each other. Between the day before yesterday and the day after tomorrow, between the opposed seasons and latitudes, between old-fashioned and immature, between a barbaric lack of form and an inexhaustible superabundance—that is how he sees a people that "does not yet have a today," in the mask of an art that is simultaneously from the day before yesterday and the day after tomorrow. The passage is the last one in Nietzsche's work in which Germanness is granted a "day after tomorrow," where something like hope is associated once more with the idea of "German," and also the last in which the *specifically German* character of a work of music is affirmed once more, even if it occurs on the most extreme verge of tipping over into a future No. A farewell is already being announced—"no beauty, no south, not a hint of grace, no dance, hardly a will to logic: something capriciously barbaric and ceremonious"—and this farewell applies just as much to Germanness in the guise of music as to music in the form of Germanness. For just as both are united here in that suspended moment between love and disavowal that is called farewell, Nietzsche's first clear estrangement from Germanness takes place at precisely the same moment in his development in which a disavowal of music takes hold of him: in *Human, All Too Human.* The great, eye-opening disappointment abruptly reveals to him: the dream of a future German-Greek culture out of the spirit of music was itself only a musical hallucination; a *culture* can never be founded on *music,* the future never on the past, the classical never on the romantic, a present never on nostalgia. And music *is* the sum of this anti-future, it is the past itself. Its romanticism, its nostalgia, its deep antipathy toward thought render it a beautiful phase of melancholy and the love of death, which must remain a phase if it is not to be an end, *the* end. *Human* gives repeated expression, half resolute, half plaintive, to this painful suspicion:

> Music as a late arrival in every culture.—Of all the arts in any given cultural landscape . . . music makes its appearance as the last of all the plants, during the autumn and the withering away of the culture that belongs to it. . . . Indeed, sometimes music sounds like the language of a vanished age echoing in an astonished and new world and coming too late. The soul of the Christian middle ages finally achieved

> its full sound in Dutch music: its tonal architecture is the late-born but legitimate and equal sister to the Gothic style. It was not until Händel's music that the best of Luther's soul and of his brethren resounded, that great Jewish heroic strain, which created the entire movement of the Reformation. It was Mozart who first lent a *golden* voice to the age of Louis XIV and to the art of Racine and Claude Lorrain. Only in Beethoven's and Rossini's music did the song of the eighteenth century finally die out, that century of dreamy enthusiasm, of broken ideals and fleeting happiness. A friend of sentimental metaphors might thus like to say that all truly significant music is a "swan song."[43]

We thus experience in music the same thing that, according to a comment in *Human,* we do while we are asleep and dreaming: we "experience once again the entire earlier development of humanity."[44] Music is in truth a revenant: "Almost all music becomes *magical* at the point when we hear it speak the language of its own *past:* and in that way all *old* music seems to amateurs to become better and all recently born music seems to be of little value: for it does not yet stir any sentimentality"[45] (*Human*). Music is the end, the opposite of any kind of new birth, of renaissance: it is the *baroque* of the soul. It is the most un-present, the truly unclassical art: "No musician has ever created like the architect that built the Palazzo Pitti[46] . . . where does all of our music belong? . . . Is it constitutive of its character that it is anti-Renaissance? Is it the sister of the baroque style? . . . Is music . . . not already décadence?[47] . . . Why does German music culminate at the time of German romanticism? Why is Goethe missing in German music?[48] Music achieved its greatest maturity and fullness as romanticism, as yet another reactionary movement against classicism."[49] (*Will to Power*). And as baroque style, as romanticism, music withers more quickly, like all baroque forms, like all romanticism: "It is part of the essence of music that the fruits of its great cultural vintages become vapid sooner and spoil more quickly than the fruits of the visual arts or even those that grow on the tree of knowledge: for among all the products of the human artistic drive *ideas* are the most durable and robust"[50] (*Human*). Indeed, Nietzsche even aligns himself, against Schopenhauer, with "civilization," with the intellectual hostility to music: "Music in and of itself is not so significant for our inner life, so deeply moving, that it could be considered as the *immediate* language of feeling; rather, its ancient connection with poetry has placed so much symbolism into rhythmic movement, into the strength and weakness of tone, that we imagine that it speaks directly to our inner being and comes out of that inner realm. . . . By itself no music is deep and meaningful. . . . It was the intellect itself that first attributed this meaningfulness to sound . . ."[51] (*Human*). And the enormous hopes from the Wagner period have made way for a half-sarcastic, half-disconsolate resignation. In the end, music reveals most clearly *that* there is no more hope for and through music: "Our musicians do not have the slightest inkling that they are setting their own history, the history of the uglification of the soul, to music"[52] (*Daybreak*). And again: "Today, only minor things can be done well, can be done masterfully. Here alone integrity is still possible. . . . What we can still experience, at best, are exceptions. No god will save music from the rule that decay prevails, that corruption is fatalistic"[53] (*The Case of Wagner*).

Thus the powers of disappointment, of an overly clear-sighted psychology, the cold stream of intellectualism seem to push the happiness of music ever farther away from Nietzsche: "I began by denying myself all romantic music on principle, this ambiguous, show-offish, humid art that robs the mind of its rigor and joy . . . 'cave musicam' is still my advice to anyone who is man enough to insist on cleanliness in matters of the mind. . . ."[54] is how the preface to the second volume of *Human* puts it. An enlightened hostility to music seems to have seized the "most disappointed of all Wagnerians."[55] "Goethe's cautious attitude toward music: very advantageous that the German inclination toward obscurity has not yet received any artistic support. . . ."[56] "In Milton and Luther, where music is a part of life, the defective, fanatical development of the understanding and the unbridled hatred and vituperation were perhaps partly caused by music's lack of discipline. . . ."[57] "Here are people who would like to make the entire world drunk with music and think that culture would then arise: but up to today something other than culture has always followed from drunkenness"[58] (Notebooks to *Daybreak*). And where it is not hostility, it still seems to be a final farewell: the farewell of someone who had sent his Genoese ship out onto oceans that were more Greek, behind him the fading shore of art in which everything that was passing away was singing its last. The Zarathustra will that was growing stronger and stronger, it appears, would have had to bring an even more decisive end to the musical passion of the romantic Nietzsche than the Voltairean positivistic suspicions had done through disappointment. For how could there be a place for the art of all counter-Renaissance, of beautiful decline, for the baroque of the soul in the new realm of Zarathustra's higher men, in the classical land of sunrise, of morning, and of every kind of beginning? Music, one thinks, now lies in the past, where the north, where Schopenhauer's metaphysics, where Christian pessimism and the hopes for a German rebirth, a German culture will slumber forever.

Instead, something else takes place. A hovering paradox, a substitution of seasons and latitudes of the soul, of the kind that only Nietzsche would dare, attains before our very eyes what we least suspected: music becomes possible again. More than that: it becomes more possible, more necessary than ever before. Nietzsche dares to take the boldest step: his will experiences the south in the form of the north, the future in the mask of the past, Hellas as super-Germanness, Zarathustra as music. His "music of the south" is a magnificent salvation of the unsalvageable, a powerful attempt to make the new, hotter south of humanity experienceable for himself by secretly northifying it, and still, in spite of his realization to the contrary, salvages music for himself by imperiously de-northifying it. A "redemption of music from the north"[59] is the dream to which he devotes an incomparable page in *Beyond* and that fills the work of his last decade with constantly renewed hallucinations of music to come. Nietzsche always has "the prelude of a deeper, more powerful, perhaps more evil and more mysterious music in his ears, a super-German music that does not die away, turn yellow, grow pale in the face of the blue, voluptuous sea and the Mediterranean brightness of sky . . . that still prevails before the brown sunsets of the desert. . . ."[60] He wants to perceive the eternal sky of Hellas by—hearing it. "Our music," he had already written in *Daybreak,* which was still rather intellectual and anti-musical, "used to take its direction from the *Christian scholar* and was able to translate his ideal into sounds; why should it not finally find that brighter, more joyous and general sound that corresponds to the *ideal thinker?*—A music that would finally be able to sway comfortably up and down in the vast, soaring chambers of his soul?—Until now our music has been so great, so good: nothing was impossible for it? Then it should show that it is possible to feel these three things simultaneously: sublimity, deep and warm light and the bliss of the highest logical consistency!"[61]

In *The Gay Science,* the vision of a Goethean music corresponds to such an ideal of a de-Christianized, a Hellenic thinker's music—"Goethe, the Exceptional German, for whom a music of equal rank has not yet been found"[62] (even in *The Will to Power* Nietzsche finds that German music lacks "that full redeeming and binding element: Goethe");[63] a music that would like to add refinement, nobility, elegance, grace, esprit to the virtues of German music, a music that, as Nietzsche hears it, is "bourgeois," moralistic, with its rapturous, scholarly, often surly "sublimity," Beethovenian sublimity. Nietzsche specifies here both kinds of music he means in the comparison of Beethoven "as he appeared, for example, during their meeting in Teplitz"[64] with Goethe: the music "Beethoven" next to the music "Goethe," "as semi-barbarism next to culture, as the people next to the aristocracy . . . as the dreamer next to the artist, as one needing consolation next to the consoled, as the exaggerator and suspicious one next to the fair and just, as the moper and self-torturer, as the foolishly ecstatic one, the blissfully unhappy, the ingenuous extremist, the arrogant ruffian—and, all in all, as the 'untamed man': that is how Goethe himself perceived and described him. . . ."[65]—in short, as the German next to the super-German, as the northerner next to the Greek—that is how Nietzsche's two "musicians" stand next to each other. There is certainly nothing that would characterize Nietzsche's own being more profoundly or comprehensively than his longing to—*hear* Goethe, to recover in him the South, the Greek, the decided Non-Christian as "equal music."

But the will to the de-northification, de-Christianization, de-Germanization of music, to the overcoming of Beethoven through Goethe, this wish to hear all music Hellenistically and to be allowed to interpret Hellenistically gains another particular form in Nietzsche: it is his increasing love of *melody* as the form of the south, and his growing hostility toward harmony as the specifically northern will to nebulousness. As early as in *Human,* one encounters the first formulation of this post-Wagnerian ideal of the reborn, Mozartean bright childish happiness, of a second innocence, whose realization Nietzsche later detected in Peter Gast's plain music: "No matter how attached one is to serious and rich music, one is occasionally perhaps all the more overcome, enchanted and almost melted away by its very opposite. I mean those extraordinarily simple Italian operatic melismas[66] that, despite all of their rhythmic uniformity and harmonic childishness, sometimes seem to serenade us like the soul of music itself. Admit it or not, you Pharisees of good taste: *it's true.* . . . Our sentiment harkens back to the first musical delights—the strongest of our lives—when we hear those Italian melismas: childish bliss and the loss of childhood, the feeling of what is most irretrievable and of the most precious possession—that touches the strings of our soul more strongly than the richest and most serious presence of art alone would be able to do."[67] The Notebooks to *The Gay Science* give even more decided expression to this preference for the southern, melodic style: "In playing the piano, the main thing is to let the song *sing* and the accompaniment *accompany.* Now I can endure music in which music and accompaniment are not distinguished in this way only as a short interlude, as a kind of ideal noise that makes us wish for the song to begin again."[68] (Indeed, Nietzsche's own playing is supposed to have been characterized by such an emphasis on *one* dominant voice, even with distinctly polyphonic music.) Notice the impatient accent with which "music" and "accompaniment" are distinguished here, so that it is actually only the leading voice, the melody, that counts as music—the harmonic remainder is tolerated only as mere accompaniment and, so to speak, as sub-musical—a very "aristocratic" valuation of melody (and perhaps psychologically not unrelated to Nietzsche's hero worship!), in any case a very southern and perfectly Greek way of experiencing music as only song, as monody, to perceive harmony, so to speak, as Scythian.[69] "The atrophy of melody," he writes in almost Platonic fashion in *The Will to Power,* "is the same as the atrophy of the 'idea,' . . . of the freedom of the most spiritual movement. . . ."[70] And he considers the Grand

Style, as he writes in a letter from the middle of his last decade, synonymous with the highest intensification of the art of melody. (It appears that in these valuations, in this Greek distinction between song and accompaniment, memories of Jakob Burckhardt's conception of Greek music unconsciously resonate; one encounters in Burckhardt's lectures exactly the same tendency: he emphasizes that only song, not instrumental music, was worthy of the wreath for the Greeks, and he speaks of the aversion of Greek poets, thinkers, and politicians to the spread of instrumental music: they had wanted to preserve music as "impassioned melody." He cites the angry voice of a contemporary of Aeschylus: "The muse has given supremacy to song! The flute should come later to the dance, for it is the servant. The flutist who wants to make himself heard above the singer should desist!")[71] The glorification of the singing melody as the "art of art," the hatred for the "flutist," find ever new expressions in Nietzsche. The Notebooks to *The Gay Science* even call the human voice the apology of music.[72] "I now judge," he writes from Genoa in 1882, "all new music in relation to the increasing atrophy of the melodic sense. Melody, as the last and most sublime art of art, has laws of logic which our anarchists would like to decry as slavery—I am certain only that they cannot reach these sweetest and ripest fruits. I recommend to all composers the most delightful of all asceticisms: to consider for a time harmony as having not been invented and to assemble collections of pure melodies, for example from Beethoven and Chopin. . . ."[73] It is highly significant as well that Nietzsche now burdens the Germans with representing the anti-melodic, anti-Hellenistic musical ideal. As early as in the fourth *Untimely Meditation,* he says Wagner attempted to interpret the Germans' promotion of music by claiming, among other things, that because they lacked the seductive instinct of a natural melodic vocal talent, they were obliged to treat music with the same profound earnestness as the Reformation had applied to Christianity. What is here still given a positive, reformatory, Lutheran value—the lack of innate "melody" is precisely what drives the Germans up to the highest "Beethovenian" sublimity—later becomes insufficiency and calamity. *The Gay Science* wonders whether the constantly growing contempt of melody and the atrophy of the melodic sense among the Germans should be understood as an example of democratic bad manners and as an aftereffect of the revolution. (One sees how even Nietzsche's political antipathies seek to become music!) "Melody, that is, derives such pleasure from lawfulness and has such an aversion to everything that is becoming, unformed, arbitrary" (but for Nietzsche, that describes everything that is "German"!), "that it seems like a sound from the *old* order of European affairs."[74] In 1880 he writes a melody-entranced letter to Gast: "I sang and whistled your melodies to myself to give me *courage.* . . . And, indeed, everything that is good in music must be able to be whistled; but the Germans have never been able to sing"—here the Wagner quote from the *Untimely* appears in a negative transformation!—"and drag around their pianos: thus the lust for harmony."[75]

Despite all of its obvious injustice, such passages undeniably reveal the passionate experience, and the equally passionate interpretation, of an objective fact of musical history: the difference between melodic and harmonic gifts and talents on either side of the musical *Limes* between north and south, between the Mediterranean and Protestant soul. But this division of music into two hostile counterpoles (which Nietzsche finally symbolized with Wagner's and Bizet's music), the burdening of the Germans, who "were never able to sing," with the curse of and lust for harmony, the salvation of melody for the south, *as* the south—this entire process is also itself only symbolic: it means that Nietzsche cannot and does not want to do without music for the construction of his new spiritual empire, for his "south," his renewed Hellas, for the new world of his overman; that very music he had recognized and described as the ages singing out their last, as a form and sign of the end, as a swan song. It is true that his disappointment with Wagner had cured him of the delusion during his enthusiastic years that he could build a completely new culture based on music. Now he realizes that in the bright, southern, more malevolent, Mediterranean, Hellenistic realm of the overman he had still not left the north, the north as music, behind, that he cannot forget the music that he *is*—and thus he does to music what he does all too violently to himself: he tears it apart by denying, mocking, damning, demonizing one half of it—and stylizing and deifying the other all the more passionately as the opposite ideal he so painfully desires. Nietzsche does to music what he does to himself, and if he suffers from the fate of music "as from an open wound,"[76] then he is suffering *from himself*. The creation of his phantom of love, of "Mediterranean music," that deeper, more powerful, perhaps more malignant and more mysterious music, this visionary hope of the fanatic of the south betrays itself as being born of the north precisely in its vast intensity that almost approaches the pain of the Passion. Just as Nietzsche's own music, such as the pseudo-Dionysian composition "Hymn to Life" (1882), in which Nietzsche imagined he was offering an anti-Romantic, super-Christian, Mediterranean, "more malevolent" music of the south—just as this music still reveals itself to the ear of a true southerner as being northern Christian, indeed as "church music," as still related to Nietzsche's earliest boyhood music and its twin-like Parsifal character. This is evidenced by a report from Peter Gast: when he played Nietzsche's "Hymn to Life" in 1887 to two Italians without revealing the text, one exclaimed, as Gast relayed it to Nietzsche: "Magnifico! . . . *Questa* è la vera musica ecclesiastica!" Gast "however rejected the word 'ecclesiastic' and translated the text for them; then one of them said that he experienced quite a surprise—he had a vision of Calvary Hill with the seven stations of the cross!"[77] That is more than an anecdote, it is a parable, this love song to life out of which a man of life hears only a Passion procession to death, this anti-Christian music, which the impartial instinct of a southerner perceives as true church music.

And what is revealed by the character of Nietzsche's own southern music against the will and knowledge is revealed *once more* by the very fact of his homesickness for southern music: namely, his deep and ineluctable northernness. For the real southerner that Nietzsche imagined himself to be, in fact to have become, the man of a new, stronger, more pagan, Hellenistic *presence,* that person would have also placed the art of the present into the center of his artistic dreams, as did Winckelmann, Goethe, and so many other lesser beings, *that* art which equally glorifies man and the moment: the art of sculpture. After all, Nietzsche himself had recognized and described music as the art of the past, indeed as the one truly spectral art, as the art in which all that is sinking and submerged sings out its last in a twilight glow but that can never announce and give voice to hope, the future, a new age. Sculpture—that is anti-music, in every sense, it is the south, presence, paganism, Greece—it is everything that *Zarathustra* would like to proclaim. But there lived in Nietzsche, Nietzsche *was* the entire hostility of the musical northerner toward the sculptural southerner: if he sees in Socrates the cause, the form of the self-destruction of Greece, then it is not coincidental that he adds (1875), with the entire contempt of his musical nature, which knows itself to be "deeper": "I believe it was because he was the son of a sculptor. If the plastic arts would ever speak, they would seem superficial to us; superficiality emerged in Socrates, the son of a sculptor."[78] What the older Nietzsche did by assigning to the music of the south, to melody understood in Greek fashion, precisely that category which was psychologically—and more than psychologically—reserved instead for sculpture, was basically the same thing that the enthusiast of *The Birth* had done, which remained the total achievement of Nietzsche's life: he preaches the most incredible thing possible, the oldest word of the heart; he proclaims the Antichrist, the third *realm*[79] of the overman, employing the rhythms of the first two testaments, like Zarathustra; he sees what is coming but he listens to what has been. He sings a new song to his lord, to the new, to the more actual man—but he sings it as a swan song. Always before we are human beings we hear music—something prehuman always expresses itself in music, as music—that was how Hebbel perceived it. Nietzsche's "tremendous hope" is based on, builds on, towers above a new cosmos—but his innate love belongs to the innermost core preceding all formation that Schopenhauer experienced as music, it belongs to the most beautiful mask of chaos—to song.

Nietzsche knew this, too, as he knew everything about himself (he was the one person who was perhaps the most fatefully clear about himself, who was demonically denied the comfort of delusion about himself: he was only "mistaken" about himself as a result of will, it was voluntary blindness in order to be able to create, because knowledge is death). Ever since his eyes were opened by the great disappointment of Bayreuth in 1876, the eyes of someone who until then had listened only with the ear of his love—ever since, he never ceased to call out to himself his mighty "cave musicam!" just as all of his writings warn of his own dangers, warn of himself. But just as he nevertheless affirms his dangers by learning to *love* them as necessary and predetermined, so too does Nietzsche also see—more and more emphatically as time goes by—his ineluctable relationship to music in light of the *amor fati:* he affirms it anew, and this time more unconditionally, more ebulliently, more ecstatically blissfully than ever before, even in the years of *The Birth of Tragedy.* He now affirms the musician in himself, as he affirms the romantic in himself, against whom he had passionately fought after 1876, as he affirms illness not only as the "instrument and fishhook of knowledge,"[80] but because it *is* all those things, and because only the absolute affirmation of his fate still seems to be worthy of himself. He battled against himself, tenaciously, bitterly, with deadly self-hatred: now, at the end, he abandons himself to himself, grateful as he had been only in his Wagnerian youth, grateful only to himself: "how could I not be grateful to my entire life!"[81] And now a truly consuming musical enthusiasm breaks out of him, a passion—there is no other word for it than this, which he wanted to be applied to his relationship to Wagner and Wagner's art: a Passion, the cultic word of those who are obsessed by it and both recognize and desire the great end toward which they are headed. An aura of such fire rises out of the last autobiographical comments Nietzsche made about his relationship to music: "Now, however, that I am in the harbor: music, music! . . . Never in my life have I needed music as much as in this year"[82] (1884 to Gast). "Music now gives me sensations as it has actually never done before. It releases me from myself, it sobers me up from myself, as if I were surveying, *sur-feeling,* myself from afar; it gives me strength in the process, and every time there comes after an evening of music (I heard *Carmen* four times) a morning of resolute insights and ideas. It is quite amazing. It is as if I had bathed in a more natural element. Life without music is simply a mistake, a burden, an exile"[83] (1888 to Gast). "I am too much of a musician not to be a romantic. Without music life for me would be a mistake."[84] "I no longer know anything, I no longer listen to anything, I no longer read anything: and despite all of that there is nothing that *would matter* more to me than the fate of music"[85] (1888 to Gast). And in *Ecce homo* he feels "the cause of music as his *own* cause, as his *own* Passion play,"[86] he suffers "from the fate of music as if from an open wound"[87]—phrases of a Passion that does not want to conceal itself any longer. A letter from his last month gives testimony to the almost unbelievable intensity with which Nietzsche experienced music during the fateful autumn in Turin, to the unparalleled, suffering happiness of his final music: " . . . An unrestrainedly beautiful autumn day. Just returned from a great concert, which basically left the *strongest* impression I have had from a concert in my life. . . . Something for the entire string orchestra alone: after the fourth beat I was in tears. A perfectly heavenly and profound inspiration, by whom? By a musician who died in 1870 in Turin, Rossaro—I swear to you: music of the very first order, of a quality of form and *of heart* that changes my entire notion of Italians. Not one sentimental moment—I no longer know what 'great' names are. Perhaps the best remains unknown"[88] (2 December 1888 to Gast). That is the Nietzsche of *Ecce homo,* who "did not know how to make a distinction between tears and music"[89] (the sudden introduction of a minor note in a major key could already move the Nietzsche of the *Zarathustra* period to tears—marginal note to Bizet's *Carmen*). And for a moment a familiar perspective from Nietzsche's earliest period opens up here once more: the birth of music out of the spirit of a tragic pessimism. Music is suffering; where music flows, there suffering resounds—that was the fundamental realization of his first book, reinforced by Schopenhauer—and it again became the experience of the last musician in Nietzsche. And, just as it is sorrow, music is also the overcoming of sorrow, as tears are both sorrow and its overcoming—that was the innermost experience of the book *The Birth of Tragedy out of the Spirit of Music,* experienced in the music of *Tristan und Isolde* as in no other—and that, too, became again the realization of the late thinker Nietzsche who only apparently had been abducted from music by knowledge. Music and pessimism belong together, for both are indications, forms, masks of the end, of every kind of end—they are in every sense something final: that was for Nietzsche both an experience and a realization. But there also lives in both an element of overcoming this final *fatum,* both are a "and yet"—both are, still, forms of life, masks of *happiness.* This, if anything, became Zarathustra's experience and realization: singing is sorrow, but as happiness; music is weeping, but as high ecstasy. "But if you do not want to weep, to weep your purple melancholy, then you will have to *sing,* oh my soul! . . . You already glow and dream, you are already drinking thirstily from all of the deep, resonant wells of consolation, already your melancholy rests in the blissfulness of future songs!"[90]

"Oh, my soul, I have now given you everything and even my last and all of my hands have become empty for you—that I enjoined you to *sing,* lo, that was my last!"[91] ("The Great Longing")

It became Nietzsche's last just as it was his first: the last letter to his musician friend Gast, written already beyond the living, reads: "Sing a new song to me: the world is transfigured and all the heavens rejoice. . . ."[92] Song leads him back into the old night, just as song accompanies his coming into consciousness, his full awakening to himself. His life, whose exemplary and portentous self-overcoming represents perhaps an overcoming of music, a longing, desire, summons for super-musical, formative powers—it never left the boundaries of a still musical world. He did not *want* to leave it, as his consoling fantasy of a music of the south proves, that vision of a world that was no longer musical subsumed under the form of music. He *could* not leave it in the end because, in truth, music was and had to remain the "more natural" breathing element of his soul. Because, beyond its boundaries, he would have perceived his life as a hideous "mistake." Nietzsche's deeply rooted aversion to the plastic ideal, to the *form* of man—an aversion that accompanied him throughout his life—is only the negative expression of an inner affinity to *that* art which, according to Schopenhauer, provides the innermost seed preceding all formation. And even when Nietzsche is forming the new man, Zarathustra's super-musical man to come, he listens with the ear of his love for that music which we, according to Hebbel, heard before we were human. The romantic and homesick cult of the past, of everything ancestral and fading away, the cult that so strangely breaks through Nietzsche's prophetically oriented will to the future again and again, proves to be basically identical to his love of music, which he always understands as the swan song of an age that is ripe for passing away, which begins to have an enchanting, magical effect only at the moment when we hear the language of the *past* speaking from it—which, indeed, sometimes rings like the language of a vanished age into an astonished and new world. Nietzsche's identification of himself with music—there is nothing that actually mattered to him more than the fate of music, the cause of music was his own cause, his own Passion—gains the importance of an identification with the forces of a disappearing world, not with one to come. It is not for nothing that Nietzsche's favorite phrases are those in which he portrays himself as a song nearing its end, as a finale. "It seems to me that I am something of a dying breed of German"[93] (Notebooks to the *Revaluation*); "me, the last anti-political German"[94] (*Ecce homo*). Even as a musician, precisely as a musician, Nietzsche regards himself as a final exception; for "no God will save music from the rule that decay prevails, that corruption is fatalistic."[95] But music is still the only force within him that prevents him from perceiving the "new life" as a mistake and exile. This new life that he announces, prepares, to which he offers himself as a first sacrifice—he would never have seen its shore if music had not kept him afloat. Like Arion in the Greek legend we read in Herodotus (another mask of Dionysus), he was kept above the waves of the unbreathable element of his "new oceans" only by the force of its inner song in the form of a helpful dolphin.[96] This is the most personal meaning of Nietzsche's confession that he suffered from the fate of music as if from an open wound: if music died for him and in him, then the creature magically bearing him would sink away beneath him. Thus the fervent gratitude for music during his exit: the gratitude for the first twilight view of the new shore, the Dionysus shore of a third *realm*, the land of a highest presence, the land without music, which is always the past, always romanticism. In this way we experience the strange but symbolic paradox that it was precisely *that* violence which most closely aligns Nietzsche with the old, vanishing world, that it alone gives him the energy, if not actually to set foot on a new continent rising up on the horizon of humanity, then at least to be the first to presage it. That the most anti-Greek of all ecstatic experiences, the ecstasy of music, could bestow on him, as *The Birth of Tragedy* had already symbolically anticipated, the most Greek dream of the Dionysian man, Zarathustra's man. ("Music as an echo of states whose conceptual expression was *mysticism*—the feeling of the transfiguration of the individual—" we read in the late Notebooks from the *Transvaluation* period, "or: the reconciliation of the inner antitheses into something new, *the birth of the third thing*."[97] But that is explicitly an ancient, an Eleusian phrase for the experience of Dionysus: this middle, third figure who is here born out of the spirit of music is the *τρίτοζ μέποζ*[98] the cultic secret name of the reborn Dionysus himself.) If overcoming music is the classic sign under whose star Nietzsche's life was fulfilled—its symbol: the Wagner experience—then there still simultaneously gleams in this overcoming an extreme loyalty and a final gratitude for what was overcome: he who has to sacrifice music follows it into the abyss. And he who already saw the realm of the new man, disdained at the supreme moment of his descent the happiness of the eye: like his dying Tristan, to whom he dedicated his last "tremendous page,"[99] he *heard* the light—"Sing a new song to me: the world is transfigured"[100] . . . "that I enjoined you to sing, my soul, lo, that was my last."[101]

6

Illness

The extraordinary things that such people accomplish presuppose a very fine organization that makes them capable of fine feelings and to understand the voices of the gods.
—Goethe to Eckermann, 20 December 1829

If therefore you see that one creature has been granted some special advantage, then immediately ask yourself where there is a lack elsewhere, and if you look with an inquiring mind, you will soon find the key to all formation.
—Goethe, *Metamorphosis of Animals*[1]

Nietzsche attested more than once to an innate, inherited Christianity in his blood. But Zarathustra knows that blood is spirit. And one would certainly not need confirmation from Nietzsche's own lips to perceive the deeply rooted Christian atavism of his mind throughout all its phases (and not just in the Schopenhauer period) as one of the strongest latent obligations of this "free spirit" and Hellenic Antichrist. If Nietzsche likes to understand himself as the first radical non-Christian in German intellectual history, which in his eyes remains disastrously bound up with Christianity ("if people do not get over Christianity, it will be the Germans' fault!"),[2] then that is perhaps the most decisive self-misunderstanding of this mind that so ardently loved to confuse the objects of his will to knowledge with the roots of his being. One need only cast a retrospective glance at the truly essential non-Christian elements of German intellectual and art history (it goes without saying that we are speaking here not about dogma and religious confession, but about fundamental inner tendencies), at the ranks of such people as Winckelmann, Heinse, Lichtenberg, Wieland, or Goethe, Hölderlin, Mozart, or Holbein, Böcklin, Marées—all of whom, despite vast tensions among them, have in common the decisive Hellenic, pagan element, the southern element, even if it is prismatically refracted entirely differently in each one—and, on the other hand, to bring to mind an opposite list of truly northern Christian representatives of Germanness—including Luther, Angelus Silesius, Novalis, Hebbel, but also Bach, Klopstock, Schopenhauer, Brahms, as well as

Grünewald and Rembrandt (whose common, deeply embedded "Christianity," as opposed to those in the first group, needs no elucidation): one would need to consider this antithesis for only a moment in order to be spontaneously certain how completely Nietzsche, with respect to his entire being, to his spiritual blood, belongs to the second order, no matter how much his own will, determination, priestly zeal and Hellenic homesickness would like to insert him into the first, "southern" group. In an isolated passage from the Notebooks, Nietzsche at one point specifies Goethe's spiritual geographical place as being "between Pietism and Hellenism":[3] that comment, like so much else in Nietzsche's stylization of Goethe, is entirely self-revealing, an autobiographical mask, and without doubt far more accurate with regard to Nietzsche than to Goethe. Nietzsche is a pupil of the Greeks (there is no one else in modern European intellectual history who is more grateful, more reverentially blissful), but a grandson of "Pietism," of northern Christianity; an elective heir of the Hellenic character, but a blood heir of the Protestant one. Despite the relative degree in him of southernization, of self-liberation, of longing for the three-dimensional, Nietzsche remains a musician bound to the north, he remained a Christian: indeed, his final exit appears to reveal him as "more Christian" than even his Schopenhauerian, Dionysian, Wagner-romanticism had been: *The Antichrist* is a theological polemic, just as *Zarathustra* is a late-Protestant Luther-poem, just as *The Case of Wagner* is the work of a Wagner disciple, of someone who knows himself to be deeply related to Wagner, a Wagner lover. (We did not need the "tremendous page"[4] about *Tristan* to teach us that.) And if no other topic so preoccupied this shrilly bursting mind at the onset of insanity as the profound identity of the mutilated Dionysus with the crucified Christ (an identity, incidentally, that is not merely historical, but also an actual, lived religious experience), then that fact almost seems to be a premonition of the projected future arc of this life that broke apart at its apex: it allows us to venture the interpretive speculation that at some point, Nietzsche would have perhaps made the knowledge of this, his own Christian identity, magnificently productive, that he would have been able to infuse the image of a crucified Dionysus, of the victoriously shattered life, with a new meaning, one that had never been witnessed before, but was ancient nonetheless—that he would have somehow unified the two great cultic opposites and ends of humanity, the Hellenic cult of the body and the Christian cult of suffering in a "new song" . . . a song that now only lies dormant and will never be awakened by any mere "knowledge."

For if the glorification and intoxication of the *body* constitutes the essence of Hellenic religiosity and the will to intoxication the hallmark of Nietzsche's Greek homesickness (Zarathustra remains the magnificently tragic testimony of this will to body-glorifying intoxication, not of intoxication itself)—then it is doubtlessly the deepening and exaltation of *suffering,* it is the Passion that provides the content and essence of Christian piety, and there is no more genuine evidence for Nietzsche's deeply ingrained Christianity than his relationship to suffering, not to the accidental, individual sorrows of life that are external and avoidable (with which ancient moral philosophy was almost exclusively concerned, with the tendency to teach its avoidance through inner intransigence, *ἀταραξία*), but rather to the inborn, twin-like suffering, which one does not experience, but which one *is,* to life as a Passion that one affirms, that one *wills.* The Christian idea of "illness" (*illness* as a designation of innate suffering, which is thus *essential* and necessary to the human condition, as opposed to mere accessory suffering as an accidental individual experience), that illness which Christ "took upon himself" in the form of his becoming human constitutes, as the Passion, the innermost cultic core of the Christian doctrine of salvation and of all Christian metaphysics and is perhaps nowhere more fervently intensified, more central to the experience of conversion, than in the Pauline epistles; and it is precisely this idea of "illness," this cult of the Passion, as significant as it is necessary, that became the central idea, or rather the centermost experience, of the Christian Nietzsche. Affirmed "illness," conceived as the Passion, is the core idea of the Christian mythos—"Love is entirely an illness: *thence* the wondrous meaning of Christianity"[5] reads one of those fragments by the Christian Magus Novalis that, with their mysteriously bold "thus's" and "thence's" have such a strangely intuitive persuasive effect, so enchanting and bewitching—(Nietzsche himself once said during the time he was writing *Daybreak:* "One should not think that health, for instance, is a fixed goal [=ideal, summum bonum]; *look at how Christianity preferred illness* and with good reason! 'Healthy' is almost a concept like 'beautiful,' 'good'—highly variable!");[6] and affirmed illness, conscious, willed, summoned Passion is equally a crucial point in Nietzsche's philosophy of homesickness for life. Nietzsche's stance toward his own "illness," toward his empirical sickness as well as toward the spiritual Passion of his own life, rests on a completely Christian foundation, it is experienced in a Christian manner, indeed it is submitted to a Christian exegesis. It was not the accident of his falling physically ill that led Nietzsche to his philosophical interpretation of suffering (he did not even believe in the "accidental" nature of his illness: one needs only to remember the fatalism with which he juxtaposed the illness and early death of his father with his own predetermined fate), just as little as it was an accident (literally an accidental opening of a book, as Nietzsche reports) that led him to Schopenhauer's magnificent Passion metaphysics long before his physical illness; rather, like the illness itself, its interpretation also lay dormant within him, its philosophical and its active overcoming as a "this is how you must be": just as every Pauline experience already lies within Saul and is not waiting on some accidental road to Damascus. It is idle to ask how Nietzsche's philosophy would have developed without his illness: because Nietzsche *was* this illness and would have formed it out of himself as a Passion in some shape or another.

Nietzsche's philosophy, this most life-affirming, life-glorifying, this most anti-Christian philosophy to come out of Christian Europe, hovering paradoxically "between Pietism and Hellenism,"[7] thus became a philosophy of suffering, a metaphysics from the perspective of Philoctetes, a cult of the Passion, and thus in its innermost meaning a thoroughly Christian philosophy, with the most daring turn of the will toward the Greek. For, to be sure, the Christian valuation of the Passion in Nietzsche becomes complicated in the most peculiar and unique way through the Hellenic valuation of intoxication, of the heightening of life, so that the Hellenic ideal is, as it were, affirmed through the medium of its negation (as indeed negation is so often in Nietzsche, purely dialectically, the technical form of expressing a Yes all the more forcefully), and so that the root Christian feeling is justified by a blossoming out into the Hellenic blue. Between Schopenhauer and the Roman Goethe, between Novalis and Hölderlin, between the St. Matthew's Passion and the spring ecstasy of the Dionysian tragedy there thus arises a strange intermediary realm, a mediating third *realm,* for which the one world is always merely the symbol and apology for the other. Only in light of this middle realm can we interpret the otherwise irresolvable contradictions that are solidified as a deep chasm between Nietzsche's utterances, between the formulas of Greek will and Christian instinct, between the ideals of suffering knowledge and ecstatically blissful being.

It almost determines a person's place in the hierarchy of values *how* deeply he can suffer—that is the Christian phrase from *Beyond.* But that is the valuation of a martyr, the instinct of Gothic Christianity; it is the valuation, nearly the words, of Paul, the same Paul that Nietzsche hated as he hated almost no other person, and he did so for precisely such words that suck triumph out of suffering, the right to "Eternal Life" out of "illness." The Christian apologist Novalis could also have written verbatim this sentence in the Notebooks on the *Transvaluation:* "The world that thinks away suffering is unaesthetic in every sense: and perhaps desire is only a form and rhythmic version of the same thing!"[8] (A thoroughly Christian sentiment, interpreted and justified by means of early Greek dialectics!) Nietzsche, who hit upon the Greek formulation: "The *body* is inspired—let's leave the soul out of it!"[9]—who posited the Greek, indeed the truly anti-Pauline demand: "To raise man beyond himself, like the Greeks—not incorporeal phantasms.[10] The higher mind bound to a weak, nervous character—to be abolished.[11] Goal: the higher formation of the entire *body*—and not only of the brain!"[12]—and the same person says again: "As concerns illness: would we not almost be tempted to ask whether we can do without it altogether? It is not until one experiences great pain that the mind is finally liberated . . . it is only the great anguish, the long, slow agony that takes its time, as if we were being burned by unseasoned wood, which forces us . . . to climb into our ultimate depths . . . I doubt whether such pain 'improves' us—but I know that it 'deepens' us."[13] We are to understand it as Christian profundity, not as Stoic shallowness, when we read in *The Will to Power:* "I wish for the people *who matter to me* to experience suffering, abandonment, illness, mistreatment, degradation—I wish that they will not remain unacquainted with deep self-contempt, the torments of mistrust of oneself, the misery of having been overcome: I have no pity for them because I wish for them the one thing that today can prove whether someone has *value* or not—*that he is steadfast.*"[14] But nothing is more "Pauline," nothing more Christian than such a wish for martyrdom: it is the specifically Christian form of turning negative suffering into the positives of trial, martyrdom, probation; it is the ethos of someone who suffers deeply and irredeemably, who admitted to himself and to his friend: "At *all* stages of my life the surplus of suffering in me was enormous"[15] (1883). In his severity toward himself and toward everyone "who matters to him," Nietzsche's ethics prove to be entirely the heir and grandchild of Christian *asceticism,* of Christian self-overcoming, indeed of Gothic self-torment, of the Pascalian *moi haïssable,*[16] the "moi" understood as the "Mere Self," as body, as "illness," as a Christian "Not-God"; indeed, even Nietzsche's metaphysics, the philosophy of the Eternal Return, *his* mythos of Eternal Life, is in the end a form of this asceticism, this self-torment and self-overcoming: it is the self-martyrdom of a being who would prefer, egoistically, to say to itself "No" and forces itself, in Christian fashion, to utter an eternal "Yes" as the most extreme sacrifice and martyrdom of which it is capable. The ultimate Dionysian "Yes" to life, contained in the doctrine of recurrence, does not rest on Greek assumptions, but rather on Pascalian ones: it is the "Yes" of a Christian to a final and most difficult asceticism—a trial extended and intensified into infinity and a forever renewed self-overcoming. (The doctrine of the Eternal Return is psychologically undoubtedly an extreme form of self-martyrdom, a heroic negation of original, Schopenhauerian existential fear. "Was that life? Very well, once more!"[17]—this exclamation at Nietzsche's end is truly not an outburst of jubilation, but rather a decision, a sacrifice, an eternal self-crucifixion.) "My self-overcoming," he writes in 1882 to Overbeck, "is basically my greatest strength: I recently reflected on my life and found that since then I have done *nothing* else. Even my 'achievements' (and particularly those since 1876) belong under the rubric of asceticism. . . .

Even the *Sanctus Januarius* is the book of an ascetic."[18] "With regard to pain and privation, the last years of my life can be measured against that of every ascetic from any period,"[19] he claims with a certain note of pride in 1880 to Malwida, and two years later, to the same person, he speaks of himself as of an eccentric saint, "who has taken on the burden of a voluntary asceticism (an abstruse asceticism of the mind) in addition to all of his other burdens and forced privations."[20]

But "what do ascetic ideals mean"? Is it not Nietzsche himself who, in the *Genealogy of Morals,* gives voice to the most pitiless words of derision, the most biting insights into this very ascetic ideal? "The ascetic ideal arises out of the instinct for protection and preservation in a degenerating life[21] . . . it points to a partial physiological retardation and exhaustion . . . it is a trick for the *preservation* of life. . . . What does it *mean* when a philosopher pays tribute to the ascetic ideal? . . . he wants to escape *from some torture.*"[22] ("My condition is unbearable and painful to the point of torture," he writes to Overbeck in February 1888, "my last work revealed something of it: when one is taut like a bow strung to the breaking point, any emotion feels good provided that it is violent—"[23] which the *Genealogy* from the previous year anticipates almost verbatim: "the release of emotion is the greatest attempt to relieve, that is to say to anaesthetize suffering, the involuntarily desired narcotic against torments of whatever sort.")[24] And who is Nietzsche talking about when he speaks of the deep pathological nature of the prevailing human type—"for man is more ill, more uncertain, more changeable, less determined than any other animal, there is no doubt about that—he is *the* sick animal: where does that come from? Certainly he also dared, innovated, defied, challenged fate more than all the other animals combined: he, the great experimenter on himself, the dissatisfied, unsated one who battles against animals, nature and gods for ultimate supremacy, the one who is eternally of the future . . . whose future mercilessly bores into him like a spur in the flesh of every present—could such a courageous and fertile animal not also be the sickest among all the sick animals? . . ."[25] Who is he thinking of, secretly, when he speaks of man as one who wounds himself, as the master of destruction and self-destruction? Of the ascetic priest as the wish-become-flesh for being different, being elsewhere, and indeed as the highest degree of this wish, as its true fervor and passion? And against whom are all of these revealing, derisively fierce negations directed? What does the vehement criticism of the ascetic type mean? Yet the entire vindictively piercing analysis of asceticism and of the ascetic ideal in the *Genealogy*—is itself asceticism, it is Nietzsche's asceticism *once more!* It is a form of Christian self-hatred, Christian self-mortification and self-overcoming—it is Nietzsche's self-sacrifice. Everything, truly everything, that this chapter of *Genealogy* contains in the form of pitiless conclusions and the most vicious disdain is really Nietzsche attacking *himself,* confessing, negating himself. What he describes there are the inner landscapes of his own domain, what he illuminates with hostile intent are the grottos and shafts in the mine of his own depths. He speaks of himself, prophesies himself, when he speaks of "triumph precisely in the final agony": "the ascetic ideal has always fought under this superlative banner; it recognized in this enigma of seduction, in this image of rapture and torment its brightest light, its salvation, its ultimate victory. Crux, nux, lux—these all belong together in it."[26] He writes the ascetic law of his life, and particularly of his life, when he says at the end of the book: "All great things perish through themselves, through an act of self-cancellation: that is what the law of life dictates, the laws of the *necessary* self-overcoming within the essence of life—the lawgiver himself is always the last to receive the call: *patere legem, quam ipse tulisti.*"[27]

Nietzsche's entire psychology of asceticism *is* asceticism. It is true of him what he thought he was saying about the atheists, anti-Christians, moralists, nihilists, skeptics of his time in the *Genealogy:* "They believe themselves to be as unencumbered as possible by the ascetic ideal, these 'free, *very* free spirits': and yet, I may reveal something to them that they cannot see themselves—for they stand much too close to themselves—this ideal is most particularly *their* ideal as well, they themselves represent it today as perhaps no one else does, they are its most spiritualized product . . . and if I am in any respect a puzzle solver, then I want to be one with *this* statement!"[28] (The passage is typical of Nietzsche's vengeful solitude with a mirror, also of his care not to destroy the sheer, gauze-like layer that still separates him from the ultimate insight, the great *tat twan asi.*) The sentence, "look at how Christianity preferred illness and with good reason!"[29] truly has, as do so many others, the value of a self-characterization, a self-classification of someone who is in many essential respects an exceedingly Christian thinker, more akin to Pascal than to Schopenhauer. In its psychological substructure Nietzsche's philosophy is a thoroughly Christian theodicy of the Passion, of suffering and illness, a veritable apologia in which Pauline ideas are juxtaposed and combined in a highly idiosyncratic fashion with romantic ones (Novalis), where mystical and Goethean notions meet, and that are finally and most peculiarly, with a power of transformation that Nietzsche alone possessed, augmented with completely Greek consistency to an even higher level of intensity.

At first glance, Nietzsche's philosophical classification of illness appears to be completely Pauline—and it is precisely Paul at whom he aims an indictment in *The Antichrist* that virtually quivers with hatred. In *The Antichrist* he quotes the verses from the first letter to the Corinthians, adding commentaries full of bitter derision: " . . . God hath chosen the weak things of the world to confound the things that are mighty; and base things of the world, and things which are despised, hath God chosen, yea, and things which are not, to bring to naught things that are."[30] He could have aligned other related passages from the Pauline letters next to this one—which he calls a document of the first importance for the psychology of all chandala morality—but that would only make clearer how closely the glorification of everything that is sown in weakness and arises in strength is basically related to Nietzsche's own defense, which he drew out of his own deepest experiences, of illness and of everything that stands with one foot beyond life. What Nietzsche says about the *artist,* about Zarathustra, about himself, is strictly speaking only a reformulation of the Pauline words about *Christians*—that is how deeply rooted in the Christian context both Nietzsche's concept of the artist and his self-assessment are. "Exceptional circumstances are what determine the artist," we read in *The Will to Power:* "they are all deeply related and linked to pathological phenomena: so that it does not seem possible to be an artist and not to be ill."[31] "To become healthier—that is a *regression* in the nature of someone like Wagner,"[32] he says in *Ecce homo* while discussing *Tristan.* And in notes for the "Attempt at a Self-Critique" from 1886, we read that *The Birth of Tragedy* is the confession of a romantic: "The person who suffers the most desires beauty the most deeply—he generates it."[33] *Zarathustra* asks: "Spirit is that form of life which cuts into life; it increases its own knowledge through its own pain—did you know that already? And the happiness of the spirit is this: to be anointed and consecrated by tears to be the sacrificial animal—did you know that already?"[34] But *Ecce homo* straightforwardly acknowledges: "In order even to begin to understand my *Zarathustra* one would perhaps have to have a constitution similar to mine, with one foot *beyond* life. . . ."[35] All of this is Pauline inheritance, which also influenced Luther's conception of the Great Man: when a magister asks him (in the *Table Talks*): "What kind of person do you, Herr Doktor, think Paul was?" Doctor Martin answers thus: "I believe that Paul was a despised person who enjoyed no respect, a poor, frail little man like Magister Philipp (Melanchthon)."[36] And on another occasion: "David must have had more dreadful devils than we do; for he could not have had such a great revelation and knowledge of God without such great challenges."[37]

Romantic Christianity, in addition to Reformation sources, helped bring Nietzsche's theodicy of illness into sharper relief. Above all, the shade of Novalis, the mystical magician and romantic apologist of illness, looms above *Zarathustra*'s "beyond life." One sentence, such as the passage in *Ecce homo* about *Tristan:* "the world is impoverished for him who has never been ill enough for this 'voluptuousness of hell': it is permitted, it is almost imperative to use a phrase from the mystics here"[38]—such a sentence is not only unthinkable without Novalis, the phrase from the mystics could just as well be in his *Fragments,* and indeed it is. And we know that Novalis wrote his own Tristan music, experienced his own "voluptuousness of hell"—in the *Hymns to the Night.*[39] Illness is magic—that was the philosophical maxim Novalis had made his own through suffering. "Illnesses," the *Fragments* tell us in proto-Nietzschean terms, "distinguish man from animals and plants. Man is born to suffer. The more helpless, the more receptive for morality and religion."[40] "Illness belongs to individualization." Indeed, illness and its affirmation are for Novalis, as for Nietzsche, more than a philosophical precondition, a goad upward, and a hook for knowledge: it is a philosophical *act,* in so far as it demands and symbolizes the negation of what is merely individual. "The genuine philosophical act," Novalis finds, "is suicide; this is the real beginning of all philosophy.—The act of leaping over oneself is everywhere the highest one, the primal point, the genesis of life."[41] "Illnesses," he says in another passage, in an almost eerie anticipation of Nietzsche's philosophy of illness, "illnesses are certainly an extremely important subject for humanity. . . . We are still imperfectly acquainted with the art of using them. They are probably the most interesting stimulus and material of our reflection and action. There are no doubt many fruits to be harvested here, especially, it seems to me, in the intellectual field, in the area of morality, religion and God knows in what other wonderful areas. What if I should become the prophet of this art?"[42] (Forty years later, and forty years before Nietzsche, Hebbel takes up this romantic idea again when he says: "Philosophy is a higher pathology.")[43] And again, almost with the apodictic sovereignty of Nietzsche in his last years: "The more forced a life, the higher it is."[44]

Such a thoroughly Nietzschean sentence, like Novalis's entire philosophy of illness, sounds as if it were infused with Goethe's instinctive, determined hostility to Christianity. And yet it indicates precisely the point where, next to Pauline-Lutheran Christianity, next to romantic mysticism, Goethe's wisdom and Greek humanism enter into Nietzsche's philosophy of illness. Goethe, whose "Metamorphosis of Animals"[45] contains a primal symbol and first basic law for every Nietzschean "Above and beyond oneself" and "Beyond life," himself outlined on several occasions what Riemer heard him say the year Schiller died: that certain operations of the mind occur only in those of a more delicate organization—which he repeated almost verbatim twenty-four years later to Eckermann, but with the gentle inclination toward the mythical realm that was typical of his final years. There one occasionally imagines one is listening to the words of *The Gay Science,* but spoken more as if in a whisper: "All of you do not sense that people who are prophetic suffer greatly."[46] In the symbolic realm as well Goethe made repeated modifications of this mystery notion of illness, which alone makes the "voices of the divine" perceptible. (Gundolf notes, in reference to figures such as Ottilie in *Elective Affinities* and Makarie in *Wilhelm Meister's Travels,* that in Goethe's works physical suffering is a sign of a fragile organism's defenseless cognitive sympathy with the laws of the universe: "Where there is much wisdom there is much suffering.")[47] And certainly Nietzsche, whose philosophy so thoroughly represents a "higher pathology," legitimately found Goethe's dictum about the productivity of what is inadequate compatible with Novalis's "individualizing illness" and with his bold formulation: "The more forced a life, the higher it is." For there are countless comments by Nietzsche that reverberate in the apologetic rhythm of Goethe's axiom that the inadequate is productive. If a hyperbolic English saying, perhaps echoing Goethe, states: "The world's work is done by its invalids,"[48] then Nietzsche makes it more pointed in the *Genealogy of Morals:* "Human history would be a far too stupid affair without the spirit that entered into it from the powerless."[49] *Human, All Too Human* translates it: "Degenerating natures are always of utmost importance wherever some advance is to occur; a partial weakening must precede every advance. The strongest natures hold onto the type, the weaker ones helped to develop it further."[50] "Europe is an invalid," he says in *The Gay Science,* "which owes the greatest debt to its incurability and to the never-ending metamorphosis of its affliction: these constantly new . . . dangers, pains, . . . finally created an intellectual sensitivity that almost equals genius, and is in any case the mother of all genius."[51] There are pages about Homer or Epicurus—secret, or only barely secret, self-portraits—that correspond precisely to his theory of the artist, who is virtually impossible without "illness": "Homer—don't you perceive the pessimist and overly sensitive soul who, for the sake of his suffering, invented the abundance and perfection of the Olympian gods!"[52] (Notebooks to *Transvaluation*). And in *The Gay Science:* "One should not hide from this fact: with the happiness of Homer in one's soul—the state in which he invented the Gods for the Greeks—no, invented *his* Gods for himself!—one is able to withstand more suffering than any other creature under the sun! And for this prize alone one buys the most precious shell that the waves of existence have thus far washed up onto the shore!"[53] Or, also in *The Gay Science,* about Epicurus: "Only someone who suffered continuously could have invented such a form of happiness, the happiness of an eye before which the ocean of existence has become calm and now cannot get enough of looking at its surface and at this gently trembling ocean skin: never before had there been such a modesty of delight."[54] True, Nietzsche is not content with such stylizations of extraordinary individual Hellenistic types into figures more appropriate to late antiquity and almost to early Christianity: in eminently characteristic form he conceives of the Greek people in their entirety as a magus of his own illness, as a people that suffers deeply and venerates illness. Even *The Birth of Tragedy* devoutly extols the Greeks as "the people so singularly capable of suffering,"[55] whose entire existence, "despite all of its beauty and moderation, rested on a veiled substratum of suffering and knowledge."[56] Therein still lies the coupling of Schopenhauerian metaphysics with a Burckhardtian philosophy of history. But the conception of the Greeks as brilliant sufferers remains the same far beyond his Schopenhauer period and is far removed from the immediate influence of Burckhardt: "Some peoples," he writes in *Human* with apparent objectivity, but with a secret love for all victorious suffering, "some peoples have created great auxiliary powers of culture out of illnesses: for example, the Greeks, who in earlier centuries suffered from great nervous epidemics (a sort of epilepsy and chorea) and transformed them into the magnificent type of the Bacchae. The Greeks, you see, enjoyed anything but robust health; their secret was to venerate illness, whenever it had any power, as a god as well."[57]

But precisely these stylizations of the Greek character as pathological, as ill in a Nietzschean sense, nevertheless also reveal something of the very particular form of his affirmation of suffering, of the theodicy of illness so peculiar to Nietzsche, going beyond the Christian context and into the Hellenic one. His affirmation of the suffering person is not open, as in the Christian manner; Nietzschean man does not admit to being a suffering being; like his Homer and his Epicurus, he invents the stirring appearance of happiness, of abundance, of health, he wraps himself in the cloak of a Hellenistic perfection. The Greek in Nietzsche, or his obsession with Greece, is ashamed of the Gothic ideal that is innate to the Christian, which is an ideal of suffering and decorporealization; and even the Christian in him darkly senses that suffering alone is not sufficient before the meaningful gaze of the godhead. The cross alone did not make the Savior—there were also thieves hanging at Golgotha. And out of this typically Nietzschean mixture of Christianity and Hellenism there arises, as a transition and bridge from one to the other, as a unification of irreconcilables, the phantom ideal of the Great Recuperation and of the Second Health. There arises the lasting inner attitude of those portraits of Homer and Epicurus, the glorification of everything great and lasting as of the art of precisely this transition, of this moment of the Great Recuperation: "Singing is for those who are convalescing; the healthy may speak"[58] (*Zarathustra*) is the insight of this new-born soul, which would prefer to sing than to speak and for whom life without music would be a mistake. There arises, finally, the cult of the artist as the Great Physician; now the artist is not merely someone who is necessarily ill; he is, like the bacchantic Greeks, a patient and physician at once, a magus who produces the magic of Eternal Life from the closest proximity to death. Thus arises Nietzsche's "central doctrine," as it is formulated in the Notebooks to *Zarathustra:* "Central doctrine: it is in *our* power to turn suffering into a blessing, poison into nourishment. Will to suffering."[59] "Apart from the fact that I am a décadent, I am also its opposite . . ."[60] *Ecce homo* repeats. "People should say of me that I was a *good* physician—and not only to myself"[61] (to his mother). "I was in every respect my own physician"[62] (to Rohde). "One must be one's own physician"[63] (to Gersdorff). This pride of someone who, like Zarathustra, knew how to brew his balm out of his poisons, the pride in having defied himself, in having created himself, resonates through Nietzsche's works and private utterances more strongly as time goes by. It becomes triumphant in *Ecce homo,* it becomes boisterous, even turning into a veritable intoxication of recuperation. But the entire foreword to *The Gay Science* of 1886 speaks of such an "intoxication of recuperation"; it is the most extensive testimony we have from Nietzsche about the importance of *his* illness and *his* recuperation for his life and work, and only *Ecce homo* comes close to matching its revealing perspicacity. "Gay science: that means the saturnalia of a mind that has patiently withstood a terrible, long pressure—patiently, austerely, coldly, without surrendering but without hope—and which now is suddenly seized by hope, by the hope for health, by the *intoxication* of recuperation. . . ."[64] "It was then," the foreword to *Human* from the same year adds, "it was then that I learned the art of *acting* cheerful, objective, curious, above all healthy and malicious. . . . Nevertheless, what perhaps constitutes the charm of these writings will not escape a fine and sympathetic eye—that the person speaking here is suffering and experiencing privations, but doing so as if he were *not* suffering and experiencing privations. Equilibrium, composure, even gratitude for suffering are supposed to be maintained here, there is an austere, proud . . . will here that has assumed the task of defending life *against* pain . . . it was then that I gained from myself the maxim: someone who is suffering does *not yet have a right* to pessimism![65] . . . In the meantime there may be long years of recuperation, years full of colorful, painfully magical transformations, mastered and reined in by a tenacious will to health, which often dared to clothe and disguise itself as health."[66] *Ecce homo,* as always, puts it more uncompromisingly, more pungently, more definitively: "I made my philosophy out of my will to health, to *life.* For one should take note: the years of my lowest vitality were those in which I *ceased* being a pessimist: the instinct of self-recovery *forbade* me from accepting a philosophy of poverty and despondency."[67] "To look out, from the perspective of illness, for *more healthy* concepts and values, and, on the other hand, to peer down from the abundance and self-confidence of the *rich* life into the secret labor of the décadence instinct—it was there that I had my most lasting effort, my true experience, and it was there, if anywhere, that I achieved mastery."[68]

From this achieved summit, in the certain consciousness of an attained Second Nature, there is no more need of the shame and disguise of that First—sick—Nature; the all-too-Christian demands made by his physical being now become a distinction even in the Hellenic sense, for they give evidence of the triumph of a long will, and that is precisely "what is most profoundly and sincerely heartening, to see the victorious god next to all of the monsters he has fought"[69] ("Schopenhauer as Educator").

In this way Nietzsche, in his final phase, openly avows the Christian-Hellenic ideal of that Great Healthfulness—"of the sort which one not only has, but which one is also constantly acquiring and must be acquired"[70] (*Ecce homo*). Even in the period of *Zarathustra* he writes, half unwillingly, to Rohde: "Very well, I have a 'second nature,' but not in order to annihilate the first one, but in order to *bear* it. I would have foundered on my 'first nature' long ago—I almost did founder on it."[71] Similarly, during the same winter, to Hans von Bülow: "What concern is it of mine if my friends claim that my current free-thinking ways are an eccentric *decision* I doggedly adhere to, one that is forced and wrenched from my own inclination? Very well, there may be a 'second nature': but I still want to prove that with this second nature I have only just entered into the true possession of my first nature."[72] But as early as 1886, in the preface to *The Gay Science,* the true "treatise on recuperation," he writes more proudly: "One can guess that I would not like to appear ungrateful in saying goodbye to that period of dire infirmity, whose benefits for me have to this day not yet been exhausted: just as I am well enough aware of the advantage I have in general with my changeable health over all those who are robust of spirit. A philosopher who has made and continues to make his way through many periods of health has also made his way through just as many philosophies. . . . And as concerns illness: wouldn't we almost be tempted to ask whether we can do without it altogether? It is only through great pain that the mind is finally liberated. . . ."[73] And in the book itself we read similarly about the great open question "whether we could *dispense* with illness, even for the development of our virtue, and whether in particular our thirst for knowledge and self-knowledge needs a sick soul as much as it does a healthy one: in short, whether the exclusive will to health is an advantage, an expression of cowardliness (cowardliness!) and perhaps an example of the most refined barbarism and backwardness."[74] Nietzsche's justification and grateful affirmation of illness is expressed perhaps most clearly in a letter to his sister: "The entire significance of the terrible physical pains that afflicted me was that *through them alone* I was roused from a false, which is to say far too *humble,* conception of my life's mission. And since I belong to that category of people who are modest by nature, the most violent means are necessary to call me back to myself."[75]

In this gratitude, in which both "Christian" humility and the Hellenic will to the heights are present, we have the true image of Nietzsche's philosophy of illness, its point of origin and its goal. A tremendous energy for generating meaning speaks out of it, as does the confession of being inadequate, which became productive here. And we would not like to dispense even with the echo of a horrible lamentation that reverberates in it, that long, disconsolate cry of an ill, reclusive soul that so often arises out of the letters (most immediately, perhaps, in the letters to Overbeck), this cry of the most unbearable suffering, which even Zarathustra's festive songs of triumph were not able to drown out, for how much suffering and inner vulnerability is "revealed by this masquerade of a reclusive invalid!"[76] (*Beyond*).

But this cry belongs to triumph, like the "Out of the Depths"[77] belongs to exemplary Christian suffering, like the lamentations of Philoctetes belong to the image of the Hellenic hero ("The 'patient sufferer' is Hellenic: Prometheus, Heracles,"[78] reads a note in the Notebooks for the Basel period.) That is what is most profoundly and sincerely heartening, to see the victorious god next to all of the monsters he fought, and the image of the victorious saint always includes the symbols of his endured martyrdom. If Nietzsche's life seems so vividly striking, as does perhaps no other in modern intellectual history, then the symbolically close proximity of terrible illness and great recuperation, of lamentation and triumphal cry, of wail and song, is perhaps the most concretely tangible cause of that impression. For how deeply affecting it is, almost like the Passion, that just behind the *Ecce homo,* that song of thanks for the most tremendous of hopes from someone enjoying a deceptive recovery, there lurks the most extreme and incurable suffering and a sacrificial end! How almost eerie the hubris with which this strong-willed physician of himself, thinking he had mastered his long infirmity after all, sacrifices his rooster to Asclepius, unaware that he was still doing the same thing Socrates had done before his final convalescence![79] And even this last, horrible hubris, which once more combines Nietzsche's ultimate illness with a final great recuperation, is justified by Nietzsche's entire fate both as a willingly suffering Christian and as a proud Greek, in accordance with the words of Hyperion: Whoever is spoken to so loudly by fate is also permitted to speak more loudly to fate; the more unfathomably he suffers, the more unfathomably powerful he is.

7
Judas

Judas is the most faithful one of all.
—Hebbel

The great apologetic problem of Judas—how were both Judas and Judas's betrayal possible, and why were they necessary—this most absorbing of all the problems of justification has preoccupied Christian thought for two millennia.[1] For Christianity, Judas's deed and fate were, next to Adam's fall, the most concrete embodiment of the eternal question about the meaning of evil, about the relationship between freedom and necessity. Every kind of interpretation has passed over the image of Judas. We have Dante imperiously sitting in judgment over him and relegating him to the innermost region of hell, delivering him to the crushing jaws of Lucifer; we have the rich store of both popular and monastic legends and mystery plays in which Judas, like the primal image—of evil itself—shimmering through him, is reduced through humorous distortion to mundanely bearable proportions, or in which his betrayal has to serve, through grotesque motifs, as a temporary relief for spectators burdened by the atmosphere of the Passion. We have Klopstock's reading of Judas's deed as the revenge of a darksome lover, performed out of desperate jealousy toward the favorite disciple, John.[2] (Renan's *Vie de Jésus* [*Life of Jesus*] also assumes jealousy of John as the motive for Judas's betrayal.)[3] In Russian literature we possess, characteristically enough, literary apologies of Judas (Hebbel, the most Russian type[4] among German writers of his century, also left a *Judas* among his dramatic plans), literary works that all serve to explain, humanize, justify Judas's treachery; some by respecting his motives but diminishing them through realistic depiction and, as if continuing the technique of the mystery plays, making Judas into the symbol of comic normalcy, the most insipid misunderstanding of a divine presence; others by letting him consciously struggle from the beginning with the inner experience of his treasonous nature and attributing the burden of having murdered God not to a blindly unsuspecting Hodur, but rather to a clear-sighted Loki,[5] a demon consumed by the evil primal fire, whose greatness consists in his acceptance of the entire terribleness of his deed and its consequences, and in enduring it with the pride of a somber but fateful accursedness. And we possess, finally, the poetic legend in which Judas appears as the other half of the balance in the great work of Redemption, as the second dark sacrifice of the New Covenant. Here Judas sacrifices himself knowing that the scripture must be fulfilled and that, if he does not do what is preordained, the work of Redemption will remain undone and the entire, breathing Creation will be condemned to meaninglessness; he sacrifices himself by consciously taking upon himself the most dreadful curse in the world and betraying him who *must* be betrayed. In this legend, Jesus recognizes the sacrifice Judas brings to him and to his work of redemption, he knows that for a moment the fate of the entire world rests in Judas's hands; if they refuse to do what is written, if they recoil at the "woe unto that man by whom the Son of man is betrayed!"[6] then the sacrifice on the cross will also remain undone. Thus, on the last evening, he sees in Judas the dark companion of his own self-sacrifice; he speaks of him in words that the other disciples do not understand and he thanks the traitor with a gesture of love that Judas merely returns in the Garden of Gethsemane. (In the Gospel of John, which is otherwise especially venomous toward Judas, there are traces of such a special commonality, of a mysterious agreement between Jesus and Judas; thus, the morsel that Jesus gives, of all people, to Judas during the Last Supper is a symbol of this community of fate, together with the bitter words: "That thou doest, do quickly."[7] When Judas goes out after his betrayal and destroys himself at the same hour as the work on Golgotha is finished, it is not done out of any kind of remorse, but out of the sense of the utmost community of fate even in extremis, out of a sense of succession and affiliation, deeper than that of all those who, at the moment of betrayal, fled and abandoned not just the master but above all themselves and their own discipleship. Whereas at that moment he, Judas, obeyed the Lord and himself most profoundly. In his last hour, he too feels a darker, "It is finished."[8]

Out of this last, already overdetermined Judas legend there emerges in perhaps concentrated form the buried meaning of all the ameliorating interpretations that the figure of Judas has undergone in twenty centuries of Christianity. In it, as in so many parables of redemption within the most varied mythic circles, there is the typical division of the redeemer into two parts, splitting him into light and nocturnal components, into angelic and diabolical halves, which only together can perform the work of renewing and redeeming the world. In all that convulses humanity, revives humanity—which is the meaning of all these myths—God *and* demon work together, and the one without the other is incapable of transforming the aged waters. The myth merely illustrates through two figures what it recognizes and wants to present to the mind as a single being; it represents only by antithesis the inexorable law that stipulates that the creator must always be a destroyer, the progenitor always a murderer, the redeemer always a traitor as well. That in every great symbolic man, Christ and Judas must always again exchange the dark kiss.

Nietzsche's life, too, obeyed this law, exemplifying it as few have done. In almost cruelly graphic fashion, his life demonstrates the struggle of the individual against a mission, against the burden of the duty of renewal. And it is a struggle against both the bright mission of the savior and of Zarathustra, as well as against the curse of treason. It demonstrates that struggle—and it also demonstrates an obedience to both, who were not brought to his attention from without, but who grew up within him, both opposing each other, both presupposing each other. It was the undoing of this life not to be allowed to obey one of these two imperatives of renewal more than the other, but rather to be forced to serve both, to *be* both. As early as in *Human,* Nietzsche had, in crucifying the ascetic in himself, come up with the skeptical phrase: "in every ascetic morality, man reveres a part of himself as a god and needs to demonize the rest."[9] And in *Ecce homo,* he tips the fateful equilibrium of this tremendous balance toward the positive, stylizes it into something sublime:

> Do you want a formula for such a fate that becomes a man? It is in my *Zarathustra.*
>
> "—And whoever desires to be a creator in good and evil must first be a destroyer and demolish values.
>
> Thus the highest evil belongs to the highest goodness: but the latter is the creative one."
>
> I am by far the most terrifying person there has ever been; this does not rule out that I will be the most beneficent. I am familiar with the joy of destruction to a degree that is suited to my power to destroy—in both I obey my Dionysian nature, which does not know how to separate doing 'no' from saying "yes" . . . I am the destroyer par excellence.[10]

In this soul there lives, terrible to itself, the need for a redemptive act of betrayal in the form of a fateful imperative to creative destruction. This soul was by its natural disposition grateful as few others are—his relationship to all of the elements of his early education attests to it: his relations with friends, with his family, and with every kind of ancestry movingly demonstrate that—but this hyper-gratitude corresponds, in fact is mysteriously linked, to an inner compulsion to disown and desecrate what is most beloved to him. Nietzsche was proudly and painfully aware that this demonic linkage between the most profound gratitude and crass betrayal was the most proper law of his life. "To attack is for me a form of gratitude,"[11] we read in *Ecce homo.* It is impossible not to hear the accent of deep satisfaction that fills his most radical renunciations, his most vicious words of disavowal—a satisfaction experienced only by a person who finally yields to an inner law after a long struggle. No one will believe that Erwin Rohde's harmless skepticism about Taine as a historian could have been even remotely sufficient to offer Nietzsche a pretext in his own eyes for a renunciation of his once most beloved friend, as his letter from 21 May 1887 presents it.[12] It is the tone of someone who had long waited for some opportunity. His letters to his mother and sister are no different. A passage about his mother in one letter, for instance, almost quivers with the joy of hatred and an intense desire to mortally wound: "How it is possible that we are related by blood counts among the puzzles that I have thought about many times."[13] (1885 to his sister). Letters to Malwida, to Rée, to Lou offer similar examples (the letters to Gast are probably the only ones that contain nothing of the kind). And common to all is the significant circumstance that in Nietzsche's eyes it is never an intended break, which for that reason he would have tried to make sound as irreversibly harsh as possible. It is always merely an articulation, an outburst of the "evil" lurking in the background of every one of these relationships: remorse does not follow the betrayal (because it arose out of necessity), nor does any retraction, but there is a wistful mindfulness of fate, an almost beseeching emphasis on their unbreakable commonality, the fateful fellowship between them. Thus after that cruel and coldly cutting letter to Rohde follows another one: "No, don't let yourself be estranged from me too easily!"[14] and after the radical rejection of his sister (letter draft December 1888)[15] the plea not to see harshness in his rejection but rather its opposite, and the plea for love.

But the great example of his betrayal, which obeyed a deep necessity typical of legend, remains the case of Wagner, and not just the pamphlet of the same name. Is there anything in all of intellectual and spiritual history more ghastly than the denials and self-abnegations of *The Case of Wagner* after the days of Tribschen? Than the image of this most loyal of disciples ("I swear to you before God that I think you are the only one who knows what I intend,"[16] Wagner to Nietzsche, 1873), who after years of struggle between the most grateful love and insistent doubt leaves the master at the moment when their common cause appears to have emerged victorious? Than the helpless, then furious, and never-overcome sorrow of the one who believed to have been betrayed, who (in the words others also put in his mouth) knew whom and what he lost ("Tell him: since he went away from me I have been alone")[17]—than the willed callousness of the younger man who could not forgive his own betrayal of the one whom he had once adored? Is there anything more tragic in the truest sense of the word than the spectacle, despite everything, of absolute ineluctability, inevitability, ultimate necessity?

Both blinded, both unjust to the point of cruelty, but both obeying themselves, both loyal to themselves and both suffering for it to their end. Who was burdened more by guilt and by the suffering from guilt? "I stand only by the one who suffered most in this matter, and that was my brother"[18] was how his sister once concluded a conversation. "I was fated to turn my back on Wagner,"[19] we read in the foreword to *The Case of Wagner*. But here, too, something emerges that had been preformed in rudimentary fashion, as it were, in Nietzsche's other relations, that rejection and betrayal even in the most radical form did not destroy the relationship itself, that attacking is a form of his gratitude and apostasy a form of his devotion. Every note sounded in his last letter to Rohde, the friend of his Schopenhauer youth, has a motivic correspondence in the years of his Wagner polemics. To the end, Nietzsche never denied his fateful connection to Wagner's person, he never disavowed Wagner's art and problem, his calamitously traitorous discipleship, his hostile confraternity, their ultimate identity; he was never able to conceal his love for him and the pain of betrayal that was remorseless (because fatalistically clairvoyant), but forever unconquerable, no matter how many guises he lent both. Indeed, one may say that even the young, Wagner-drunk Nietzsche did not express such accents of love and innermost affiliation as the apostate of *The Case of Wagner*, the master who wrote the most fanatically destructive polemic we possess in the German language. "I loved and revered Richard Wagner more than anyone else,"[20] he wrote in the preliminary studies for *The Case*, and that one will notice by his judgment that he loved Wagner deeply: for an opponent would never take his adversary so seriously. *Ecce homo* attests to this fact with heavy testamentary seriousness: "Without any doubt, what most profoundly and sincerely restored me in my life by far was the intimate relation with Richard Wagner. I rate the rest of my human relationships low; I would not want to forfeit for any price the days in Tribschen, days of trust, of cheerfulness, of sublime coincidences—of deep moments. . . . I do not know what others have experienced with Wagner: a cloud never darkened our sky. . . ."[21] "I would not have endured my youth without Wagnerian music. . . . I call Wagner the great benefactor of my life. The point where we are related, that we suffered more deeply, also from each other, that we were able to suffer as people of this century will forever bring our names together. . . ."[22] In the late Notebooks to the *Transvaluation*, there is a painful eruption: "I loved him and no one else. He was a man after my heart.[23] . . . It needs no explanation that I will not easily grant to anyone the right the make my (current) estimation of Wagner his own, and the impudent rabble that teems like lice on the body of today's society should not even be permitted to take such a great name as that of Richard Wagner in its mouth, either in praise or in contradiction."[24] And even in the final twilight years in Weimar, as his sister reports, the name of Wagner could never be mentioned without Nietzsche adding: "I loved him very much."[25]

Nietzsche himself painfully glorified his life's tragic betrayal as an act of Judas, of Brutus, by clothing it in the mask of an aphorism: "In Praise of Shakespeare,"[26] which is found in *The Gay Science.* With his entire being, he thanks Shakespeare for having legitimated Brutus, whom Dante had consigned along with Judas to the jaws of Lucifer: the tragedy of Caesar's death is to him a kind of acquittal of both himself and his betrayal of Wagner:

> The most beautiful thing I could say in praise of Shakespeare the person is this: that he believed in Brutus and cast not a single grain of mistrust onto his type of virtue! He devoted his best tragedy to him—it is today still called by a false name—to him and to the most terrible incarnation of high morality. Independence of the soul—that is what matters here! No sacrifice can be too great: one must be able to sacrifice even one's dearest friend to it, even if he may also be the most magnificent person, the paragon of the world, an incomparable genius—that is what Shakespeare must have felt! The height to which he elevated Caesar is the finest honor he could have shown Brutus: only in that way did he raise Brutus's inner problem to the level of a monstrosity, together with the inner strength needed to cut through *this* knot! . . . Do we not perhaps stand before some dark event and adventure from the poet's own soul that has remained unknown and which he wanted to speak about only through symbols? What is all of Hamlet's melancholy compared to the melancholy of Brutus—and perhaps Shakespeare was familiar with that kind of melancholy, as he was familiar with the other one, from experience! Perhaps, like Brutus, he also had his dark hour and his evil angel![27]

But, as certainly as the Brutus-relationship to Wagner was the most profound, transforming, the most fateful event of his personal life, it is nevertheless only the reflection and allegorical image of Nietzsche's place and destiny within the intellectual, and more than intellectual, crisis of European culture, into which he, like Wagner, was born and which he desperately and heroically attempted to solve and redeem, just as Wagner, at least in his highest achievements, represents such an attempt, but by more impure, because more egotistical, means. The love of Wagner and the betrayal of Wagner are the parables of every love and every betrayal in Nietzsche's life; their trajectory is entirely the same as that of his love-betrayal of romanticism (Schumann, Schopenhauer, Hölderlin), of music, of morality, of Germanness, of the Lutheran heritage—of the Lutheran God. Zarathustra is the murderer of God (like his "ugliest man"), as Nietzsche is the traitor of Wagner. Just as he deliberately discovers and invents Bizet's *Carmen* as a "more evil" contrast to the artistic Wagnerian heavens of his youth, and just as the Frenchman's art can only help him to elucidate Wagner more extremely ("You should not take what I say about Bizet seriously; given the way I am, Bizet is unsuitable to me in a thousand different ways. But as an ironic antithesis to Wagner it has quite an effect"[28] [1888 to Fuchs]), so, too, he invents his anti-Christianity as a means and medium for making Zarathustra's new divinity visible.

In the Notebooks to *Zarathustra* there is a significant note: "I intentionally lived in precise opposition to a religious nature. I know the devil and his perspective regarding God."[29] (Precisely the same basic feeling is active here as, more narrowly, in his relationship to decadence: "To look for more healthy concepts and values from the vantage point of illness—that was my most lasting effort, my true experience, it was there, if anywhere, that I achieved mastery. . . ."[30] [*Ecce homo.*]) Intentional opposition to a religious nature (and thus undoubtedly to his own unintentional nature)—a light falls here on the importance of the cult that Nietzsche, characteristically enough just at the moment of his falling away from Wagner—namely while writing *Human, All Too Human*—entertains with the "mind," with the free spirit of every sort of enlightenment, with a new and more radical Voltaireanism. Here, the mind does not take on the meaning of a new and free devotion, it has nothing of the idea of Pascal or Goethe—who both come into closer proximity with the later Nietzsche—but, rather, it is a means of intentionally living out the exact opposite of a religious nature. Nietzsche's Voltaireanism serves as a perspective for God. And if, just at this epoch of his life when he was most obsessed with renunciation—and only then—he enthusiastically takes sides with knowledge against life (Nietzsche's beginning and end, however, stand under the sign of his pronouncement in the second *Untimely:* "Only insofar as science [and knowledge] serves life do we want to serve it"),[31] then his betrayal of the concept of life at this moment, at the moment of his betrayal of Wagner, of his own youth, of the deepest experience of his existence, is symbolic for his intention to know the devil and his perspective for God. For it is always the mind that dangerously tends toward the betrayal of life: "The mind is that life which itself cuts into life,"[32] Zarathustra says. And it is always the mind that feels called upon from afar to defend evil, to offer an apology for Satan—and is thus itself evil twice over. For the most wicked degree of evil, according to Swift, the true Judas-degree of evil and as such worthy of the depths of hell, is the *defense* of evil.[33] But it was such a defense, and precisely that, which Nietzsche felt was his proper task and mission. "We are the defenders of the devil's honor,"[34] he writes triumphantly in *The Will to Power,* and not only there. The integration, the incorporation of as many powers as possible that count as evil in Christian ethics into the organism that Nietzsche calls culture, the rehabilitation of the nourishing and rejuvenating forces of the subterranean currents of "evil" for the tree of life: that is the meaning of Nietzsche's initially skeptical, and in its roots and full blossoming passionate, immoralism. "Everything good is the transformation of some evil; every god has a devil as his father"[35]—this statement, from the paralipomena to *Zarathustra,* gives perhaps the most passionately one-sided voice to this fundamental sense. It is the strongest thesis of an *advocatus diaboli.*[36] Nietzsche's immoralism is expressed more justly, with a deeper feeling for the great balance of the world, in Zarathustra's parable of the tree on the mountain: "But it is with man as it is with the tree. The more he wants to go up into the heights, into the light, the stronger his roots tend toward the earth, down into the dark, the deep—into evil."[37] It is the superhuman element that seeks to drive its roots deeper into the subhuman sphere. It is the man who is most desirous of God who is most ardently drawn to the sources of evil, and it is perhaps God who most painfully seeks the black angel. Nietzsche himself attests to how closely these notions are tied to his character when he mentions his childish theological speculations in the preface to *On the Genealogy of Morals:* "Even as a thirteen-year-old boy I was preoccupied by the problem of the origin of evil: at an age when one has 'half childish games, half God in one's heart'[38] I devoted my first childish literary game to it, my first philosophical writing exercise—and as concerns my 'solution' to the problem at the time, well, as is only fitting, I gave God the honor and made him the father of evil. Did my a priori want that from me?"[39] (Similarly, in the preface materials from the years 1885 to 1888: "When I was twelve years old, I invented a peculiar trinity: namely, God-Father, God-Son, and God-Devil . . . with that I began to philosophize.")[40] There truly was an a priori secretly active here: we already have the late Nietzsche in that child's game—one of the strangely predictive elements in Nietzsche's development—who wants to subsume God and Satan into a higher unity beyond both, we have that Nietzsche for whom evil is of divine origin, indeed a highest characteristic of everything that he calls divine. Thirty years later, in a playfully malicious manner, but certainly not in an unserious one, *Ecce homo* again makes God the father of evil: "Speaking theologically—one should listen, since I rarely speak as a theologian" (perhaps not so rarely as Nietzsche here imagines)—"it was God himself who at the end of his day's work laid himself under the tree as a snake: thus he rested from being God. . . . He had made everything too beautiful. . . . The devil is merely God's idleness on every seventh day. . . ."[41]

Nietzsche's theology of evil leads him far into trains of thought, into modes of feeling, that we are accustomed to perceiving and identifying as Russian. Thus the Russian soul had generally shielded itself from the deep and passionate openness for all manner of evil that makes Asia's primal instinct so completely and categorically distinct from Europe's Socratic goal-oriented drive toward the "good": Russia's poets, those preachers of goodness, are at the same time the most profound connoisseurs and preachers of all human evil. In *The Antichrist,* Nietzsche says that the words "resist not evil" (Matthew 5:39) "were the deepest words of the Gospels, in a certain sense their key"[42]—an exegesis that sounds as if Tolstoy had formulated it, a saying that seems to pertain entirely to that Judas of legend whose particular form of piety was not to resist the greatest evil because only it made the Gospel possible. And a sentence from the Notebooks to *Transvaluation* also sounds as if it were written under the impression of Tolstoy: "The deepest misunderstanding of religion: that evil people have no religion."[43] He contemptuously calls the "odd and sick world of the Gospels," which he instinctively hated, "a world as if from a Russian novel"[44]—in the epilogue to *The Case of Wagner* he even states outright: "The Gospels present to us exactly the same psychological types that Dostoyevsky's novels portray."[45] Nevertheless, an uncommon sympathy draws him toward the sick and wild genius in which the humility and goodness of the Gospels combine so strangely with the power-hungry fanaticism of the church fathers; and his admiration for the *psychologist* Dostoyevsky, the "only one from whom I had something to learn,"[46] whose discovery he counts among the happiest finds of his life—even that admiration is the expression of a will not to resist evil: for Nietzsche's own "psychology" is also only a form of his surrender and devotion to evil.

The Nietzsche of *Human* already demands and defends an art of the evil, ugly soul: one draws far too narrow boundaries around art, he says, if one expects that only a well-ordered, virtuous, and balanced soul may express itself in it. "As in the visual arts, so too in music and poetry there is an art of the ugly soul, next to the art of the beautiful soul;[47] and the most powerful effects in art, the breaking of souls, the moving of stones, the anthropomorphizing of animals, is perhaps best accomplished by that former art."[48] If Orpheus is being demonized here (Nietzsche once called Richard Wagner the "Orpheus of all clandestine misery"),[49] then *Daybreak* makes the evil man the most grateful listener of music in the aphorism "The Evil Ones and Music": "Should the full bliss of love, which lies in unconditional trust, ever have been granted to people other than to those who are deeply suspicious, evil and bitter? For they derive from it the tremendous joy in a disbelieved and indeed unbelievable privilege of their soul . . . like a precious mystery and miracle full of golden brilliance and beyond all words and images. Unconditional trust renders one mute; indeed, there is even a suffering and gravity in this blissful muteness, which is why such souls also tend to be more grateful for music than all the other, better ones. . . ."[50]

It is Zarathustra who first turns the apology of evil entirely into a positive: "This alone I have learned thus far, that the most evil part of man is necessary for his best, that his most evil energies are his best power. . . ."[51] Indeed, "everyone who has mattered so far was evil"[52]—that is the sharpest, most Luciferian intensification of the point from the *Transvaluation* period. Nietzsche's historical-philosophical advocacy thus primarily applies to the great evildoers. He defends Loki and Cain in their historical masks. And his glorification of power? We recall the phrase that Jacob Burckhardt borrowed from Schlosser and turned into a kind of pessimistic leitmotif of Schopenhauerian musicality in his *Weltgeschichtliche Betrachtungen,* whose decisive impression on Nietzsche even in the most minute details becomes ever clearer to the reader who carefully compares both Basel humanists: "Power in itself is evil."[53] "The worldly regime comes from Cain,"[54] is how Luther expressed it. Nietzsche's original conception affirms it not because it is power, but because it is evil; and if, in the idea of his fragmentary major work he makes the will to power the burning heart of the world, then this is not only a reverse affirmation of Schopenhauer's metaphysics of the will; it is also a secret Yes to Schopenhauer's valuation of the will—as the primal evil. The synthesis of overman and savage shocked him in the phenomenon of Napoleon. Leonardo, who "saw too large a measure of good and terrible things,"[55] the powerful amoralism of the Hohenstaufen Emperor Frederick II, in the twilight of his Judas-aphorism about the three great deceivers; the Mephistophelian side of Goethe (gladly and consciously exorcized by the solely Faustian one)—these are the typical models he longed for again and again. And a favorite parable, his preferred example of living beyond good and evil[56] is the notion "Cesare Borgia as Pope" (in *The Antichrist*): "I see before me a possibility of a perfectly supernatural magic and charming color—it seems to me that it gleams in all the shudder of refined beauty, that in it there is an art at work, so divine, so devilishly divine, that one searches through centuries for another such possibility . . . Cesare Borgia as Pope . . . do you understand me?"[57] Do we understand him? Do we have an inkling of what originally underlies this blasphemous vision? For it is the image of the identity of the greatest evil and the highest purity, of the primal will and the primal idea (as in Schopenhauer's music), of eternal scornful laughter and of eternal hymns of praise—it is the image of Judas and of Christ in *one* incarnation. The sublime cynicism of this arch-romantic historical irony forms only the foreground to the spectacle that attracts him. Behind it is the will to see two worlds united, both of which he knows reside within him but are eternally separated—one betraying the other, one painfully blessing the other.

Zarathustra himself also clearly bears the traits of Lucifer and Loki in addition to those of a coming savior. One need think only of the Ass's Litany,[58] of the Luciferian cry: "If there were gods, how could I bear not being a god?"[59] Indeed, the entire style, the rhythm of Zarathustra, that Dionysian fiend, as Nietzsche characterizes him, displays the stigma of this romance with the devil. All of the garishness, the parodic, malicious derision, the self-conscious blasphemy that suddenly burst through the solemn rhythms of the Old Testament style, the softly tempered speeches in the manner of the Sermon on the Mount—all of these elements of Zarathustra's style, which is Nietzsche's style *once again,* are rooted in the pleasure of betrayal, but the betrayal of what one holds most dearly; the creative and parodic brilliance of this style, which forces together the most unheard-of things with those that have been heard forever into a unity of singular greatness and irresistible force (and in that truly represents a "third stage" beyond Luther and Goethe), it is the truest symbol of what its creator, in a moment of self-interpretation, defined as genius: "A person is in an inspired state when he finds himself to be simultaneously in a state of love and derision toward one and the same thing"[60] (Notebooks to *Human*). (The malicious elements of this style have entirely the same formal and psychological necessity as do the incomparably grotesque chimeras that grew out of the most ardent pleasure in evil that we find on the most passionately devout structures in the world—the cathedrals of northern France: their extreme demonic malevolence gives testimony to the pure, fervent power of longing out of which these works arose.) The object of this inspired love and derision, however, both in *Zarathustra* and throughout the rest of Nietzsche, is always one and the same: man himself, double-souled, wretched and divine man.

The fate of Judas is inseparable from Judas's betrayal. To be destroyed through oneself—that is the final seal on the traitor's hidden identity with Christ. We know the word with which Zarathustra tortures himself in his final solitude, with which, in both senses, he *betrays* himself and his seemingly bright, cheerful, generous divinity, the evil word of Judas: self-executioner.

> O Zarathustra
> Cruelest Nimrod![61]
> Only recently still the hunter of God,
> The trap of all virtues,
> The arrow of evil!
> Now—
> Hunted down by yourself,
> Your own prey . . .
> Strangled in your own snares,
> Self-Knower!
> Self-Executioner![62]

A presentiment of his self-sacrificial exit is always awake in Nietzsche: "One is never destroyed by anything other than by oneself";[63] "going to ruin presents itself as ruining oneself."[64] As a pupil at Pforta he had already admired nothing more than the voluntary end of Empedocles ("the entire work always moved me particularly deeply whenever I read it").[65] And *Ecce homo* delivers a maximum of self-condemnation amid grim self-deification: "I have a terrible fear that one day I will be canonized. . . . I don't want to be a saint, if anything a buffoon. . . . Perhaps I am a buffoon. . . ."[66] Even the last, pitiless rejection of European nihilism and of European decadence in the first book of *The Will to Power,* the damning characterization of the nihilist as the Last Man—that, too, is a form of self-condemnation: for who would have abandoned himself more completely to all of the ecstasies and dangers, all of the delights and the boundless pessimism of European nihilism in the second half of the century, than Nietzsche himself, the disciple of Schopenhauer and Wagner, the burdened heir of romanticism, he who calls himself a decadent and was only too conscious of his "existence that for a hundred reasons was eternally problematic"?[67] Decadence, nihilism were for him truly diabolical, the essence of evil; but he fought against those forces, he overcame them by surrendering himself to them, by suffering from them more deeply than anyone else—and finally by condemning himself *for* having surrendered to them. The victory over European decadence-nihilism occurred in an exemplary way *in* him, just as it occurred *through* him. "Resist not evil"—if, as Nietzsche says, these are the deepest words of the Gospels, then Nietzsche's intellectual fate, as he prepared it for himself, is just as deeply evangelical as was Judas's betrayal in the legend: in the midst of an entirely hopeless, entirely skeptical, entirely godless late humanity, it made a new Dionysian Gospel, the new and ancient Gospel of *man,* possible again. That is the meaning of the words in *Ecce homo* in which he calls himself the man of doom, the destroyer par excellence, by far the most terrible man who had ever existed—and at the same time the evangelist, a bringer of glad tidings such as there had never been before. What was the horrible triumphal name that he gave himself and his last book even as he had begun his descent? It was the name whose first incarnation Judas had been, the name of the great counter-savior, of the prophesied last counter-deity—the name of the Antichrist.

Thus Nietzsche's *exitus* shimmers in a strange double light: half Judas-like self-execution, half proud Promethean self-sacrifice; both connected by the consciousness of an immense necessity that unites both with a decisive turn in human destiny, with the coming of some new covenant and new fire; and in such a way that he himself is not the bringer of the new salvation, but so that without *his* sacrilege, without his murder of God, the iron gates to the New World would remain forever barred. It is a Luciferian end, not in despondent remorse like that of the Judas of scripture, but rather in the sublime remorselessness of someone who sees and affirms himself as the darker victim of a new salvation: "The best and highest things humanity can obtain are acquired through sacrilege. . . ."[68] (*The Birth of Tragedy*). We admire in the legend of Nietzsche's life the symbol of faith in the form of an ultimate betrayal of that faith, a salvation of the divine through a murder of God. His grandly Promethean hostility toward Jehovah is his praise of God; his murder of the old God—which was, by the way, purely philosophically speaking, much more Kant's deed than Nietzsche's—is the preparation and prediction of a new divinity that in the vision of Zarathustra casts the first shadow on the path in the desert. (Perhaps Nietzsche felt that the words of Rénan, which he knew, were directed at him, pointing toward Zarathustra: "Les dieux sont une injure à Dieu. Dieu sera un jour une injure au divin."[69] We honor his voluntary and conscious Cain-ship, which is able to sacrifice what is most fraternally dear to him and to wear the mark as a stain and crown simultaneously. Confronted by images such as his, we recall, with Hebbel, that the best thing about religion is that it brings forth heretics, and we remember that the power of eternal resurrection does not reside in the reigning God shrouded in incense, but rather in the repudiated and dismembered one, only in the dead God—when the old God dissipates the new one awakens—and that whoever kills God thereby preserves him for humanity.

8
Mask

After all, we do not always speak to ourselves the way we think, and it is our duty to say to others only what they can absorb.[1]
—Goethe

A noble appearance has a significant effect.[2]
—Goethe

"The problem of the actor has troubled me for the longest time,"[3] Nietzsche admits in *The Gay Science.* Despite this confession, which obviously touches on a fundamental psychological trait in Nietzsche, the problem of the actor does not initially seem to be one that necessarily emanated out of his primary constitution. It was *not* at first an eminently "autobiographical" problem for him. With respect to his entire nature, Nietzsche was unactorly and untheatrical to the core, even if one may observe traits of a certain intellectual coquetry throughout all his phases, and particularly in his late period. A friend from his youth, Deussen, confirms: "Nietzsche was by nature a deeply serious person, everything having to do with acting in both the pejorative and positive sense was completely foreign to him."[4] Nietzsche is scarcely posing when, a few pages after the confession he offered above, he says: "My melancholy wants to find repose in . . . *perfection:* for that I need music. What do I care about drama! The cramps of its moral ecstasies . . . the whole gestural hocus-pocus of the actor! You can tell that I am essentially anti-theatrically inclined—Wagner, however, was on the contrary essentially a man of the theater and an actor, the most enthusiastic lover of mime who ever existed, even as a musician!"[5] There is an anti-theatrical pride in a statement he makes in an isolated passage in the late Notebooks: "To be truthful is a distinction";[6] or in an etymological derivation from the time of *Daybreak:* "The noble ones, ἐσθλοί,[7] the truthful ones who *do not need to dissemble!* As individuals and the powerful!"[8] But "not to need" to do something always means at the same time "not to be able" to do it as well: Nietzsche's powerful individuality could have allowed itself to say what Napoleon admitted to himself: "I cannot disguise myself—I am recognized behind every mask."[9] Certainly, as an essentially Protestant nature, Nietzsche was at heart essentially untheatrical (the young Nietzsche's naïve enjoyment of opera is not proof to the contrary): how unaffected his rigidly egocentric letters are in spite of all of their touchingly transparent pet gestures, especially where the letters *would like* to transform themselves into something else for the sake of their addressee! Or compare all of his almost defenselessly autobiographical writings *εἰζ ἑαυτόν*[10] with Wagner's typical actor's memoirs that display such a naïvely sophisticated pleasure in dissimulation and such skill in the stage-managing of his self that it almost seems instinctive! Only after experiencing "Wagner" did the wave of this question, this problem of the actor, wash up to the hem of his inner existence. Only after being enchanted by Wagner's art and powerful personality did the mystery of the "mask" appear to be one that mattered to him. Only in Wagner, *as* Wagner, did the problem of transformation trouble him, a problem that would truly trouble him "for the longest time," into the sleep of his mind.

The Birth of Tragedy (together with the fragments of the Notebooks that surround it) is the first magnificent testament to that trouble; an almost poetic attempt to make sense of the mystery of how the phenomenon of acting arose. What forces create the Transformed Man?—this question forms the core of the book. Dionysus is a name for the transformative power that forces people to become masks, masks of a superpersonal, "divine" being. But at the same time, this work also reveals that the problem of transformation and of the enchantment of masks is still being seen and interpreted by an observer, not by someone who has himself been transformed; it is being experienced theoretically, *not* Dionysically. It is *poetic* philology, without a doubt, but still philology, or rather it is a philological-historical method that wants to go beyond itself. "How unfortunate that I did not dare to say what I had to say then as a poet: I might have been able to do it!"[11] Nietzsche lamented in his own preface to *The Birth* in 1886. That is the lament of someone who is disenchanted, who is ashamed at having spoken about matters of enchantment *other* than in the state of enchantment. Spoken—not sung, as it would have been appropriate to the "transformed man": "It should have *sung*, this new soul—and not spoken!"[12] thus the self-reproach from the same preface. Nietzsche later perceived with agonizing certainty the inner dichotomy of this book, which basically talks about the longing for enchantment by seeming to speak from out of enchantment itself.

"Enchantment is the prerequisite of all dramatic art"[13]—that is the central sentence of the book. But hear how completely it is the analyst, *not* the actor, not the dramatist, not the self-enchanter who speaks of this phenomenon: "we speak so abstractly about poetry because we all tend to be bad poets. The aesthetic phenomenon is basically simple; if one has the ability to see continuously a living play and to live constantly surrounded by hordes of spirits, then one is a poet; if one has the urge to transform oneself and to speak out of other bodies and souls, then one is a dramatist."[14]

> The Dionysian state of excitement is capable of communicating to an entire crowd this artistic gift of seeing oneself surrounded by such a horde of spirits with which it knows itself to be inwardly unified. This process of the tragic chorus is the originary *dramatic* phenomenon: to see oneself transformed before one's own eyes and now to act as if one had actually entered into another body, into another character. . . . And indeed this phenomenon appears epidemically: an entire throng feels enchanted in this way. . . . The dithyrambic chorus is a chorus of *transformed* people whose entire civic past and social status have been completely forgotten: they have become timeless servants of their God, living outside the spheres of society. All other choral lyric poetry of the Hellenes is merely a tremendous intensification of the individual Apollonian singer; whereas in the dithyramb a community of unconscious actors stands before us, who regard themselves as transformed.[15]

Nietzsche's conception of this epidemic of transformation, of the ecstatic enchantment of the oldest choral society into the first community of unconscious actors, becomes clearer in a preparatory study for *The Birth,* an essay on the Greek musical drama from 1869/70. Here the Dionysian intoxication is directly described as the womb of drama, the portrayal of the enchanted state reveals even more noticeably the influence of Schopenhauerian aesthetics:

> The soul of the Athenian who came to watch tragedies during the Dionysia[16] still had in it something of that element out of which tragedy is born. It is the overpowering instinct of spring bursting forth, a storming and raging of mixed emotions . . . the omnipotent effect of spring, which announces itself so suddenly, intensifies the vital forces here to such an immoderate degree that ecstatic states, visions and the belief in one's own *enchantment* emerge everywhere, and similarly attuned beings travel through the countryside in droves. And here is the cradle of drama. For it does not begin with someone disguising himself and wanting to create an illusion in others: no, it begins, rather, with people who are beside themselves and believe that they *have been transformed and entranced.* In this state of "being-beside-oneself," of ecstasy, there is only one more step that is necessary: we do not return back into ourselves, but rather go into another being, so that we behave as "entranced" people. That is where the deep astonishment in viewing drama basically comes from: the ground—that is, the belief in the indissolubility and solidity of the individual—is shaken.[17]

That is Schopenhauerian terminology applied to Wagner's theories, but it is not actually a confession; and this reexperiencing of Schopenhauer in the contemplation of Wagner becomes completely evident in another passage in the *parerga* for *The Birth of Tragedy:*

> Piousness, the most marvelous mask of the life instinct! Devotion to a perfect *dream world,* which is granted the highest moral wisdom! Flight from the truth in order to worship it from afar, wrapped in clouds! Reconciliation with reality *because* it is mysterious! Aversion to unraveling the mystery because we are not gods! . . . Glorification and transfiguration of the terrors and horrors of existence as the means of salvation *from* existence! . . . The triumph of the will in its negation! . . . The terrible or the absurd is uplifting because it is only *apparently* terrible or absurd. The Dionysian power of *enchantment* proves its potency here again at the very height of this world view: everything real dissolves into appearance and behind it the unified *nature of the will* reveals itself, wrapped up in the glory of wisdom and truth shining in blinding brilliance. *Illusion, delusion has reached its summit.*[18] ("The Dionysian World View," 1870)

One cannot simplify and, as it were, Schopenhauerize the difficult, multifarious problem of the theater and of the mime more enchantingly than is done here. The illusion of the Wagner-entranced Nietzsche is at its summit. But the same essay also contains the first step toward separating the narrower problem of the actor from that of Dionysian enchantment. The play with intoxication instead of intoxication itself, the actor in place of the ecstatic celebrant, the egotistical, mask-loving individual in place of the one lost in God—that indicates the origin of the actual model of the actor. A middle world arises, in exceedingly Nietzschean fashion, between God and the individual, between Dionysus and Socrates: "This *middle world* between beauty and truth reveals itself in a state of play with intoxication, not in a state of complete possession by it. We recognize in the actor the Dionysian man, the instinctive poet, singer, dancer, but as someone *playing* Dionysian man. He tries to match his model by moving the passions through sublimity or moving them through laughter: he goes above and beyond beauty and never even seeks the truth. He remains hovering between the two."[19] And Nietzsche's estimation of the actor as such, of the person only playing the role of Dionysian man, already reveals itself in unmistakable terms of contempt: "Even in the mouth of an actor who is supremely convinced of his role, a profound thought, a simile, in fact basically every word sounds to us as if it were weakened, atrophied, profaned; we don't believe in this language, we don't believe in these people, and what would otherwise touch us as the deepest revelation of the world now seems to us to be a disgusting masquerade. . . . One senses something like a desecration" (*Music and Tragedy,* 1871).[20] (Which remains his instinctive objection to *Parsifal* seven years later as expressed in a letter to a friend: "Much of what is bearable for the inner eye will hardly be endurable in performance: just imagine our actors praying, trembling and in ecstasies.")[21] The negative estimation of the actor—of the professional actor cut off from all religious roots and sunk in egoism and self-satisfaction—is thus not at all the result of his turn away from Wagner; it is, as we see, already fully formed during Nietzsche's most Wagnerian period. A passage from a letter to Deussen (February 1870) demonstrates only the practical counterpoint, so to speak, to this thematic pattern: "It is sad, but characteristic of the unspeakably feeble quality of German sociability, that you enjoy the company of actors. It was the same with me as well. The aura of art also envelops even its most unworthy servants. In addition, we idealize this segment of society: and sometimes the little daemon speaks up whom Sophocles so delightedly thought he had escaped. . . . At the moment I find this breed abhorrent."[22]

What kind of process necessarily had to occur in Nietzsche's relationship to Wagner's personality and work for his recognition of the magnificently theatrical soul of this man and his work to break through the gratitude of blind love? What happened was precisely what Nietzsche's theoretical estimation of the actor had already, as it were, prophetically predicted: the arc is repeated from the Dionysically enchanted celebrant to the actor *whom one does not believe:* Dionysus and the Dionysically transformed person, as a mask of the god, becomes an actor; the Dionysian magician of music becomes a wily Pied Piper, the powerful leader of a dance of souls becomes an ambitious seducer; the wise master: a clever maestro; God—a director. That was the experience Nietzsche never got over. We are familiar with the tragic stages of this rapidly occurring process. In the works published during Nietzsche's lifetime we encounter the first allusion to Wagner's theatrical nature in the wrenchingly panegyric poem "Richard Wagner in Bayreuth," an offering of a disciple who is already disenchanted, already slipping away, a mind already sliding toward apostasy but offering one final display of ardent gratitude in the last hour of departure. "If one has attempted," reads the highly significant passage in the fourth *Untimely,* "to derive the most magnificent developments from inner inhibitions or deficiencies, arguing for example that for Goethe writing poetry was a kind of outlet for a failed career as a painter, or that one can speak of Schiller's plays as if they were the transposed eloquence of the people . . . if one wanted to draw a line in similar fashion between Wagner's development and such an inner inhibition, then one would probably be permitted to assume that his fundamental talent is that of an actor, which refused to be satisfied by the most immediate, trivial means and found its outlet and salvation by drawing on all the arts to form a great theatrical revelation."[23] The fact of Wagner's fundamental talent being that of an actor is still delivered here in an emotionally neutral tone. That Nietzsche had in reality already inwardly moved on to decided negation, to aversion, is now proved by the notes left in the Notebooks. In the earliest *critical* comments on the Wagner problem we have from

Nietzsche, in notes from as early as January 1874, more than two years before the decisive disappointment of Bayreuth, namely the "Thoughts on Richard Wagner," the problem of the actor, of the theater, already occupies a strangely central place, and in an entirely skeptical vein. One clearly notices how Wagner's uprooting within Nietzsche begins with a consideration of the theatrical in Wagner and in his art. "Wagner attempts tyranny by using the theatrical masses. There is little doubt that Wagner would have achieved his goal if he were an Italian. Germans have no respect for opera and always view it as an import and as un-German. Indeed, they don't take theater as a whole seriously.[24] . . . There is something comical about it all: Wagner cannot persuade the Germans to take the theater seriously.[25] . . . Someone who claps applause in a theater today is ashamed about it tomorrow: for we have our domestic altar, Beethoven, Bach—memory blanches before them.[26] . . . One of Wagner's qualities: lack of restraint, immoderation . . . the other quality is a great theatrical talent that is displaced, which is pioneering in many ways except for the most logical one: for that he lacks the form, voice and requisite moderation.[27] . . . Wagner is a born actor, but, like Goethe, a painter without a painter's hands, as it were. His talent seeks and finds alternatives. Now imagine these frustrated drives working together.[28] . . . Wagner's stance toward music is that of an actor: for that reason he can, as it were, speak out of various musicians' souls and place completely different worlds (*Tristan, Meistersinger*) next to each other.[29] . . . As an actor he wanted to imitate human beings only in their most effective and most real guise: in the throes of the most intense emotion.[30] . . . Wagner wanted to reproduce for others what had a strong effect on himself. He understood from his models only what he could imitate. The soul of an actor. . . ."[31] In Nietzsche's eyes, Wagner's actorly soul is ostentatiously and disastrously expressed not only through his work; it is not only toward music that he stands as an actor. That Wagner remained a brilliant actor as well and above all to himself, which his meticulous and cleverly veiled old-masterly style, even in his letters, reveals him to be—that is what Nietzsche could least forgive him. As early as "Richard Wagner in Bayreuth," the notion of comedy is raised for Wagner's life: "Wagner's life, seen from up close and without affection, has . . . a great deal of comedy about it, and indeed of a remarkably grotesque variety."[32] That is still expressed without the suspicion that Wagner himself may be the master comedian of this remarkably grotesque comedy. But the all-too-close view of the Festspiele of 1876 causes the already thin partitioning wall to finally collapse: "I am incapable of acknowledging in someone any greatness that is not combined with *sincerity toward oneself,*" reads the Notebooks to *Daybreak;* "playacting before oneself fills me with disgust: if I discover that in someone, then all accomplishments count for nothing to me."[33]

Genealogy takes up the same theme: "We have been promised an autobiography of Wagner: who doubts that it will be a *prudent* autobiography?"[34] And *The Case of Wagner* ruthlessly sums up: "What has been circulating up to now as 'Wagner's Life' is a *fable convenue*,[35] if not something worse. I admit I distrust every point that is documented only by Wagner himself. He did not have enough pride for any truth about himself . . . just like Victor Hugo, he remained true to himself even in relation to his biography—he remained an actor."[36] (One has to remember here that Nietzsche, as one of the small number of Wagner's closest intimates, had firsthand knowledge of his memoirs, which appeared as *My Life* in 1911: Nietzsche had corrected the proofs for an earlier private printing in Basel. The comedic aftertaste of this book must have been very strong for Nietzsche: the passages he wrote more than a decade later about Wagner's *vita* certainly suggest that.) Indeed, one may doubt whether it was Wagner's music or his personality that *first* revealed to Nietzsche the magnificent, primary element of the actor in his being. Sometimes it appears that it was not the master who followed the mantle of his music, but rather that the music trailed after its duke. What is certain is that the life-threatening crisis of 1876 was brought on solely by the revelation, which was long in coming but sudden nonetheless, of the fundamentally theatrical nature of Wagner's person and his music—this music that was more conscious of its effect, enjoyed, indeed was obsessed with, its effect more than any other. The distortion of the beloved image of a Dionysian nature into that of a comedian, of a primal Orphic music for the Dionysically transformed man into a massive romantic magic opera for the bourgeois of the new German empire became an almost deadly self-revelation for Nietzsche: *thus* he had let himself be deceived, or rather had deceived himself, in the most essential, the most substantial part of his being! If *this* experience had been the effect of an actor, a theatrical deception, what was henceforth real, what was *his* reality? We have an example of smaller proportions of the poisonous, life-threatening effect this lifting of Nietzsche's self-deception had on him in the encounter with Lou Andreas-Salomé in the years 1882 and 1883. "Who could have suspected that her words 'heroism,' 'struggling for a principle,' her poem 'To Pain,' her tales about struggling for knowledge were simply a fraud?"[37] (To Rée about Lou.) "A poem such as 'To Pain' is, in your mouth, a deep untruth"[38] (to Lou). What made *this* disappointment so terrible for Nietzsche that it avowedly brought him to the brink of madness and suicide was the recognition that here *his* "typical experience, which is repeated again and again"[39] had touched him: namely, to fall victim to the actor at precisely the place where he looked for and thought he beheld the most living person, to see through the mask where he yearned to believe in a face. "To look for love—and always be forced to find and destroy masks, accursed masks!"[40] is the constantly repeated lament of this soul preordained to disappointment ("Speeches, Allegories and Images," 1882–88). Everything that Nietzsche had ever theoretically expressed as an insight into the necessity of illusion and lie, into the life-preserving function of delusion, into the deadly effect of clear-sightedness, arises out of the pain caused by the experience of seeing Dionysus reduced to an actor's mask, of having venerated the great actor as a god. With the shudder experienced by the "nihilist" on discovering the "falsehood" of the "true world," *The Will to Power* still draws the final epistemological, practical conclusion from *this* shock: "whether the lie is something divine? whether the value of all things does not rest on their being false? whether one should not believe in God not because he is not true, but because he is false?— . . . whether it is not precisely lying and distorting, adding meaning that is itself a value, a meaning, a purpose?"[41] *Beyond* adds: "Why couldn't the world that matters to us—be a fiction?"[42] And everything Nietzsche adduces and discloses regarding his extreme distrust toward the categories of the artist, the prophet, the faithful—categories that describe himself—everything has its origin in the poisoning experience of the actor, which Nietzsche never got over, never overcame, from which he never recovered. "Pardon? A great man? I never see any more than the actor of his own ideal"[43] (*Beyond*)—that now became the instinctive mistrust of this mind that yearned to venerate, for whom veneration was the mark of humanity ("Man is the *venerating* animal").[44] "In my youth I was unfortunate," reads a passage in the late Notebooks; "a very shady person crossed my path. When I recognized him for what he was, namely as a big actor who had no true relationship to anything (not even to music), I was so disgusted and ill that I believed that all famous people had been actors, otherwise they would not have become famous—and that the main thing in what I called an 'artist' was *actorly* energy."[45] That refers to the passage in *Beyond* that Nietzsche also incorporated into *Nietzsche contra Wagner:* "The 'work,' that of the artist, of the philosopher, is what invents Him who created it, who is supposed to have created it; the 'great men,' as they are venerated, are minor, poor fabrications after the fact. . . . Those great poets, for instance, such as Byron, Musset, Poe, Leopardi, Kleist, Gogol—I don't dare name even greater names, but I am thinking of them—[46] . . . what a torture these great artists and in general higher human beings are for the person who at one point figured them out!"[47] One hears the lingering rancor of this most incurable disappointment, the bitterness of someone whose venerating power has been paralyzed and poisoned, in all of the Wagner passages in *The Case* and in the later Notebooks: it is none other than the notion of the actor that is uttered with the accents of an unquenchable hatred with which a creature would pursue only what is completely inimical to itself, what it perceives as truly life-threatening: "You don't know who Wagner is: a very great actor! . . . Wagner the actor is a tyrant, his pathos undermines all taste, all resistance. . . . Was Wagner even a musician? In any event he was something else *more:* namely an incomparable histrio,[48] the greatest mime, the most astonishing theatrical genius the Germans have ever had. . . . He belongs somewhere else than in the history of music: one should not confuse him with its great genuine figures. Wagner *and* Beethoven—that is blasphemy. . . . Even as a musician Wagner was merely what he was in general: he *became* a musician, he *became* a poet because the tyrant in him, his theatrical genius, forced him to. One understands nothing about Wagner as long as one does not understand his dominant instinct. . . . Wagner wants to create an effect, he wants nothing other than to create an effect. Therein he has the unscrupulousness that every theater person has. . . . Even in his plot designs Wagner is above all an actor.[49] . . . Wagner signifies . . . the rise of the actor in music . . . never before had the integrity of musicians, their 'genuineness,' been so dangerously tested. . . ."[50] In the postscript to *The Case* the sentence: "Discipleship to Wagner comes at a high price,"[51] is repeated five times; and the three concluding demands that Nietzsche says "opened his mouth" are "that the theater does not become master of the arts. That the actor does not become the seducer of those who are genuine. That music does not become an art of lying."[52] Even more unsparingly than in *The Case of Wagner,* where a malevolently jocular tone of strained lightness and forced gaiety is maintained, the whole business of acting is indicted in the Notebooks notes: here the actor is a Cagliostro,[53] a brilliant charlatan lacking any intellectual character, an old, experienced Pied Piper, an unscrupulous demagogue and people's tribune in matters of art and not only of art. "A democratic age pushes the actor to the top—in Athens and today as well. Richard Wagner has surpassed everything in that regard and awakened such an elevated notion of the actor that it can cause one to shudder. Music, poetry, religion, culture, book, family, fatherland, commerce—everything above all *art,* that is to say stage pose!"[54] "Wagner was a great actor: but without a core and inwardly prey to anything that has a strong intoxicating effect."[55] And in an analysis completely lacking in mercy, full of the most extreme lust for vengeance: "Wagner, under the spell of an unbelievably pathological sexuality, knew all too well *what* an artist thereby forfeits, that he loses his own freedom, his *respect* for himself. He is condemned to be an actor. Even his art becomes a never-ending attempt to flee, a means of forgetting himself, a self-anesthesia—it changes, in the end it determines the nature of his art. . . . Someone who is so 'unfree' requires a hashish world . . . he needs Wagnerian music . . . a certain catholicity of the ideal above all is virtually proof of self-contempt, of a 'morass,' in an artist."[56] This *last* Wagner, the Wager of *Par-*

sifal—"basically a broken and overcome man, who nevertheless could not leave off the grand play-acting"[57]—is called to account by Nietzsche in poetic form in *Zarathustra,* in the scene and figure of the Magician, who with his art and "touching gesture"[58] wants to worm his way into Zarathustra's affections and to whom Zarathustra calls out: "Stop, you actor! You counterfeiter! You bottomless liar! I know you well! . . . You peacock of peacocks, you ocean of vanity, what are you performing before me, you miserable magician, in whom should I believe? . . ."[59] "The penitent of the spirit," the old man says, "it was *him* I played. . . . And go ahead and admit it: it took a long time . . . before you caught on to my art and lie! You *believed* in my suffering. . . . I heard you wail 'they loved him too little, loved him too little!' My own malevolence inwardly rejoiced over deceiving you so successfully."[60] "You may have deceived more subtle ones than me," Zarathustra says severely. "I am not on guard against deceivers, I *must* be without caution, thus my fate wills it. But you—*must* deceive: that well do I know you! . . . I have figured you out: You became an enchanter of everyone, but you have no lie or trick left over for yourself—you are disenchanted to yourself! You have harvested disgust as your One Truth. Not one word about you is genuine anymore, except your mouth: namely the disgust that sticks to your mouth."[61] "Who are you, then!" the old magician cried out at this point . . . "who may speak thus to *me,* the greatest man alive today?"—and a green lightning bolt shot out of his eyes toward Zarathustra. But immediately thereafter he transformed himself and said sadly: "O Zarathustra, I am tired of it all, I am disgusted by my arts, I am not *great,* why do I pretend! However, as you well know—I sought greatness! I wanted to portray a great man and convinced many: but this lie exceeded my powers. I foundered on it. O Zarathustra, everything about me is a lie; but that I founder—my foundering is genuine!"[62] This passage, and even more Zarathustra's response, both reveal how Nietzsche would have wished Wagner's end to be, an atonement of Wagner the actor: "You miserable magician, *that* is the best and most honest thing I respect about you, namely that you grew tired of yourself and announced it: 'I am not great' . . . and even if it was only for the briefest, fleeting time, in that One Moment you were—genuine."[63] But Nietzsche was not to experience this genuine moment of his magician, and thus the most bitter utterance that Nietzsche ever dared make about life was secretly directed at his own most difficult experience, the enormously fateful encounter with the old magician—that declaration in the preface to *Zarathustra:* "Human existence is uncanny and still has no meaning: a clown can be one's undoing."[64]

A clown—that would be the final transformation of the Dionysian sorcerer that the enraptured disciple of Tribschen saw in Wagner. A charlatan—that was the tragic, in every sense of the word, life-threatening final judgment of a disappointed lover about the phantom of his former affection. A charlatan who wants to have an effect because he cannot *be,* a clown who hides his actual, suffering self while prancing and parading the one he hopelessly yearns for—that is the Wagner of *The Case.* It seems to be the end of the problem of the mask for Nietzsche, which after all troubled him first and for the longest time in Wagner, as Wagner. But everything that Nietzsche pursues and unmasks with thankless, self-tormenting psychology exacts a spectral vengeance: driven into a corner, it turns half beseechingly, half threateningly toward him and shows him its face—his own face. Even Zarathustra's Magician conceals just as many secret traits and self-recriminations of Nietzsche as he bears features of Wagner. For it is not for nothing that Zarathustra knows: "The worst enemy you can meet will always be you yourself; you lie in wait for yourself in caves and forests."[65] And the mask of the Magician also looks back at him with the glance of his own self. In *The Case of Wagner* he writes: "One is an actor by having one insight that the rest of the people do not have: what is supposed to seem real cannot be real. The sentence is a formulation of Talma's:[66] it contains the entire psychology of acting, but it also contains its ethics. Wagner's music is never true.—But people think that it is: and that is how it should be."[67] This doctrine and guiding principle of a great actor, from whom Napoleon learned how to walk like an emperor, contains not only the entire psychology and ethics of an actor: it is the guiding principle of Nietzsche's own practice of the knowing teacher, all of his applied and communicable knowledge; it is the fundamental tenet of his Socratic epistemology, which always wanted, and was intended, to be a valuation of experience at the same time: "What is supposed to seem real cannot be real"—this statement, the recognition of its validity for Nietzsche himself became Wagner's revenge. The disciple was permitted to surrender himself as he was, which is the charming prerogative of youth. The man who has become a master himself recognizes that the mask is appropriate to the master, indeed even to the wisdom and the art of the master, for the mask is the sad prerogative of old age. For the aged no longer live for their own sake but rather must live and want to live in many others. For it is the mask alone that seems to be real. It is only behind the mask, only as illusory image that all life seduces to life. This recognition was already slumbering in the Dionysian hope and faith of the disciple who wrote *The Birth;* sketches from the Notebooks for this book already articulated it: "*Cultivation* is a continuous exchange of hallucinations toward more refined ones.[68] . . . What is education? That one immediately grasps everything one experiences according to certain hallucinations. The *value* of these notions determines the value of the cultivation and education in question. . . . These hallucinations are communicated only through the *force* of the respective *personality.* . . . A magical influence by one *person* on *another.* Every *new creation of a culture* thus occurs through strong, exemplary natures in which hallucinations generate themselves anew."[69] But only for the mind that has become independent, for someone thirsting in the wasteland of disappointment for a mirage on the horizon, does mere recognition become lived experience: the mask is unavoidable, it is necessary.

During the time of *Human, All Too Human,* this consciousness of the *necessity* of the mask is initially expressed with unvarnished bluntness, not without a certain bitterness and still partially in Schopenhauerian terminology: "Mediocrity is the most fortunate mask that the superior mind can wear because it doesn't cause the vast majority, that is, the mediocre, to think of disguises—and yet he puts it on precisely for their sake—so as not to upset *them,* indeed not infrequently out of compassion and kindness."[70]—"Deep-thinking people feel they are actors in their relations with others because, in order to be understood, they always first have to feign superficiality."[71]—"One must either hide one's opinions or hide oneself behind one's opinions. Whoever does otherwise either is ignorant of the ways of the world or belongs to the Order of Holy Foolishness."[72] In these statements the negative aspect, the precautionary note, the mimicry of the mask still predominate; they are still "aphorisms on worldly wisdom." But the notion of the necessary mask also finds itself raised up into the positive realm, elevated for the first time into the consciously pedagogical sphere in another aphorism from *Human, All Too Human:* "*The active man is a phantom, not a reality.*—A person of significance gradually learns that, insofar as he is active, he is a phantom in the minds of others, and he perhaps finds himself confronted by the subtle inner torture of asking himself whether he ought not to maintain that phantom for the good of his fellow beings."[73] That is the actor who has learned through experience that what is supposed to seem real cannot be real. But "when a person begins to discover to what extent he is playing a role and to what extent he *can* be an actor, he *becomes* an actor,"[74] according to *The Gay Science.* The deeper the nature in question, the more inevitably a protective mask will grow around it. "Our doubts about the communicability of the heart are profound," read comments in *The Will to Power;* " . . . always disguised: the higher a man's nature, the more he requires an incognito.[75] . . . To makes oneself understood by the masses is impossible. *Every* action is misunderstood. And, in order not to be perpetually thwarted, one must have a mask. Also in order to seduce."[76] And with more finality in *Beyond:* "Everything deep loves the mask . . . should not the *opposite* be the true disguise in which the modesty of a god could stroll about? . . . Such a dissembler, who instinctively uses speech to be silent and to conceal and is inexhaustible in evading communication, *wants* and demands that a mask of himself walks around in the hearts and minds of his friends in his place; and provided that he does not want it, then one day his eyes will be opened to the fact that a mask of him is there anyway—that that is how it should be. Every deep mind needs a mask: even more, a mask is continually growing around every deep mind, thanks to the constantly false, namely *shallow* interpretation of every word, every step, every sign of life he makes."[77]

But a deep mind is always a suffering one as well—"it almost determines a person's rank in the hierarchy how deeply he can suffer"[78]—and thus the mask of the active person always becomes the mask of someone who suffers, who has to hide his suffering from everyone since he wants to seduce them to live—and we believe only those who are happy, who seem to be happy. " . . . The silent intellectual haughtiness of those who suffer, this pride of those chosen for knowledge, of the 'initiates,' the nearly sacrificial victims, finds every form of disguise necessary to protect themselves against being touched by intrusive and sympathetic hands and in general against everything that is not their equal in pain. Deep suffering ennobles; it creates distance. One of the most subtle forms of disguise is Epicureanism and a certain . . . demonstrative boldness of taste . . . there are cheerful people who employ cheerfulness because they are misunderstood on account of it. . . . There are 'scientific people' who employ science . . . because a scientific character suggests that a person is superficial. . . . There are free, audacious spirits who would like to conceal and deny that they are broken, proud, incurable romantics . . . and occasionally foolishness itself is a mask for abject, all-too-certain knowledge.—Which shows that it belongs to finer humanity to have respect 'for masks' and not to indulge in psychologizing and curiosity in the wrong place"[79] (*Beyond*).

Respect for masks—with this demand the role of smashing accursed masks comes to an end. Respect for masks is a demand that he wants to make applicable to himself above all. "There are people who do not want to be seen in any other way than as shimmering through others. And there is much wisdom in that"[80] (*Daybreak*). With that, Nietzsche reveals the wise maxim, the peculiar technique of disguise, which turns his descriptions of other souls and minds into strangely cryptic portraits of himself. Nietzsche speaks most clearly, most openly about himself precisely at those points where he seems to be speaking least about himself. "Not to speak of oneself at all is a very refined form of hypocrisy,"[81] *Human* says. Nietzsche is especially fond of succumbing to this refined form of hypocrisy by letting himself speak through the masks of others. In *Ecce homo* "where he leaves nothing to doubt," he "had also in that respect the courage to go to the extreme,"[82] in that he revealed, admitted to himself this, his most often used technique—for this lover of masks also wore one final protective mask before himself. "In all of the psychologically decisive passages of 'Richard Wagner in

Bayreuth,' I am speaking only of myself—one may freely place my name or the word 'Zarathustra' wherever the word Wagner appears in the text. The whole portrait of the dithyrambic artist is the portrait of the preexistent poet of *Zarathustra,* drawn with unfathomable depth and without even touching Wagnerian reality for an instant. Wagner himself had an inkling of that; he did not recognize himself in this work. . . . That is the strangest kind of 'objectivity' it can offer: the absolute certainty about what I *am* was projected on some arbitrary reality—the truth about me was uttered out of terrifying depths."[83] "Speaking broadly," he writes in another passage of *Ecce homo* about the last two *Untimely* essays, "I seized two famous and still entirely diffuse types, in the same way one seizes an opportunity, in order to express something, in order to have a few more phrases, signs, linguistic means at my disposal. . . . In the same way Plato made use of Socrates as a semiotics for Plato . . . I do not wish to deny now that these works basically speak only about me. The book *Richard Wagner in Bayreuth* is a vision of my future; by comparison, my innermost history, my *becoming*—above all my *solemn vow!*—are written into *Schopenhauer as Educator.*"[84]

It was for just such a "semiotics for Plato" that Nietzsche, with his Socratic love of masks, made similar use of almost all the great types, and by no means only of his two great teachers, that reappear in his works. Among Nietzsche's masks stands, before all others, Socrates. Then Heraclitus, Empedocles, Epicurus; among the moderns Leonardo, Shakespeare, Pascal, Napoleon. And, not least, Goethe as well. Whoever goes to the trouble of looking up the almost innumerable passages in which Nietzsche comments on Goethe will perhaps be astonished by the autobiographical significance of these comments but will certainly be in no doubt: Nietzsche was using this Olympian mask with the boldest predilection as an expressive, self-expressive, mouthpiece. There are some passages in which the self-portrait–like nature of Nietzsche's Goethe suddenly bursts through with prophetic force, double visions against which Nietzsche, with his deep instinctive fear of beholding himself, with the great wisdom of his will to conceal himself, holds up the protective Goethe mask, even if it is with some difficulty. The most salient example of this is the section in the second volume of *Human* on Goethe's errors. Here, Nietzsche both concealed and expressed the great balance of his own nature, his dual fate hovering painfully and dangerously between artistry and knowingness, under the image of Goethe's dual disposition to poetry and science. He commends Goethe as the great exception among the great artists for not having lived within the narrowness of his actual abilities:

> Twice he thought he possessed something higher than what he actually did possess—and was mistaken, in the second half of his life, where he appears completely filled with the conviction that he was one of the greatest scientific discoverers and bringers

> of light. And similarly in the first half of his life: he *wanted* something higher from himself than what poetry seemed to him—and was mistaken there, too. He thought nature wanted to make a *plastic* artist out of him—that was his inwardly burning and scorching secret, which finally drove him to Italy so that he could give full vent to this delusion and sacrifice everything to it. Finally, after he had come to, he discovered . . . that he had to bid *farewell* as if to the greatest passion of his desire. . . . The painfully sharp and gnawing conviction that it was necessary to bid farewell completely reverberates in the mood of *Tasso:* there lies over him, the "intensified Werther," the premonition of something worse than death, as when someone says of himself: "now it is over—after this farewell; how is one supposed to go on living without going mad!" These two fundamental errors in his life gave Goethe . . . such an unselfconscious and almost unreflective attitude toward poetry. . . . Goethe seems like a Greek who visits his beloved now and again, uncertain whether she might not be a goddess for whom he can't quite find the right name. One notices in all of his writing the breathing proximity of plastic form and nature . . . he thought he was perhaps always on the trail of the transformations of a single goddess. . . . Without the diversion of his error he would not have become Goethe. . . . [85]

Nietzsche was obviously inscribing his own perilous battle between the "scientific discoverer and bringer of light" and the poetic and musical, if not plastic, artist into the image of this Goethean conflict, this mournful farewell from himself, from the favorite phantom of himself. A heightened Werther-mood, Tasso's despair, a presentiment of something worse than death—these are masks of Nietzsche taking bitter leave of Wagner and his Wagner illusions: "Now it is over, after this farewell; how is one supposed to go on living without going mad!" Goethe's unself-conscious and almost unreflective attitude toward poetry is the same attitude in Nietzsche toward philosophy, knowledge, toward "truth." Goethe the Greek who visits his beloved now and again uncertain whether she might be a goddess—that, too, is Nietzsche, in all of whose thinking and writing one perceives the breathing proximity of music; he also thought he was on the trail of the transformations of a god—of Dionysus. And without the tragic diversion of his error Nietzsche would truly not have become Nietzsche—even this, the thinker's innermost destiny of *transformation,* is still expressed by his hidden and secretive Goethe mask. But even shorter casual characterizations turn out to be secret self-portraits: thus, for example, the striking description of Herder in the second volume of *Human.* There, Nietzsche delivers one of the most sophisticated specimens of his pleasure in masks and his technique of employing them: here we even have an example of a double proscenium, a "play within a play" *once more.* In the foreground we see the characterization of Herder and his St. John–like fate as a tragic precursor: namely, to have been the greatest and most prolific initiator whom his nation had ever produced before the group of early romantics around

Friedrich Schlegel—and before Nietzsche—but never to have experienced any completion of himself. Out of the middle-ground we hear an allegory of Wagner, in which even his relationship to the young Nietzsche does not go unmentioned: "Herder is not everything he wanted others to see in him (and wanted to see in himself) . . . he probably suspected as much from time to time and yet did not want to believe it himself, he, the ambitious preacher who would so much have liked to have been the supreme intellectual authority of his time . . . he seems to have lived for a long time as the claimant to several kingdoms of the mind, indeed to a universal realm and even had an entourage that believed in him: the young Goethe was below him . . . more than any other of our so-called classical writers he lacks a simple, upright manliness."[86] Far off in the background of this portrait, however, we can make out the unacknowledged secret self-portrait, that "Self-Portrait with Death," with the death of self-knowledge, which opens its sad and faithless eyes in so many passages of his works; what he says about Herder and Wagner he says in his innermost, unknowing heart of himself: "He saw and picked the first growths of the seasons earlier than all the others . . . his mind was between light and dark, old and young and was everywhere like a hunter lying in wait where there were transitions, breaks, convulsions, signs of inner stirrings and growth: he was driven by the restlessness of spring, but he was not the spring itself!"[87] That is the eternal wanderer Zarathustra. And this, too, is still Zarathustra: "Especially when he doubted himself he wrapped himself in dignity and enthusiasm: too often these were garments that denied a great deal, that deceived and consoled only him. He actually had enthusiasm and fire, but his ambition was much greater! It blew impatiently into the fire so that it flared up, crackled and smoked—his *style* flares up, crackles and smokes—but he wished for the great flame and it never burst forth! He did not sit at the table of the truly creative ones: and his ambition did not allow him to seat himself modestly among those who are happy to consume. He was thus a restless guest, a taster of every intellectual dish . . . never really satisfied and happy, Herder was in addition all too often ill . . . something raw and unfree never really left him. . . ."[88] No doubt, *Ecce homo* is such a characterization, an "Ecce homo" of his self-tormenting, self-doubting hours. "If you could only know how despondent and melancholy I *basically* am when I think of myself as a productive being! . . . I am indignant about how much, how unspeakably much there is about me that is unfree. There can be no talk of true productiveness as long as one is still stuck in unfreedom, in suffering and feeling burdened: will I ever make it? Doubts upon doubts. . . ."[89] That is a confession Nietzsche made to a friend during the period in which he wrote this description of Herder: do not both basically say the same thing? The Notebooks are rich in such transparent characterizations of artists and writers in which Nietzsche elaborates the "second face"—usually unconsciously and unintentionally, as evidenced by the fact that such characterizations are often also sharply polemical (on Sainte-Beuve, Rénan, Flaubert). He notes, for example, after reading Taine about the late English successor of Nietzsche's favorite, Claude Lorrain, namely the "great landscape painter Turner, who wants to speak to the soul and the mind instead of to the senses, and paints philosophical and humanitarian epics. He counted himself first among men and died mad . . . 'As a result of his profound attention to the moral in man his optical sensibility is désaccordée.[90] . . . Exaggerated, brutal, garish, hard, dissonant'"(Taine).[91] Or as he notes about Balzac: "'Profound contempt for all masses.' 'There are inner calls that one must obey: something irresistible draws me toward fame and power.' 1832 'Mes deux seuls et immenses désirs, être célèbre et être aimé.'"[92] Those are doubtlessly masks of Nietzsche's own being or certainly parts of his being.

One finds a "musical" example of this complicated mask technique, for instance, in the wonderful passage on the prelude to the *Meistersinger* in the eighth section of *Beyond.* To begin with, it is itself actually technically an overture in that it masterfully concentrates the motifs of the entire section and anticipates them as "music." It is, secondly, an analysis of the prelude to the *Meistersinger* itself—and in fact the most perfect one imaginable—or rather, it is the prelude *once more* in words; it is, viewed from a preliminary distance, a definitive characterization of the German essence, which it also admits to being in the very first bars (when "the curtain rises," as it were), and in the perspectival background it is a self-description of Nietzsche, of his mixed and magnificently equivocal being, of his work that points both backward and forward, in his ancestrally predetermined, extravagantly untimely character, with all of his day before yesterday and his day after tomorrow. It is in every sense a masterpiece of his equivocal style.

And Nietzsche even reveals the ambition of this equivocal style itself from behind a mask, namely behind the mask of his characterization of Sterne,[93] in *Human,* where Nietzsche is speaking about his own stylistic ideal at the time. The "endless melody," which he praises there in Sterne—"if with this phrase one can label an artistic style in which the definite form is continually broken, delayed, translated back into indeterminacy so that it means one thing and simultaneously another"[94]—this endless melody is that of his own new stylistic ambition, of his new music beyond Wagner. He is himself the great master of ambiguity that he describes Sterne to be—"this word understood much more broadly than is usually the case. . . . The reader is to be given up as lost who always wants to know precisely what Sterne actually thought about a matter, whether he is wearing a serious or a smiling expression: for he knew how to do both with a single fold of his face, just as he knows and even intends to be right and wrong at the same time, to entangle profundity and farce. . . . In this way he produces in the right reader a feeling of uncertainty about whether he is walking, standing or lying down: a feeling that is most closely related to that of hovering. He, the most supple of writers, also communicates something of this suppleness to his reader. Indeed, Sterne will unexpectedly switch roles and is just as much a reader as he is an author; his book resembles a play within a play, an audience in front of another audience."[95]

This stylistic ideal (which entirely accords with the ironic one of the romantic theoreticians: gravity must be cheerful, wit must sparkle in earnest, says Novalis)[96] is entirely in keeping with the style of Nietzsche the *writer,* and even as a poet Nietzsche tries, like Jean Paul, to make it possible in heightened form for poetry. It is itself, on the other hand, the style of the ironic mask, the double herm that combines the Socratic grimace with the Platonic countenance, this exquisitely cunning, ambiguously iridescent romantic style in which the disciple of Wagner had already wanted to tell the philosophic story of Socratism: "There is also a way to tell this story, *ironically* and *full of sorrow.*"[97] (It is the style with which the *writer* Nietzsche had the strongest and widest European effect, the same one as well that attracted so many imitators: it was the part of his prose that could be learned, the element that brought him in closest contact with the pervasive European skepticism.) It is, in the final analysis, the style of Socrates that exerts its fascination on Nietzsche, the style of "sly self-belittlement," of the ironic mask, of that Socrates whom a fragment in the late Notebooks characterizes yet again in the mode of a veiled self-portrait:

"Always ironice:[98] it is an exquisite sensation to watch such an honest thinker. But it is even more pleasant to discover that this is all foreground and that he basically wants something else and wants it in a very daring way. I believe that the magic of Socrates was this: he had his soul and behind it another one and behind it yet another. Xenophon laid himself to sleep in the foremost one, in the second one Plato laid himself to rest and Plato was there in the third one as well—but Plato with his own second soul. Plato himself is a person with many backdrops and foregrounds."[99] It is Plato as the great Cagliostro (as the *Will to Power* calls him, with a significant accent of Wagner hatred) who is seductively imagined in this style: "Is perhaps Plato's integrity beyond question?" the *Will to Power* asks. "But we know at the very least that he wanted something *taught* as absolute truth that he did not consider to be even relatively true: namely the separate existence and the separate immortality of the 'soul.'"[100] Does this not suddenly throw light on the meaning of the doctrines of the overman and the Eternal Return as being great pedagogical lies in the mask of "absolute truths"?

The only thing that seems certain is that it is precisely these characterizations of Socrates and Plato that demonstrate most clearly how Nietzsche's being and work, his stylistic foreground and the final secret background and reserve of his doctrine, *had to* succumb to the Socratic demon of the mask that he had so passionately hated as Wagner's theatrical nature.

Every line of his work reveals the person who did not want to reveal himself, the "wanderer" of *Beyond,* who had only one request: "one more mask! another mask!"[101] Who sought the "more intellectually gifted man, who has occasionally seen behind the masks and knows how to do so, who in general has understood how much everything is a mask . . ."[102] (Notebooks to *Revaluation*), whose final, cunning gratitude, like that of the dying Socrates in his "cloaked and ghastly words," is for his mask: "We don't want to become attached to anything else, we want to pray to the mask as to our ultimate god and redeemer"[103] (Notebooks on *Transvaluation*). Both as sufferer and as creator, Nietzsche loved the redemptive and seductive power of the mask as the form of his *own* suffering and creation. The Dionysian sufferer, the "conflicted one," the Pauline *ἀνὴρ δίψυχος*[104] in him viewed the blessing of the mask as a condition of his "resurrection": the value and attraction of his writing consisted precisely in this: "that here someone who is suffering and deprived speaking as if he were *not* suffering and deprived."[105] And the Socratic creator conceals himself in the changing masks of his "foregrounds" in order to be *permitted* to create: to live while remaining nice and silent about his final intentions is the desired form of his humanity and is, moreover, a matter of prudence and self-preservation—"who wouldn't run away from me if he were to realize the obligations that grow out of my way of thinking."[106] Indeed, the most cunning of all masks grows around this mind whose acuity is Socratic and whose depth is Dionysian, all the more so in that he interchanges his two most important masks: so that the suffering mind holds up the mask of Socratic will, and the creative will holds up the mask of Dionysian suffering. So that Zarathustra becomes a mask of Socrates, and the immoralistic critic a mask of the musician. So that the musical man, the "German" in Nietzsche becomes the mask of Hellenic man, the super- and anti-German man in him became the mask of the profoundly German one. It is like a final allegory of this dual herm in which every face is, and is supposed to be, the mask of the other that Nietzsche describes, the two peoples whose characters serve his own as a parable, as mask-loving, as profound actors of their own ultimate possibilities: he considers the Germans as well as the Greeks, each in their own particular way, to be *actors.* The famous passage in *Beyond* on the Germans characterizes them as the most consciously cunning, heterogeneous, contradictory people; a note in the *Transvaluation* characterizes Leibniz, the most European among the German philosophers, as a mask of Germanness *and* at the same time of Nietzsche himself:

"Leibniz is more interesting than Kant—typically *German:* good-humored, full of noble words, sly, supple, pliant, a mediator (between Christianity and the mechanistic world-view), incredibly daring for himself, hidden behind a mask, and importunate in a courtly fashion, seemingly modest.[107] . . . Leibniz is dangerous, as a true German who needs foregrounds and foreground philosophies, inwardly daring and secretive to the extreme. . . ."[108] Nietzsche says nothing more often about the Greeks than this: what actors they are! For him the mask is the symbol of the entire southern, Hellenic character:

"In the European south, the *mask* is and remains integral to the life of ordinary people! . . . And what of life in antiquity! What can one understand about it if one does not understand the pleasure in masks, the good conscience attached to masquerade! This is where the spirit of antiquity is refreshed and restored—and perhaps the exceptional and superior natures of the ancient world required this refreshment more than the ordinary ones"[109] (*Gay Science*). With that, as so often, Nietzsche joins under the sign of the mask the two opposing tendencies of his being and will, the German and the Hellenic tendencies, into the dual herm of a mysterious identity that in its disturbing duality itself remains the mask that is his alone. The question about which of the two polar tendencies was the truly dominant one in Nietzsche, about which one might have used the other in Platonic fashion as a semiotics for itself, remains unresolved: each one used the other to maintain a wise Socratic silence.

9
Weimar

Weimar . . . like Bethlehem in Judea . . . [1]

Love does not dominate, but it does educate,
and that is more.[2]
—Goethe

Among the minor prefigurative inclinations and desires Nietzsche had as a child there is a dream, reported by his sister, that the boy entertained for years: that he would like to round out and complete his later years (which at that point he probably still imagined within a "theological" framework he basically never renounced) in a modest house either on the *Rhine* or in *Rothenburg ob der Tauber* or, finally, in *Weimar.* This childish dream has something touchingly clairvoyant about it with regard both to Nietzsche's future as well as to the fundamental predispositions of his intellectual character. First of all, we see in it the early, unassuming penchant for refined seclusion, that same tendency that later bore the plan for the "Muses' Monastery" and made Stifter's *Indian Summer* his favorite book; that led the mature Nietzsche instinctively to avoid the atmosphere of the great capital cities (he never even saw his beloved Paris); and that finally produced the recluse of Sils-Maria. It is entirely the same mood and fundamental tendency that he puts into words in a letter to Rohde during the summer he spent in Basel in 1872: "I have always had only *one* wish: not to become hurried. . . . I prize Basel because it allows me to live quietly, as if on a small country estate. By contrast, I detest the very sound of a Berlin accent as much as a steam engine."[3] More toward the middle of his life, however, an image actually slumbers within the triply veiled childhood dream of the three great cultural spheres whose combination and peculiar synthesis would later determine the intellectual figure of "Nietzsche." *The Rhine:* even if it is still seen from a romantic point of view, this is already the enticing phantom of the south, a German-Italic south; it is perspectivally the closest visual form of the Roman landscape. Especially for those from the more eastern parts of Germany, the banks of the Rhine have a distinctly southern charm; the first generation after Goethe, which was still unspoiled by travel, perceived that, of course, much more keenly. While in Weimar, Goethe strongly felt the Italian, or better the southerly German, aspect of the Rhine-Main region where he grew up, its immediate ties to the Roman cultural legacy, its connection to all of the regions within the great *Limes Romanus.*[4] (It is no coincidence that until the middle of the nineteenth century, the great English and German collections of landscape engravings typically grouped views of Italy and the Rhine together, often with titles such as "The Rhine, Italy, and Greece": the northern European traveler of that time, whether engaged on a real or imaginary journey, still viewed this progression with naïve freshness.) Thus something of the music of the south, which he later learned to love so passionately, may have echoed in Nietzsche's ears when he heard the word Rhine as a boy, just as the young student had a first intimation of the more sculpted southern landscapes when he beheld the contours of the Siebengebirge,[5] the Alban Hills of the Roman Rhineland. There is nothing more indicative of this than the first Rhine letter by the *mulus*[6] beginning the semester in Bonn, which sounds as if the twenty-year-old were imagining an Italian journey in the manner of Goethe. "Old Roman roads still run through the area; last night we sang 'integer vitae' by the light of the moon sitting on the ruins of an ancient Roman fort. My views on the life and mores of the people are being enriched every day. I make note of everything, the peculiarities of diet, occupation, agriculture, etc."[7] The ideal of a chosen home in the Rhineland thus really does seem to be a premonition of the later wanderer's Italic exile and of everything that Nietzsche's intensive notion of the south came to embrace.

Rothenburg—this is the symbol of the second cultural sphere that became decisive for Nietzsche, even if it did not seem decisive to him. The Germany of the late-Gothic period and of the Reformation is represented by this more secluded, more intimate, miniature version of Nuremberg (the previous generation would have said, with Wackenroder,[8] "Nuremberg," where Nietzsche mentions the more virgin Rothenburg); the Germany of Luther, of Dürer, and of the oldest German music, the quaintly pious and simultaneously staunchly Protestant Germany out of which Nietzsche drew his oldest ancestral powers, to which he owes the particular rhythm of his theological and Reformation blood—the Germany of the *Meistersinger,* for which he fashioned the most beautiful monument in *Beyond* with the magnificent analysis of the opera's overture as a parable of German character and, in its innermost secret shadow, of himself.

Weimar, however—geographically, intellectually, and symbolically the closest to the young man from Thuringia—Weimar represents among the boy's three fabulous wishes the one closest to reality and fulfillment. And just as it was the one of the three that actually did come true—tragically, in more senses than any other innocent boy's dream had ever been realized by fate before—so, too, the cultural sphere that the magical word Weimar opened was perhaps not the most important for the entire intellectual phenomenon we call Nietzsche, not the most visible or most conscious, but certainly the most comprehensive of the three, the one that absorbed the most currents within it. The Lutheran, Protestant element remained a blood memory and atavism in Nietzsche; the southern Romanic yearning for the beyond, an enticing and fruitful danger, remained the vision of his future—a romanticism projected, as it were, into the future. Weimar, however, is the atmosphere of his life, a *presence* that is evident or latent everywhere in his work; and it is a presence in an intensive, a classical sense, which will have to be described more precisely. The Christian Protestant, northern moralistic element of his ancestral inheritance became condensed in his youth in the imitation of his great teacher, the pessimistic Christian ethicist, Schopenhauer. His belief in the future, his Greek hopes, his forward-facing romanticism, all crystallized in the experience of Wagner. But his intellectual present, the formative atmosphere of his youth, the humanistic concept of culture from his years in Basel, the industrious, life-affirming, life-transforming will to culture of his maturity—indeed even the secular epoch into which the entire phenomenon retrospectively seems to fit and whose tremendous finale it forms: all of this is suffused with the atmosphere of Weimar, it circles around Weimar's physical and symbolic center, around the name of Goethe.

These three names always belong together when and however one wants to describe and interpret Nietzsche's image. He says it himself in a fragment in the Notebooks from the year 1874: "The most important events that have happened to philology" (which is to say, that have happened to him, the philologist and more-than-philologist), "are the appearance of Goethe, Schopenhauer and Wagner: with them one is lent vision that has a greater range."[9] Today we call this long-range vision Nietzsche. But if the experience of Schopenhauer was the earliest, the most deeply and decisively stirring one, and the experience of Wagner was the most profound, the most sweetly and painfully transformative one, then the experience of Goethe was the longest, most durable, and quietly sustaining one of his life. Whereas Schopenhauer's testament and teachings are soon counted among the things he overcame, dismissed as atavism and relegated to the past, and whereas the romantic phantasm of love called Wagner's music of the future is unmasked by bitter, festering disappointment as a northern delusional phantom and a counterfeit future (in its place steps the magician of the east, Zarathustra, and the music of the south)—whereas he overcame and transformed these experiences, Goethe remained until the end a present power, an atmosphere he breathed with veneration, Goethe remained a *form* for Nietzsche, the only one he never shattered because, by transforming itself, this form of Goethe remained, was able to remain akin to him. Nietzsche's ardent vision—further-reaching, further-desiring—was cast into future landscapes that stretched into blue distances far beyond the horizon of Weimar; but his feet never left the radial border of the circle whose center is called Goethe.

The relationship of the poet of *Zarathustra* to his Goethe experience is far more intricate and convoluted than the almost graphically simple and obvious fable of his love for Wagner or of his discipleship to Schopenhauer. It is, with the sole exception of Socrates, perhaps the most complicated relationship to an intellectual forebear that we can observe in Nietzsche. It refuses to be cast in an unambiguous image or an easy formula. Yet one delimitation can immediately be made that is clear both as an image and as a phrase: Nietzsche's experience of Goethe is completely contained in the name of Weimar. So much so that the totality of his image of Goethe is completely absorbed by it. The pre-Weimar Goethe hardly ever comes into view: in the virtually countless comments and declarations about Goethe that are scattered throughout his works, the Notebooks, his letters, the Goethe of the Strasbourg period is almost never mentioned, the Goethe of *Werther* only negatively.[10] Nothing of the Faustian happiness and fantastic abundance of the youthful poetry, nothing about the *Sturm und Drang*.[11] Nowhere does he seem to be close to *the* poet for whom a full heart, a heart completely full of emotion, makes the poet. (He occasionally cites corrupted lines from the "Journey through the Harz in Winter," while revealing that he is unaware who the author of the passage is.) Nietzsche's earliest Goethe is none other than the wise man from Weimar, the world-embracing, world-interpreting, world-withholding Goethe of Eckermann and of the Eckermann years.[12] And where he speaks of the *poet* Goethe, it is almost exclusively the classically serene, the magisterially wise artist of the late period, of the true Weimar style, who tranquilly rests beyond the powerful reality of youth in the didactic realm of allegory. It is very indicative that in 1887 Nietzsche still acknowledged to Peter Gast that the "earliest and *strongest* impression" he ever had from Goethe was the "Lion Novella";[13] the novella that is one of the most calculated, indirect, artistically clever, and carefully constructed works that Goethe's selective classicism ever brought forth; it is entirely a didactic exercise, a formal composition, a cleverly graduated organization of effects, allusions, symbols; and whose "initially very realistic and in the end entirely idealistic character"[14] (Goethe) points to the allegorical value and allegorical intentions of his late art. If an epic structure of this kind and intention among all of Goethe's works could make the earliest and strongest impression on Nietzsche, then that says something, it says a great deal about his particular conception and love of Goethe. In his preference for this work, virtually everything has an elective affinity characteristically to himself:

the graduated symbolism, the deliberate classicism, the play with surfaces and depths, the false realism, the meaningfulness, the sublime art of the concrete, mystical ending—all of this could have had for the young Nietzsche the seductive power of a premonition, the secret anticipation of his own possibilities. That is the only explanation for the child's love of this late work, in which a person just awakening to the experience of poetry would hardly ever have sought his earliest encounter with Goethe, much less found his deepest gratitude for Goethe. Not coincidentally, the aesthetic negotiations about the "novella" in the conversations with Eckermann occupy a significant amount of space: this work is a symbol of Eckermann's Goethe world. But this Eckermann world, which Heine ridiculed, this late Weimar world is Nietzsche's true Goethe sphere. Schopenhauer's image of Goethe obviously had a strong and in a certain sense limiting effect on Nietzsche. But above all it was the predetermination of his own nature by which he gave himself the gift of this particular image of Goethe. No other book, next to Luther's Bible and *The World as Will and Representation,* had, or could have had, such an influence on Nietzsche as "the best German book there is"[15]—Goethe's *Conversations with Eckermann.* The declarations on behalf of Eckermann's Goethe accumulate in the early years: "Someone recently wanted to instruct us that at 82 Goethe had outlived himself: and yet I would gladly trade a few years of the outlived Goethe for entire wagon-loads of fresh, ultramodern biographies in order to take part in conversations such as those Goethe had with Eckermann and thus be spared all the up-to-date instruction by the legionnaires of the present moment. How few people alive today, compared to such men, even have the right to live!"[16]—that is Nietzsche "On the Use and Disadvantage of History for Life" in the *Untimely Meditations;* and in the Notebooks to the same work we read: "Goethe is exemplary: unbridled naturalism gradually becoming austere dignity. He went higher, as a stylized being, than any other German before him. Today people are so narrow-minded as to turn this into a reproach and even to accuse him of becoming old. They should read Eckermann and ask themselves if anyone in Germany has ever come so far in noble form. From there it is still a big step, to be sure, to simplicity and greatness, but we should certainly not imagine we can skip over Goethe; instead, we always have to begin again, as he did."[17] Nietzsche liked to quote passages verbatim from Eckermann up until *Human* (even in academic lectures), and the quotations from Goethe's late period in general seem almost innumerable. One notices the influence of the *Conversations* everywhere one looks in the early Nietzsche: in value judgments and preferences (Claude Lorrain, Napoleon, Lord Byron), in objections (the revolution, nationalism, everything all-too-German), in his whole pedagogical orientation, in his stance toward Greece, toward the Hellenic problem of "culture and barbarism." Nietzsche's entire didactic cultural enthusiasm during his years in Basel, as much as it was awakened by Wagner, as much as it signifies an active, youthful reaction against Schopenhauer's anti-developmental pessimism, is nevertheless completely rooted in the cultural soil of Weimar. During the crisis of 1870, Goethe's attitude, for whom the only things of importance were culture and barbarism, stood as an example before Nietzsche. (One need only think of the scene in which Nietzsche and Burckhardt were found together in tears when they received the—as it turned out, false—report of the burning of the Louvre—that was "Weimar.") The conversation Goethe had with Eckermann in March 1830 stayed with Nietzsche all his life: "How could I, for whom the only things of importance are culture and barbarism, have been able to hate a nation that belongs among the most cultivated on earth and which I owe such a large part of my own formation! In general, national hatred is a peculiar thing. You will always find it strongest and most vehement at the lowest level of culture. But there is a level where it disappears entirely and where one stands, as it were, *above* nations and feels the happiness or sorrow of a neighboring people as if it were one's own. This level of culture suited my character and I had settled there before I had reached my sixtieth year."[18]

There is an echo of this in Nietzsche that sounds almost Eckermannian even in its inflections: "I have the deepest misgivings about the coming state of culture. If only we do not have to pay too high a price for the extraordinary national successes in a sphere where I, in any case, would not be prepared to suffer any losses. Confidentially: I consider the Prussia of today to be an extremely dangerous force for culture. . . . It is often quite difficult to do so, but we have to be philosophers enough to remain level-headed amid the general frenzy—so that a thief does not come and steal from us or diminish what in my eyes cannot be compared with the greatest military deeds, indeed even with any national uprisings"[19] (to Gersdorff, November 1870, following his return to Basel from the battlefield). "When I heard about the fire in Paris" (the ostensible burning of the Louvre during the commune), "I was completely devastated and dissolved in tears and doubts for several days: the entire notion of a scholarly and philosophical-artistic existence seemed to me to be an absurdity if a single day could eradicate the most magnificent works of art, even entire periods of art . . ."[20] (to the same, June 1871).

And even Nietzsche's "good European" is in the end a Weimar reminiscence, a *memory* at least as much of the classical German epoch of world culture, of world literature, as it was a future vision of the coming European man who, in Goethe's sense, stands *above* nations by raising his own up to its highest possible level within himself. And if Eckermann hears Goethe say again and again: "One should, before everything else, study the ancient Greeks and the Greeks again and again . . ."[21] "in our need for something exemplary we must always return to the ancient Greeks, in whose works the beautiful human form is always represented. We must view everything else as merely historical . . ."[22]—then that is precisely the governing notion in Nietzsche's youthful, enthusiastic concern for the future of German culture. In his 1869 inaugural address in Basel about Homer and classical philology, Nietzsche lends words to this concern that echo Eckermann and Weimar: "The sword of barbarism hangs over the head of everyone who loses sight of the inexpressible simplicity and noble dignity of the Hellenic character; no matter how brilliant the advances may be in technology or industry, how modern the organization of schools, how widespread the political education of the masses, they cannot protect us from the curse of ludicrous and Scythian aberrations of taste and from annihilation by the terribly beautiful Gorgon head of classicism."[23]

One of the strangest manifestations of the deeply embedded duality of Nietzsche's character is that, of all people, this young arch-romantic, the disciple of Schopenhauer's fusion of Christian and Indian pessimism, the mystagogue of Wagner's new Eleusis, that of all people it was he who abandoned himself with such intensity to the most anti-romantic figure imaginable, the figure of the classical Goethe, while studiously eradicating all the "romantic" traits from his image that had guided and enriched the early romantics themselves. In spite of his occasional irascible polemics against the conception of Goethe as the "Olympian," no one else had ever emphasized with such force and agitation the "classical" aspect in and of Goethe's life and character, of his being and art, from such a deliberately narrow perspective, no one had elevated the strange exemplariness of his will to Hellenism, of his de-Germanized super-Germanness as had this heir of the most Goethe-distant romanticism, whose own intellectual path (symbolized by his style) led away into ever more unclassical regions until it reached the baroque dissolution of an ecstatic logic. The person who was destined to find an intellectual end as the fantastic-tragic radical and transvaluer, as an aristocratic revolutionary—the person who thought he would "convulse the world with the devastating lightning strike of transvaluation,"[24] even though Goethe disavowed "violence even in major matters"[25]—nevertheless a dark counter-instinct bound him admonishingly to Goethe, not to the youthful, god-defying Goethe of the Prometheus poem but rather the humbly proud Goethe who, "walking enwrapped in secrets," felt himself to be the voice of his century, who, both profoundly disenchanted and enlivened by Rome, watched as a new, untitanic world rose before him and from there wrote to Herder, his teacher and "humanus": "All paths lie paved before me because I walk in humility."[26] Following secret laws of even more secret kinds of attraction and fertilization, this most un-Nietzschean Goethe had to become Nietzsche's Goethe: in no period of this thought was he able to acknowledge Goethe even fleetingly in any other guise than that of the classical, even classicistic sage of Weimar, when Goethe felt most consciously the burden and responsibility of inheritance, saw himself as the defender of tradition who, while turned reverently toward the past and with noble mistrust toward the future, remained faithful to the genuine fate of all humanity. In the section on "the revolution in poetry"[27] in the first volume of *Human,* we have Nietzsche's most important, most unrestrained affirmation of the classical Goethe of Weimar, of the heir of humanistic antiquity ("Goethe imagined a European culture which the full inheritance of an already achieved humanity produces,"[28] [*The Will to Power*]) and of the "ancient" style, the style of grand and resigned convention. It is the most decisive affirmation of the wisdom of metamorphosis, that namely perfection was only ever possible in a limited sphere; an affirmation of the Goethe of *Pandora* and of *Achilleis,* for whom it was beautiful to be an heir of Homer, even if one were the last one. No comment Nietzsche ever made about art is more anti-Shakespearean than this; none that emerges more clearly from a spirit of Atticism that is less French than it is Goethean with a French accent. Here, Goethe is stylized in the direction of Voltaire, just as Voltaire's image is lent Goethean traits. "One need only read Voltaire's *Mahomet* from time to time in order to appreciate fully what European culture lost forever by that break in the (classical) tradition. Voltaire was the last of the great dramatists who tamed his multi-faceted soul, which could withstand the greatest tragic cataclysms, by submitting to Greek moderation . . . just as he was also the last great writer who in his treatment of prose displayed a Greek ear, a Greek artistic conscientiousness, Greek simplicity and grace; indeed, just as he was one of the last people who were able to combine in themselves the highest intellectual freedom and completely unrevolutionary convictions without being inconsistent and cowardly."[29] (How much more does such a sentence characterize Goethe's type than it does Voltaire's!) Yet this remaining ancient tradition comes to an abrupt and fateful halt: "Lessing turned the French form, that is, the only modern form of art, into an object of ridicule in Germany and pointed to Shakespeare; and thus we lost steadiness . . . and plunged into naturalism—that is, back into the beginnings of art. Goethe tried to save himself from that by always being able to limit himself anew in different ways; but even the most gifted person goes no further than continuous experimentation if the thread of development has been broken."[30]

Thus the deliberate and conscious self-constraint, self-limitation of the Roman Goethe acquired in Nietzsche's eyes the shimmer of a quietly mourning Too Late. What has become severed can never be reconnected. Goethe's "mature artistic insight during the second half of his life"[31] thus becomes more an expression of wisdom than of productivity, more a "twilight of art" than a new day—that most mature insight that Nietzsche nevertheless, despite its "beautiful 'In Vain,'" values as untimely and promising for the future: "With it, he leapt so far ahead of several generations that one can, broadly speaking, claim that Goethe has not even had any influence yet and that his time is yet to come."[32] And there follows here the powerfully vivid description of Goethe's late style, of the classicism of *The Elective Affinities,* for example, or of *Pandora,* the *East-West Divan,* and *Wilhelm Meister's Travels;* it is perhaps the most beautiful mask of the Weimar Goethe that Nietzsche made, and not without runes of his own character and desires:

> Precisely because Goethe's nature kept him for so long on the path of poetic revolution . . . his later transformation and conversion counts for so much: it means that he felt the deepest longing to recapture the tradition of art, and with the eyes of his imagination to project poetically onto the temple's remaining ruins and colonnades its old perfection and wholeness. . . . Thus he lived in art as in the memory of true art: his poetry had become an aid to memory. His demands were, to be sure, unfulfillable with respect to the energy of the new age; but his disappointment over that fact was more than compensated by the joy in knowing that they had once *been* fulfilled and that we, too, can still take part in this fulfillment. Not individuals, but rather . . . ideal masks; not reality, but an allegorical generality; historical specificity, local color were muted almost to the point of invisibility and made mythical; the perceptions and problems of contemporary society were reduced to their simplest forms, divested of their charming, exciting, pathological characteristics and made inert in every other sense but the artistic one; no new subjects or characters, but instead the old, long-familiar ones in everlasting revivification and remodeling: that is art as Goethe *understood* it late in life and as the Greeks, and even the French, *practiced* it.[33]

Weimar classicism has never been described more perfectly, more affectionately, more painfully clearly in its greatness and tragic limitations than it is here. It is impossible not to recognize features of his own ideal, for truly many traits of the stylistic model sketched out here were incorporated in Nietzsche's aphorisms, even in the idealistic masks of his *Zarathustra.* One could even say that these Goethean stylistic demands are basically already clearly articulated in a compact comment in the Notebooks to the second *Untimely* essay: "The path to style has to be taken, not skipped over: one will not be able to avoid the hieratically determined 'style,' that is, convention. Goethe's theater direction."[34] A note for *Daybreak* already defends Goethean classicism against the revolutionary, romantic stylistic ideal with the sharper accents of Nietzsche's later period: "Germans think that strength has to manifest itself in hardness and cruelty, they then like to subjugate themselves and do so with admiration . . . it is not easy for them to believe that there is strength in moderation and tranquility. They cannot find strength in Goethe and think Beethoven has more: and in that they are mistaken!!"[35] An antithesis, which is taken up again in a famous passage in *The Gay Science,* in the juxtaposition of the northern-romantic and southern-classical man, embodied in the meeting in Teplitz.[36] Such passages already indicate the direction in which Nietzsche broadens, extends, interprets Weimar classicism in order to preserve its exemplarity in his eyes so he will not have to watch it slip backward away from him, as happened with Schopenhauer, with Wagner, and so many others. It is the more and more decisive direction toward the super-German, super-Christian, Hellenistic sphere, toward the sublime solitude of Zarathustra, that Nietzsche seems at pains to lend this classicism. It is as if Nietzsche's thinking and experience, which become increasingly lonely, more and more distant from any kind of community (but all culture is community), found confidence and strength through an increasingly ardent gratitude, a kind of exclusive feeling of refuge, which one otherwise never senses in him, in sounding out a secret resonance with Goethe's nature. The classical Goethe becomes a companion in fate with the Dionysian Zarathustra, the Roman German joins with the super-German, the enemy of the revolution with the hater of democracy, the opponent of romanticism with the adversary of Wagner, the "decided non-Christian" with the Antichrist, the pupil of the Greeks with the disciple of the Greeks. "Goethe's noble isolation—the highest born need a kind of castled knighthood and robber barons. . . ."[37] (Notebooks to *Transvaluation*)—that is an apology for Zarathustra's seventh solitude through Goethe. "To be a good German means to rid oneself of Germanness . . . no one will grant me that today. Goethe perhaps would have agreed with me"[38] (ibid.). "Goethe stood above the Germans in every respect and still stands there today: he will never belong to them. . . . Just as Beethoven made music over and above the Germans, just as Schopenhauer philosophized over and above the Germans, Goethe wrote his *Tasso,* his *Iphigenie* over and above the Germans"[39] (*Human*). "The Germans did not need Goethe, they thus do not know how to use him, either. One should take a look at our best politicians and artists in that regard: they all did not have Goethe as a teacher, nor could they have had"[40] (*Human*). "Goethe stands in a relationship to his nation that is neither vital, nor novel, nor obsolete. He lived for only a few and lives for them still: for most he is no more than a fanfare of vanity that is blown across the German border from time to time. Goethe, not just a good and great man, but a *culture*—Goethe is an incident without consequence in the history of the Germans: who would be able, for example, to point to a single element of Goethe in the last seventy years of German politics! (whereas an element of Schiller, and perhaps a tiny element of Lessing have been at work there)"[41] (*Human*). "What did Goethe actually think about the Germans? But there were many things all around him that he never clearly spoke about, and throughout his life he understood the fine art of remaining silent: he probably had good reasons for it. . . . There are comments by Goethe in which, as if from the perspective of a foreigner, he speaks with an impatient severity about the things that Germans are proudest of. . . ."[42] (*Beyond*). "Goethe is an exception: he lived among the Germans finely concealed and disguised.[43] . . . Goethe, isolated between pietism and Hellenism; uncertain whether he should write in French or not"[44] (Notebooks from the *Revaluation* period). No doubt, those are all finely disguised moments of Nietzsche, masks of Zarathustra, justifications of the Hyperion loneliness among the Germans to which Nietzsche was condemned ("I was always condemned to Germans"),[45] who laments in *Ecce homo:* "Ten years—and no one in Germany made it a matter of guilty conscience to defend my name against the absurd silence under which it was buried,"[46] the same Nietzsche who wrote to Burckhardt and others that his last works should not have been written in German but rather in French—and that to a certain degree they were written in French, and in any case that it would be easier to translate them into French than into German. In his disgust with the dogma of equality, Nietzsche found himself united with the most unrevolutionary mind among the Germans: "The doctrine of equality!—but there is no more poisonous poison: for it *seems* to be preached by justice itself, whereas it is the *end* of justice . . . the fact that this doctrine of equality was surrounded by so much terror and blood gave this 'modern idea' *par excellence* a kind of glorious halo so that the revolution as *theater* seduced even the finest minds. In the end, that is not a reason to respect it more. I see only one person who perceived it as it had to be perceived: with *disgust*—Goethe . . ."[47] (*Twilight*). "What would Goethe have thought of Wagner?" *The Case of Wagner* asks; "Goethe once put the question to himself what the danger was that hung over all romantics: the romantic fate. His answer: that they would suffocate on the regurgitation of moral and religious absurdities. More concisely: *Parsifal.*"[48] And even Nietzsche's conception of romanticism as typical decadence, of the romantic artist as a decadent, appears to be an extension of Goethe's famous definition in his conversation with Eckermann in April 1829 in which he labels the classical as healthy and the romantic as sick.[49] It can be no surprise that the passionate Antichrist claims the classical Goethe as a determined non-Christian, failing to recall, for instance, Goethe's comments to Eckermann about Luther and Protestantism, about the culture of the Gospels. "A test of whether one possesses a modicum of *classical taste* is how one stands toward the New Testament—see Tacitus—whoever is not revolted by it . . . does not know what is classical. One has to perceive the 'cross' like Goethe"[50] (*The Will to Power*). "I remember how the last German with refined taste, how Goethe perceived the cross"[51] (*The Case of Wagner*)—a reference above all to the sixty-sixth of the *Venetian Epigrams,* probably as well to passages in the *Wilhelm Meister's Travels* (II, 2) and to the paralipomena to *Faust* ("Country Road. A Cross along the Path"). "Goethe is the last German for whom I have respect: he might have felt three things that I feel—and we agree about the 'cross'"[52] (*Twilight of the Idols*).

The classical Goethe is stylized everywhere here as the powerful *exception,* as the lonely companion of Zarathustra. And he is a powerful exception in one respect above all—as the Greek nature among the Germans. For Nietzsche, Goethe understood and experienced the noble secret of the Hellenic character more deeply than anyone else—Nietzsche does not exempt even the favorite of his earliest years, Hölderlin—namely the competitive love of life that speaks with such enthusiasm out of Plato's dialogues: "The measure of study lies therein: only what is seized by love and desires to procreate should be studied . . . in *that* way Goethe apprehended antiquity: always with a competitive soul. But who else?"[53] (*We Philologists,* 1874–75). Or more mysteriously, with more chiaroscuro, in the Notebooks to *The Birth of Tragedy:* "The Greeks are the artists of *life;* they have their gods in order to be able to live, not to alienate themselves from life. Important is the idealism of the living for life. A cross surrounded by roses, like Goethe in the 'Mysteries.'"[54] (Here we already catch a very early glimpse of Nietzsche's final vision of Dionysus, the suffering and dancing god, the "Christ Dancing": "I would believe only in a god who knew how to dance,"[55] Zarathustra confesses. Perhaps Nietzsche's pedagogical powers of prophecy had never been in such close proximity to Goethe's as at the moment he made this phrase, which already anticipated the Nietzsche of the final Dionysus Dithyrambs, a phrase that bears a significant resemblance to Goethe's fragment on the Humanus, the Saint, the Sage—"the best man I have laid eyes on";[56] to that profoundly secretive Rosicrucian poem that begins with the verses: "A wonderful song is brought unto you. . . .")[57] To be sure, we encounter comments by Nietzsche in which Goethe is not Greek enough for his prophetic impatience, where his classicism is all too Weimarian, all too bright, too conscious, too historical—too inward without any new, tremendous hope. Thus in *Twilight of the Idols,* for instance, he rather sharply draws the boundaries between Goethe's antiquity and the "true," that is, Nietzsche's own, Hellenism: "When we examine the concept 'Greek' that Winckelmann and Goethe elaborated for themselves, we find it incompatible with that element out of which Dionysian art grows—the orgy. In fact, I do not doubt that Goethe on principle excluded everything of the sort from the possibilities of the Greek soul. As a result, Goethe did not understand the Greeks.

For it is only in the Dionysian mysteries, in the psychology of the Dionysian condition, that the fundamental fact of the Hellenic instinct is expressed."[58] Similarly, we read in *The Will to Power* that the Dionysian experiences represent, for all that is Greek, the Great Depth, the Great Silence; without access into the concealed, subterranean realm one cannot know the Greeks. Even the noble zeal of such friends of antiquity as Goethe and Winckelmann retained in this respect something immodest, almost illicit, about it. Indeed, Nietzsche occasionally even calls Goethe's Greece historically false and "too soft and unmanly."[59] (It is not for nothing that Nietzsche believed he had a "more severe, masculine style"[60] than Goethe, the linguistic artist.) One thing is certain: in the ill clairvoyance of his final, transvaluing period, it became difficult to bear an un-Greek material remnant in Goethe's classicism. Nietzsche's sensibility perceives a final barrier of resignation (as in the section of *Human* on revolution in poetry), indeed of fear, a trace of the German "cowardice before reality"[61] in Goethe's character, in Goethe's Greek classicism, even in his historical understanding of Hellenism. He sometimes seems to think that a fear of the deepest tragic and heroic substrata of all things human fuels this Weimar classicism, that its artistry has an aversion to the most extreme knowledge: he quotes as significant Goethe's admission that it would destroy him to produce a tragedy. "What Goethe perceived in Heinrich von Kleist was his feeling for the tragic, which he turned away from: it was the incurable side of nature. He himself was conciliatory and curable,"[62] he wrote in the second half of the 1870s and, more succinctly, as early as 1873: "Goethe on Kleist: *afraid*."[63] In *Human* he parodies the Faust notion rather dismissively as the ostensibly greatest German "tragic idea"—"as one hears the Germans say";[64] and here, too, the final sentence quotes: "Goethe once said that his nature was too conciliatory for the truly tragic."[65] As early as in the preliminary studies for *The Birth of Tragedy*, he detects this protective barrier against tragic knowledge in Goethe's classicism—the living barrier of the self-organizing sage, but not of the self-sacrificing hero, against the ravenously formless, chaotic darkness: "With Goethe, in accordance to his epic nature, poetry is the remedy that *protects* him against full knowledge: in tragic natures, art is the remedy that liberates them from knowledge. Such a person finds life disturbing: it immediately retreats from him like an image, and he finds this disturbed life worth depicting."[66]

Common to all of these references to Goethe is obviously the open or implied reproach that he had an untragic, un-Dionysian constitution and attitude; and it is not accidental that the young Nietzsche valued Schiller, as the expression of a tragic culture, more highly than Goethe, who to him was the expression of an "epic culture."[67] For the Nietzsche of "Richard Wagner in Bayreuth," the only hope and only guarantee for the future of man is "that the tragic sensibility does not die out."[68] No question: the young Nietzsche's own image of Goethe was not completely compatible with the Dionysian ideal. But in his maturity he was driven by a deep identificatory desire to have the two concepts, which seemed to exclude each other in the mentioned references, flow into a final Goethean and Dionysian union. Indeed, at the end of Nietzsche's two decades as a philosopher, Goethe's classical Greekness, despite such skeptical individual fragments, is less questioned, it is stylized more powerfully, more imperiously, than in the period of *The Birth.* If, for the young Nietzsche in Basel, Goethe is essentially still the very model of the *contemplative* man, more of a conservative and peaceable force than an active and creatively affirmative nature, more of a classicistic than a classical man, then the image of Goethe during the years in Sils-Maria is unrecognizably intensified into the yea-saying, yea-doing realm of an overflowing devotee of life—clear traits of Zarathustra estrange the familiar portrait by Eckermann, and even the highest name of Dionysus becomes combined with the circumspectly Apollonian seer and creator of Weimar into a mysterious identity. Now, the final ecstatic ideal of a great, Hellenistic totality of all life forces, of their inclination toward cheerfully fatalistic, toward an active and trusting affirmation of all that is vitally human, is symbolized in Goethe: "What he wanted was *totality;* he fought against the disaggregation of reason, sensuality, feeling and will (—advocated in the most repellant form of scholasticism by Kant, the polar opposite of Goethe); he disciplined himself toward wholeness, he *created* himself . . . he made use above all of practical activity; he surrounded himself with nothing but closed horizons; he did not separate himself from life, he placed himself into it; he did not lose heart and took as much as possible onto himself, over himself, into himself"[69] (*Twilight*). "Totality," as the pinnacle and meaning of Goethean classicism, is also celebrated in *The Will to Power:* "In Goethe there is a kind of almost joyful and trusting fatalism, which does not revolt, does not tire, which seeks to form out of itself a totality in the belief that only in totality everything is redeemed and appears to be good and justified."[70] Nietzsche finds it characteristic of Hellenic physical and spiritual perfection—the condition of being "well-rounded"—when someone, like Goethe, becomes attached to the things of the world with ever greater pleasure and heartiness—"in that way, you see, he retains a generous conception of humanity, so that man becomes the transfigurer of existence when he learns to transfigure himself."[71] But the expression of such a well-turned-out being, the form of such a transfiguration of existence, becomes—as always in *The Will to Power*—classical art, the "art of apotheosis"[72] (as opposed to an art of suffering and revenge, of a basically romantic and Christian pessimism), that comes "out of gratitude and love": "dithyrambic, perhaps, with Rubens, serene with Hafis, bright and benevolent with Goethe, and spreading a Homeric halo over all things."[73] Until, finally, in *Twilight of the Idols* he calls the joyful and trusting fatalism of the Goethean man—the belief that only what is individual could be objectionable, that in totality everything is redeemed and affirmed—Nietzsche calls this belief that can no longer negate the highest of all possible beliefs: "I have christened it with the name of Dionysus."[74] With that, Nietzsche saved the man of the Goethean ideal, and thus Goethe himself, for his own Dionysian ideal, he married Weimar classicism, which intermittently seemed too Winckelmannian, too un-Dionysian, too intellectually nostalgic, with his own vision of Hellas. That, too, is an example of the art of reconciling contrasts, which Nietzsche admitted he knew was his greatest creative gift. If even the notion of a "German classicism," of "classical German man," was an example of the unification of what cannot be unified—for "classical" and "German" seem to be self-canceling concepts, not just for Nietzsche, but also objectively, as are classic and romantic, plastic and musical—then the image of the Greek Goethe unifies yet another pair of opposites: the opposition between Apollo and Dionysus, as *The Birth of Tragedy* thematically develops it. Despite his own definition of Goethe, Nietzsche allows the secret of Dionysus and his orgiastic totality of life to flare up behind the Apollonian head of Goethe, that wisest, most controlled Apollonian man, the faceless mystery behind the classical mask, Hölderlin's Dionysian Eleusis behind Goethe's Apollonian Rome. "Goethe's man"—belonging both to Weimar and orgiastic classicism—becomes a symbol for Nietzsche's will to incorporate the elements of his ancestry, his education, his cultural sphere of Eckermann's Weimar into the hope and demand of his New Man, the Dionysian Greek man, whom the historical Goethe, in Nietzsche's opinion, "did not understand."[75] It is a symbol for Nietzsche's longing to have the New Man be born out of the day before yesterday and the day after tomorrow, out of the German urge for formation and for taking form, out of a Hellenic formative ecstasy and delight. A mask of this future man, yet another Zarathustra mask—that is Nietzsche's double-faced classical Goethe.

And this love for the Weimar Goethe tells us one last thing: if one surveys the legend of Nietzsche's life in its entirety, then the fact that the arc of this rare, so eminently allegorical life turns back to where it began, takes on the value of allegory; that *Weimar* should be the final return home from this odyssey of knowledge, and that the childish wish should be fulfilled in such an eerily ambiguous fashion, by completing his days in the city of Goethe. Just as Nietzsche physically returns once more to his Thuringian homeland out of the deadly south in order to see the sun set over the hills of Weimar, so too does his intellectual being, as we now see it slowly finding its place in the continuity of German and European intellectual history, appear to be bound by a predetermined return to

Weimar. The peculiar tendency of Nietzsche's thought, even up to the threshold of his exit, to legitimize itself by constant reference to Goethe as the only one who remained "akin to him by transforming himself," remains as it were Nietzsche's own passkey allowing his entry into the more properly termed Weimar period of German history. In fact we already see today the entire phenomenon of Nietzsche becoming more clearly aligned with the epoch of German humanism that ended through and with him, reaches from Herder to Nietzsche and within which German romanticism, the daughter of Herder and Goethe, represents only a brief, well-defined episode, a beautiful moment within a world-embracing abundance. Nietzsche, despite his more immediate origins in romanticism—even his intellectual father Schopenhauer, after all, unified arch-romantic elements with completely classical, anti-romantic ones—Nietzsche is a child of that same classical cosmopolitanism, of the century of *cultivation* in Goethe's sense: cultivation, de-barbarization, assuming form through the love of Hellenism. He represents this epoch of cultivation and humanism one last time, in unforgettable style, by simultaneously analyzing and undermining it. He belongs to it in the same way in which Wagner (together with Brahms) belongs to the epoch of German music: he is the one who, in his sphere, *has no succession.* This relationship becomes most clear in the admittedly much more limited example of Heine and his stance toward genuine German romanticism. Just as Heine, consciously and with all of the hyperintellectualism of his blood inheritance, that makes him so fatefully akin to Nietzsche, dismantles German romanticism with the very tools this romanticism had created, just as his "sweet and passionate music and divine malice"[76] (a comment about Heine from *Ecce homo,* which is just as valid for Nietzsche himself) sings to romanticism its final free forest song: in the same sense and with more intensified effect, Nietzsche sang the end of Goethe's century, brooded over and caustically derided the century of Eckermann's sage of Weimer until it was no more. More passionately, more mournfully, more powerfully, and above all more purely than Heine—but nevertheless with the historically identical stance overall. And also with a fate similar to that of the all-too-clear-sighted cynic, who productively reduced the romantic, classical cosmos of the Faust problem into a mere dancing song: the productive, positively creative development did not extend beyond himself. He made a new world possible, but he did not create it; he sang the end of a world, but he did not compose a new one; he demolished temples, but he built none, for "one should not build when there is no more time."[77] And what he retained was the sense that someone was coming who would be "the deed of his thoughts"[78]—whether one calls him the overman or lends him more human names. For as much as his *Zarathustra* was supposed and intended to be the third great German step, and not merely in linguistic terms, the step "above and beyond Goethe,"[79] as he wrote to Rohde: Zarathustra himself knew, despite all of the ecstatic self-stylizations in the manner and intention of *Ecce homo,* all too well that even he was only the call for the great midday, but not the midday itself. He knew that he was still bound to the old world whose god he had buried. That—as the young enthusiast of *The Birth* had said of the Weimar Hellenism of Goethe and of his friend—he had, with *his* "most daring struggles, not come further than that longing glance which Goethe's Iphigenie sends from barbaric Tauris toward her home and across the sea."[80] Zarathustra, he of the great downfall, knew in his heart of hearts that the words applied to him with which the last *Untimely Meditation,* "Richard Wagner in Bayreuth," prophetically ends: that he could not be, "as he may perhaps appear to us,"[81] the seer of a future for his people, but rather the interpreter and transfigurer of a past, of the most beautiful and most perfect moment of our intellectual past, which we call by the name of the town where Nietzsche died.

10

Napoleon

He had it, and one saw by looking at him that he did; that was all. . . . He had to an eminent degree a thoroughly demonic nature, so that hardly anyone else can be compared to him. The Greeks counted demonic natures of that sort among the demigods. . . . His life was the procession of a demigod. . . . One may very aptly say of him that he found himself in a state of perpetual inspiration. . . . He was one of the most productive men who have ever lived.[1]

—Goethe on Napoleon

Nietzsche proves he is a pupil of the Greeks when he says that for him, as was true of his teachers as well, "the most abstract idea always coalesces into a person," whereas for the moderns, "even what is most personal is sublimated into abstractions."[2] "The Greeks," he writes in the fragment from 1873 on "Philosophy in the Tragic Age of the Greeks," "were the opposite of realists in that they believed only in the reality of men and gods and viewed the whole of nature as if it were only a disguise, masquerade and metamorphosis of those divine beings. To them, man was the truth and center of things, everything else was merely appearance and an illusory game."[3] To be sure, only one other person among the moderns not only thought but also felt and believed the same way, in such an eminently Greek way—only Hölderlin. "For always to seek and fail to find, always to *need,* as heroes do the laurel, the hearts of feeling people, the consecrated elements for fame. . . ."[4] "What would the sky and the sea be and the islands and the stars and everything that human eyes behold, what would it all be, this dead song, if I did not give it music and language and soul?"[5] That is Greek. Nietzsche's mediated and northern Hellenism is less present than Hölderlin's; not naïvely innate and ethereal like that of the Swabian[6] Greek. But in the midst of the merely natural realm, Nietzsche also perceives with a Greek sensibility, anti-romantically, the ancient question: "Tell me, where is Athens?"[7] "Your gaze toward distant seas," he writes during the time of *Zarathustra,* "your desire to touch the rocky cliff and its peak—that is only the language for your longing. Your gaze and your desire seek only man and that which is more than man!"[8] And again: "We want to infuse nature with humanness . . . we want to extract from it what we need in order to dream *over* and above man. Something that is *more magnificent* than storms and mountains and seas shall yet arise—but as the son of man!"[9] Just as nature here coalesces in eminently Greek fashion into the image of man and of divine man, so too does Nietzsche's intellectual landscape. His intellectual world, the second or almost the "first nature" for his entirely inwardly directed eye, with all of its inner storms, mountains, and seas, indeed even with the rocky abstractions it contains, this world reveals again and again the same Hellenic longing to coalesce into a *person,* into some human embodiment. The "metaphysical" mountain backdrop of the Engadin, the Greek coast of Portofino, combine to form the vision of the overman; the landscape of Nietzsche's philosophical thought, in his guise both as a critic of morals and as an author of an ethos, as a believer in art and as an analyst of religion, is always condensed into heroic figures of superhuman proportions. Nietzsche involuntarily thinks in great human visualizations. He even mythologizes the results of his analytical labors into powerful representative types. His gratitude respects virtually no critical boundaries to such mythologizing, wherein historical figures appear to him as crystallization points. His entire view of history and the philosophy of history is determined by this will to heroization. Just as he thinks that an entire people is merely the detour nature takes in order to arrive at five or six great men, he also seems to think that a historical epoch, a particular period in the development of philosophical, religious, or artistic life occurred only so that it would anthropomorphize into one or more super-life-sized types. Thus the seductive power of certain epochs in history for Nietzsche, particularly pre-Socratic Greece and the Italian Renaissance. He is, even more than Carlyle,[10] the typical representative of a historiography based on enthusiasm in Goethe's sense, whose maxim Jakob Burckhardt formulated with the remark that the power to venerate is as essential to us as is the object of veneration itself.[11]

This enthusiasm in Nietzsche can be formally quite critical, just as it can very frequently veer over into a crassly negative over-stylization; even then, however, the original tendency toward magnification, toward a "tremendous amplification," remains the same, as for example with regard to Socrates, Paul, Luther, or Wagner. Here, as we know, the anti-stylization tips over into the grotesque; but the scale of the caricature always remains the same in its colossal exorbitance. One observes this tendency of Nietzsche's thought—in its form romantic and heavily determined by Schopenhauer's doctrine of the genius, at its roots Greek—one can observe it at its purest in the conception of Zarathustra and his overman. Here, where there was hardly any historical substratum given and where a crystallization point had to be artificially created by splitting something into two halves, one sees Nietzsche's heroizing, mythologizing tendency at its most unrestrainedly active, its most powerfully vital. (*Ecce homo,* by contrast, presents the opposite of such extremely negative caricatures: namely in its extravagantly superlative caricatures.) Freed from all the constraints of historical fact, the mythologizing will to intensification reaches here its upper limit at the strictly divine, where the mythic intensification, the heroization, passes over into the mythical superlative, the identification with god. Analogously, the comparative affirmation of life is simultaneously intensified into the absolute superlative of the will to the eternal recurrence of life—"was *that* life? Very well: once more!"[12] The overman, of which even Zarathustra was only supposed to be the pre-dream, the bridge and transition, is the highest level of objectification (to use Schopenhauer's terminology) of the will to mythologize everything, which testifies to the Greek in Nietzsche. Just as the Greeks conceived of physical nature as only a "disguise, masquerade and metamorphosis of the divine being,"[13] so too Nietzsche understands the entire intellectual world, including his skeptical, analytical, positivistic insights and inclinations, as only a mask and material for the formation of the overman, as "the truth and center" of *his* concerns; his *thoughts* are for him merely the "appearance and illusory game"[14] of his *will,* a will to the highest Greek reality: to *form.*

If the conception of the overman is the purest formation—purified, so to speak, of all elements that are still historical—of Nietzsche's Hellenically mythologizing thought, then the grandly conceived heroic types are obviously preliminary stages on the way to the overman, less distinct, prophetic phantasms, as it were, and experiments, similar to the series of subordinate, less distinct demigods and nature gods in the Greek mythological hierarchy that underlie the forces concentrated within the major deities. In the intellectual ancestry leading up to Zarathustra, who is the highest preliminary stage on the way to the future overman, all of Nietzsche's great human types unmistakably line up, and indeed already do so at a time when the form of Zarathustra had not even remotely occurred to Nietzsche yet. This becomes perhaps clearest in the series of pre-Platonic philosophers to whom Nietzsche devoted the wonderful fragment on "Philosophy in the Tragic Age of the Greeks." Figures such as his Empedocles, and above all Heraclitus, are already the immediate ancestors of his later son, Zarathustra. Early on, other anticipated traits of Zarathustra already make his mythological portraits of Wagner and Schopenhauer strange and alien, as do his poetic superelevations of Frederick the Second of Hohenstaufen, Leonardo da Vinci, even of Cesare Borgia; Goethe is mythologized in magnificent fashion and his Apollonian head is made to resemble Zarathustra's through the addition of Dionysian traits. Now, these great individual figures are not actually "supermen" in Nietzsche's eyes, at least not according to the meaning of the word in *Zarathustra:* the overman is an entirely future reality, never an actually existent one, he is a postulated figure, not historical. It is perhaps even fundamentally the case that the overman, like the idea of the Eternal Recurrence, is not so much an idea out of some (future or metaphysical) higher reality for Nietzsche, but rather was pedagogically posited as an *εἴδωλον ἡγεμονιχόν,*[15] a governing illusion. The great ones, who are "successful," as Nietzsche calls the powerful and exceptional guides among men, are themselves only silhouettes, promises, and metaphysical memories of the Platonic primal form of the overman. We should not be confused by the occasional application of the term overman to them.

Nietzsche's great men—demigods in the Greek sense, prophetic figures according the Christian Old Testament conception—are prismatic refractions of the Platonic primal light called "overman": even their sum total would not yield the original image, but only a rainbow bridge leading over to it. Yet there are for Nietzsche degrees of approximation to the ideal of the overman; singular historical incarnations through which the original image shines through more brilliantly than through other great beings. This is how Nietzsche almost always views Heraclitus; at times Goethe—Mephistopheles; above all, however, the great "ancient" phenomenon of modern history: Napoleon. Not Napoleon as Bonaparte, but as Caesar.

Nietzsche's powers of veneration often rise up to Pindaric praise when he speaks of Napoleon. He never talked about anyone who lived in the post-ancient world in the same way. "The major event of the last millennium is the appearance of Napoleon";[16] "Napoleon, the first and most advanced person of modern times";[17] "the history of Napoleon's influence is virtually the history of the higher happiness that this entire century achieved in its most worthy people and moments";[18] "we owe almost all of the higher hopes of this century to Napoleon,"[19] and so forth. It is temporally the closest, the singularly colossal embodiment of the ancient ideal that so deeply affected Nietzsche in the phenomenon of Napoleon. His Napoleon has no romantic traits and no revolutionary ones, he is a brother of neither Byron nor Beethoven. He is most closely related to the demonically violent but sovereignly mastered natural force that Goethe also experienced in Napoleon.[20] But even more than for Goethe, here Napoleon more decisively partook of *actual* antiquity—just as, in an entirely different, incommensurable sphere Hölderlin's experience partook of a late-born Hellenic reality; we recall the late, stammered lines in which Hölderlin's mind, already drowning in chaos, seems to sense the indescribably *foreign* ancestry of his mighty contemporary, and which begin:

> I would like to ask whence he comes?
> Lodi, Arcole . . .
> Ha, he prophesied not in vain
> When he stood above the Alps
> Looking down toward Italy and Greece . . .

and the others in which Hölderlin, like Nietzsche, also views "Buonaparte" as a return to nature:

> The poet should leave him untouched
> Like the spirit of nature . . . [21]

Napoleon is nature—ancient nature, living antiquity—thus his unparalleled exceptional status among Nietzsche's historical valuations. *On the Genealogy of Morals* puts it perhaps most decisively: "The ancient ideal stepped *bodily* and with unparalleled splendor before the eyes and conscience of humanity. . . . Napoleon, the most unique and latest-born man there ever was, appeared like a final gesture toward the *other* path, and he seemed to be the problem of the noble idea in itself become flesh—one should consider carefully *what* kind of problem that is: Napoleon, this synthesis of monster and overman. . . ."[22] (This is, by the way, tellingly enough, the only passage in the writings of these years in which the word overman is connected with a particular historical name.) *Twilight of the Idols* says: "Napoleon was an example of the 'return to nature,' as I understand it";[23] a return to ancient nature, not to Rousseau's. "Napoleon belongs to antiquity in his entire contempt of 'Christian virtues' and of moral hypocrisy as a whole (Thucydides),"[24] reads a passage in the Notebooks from the *Transvaluation* period. Precisely for that reason, he is characterized there as the most extreme opposite of Rousseau: " . . . ancient, contemptuous of man . . . he thought nothing of the Christian virtues, did not even register them as present."[25] The return to the egocentric morality of antiquity, as Nietzsche understands it, places Napoleon, so to speak, among the great philosophical figures of the Hellenic spirit; it thereby also puts him in proximity to Zarathustra: "With people such as Napoleon," he writes in a late passage from the Notebooks, "every disregard for *oneself* is a danger and a loss: they have to keep their heart closed; just like the philosopher—Zarathustra."[26] The tremendous simplicity, the clear outline of his figure and of his fate, is ancient as well; this sublime simplicity also relegated him, on the one hand, to the mythic heroes; on the other, it recalls the powerful one-sidedness (Nietzsche says "monocularity,"[27] citing John Stuart Mill) of early Greek philosophy, which intellectually creates and constructs the world out of One Principle (that is, out of a single imperious act of will). "Napoleon, as the type of an instinct that has been perfectly thought through and completely developed, belongs to the humanity of antiquity: whose qualities—simple constitution and the inventive cultivation and elaboration of one motif or of a few motifs—are easy enough to recognize"[28] (*Daybreak*).

Napoleon's character also displays the ancient quality of great deterministic fatalism, a Caesar's belief in the stars, the heroic hubris by which he aligns himself with the exalted Promethean figures in the ancient store of myth: "Napoleon's character," *Human* finds, "certainly grew precisely through his belief in himself and in his star and through the contempt for men that flowed out of that into the powerful unity that raises him up out of the mass of all modern people, until finally this same belief turned into an almost mad fatalism, robbed him of his quick and sharp eye and became the cause of his downfall."[29] It is precisely this element of the *sacrilegious* that is thoroughly ancient; for "the best and the highest things that humanity can obtain are acquired through sacrilege"[30]—that, in the words of *The Birth of Tragedy*, is a fundamentally Greek conviction.

That Napoleon was a man of ancient sensibility—that alone makes him a measure of value for Nietzsche, a counterweight, a judge of all modern culture. "Everything that we now call culture, education, civilization, will one day have to appear before the infallible judge Dionysus,"[31] proclaims *The Birth of Tragedy;* for the *Zarathustra* period the idea of the overman is such an image of judgment. But among all historical approximations to the overman-Dionysian form of human existence, Nietzsche seems to think that Napoleon came closest to being identical with a judging "measure of things." His existence cannot be evaluated and measured by the moral standards of the moderns (that was also Goethe's opinion when he said to Riemer in 1807 that extraordinary people such as Napoleon stepped out of morality, and that in the end they acted like physical elemental causes, like fire and water);[32] rather a nature such as his evaluates and measures all other existences through their mere being, in the same way the early Hellenic philosopher whom Nietzsche most revered thought that fire *judges* things.[33] "The revolution," a passage in the late Notebooks reads, "made Napoleon possible: that is its justification. One would have to wish for the anarchic collapse of our entire civilization for a similar reward. Napoleon made nationalism possible: that is its exculpation."[34] In Nietzsche's view, Napoleon placed a new secular weight in the balance of the centuries: after Napoleon, through him there is a new valuation of life, or rather the old one, the ancient one has had its validity restored. A new epoch in world history begins with him, the events of coming centuries will gravitate around his granite core, Europe's fate will be nourished by his own. These notions and their historical consequences were not unknown even to Napoleon's contemporaries; they are hyperbolically concentrated in Hegel's dictum, after Jena: "I have seen the world soul on horseback!"[35] For Nietzsche such a concentration is more than hyperbole: Napoleon, that "ens realissimum," as he likes to call him in a phrase borrowed from Spinoza, *was* for him the incarnation of the fate of the European world.

"We owe it to Napoleon," *The Gay Science* says,

> and not at all to the French Revolution . . . that several belligerent centuries will now follow on each other that have no equal in history, in short, that we have entered into the classical age of war, of both intellectual and traditional war on the largest scale (war of resources, of talents, of discipline). . . . For the national movement out of which this glorification of war is growing is only the aftershock against Napoleon and would not be present without Napoleon. Thus one day he will receive credit for the fact that *man* in Europe has again become ruler over the merchant and philistine; perhaps even over "woman," who has been cosseted by Christianity and the enthusiastic spirit of the eighteenth century and even more by "modern ideas." Napoleon, who saw in modern ideas and particularly in civilization something like a personal enemy, and by this hostility proved himself to be one of the greatest among those who have continued the Renaissance: he brought an entire element of the essence of antiquity, perhaps the most decisive one, the element of granite, to the surface again. And who knows whether this element of antiquity will not finally become master of the national movement and thereby come to inherit Napoleon's legacy in an *affirmative* sense—as the one who wanted a United Europe, as we know, and that it should be the *ruler of the earth.*[36]

(This "personal hostility" of Napoleon toward civilization, an opposition that Nietzsche here sees as the actual greatness of his hero, is still clearly echoed in a paralipomenon to the same work: "Basically all civilizations have the same deep fear of the 'great man' that the Chinese alone have admitted to themselves in their saying: 'The great man is a public misfortune.' Basically all institutions are organized so that he arises as infrequently and under circumstances that are as unfavorable as possible.")[37]

All of these elements of "Napoleonic antiquity"—one sees to what degree they are also elements of the new Zarathustra ideal: here, before *Zarathustra,* Napoleon's status as a precursor is already clearly delineated as that of an ancient Baptist before the coming overman and divine man. "To inherit and continue Napoleon's legacy in an *affirmative* sense," to say Yes to everything that was decisive, that was granite, ancient in Napoleon, which did not achieve its final affirmative perfection itself—just such an ambition slumbers in the phantasmagoria of *Zarathustra.* The United Europe as ruler of the earth stands only as the modern disguise, as the political expression for the ancient Greek ecumene, for the renewal of the world-uniting Hellenic spirit.

Napoleon's Roman Caesarism was itself no more than such a political symbol for the longing for an even deeper, a spiritual *new world unity.* From out of Hellenic antiquity extended the last connection that still linked the peoples of post-antiquity to an ecumenical community: the Christian, "Catholic" community, whose political expression had been the Holy Roman Empire of the German Nation. The Reformation destroyed this last Hellenic unity, the revolution finally did away with its petrified political symbol. With the ancient inheritance of his being, Napoleon once more raised the possibility of an ancient foundation (just as, significantly, Goethe and Hölderlin at the same fateful moment made their way through the rubble of a Christian millennium to the same ancient granite)—and in Nietzsche's view of the world, oriented as it was to antiquity, the tragic German sin was to have turned Napoleon's existence into a magnificent "In Vain," in the same way that "Goethe became an incident without consequence in the history of the Germans"[38] (*Human*), a "mere incident, a beautiful In Vain"[39] (*Twilight of the Idols*). Here one of the deepest roots of Nietzsche's passionate hatred of the Germans is laid bare, a tragically aristocratic, thoroughly German hatred, which may be compared psychologically, and more than psychologically, only with the laments and indictments of Hyperion and, like these, stems from the most devout reverence for German possibilities and futures. That the Germans suffocated the Greek spirit in themselves, the Germans, in whom something sleeps that *could* be Hellenic—that is the lament that both make about the German "reality." And a symbol of this deep culpability toward themselves—the true original sin of the German character—is, for Nietzsche, the behavior of the Germans toward Napoleon in that fateful moment when they, among all the peoples of Europe, who were the only one that was ecumenically worldly, universal in Goethe's sense, ancient in Hölderlin's, chose and opted for egotistical narrowness, for a minor Only-Germanness, for "nationalism." All of this rumbles angrily in the indictments of *Ecce homo:* "When a *force majeure* of genius and will became visible on the bridge between two centuries of *décadence,* one strong enough to create out of Europe a unity, a political *and economic* unity, for the purpose of ruling the earth, the Germans, with their 'wars of independence,' robbed Europe of its meaning, the miraculous meaning in the existence of Napoleon—they thus have everything that came thereafter, everything that we have today, on their conscience, this *most anti-cultural* sickness and unreason that there is—nationalism—this *névrose nationale* which afflicts Europe, this perpetuation of Europe's division into minor states, its *minor* politics: the Germans robbed Europe itself of its meaning, of its *reason*—they led it into a dead-end.—Does anyone apart from me know a way out of this dead-end? A task great enough to *unite* the peoples again? . . ."[40]

For *unity,* this most Greek idea, a renewed unity was Napoleon's great mission, in Nietzsche's eyes. He was the mightiest one among the "Anti-Alexanders," whose necessity is mentioned in "Richard Wagner in Bayreuth": Anti-Alexanders who "have the greatest power to pull together and unify . . . to protect the fabric from being blown apart. Not to undo the Gordian knot of Greek culture, as Alexander did, so that its ends flutter in all directions of the world, but *to tie it after it had been undone*—that is now the task."[41] Wagner seemed at that time to be such an Anti-Alexander; in *Ecce homo,* where Nietzsche is conscious of having expressed about himself what he imagined in his earlier blind gratitude he was saying about Wagner—in *Ecce homo* Nietzsche feels alone in his role as such an Anti-Alexander, alone in his knowledge of the only way out of the dead-end, his knowledge of the task, enormous enough, of *unifying* peoples again. Here, too, Nietzsche is an heir of the Napoleonic idea, as a "simplifier of the world,"[42] as he calls Wagner in the early work while unknowingly already meaning himself. The great simplifier of the world—its redeemer through re-antiquating, neo-Hellenization: that is how Napoleon stood in Nietzsche's stylizing eyes; that is how he, as a tragic predecessor, entered into his historical worldview; that is how he helped in forming the traits of Zarathustra and his overman. Without Napoleon, no Zarathustra; without this "ens realissimum," no overman.

Nietzsche reveals how deeply he delighted in contemplating the great image of Napoleon when he, the cunning lover of all indirection and masks, interprets Goethe's relationship to the phenomenon of Napoleon. The audience in Erfurt in 1808 always remained for Nietzsche one of the most fascinating, symbol-laden moments of world intellectual history; just as for the philosophically inclined observer, those rare symbolic meetings of two intellectual realms in the person of great representatives have always presented a magic magnet for synthetic speculations—Alexander and the Cynic philosopher,[43] Jesus before Pontius Pilate, Savonarola and Lorenzo de' Medici, Luther before Charles V, Bach with Frederick the Great, Wagner and the romantically morbid German King.[44] If after that meeting (about which, as we know, Goethe liked to maintain a significant silence) he himself "freely admitted that nothing could happen to him in his life that would be greater or more pleasing than to stand before the French Emperor and, moreover, in such a way"[45] (to Cotta, 1808), then Nietzsche stylized this feeling into the single most decisive moment in Goethe's life, into the confession of the greatest symbolic instant of his existence. He sees in Goethe's experience of Napoleon—which, in accordance with Nietzsche's Greek perspective, must have been concentrated most movingly in the physical meeting of 1808, as that was indeed most appropriate to Goethe's visual nature—he actually sees a transforming experience of the greatest German: "The event that caused Goethe to *rethink* his *Faust,* indeed the entire problem 'man,' was the appearance of Napoleon,"[46] he writes in *Beyond.* Just as Goethe's existence is for Nietzsche a justification of the German character, the apology and theodicy of German misdeeds, so too the scene "Goethe before Napoleon" once more turns into a justification of the Germans before the example of the ancients, before Napoleon's man-measuring eye. "We should understand," he says in *Beyond* with characteristic impatience, "we should finally understand fully Napoleon's amazement when he laid eyes on Goethe: it reveals what people had thought for centuries about the 'German spirit.' 'Voilà un homme!'—that meant: 'But this is a man! And I had expected only a German!'"[47]—The deepest gratitude Nietzsche felt for Goethe is nourished by this source: Goethe, by physically legitimating himself at Napoleon's first glance as a nature, simultaneously made the German essence legitimate again before the tribunal of antiquity, he proved by his very existence that there was truly, in Nietzsche's words, something in the Germans that could be Hellenic. "Voilà un homme"—that meant an anti-Christian, an Hellenic "Ecce homo"; that meant to say: finally a man like me, a man of ancient measure. Nietzsche read into that hour in Erfurt something like an encounter of two brothers who recognize each other: the moment when he speaks most reverentially, most gratefully of Goethe is when he stylizes him as the utterly unrecognizable German half-brother of Napoleon—it is the greatest thing he can say about Goethe. Like Napoleon, Goethe is not a national, but rather an ecumenical event, like him he is a *return* to nature understood as the ancients did; like Napoleon, he is a man of ancient wholeness, of the most intensive reality, like him he is a Hellenic, positive fatalist; and like Napoleon, Goethe, too, is a mask of the great god, a mask of Dionysus.

Here is *Twilight of the Idols:*

> Goethe—not a German event, but rather a European one: a magnificent attempt to overcome the eighteenth century through a return to nature, through a resurgence of the naturalness of the Renaissance. . . . What he wanted was totality; he fought against the disaggregation of the person into the components of reason, sensuality, feeling, will . . . he disciplined himself to wholeness, he *created* himself. Goethe was, in the midst of an age that was ill-disposed toward reality, a convinced realist: he said Yes to everything that was akin to him in that regard—*he had no greater experience than that of the "ens realissimum" called Napoleon.* Goethe conceived of a strong . . . man who would dare to grant himself the full wealth of naturalness . . . because he would know how to use profitably what would destroy an average nature; a man to whom nothing would be forbidden except for *weakness* . . . such a liberated spirit stands with his joyful and trusting fatalism in the middle of the universe in the belief that only the individual is objectionable, that within totality everything is redeemed and affirmed—he no longer says no. But such a belief is the highest of all possible beliefs: I christened it with the name of Dionysus.[48]

Here Napoleonic and Goethean traits are unmistakably fused into an image of an ancient ideal type in which Heraclitean philosophy and a Dionysian heightening of life are unified: the two greatest instances of modern humanity and the two most powerful guiding idols of Nietzschean Hellenism in a twofold marriage—a genuinely Nietzschean synthesis that found its poetic form in *Zarathustra.* Indeed, if the image of Goethe—as in the passage from *The Twilight of the Idols*—is visibly stylized toward a realistic antiquity, toward activity, toward the Napoleonic realm, is made to approximate a demigod, then Nietzsche lets Napoleon, as if in compensation, merge into Goethe's most proper sphere by placing the classical author of Caesarean memorabilia next to Eckermann's self-portraitist. In his notes on the *Transvaluation,* he names "the two good books that will survive this century, more accurately: whose branches will reach beyond this century as trees that do not have their roots in it"[49] as being: the *Mémorial de Sainte-Hélène* and Goethe's *Conversations with Eckermann.*

Indeed, Napoleon's writings had a strong influence on the formation and even on the articulation of Nietzsche's own intellectual world, just as the most powerful effect that Goethe had on him did not come from the poet but from the sage, the image of the ancient philosopher in the conversations with Eckermann. It even seems that one can detect direct borrowings here and there in his writings. Thus, in the sections on the "basic problem 'man and woman'" in *Beyond,* which occasionally display a word-for-word agreement with comments by Napoleon ("a man who has depth, both to his mind and to his desires . . . can think about woman only in an *oriental* fashion . . . in this he has to adjust to the immense reason of Asia, its superiority of instinct, as the Greeks once did, those consummate heirs and pupils of Asia . . ."),[50] or in certain political judgments, distinctions, characterizations of peoples, for example about England or about the future of Russia. He is entirely Napoleonic in his estimation of Shakespeare, the "great barbarian,"[51] a "wild genius," against which "his artistic taste wrathfully defends the names of Molière, Corneille and Racine,"[52] whereas he thought that "Voltaire was the last great dramatist who tamed his own multifaceted soul, which could withstand the greatest tragic cataclysms, by submitting to Greek moderation."[53] Napoleon put it thus: "Shakespeare was forgotten even by his compatriots for two hundred years, and then Voltaire, in order to flatter the English, deigned to elevate him; and since then everyone reiterates that Shakespeare is the first dramatic poet in the world. I have read him; there is nothing in his oeuvre that approaches Corneille or Racine. It is not even possible to read his plays to the end without shrugging one's shoulders."[54] Napoleon's dictum—"One must be strong to be good"[55]—sounds like a motto for *On the Genealogy of Morals.* And the "synthesis of monster and overman,"[56] as Napoleon is called in the same book, seems to be borrowed directly from Napoleon himself: "A man such as I am is always either *un dio* or *un diavolo.*"[57]

The Notebooks of the final years are otherwise rich in excerpts of Napoleonic dicta and psychologica that were intended to have a place in his major work. But one sentence that Nietzsche wrote out verbatim and without translating it sounds more ancient, more Greek than all the others, and which Nietzsche, in the pride of those last years, the pride of Zarathustra submitting to Empedocles's fate, was happy to take up symbolically: "J'ai refermé le gouffre anarchique et débrouillé le chaos. J'ai ennobli les peuples."[58] Only Zarathustra knows, like Napoleon, a retreat out of the dead-end of "European nihilism," out of the chaos of the anarchic "Last Man"—"No herdsman and One herd"—knows the task, great enough to ennoble peoples again by *reunifying* them. ("After the recuperation of Zarathustra there stands Caesar,"[59] reads a mystical abbreviation in the *Zarathustra* Notebooks.) Out of his proud, ancient phrase "*amor fati*—that is my innermost nature"[60] we hear something like the echo of Napoleon's laconic: "I was a fatalist from the start";[61] and the prevailing mood of the retrospective *Ecce homo,* with its Promethean hubris, sounds even darker in the words of the Corsican Prometheus chained to his rock: "All in all—what a ballad my life was."[62]

11

Jest, Cunning, and Vengeance

. . . You should deliver your tale drolly.
—Goethe, *Hans Sachs's Political Mission*

. . . There is hardly a page in this thoroughly ambiguous life that is so serious as to preclude a passage devoted to jest . . .
—Schopenhauer, preface to *The World as Will and Representation*

The mystical and didactic inheritances within German literature are the two strongest and oldest forces of continuity that have exerted an uninterrupted influence since its old-High-German beginnings. Initially, they were fused together; then they diverged, the former culminating, before Luther, in the works of Eckhart,[1] Suso,[2] and Tauler,[3] and in the spiritual poetry of the hymns; the latter, with roots in ancient runes, riddles, and rhymes, blossoms in an abundance of popular verse. Both also merge to nourish here and there a work of a higher order, such as Wolfram's *Parzival,* or the religious plays about the Passion of the Lord and the Death of Man. The great narrows through which the river of the Reformation passes, which is where our tradition properly speaking begins, clearly demonstrates the force of the two basic currents: the mystical linguistic power that gave us the German of the Bible and the church song, and the didactic one that is expressed in the poetry of Hans Sachs[4] and the satirists; and thus the two atavistic types to whose legacy all of our poetry and elevated prose can in some fashion, if not exclusively, be genealogically traced.

As a stylist, Nietzsche, like Goethe, demonstrates an adherence to both ancestral types that is clearly visible in the form of his language; even if, also like Goethe, it is in his masterpiece that both currents achieve a new, and in both cases extremely German and unique, combination and fusion that is audacious in every respect. The language of *Zarathustra* is a great-grandchild within the spiritual bloodline that runs from the mystics through the language of the Bible; but the worldly and didactic pleasure in rhyme and riddles from the tradition of Hans Sachs, the old *Eulenspiegel* element of the German language, is no less alive in Nietzsche's predilection for the coarse German *Knittelvers,*[5] the old "Reformation" verses with didactic, comic, and punitive intent. It is significant that Nietzsche's work, like Goethe's, comes into closest contact with folk tradition at its highest and most rigorous consummation and again in the carefree formlessness of the naïve moment, which is to say, at both of its extremes; what lies between these two poles is, in both instances, the most "un-German" part: Nietzsche's aphorisms and expository prose are far more indebted to the Latin, and particularly the French, linguistic universe than to the German one, just as Goethe's narrative and didactic prose never denies nor wants to deny its essentially French paternity.

The course of the two "reformatory" traditions obviously runs through Goethe toward Nietzsche himself; indeed, the Hans Sachs microcosm of his aphoristic wisdom betrays the Goethean intermediary stage even more clearly that the language of *Zarathustra,* which Nietzsche himself thought represented the third major juncture in the German language after Luther and Goethe. Just as Goethe's aphoristic sayings in verse represent a more developed, more humanized Hans Sachs–world (whereby the name of Hans Sachs is also representative for many smaller and related folk figures), so, too, the province of German *Knittelvers* in Nietzsche's expansive linguistic realm is colonized by passing through Goethe's territory. Even down to their particular details, Nietzsche's *Knittelvers* and his satiric rhymes are a more or less conscious continuation of Goethe's technique of old German verse, but a continuation that is more shrill, more nervously witty, Heinesque, indeed it even veers over into a consciously parodic, distorted, grimacing mode—perhaps the clearest example on a small scale of the tendency toward the decomposition of style in Nietzsche's development as a writer.

There is evidence of this conscious reliance on Goethe's use of old German verse forms in the Goethean title of his *Singspiel*[6] "Jest, Cunning and Revenge," which Nietzsche gave to the verse prologue "in German Rhymes" to *The Gay Science.* The rhymed verses of the prologue, written one year before *Zarathustra,* constitute, with a few other additions from the Notebooks, what one might call a positive parody of Goethe. The most famous of these verses are linguistically the most obviously indebted to Goethe's model. The magnificent "Ecce homo," with its eruptive "Yes! I know whence I came!" is an entirely Goethean form ("Yes! I consider it an honor, That I continue to travel alone!"[7] "Yes! Who doesn't know of your admiration! You build monuments to yourselves, not to him").[8] Other verses of the "Prologue" begin: "Yes! Sometimes I make ice . . ."[9] "Yes! my happiness—wants to make others happy."[10] Goethe's "Step Verse," for instance, proves to be "pre-Nietzschean" in rhythm and imagery:

They have to gripe here and there
And pester from the outer fringe,

Involving me in petty skirmishes,
But you do harm to your own reputation:
By staying on the lower step,
Which I've already left behind![11]

That is of the same type as Nietzsche's maxims "Invitation,"[12] "Dialogue,"[13] "Ecce homo,"[14] "End Rhyme,"[15] and "To the Disciples of Darwin"; and it is simultaneously the model for "My Severity."[16] Nietzsche's "Roman Sigh": "Only German! Not Teutonic! That is the modern German way! . . ."[17] is an imitation of Goethe's "To the T . . . and G . . .": "Accursed people! You are hardly free . . ."[18] And "The Word," for example, is entirely beholden to Goethe's verse poems in the manner of Hans Sachs:

I mean well to the living word:
It gambols about so cheerfully . . .
But the word remains a delicate creature,
Quickly ill and just as quickly recovered,
If you want to preserve its little life
You have to grasp it with a light and delicate touch,
And not clench and touch it roughly,
It will often die from harsh glances alone—
And then lies there, so misshapen,
So soulless, so destitute and cold,
Its little corpse terribly transformed,
Mishandled by death and dying . . .[19]

And certain kinds of folksy German earthiness, which Goethe liked to borrow from the German of the Reformation period and which sound quite forced and questionable in Nietzsche's mouth, are clearly adopted solely for the sake of their traditional rhyme.

The greatest refinement that German rhymed verse undergoes at the hands of Goethe is displayed by the *Westöstlicher Divan:* here, partly using the archaizing (*Knittelvers*) technique of rhyme, a balance is achieved between wisdom and poetry, between exuberance and reflection, between raillery and rapture, that mysterious double harmony of mystical didacticism that is entirely singular in German poetry. Out of the most intimate elective affinity, Nietzsche also raised his aphoristic verse up to such knowing lyricism, to such ecstatic aphoristic wisdom, here, too, gratefully building upon Goethe's form and technique. The aphoristic poem "To Hafis," for instance, exhibits this west-eastern type in Nietzsche (renewing the sphere of the *Divan* even in his choice of subject):

. . . You are everything and nothing, you are cup and wine,
Your are phoenix, mountain and mouse,
You fall eternally into yourself,
You fly forever out of yourself—
You are the absorption of all heights,
You are the illusion of all depths,
You are the intoxication of all those intoxicated
—Why, why *to you*—wine?[20]

Or the related "The Kingfisher":

Thus a woman spoke demurely
To me in the morning sun:
"If you are so blissful in sobriety,
How blissful will you be—intoxicated!"[21]

Nietzsche's most perfect verses are perhaps those that are like the *Divan* in this way: "Preordained to the Starry Path . . .,"[22] "Whoever has much to proclaim one day . . .,"[23] "To New Seas,"[24] "All Eternal Wellsprings Spring Forth Eternally,"[25] "Pine Tree and Lightning;"[26] the final strophe of the "Music of the South"; and above all the poem "Ecce homo": "Yes! I know whence I came! . . ."[27] which belongs entirely to the mystically didactic genre, to which also the most profound poem in the *Divan* belongs, "Sacred Longing": "Tell it to No One, Only to the Wise . . ."[28] Even technical details are inspired by the *Divan,* such as the rich rhyme scheme.

The further developments Nietzsche imports into Goethe's technique of rhymed verse are at the same time (as one would hardly expect otherwise) elements of decomposition, a decomposition that yields a style that is more colorful, ambiguously witty, overrefined, and occasionally striving ineffectually for effect. What in Goethe still belongs to the Hans Sachs of the Reformation is in Nietzsche already a Wagnerian Sachs (occasionally even Beckmesserish);[29] what is purified folksiness in Goethe is parodistically popular in Nietzsche; what is humorous there becomes burlesque here, what is cheerfully mocking there, here becomes ironically malicious; intelligence becomes cleverness, brilliance becomes glaring, ambiguity becomes antithetical; laughter turns into a guffaw, movement into nervousness, superiority into the consciousness of superiority; everything becomes more dazzling, more effective, more pointed, more colorful, and more clever—everything less simple, less German, less Goethean. A process of disintegration takes place, comparable to what happens to the romantic element (more precisely to the folksier side of the romantic character) in and through Heine: a disintegration into parody, as parody. An example of this conscious tendency toward parody is the introductory verse "To Goethe" to the "Songs of Prince Vogelfrei" ("Prince Outlaw"), in the appendix to *The Gay Science:*

> The indestructible
> is but your invention.
> God, the ineluctable,
> poetic pretension . . .
>
> . . . The imperious play of the world,
> Mixes being and appearance—
> The eternally foolish
> Mixes *us*—in, too![30]

Typical of Nietzsche's rhymed verse, here as elsewhere, is the entirely un-Goethean inclination toward a surprise conclusion (which was also so peculiar to his prose rhythm), which is concretely expressed by his beloved hyphen before the last word of the last rhymed verse: "Forever below is—hell!"[31] "You are lost, you believe—to danger."[32] "Like everyone who once wore chains he hears everywhere—the clanking of chains."[33] "All meadows curse the sun; to them, the value of trees is—shade!"[34] "Whoever intends to ignite lightning one day, Must long be—a cloud."[35] This tendency toward "Latinate" antithesis, which is so much more suited to French prose aphorisms or to imitations of the classical distich than to the more guileless rhymed verse of the German *Knittelvers,* becomes characteristic—an inclination that not infrequently makes Nietzsche's rhymes strangely similar to certain verses of Conrad Ferdinand Meyer's antithetical poetry:

> . . . His superhappiness became uncomfortable for him,
> His superlight pursues your darkness.[36]
>
> . . . I cannot be my own interpreter.
> Yet whoever climbs on his own path
> Also carries my image up to a brighter light.[37]
>
> Predetermined to a starry path
> What do you, star, care about the dark?
> Roll blissfully on through this time!
> Its misery is foreign to you and far! . . . [38]
>
> No retreat? And no advance?
> And no path even for the chamois?
> . . . Ground five feet wide, a red dawn,
> And *below* me—world, man, and death![39]

Whoever will have much to proclaim one day,
Must long remain silent unto himself . . . [40]

The most perfect type here as well, once again, is the wonderful "Ecce homo": "Yes! I know from whence I come! . . ." next to the mystical "Sils-Maria," which hovers on the border to the poetry of the *Divan:*

Here I sat, waiting and waiting—yet for nothing,
Beyond Good and Evil, now enjoying
The light, now the shade, entirely play alone
Entirely sea, entirely midday, entirely time without goal.

Then suddenly, friend! One became Two—
And Zarathustra passed by me . . . [41]

In addition, there is an entire series of characteristic tics that overburden Nietzsche's late prose with so many dangerous little pleasures. There is the travesty of familiar quotations and idioms:

Whoever loves his "God," chastises him.[42]

His head went to hell—no! no! to woman![43]

Even the purest holiness
Does not get the worm.[44]

There is the predilection for playing with sound associations, "I rolled myself, round rolling barrel,"[45] "Minerva's Darling Ow—ow—owl."[46] "The A and O of my wisdom . . . only the eternal Hey! and Oh! . . ."[47] There is the interjection of foreign words and phrases into lines of verse: " . . . Unenthusiastic, unjovial, indestructibly mediocre, *Sans génie et sans esprit!*"[48] "*O peuple des meilleurs Tartuffes,* I will be true to you, certainly!"[49] " . . . *amor dei,* blessed through reason . . ."[50] "To place Darwin next to Goethe means: *lèse majesté—majestatem Genii!*"[51] "He writes and writes his unbear-Able nonsense, As if the rule were *primum scribere, Deinde philosophari,*"[52] an Alexandrianism that entered into Nietzsche's later prose especially, a style that even tore apart one of his most beautiful purely lyrical strophes—one thinks of the almost incomprehensible frivolity that tarnishes the third strophe of the Venetian song "My Happiness" with a witty Gallicism:

You severe tower, with what lion's strength
Did you rise up here, victorious, with ease!
You send out over the square a deep sound—
In French would you be its *accent aigu?*[53]

All of these elements of a colorfully iridescent decomposition visibly enter into his more serious poetry; the two separated species in Nietzsche's "motto": "A song is 'words as music' . . . an aphorism is 'sense without song'—may I bring to you something of both?"[54]—fuse together to form that dangerous Perhaps, the philosopher of which Nietzsche proclaims himself to be and which he loved so well even as a poet ("What a pity that I did not dare to say what I had to say at the time as a poet—I might have been able to do it").[55] It is no coincidence, but rather the most vital expression of his nature, which was born under the sign of Libra, that Nietzsche's most perfect poems are precisely those that incorporated the aphoristic element of "Jest, Cunning and Revenge"—in which irony, the pleasure in masks, and a self-hating, self-overcoming didactically break or threaten to burst their lyricism; and the most perfect of his proverbs are those that, like the hermaphroditic constructions of the highest sphere of the *Divan,* seem to approach the lyricism of a mystical secret doctrine. "Whenever I have a few minutes to think about whatever I want," he wrote to his mother and sister during his last year at Pforta, "I look for words to a melody I have and a melody to words I have, and what I have in both together is not right, even though they came from *one* soul. But that is my lot!"[56] Nietzsche never expressed anything more intuitively definitive about himself in his late, probing self-analyses than what the pupil here revealed, almost presciently, about the lot of a "new soul." Nietzsche's most genuine constructions hover between word and melody, between singing and speaking, between sense without song and words as music, suspended in a sphere of supreme, unending tension and an eternal balance of illusion, remaining all the while conscious of this, their fate, their "Centaur" fate (as he put it himself).[57] The form of Nietzsche's aphorisms, his entirely individual development of the *Knittelvers* tradition from the Reformation through Goethe, is only *one* reflection of this constant search for the Other that is Nietzsche's inner fate, the search for a melody to words, for words to a melody.

And just as Nietzsche dared to undertake the magnificent experiment in *Zarathustra* of merging *for once* sense without song and words as music, allowing that which "came from *one* soul" to become one again in the work, he also made a similar attempt within the narrower precinct of his aphoristic technique to create his own new form, which could resolve within itself the inner dualism of meaning and song. Characteristically enough, it is precisely while writing *Zarathustra* that it occurs to Nietzsche to undertake this renewal of aphoristic wisdom. As if this, too, were a symptom of the most extreme de-Germanization and of the most impatient will to Greece that mark his final years of disintegration, he now, from 1882 on, tosses aside the aphoristic form he had so lovingly cultivated in the tradition of Hans Sachs and Goethe as if it had become an empty vessel, like one of his many "snakeskins"; and the aphoristic form he created from then on displays, insofar as it was not incorporated into *Zarathustra,* a completely different, new character, one entirely removed from any German tradition. These are the "Speeches, Parables and Images" from the years 1882 to 1888, which one finds under "Poetry" as fragments to the "Dionysus Dithyrambs." Formally they are indeed fragments, unfinished pieces of Dionysian character, obviously influenced by Pindar's hymns, as are the great "Dionysus Dithyrambs" from the year 1888. But at the same time, they form self-contained individual aphorisms, aphoristic dithyrambs, so to speak, which have unmistakably assumed the inheritance of "Jest, Cunning and Vengeance" and are the successors of Nietzsche's earlier German *Knittelvers* in a more Greek climate. All of the elements of Hans Sachs's aphoristic style are reunited here, but in a new, more intimate fusion, which from the start "brings something from both," as it were, namely by synthetically dissolving the opposition between song and sense. At once more concise and "less quantifiable" than those cozy rhymed sayings; at once less German and more Nietzschean; in type a "final form," like Hölderlin's latest hymns; the expression of an inner tension that, compelled by an immoderate urge toward self-expression, inexorably verges on the brink of nonsensical babble. It is no accident that the fatalistic element in these adages seems so eerie; they are the foam-flecked waves of a stream that is more and more unmistakably rushing toward a cascade roaring in the distance, being sucked into a fate in which willing and being willed are one and which already recognize each other as one:

THE SPHINX

Here you sit, unrelenting
Like my curiosity,
Which forced me to you:
So be it, Sphinx,
I ask questions, like you;
This abyss is common to us both—
It is possible that we speak with the same mouth![58]

What is happening? is the ocean receding?
No, my land is growing!
A new fire is lifting it up![59]

Such is now my will:
And since it has been my will
Everything occurs according to my wishes—
This was my final wisdom:

I willed that which I must do:
Thus I subordinated every "necessity" . . .
Ever since there is no "necessity" for me . . . [60]

But the antithetical technique familiar from the rhymed proverbs is also otherwise present:

They created their God from nothing:
It's no surprise that he means nothing to them anymore.[61]

And only when I am a burden to *myself*,
Do I find all of you insupportable![62]

All of you who despair! How much rage
Do you cause those who observe you![63]

We are certain of his death:
Why wouldn't we want to be cheerful?[64]

This alone liberates us from all suffering
(—choose now!):
A quick death
Or a long love.[65]

The pointed concluding surprises are there, as in the earlier rhymed verses:

"Love thine enemy,
Let your robber rob you":
Woman hears—and obeys.[66]

The most beautiful body—merely a veil
Which modestly conceals—something more beautiful still.[67]

The earlier games with sounds and associations—occasionally almost reaching the level of an unintentional caricature of Wagner's style:

I am someone to whom people swear oaths:
Swear that to me![68]

What lives around you
Soon comes to live within you:
From that comes habit.
It is what we're grow accustomed to
That turns into our customs.[69]

Milk flows
In her soul; but beware!

Her mind is milky.[70]

One runs to ruin
If one always rushes.[71]

And here, as well, all of the idiosyncrasies of Nietzsche's late prose: the inclination to underline and emphasize individual words, the preference for the interrogative form, for the willful transformation and coinage of words, for parodistic quotation:

When money jumps into the pot,
The soul always jumps in right after![72]

A wolf . . . said: "You howl even better than we wolves."[73]

Where there is danger . . . I grow out of the earth"[74] (no doubt a play on Hölderlin's "But where there is danger, there salvation grows, too").

I want to pave the way to my hell with good inventions.[75]

Thus Nietzsche's latest aphoristic form proves to be capacious enough to absorb all the possible peculiarities of his prose without running the risk of being broken apart or undermined like the more traditionally bound verse form, because it arose out of a single, unified rhythm from the beginning. But, as if even this more unified linguistic type still seemed too painfully dualistic to Nietzsche, as if he still felt the aphoristic quality of its form to be a vague reproach, a muted complaint, he forced even this more Greek, unrhymed, de-Germanicized high aphoristic form, significantly, into *song*, as he in the end forced everything in himself toward the solace and redemption of song—"that I called upon you to sing, my soul, behold, that was my last"—and thus the most moving, the most perfect aphorisms of this last type—the dithyrambic fragment—are those that "hover, always softly knocking"[76] at the door of song. Not yet song, but already beyond speech, not yet mysticism, but already beyond "knowledge," a reflection of Nietzsche's twilight soul, a touching and dangerous "Perhaps." Thus, for example, the aphorism "Industry and Genius" that ends in Greek lyricism:

I am envious of the industry in the industrious:
Bright as gold and constant the day flows up to him
Bright as gold and constant back
Down into the dark sea—
And around his bed blossoms
Relaxing forgetfulness.[77]

So, too, "the iron silence," with the two-facedness of its refrain, a perfect symbol:

Five ears—and no sound therein!
The world became mute . . .
I listened with the ear of my *curiosity:*
Five times I threw the rod over my shoulder
Five times I pulled up no fish.
I asked—no answer swam into my net . . .
I listened with the ear of my *love*—[78]

Or, finally, the most melancholy evening aphorism of "The Loneliest Man" full of uncomplaining questions:

Now, as the day
Has become tired of day, and the streams of all longing
Splash with new consolation
And all the skies, caught up in nets of fine-spun gold,
Call out to everyone who is tired: "Rest now!"
Why do you not rest, you dark heart,
What impels you on to foot-sore flight . . .
Whom are you awaiting?[79]

Here Nietzsche, already visibly, willingly abandons his final aphoristic form to song, to the dithyrambic evening bliss of the latest Nietzsche, which radiated perhaps most beautifully in the three-part Dionysus dithyramb "The Sun Sets," still aphorism but simultaneously pure song, in a strange unity for which we know only the name "Greek," dictum *and* song, wisdom *and* music:

Cheerfulness, golden one, come!
You, the most secret,
Sweetest foretaste of death!
—Did I travel too quickly down my path?
Only now, when my feet became tired,
Did your glance finally catch up with me,
Did your *happiness* finally catch up with me.

. . . *Seventh* Solitude!
Never have I felt
Sweet certainty closer to me,
The sun's rays on me warmer.
—Does the ice of my peaks not still glow?
Silvery, light, a fish
My boat now swims out . . .[80]

12
Anecdote

History is one great anecdote. An anecdote is a historical element, a historical molecule. . . . A master of anecdote has to know how to turn everything into an anecdote.[1]
—Novalis

"Only what is personal is forever irrefutable. It is possible to render the image of a person with three anecdotes; I try to extract three anecdotes out of every system and discard the rest."[2]

Thus Nietzsche wrote in a later preface to the work that remained a fragment, the "Philosophy in the Tragic Age of the Greeks." Just as he lends poetic amplifications of his own philosophical potential to the philosophers in this fragment, so, too, do these sentences from the preface offer the aphoristically concentrated kernel of his philosophical method. Out of three anecdotes an image, out of three anecdotes a system—and discard the rest: that is indeed a valid formula for Nietzsche's procedure of imagistic thinking, his philosophical rhythm.

Nietzsche was, as were few other great figures in so pronounced a way, a thoroughly "anecdotal nature." For such a nature it is simultaneously a gift and a limitation that, in order to gain mastery over a phenomenon, he does not simplify it by submitting it to patient organization and by constructing an architectonic system, but rather by experiencing it most clearly in the heat of the moment, by imagining it in the form of the absolutely unique instant. It is the gift and limitation of the romantic, of extreme romantic individualism. Novalis, Friedrich Schlegel, and Jean Paul are, in three different refractions, the great representatives of the romantic mastery of anecdote. And at the outermost boundaries of romanticism, where it engages in a bitter conflict with one of its most hostile intellectual principles, both conquered and unconquerable, namely, in Heine, Hebbel, and Nietzsche, the fundamentally anecdotal character of all romanticization shows forth a second time. Indeed, it emerges all the more distinctly at precisely the point where romanticism struggles with skepticism, enthusiasm battles cynicism, where extreme individualism triumphs, as it were, in both of its guises: that is where anecdote (in its most intensive sense) becomes the legitimate form, even the necessary and unavoidable expression, the only one that can simultaneously contain both tendencies. Forms such as *Atta Troll* or *Germany, A Winter's Fairy Tale,* such as Flaubert's *The Temptation of St. Anthony,* and above all *Bouvard and Pécuchet* indicate the possibilities of this anecdotal type. (An example of a narrower sphere, but of a very pure type, is offered by the person and art of Theodor Fontane,[3] the classical master of the anecdote, whose skepticism does not disavow the late-romantic roots of his ballads.) But at this juncture, at the outermost border of the old romantic land, is where the pyramid of Nietzsche's life's work rises up, occupying equal parts of territory on either side of the divide.

Nietzsche's entire technique, so much is evident, consists in implementing the romantic mastery of anecdote that Novalis extolled. For Nietzsche, too, the anecdote is an element and molecule of both his thought and his style. To understand his use of aphorism as a form and aid born of need, made necessary by his illness and his peripatetic life, could lead only to a complete misperception of the contours of his mind. Rather, it is the authentic form of his soul, as is the sibylline fragment to Novalis,[4] the *Streckvers* to Jean Paul,[5] the anecdotal symbol in Hebbel's diaries. Its paternal origins, so to speak, in the skepticism of the French aphoristic tradition essentially influence only its form; what is decisive is the maternal inheritance of romanticism. (Here, too, Nietzsche's warning from the Notebooks to the *Zarathustra* period is valid: "You shall show me respect for the maternal: the father is always merely an accident.")[6] And if it is true, as those who argue that it was a form born of need would have it, that a note of resignation shines through his aphorisms, then it is one that is anchored much more deeply than in specific external limitations and constraints; it would stem instead from the primal feeling arising from sibylline knowledge that a fragment from the ruins of *The Will to Power* puts into words: one should not build when there is no more time—or, in the words of *The Case of Wagner:* "What today can be done well, done masterfully, is of necessity small. Here alone sincerity is still possible."[7] We should not view the earliest works, which seem to be composed more architectonically, as an exception or still less as an objection. For it is precisely these works in which the ambition to build is unmistakable, to compose symphonically in Schopenhauerian fashion, to erect soaring vaults, it is precisely these works that manifestly betray how constructed they are, how purposefully they are erected out of hundreds of individual intuitions and short, intersecting intellectual arcs, out of nothing but small, "sincere" perfections. They are mosaics, no doubt, and that they are is what constitutes the ineffable, shimmering, unsettling charm that is so peculiar to *The Birth of Tragedy,* "Schopenhauer as Educator," and "Richard Wagner in Bayreuth." If one really reads them with an eye toward strict intellectual architecture and logical progression, they seem almost embarrassing through their constant self-interruptions and pauses; but in reality one involuntarily reads them as if they were already the later books, which openly acknowledge their mosaic character, their technique of creating the whole out of individual fragments. And it is no different with the books from the last years that are not so obviously aphoristic: *Beyond, Genealogy, The Antichrist,* the polemics against Wagner, *Ecce homo;* their technique is one of virtuoso accretion, which is lent the illusion of structure, of composition, only through the skillful use of a leitmotivic return to certain concepts, through a spiral return to connecting ideas. Above all, however, *Zarathustra:* no structure, but rather a gigantic agglomerate, no architecture, but rather a series of dreams and ecstatic visions, no mountain massif rising up to a majestic peak, but rather a landscape of volcanic craters. And as with the whole, so too with its parts: one should try reading *Zarathustra* while paying attention to how many of its chapters are crystallized exclusively around an anecdotal moment, or rather build on top of it, as over a crypt. (Even their titles often demonstrate that.) The foreword, for instance, is entirely organized around the anecdote about the tightrope walker—an experience Nietzsche had as a boy on the market square of Naumburg—extending even to the adoption of its episodic origin. How many of the individual chapters are glorifications of an elevated moment, interpretations of an instant in time concentrated into a forceful image, into an anecdote with symbolic potential! Even Nietzsche's letters overflow with his pleasure in anecdote, in swift and salient comparisons, leitmotifs, and parodic quotations. And this predilection for the pointed moment, for the accumulation of small, individual tidbits follows him into the philological sphere: "Unfortunately, I have a predilection for the Parisian feuilleton, for Heine's *Reisebilder,* etc., and I prefer to eat a ragout than a roast beef,"[8] the young philologist coquettishly sighs in a letter to the wife of his teacher, Ritschl. And Ritschl himself thought that Nietzsche wrote even his philological treatises in an absurdly entertaining fashion, in the manner of a Parisian *romancier.*

But the strangest and yet most characteristic thing of all is that even his relationship to music, that most fluid and unanecdotal, because unintellectual, art, is marked by his predilection for the anecdotal emphasis on particularly beautiful passages, minor idiosyncrasies, and self-enclosed moments. Thus, when he says about Wagner, for example (who, as always, serves here as well as an unconscious allegory of himself) that he was admirable and charming only in the invention of the smallest things, in the poetic elaboration of details. He was, Nietzsche said, our greatest musical *miniaturist,* who forces an infinite amount of meaning and sweetness into the smallest space. "If I am to be believed, then one cannot obtain the highest notion of Wagner from what people like about him today . . . there is another Wagner, who sets aside little delicacies: he is our greatest musical melancholic, full of glances, tendernesses and words of comfort that no one anticipated before him. . . . A lexicon of Wagner's most intimate words, nothing but short pieces of five to fifteen bars, nothing but music that *no one knows*"[9]—or when he recommends assembling collections of pure melodies from Beethoven or Chopin. Even his way of experiencing music symbolically still reveals the cult of the heightened moment. *Human* describes the impression of Chopin's *Barcarole* thus: "Almost all circumstances and ways of life contain one blissful moment. Good artists know how to fish it out. Even life at the edge of the sea has such a moment, a life that is so monotonous, dirty, unhealthy and that takes place in the proximity of the noisiest and greediest riffraff. Chopin, in his *Barcarole,* made this blissful moment resonate in such a way that it could make even the gods want to spend long summer evenings lying in a skiff."[10] And perhaps his early love of Schumann was felt most deeply for the master of the smallest musical form, the musical novella, of the most evanescent moments full of high spirits, fleeting happiness, or tender pangs of the heart, this greatest master of the musical moment that German music, at least, has ever possessed. But his late musical love for Bizet's music to *Carmen* stands entirely under the sign of gratitude for the smallest element, for the most fleeting moment: the comments Nietzsche made in the margins of a piano score for *Carmen,* which he sent to Gast in January 1882, are exceptionally indicative of this very thing (the copy is located today in the Nietzsche-Archive). Almost all of his notations and marks refer to individual harmonic or melodic moments. The note on the tragic D-minor motif in the overture thus reads characteristically enough: "An *epigram* on passion, the best thing that has been written *sur l'amour* since Stendhal"; on the "inexorable" in the card-reading scene he writes: "This major key is completely horrifying"; on the fortissimo introduction of the major key in the intermezzo to the fourth act: "This major key moves me to tears"[11]—and so forth.

In *The Case of Wagner* Nietzsche himself characterizes the transformation and decomposition of style in a way that allows us to recognize the romantic master of anecdote, the extreme individualist. And what distinguishes every literary decadence? he asks. And his answer (which is, as has undoubtedly been noticed, a paraphrase of sentences from Bourget's *Baudelaire* of 1883:[12] that life no longer resides in the whole. "The word becomes sovereign and jumps out of the sentence, the sentence spreads out and obscures the meaning of the page, the page gains life at the cost of the whole—the whole is no longer a whole."[13] (One may compare in passing the French model of this passage, which reads in Bourget: ". . . . Une même loi gouverne le développement et la décadence de cet autre organisme qui est le langage. Un style de décadence est celui où l'unité du livre se décompose pour laisser la place à l'indépendence de la page, où la page se décompose pour laisser la place à l'indépendence de la phrase, et la phrase pour laisser la place à l'indépendence du mot.")[14] "But that is," Nietzsche goes on, raising Bourget's cool observation to the level of passionate complaint and accusation, "that is the symbol for every decadent style: in every case an anarchy of atoms, a disaggregation of the will, the 'freedom of the individual,' in moral terms—expanded to the realm of political theory 'equal rights for all.' Life, the same liveliness, the vibration and exuberance of life, forced back into the smallest forms, the rest bereft of life. . . . The whole . . . constructed, calculated, artificial, an artifact."[15]

What Nietzsche employs here to characterize and interpret Wagner, he also says (and laments) at the deepest level about himself. With Wagner, he says, there is in the beginning a hallucination: created not by sounds but by gestures; only later does he look for their tonal elaboration. But that holds true for Nietzsche's intellectual music as well: in the beginning is the moment, the mystical flash of lightning, the individualized and unleashed instant, inspiration, an occasionally grotesque obedience—one thinks of his description of "inspiration" in *Ecce homo,* that magnificent transfiguration of the prophetic moment. Or, as he writes in *The Will to Power:* "Here is a small ideal that I realize once every five weeks during a wild and lonely walk, in an azure moment of outrageous fortune."[16] No doubt this "azure moment"—"a thought flashes up like a bolt of lightning, full of necessity, without hesitation in its form—I never had a choice . . . one listens—one does not search; one receives—one does not ask who is giving. . . ."[17] That moment designates the classical origin of the Nietzschean "idea"; "in the beginning there is an hallucination" here: not of the idea, but of the metaphor, the image ("the involuntary character of the image, the metaphor, is the strangest thing; one no longer has any idea what is an image, what is a metaphor, everything lends itself as the nearest, the most important, the simplest expression")[18] as the chaos of an evolving world in the state of the productive "anecdote," the decipherable moment. And just as Wagner, according to Nietzsche, searches for and invents a tonal semiotics only after the primal hallucination of gestures, just as he imperiously elaborates and transforms the motif into a leitmotif, so too Nietzsche: his books, like Wagner's agglomerates, are also formed out of an "anarchy of atoms, a 'freedom of the individual,' in moral terms,"[19] to an artifact of wholeness, artificial, constructed, indeed calculated to be constructed by the ideal listener who recognizes them; a whole consisting of sovereign leitmotifs, every one of which has to be sought out and have its deeper meaning divined—indeed out of such a whole in which the author himself seems to be painfully seeking the true, most sovereign leitmotif. (Is it a coincidence that Nietzsche's only book in which a single, dominant leitmotif is unmistakably supposed to govern and order the whole, *The Will to Power,* remained an awe-inspiring chaos of ruins and fragments?) The exuberance of life forced back into the smallest forms, the rest *poor* in life . . . the whole no longer alive at all: it is constructed, artificial, an artifact—is not this characterization of the decadent style in general and of Wagner's style in particular above all—a critique of *Zarathustra,* that is of Zarathustra as a figure, as a living instantiation, as the visualized unity of his speeches and parables? Is not Zarathustra to an eminent degree such an artifact on the most magnificent scale, with an exuberance of life and the will to life in even his most minute constituent parts, as a whole, however, a sublime abstraction, a silent contour instead of a living, full, and fully realized figure, a flickering mosaic instead of the body of a prophet? *Zarathustra* became a vessel for thousands of moments of inspiration, an empty framework for countless anecdotal miniatures, each one unique in itself and deeply experienced and suffered; it became a musical drama designed for a profusion of individual philosophical motifs, full of short pieces of five to fifteen bars, all delicacies that no one knows—but he did not become a mouth, a person, a figure who is simply *there,* but merely one that is *supposed* to be there because it emanates from the imperious will of the man who invented it; just like Wagner's "musical drama," as genre and type, owes its existence solely to Wagner's imperious will, not to its own fullness of life. Figaro, Don Juan, Fidelio *are*—the Nibelungs, however, born out of the most powerful ambition, are *supposed* to be: that is also the relationship between both Luther's Bible and *Faust* and *Zarathustra.* Both the *Nibelungen* and *Zarathustra* are artifacts of an immense, synthesizing will, not births; demonically over-vital in their particulars, stiff as a whole; and, like everything that is artificial, "demands an enclosed space"—namely the presupposed and necessary individual world of their inventor, the glass dome of that particular soul and that one alone. It is highly indicative how Nietzsche imagines the birth of Beethoven's songs. He thinks that they arose like his own works: out of the spirit of musical anecdote as a mosaic of the smallest delicacies, of five to fifteen bars—just as the symphony *Zarathustra* later actually came into being. And yet at the same time, strangely enough, he tries to deny here, during his most positivistic period, that inspiration which he later, instinctively realizing that it alone legitimated a work of *Zarathustra*'s rank, declared to be the mother of this book, which is simultaneously his most ambitious and most self-hating work. "One now sees from Beethoven's notebooks," he wrote in the first post-Wagnerian period, "that he gradually collected the most magnificent melodies and chose from among several inceptions, as it were."[20] And in another passage, even more clearly and less ambiguously autobiographical: "Beethoven's music frequently seems like a deeply felt *reflection* occasioned by the unexpected rehearing of a piece one had thought vanished long ago called 'Innocence in Sound'; it is music *about* music. In the songs of beggars and children on the street, in the monotonous ditties of wandering Italians, at a dance in the village tavern or in the nights of Carneval—that is where he discovers his 'melodies': he collects them like a bee by snatching a sound, a brief passage here and there. They are to him transfigured *memories* from the 'better world': similar to the way Plato thought of the Ideas.[21] . . . One might call Beethoven a minstrel's ideal listener."[22] Does one not hear in this characterization of Beethoven's music the confession of the future composer of *Zarathustra,* who really thought that *Zarathustra* seemed to belong "among the symphonies"?[23] Not just "a minstrel's ideal listener," the reflective "music about music," the "second innocence," are all clearly Nietzschean traits. Above all, the image of the lonely musician in search of the fragments of an originary Platonic music is secretly Nietzschean, someone who collects his melodies, like so many scattered distant bolts of lightning from the rumbling primal fire, in tiny snatches on the streets of his travels, transfigured memories of a better world; Nietzschean, too, and self-revealing, his imagining the origin of the great, lonely, triumphal songs that Beethoven sang to himself in the *Missa solemnis* as the final results of patiently and ascetically collected visions, of tiny, isolated, originary motifs, of mystical musical anecdotes. If the Ninth Symphony, if indeed the *Missa,* is such a Platonic mosaic for the poet of *Zarathustra,* why should *Zarathustra* itself not originate the same way—a "memory of something more beautiful than me,"[24] as he wrote in his "Autumn" poem, a memory that was collected with a bee's patience in thousands of individual flights and excursions. But, for Nietzsche, there existed a higher level of artistry than the Beethovenian-Platonic one described here; and it is not by chance that this passage on Beethoven concludes with a consideration of the opposite of Beethovenian music, the music that Nietzsche himself would have liked to have been: "Mozart stands in an entirely different relationship to his melodies: he finds his inspirations not by listening to music, but by viewing life, the most turbulent Mediterranean life: he always dreamed of Italy whenever he was not there."[25]

Nietzsche was aware of his all-too-romantically anecdotal, mosaic-like intellectual nature—he seems to admit as much in this analysis of Beethoven. But it also points, in exemplary fashion, to the place where Nietzsche escapes the curse of the individualistic leitmotif, the anarchy of atoms. He is, with Novalis, the true master of anecdote, who knows how to transform everything into anecdotes; but he also knows, on the other hand, how to transform the anecdote into history, into idea. "It is possible to render the image of a person with three anecdotes"[26]—that is, to be sure, a romantic technique and an inclination toward decadence. But "apart from the fact that I am a *décadent,* I am also the opposite,"[27] Nietzsche says. Above all, the opposite. For with Nietzsche, unlike with a romantic skeptic epitomized by Fontane, the stress is not ultimately on the three anecdotes. Rather it is on the image; and on the image in its Platonic intensification, as εἶδος, as idea. That is precisely what shines through the passage on Beethoven. "A memory of something more beautiful than me"[28]—such Platonic ebullience rises above his anecdotal individualism. Nietzsche's aphorism, his psychological anecdote proves to be a musical original form by virtue of its innate Platonic homesickness. Every tone is homesickness, parable. And all of the psychological resoluteness, all of the ascetic cynicism, all "cave musicam!" in Nietzsche's aphoristic self-descriptions cannot hide the fact that a musician, a Platonist had created a musical form for himself here, a secret dialogue: beyond Schlegel's romantic fragment, beyond the mystical-realistic union of opposites in Novalis's visions and premonitions, he created the more sober and yet more passionate type of aphorism that achieves its pinnacle in the anecdotal imagistic speech of *Zarathustra,* consisting of nothing but self-contained little worlds, yet full of a secret conflict, perfect unto themselves, and yet, like everything perfect, expressive not just of themselves but also of an entire interrelated world. Nothing but miniature delicacies, from five to fifteen bars, but possessing a symphonic power ("my ambition is to say in ten sentences what everyone else says in a book—what everyone else does *not* say in a book").[29] Here anecdote meets parable, cynicism meets the symbol of faith, the historical molecule meets historical philosophy. Three anecdotes render the person, the image, the music. There is Socratic music in this aphoristic style, just as that music lies dormant in the pseudo-rationalism of the Platonic dialogues to which Socrates offers a sacrifice only in the face of death. Socrates, the true master of anecdote, who had invented the pedagogical anecdote and kept it as an ironic secret, who knew how to transform everything into anecdotes, is the secret model here, as he is for all those in whom "skepticism and longing are conjoined."[30] *Ecce homo* became perhaps the masterpiece of this ambition to achieve Socratic music, the mystical anecdote. Dissolved into so many fragments of an almost purely anecdotal character, it is the perfect example of the sovereignty of the individual sentence and individual word in the manner of all decadence, yet the entirety of this extraordinary self-confession still demonstrates a totality, an inner unity and even rigor that is the complete opposite of an anarchy of atoms. *Ecce homo* thus becomes a reflection of Nietzsche's effect as a whole: a life laboriously wrested or consciously stylized out of individual moments, individual flights, individual inspirations, a work composed of new starts, disappointments, paradoxes, ascetic self-denial—and yet, the whole resting incomparably within a majestic unity. A thunderstorm full of lightning—and yet radiating the clarity of a continuous day. Carrying the sharp, individualistic charm of the personal anecdote and the unique intellectual adventure—and simultaneously, indeed simultaneously in a way that is difficult to explain, full of the fascination of a depersonalized fate, the aura of parable and the stillness of an imperishable image.

In the end, even Nietzsche's doctrine of the Eternal Recurrence, the idea of the Eternal Return, is itself the epitome and glorification of a highest moment: his "eternity" is the cult of the mystical moment, of such a moment as he experienced next to the pile of stone at Surlei, on the lake of Silvaplana in August 1881. We experience all eternity *only* in the form of the Dionysian moment, we affirm all eternity only in the Yes of the justifying instant, to the fateful Faustian moment of the "Tarry awhile!"[31]—that is the ultimate conclusion that Nietzsche's eternity-obsessed will draws from his own fundamentally anecdotal disposition, the boldest intensification of his Socratic individualism toward Platonic metaphysics: the Platonist in him forges the golden moment for Zarathustra's "nuptial ring of rings, the ring of recurrence"[32]—that is put most beautifully, apart from in *Zarathustra* itself, in the fragments that were intended to form the final chapter "Dionysus" to *The Will to Power:*

"Granted we say Yes to a single moment, then we have thus said Yes not just to ourselves, but to all of existence. For nothing stands on its own, neither in ourselves, nor in things: and if our soul has trembled and resounded with happiness once and only once, then all eternities were necessary to cause this singular occurrence and all of eternity was endorsed, redeemed, justified and affirmed in this single moment of our saying Yes."[33]

13

Indian Summer

The autumnal day now rests in its fullness,
The grape is purified . . . [1]
—Hölderlin

Enough is not enough. Praise be to Autumn.[2]
—Conrad Ferdinand Meyer

Nietzsche, who disdained Mörike[3] and who thought "the highest notion of a poet" was represented not by Goethe or Hölderlin but by Heine's "sweet and passionate music and divine malice,"[4] loved Adalbert Stifter—that is one of those symbolic paradoxes, sometimes themselves almost malicious, that even superficially give his life the allure of extremism, of romantic inconsistency. It was not an early attachment of Nietzsche, like the love for Schumann he later disavowed and bitterly ridiculed, whose music is so close to the writer of the early *Studies,* the "The Condor" and "Wild Flowers"[5] (both artists occupy a province in the great kingdom of Jean Paul)—but rather a love of the mature Nietzsche, and it was directed solely at the autumnal poet who wrote *Indian Summer* (*Der Nachsommer*). The oft-quoted passage from *Human* is well known, where Nietzsche enumerates the few books of German prose that deserve to be read and reread; apart from Goethe's words, and particularly the conversations with Eckermann—"the best German book there is"—what does he mention? Four books by minds that were worlds apart from each other but who were all linked to him by deep consanguineous ties: the skeptical aphorisms of his moralistic predecessor Lichtenberg,[6] the pietistically devout youth of Jung-Stilling,[7] the Epicurean golden laughter of the Higher Man in the People of Seldwyla[8]—and Adalbert Stifter's transfiguration of homesickness in a super-German community seen through the lens of a stylized antiquity at the end of Goethe's century.

One of those guiding coincidences that occur so frequently in Nietzsche's reading led him to this so-little-known book, which even today still has an almost apocryphal afterlife (often the fate of the most fervent German creations and compositions), indeed which to this day is still considered inaccessible even in the unmutilated original form in which Nietzsche read it:[9] a friend of Nietzsche discovered in it the most beautiful love story he had ever read—and from that point on, a deep elective affinity united the poet of *Zarathustra* with the sculptor of a post-Goethean, late, melancholy happiness. Letters to his musician friend give testimony to this elective affinity: "As soon as I imagine you reading 'Indian Summer,' I am happy," Nietzsche writes to Gast; "I had actually wanted to save it until we were together; ever since I got to know the book, I had intended it for you."[10] Even eight years after this letter, he still describes the "lion's music" of his "Venetian maestro" as refreshing, restorative, sincere, cheerful, radiant, comparing it to Goethe's *Novella* of 1826 and Stifter's *Indian Summer.* "In *this* direction," Nietzsche adds, "there is still an entire world of beauty."[11] For a "delightful adagio" by Gast, he suggests the title "Indian Summer Music"—his friend's Venetian music and the Austrian writer's late work are in his eyes delights from the same world of a new beauty. And he writes to Gast that he would like to get to the bottom of *why* that is so.

Why did Nietzsche love this book so much, this book by a poet who is so unlike Nietzsche himself? Why did it become a parable in his eyes? Does not such a love, like all love, also reflect on the character of the lover? There is more than just one congruity in the characters of these two poets, who appear to stand on opposite ends of the broad spectrum of the German character. There is a hidden confraternity of souls that often binds precisely the most hostile minds together—such a confraternity united the poet of *Indian Summer* with the sage of Sils-Maria. In what could it have been rooted?

An innate autumnal mood of the soul, a profound October serenity—to take up a word of Nietzsche's—is obvious in Nietzsche's character from the beginning, and that is what predestines him to the kind of Indian summerly pleasures that Stifter's mature art radiates most magically of all. (In German literature the magic of Indian summer finds a similarly intensive expression in perhaps only one other work, if of a completely different sort—in certain autumnal poems in *The Year of the Soul.*)[12] Even as a student at Schulpforta he had already written to his mother (in September 1863): "I love the autumn very much, even if I know it more through my memory and though my poems" (the qualification is highly characteristic for the non-experiential, but rather predestinational nature of the young Nietzsche's love of autumn!); "but the air is so crystal-clear, one can see so freely from earth to the heavens, that the world seems to be lying naked in front of one's eyes."[13] Six years later, in autumn letters to Rohde, Nietzsche is even more deeply aware of the significance and implications of his innate autumnal blissfulness. In September 1869, he writes, for instance: " . . . Zeus knows, as does the pure autumn sky, that I am so powerfully lifted up into the positive realm at precisely this time, that I experience so many rich hours of abundant insight and true vividness. . . ."[14] "It is a pure, blue, cool autumn morning, one *entirely* forgets the stunted volatility of one's soul."[15] And one month later he returns to the theme, now sounded in a deeper, more classical, more Nietzschean vein:

"Outside, before the windows, lies the thoughtful autumn," (thoughtful!) "bathed in clear, mildly warm sunshine, the northern autumn that I love as I love my best friends, because it is so mature and unconsciously lacking all desire. Fruit falls from the tree without a breath of wind.

"And thus it is with the love of friends: without admonition, without shaking, in perfect calm it descends and pleases. It desires nothing for itself and gives everything of itself. . . .

"I should also think that someone who truly loves autumn, a few friends, and solitude may also be permitted to predict for himself a great, productive, and happy autumn of life:

Thus allow that one of the Fates
Shall spin my autumn for me, lovely and long,
Out of half-cooled sunshine
And leisure

"But you know what leisure we mean: we have already experienced it together, as *true σχολαστικοί*, that is, as idlers."[16]

That is already the tone of late, halcyon happiness that is repeatedly struck in Nietzsche's works and letters from then on, and is always a reflection of his most grateful, most intensive moments; it is already a prophetic presentiment of the highest moment in the great, productive, and happy autumn of his life, when he strolls in the high "idleness of a god along the Po,"[17] when, in the introductory words of *Ecce homo,* he looks back on his life "on this perfect day when everything is ripening and not only the grape is turning brown": "I looked back, I look out, I never saw so much and so many good things at once. . . . How could I not be grateful to my entire life?"[18] And it is already an anticipation of the profound October gratefulness that flows forth in a letter to his friend during his last autumn: "The purest light of October everywhere. . . . I am now the most grateful person in the world—in an autumnal frame of mind in every good sense of the word: it is my great time of harvest. Everything is becoming easy for me, everything I do is turning out well, although it is doubtful that anyone has ever had such great things entrusted to him before. . . ."[19] And even the idea of "idleness" is already circumscribed here, that "Greek" idleness that is glorified in both *Zarathustra* and in *Ecce homo,* and whose actual transfiguration is represented in Stifter's *Indian Summer* as in no other literary work in the German language; a reflection of Arcadian, ancient happiness of the gentlest Epicureanism, the symbol of which

Nietzsche loved in Claude Lorrain's paintings. (But Stifter also especially loved Claude Lorrain's "quiet greatness and dignity.")[20]

The "perfect autumn day" that rests in its plenitude, a "Claude Lorrain thought into infinity,"[21] remains a favorite conception of Nietzsche in his role as both poet and composer. His lecture "On the Future of our Educational Institutions," which often strikes a poetic register, presents a philosophical conversation of an invented sage (in Schopenhauer's mask) taking place on such an Arcadian day at Rolandseck:[22] "It was one of those perfect days which are only possible, at least in our climate, at the very end of summer: heaven and earth calmly flowing in harmony next to each other, a wonderful combination arising from the warmth of the sun, the freshness of fall, and blue infinity"[23] (here, too, one hears even in the choice of words the details of his last autumn in Turin). And twelve years later, abstracted into Zarathustra's twelve happy isles: "Autumn is upon us and a pure sky and afternoon. See what plenitude surrounds us! And it is good to look out of such abundance toward distant seas."[24] And in the essay on "Richard Wagner in Bayreuth," even the pleasure in Wagner's music, which he still thought of as an art of the future, is given an autumnal twist and experienced as an inner autumn: "We have a feeling of great distance, as if Siegfried were narrating his deeds: the profound sadness of late summer is woven into the most moving happiness of remembrance, and the whole of nature lies quietly in the yellow evening light."[25] Nietzsche's own musical production still pays homage to the god of autumn as his patron muse: a letter to Gersdorff in the fall of 1871 reports a larger composition for four hands that reverberates with all the sounds of a beautiful, sun-filled autumn: "I had not composed anything for six years and *this* autumn stimulated me again!"[26] Finally, this inner autumn, both poetically enchanted and enchanting, resounds most purely in the Dionysus Dithyramb "The Sun Sets":

> . . . You will not thirst much longer,
> Parched heart!
> There is promise in the air . . .
> The great chill is coming . . .
> Hail to thee . . . you cool spirits of the afternoon.
>
> My life's day!
> It inclines toward evening . . .
> Golden cheerfulness, come!
> You most secret, sweetest foretaste
> Of death . . .
> My raft now stands idle.

How it forgets storm and sail!
Hopes and wishes have drowned,
Sea and soul lie flat.

Seventh solitude!
Never have I felt
Sweet security nearer to me, or
More warmly the glance of the sun . . . [27]

The golden cheerfulness of such inner autumnal happiness, into which the portent of the great chill and the most mysterious foretaste of death are woven: that is, above all, what drew Nietzsche to Stifter's poem of autumn, over which Jean Paul's words hover: "O calm, you gentle word! Autumnal bouquet from Eden! Calm of the soul, when shall you hold our head so that it quietly rests and our heart so that it does not pound?"[28] All the masks that a preordained autumn of the soul had used to seduce Nietzsche are collected here. Here there reigns, to quote the words of *Hesperus* again, that "inner windless calm which is never so great and so magical as in souls that have been tossed back and forth by churning hurricanes."[29] Here the magical image of a life that has been raised up to an ultimate Epicurean ripeness and ethereal modesty, as it first appears as "Muses's Monastery" in the early correspondence with Rohde and, seen with the eyes of love, became something like reality for Nietzsche perhaps only once as the days in Tribschen. One feels the seduction of an extreme aristocratic conception of life here, an almost childlike refusal to cast even a glance at the vast social substructure that supports and enables the life of his Higher Men, this life of tranquil beauty, of grateful proximity to nature and ancient leisure, of the most refined humanistic culture, of the transcendent peacefulness of evening. It was an ideal that filled Nietzsche's hopes and dreams; during his first years in Basel he writes—years before he got to know *Indian Summer*—that he had only *one* wish: not to become hurried, "and such cheerful late-summer weather preaches this doctrine in the most vivid manner, colored blue and gold";[30] that he loves Basel so because it allows him to live quietly, as if on a small country estate. And in Sorrento, in that same fall and winter of 1876–77, he actually attempted to realize, beyond the real world, such a shared humanistic Indian summer happiness.[31] A deeper, purer love for the works of the ancients, a love that flows out of the most profound masculine homesickness, makes this lover of the Greeks feel grateful, as only a shared cult of love can make one feel grateful and allied. One recalls the incomparable passages on the Greek statue, the Cumaean Girl, in the stairwell of Asperhof,[32] or the cameos. Even the amateurish art historical musings, which as such were the last thing Nietzsche was interested in, still give off a hint of that atmosphere he associated with Eckermann, indeed with Burckhardt, and had to strike him as familiar: the delicate sensuous humanism and historicism that surrounded him in Basel as well, the truly Stifterian philology of the eye, which in Nietzsche merely retreated into de-sensualized, more abstract intellectual regions of sight.

But something must have affected Nietzsche more strongly than the Eckermann mood of this late classicism and humanism, which Nietzsche knew was coming to an end, whose melancholy transfiguration *Indian Summer* is intended to be; this work must have affected him even more strongly as an entirely unique pedagogical utopia—for the book presents itself as such, which even within a literary tradition that is so "pedantic," so pedagogically serious as is the German one, has a parallel only in *Wilhelm Meister's Travels,* at most in certain parts of Gottfried Keller's work[33] (which not coincidentally was also one of Nietzsche's favorites). The image of an educational idealism of the first order, of Platonic seriousness, of Goethean sobriety, of Jean Paulean fervor, had to have made an impression on the great impatient educator of the overman with the force of a comforting phantom and ideal. And it did, and evidence that it did is provided by the same book in which Nietzsche singles out *Indian Summer* for special honor among German works of prose. The aphorism about the poet of the future clearly arose under the lasting impression of Stifter's pedagogical late work. "Just as, in former times, artists constructed their tales around the images of the gods, so too will the poet construct his tale around the image of beautiful humanity, and search out those instances where . . . a great beautiful soul can even today be incorporated into harmonious, well-proportioned circumstances through which it acquires visibility, permanence and exemplarity and thus, by exciting imitation and envy, helps to create the future. Literary works by writers of this sort" (here the proximity of Stifter becomes especially clear) "would distinguish themselves by appearing to be closed and inaccessible to the heat and flame of passion: the irremediable mistake, the demolition of the entire human enterprise, derisive laughter and the gnashing of teeth, and everything tragic and comic in the old customary sense would be perceived next to this new art as . . . a coarsening of the human image. Strength, kindness, mildness, purity and unforced, innate moderation in people and their endeavors: a smoothed ground that offers the foot rest and delight: a brilliant sky reflected in their faces and actions . . . all of this would be the inclusive, universal, gilded background against which the gentle differences among the embodied ideals would form the actual portrait—that of the continual growth of human majesty."[34] That is, knowingly or not, a portrait of *Indian Summer,* without a doubt. But the conclusion of this aphorism sounds as if it has been taken out of Stifter's aesthetic writings, as when he writes: "Many a path leads from Goethe to this poetry of the future: but one needs competent guides and above all a much greater power than the current writers possess, those unthinking portraitists of those brutes and immaturity and immoderation which they confuse with strength and nature."[35] (One recalls here Stifter's preface to *Bunte Steine* [Colorful Stones] and his letters to Heckenast[36] from the 1850s.)

But beneath the secret sign of autumn, this pedagogical-poetic signpost also points the way into a Goethean future. For the educational passion (and Nietzsche knew this through painful experience, even if he sought to deny it himself) always awakens at the first hint of autumn, of the great chill, of the end. That passion stands, finally and secretly, under the sign of death, like everything that serves what is to come more passionately than it serves itself; it is a promise that hangs in the air and is almost itself a form of the end. It becomes a dominant obsession only when someone knows that he stands at the edge of life, indeed "with one foot beyond life."[37] It becomes a passion and natural urge to form, to immortalize, at that moment in which a living being recognizes itself to be an end, an extreme point that no longer serves any chain as a natural link, but rather must posit itself as the first link in a more spiritual chain if it does not want to feel annihilated—and such "moments" can assume the form of an entire human life (the most inward meaning of priestly celibacy, and the ultimate cause of that deep sympathetic mistrust, that reserve which arises from a perpetually renewed mixture of contempt and respect with which a vital living being, a being that knows itself to be part of a chain, looks both at and up to those who posses a pronounced pedagogical and didactic nature). Stifter's pedagogical passion, which fills all of his literary works—none so completely as *Indian Summer*—was entirely of this kind. It came from an initially unconscious, later painfully distinct, feeling of an innate and predetermined "childlessness," a feeling of representing an end, of being an end. Stifter gave the most profoundly moving expression to that feeling in "Der Hagestolz" (The Bachelor) (particularly in the conclusion), which a contemporary of Stifter called, not without reason, the most profound story in German, and he lent it the most magnificent voice in his reformulation of the legend of the Wandering Jew, "Abdias."[38] But all of his works are basically an expression of this basic experience; this *fatum* of the end extends even into his narrative technique. And this is what Nietzsche experienced in *Indian Summer* as something deeply related to his own destiny, he who is also "childless," an exit and final chorus, as a mask of the end and nearly a will to the end, as passionately as he—the great, exemplary willed sacrifice of his life—interpreted himself into the opposite. (There is an eminently Stifteresque sound to the motifs of "Ahasverus"[39] and "Hagestolz"[40] in the deeply earnest letters to Rohde from 18 July 1876 and 22 February 1884. "No, wanderer, no! I shall not greet *you* in *that* tone. I sing because the night is so beautiful: but you shall go forever more And never shall you understand my song! Go, go hence—And if your step shall sound from afar I shall raise my night song again. . . . Farewell, you poor wanderer!"[41] . . . "Oh, friend, what an odd, silent life I lead! So alone, alone! So without 'children'!")[42] He, too, is an educator by fate and passion, a dreamer of the most noble forms of human cultural community and of a happiness brought on by eagerly assumed responsibility and willing sacrifice. Over him, too, in him, there is something of that indescribable autumnal Edenic glow, the magic of the end, which constitutes the most profound spell cast by Stifter's works and, perhaps, will one day emanate from the entire phenomenon of Nietzsche. Nietzsche knew (and with deep emotion recognized in *Indian Summer*) the gratefully resigned, twilight happiness of an innate season of the soul that sings its last in song and that perhaps does not know but senses it has arrived at the end; he knew the aging Stifter's prevailing mood after the terrible disappointment of the revolutionary year[43] (until then, he had been, according to his own testimony, as "serene as the ancient peoples"),[44] which decisively and conclusively drove the disciple of Jean Paul into the sphere of *Indian Summer:* the prevailing mood of "irretrievability."[45] Stifter's highly conscious sense of having immortalized something that was already irretrievable, something that had been lost forever as a vital way of living with his vision of a late-Goethean existential utopia, his transfiguration of a German-humanistic educational ideal, this composed state of mourning, which was also not foreign to Eckermann's Goethe (he writes to Zelter in 1825: "Let us retain as much as possible the convictions we started out with; we, together with perhaps a few others, will be the last ones from an epoch that will not return again any time soon"),[46] that sense gives *Indian Summer* that pungent "roseate odor of irretrievability" that Nietzsche painfully loved most in all things concerning existence: "Basically," he wrote in a letter from his last years, "basically this autumn was also nice again . . . slightly melancholy, but just in the way that people like us find all the enjoyments of life spiced with an old, faint roseate odor of *irretrievability.*"[47] It is the ancient, melancholy, mature happiness of Epicurus that Nietzsche encounters again in Stifter as a partner in fate, and perhaps the passage in *The Gay Science* that speaks of this Epicurean happiness could also not have arisen without a glance at the gentle melancholy of *Indian Summer:* "Such happiness could have been invented only by someone who constantly suffered, the happiness of an eye before which the ocean of existence has become calm, and now cannot look long enough at its surface and at this colored, gentle trembling skin of the ocean: never before was there such modesty of delight."[48] That the noblest happiness is an autumnal fruit on the tree of suffering—this favorite notion of Nietzsche, so redolent of late antiquity, is also the perfect motto for the Indian summer world of his favorite literary work.

But the innermost identity that Nietzsche's elective affinity with Stifter displays rests no doubt on an ultimate homesickness, on the most unquenchable kind there is: on the homesickness both felt for *perfection.* After the autumnally serene rest on the seventh day, in the Sunday stillness of creative leisure and a wishless presence, after the nuptial "And, behold, it was very good,"[49] with which *Indian Summer* closes and into which Nietzsche also had the poem of his life flow, in the high October happiness of his *Ecce homo.* Perfection—that, too, like the educational ideal, is a dream-form of death, indeed its closest, most immediate pre-form, the figure of Hermes, in which it leads and seduces the death-ready soul to the underworld—perfection, not for nothing the favorite word of the late, already secretly death-drunk Nietzsche ("On this perfect day"[50] [*Ecce homo*]. "Yesterday and the day before the highest perfection on earth and the Engadine"[51] [August 1888]. "What we miss in Wagner: . . . the shimmering light of the south, the smooth sea—perfection"[52] [*The Case of Wagner*]. "What alone can restore us?—The sight of perfection"[53] [Notebooks to *Transfiguration*])—and the earnest symbol of his inner insatiability, of his great dissatisfaction with himself, of his Greek homesickness—perfection is also the guiding dream and painful ardor of Adalbert Stifter, who labored like almost no other German artist did on the verbal realization of his homesick dreams that were unsullied by reality, who worked on his half ancient, half monkish vision, to use Nietzsche's expression, as if on a sculpture, and who movingly lived his life according to Hölderlin's appeal to young poets to "Be only pious, like the Greeks were!"[54] In his own aloof, bourgeois, unintellectual, dreamily pedantic German fashion, Stifter also harbored and cherished a dream of Greece, as did Goethe, Hölderlin, or Nietzsche in higher, but not in purer, spheres. He also created himself and his softly glowing Indian summer world out of a Nevertheless; like Hölderlin in more solemn Pindaric fashion, and Nietzsche in a more impatient Lutheran manner, he also forced an inner autumn into an unfadable realm—Nietzsche gleaned that from *Indian Summer* and paid his respects. For him, this work was one of those encounters with himself, which are characterized by the names Schopenhauer and Schumann, Stendhal and Bizet, encounters, the most humanly endearing of which carries the name Rohde, the most tragically fateful that of Richard Wagner. It was a piece of himself, whose intensification explained himself to himself, whose transfiguration made him feel grateful, whose danger and boundary were also his own.

Indeed, if one were permitted to pinpoint and elucidate the predetermined fate of a soul *more geometrico* by reference to a particular spot, then the phrase

"Indian summer," in its Stifterian resonance, would perhaps encompass most perfectly the fateful point, the moment of predestination, from which Nietzsche's inner life's journey began and to which it arched back. Nothing, certainly, can be superficially further from Stifter than Nietzsche's intellectual Ahasverus legend. But no matter how Nietzsche interpreted himself, to what heights he raised himself, to what degree he transformed himself, whether he felt himself to be the Föhn[55] storm, the thaw heralding new, hotter summers of humanity, as an impudent mistral,[56] or as a stifling, high-noon brooding decision—there is always nevertheless, as in his *Ecce homo,* as in his favorite Claude, something in the innermost landscape of his being that is mournfully mindful of the end, but in this consciousness itself an all the more intense present-embracing afternoon light, an autumnal happiness of the highest moment in the presentiment of the great chill, but of a moment "thought into infinity," mature and mature-making, with a grateful and transfiguring eye ("I never saw so much and so many good things all at once,"[57] "I never thought such a thing was possible on earth"),[58] an autumnal happiness singing a blue, serenely profound late music ("what I really want from music: that it be serene and profound, like an afternoon in October"),[59] and full of a perhaps deadly but "unbridled" and purest perfection.

14

Claude Lorrain

Every person is born with his own north or south, whether he is born into an external one as well—is of little consequence.[1]
—Jean Paul

We are nothing; what we seek is everything.[2]
—Hölderlin

For several hundred years, ever since *Faust* and Luther's Bible gave us our German foundation, one question has stood as a familiar symbol of our forever conflicting German possibilities: Luther's or Goethe's journey to Rome and what became of it, Luther's or Goethe's image and concept of Rome—which one seems to be the *more German* solution to the thoroughly German problem, to the German fate that remains inescapable in its repetitions and variations: that of the "northern man in the south"? Both figures, owing to everything that drew them to these southerly spheres of their existence, are perfect symbols of the noble self-dissatisfaction that has always characterized all higher forms of Germanness. Whose attitude, whose decisive transformation "in Rome" seems to us more German will always necessarily be determined by one's own inner predestination, one's inner succession, and thus in a highly personal way, in an unequivocally unjust fashion, as must always apparently be the case in life. But for certain epochs and a number of people, the great magnetic mountain of the German soul will always threaten and beckon from the *south,* a longing for the south will waft a feverish happiness and feverish danger, a seductive Föhn, into German souls. What Goethe, as a seventy-nine-year-old, confessed to Eckermann will also always sound very German in a particular sense, as a possibility of the soul available only to Germans: "I can say that I felt only in Rome what a human being actually is. Thereafter I never reached that height again, that happiness of sensation; compared to my state in Rome, I have never actually been cheerful again."[3] This will always sound just as German as Luther's disappointed, powerfully Protestant pronouncement: "The closer to Rome, the worse the Christians"; or as the judgment that still rumbled in his *Table Talk:* that when Germans go to Italy they become worse than the Italians themselves, which led the Italians to the saying: a German foreigner is a *diabolo incarnato.* "Thus beware a German foreigner!"[4]

Today the figure of Nietzsche the wayfarer—asking the way, pointing the way—stands as the most recent addition to the long ancestral line of German preachers of the south. The thousand-year history of the soul of our people is repeatedly concentrated in pioneering figures who testify to this happiness in the south, and the longing for it, as their determinative German experience. Nietzsche's deep inner beyond-ness, his super-Germanness that brimmed with an "ultramontanism" of the soul, his anti-Germanness in the highest sense itself ("to be a good German means to rid oneself of Germanness"[5] he says to sharpen his point, and lives in the serenely certain belief that Goethe would have agreed with him)—everything, as keenly personal as it is for him, is still merely a symbolic enactment of a recurrent fundamental attitude of the noblest German spirit, the oldest German tragedy.

Such a northern person, born and raised just north of the great wine border of humanity, endowed with the whole self-governing conscience of the Gothic northern spirit, but richly and dangerously gifted with the darker-blooded drives and instincts from old ancestral mixtures: does he not embody a German fate precisely in his *mixture,* which as such always becomes a problem and a task: cope with yourself—become One out of the conflict that you are? Nietzsche's overbearing and deadly homesickness for the south is only apparently a personal *fatum;* his Gothic collapse in the ecstatic happiness and hubris of the south is strictly speaking typical, it is a solemn symbol of the eternally renewed Gothic downfall, which remains a predetermined Germanic fate of the soul. The painfully accusatory disownment of the all-too-northern homeland is German, as is the magnificent, violent self–de-Germanification, and German, too, is the creation of an inner south of the soul, for which the external, geographical south, the south of "common reality," signifies only a parable, an incentive, and a promise.

For it is never the south that one actually experiences, but rather the south that one yearns for and wants to incorporate, which is primary and decisive for the man of the north. And Nietzsche's will to the south as well was not determined by present experience. Even more than was the case with Goethe, *his* Italy was a preordained fact, a desire for experience and a necessity: the secret south of his most veiled nature craves fertilization. And however powerfully it may be confirmed by the happiness felt in the presence of the Italic sky, this inner south still recognizably remains a governing idea brought from the north. The south is not an experience, but rather a *condition* of the German soul, and perhaps its most mysteriously fruitful, its tragically noblest one of all: in the state of homesickness, it always bestowed its most lasting gifts. It pays for its true homecoming, the fulfillment of its Nordic dream, by being doomed to succumb somehow to the "Roman fever." The happiness of the south and the danger of the south are inseparable. And perhaps never before has a German experienced that very danger of the south, of his own south, so much as happiness as did Nietzsche. His longing for the south has something about it that is conscious of that danger and proud of it; it contains a death-defiant "nevertheless." The wonderful yearning pulls him, like Hölderlin, toward the abyss. The south as *lethal perfection,* as complement and poison, as conquest and ruin—Nietzsche adopts this Gothic fate into his will: *amor fati,* the affirmative will to fate is what he perceives and pronounces himself as his innermost nature; and this, his *fatum* bears the traits of the fever of the south, which gradually become ever more recognizable. But pure Germanness that restricts itself to itself, that protects and shields itself from the danger of the south, seems cowardly to him, as a flight and thus in the end as un-German (for it is un-German, in good as in evil, to preserve oneself instead of extravagantly giving oneself), it seems to him to be timidity before one's own, ineluctable fate. The south for him becomes the formula and the magical keyword for everything that is super-German, for the de-realization toward a higher reality, for the fulfillment of his innermost German nature, which, like Nietzsche's ideal landscape, the Engadin, basically incorporates "all of the middle regions between the ice and the south."[6] "The Germans," reads a passage in the late Notebooks—at a time when he gives voice almost exclusively to pitiless rejections of the German character out of a bitterly disappointed love—"the Germans landed perhaps in the *wrong* climate! There is something in them that could be Hellenistic—it awakens on contact with the *south*—Winckelmann, Goethe, Mozart. Finally: we are still very *young.* The last thing that happened to us is still Luther."[7] Or a critical observation on *Faust* from the same period says that the true German Mephistopheles crosses the Alps believing that everything belongs to him (Luther's *diabolo incarnato!*). "For that reason he [Goethe] felt at home there, just as Winckelmann felt at home, as did Mozart. He views Faust and Hamlet as caricatures that were invented to be laughed at, the same with Luther. Goethe had good *German* moments, in which he laughed inwardly at all of that. But then even he fell back into damp moods."[8] Thus, at bottom it is always a feeling of an intensified *German* presence or possibility that Nietzsche senses and loves in his south, as if it were a premonitory phantom of German futures. No doubt, the gratitude, the sigh of relief, the pleasure in the present, all of this is familiar to him, the feeling of having escaped the "detested fog of the dismal north,"[9] which weighed down so massively on Goethe; that overflowing feeling of intoxication in the early giddiness of first happiness in the south as one recuperates from the north, feeling that one's entire previous life has been suddenly left behind like some ghostly existence: "I do not have enough strength for the north," we read in an antithetically refined comment: "it is dominated by ponderous and artificial souls that labor as steadfastly and compulsively on precautionary measures as beavers do on their dams. I spent my entire youth among them! That occurred to me when I saw night fall over Naples for the first time, with a velvety gray and red in the sky. You could have died without seeing this—a shudder, pity for myself that I began my life being old, and tears and the feeling of just having been saved at the last moment. I have enough spirit for the south."[10] Or on another, later, occasion to Brandes from Nice: "I admire nearly everyone who does not lose faith in himself under an overcast sky. I would be a nihilist in St. Petersburg: here I believe, like a plant believes, in the *sun.*"[11] And poetically in the verses "In the South" from the "Songs of Prince Vogelfrei":

> . . . Where am I then? Oh, far away! Oh, far away!
> The white sea lies fast asleep,
> And above it rises a purple sail.
> Cliffs, fig trees, tower and harbor,
> Idyll all around, the bleating of sheep—
> Innocence of the South, take me in!
>
> Only step by step—that is no life,
> Always one foot in front of the other makes one heavy and German.
> I called on the wind to lift me upward,
> I learned to float with the birds—
> I flew across the sea to the South.[12]

But it is precisely these "merely present" moods of gratitude that are fairly rare in Nietzsche. It is, instead, characteristic of his predestined stance toward the south that the objective presence of a *landscape,* for instance, has very little to do with the essence of his southern happiness. For Nietzsche a landscape occasionally seems to hold importance only as a symbolic value: thus he calls the Upper Engadin *his* landscape, "so far from life, so metaphysical";[13] or he speaks elsewhere of the anemic beauty of Lake Maggiore in the late autumn, which spiritualizes every contour and almost turns the entire region into a vision: "It doesn't delight me, but it does speak to me in a familiar and sad way—I experience that kind of thing not only in nature"[14] (Notebooks to *Daybreak*). That certain landscapes can appear to be a premonition and a double dream of one's own experience is a notion with which Nietzsche was well acquainted: "There are places in nature in which we encounter ourselves, with a pleasurable shudder; it is the best kind of *Doppelgänger.*"[15] (An experience that Hebbel noted in very similar fashion in a passage in his diary: "I often think that I have already seen something that I am demonstrably seeing for the first time, particularly landscapes"[16] [1837].) His frequent cloaking of his perceptions of nature in the allegory of Claude Lorrain's wistful landscape fantasies is characteristic of this *mediacy* and parabolic translation. Even his fondness for this painter, the only one Nietzsche occasionally mentions, and always with affection, is itself mediated: he is clearly indebted, in the first place, to Goethe's *Conversations with Eckermann,* his favorite German book, in which one often encounters observations on Claude Lorrain's landscapes and consistently in a tone of deep admiration—Goethe calls Claude Lorrain "a perfect human being,"[17] an accent that must have made Nietzsche prick up his ears, and Goethe says of his paintings, employing an antithesis that would certainly have sounded familiar to the young Schopenhauerian Nietzsche, that they contained the highest truth but not a trace of reality. Second, however, Nietzsche obviously owes this characteristic predilection as well to his association with Jakob Burckhardt, who particularly admired Claude Lorrain and even occasionally liked to compare various impressions to his landscapes—"this melody is a Claude Lorrain in sound,"[18] he writes at one point about Gluck's *Armida.*[19] In exactly the same way, Nietzsche refers to two movements of a symphony by Peter Gast as the "most beautiful Claude Lorrain in music I know . . ."[20] (It appears entirely typical for the type of mind on whom Claude Lorrain's art—this art of "the highest truth but without a trace of reality"—makes a determinative impression that yet another contemporary artist, a poet and psychologist like Nietzsche, a Swiss lover of the south and interpreter of history like Burckhardt, esteemed in Claude Lorrain a master who was particularly close to him: namely Conrad Ferdinand Meyer. The psychological effect of the painter's art on these three glorifiers of the south, who were linked by fate with one another in more than one respect, must have had something of the magic about it that Schopenhauer attributes to music as the metaphysical art: its inexpressible inner essence, thanks to which it represents in itself a paradise that is so utterly familiar and yet eternally remote, seems to rest on the fact that it reflected stirrings of their own innermost being "but entirely without reality and far from its pain.")[21] The landscape dreams of this Lorrainese[22] pre-romantic filled with southern perspectives, which "excite boundless longing" with the faint sounds from their distant backgrounds, are truly a perfect symbol for the transmuted southern happiness experienced by the northerner, for that homesickness for the south that is experienced from an inward northerliness and that Nietzsche felt all his life. "Two days ago, toward evening," he writes as early as the 1870s, "I was entirely submerged in Claude Lorrainesque delights and finally broke down in sustained and violent weeping. That I was still able to experience that! I had not known that the earth offered such a display and had thought that the good painters had invented it."[23] And he continues, gratefully catching his breath in the strangely cool air of a Greek momentary presence: "The heroic idyll is now the discovery of my soul: and with a single blow the bucolic element of antiquity has now been unmasked before me and made obvious—until now I did not understand a thing about it."[24] But even at the end, in 1888 in *Ecce homo,* he similarly writes, with the same sigh of late happiness—"Never—until today . . ."—again, characteristically, with a comparative glance at Claude Lorrain: "I have never experienced such an autumn, nor did I ever think such a thing was possible on earth—a Claude Lorrain thought into infinity, each day of the same unbridled perfection."[25] Or, from the same time, to Gast: "In terms of its landscape, Turin is so much more agreeable to me than that limestony, treeless and dull stretch of Riviera that I cannot stop being upset with myself for waiting so long to leave it. I will not say a word about the contemptible and cheap sort of people there—not excluding the foreigners. Here there arises day after day with the same unbridled perfection and sun-filled plenitude: magnificent trees in blazing yellow, the sky and the great river a delicate blue, the air of utmost purity—a Claude Lorrain as I never dreamed I would see it."[26]

Even this last passage demonstrates, incidentally, how skeptical Nietzsche's comments about the immediate, objective reality of the south can be. He is no stranger to the contempt that can swiftly befall a northerner, even Goethe, in the south like a wave of disgust.[27] "A complete and sudden repugnance toward Italy forced me to return quickly from Bergamo,"[28] he wrote to Malwida in 1872, and in the following year he assures her: "I would have come to Florence in any case *only* because of you (and not for the sake of some paintings)."[29] The famed beauty of the contours forming the classical gulf causes him to be fastidious: "It is difficult for me to persuade myself about a region, no matter how famous its name. I saw imperfect lines near Sorrento."[30] During his time in Nice he writes (to Malwida in 1885): "I do not like this coast, I despise Nice, but in winter it has the driest air in Europe."[31] And at the same time to Gast: "I am weary of Nice, a noisy disgusting French town, from the bottom of my soul."[32] That does not sound very much like respect for Latin *reality,* which one would actually expect given the emphatic reverence the late Nietzsche shows toward everything French; he simply does not know "how to avoid it since, as I know after extensive research, the climatic conditions of this place are not to be found anywhere else in Europe."[33]

Here, as in many other passages, it becomes evident that Nietzsche's relationship to *French* culture is also constructed entirely on the basis of the ideal antithesis "north against south, north *in* the south." The fact that the trip he planned to take in 1869 with Erwin Rohde to Paris—the "university of existence"[34] (as he wrote as a twenty-four-year-old)—did *not* occur, no doubt strongly promoted the pronounced stylization of all French things that marks Nietzsche in his middle and late periods. A fateful instinct perhaps led him thereafter to avoid the reality of "Paris" he revered from afar, just as he also very reluctantly made contact with the reality of Rome, "this most obscene place on earth for the poet of *Zarathustra.*"[35] The French people, as Nietzsche imagined them out of cultural gratitude and a very distant acquaintance (and peoples, as a whole, are always imaginative constructs based on love, pride, or envy), this beautiful, otherworldly France has something about it of a transfigured, wishful ideal of German possibilities. For it demonstrates, above all, that ideal balance of northern and southern elements that Nietzsche simultaneously misses in the German character ("there is something in it that could be *Hellenic*")[36] and demands as the fulfillment of a primal disposition. "Within the character of the *French,*" he writes in *Beyond,* "there is a halfway successful synthesis of the north and south, which allows them to grasp many things and leads them to do other things that an *Englishman* will never grasp; their temperament, which periodically turns toward and away from the south, in which Provencal and Ligurian blood bubbles over from time to time, protects them from the ghastly northern gray on gray and from sunless conceptual phantasms and spiritual anemia—that is, from our *German* illness of taste. . . . Even today there still exists in France an appreciation and accommodation for those rarer people who know how to love the south in the north, the north in the south—for the born 'middlelanders,' the 'good Europeans.' Music was created for them by Bizet, that last genius who saw a new beauty and seduction—who discovered a part of the *music of the south.*"[37]

The southernization of music, whose possibility Nietzsche delightedly hears in the "African aridity and fervor" of *Carmen,* a promise of "unheard-of"[38] southern charms, is particularly in his last years an article of faith and a deeply certain hope, and a symbol and guarantee for the coming new southernization of Europe that was becoming all too northern (for he sees even France threatened by this danger). A late note in the Notebooks audaciously states this idea in French: "Il faut méditerraniser la musique."[39] He admonishes his friend Gast, his musician of the south: "*Stay southern,* and even if it be only in belief!"[40] The poem "Music of the South" from the autumn of 1884 concludes with the related wishful ecstasy:

> Oh, do not hesitate to turn the ship's desire
> To Southern climes To Blessed Isles
> To the games of Greek nymphs—
> No ship ever found a more beautiful destination![41]

In *Beyond,* he then composes a fugue in which these two leitmotifs, "music" and the "south," become a vision of the ear, a premonitory dream of a future "Mediterranean" music:

"Assuming that someone loves the south as I do, as a great school of recuperation, in the most intellectual and sensual sense, as an unbridled abundance and transfiguration of sun spreading out over an insolent, credulous existence: well, such a person will learn to be on guard against German music . . . Such a southerner, not by birth but by belief must, if he dreams of the music of the future, also dream of music's redemption from the north and he must have the prelude to a deeper, more powerful, perhaps more evil and more mysterious music in his ears, a super-German music that will not fade, turn yellow and pale before the sight of the blue voluptuous sea and the Mediterranean brightness of the sky the way all German music does, a super-European music that will be right even when confronted by the brown sunsets of the desert."[42]

Here, at just this point in *Beyond,* the south clearly gains a meaning that appears to go beyond the significance Nietzsche had previously ascribed to it. That strange mediacy of his experience of the south acquires its meaning: it becomes seemingly transparent and lets something like a deeper south shimmer through; an *Oriental* element becomes visible in it, a secret, inner Orient. We can observe in Nietzsche's final years something similar, although more compressed, to what happened to Goethe, whose *Westöstlicher Divan* (West-Eastern Divan)[43] is a testament to a second great journey to the south, albeit only an inward one, a higher spiral turn up above the Italian journey. "Flee so that you may taste the patriarchal air of the pure East"[44]—the motto of the *Divan* accompanies Nietzsche throughout the *Zarathustra* decade. What he now admires as the highest possibility of the Italian genius is precisely its eye for the grandly Oriental: "Leonardo da Vinci was perhaps alone among the artists of the Renaissance in having a truly super-Christian eye. He knows 'the Orient,' the inner as well as the external one. There is something super-European and discreet about him, something that distinguishes anyone who has seen too broad a spectrum of good and bad things."[45] *The Gay Science* trains such a Leonardo eye on southern Catholicism with its opposition to the "always more genial and shallower north": "The entire Roman Church rests on a southern suspicion about the nature of man, who is always misunderstood from the perspective of the north: in this suspicion the European south assumed the inheritance of the deep Orient, of ancient, mysterious Asia and of its contemplation."[46] Even early on, in his inaugural lecture in Basel in 1869, Nietzsche speaks, with an eye toward the symbolic value of whole epochs and cultures, of the ideal of Greek antiquity as "perhaps only the most beautiful outgrowth of the German love affair with the south."[47] Now, after *Zarathustra,* this ideal of antiquity also takes on an ever more distinct Oriental background and undertone that come out of a northern homesickness for the south:

"To rediscover the *south* in oneself and to spread out over oneself a bright, radiant, mysterious southern sky; to reconquer for oneself the southern health and hidden strength of the soul; to become, step by step, more extensive, more transnational, more European, more trans-European, more Oriental, finally more *Greek*—for the Greeks were the first great absorption and synthesis of everything Oriental and thus the *beginning* of the European soul, the discovery of *our* 'new world'—who knows what can happen to someone who lives according to such imperatives? Perhaps—a *new day!*"[48]

It is not without a deeper symbolism that, in Nietzsche's final years, his taste in landscapes displays a pronounced proclivity for progressively browner, yellower, more fiery desert tones; characteristically enough, he seeks to go beyond the merely Italic south in making his travel plans; he seriously wants to go to Corsica, to Spain, to Tunis, to the oasis at Biskra;[49] he would like to live for a while among Muslims in order to sharpen his eye for everything European; his predilection for certain brown desert moods is unmistakable in the latter parts of *Zarathustra.* Because none of these travels could be realized, he is able to stylize in his own mind the sensuous impression of the Italian present into something more fiery, more Oriental, more African; thus he writes to Gast in 1886: "During the journey to Nice I saw and very clearly felt that after Alassio something new begins in the air, the light, the colors: namely, something *African.* The expression is very precise: I have consulted the opinions of the best experts on Africa. . . . Everything is a hundred times finer, more delicate, white-yellowish, more un-German, more indifferent than even Genoa and its environs."[50] (That this is no momentary notion of Nietzsche's is demonstrated by a letter two years later to Seydlitz from Nice: "The days are going by here in shameless beauty; there has never been a more perfect winter"—one notes the superlative tone of the last year!—"All of the colors are shot through with a brilliant, silvery gray; intellectual, sophisticated colors; not a remnant of the brutality of the bottom shades. The advantage this little piece of coast between Alassio and Nice enjoys is a license to indulge in Africanism in color, flora and aridity: that occurs nowhere else in Europe."[51] A few years earlier, he turns the experience of the promontory near Portofino into something Greek, tropical, Robinson Crusoesque: "Imagine an island in the Greek archipelago, with a forest and mountain arbitrarily tossed on and which accidentally washed up to the mainland one day and never drifted away. There is something *Greek* about it, no doubt: on the other hand, something pirate-like, sudden, hidden, dangerous; finally, on a lonely bend, a bit of *tropical* pine forest that takes one out of Europe, something Brazilian, as my dinner companion says who has traveled several times around the world. I have never lain about so much, in true Robinson insularity and oblivion; I also frequently build large fires and watch them burn."[52] These archipelago landscapes and these childishly lonely fires were what surrounded the writing of the great Robinsonade of Zarathustra's loneliness. And here, too, one strongly senses the allegorical aspect of the enjoyment in landscape, the need for interpretation and alienation, a flight into the pure east, into the innocence of an outermost south.

And thus it becomes clear on many levels: every south is in Nietzsche's experience a de-realized symbol of a higher reality, a mysterious medium though which he senses and reveres the first homeland of *his* humanity and, beyond that, of his German humanity. Just as he loves in his favorite Claude Lorrain not so much the painter as the interpretive artist who, among all the landscape painters, captures most intensively the perspectival character of existence that *The Gay Science* considers, and who also knows how to raise the sensuous present to the level of allegory, thereby awakening homesickness. "Three landscapes by Claude Lorrain made me think,"[53] he wrote from Rome in 1883. *Made me think*—this phrase expresses and demonstrates a great deal about Nietzsche's strangely metaphorical and intense experience of paintings and landscapes. It gives a sense of the unsensuous mediacy, the intellectually non-present, the Nordic brooding of his southern happiness—a very un-Goethean southern happiness. Such a Lorrain landscape, a landscape more of interpretation than of being, of northern-Norn[54] allegory more than of present happiness, is the mighty south bordering on the desert of silence that Nietzsche proclaims and glorifies, and whose victim he himself became a few weeks after the last southern ecstasy of the autumn in Turin: "I have never experienced such an autumn, nor did I ever think such a thing was possible on earth—a Claude Lorrain thought into infinity, each day of the same unbridled perfection."[55] An Italic land, whose ancient sky had so often been given a deeper blue by northern gratitude, is only an *allegory* here as well, only a transition and an exit to the "inner Orient"; it is only the soul's bridge from the wineless landscape of the northern homesick man who is never drunk on the present into the presentless present allegorical land of the pure East, which is the homeland of Zarathustra, the homeland of all that longed to be Zarathustra.

15

Venice

. . . There, for the first time, the meaning of song was unlocked for me. From a distance a voice sounds exceedingly strange, like a lament without sadness, there is something unbelievably touching about it, that even moves one to tears. . . . And yet one can imagine that a listener up close would derive little pleasure from such voices that have to fight with the waves of the sea. . . . It is the song of a solitary person sent out into distant reaches so that someone of like disposition may hear it and respond.[1]
—Goethe, *Italian Journey*

Inscribed in the legend of Nietzsche the wanderer are four cities on whose names there now falls a reflection of his own like a gift of belated gratitude. These four cities alone are more than the accidental backdrops to a heroic drama played out entirely within himself, more than mere milestones on the path of the philosophic pilgrim. Their names designate and truly embody distinct directions in his intellectual landscape, their outlines mark the extreme ends of his inner universe.

There is Basel, an island of belated aristocratic humanism, one of the last of the venerable and refined city-republics in pre-revolutionary Europe and still the most spiritual one of all. The city conscious of straddling the frontier between Germanness and super-Germanness in Nietzsche's sense, who thought that all the good qualities formerly considered "German" were now to be found in purer form and more often in Switzerland than in the "empire"—"the noblest example Jakob Burckhardt." Basel, which honored itself with an imperishable wreath by appointing the young Nietzsche to a university chair, represents in Nietzsche's life the entire store of tradition that always nourished all that was radically new and unprecedented in this transvaluer. "Basel gave me your image and that of Jakob Burckhardt"[2] he says in his confession of gratitude to Overbeck, the church historian in Basel. And to Burckhardt himself, the most distinguished son and representative of Basel who, in the words of Cosima Wagner, "was the only thing in Basel that mattered" to Nietzsche: "I know no one apart from you who has so much in common with me."[3] Basel—that signifies the foundation Nietzsche acquired in Schulpforta in a freer and purified sphere, lent the most magnificent long-distance vision; it signifies exquisite humanistic tradition and the philosophy of history deepened by skepticism, labor in the service of memorializing the highest, Hellenic humanity, and not merely memorializing it. Basel—that means for Nietzsche, to whom everything "illegitimate" remained repugnant to the end, the last time he experienced an intellectually aristocratic bourgeoisie, where the bourgeois had a home (how expressive of his never-extinguished homesickness for the bourgeoisie he left behind is the copy of his last letter to Jakob Burckhardt, which he wrote as the catastrophe in Turin began: "You may make use of this letter in any way that will not lower me in the esteem of the citizens of Basel");[4] Basel means for the last time a positively valued and interpreted Germany, one stylized along the lines of the *Meistersinger,* without the flamboyant scorn of his late super-Germanness, but already with all of its noblest impatience (it is not for nothing that he sees Böcklin's art as a symbol of a desirable Swissification of German culture); it also means Tribschen, the birth of a tragedy out of the spirit of music, it means a tremendous hope for reformation, "Muses' Monastery," the cult of friendship, "bliss *inter pares*"—it means, finally, farewell, the bitterest farewell to all the piety and faith of his youth and from the rapturous delusional fantasies of an all-too-extravagant gratitude: from the delusion, above all, of the most fruitful and decisive bond of his life—that with Richard Wagner. Basel—retrospectively it was for Nietzsche the necessary transformative threshold to himself ("'I yearn for myself'—that has actually been the continuous theme of my last ten years,"[5] he writes of Basel in 1877)—but the threshold to someone who was henceforth unavoidably solitary. Basel means in his life *The Birth of Tragedy*—"incipit tragoedia."

But farther down to the south, *Genoa* already beckoned, the city of Columbus, the port to new oceans, where "the will expands," where one "no longer has the courage to be cowardly."[6] The city that for Nietzsche is the *face* of brave and lordly generations past, and an image of similar ones to come. Above all, a reflection of his own boldest, most adventurous, and solitarily triumphant moments:

> I can always see how the architect trains his gaze on all the structures built around him near and far, and on the city, sea and mountain silhouette, how he exercises violence and conquest with this gaze: all of this he wants to incorporate into *his* plan and in the end make his possession. . . . Just as these men recognized no boundaries abroad and, in their thirst for novelty, erected a new world next to the old one, so too everyone continued to struggle against everyone else back at home, trying to discover a way of expressing his own superiority and to place between himself and his neighbor his personal boundlessness. Everyone conquered his homeland once more for himself by overwhelming it with his architectonic ideas. . . . In the north, one is impressed by the order and the general enjoyment in orderliness and obedience when one observes how the cities are built. . . . Here, however, when you

> go around every corner you find an independent person, someone who knows the sea, adventure and the Orient, someone who is averse to order and to his neighbor: . . . he would like . . . to found all of this anew, at least in his thoughts . . . invest it with his own meaning: even if this were only for the moment of a sunny afternoon. . . .[7] (*The Gay Science*)

That is Genoa, the city with a view of the most majestic promontory in Europe, of Zarathustra's Greek and super-Greek peninsula, the city from which the new tone, the Zarathustra tone, makes itself heard in Nietzsche's letters for the very first time: "Here in Genoa I am proud and happy, entirely Prince Doria[8]—or Columbus? I wander . . . exultant with joy over the heights and with a view of the future that no one before me has ever dared . . ."[9] (1881 to his sister). Genoa—that means the sea, it means the secretiveness of the sea, the happiness and the dread it evokes; it means daybreak and beyond, hope without horizon and the most daring adventurousness, godlessness out of profundity, solitude out of a belief in humanity, cynicism out of the will to the highest reverence—Genoa, that means *Zarathustra.*

Then, far from the sea and close to the ice, *Turin* glistens, its self-confident present, its royal certainty in possessing masterful maturity, in having fulfilled its predestination, in dominion—"my residence from now on":[10] "when one feels at home here, one becomes king . . ."[11] not only of Italy. Nietzsche's "classical place," and not only "for my feet and eyes."[12] Not a new metropolis, like the new cities of the "empire" ("those manufactured vices"), thoroughly unmodern, a "seventeenth-century royal capital,"[13] embodying dignified gravity, ceremonial legitimacy, full of aristocratic serenity and a uniformity of taste—the final, worthy setting for a fate ending in tragedy, the last benefaction of the Italic south to its northern celebrant, the ecstasy of a deceptive perfection and of Hellenic hubris, the "leisure of a god along the Po"[14]—Turin, that means: *Will to Power* and *Ecce homo.*

The last city, however, lying far removed in a fantastical twilight, is Venice. It is the city that remained to the end closest to Nietzsche's heart. The city of his love. "Venice, the only place on earth that I love,"[15] he writes to Overbeck in 1887, and in 1885 to Gersdorff: "In the end, Venice is the only city I love."[16] 1884 to Gast: "Apart from Capri, nothing in the south made such an impression on me as your Venice."[17] (It also seems to him, as Platen[18] put it in an expression that was one of Nietzsche's favorite phrases, to be the perfect city, the city in itself, compared to which Rome is "crude and too gaudy, and Naples is a pile of houses.")[19] One year later: "I have discovered that so far I have liked and benefited from Venice alone";[20] and in his final year, from Turin: "Venice—a consecrated place for my feeling . . ."[21]

It is not immediately obvious, as it is with Nietzsche's other three cities, how to delineate the spheres of his being that coalesce into the symbol, the magic cipher

"Venice." A strange twilight falls not only on Nietzsche's own comments about Venice, it also envelops, it seems, the essence of this love, of this "consecration" itself. If Basel, Genoa, and Turin call forth very particular, unequivocally clear associations within the legend of Nietzsche's life, then various twilight tones reverberate in the name of Venice in a mysteriously ambivalent way. Indeed, it truly seems as if everything Nietzsche's being and fate contains by way of an ultimate irresolvable ambiguity surrounds the word Venice as if it were a prism. It is the only city he loved, but he still counted it among his forbidden places. It is the city in which Richard Wagner, hated and beloved, died at a "holy hour," and it is also where *his* musician, Peter Gast, lived, his anti-Wagner and herald of a super-German, Mediterranean southern music, where he created that "lion's music" that to Nietzsche "is itself in many respects a kind of idealized Venice":[22] "it is possible that twenty of its enchanting melodies may one day come together in the word and notion of 'Venice.'"[23] It is the city where *Tristan* was born, the work most shrouded in twilight, whose fascination for Nietzsche is without parallel in the history of art, and at the same time where the bright "lion's music" was born, the music of the south, the most anti-Wagnerian, anti-romantic of all possible music envisioned by Nietzsche. It is the city whose solitude is magically deeper and more irrevocable than that of any other: "a hundred deep solitudes together form the city of Venice—that is its magic,"[24] he writes during the time of *Daybreak;* but it is also the city of the most gregarious enchantment, the most entrancing of all forms of magic that create the illusion of intimacy: of music. "If I search for another word for music, then I always find the word Venice,"[25] *Ecce homo* says. Music, however: that is the sweetest form of *that* delusion which Nietzsche "desperately needs" like no other—the delusion of "not being so isolated":[26] "How delightful it is that words and tones exist; are words and tones not rainbows and illusory bridges between what has been eternally divided?

"For every soul there is another world. . . . Between things that seem most similar it is, above all, semblance that creates the most beautiful illusion; for the smallest divide is the most difficult to bridge.

"For me—how could there be an Outside-of-me? There is no Outside! But we forget that in listening to all the tones; how delightful it is that we forget! . . . How delightful . . . the whole lie of tones!" (*Zarathustra*).[27]

For Nietzsche, Venice became a city of symbol like no other. Symbol of all that "mattered most to him"—like the "fate of music"[28]—symbol, above all, of his own innermost ambiguity and duality of soul. Just as, according to Nietzsche himself, the Engadin, by embracing all the points midway between the ice and the south, is his *proper* landscape, related to him by blood, even more, "so far from life, so metaphysical"[29]—in precisely the same way Venice, the middle and mediator between Orient and Occident, half Byzantium, half Bruges, formed by amalgamating land and lagoon in an enigmatic double existence, the consanguineous city of his soul, the only one he *loves*—can love. It is truly his *civitas metaphysica,* just as *Tristan,* which was born in Venice, of Venice, appears to him as "the true *opus metaphysicam* of all art."[30] The world, he says, is *forgotten* in Venice. With that, the mood of *Tristan* is struck as Nietzsche tries to capture it in words in the fourth *Untimely Meditation.* What he expresses there about Wagner's most profound work, the one nearest to death, is true as well of his Venice: it is the city "on which rests the glance of a dying man with his insatiable, sweet longing for the secrets of the night and of death, far away from life, which appears as evil, deceptive and divisive, illuminated by a ghastly, spectral morning light and clarity. . . . Appropriate to the secret of which it speaks, of being dead in a living body, of being one within duality."[31] A deep coincidence, if not something more than that, also allowed one of Nietzsche's favorite works of literature, Byron's poem full of the wish for forgetfulness, the desire for death—*Manfred*—to be completed during the three years this restless wanderer spent in Venice[32]—"forgetfulness!" is his mournful Tristan plea to the spirits—in exactly the same years that witnessed the creation of *The World as Will and Representation;*[33] and, not coincidentally, Nietzsche speaks about this Venetian poem in accents that he otherwise employs solely for *Tristan:* "I must be deeply related to Byron's *Manfred:* I found all of the same chasms in myself—at thirteen I was ready for this work."[34] The magically seductive Tristan-ambiguity of Venice, a metaphysical ambiguity commingling the closest proximity to death with an ultimate sweetness of life—it is this masqueraded beauty of Venice to which everyone has always succumbed who, like Byron, like Nietzsche, are half conscious of a tragically incurable dualism in the fundamental disposition of their being and who encounter in the miracle of the lagoons a half-confounding, half-delightful *Doppelgänger* symbol of their own existence—within German literature one thinks of Platen's *Venetian Sonnets,*[35] Conrad Ferdinand Meyer's "On the Grand Canal,"[36] or Thomas Mann's *Death in Venice*—all instances in which beauty does not, as with Plato, only seduce us to the highest life, but also where it simultaneously, mysteriously simultaneously, must signify a seduction toward death: "Whoever has viewed beauty with his own eyes, Is already consigned unto death"[37] is how the poem by Platen begins that, significantly and almost clairvoyantly, he gave the title "Tristan." They all truly experienced here, if anywhere, how "the ambiguity of life coalesced as if in its proper body"[38]—so says Georg Simmel in a short, Nietzsche-inspired study on Venice, the "artificial city," the city of the most extreme tension between appearance and reality, the city that like no other on earth is a tragic and dangerous lie. Everything here is ambiguous—public squares, bridges, facades—"the dual life of the city is ambiguous, first in the context of its streets, then in the context of the canals, so that it belongs neither to the land nor to the water—rather each one appears to be the Protean garment behind which, in each case, the other beckons as the actual body; ambiguous, too, are the small, dark canals whose waters flow and surge so restlessly—but without flowing in any discernable direction, in constant motion, but going nowhere. That our life is actually only a foreground behind which death stands as the only certainty—that is the final reason why life, as Schopenhauer says, is 'thoroughly ambiguous'. . . ."[39] What is seen here purely analytically and formulated in Schopenhauerian terms regarding Venice's ambiguous character, its metaphysics, is the same thing that Nietzsche experienced in music and expressed in Wagnerian accents. His love for this city, a love that swims like a forgotten island from the earliest Schopenhauer landscape of his youth, floating so strangely, so paradoxically and apparently rootlessly in the completely differently directed philosophy of his final "Genoese" decade—it is ultimately identical with his love for *that* art which he himself calls ambiguous: for music, for a music he experienced in Wagnerian fashion (affectionately or antagonistically in Wagnerian fashion). Even the latest Nietzsche, the restless wanderer, repeatedly flees the changing landscapes of knowledge to the landscapeless calm of Venice, to the seasonless dream of a city in which "the world is forgotten," to *that* art which, in Luther's words, "has nothing to do with the world"[40]—to music, for which Venice to Nietzsche is only another word. Again and again, his love returns from the more southern, sunnier, more sinister world, which he thought he could also hear in the music of his Venetian maestro "Pietro Gasti," back to the most truly Venetian work of tonal art of all times, to the "secrets of the night and of death, far away from life"[41]—to Wagner's *Tristan.* Even the last time he reviewed his life he still admitted: no other art, no bright Mozartean music, no livelier art of "the day" stayed as close to his heart as the music of this work, on which rests the glance of a dying man, which speaks of being dead in a living body, of being one within duality: "I am still looking," *Ecce homo* says, "for a work of equally dangerous fascination, of an equally horrifying and sweet infinity, as *Tristan*—I look to all the arts in vain."[42] The "danger," the magic, the horrifying and sweet infinity, the unity in duality—these *Tristan* formulae characterize his experience of Venice: the oppositions of his being flow together here into a mysterious, otherworldly, metaphysical identity. And everything that he long yearned for on his many paths as the goal, as the final happiness and final meaning—the happiness and secret of the south, of danger, of suffering, of music, even the horror of the nearness of death: he finds that everything is somehow enigmatically unified in the "Beyond Day," in the night that is called Venice. This is most stirringly expressed in the strangely Venetian passage of the *Ecce homo* confession: "If I say: 'on the other side of the Alps,' I am actually saying only 'Venice.' If I look for another word for music, then I always find only the word Venice. I don't know how to make a distinction between tears and music—I cannot think of happiness, of the *south,* without a shudder of fearfulness."[43] Here we are at the innermost threshold to Nietzsche's musical sanctuary; at the root of his *fatum,* which makes him "suffer from the fate of music as from an open wound."[44] Here Nietzsche enters into something like a constantly renewed birth of music out of the spirit of Venice, comparable to a nocturnal experience that a letter to Gast touches on: "The night on the Rialto Bridge brought music to me that moved me to tears, an incredible, old-fashioned adagio *as if there had never been any other adagio before.*"[45] The incredible adagio was the music of Venice, it was Venice itself. Even the antimusical, plastic mind of a Goethe heard it, he whose south was otherwise called Rome and not Venice; he confessed that in nocturnal Venice "the meaning of song was unlocked for me for the first time," where he speaks of the calling night-songs of the gondoliers: "From a distance a voice sounds exceedingly strange, like a lament without sadness, there is something *unbelievably touching about it, that even moves one to tears.* . . . It is the song of a solitary person sent out into the distant reaches so that someone of like disposition may hear it and respond."[46] (The Wagner of *Tristan* also heard it, this ancient, strange voice of Venice, echoing out of distant canals in the silent nocturnal city, and it entered his work. While he was working on *Tristan* he wrote in a letter to Mathilde Wesendonk: "The melodies of the gondoliers are in any case ancient, as ancient as Venice. . . . These deeply melancholy melodies, sung with a resounding, powerful voice, carried over the water from afar, fading away even farther away, sublimely moved me.")[47] The same impression elicited similar words from the most dissimilar minds imaginable. What Goethe says about Venice, almost unwillingly ("I attributed it to my mood; but my companion said: é singolare, come quel canto intenerisce . . ."),[48] is almost a symbol for the fate of Zarathustra's soul, which is all-too-close to music, a soul that was never permitted to dissolve fully in its "music" and "to be one," but that instead remained imprisoned in the hopeless solitude of the word, and of the word alone, up to the threshold of madness—"it should have sung this new soul, and not spoken,"[49] is the painful word the late Nietzsche repeatedly says, mourning the youth who produced *The Birth of Tragedy out of the Spirit of Music,* out of Wagner's transformative proximity. Zarathustra's voice, too, is a voice from afar, and one may well hear the exceedingly strange sound of a lament without sadness arising out of its painfully heroic will to that which is eternally renounced, to the most vital life. His solitary voice is also a song sent out far and wide, a "song of a lover," so that someone of like disposition may hear it and respond. Out of the hundred solitudes that together form the city of Venice, out of the most incommunicable seventh solitude of his spectrally lurid, hyperconscious day, he hears "with the ear of his love"[50]—but "no sound of love reached him anymore." Again and again, music, and music alone, creates for him a deceptively gladdening rainbow, an illusory bridge between what is eternally divided to the yearned-for "unity in duality,"[51] out of the dungeon of a Schopenhauerian, incommunicable individuality. "For me—how could there be an Outside-of-me? For every soul there is another world. But we forget that in listening to all the tones. How delightful the whole lie of tones!"[52] And whenever Zarathustra bids his soul to sing ("That I bade you to sing, my soul, behold, that was *my last!*"), it always occurs on the brink of the most extreme, unbearable loneliness, it is an ecstatic call into the outermost expanses, asking whether someone might finally be listening, whether someone might not perhaps answer after all. The short poem "Venice," which Nietzsche inserted immediately after the passage in *Ecce homo* in which he speaks about Venice as only another word for music, concludes with such a questioning song of a lonely man sent into the distance, the same kind that Goethe heard in tears:

> I recently stood on the bridge
> During a dark-brown night.
> From afar came a song;
> It surged like a golden drop
> Over the quivering surface.
> Gondolas, lights, music—
> Drunkenly it swam out into the twilight . . .
>
> My soul, a stringed instrument,
> Secretly sang along to itself,
> Invisibly moved, a gondola song,
> Trembling with radiant bliss.
> —Is anyone listening to it?[53]

Did anyone listen to it? . . . This question, half lament, half joy, gliding drunkenly out into the twilight from a loneliest soul that feels invisibly moved—this question, which is also raised in the overture to *Tristan,* solemnly strange, and like a lament without sadness—which hears and answers only a second, more distant question of like mind—this *Tristan* question with no other answer except an otherworldly, metaphysical one: that is Nietzsche's Venice. "Venice"—there is no concept, no name, no idea, no hope that answers to this sound in his legend—rather, a waft of music, a distantly questioning song full of ambiguous melancholy, a moving and incredible adagio over evening waters.

16

Portofino

We are close to waking up when we dream that we are dreaming.[1]
—Novalis

Visit Herder's creations, where Greek vitality and Indian lassitude are oddly conjoined, and you will be bathed, as it were, by moonlight on which daybreak is already encroaching—but a hidden sun illumines both.[2]
—Jean Paul

Two landscapes live on in the poem about Zarathustra's downfall. One, containing "all the points midway between the ice and the South,"[3] the most remote, high-lying valley on the continent, the Engadin, where "Italy and Finland form an alliance,"[4] where a "constant sunny October wind"[5] blows: this, Nietzsche says, is "*my* landscape: so far away from life, so metaphysical."[6] Here, according to his own testimony, "the basic conception of *Zarathustra,* the idea of the Eternal Return, that highest formula of affirmation,"[7] came over him with the force of an ecstatic vision. The other landscape, however, is that of the Gulf of Rapallo, which is dominated by the noble promontory of Portofino—"a small forgotten world of happiness,"[8] as Nietzsche still gratefully says in *Ecce homo.* During extended walks through this landscape, "the entire first part of *Zarathustra* occurred to me, above all Zarathustra himself, as a type: or more accurately, he *descended* upon me . . ."[9]

Both landscapes, as image and atmosphere, achieved intellectual immortality in *Zarathustra.* What Nietzsche says about the Engadin applies to both: he feels he is related to that landscape by blood, indeed even closer. Both gain for him the highest degree of reality and forcefulness that any sensual impression could ever give him: they became for him allegorical, symbolic, decipherably ambiguous. He experienced them as sensual allegories of himself: "we see many landscapes again when we encounter them for the first time."[10] If the Engadin is Nietzsche's "landscape of the middle," in whose cool and high symbolism all of the extreme opposites of his nature are unified, becomes an allegory of the power in him to wed opposites, then the landscape of the Gulf of Rapallo is the natural symbol of all the forces in his being that tend toward the extreme. And the magic of this landscape, as Nietzsche perceived it and as it is carried over into *Zarathustra,* that magic is foremost one of extremes. "The magic that fights for us is the *magic of the extreme,* the seduction that every extreme performs,"[11] he writes in *The Will to Power.* That is precisely the magic of this landscape as well. Whenever Nietzsche talks about it he interprets it into the extreme, as if he were enraptured by a strange ecstasy. He does not believe he is in Italy there: he stylizes the coast of the Genovese gulf into the coast of the noblest sea, that of the Greek archipelago; the promontory becomes in his eyes a Greek island that possesses something pirate-like, something sudden, hidden, dangerous. Indeed, he thinks he feels something tropical, Brazilian, a true Robinson Crusoe insularity and oblivion. Above all, however, it is the visibly extreme element of this landscape that enchants him with the seduction of all extremes: the powerful promontory of Portofino itself, falling into the sea in the boldest and noblest line formed by the entire coast, when viewed from the Genovese side, made an indelible impression on Nietzsche's imagination. The original model of the "high pass between two seas," on which Zarathustra "strolls full of the prophetic spirit,"[12] is the pass in the promontory high above Portofino, between the two gulfs of Genoa and Rapallo, where on overly clear days heralding a storm one can see the coast of Corsica surfacing at the extreme edge of the sea, which does not appear to lie flat but, in its unnaturally broad expanse, seems to rise up toward the horizon like a wall, the entire spectacle fantastically unreal from the distorting perspective of the promontory's height and almost dreamlike in its notional symmetry and rigidity. It is Zarathustra's dream landscape, not the one in which the revelation of the Great Midday comes to him, the thought of the Eternal Return of all things in themselves, the thought that the willing man stands in the high middle of all time for all eternity, which joins Formerly and Yet to be, animal and overman, in an ever renewed union—that is the landscape of Sils-Maria—but rather the landscape of a "final morning dream": "In a dream, in a final morning dream, I stood today upon a promontory—beyond the world, I held a pair of scales and *weighed* the world"[13] (*Zarathustra*). This promontory beyond the world is also a heightened vision of Portofino, and strangely combined with it, within and outside of *Zarathustra,* the atmosphere of the final dream, immediately before waking into a new day. That atmosphere of "daybreak," the magic of twilight—one does not know if it is a morning or evening twilight—which constitutes perhaps the most fascinating allure of Nietzsche's works, is in truth a magic of the extreme, the trickling dream shudder of initial doubt about the apparent reality, how it begins to stir under the thin and increasingly colorful surface of the morning dream announcing awakening, in fact already the first breath of awakening itself. The entirety of Nietzsche's oeuvre radiates this exquisite and dangerously bewildering magic of the half-dream, in its slightly unsettling mixture of joyful doubt about the reality of what has thus far been taken as true, and about the dream in which we all dream and are dreamt. "How wonderful and new and simultaneously dreadful and ironic my knowledge makes me feel toward the whole of existence! I discovered for myself that ancient humanity and animality, indeed the entire expanse of time and the past of all sentient being continue to create, love, hate, reason in me—I have suddenly awakened in the middle of this dream, but only to the consciousness that I am dreaming and that I must go on dreaming—in order not to be destroyed: as the sleepwalker has to go on dreaming in order not to fall"[14] (*The Gay Science*). "You don't even feel that you are dreaming: oh, then you are very far from waking up!"[15] reads a late passage in the Notebooks, in very peculiar agreement with a fragment by Novalis. The control that someone who is still dreaming, but in the process of waking up, has over both the dream and wakefulness, the twilight of voluntary delusion and knowing awakening—this unites here the earliest romantic with the final one: both are wizards of the extreme, magicians of "crossing," bridge builders into the unknown and masters of the end. A master of the end, a dream reader of every kind of end and extreme, which simultaneously hints at a new beginning, some sort of awakening, a crossing—if anywhere, Nietzsche could claim mastery in that regard, as Novalis could, too, before all the other romantics. The virtuosity of his psychology is a mastery of the end, one that is and wants to be, above all, a psychology of the end. "I have a finer nose for the signs of rise and fall than anyone has ever had, I am the teacher par excellence for that . . ."[16] (*Ecce homo*). Like Novalis, he is enchanted by all things that are already surrounded by the magic of death; indeed, he experiences them most gratefully, most deeply, by interpreting them as an exit, as a form of the end, as a seductively attractive death—the classical example is the gratefully melancholy passage in *Human* on the last art: "Just as one thinks back on one's youth in old age and celebrates festivals of memory, so, too, will humanity soon stand toward art in a relationship of *touching memory* of the joys of youth. Perhaps art has never before been understood as profoundly and soulfully as it is today, when the magic of death seems to hover over it. One thinks of the Greek city in southern Italy that still celebrates its Greek festivals on one day of the year amid sorrow and tears that foreign barbarism is steadily winning out over their received customs; never has anyone enjoyed Hellenic culture as much, nowhere has this golden nectar been savored with such delight as among these dwindling Hellenes."[17] But that is undoubtedly how Nietzsche himself enjoyed all art; in the Notebooks to *Human* from the same time we find the comment: "We are experiencing the decline of the *last art:* Bayreuth convinced me of that."[18] And throughout his life no art was ever as close to him as the one in which he perceives the ages singing their own end: "Every truly significant music is a *swan song.*"[19]

Nietzsche is completely conscious of his passion for everything that sings its own finale, everything that is the most extreme example of its kind, for everything that is perfect which, to speak with Goethe, goes beyond its kind in order to become something else, something incomparable—he is conscious of this promontory type of his entire psychological vision, and he consciously cultivates it as the form, as the style of his thinking and reading. Indeed, in the consciousness of his mastery of the end and of ending, he even turns this particular mastery into the criterion of any kind of mastery in general, and in *The Gay Science* he erects an ideal that bears the name of Portofino: "Masters of the first rank reveal themselves by showing that they know how to find the end in major and minor matters in a perfect way, whether it be the end of a melody or of a thought, be it the fifth act of a tragedy or a political action. The leaders of the second order always become restless toward the end and do not fall into the sea in such proud, calm equilibrium, as does for example the promontory near Portofino—where the Gulf of Genoa sings its melody to the end."[20] (Characteristically enough, he thought, as he wrote in contemporary marginal notes to *Carmen,* that the *final* scene was "a dramatic masterpiece—to be studied! With a view to intensifications, contrasts, logic, etc.")[21] That Nietzsche finds this mark of mastery of the first rank in his own works above all is a matter of course. Every memory of some chapter, some segment, of some longer aphorism offers an example of his conscious art of the end. This art of the end even has an effect on the construction of his sentences: one of Nietzsche's favorite forms is the sentence that extends and turns the balanced spine of thought beyond its apparent conclusion toward a cape that abruptly affords a new perspective pointing toward new coasts like the first pier of a bridge—and already simultaneously slopes down toward the surface of silence. One encounters this promontory type of sentence everywhere: "My ambition is to say in ten sentences what everyone else says in a book—what everyone else *does not* say in a book."[22]

"The actor has spirit, but little of the conscience of spirit. He always believes in what he makes others believe most—in what makes others believe in *him.*"[23]

"And when I saw my devil I found him to be serious, thorough, deep, solemn: it was the spirit of gravity—all things fall through him."[24]

"It is a mark of subtlety that God learned Greek when he decided to become a writer—and that he did not learn it better."[25]

"Whoever is fundamentally a teacher takes all things seriously only with respect to his students—even himself."[26] Even his word coinages are determined by the urge toward the conclusion and promise of "crossing over," the most famous example being the word "overman": super-German, super-Hellenic, super-historical, super-national, super-animal, hyper-Hellenes. And, finally, the unusual frequency of using the word "extreme" in his last stylistic period, or his beginning sentences with "Finally," are merely the smallest crystallization of the magic and seductive power of the extreme, itself small but symbolic as well: in style, too, there are no coincidences, least of all in such a thoroughly "fateful" style as Nietzsche's.

"Always intent on the most extreme expression"[27]—that is one of Nietzsche's characterizations of Wagner's music. It applies in every sense—more intensively than almost everything else that Nietzsche contributed to his self-characterization while speaking about Wagner—to Nietzsche's "music." Not only in the sense that he always strove for the most extreme expression of every thought, but also in that he was always keenly intent on the extreme, the conclusion, the finale of that expression itself—as, incidentally, Wagner himself was, the magician of all intensified endings, of all final refrains and beyond. Indeed, even in the sense that the sum of all his works, that his entire life became the most extreme expression imaginable of his being and of his possibilities. And did anyone ever give such extreme expression to the meaning of his own existence as did Nietzsche in *Ecce homo?* If the essence of a grand style, according to Nietzsche, consists in the wholesale exorcism of details, then this life that exorcized so much, that was so immoderately expressed, certainly bears all the marks of grand style. The conception of the overman already displays in the word itself the stigma of the extreme, just as the idea of the Eternal Return is merely the most extreme pseudo-metaphysical exorcism of a simple "yes" to life (as opposed to the theoretical "no" of Schopenhauer's pessimism). The titles of his books, with their all-too-picturesque refinement, are all exceedingly conscious of the seduction that all extremes exude; in all of them there is a stretching, a straining of expression, including the titles of the individual aphorisms as well. *Beyond Good and Evil, Daybreak, Human, All Too Human,* the *Untimely Meditations,* all have the inner "crossing over," *Antichrist, Revaluation of all Values, Twilight of the Gods, Ecce homo,* the most extreme, shrilly exaggerated hubris devolving into parodic quotation; *The Birth of Tragedy out of the Spirit of Music* has the pompously stepped-up Händel-finale of its theme, proud of finding the perfect ending, the *Untimely Meditation,* "On the Use and Disadvantage of History for Life," the later subtitle to *The Birth:* "Greece and Pessimism," *The Gay Science,* all exhibit the tension of polar attraction between opposite extremes. But *Zarathustra* is in every sense the embodiment and unification of all extremes, of all the Beyonds in Nietzsche's being, it is the name for a "Beyond all previous lands and corners of the ideal,"[28] to use a phrase from *The Gay Science.* It is characterized by the most massive exorcism of all singularities that we possess in any work of high style in German; its style is the extreme in itself, its dynamic is intensification in itself, its ambition a constant going-beyond-itself. "Zarathustra saw further, willed further, was more *capable,* that any other human being . . ."[29] is how the superlativism of *Ecce homo* puts it; and the language of *Zarathustra* is a reflection, a symbol of this ambition to be the most extreme, the boldest promontory of humanity up to that point, the language with which Nietzsche thought he flew "a thousand miles above what has previously been called poetry."[30] And Nietzsche's entire life, for which *Zarathustra* was only the most extreme expression, is it not itself once more composed and formulated as if toward the most extreme accent of his tragic, hybrid end? Is the manner of his intellectual exit not something like a final testimony to his mastery of the end, which also, in this fifth act of the tragedy of his own life, still knew how to find the perfect ending? Certain phrases in *Ecce homo* and in the last letters sometimes sound so odd that it seems as if a master of the first order were speaking here as the master of his own end, over which his will is sovereign; as if "on this Perfect Day on which everything ripens . . . I saw backwards, I saw outward, I had never seen so much and so many things at once. . . . How should I not be grateful to my entire life?"[31] (*Ecce homo*)—as if the contour of this life were sinking by following an inner, if only darkly conscious *will,* in such proud, calm equilibrium into the sea as the hills near Portofino—there, where the Gulf of Genoa sings its melody to the end.

But even if all that remains in the twilight—what is certain is that Nietzsche's life as a whole, insofar as he can be classified within intellectual history and among related minds, that the entire profile of his life recalls Zarathustra's symbolic landscape in fantastical fashion, that it seems to be "related by blood, indeed even closer" to it. The entire phenomenon of Nietzsche is itself such an extreme promontory, a mighty, final foothill of the great high mountain range stretching from early German romanticism, as well as from the classical, idealist-humanist cultural epoch, a cape and landmark jutting far out but rooted deep in the mainland, nobly sinking down in a magnificent, steep decline toward the surface that until now has reflected only hints of new shores of the mind. But just as this promontory is a final foothill and an extreme decline, a proud and beautifully tragic finale of tremendous moving forces, so, too, is it a gesturing promise, a setting forth from old shores, already an island, a first pier of the bridge over new seas and to new strands. "I am a prelude,"[32] *Zarathustra* says, a soothsayer, "full of that soothsaying spirit that strolls on the high pass between two seas—strolls like a heavy cloud between what has passed and what is to come . . ."[33] And Nietzsche's entire intellectual stance is characterized by the unsettled, indeterminate dream-state shortly before awakening, so close to waking up that the dream is already conscious of dreaming, but pleads all the more fervently for a moment longer, for staying a while. Between the old romantic night and a new brilliant day, between the homestead and Columbus's unknown seas, half an extreme boldness of desire and knowledge (knowledge is always a form of desire in Nietzsche), and half final tender homesickness that cannot leave the shores of his own youth; the unsettled "Or?" of a moment between two worlds, both of which, neither of which, he belongs to—that is how we see Nietzsche.

That is how he saw himself in all of his extreme moments (which were always his most authentic), in those clairvoyant moments in which he always strolls on the high pass between two seas. The moment of this extreme, unsettled inner "Or?" finds its classical expression perhaps in the last sentences of *Daybreak,* which are also, simultaneously, a classic example of his mastery of the end, of that virtuosity of cadence of which Nietzsche was so proud and in which he, knowingly and unconsciously, gave and revealed the most of himself: in *Ecce homo* he significantly says of *Daybreak* that it is the only book that concludes with an "Or?" But, no matter from which direction we approach him, even Nietzsche's mighty torso always rounds out his intellectual silhouette with a final "Or?" just as all of his works from the *Birth* to *Ecce* finish in the doubling of such an Or. Hardly any of them, however, do so with such calm pride, such regal surrender, such masterly confidence in the face of all "Beyonds" as *Daybreak:*

"All of these daring birds that fly out into the distance, the farthest distance—certainly! at some point they will be able to go no farther. . . . But who could thereby conclude that there is no longer *any* open space before them, that they flew as far as one *can* fly! All of our great teachers and predecessors finally came to a halt . . . the same will happen to me and you! But what concern is that of mine or yours! Other birds will fly farther! These, our insight and belief, try to outdo each other at flying farther and higher . . . there, in the direction we went, and where everything is still sea, sea, sea!"[34] Thus the great curve of affirmative resignation in which Nietzsche's landscape sinks, full of proud equilibrium, down into the sea of the future. But before it takes the most extreme plunge, the contour turns upward once more, as if in a last, questioning effort, toward an inquisitive Crossing over, a searching Perhaps—almost cast off from the shore that it is singing its last in him, almost an island already, almost a pier on a bridge to an unknown shore, the home shore of the Great Man, that coast which is over there, which *must* be over there, where the *eye* sees the sun descending into emptiness:

"And where do we want to go then? Do we want to go *over* the sea? Where are we being pulled by this powerful desire that means more to us than any pleasure? Why, of all directions, this one, where all the suns of humanity have previously *gone down?* Will people perhaps one day say of us that we also *hoped to reach an India by steering toward the West*—but that it was our fate to founder on infinity? Or, my brothers? Or?"[35]

17

Prophecy

. . . For because
The most blessed ones feel nothing on their own,
Another must feel sympathetically
In the name of the gods—
They need him; but their punishment
Is, that his own house shall collapse
and curse what is dearest to him
as if it were the enemy and bury
father and child under the rubble,
If someone, in his zeal, wants to be like them
and not bear unequal stations.
—Hölderlin[1]

The life of a truly canonical person must be thoroughly symbolic.
Under this condition would not every death be a death of reconciliation?[2]
—Novalis

The prophetic flourishes only in half-light. It was not obscurantism, as the entire eighteenth century suspected, that spoke in favor of the sacred dusk. Just as crystal grows only while it is in the mountain and, once touched, rigidifies its growth, so too the prophetic word with the power to transform people develops only in sleep. It is part of Nietzsche's tragic transitional fate that his intellectual calling and his "spiritual election"—to express it theologically—occurred precisely during what were perhaps the most irreverent decades ever witnessed in intellectual history; at the height of the "historical" century, which so often praised its own historical piety, and was inwardly more profane in the Goethean sense than any other century before. To us, the painfully glaring illumination cast on Nietzsche's development seems almost excruciating, wrenching it out of legend's twilight, flooding it with a harsh spotlight, owing to the wealth of personal documents we have thanks to the historical training of his contemporaries and for whose tiniest chronological detail only the historian in us, as heirs of the nineteenth century, is grudgingly grateful. It strikes us as almost symbolic that the all-too-bright daylight of inner intellectualism that repeatedly set off an inner struggle within Nietzsche between the prophetic man and the great European writer, that this daylight now also disturbs the development of his external image. Not that Nietzsche's almost uncannily *pure* form—pure to an almost stylized degree, as with Hölderlin—could not "endure" such brightness. But the spectacle of the immanent battle of his own most proper and pure ambitions against the tendencies and odors of decay emanating from the 1870s and 1880s, which "helped to strangle him," is as thoroughly poignant and excruciating to witness as the sight of any struggle in which one partner is missing. Greatness thrives where nobility fends off a noble foe. But here a noble adversary is missing; thus, the weapon is turned on its owner. And given the all-too-great proximity of his sufferings and the deceptive triumph rising up before us, it occasionally seems as if we were witnessing something that should not be beheld. "We make no secret of it; but we pull a veil over that suffering precisely because we venerate it so highly"—thus the answer of the journeymen in the *Wilhelm Meister's Travels* to the question why the Passion is missing among the pedagogical mural paintings.[3] The spectacle arising out of the documents of his life is simultaneously gruesome and symbolic, showing how here, in the midst of the most crass and skeptical modernity, in the midst of cynical radicalisms and faithless disappointment, a prophetic calling takes place. How the one who is called hesitates, just like the other fearful chosen one hesitated, before the gates of the great, insolent city that has already been marked for destruction, how he resists "why me of all people?" how, borrowing the words of Annette von Droste-Hülshoff,[4] "the prophet, a desperate animal at bay, fights against the gradually rising image"[5]—the image of his task, his mission, his martyrdom. "Those born later," he writes in the Notebooks of the final years, "say of him: 'He has climbed higher and higher ever since.' But they understand nothing of this martyrdom of climbing: a great man is shoved, pushed, forced, tortured up to *his* height."[6] We had never before seen a great, pathbreaking, and representative life, a martyrdom of climbing from such a horrible proximity (notice how every image of the old saints and sages wraps itself in silence with the vivid images of their legend! How Dante surrounded himself with images, how enigmatic Leonardo and Shakespeare made themselves, how Napoleon cloaked himself in deception, how Goethe concealed himself in reticence!)—we will perhaps never observe a life from such proximity again. But *that* we see it is a part of Nietzsche's particular and unique figure and tragedy; this proximity of the viewer is in fact part of *his* fate, this shameless brightness of his time on this solitary fugitive is already part of his own timeless image—and for that reason we need not avert our eyes from this life that is all-too-brightly lit, all-too near to us.

On the surface, his childhood betrays nothing prophetic. Beautiful, calm, cheerful, conventional, and a little too restrained, too protected in an entirely female atmosphere and not lacking girlish traits. Nevertheless, there are some childish premonitions of Nietzsche's most characteristic future quality: the *amor fati,* the obedience to the law absorbed into his own will, the affirmation of necessity. (The anecdote about the slow journey home, according to school regulations, in pouring rain;[7] about the self-martyrdom after the model of Scaevola.)[8] There is also the faint shimmer of an indescribable foreignness and hidden majesty that later so moved his friend Rohde after a decades-long separation ("an indescribable atmosphere of *foreignness,* something I found completely *uncanny,* surrounded him. There was something in him that I had never encountered before. . . . As if he came from a country in which no one else lived"[9] [Rohde to Overbeck in 1886]). Just as fellow students of Hölderlin felt "as if Apollo were striding through the hall," so too an "otherwise very broad-minded" and skeptical former student during his last year at the Naumburg *Gymnasium* confirmed that he thought that the young Nietzsche, then in his second or third year, "always seemed like the twelve-year-old Jesus in the temple."[10] ("At age twelve I saw God in his glory,"[11] reads a mystical comment by the late Nietzsche.) It is reported that his fellow students dared not utter a coarse word in his presence: a boy is said to have slapped himself on his mouth and exclaimed: "No, one may not say that in front of Nietzsche!" "What will he do to you, then?" "Oh, he just looks at you in a way that makes the word stick in your mouth."[12] Indeed, a story is even told about Nietzsche in his very first year at the general public school in Naumburg in which the six-year-old, serious, reflective, with "dignified, polite manners," was so alien to the other rough and noisy boys that no one attempted to approach him; his little fellow pupils only wanted to listen: they related that "he could recite Bible verses and sacred songs with such expression that one was almost forced to cry," and they tended to call him the "little pastor." The essays that Nietzsche presented at the "synods" of the Germania Association that he cofounded with two friends—a preamble to the later idea of a Muses' Monastery—already unmistakably presage the later Nietzsche. And even the peculiarly early love of Hölderlin, his favorite during his time at the *Gymnasium,* as he once wrote to Rohde,[13] indicates an early inkling of his own fate that is so eerily foretold, foredreamed by Hyperion and Empedocles. The seventeen-year-old even dedicates an (extant) essay to his favorite poet, which understandably earns him the "friendly advice" from his teacher "to stick to a healthier, clearer, *more German* poet."[14] Finally, the premonition of having been predestined and reserved to serve a new, as yet unknown god, is movingly expressed in the poem that the future student of theology sings on leaving Schulpforta to his unknown leader:

THE UNKNOWN GOD

Once more, before I move on
And train my eyes forward,
I raise my hands in solitude
Up to you, to whom I am fleeing,
To whom I solemnly consecrated
Altars in the deepest depths of my heart,
So that your voice
Should always reach me.
Thereon, deeply engraved, glows
The word: to the unknown god.
I am his, even though I have until this moment
Also stayed among the horde of the wicked.
. . . I want to know you, unknown one,
You who delves deeply into my soul,
Who blows through my life like a storm,
You incomprehensible one, related to me!
I want to know you, even to serve you.[15]

The Dionysus-dithyramb of 1884, which is put in the mouth of the "magician" Zarathustra and one year later transformed into an independent poem, still resonates like a ghastly intensified echo of this youthful poem:

. . . Nameless! Cloaked! Awful One!
You hunter behind clouds!
. . . Cruelest hunter,
You unknown—god!

Strike deeper!
Strike once more!
. . . Why torment—me,
You spiteful unknown god?

. . . Speak at last!
What do you, thief, want from—me?
You, cloaked by lightning! Unknown! Speak!
What do you *want,* unknown—god?

Me?—you want me?
Me—all of me?
. . . Give, yes, surrender to me,
Cruelest enemy—*yourself!*

Gone!
He has fled,
My one and only companion,
My great enemy,
My unknown,
My executioner-god!

No! Come back!
With all your torments!
To the last among the lonely,
Oh, come back,
My unknown god! my pain! My ultimate—happiness![16]

But the unknown god still slumbered in the cradle of a cheerful and undisturbed youth. The testimonials of his life, the letters of the young student reveal that he retained a naïvete, an occasionally almost touching ingenuousness that in light of his coming fate is more moving than a heroic or unhappy childhood would have been. Even the faint hints of an untimely turn away from his student environment (even though he otherwise tried his best to assimilate) are still of a thoroughly harmless nature and are not devoid of a certain humor: thus, when instead of visiting the carnival in Cologne in 1865, "to the great astonishment of his friends and acquaintances,"[17] he retired to his room to work—during his first semester—on his speech for the Gustav Adolf Club on the ecclesiastical circumstances of the Germans in North America. Or when in October of the same year after leaving the Rhineland he announced his resignation from the student organization of Franconia with the odd, half childishly inept, half strangely arrogant letter that understandably so outraged the association that it expelled Nietzsche: " . . . may the Franconia soon recover from the stage of development in which it now finds itself,"[18] the second-semester student writes. Such language heralds *The Untimely Meditations,* the Basel lectures "On the Future of our Educational Institutions."

The year spent on the Rhine was the last year of Nietzsche's childhood. His sister compared it to a state of sleeping or dreaming in which the truly personal powers ripen in advance of waking. Nietzsche himself called it his lost year. He felt that he was not yet himself, he searched and found himself nowhere. "I left Bonn like a fugitive,"[19] he still wrote two years later. Not until Leipzig did fate call unmistakably, repeatedly, insistently, for him to awaken. Nietzsche's development, which until then, in Nordic fashion, had been late, ripened with fantastic speed toward its extraordinary florescence. With a strange apparent intentionality, all circumstances promoted the necessary path of the young student. Even the ugly philological bickering that caused his teacher in Bonn, Ritschl,[20] to move to Leipzig was such a cue (characteristically enough, given the young Nietzsche's love of justice, as well as his obedience, he followed his teacher to Leipzig because he believed he would learn more from him, even though he felt himself personally and factually on the side of Ritschl's opponent, Jahn, in the professorial dispute). He followed his fate in his teacher. On the soil of his homeland, Saxony, the first deep love of his life, Erwin Rohde, awaited him. There awaited the intellectually decisive and agitating experience of *The World as Will and Representation* (we remember how Nietzsche mentioned that it was a kind of *daimonion*[21] that led him to this book he picked up somewhere); there awaited, above all, the great turning point of his life, the personal contact with the powerful personality of Richard Wagner. (This, too, does not occur without strange coincidences and "signs" of the sort that the later Nietzsche loved to memorize: one thinks of the half-scurrilous, half-eerie E. T. A. Hoffmannesque scene in which one snowy and rainy night in 1868, a grotesque little tailor tried to prevent Nietzsche from accepting an invitation that would lead to his first acquaintance with Richard Wagner;[22] one thinks of the almost fantastically improbable appointment of the student as a professor in Basel, even before he received his doctorate, a promotion that alone made Tribschen possible and without which Nietzsche's life and work would have been driven in incalculably different directions.)

Wagner—that means, from whichever direction one may view Nietzsche's life and work, his baptism and his calling. His intellectual personality dates from this truly transforming moment. "I have had the experience," the twenty-two-year-old Hebbel notes in his diary, "that every capable person has to disappear in the great man if he ever wants to achieve self-knowledge and the confident use of his powers; one prophet baptizes the other and the person whose hair is singed by this baptism of fire was not truly called!"[23] That was also the experience of the twenty-four-year-old Nietzsche. His letters from this period overflow with the intoxicated happiness of disappearing in a great man and receiving his true self out of this bath of fire, made deeper, more aware, more active, and eternal: "I found a man who reveals to me like no other the image of what Schopenhauer calls 'the genius.' . . . It is none other than Richard Wagner. . . . *No one* knows him and can judge him, because the entire world stands on another foundation and is not at home in his atmosphere. In him, there is such an unconditional ideality, such a deep and moving humanity, such a sublime seriousness toward life, that I feel in his presence as if I were in the presence of the divine"[24] (1869 to Gersdorff). "I have the inestimable fortune of possessing as a real friend the true intellectual brother of Schopenhauer, whose relationship to him is like that of Schiller to Kant, a genius who was given the same terribly sublime fate of coming a century earlier than he could be understood. . . . I notice how my philosophical, moral and academic ambition is striving toward a *single* goal and that I—perhaps as the first philologist ever—am becoming whole. How wonderfully new and transformed history looks to me, particularly Hellenism!"[25] (1870 to Deussen). "I also have my Italy . . . it is called Tribschen. . . . Dearest friend, what I am learning and seeing there, hearing and understanding, is indescribable. Schopenhauer and Goethe, Aeschylus and Pindar still live, believe me"[26] (1869 to Rohde). "My listening to Wagner's music is a jubilant intuition, indeed an amazing self-discovery"[27] (1868 to Rohde).

We may regard Nietzsche's baptism in the bath of his Wagner experience as a marvelous self-discovery, a first jubilant intuition of his prophetic duties and possibilities. Their abiding monument is *The Birth of Tragedy*, one of the most peculiar books of love of all time and perhaps even today still the most heartfelt, purest, and most moving of Nietzsche's works, even if it is neither the most important nor the most beautiful one. His "foreign voice"[28]—that is what the Nietzsche of 1886 called it—was not only a "dialogue with the great artist Richard Wagner";[29] it was also the first conversation of his soul with itself, a half-brooding, half-ecstatic exchange of questions: "Who are you?" "Who am I?" "Do people understand," Nietzsche asks at the end, "what task had I already dared to approach with this book? . . . Dionysus spoke to me . . ."[30]

If *The Birth of Tragedy* contains the first annunciation of the prophet in Nietzsche, then the *Untimely Mediations* offer the first testimony of his "wrath." Both, annunciation and wrath, are inseparable from the prophetic mission; each is only the other half of the other. There is no visionary office for the annunciation of something to come that would not find its expression, indeed its legitimacy, in the inevitable opposition to the mere present as that which is not coming into being, as that which should not be. "Praise and censure"[31] are only the two wings of the prophetic ascent. The right to the one is the duty to perform the other. "Every high lament and tears about some historical period indicates, like a spring on a mountain, there is an even higher mountain or peak"—that is how Jean Paul's *Levana*[32] expresses this law of all prophecy. The high lament and tears of the *Untimely Meditations* are to be understood as such a spring on a higher mountain. These four books, especially the last three, are the first survey, the first amazed and alienated overview of a mind that was slowly returning to itself after its earliest ecstatic perturbations and now finds the surrounding world changed. "Where am I, then—oh, far, oh, far."[33] They are the expression of a high impatience that has seen farther, that has been farther, than everyone around him and now finds itself transferred back into the present that cannot be a present to it any longer, forced into a time in which it has to seem untimely to itself.

The strange, untimely inner discontent, the searching and groping, the knowing neither up nor down, which characterize his utterances during this period in particular, provide further testimony. For, after the truly magnificent eruption of *The Birth of Tragedy,* that gift which an unparalleled ecstatic happiness made to Nietzsche's mind, the period of the *Untimely Meditations* indubitably seems to indicate, externally, almost a regression. If the young Nietzsche, during the time of *The Birth,* appeared even personally "elastic, fiery, self-confident, like a young lion"[34] (Deussen's memoirs), if the letters from this period overflow with pride in his friendly proximity to the genius, with the "bliss inter pares," there creeps into the letters from the following years a diffident, tentative, often deeply dispirited tone, as if signaling the slowly eroding belief in Wagner's humanity and art. He seems continuously disturbed by doubts about the inner justification for the Dionysian happiness of the time together in Tribschen and about their artistic and philosophical expression, an uncertainty where his task lies, and whether he even has a task in the strict sense. "If only you did not have a far too high opinion of me!" he still writes in 1874 to Gersdorff. "I almost think that one day you will be slightly disappointed in me. . . . If you could only know how despondent and melancholy I *basically* become when I think of myself as a productive being! I seek nothing further than freedom, a little real air of life, and I resist, I revolt against the many, incredibly many elements of unfreedom that inhere in me. But there can be no talk of true productiveness as long as one is still stuck in unfreedom, in suffering and in the oppressive feeling of being caught: will I ever make it? Doubts upon doubts. . . ."[35] And two years later, to the same person: " . . . I am increasingly forced to seek my happiness in the happiness of my friends. All of my own plans are like smoke; I see them close to me and would like to seize them. For it is sad, indeed hardly possible, to live without them."[36] In 1874 he writes similarly to Rohde about his "agonizing despondency": "Actually, I live through you, my friends, I go forward by leaning on all of you; for my sense of myself is weak and pitiful and *all of you* have to continue to vouch for me to me. You are the best models . . . both you and Overbeck . . ."[37] Indeed, even in 1877 he writes to Seydlitz: "Will you not have been mistaken (about me)? Heaven knows you will find a very simple person who has no great opinion of himself."[38] How painfully modest, how uncertain of himself, he sounds in a letter to Malwida in 1873: "My Parnassus of the future, if I try very hard and have some luck, as well as a lot of time—is to become perhaps a middling writer."[39] And what a testimony to the most tormenting doubts about himself is found in the passage of *Daybreak,* where they are objectified and mediated in a psychological aphorism: "Who dares to cast a glance into the wilderness of the bitter torments of the soul in which perhaps the most productive people of all times . . . have languished! to hear the sighs of the solitary and distressed: 'Oh, grant me madness, you gods! Madness so that I may finally believe in myself! . . . Doubt is consuming me, I have slain the law . . . if I am no *more* than the law, then I am the most abject of all. . . .' And all too often this fervor achieved its goal too well . . ."[40] That is a Second Vision of the affliction out of which works such as *Zarathustra,* gestures such as those in *Ecce homo* arise. Out of such doubts, out of such a prayer for the madness of belief in oneself, Nietzsche rose, leaving behind as the stages to himself the role of disciple, skeptic, European writer, and moralist, to reach finally that of prophet.

Beneath the surface of doubt, ever since the days in Tribschen, the slow, seemingly subterranean development and crystallization of belief in himself is unmistakably recognizable. As early as spring 1871, the young professor feels that, regarding philology, he is "in a state of exuberant alienation that you cannot begin to imagine being any worse"[41] (to Rohde). Praise and censure, indeed all of the highest honors in this arena make him shudder. "Thus I am gradually growing into my calling as a philosopher and already believe in myself; in fact, if I should still become a poet, then I am ready even for that."[42] But the higher the waters of belief in himself rise in the underground chambers of his soul, the more his playfulness subsides, the more serious everything that happens to him seems to become. A kind of fear becomes palpable: "Who am I? and what is happening to me?" As early as one year after the exuberant alienation, the first note of this new seriousness is struck: he writes to Rohde that a tremendous seriousness overcomes him in everything he is hearing about *The Birth of Tragedy*—"because in those voices I glean the future of what I intend to do. My life will be very difficult."[43] The premonition of a path that no one apart from him can take, and which for that reason he must take, gradually opens up before him: "there is a single path in the world that no one else but you can take: where does it lead? Ask not, take it"[44]—he writes in "Schopenhauer as Educator." His jubilation over an inner development, a secret mountain ascent within him, is barely suppressed by his reticence to betray this elation before it could burst forth (*Zarathustra* is this elation). The simultaneous happiness and dread of someone who is persistently transforming himself and feels elevated, without certainty, even without an inkling in which direction he is changing, to what height he is being elevated, the fearfully joyous "Why me of all people?" that we recognize as the preliminary stage of every prophetic character, that is expressed in uncounted remarks during these crisis years, the symptom of which, but not the cause, is the final alienation from Wagner in 1876 and the dangerous "lowest point of my vitality"[45] (winter 1879–80). Even retrospectively, Nietzsche felt very strongly the preparatory transformative nature of the years before the call of Zarathustra.

"What was actually happening to me at that time?" he writes in the preface materials for the years 1885 to 1888. "I did not understand myself, but the impulse was like a command. It seems that our distant unique destiny has control over us; for a long time we experience only puzzles. Our choice of events, our grasping at opportunities and sudden desires, a rejection of what we find most pleasant, often of what we revere the most: those sorts of things frighten us, as if we were occasionally emanating something arbitrary, capricious, foolish, volcanic. But that is only the higher reason and precaution of our future task. Does the long sentence of my life perhaps want—thus I anxiously asked myself—to be read *backwards?* There is no doubt that by reading forwards at the time I found 'words without meaning.'"[46] But even in *The Gay Science* we read similarly: "If we engage in criticism, it is not something arbitrary and impersonal—it is proof that there are vital, driving forces within us that are sloughing off an outer skin. We reject and must reject things because there is something in us that *wants* to live and affirm itself, something that we perhaps do not yet know, do not yet see!"[47] Slowly, very slowly, with the most cautious self-unveiling, Nietzsche's inner transformations take on their own peculiar meaning. " . . . From month to month," he writes in August 1875, "I see some things about my mission in life more clearly without yet having had the courage to tell them to anyone. A calm but very determined pace from step to step—that is what guarantees that I have a long way to go still. It seems to me that I am a born *mountain climber.*—See how proudly I can speak."[48] The reference to his life's *mission* acquires a resonance that becomes ever stronger, especially after the crisis of 1876, which definitively washed away the final remnant of his illusion that he was serving someone else's mission—whether as Wagner's successor or as the philological curator of antiquity, merely preserving and explicating the most exquisite cultural treasures. All of that now takes on for Nietzsche the perspective of a mountain trail, a path from stage to stage, on the way to his proper height, to himself. "I know, I feel that there is a higher destiny for me than is contained in my so very respectable position in Basel; I am also more than a philologist, as much as I can use philology for *my* higher mission. I yearn for myself—that has actually been the continuous theme of my last ten years"[49] (1877). The preface from 1886 to *Human* still looks back to this time with a certain fatalistic pride: "That hidden and imperious Something for which we long have no name until it finally proves to be our *mission*—this tyrant in us exacts a terrible retribution for every attempt we make to evade or escape it, for every premature moderation, for every time we equate ourselves with people to whom we do not belong, for every activity, no matter how respectable, that distracts us from our main task, indeed even for every virtue that would like to protect us against the hardship of our own responsibility."[50] And in 1887 he writes to Fuchs about his task: "That *passion*, for which one long has no name, saves us from all digressions and dispersions, that *task* whose involuntary missionary one is."[51] This tone of a mission and fate that announces *Zarathustra* emerges for the first time in 1878: "I must live for my office and for my *mission*—at once a master and a lover and a goddess: much too much for my weak energy and deeply ravaged health. Viewed externally, my life is like that of an old man and hermit. . . . Nevertheless, I am courageous, forward, excelsior!"[52] (to Seydlitz.) Mixed in with all of this, there is still, up to the threshold of *Zarathustra*, something like a frightened refusal of this office, of his new master, of this mission, his lover and goddess; there is still an incredulous amazement over so many subterranean sources within a nature that, as he repeatedly admits to himself and to his friends, does not count among the richest; it still sounds like "much too much for me," and he still asks for his friend's help to find his own belief in himself and in his calling. "On the whole I am astonished, frankly,"—he writes to Rohde in March 1881, "*how many* sources a person can have flowing within him. Even someone, such as me, who does not count among the richest. I think that, if I possessed all of the qualities that you have in addition to mine, I would become arrogant and insufferable. There are already moments when I wander around the heights above Genoa with visions and feelings that perhaps from this very spot the radiant Columbus once cast out over the sea and into the future. . . . Friends such as you have to help me to maintain my belief in myself." But in the same letter we also encounter the sentence: " . . . I wish on no one the fate to which I am now beginning to accustom myself, because I am beginning to understand that I am equal to it."[53] Or, a few months later, to his sister: "It cannot be said with a single word where everything in me is going—and if I had that word, I would not say it . . ."[54] But he already says it, it already imperiously forces itself out of him in a presentiment of coming ecstasies: "Whether I will be able to resolve my great mission depends on conditions that do not belong to me but rather to the 'nature of things.' Believe me: I am now the tip of all moral reflection and work in Europe and of many other things as well. There will perhaps still come a time when even the eagles will have to look up timidly to me as in that image of St. John that we loved so much as children."[55] And again: "Oh, my good, dear sister, you think it is just a *book?* do you also still consider me to be a writer? My hour is here."[56]

My hour is here—not coincidentally, that is the language and inflection of the Gospel of St. Matthew.[57] My hour is here—only a prophet speaks thus, who knows that his years in the desert, the years of silence or of mistaking his own identity, are behind him and who leaves his cave, blazing and strong like the morning sun that rises out of dark mountains. It is the hour of Zarathustra. And the mood of this letter literally entered into the conclusion of his prophetic masterpiece: "Do I aspire to happiness? I aspire to my work! Very well! Zarathustra has become ripe, my hour has come . . . my day commences: arise now, arise, you great midday!"[58] Zarathustra indicates the moment of his "calling," the moment from which Nietzsche begins to read, begins to understand, the long sentence of his life backwards, at which his "mission," that mysterious cultic image of the preceding years, unveiled itself to him. "Has anyone, at the end of the nineteenth century, a clear notion of what poets in stronger ages called inspiration? If not, I will describe it. If one retained the slightest remnant of superstition, one would in fact hardly know how to dismiss the thought that one is merely an incarnation, merely the mouthpiece, merely the medium of overpowering forces."[59] (How clearly his own prophetic role is announced here, almost completely unrestrained by intellectual self-control.)

> The concept of revelation in the sense that suddenly, with utter certainty and precision, something becomes visible, audible which profoundly moves and overpowers one, simply describes the facts. One hears—one does not seek; one receives—one does not ask who is giving; like a bolt of lightning a thought flashes forth, with necessity, without hesitation in its form—I never had a choice. A rapturous transport, whose enormous tension is occasionally discharged in a flood of tears, in which the pace involuntarily becomes sometimes furious, sometimes sedate; a sense of being completely outside of oneself with the most distinct consciousness of a myriad fine shudders and shivers down to the tips of one's toes; a profundity of happiness in which the most painful and darkest things do not act as opposites, but rather as a necessary color within such a superfluity of light; an instinct of rhythmic relationships that spans broad expanses of forms (the length, the need for a broadly spanned rhythm is almost the measure of the force of inspiration . . .). Everything happens involuntarily in the highest degree, but as if in a torrent of a feeling of freedom, of absoluteness, of power, of divinity. The involuntary nature of the image, of the symbol, is the most remarkable thing; one no longer has any notion what an image, a symbol is, everything offers itself as the nearest, the most accurate, the simplest expression. It truly seems, to recall something Zarathustra said, as if the things themselves came up and wanted to be a symbol . . . "all being wants to become word here, all becoming wants to learn from you how to speak." This is *my* experience of inspiration; I have no doubt that one would have to go back millennia to find someone who could say to me: "it is mine, too!"—[60]

Never before had such sounds been attempted in German prose—they seemed reserved for the uppermost pinnacles of German music, whether it be the ecstatic communal reveries of the Mass in B Minor[61] ("Cum sancto spiritu," "Sanctus") and of the *Missa Solemnis*[62] ("Cum sancto spiritu," "Et vitam venturi saeculi") or the ardently sacrilegious individualism of the late quartets and sonatas. And only the rarest eruptions of the poetic word betray anything like the prophetically explosive inner force that speaks in this declaration: the young Goethe's "Ganymede," the Pater Ekstaticus in the transfiguration of Faust, Novalis's *Hymns to the Night,* Hölderlin's final hymns, "Entrückung" in *The Seventh Ring.*[63] After experiencing this flood of revelation (which achieved its highest moment in the conception of the idea of the Eternal Return), after this moment, Nietzsche's entire estimation of himself appears permanently transformed, raised up to prophetic rank. If he previously seemed "very reticent about all of his principal concerns" (we remember the almost diffident way in which he admits to the first glimmer of the idea of the Eternal Return at the end of *The Gay Science*), an overpowering sense of himself now snatches the confession of his mission from his lips. His comments from the *Zarathustra* years overflow with the old happiness of a calling, with the new bliss at being chosen:

"Everything that I have thought, suffered and hoped can be found there and in a way that makes me think that my life now seems *justified.* And then, once again, I am ashamed of myself: for I have thus reached out my hand for the highest crowns that humanity has to confer" (Rome, 1883).[64] "The time for staying silent is *over:* My *Zarathustra,* which will be sent to you in the coming weeks, may reveal to you *how* high my will has flown. . . . It is a beginning in letting myself be known—no more!—I know very well that there is no one alive who could make something like *Zarathustra*" (Sils-Maria, 1883).[65] "My task is enormous; my determination however is no smaller. My son Zarathustra will not tell you what I *want,* but he will call on you to guess; perhaps it can be surmised. And this is certain: I want to force people to make decisions that will determine the entire future of man . . ."[66] (Venice, 1884). If he had previously kept himself hidden, behind masks and foregrounds, now he delights in being found out. He is happy that Heinrich von Stein proved to be sensitive regarding the hidden pathos of the lonely wanderer: "In his presence I felt the way Philoctetes did on his island when visiting Neoptolemos—I mean, he guessed something of my *Philoctetes-faith* 'without my bow no Troy will be conquered!'" (1884 to Gast).[67] (How much is expressed by the choice of this particular symbol for Nietzsche's innermost feeling—it envelops the Philoctetes cry of *The Gay Science:* "You have no feeling for how prophetic men are greatly suffering men."[68] In all of these comments, the highest degree of self-esteem and self-confidence is obviously achieved, the regal stage of the highest philosophical pride attained, the same pride that Nietzsche anticipated in his premonitory description of Heraclitus (1873): "Heraclitus was proud: and if a philosopher attains to pride, then it is a great pride. . . . His talent is of the rarest sort, in a certain sense of the most unnatural sort, while at the same time exclusionary and hostile even toward similar talents. The wall of his self-sufficiency must be made of diamond if it is not to be destroyed and broken, for everything is in motion against him. . . . Inattention to the present and to the momentary belongs to the essence of a great and philosophical nature. . . . It is important to learn from such people that they once lived. No one would ever be able to imagine the pride of Heraclitus . . . no one could believe, if one were not been informed by history, in such a regal self-regard and the conviction that he was the sole, fortunate suitor of truth."[69] Now Nietzsche himself had reached this degree of pride; indeed, it is a height and plenitude of pride, an exuberance of self-certainty and pleasure in giving for which the name of philosophic pride no longer suffices, but rather is appreciable only as prophetic pride. Now he himself counts among those who, in a phrase from the Notebooks, "are walking legislations."[70] The notion of the *mission* only now gains its entire fullness and fatefulness. "The mission that rests on me is nevertheless my nature—so that only now do I have an idea of what *my* predetermined happiness was. I am playing with a burden that would crush any mortal . . . for what I have to do is terrible in every sense of the word . . ."[71] (1888 to his sister). "If I could give you an idea of my feeling of *loneliness!* I have no one among the living or the dead to whom I feel related. This is indescribably horrible. . . . Otherwise the *mission* for which I live stands clearly before me—as a fact of indescribable sadness but transfigured by my knowing that there is greatness therein, if ever there has been greatness in the mission of a mortal."[72] (1886 to Overbeck). The valuation of his own work takes on accents that not even the high self-esteem of an artist dares assume, that only the consciousness of a prophetic mission can keep from descending into grotesque pretension: "Whoever has the slightest idea about me assumes that I have experienced more than anyone else. Proof of that is even written in my books: line for line they come from new realms of life and thus, as substance, represent a real increase, an addition to the concept of life itself"[73] (1888 to his sister). Even the "indescribably horrible loneliness" he suffered is transformed into a legitimate untimeliness; like Schopenhauer, he enjoyed the delights of a sublime incognito, the sweet bitterness of knowing that the world, according to Hebbel, is the innkeeper who turns on the lights only when the emperor has already departed again. "My work has *time*—and I do not want to be confused with what this present has as its task. Fifty years hence there will perhaps be a few people (or one—it would take a genius!) who would have eyes for what *happened through me.* At the moment, however, it is not only difficult, it is completely impossible (according to the laws of 'perspective') to speak publicly of me without remaining constantly *behind* the truth"[74] (Venice, 1884). "Who knows how many generations will have to pass in order to produce a few people who will feel what I have done in its entire profundity!" (1884 to his sister).[75] "It is owing to the indescribable foreignness and dangerousness of my ideas that only a long time from now—and certainly *not* before 1901—will ears be open for these ideas" (1887 to Malwida).[76] "Remember that the present can *never* be just toward a person such as I am and that every compromise for the sake of one's 'good reputation' is not worthy of me" (1883 to his sister).[77] "I am also enough of a judge of human nature to know how the judgment of me will have turned around in fifty years and what a halo of *respect* the name of your son will shine because of the *very same* things for which I have so far been mistreated and abused" (1887 to his mother).[78] "Was there ever a person who stood more audaciously toward things than I do? One has to be able to *endure* it: that is the test; what people 'say,' what they 'think' about it is of no concern to me. After all—I do not want to be right for today and tomorrow, but for millennia" (1886 to Deussen).[79] The highest intensification of his secular self-esteem emerges more and more uninhibitedly: the word "millennium," which also concludes the description of inspiration in *Ecce homo,* appears with increasing frequency together with the word "fate": "Between the two of us—it is not impossible that I am the first philosopher of our age, indeed perhaps even something a little more, something decisive and fateful that stands between two millennia" (1886 to Seydlitz).[80] "My philosophical stance is by far the most independent, as much as I also feel I am the heir of several millennia: present-day Europe still has no inkling what terrible decisions my entire being revolves around and what wheel of problems I am tied to—and that with me a catastrophe is developing whose name I know but will not utter" (1887 to Overbeck).[81] Finally, in *Ecce homo,* with horrifying hubris, in the chapter "Why I am a Destiny": "I know my lot. One day the memory of my name will be tied to something immense—to a crisis that has no precedent on earth, to the most profound collision of conscience. . . . I contradict as no one has contradicted before, and nevertheless I am the opposite of a nay-saying spirit. I am a *joyful messenger* with no precedent, I know missions of such a height that not even a notion of them existed before; beginning with me alone hopes exist again. Given all of that, I am also necessarily the man of fate."[82]

This pride, this unconditional certainty of a secular height, of a thousand-year mission, now breaks out in an ecstatic glorification of *fatum,* expresses itself as an unconditional and passionate affirmation of the events that carried him up to this inner height. There is no longer any mistake: behold, everything was very good, everything is perfect, everything *is good*—that now becomes the predominant feeling. "Amor fati—that is my innermost nature"[83] he writes in the epilogue to *The Case of Wagner;* "fatum is an elevating thought for the person who understands that he belongs *to it,*"[84] the proud sentence says in the Notebooks to the *Transvaluation.* And in *Ecce homo* there is an echo: "My formula for human greatness is amor fati; that one does not want anything to be different, not forwards, not backwards, not in all eternity. Not merely to endure what is necessary, much less to deny it—all idealism is dishonesty in the face of necessity—but rather to love it . . ."[85] In reading such strains, one is involuntarily reminded of a similarly late glorification of necessity in Beethoven's final work, the Quartet in F Major, op. 135, where the bleak fateful question "Must it be?" changes into the fanatical cry of triumph "It *must* be! It must be!" sounding the same boundlessly ecstatic prophetic fanaticism that arises out of such passages in Nietzsche. (Nietzsche's final style, that of *Twilight of the Idols* and *Ecce homo,* seems in general to betray a peculiar psychological relationship to the style of Beethoven's last quartets, about which Nietzsche said during the period of *Zarathustra* that in some passages the sky stood more open than anywhere else.) It is the mood in which Nietzsche gave the motto from Emerson to the completed *The Gay Science*: "To the poet, to the philosopher, all things are friendly and sacred, all events profitable, all days holy, all men divine."[86] No shudder of doubt, no hint of skepticism, no shadow of inner hesitation reach up to this height. A protective hypertrophy of self-confidence preserves him from any fatal relapse into self-doubt—no skeptical self-address reaches the sleepwalker anymore. Even his feeling of instinctive defense, the knowledge "I *must* not be mistaken anymore," which appeared so strong after the disappointment with Wagner and was sharpened by his experience with Rée and Lou to an extreme excitability toward mistrust, even this has disappeared. A strong, victoriously cheerful "I *cannot* be mistaken anymore" has replaced it with the fatalism of someone who knows he has been chosen, and now turns every new experience, every encounter, and every coincidence into what is necessary, beneficial, and joyfully affirmed. "Everything is connected," he writes to Brandes in May 1888 about the conception of his masterpiece, "for years everything had been taking its proper course, one builds one's philosophy like a beaver, one is necessary and doesn't know it: but one has to *see* everything as I have seen it in order to believe it."[87] Even all of the coincidences of his external life now become meaningful, documents of a directed fate, proofs of a demonic guidance (his last letters are full of that): Nietzsche has reached that final peak on which, according to Hebbel, coincidence is the expression of divine will,[88] on which "the apparent intentionality in the fate of the individual,"[89] which Schopenhauer brooded about, has become a magnificent reality, the most immediate experience, as *that* person who knows himself to be led by religion, perceives the "finger of God" in every turn of his personal destiny. "Whoever can exert his own will on things will not be subservient to things; in the end, even coincidences arrange themselves according to our most proper needs. I am often amazed how little influence the most extreme adversity of fate has on a will. Or rather: I say to myself how much one's will itself must be fate so that it will always be right even *against* fate, *ὑπὲρ μόρον*—" (1888 to Deussen).[90] Indeed, this fatalism goes so far in its affirmation that, through a tremendous narrowing of perspective, it practically obliterates the period of doubt, the years of vacillation, the hours of desperate struggle. Thus, in *Ecce homo* he writes in the most audacious simplification of the empirical journey to himself: " . . . The organizing 'idea' that is destined to gain predominance grows in the depths . . . it successively develops all of its supporting abilities before it reveals anything of its governing mission, its 'goal,' 'purpose,' 'meaning.' In this regard, my life is simply wonderful. . . . I never even suspected what was growing within me. . . . I have no memory of ever having made an effort—there is no trace of *struggle* in my life, I am the opposite of a heroic nature. To 'want' something, to 'strive' for something, to have a 'purpose,' a 'wish' in view—I have no knowledge of any of that from experience. . . . I absolutely do not want for anything to become different from what it is; I myself do not want to become different. . . . But I have always lived that way. I have never had a wish."[91]

That is probably Nietzsche's ultimate self-stylization into his opposite, projecting his *amor fati* into his very beginnings. He even denies the psychological provenance of his own prophetic role, culminating in his rejection of the name of prophet, in the sentences about *Zarathustra* in *Ecce homo:* "It is not a prophet speaking here, not one of those horrible amalgams of illness and the will to power who are called founders of religion . . ."[92] But was it not precisely this horrible amalgamation and amalgamated fate made up of illness and will in which Nietzsche himself saw the essence and roots of his philosophy, even as late as the prefaces he wrote in 1886, for instance? The narrowing of perspective so characteristic of the prophetic type, which curiously enough one observes from *Human* onward, becomes completely unmistakable here; the radiant eye, which has only to illuminate his own dangerous fated path, puts everything he has gone through and left to one side in an even blacker darkness: more and more things and experiences "do not concern him." The temporal element disappears. The mood of Goethe's dictum is predominant: "Nothing transient interests us, no matter how it happened: We are here, after all, to immortalize ourselves!"[93]—"Come l'uom s'eterna . . ."[94] That is the motto from Dante's *Inferno* that Nietzsche inscribes on the last chapter of *The Will to Power.*[95] A consciousness of being bound to his own time, to his own age, even recedes before the intoxication of his prophetic moments that create gods. Thus, in the final notes to this same last chapter of *The Will to Power,* he writes: "How many new gods are still possible! How dissimilar, how different was the divine every time it was revealed to me—to me, in whom the religious instinct, that is the instinct for *creating* gods, sometimes stirred at inconvenient times! So many strange things have already crossed my path during those timeless moments which descend into our life as if from the moon, in which one simply no longer has any idea how old one already is and how young one will still be . . ."[96] *Come l'uom s'eterna*—the great depersonalization begins. A process of prophetic divestment of individuality, a disintegration into the superpersonal, a loss of the sense of singularity, the "incremental retreat from appearance,"[97] as the aged Goethe put it, the "retreat of the victorious individual into god,"[98] as the young Nietzsche called it. Even in *The Will to Power* he writes, albeit still skeptically, with apparent detachment: "Poets and seers . . . place great store in not being viewed as individuals at all, but as mere mouthpieces"[99]—but in truth this same tendency unconsciously becomes ever more powerful in him after *Zarathustra.* "The vehemence of my inner oscillations has been appalling throughout the last several years," reads a passage in a letter from 1887; "now that I have to make the transition to a new and higher form, I first need a new alienation, an even higher *depersonalization.*"[100] The preface to *On the Genealogy of Morals* says: "We philosophers have no right to be individual in any respect: we may neither be mistaken individually, nor reach the truth individually."[101] Portentously, the idea of an inner plurality already occurred to him during his positivistic period: "Strange! I am constantly preoccupied by the thought that my story is not just a personal one, that I am doing something for many others when I live this way and form myself and note: it is always as if I were a plurality, and I speak to it in an intimate, serious, comforting way"[102] (Notebooks to *Daybreak*). And Zarathustra finally becomes the highest symbol of that virtue that divides itself, apportions and gives itself away, saying: "What do I matter?"

"What do I matter?"—that is a leitmotif that occurs ever more frequently in his final half decade. "It does not matter at all," he had already written to Gast in 1882 about *The Gay Science,* "what my readers of today think about this book and about me—but it does matter that in this book one can read what I thought about myself."[103] One year later, the year of *Zarathustra,* he writes to the same: "I presented my soul with the following consideration: the more I will be forgotten, the better my son will have it, who is called Zarathustra."[104] What do I matter?—that is the finest formulation of an extreme pride, in the mouth of the person who preached the highest possible intensification of self-esteem and the will to be himself, as opposed to Christian self-denial. Characteristically, it first appears at the moment of prophetic self-certainty, and that fact indicates that he thinks only the highest forms of humanity have the right to depersonalization, that only the prophetic man may sacrifice himself, because he alone has value enough to be sacrificed. The annihilation of the prophetic individual was a familiar theme of the adolescent enamored with Hölderlin. The Nietzsche of *The Birth* already exhibited, with regard to his personal fate, the heroic indifference of the mouth that serves god. "Even if the individual out of whom, owing to a higher instinct, flows an aversion toward the barbarism of the present, may perish: the Pythian god was not at a loss to find a new tripod, a second Pythia as long as the mystical vapors arose from the depths"[105] (lecture "On the Future of our Educational Institutions," Basel 1871/72). Now he experienced within himself, he suspected for himself, how the depersonalization demanded by fate, the individual's retreat out of appearance inexorably will take its course to the end: to the demise of the visionary voice, to the fulfillment of the prophetic law that is written. For the prophetic word kills the mouth that utters it; and the man who expresses himself entirely, and causes the entire world that pulses in and through him to become word and form—that man dies. And thus, ever since his earliest awakening to the sense that he possessed prophetic powers, there is in Nietzsche, simultaneously, the foreboding of a demise according to prophetic laws, a foreboding that constantly grows until it achieves its ghastly fulfillment. As a student of the Greeks, he knows how all hubris ends and secretly *wants* to end; prophecy, however, predicting, summoning, coercing the future—however much one is a tool of that very future—prophecy among men is always the strongest hubris—and also the deadliest.

Nietzsche himself felt that the conclusion of his composition "Hymn to Life" is, as he wrote to Gast in 1887, "the strongest example of *hubris* in the Greek sense, a blasphemous challenge to fate through an excess of courage and arrogance—every time I see (and hear) the passage, a small shiver goes down my spine. People say that the Furies have ears for such 'music.'"[106] The feeling of having a group of Eumenides following him, of having a realm of spirits under his feet that, softly listening, would one day storm to the surface, hardly ever left Nietzsche. That humanity acquires its highest and best things through sacrilege, that the pointed tip of truth turns against the wise man because wisdom is a crime against nature—these notions from the sphere of Prometheus already permeate his first work and are still uncannily urgent in *Ecce homo:* "There is something that I call the *rancune*[107] of the great: everything great, a work, a deed, once it is done, immediately turns against the one who did it."[108] The entire decade after *Daybreak* especially lies under the growing cloud of the mystical notion of the revenge of the work on its creator, of the deed murdering the one who performs it: "I consider it possible that a mind that is richly stocked with facts and logically masterful can, in a tremendous agitation of the intellect, draw an enormous number of conclusions and thus achieve results that will take entire generations of scholars to catch up: it is also a kind of delirium that he will have to expiate"[109] (Notebooks to *Daybreak*). In his letters, it emerges even more immediately, with more foreboding: "Oh, my friend, sometimes the apprehension goes through my mind that I am actually living an extremely dangerous life, for I count among the machines that can *burst apart!* The intensity of my feelings makes me shudder and laugh . . ."[110] (1881 to Gast). After the second part of *Zarathustra,* in July 1883, he writes to him again: "The thought also came to me that I will probably one day die of such an explosion and expansion of feeling . . ."[111] In February 1884 to Overbeck: "*Zarathustra* in its entirety is an explosion of forces that accumulated for decades: with such explosions the originator himself can easily be blown up. I often feel that way—I don't want to conceal that from you."[112] And as late as the middle of December 1888, to Gast: "Now I sometimes fail to see why I should further hasten the *tragic* catastrophe of my life that begins with *Ecce homo.*"[113]

Such a feeling of being "from the family of decline"[114]—to use a phrase from a letter by Novalis to Friedrich Schlegel—slowly becomes concentrated into a great prophetic longing in Nietzsche for decline, as if it were the validation of his mission. "I know of no better purpose in life than to perish under something great and impossible . . ."[115]—that is the proud and prescient confession of the young Nietzsche of the *Untimely Meditations,* in which there appears to be an echo of the Faustian "I love him who desires the impossible."[116] The preparatory sketches to *Richard Wagner in Bayreuth* celebrate almost with the drunkenness of Novalis the "wonderful meaning of death," of the heroic end: "Death is the *judgment,* but the freely chosen, the longed-for judgment, full of horrible attraction, as if it were more than a portal to nothingness. Death is the seal on all great passion and heroism. . . . To be ready for it is the highest thing that can be achieved, but also the most difficult and gained through heroic struggles and suffering. Every death of that kind is a gospel of love . . ."[117] A strange note from 1882, before *Zarathustra,* reads: "*That which comes.* A prophecy.—The self-conquest of morality.—Liberation.—Middle and beginning of decline.—A characteristic of midday.—Voluntary death."[118] "I will not conceal that I have an increasingly profound desire for death," he writes to Overbeck in 1887. But it is not just death as such, not just any release he desires, but rather the wish to end in some great fashion. "For the death of the great is also great,"[119] Hölderlin wrote in *Empedokles,* the same work that had "always especially moved" Nietzsche even as a pupil as the glorification of prophetic death; a surviving note from his school days reads: "Empedocles's death is a death occasioned by divine pride, by disdain for man, by weariness with the world and pantheism."[120] In the *Zarathustra* poem, the Empedoclean great decline—"Thus you decline, you, the star, and the valleys shine drunkenly from your light"—is glorified and longed for, in the *Zarathustra* poem, which sings above all else the decline of Zarathustra, which begins with the wish and will to decline: "You great star . . . like you, I must go down, as people say, to whom I want to descend. . . . Bless the cup that wants to overflow, so that the water may flow golden from it and take with it everywhere the reflection of your bliss. Behold! this cup wants to become empty again. . . . Thus began Zarathustra's descent."[121] The benedictions in the prologue to *Zarathustra* are devoted to the will to voluntary decline, to prodigal death:

"What is great about man is that he is a bridge and not an end: what can be loved about man is that he is a transition and a decline.

"I love those who know not how to live, be it as people in decline or those in transition.

"I love him who justifies the people to come and redeems those of the past: for he wants to perish from those of the present . . .

"I love him who castigates his god because he loves his god: for he must perish from the wrath of his god . . .

"I love him whose soul is overflowing so that he forgets himself and that all things are in him: thus all things become his decline . . .

"I love all those who are like heavy drops, falling individually out of the dark cloud hanging over men: they predict the coming of lightning and perish as prophets.

"Behold, I am a prophet of lightning and a heavy drop from the cloud . . ."[122]

Before the lightning—that is, in every respect, the prophetic condition of the final Nietzsche. Before the lightning that he himself must herald and that will consume him. It is, in the words of his own word-poem, the waiting of the cloud ("Whoever will have much to proclaim one day, Must long remain silent unto himself, Whoever intends to ignite lightning one day, Must long be—a cloud"),[123] and at the same time the waiting of the pine tree ("I grew too lonely and too high, I wait—what am I waiting for? The clouds' seat is too close to me: I am waiting for the first lightning").[124] But in both instances, it is *the same* lightning: the prophecy is simultaneously the demise of the prophet, according to the law of all prophecy and the fate of all prophets: they augur the coming of the lightning and they perish as augurs. Zarathustra himself utters the name of his deadly lightning of prophesy in the benedictory prologue: "Behold, I am a prophet of lightning . . . but this lightning is called *Overman.*"[125] And in the fantastic-mystical late poem about the lament of Ariadne, the final introduction of the god from the cloud reads: " . . . A bolt of lightning. Dionysus becomes visible in emerald beauty."[126]

Overman or Dionysus—two names for the same vision: for the future image, the future certainty of the New Man. Two names that wed the German idea of the highest becoming with the Greek happiness of the highest being. Two of Nietzsche's words for the content of his prophecy, which found its most powerful poetic expression in *Zarathustra,* but which imbue his entire oeuvre from *The Birth* to the final pages of *Ecce homo* and *The Will to Power* in all degrees of clarity and self-certainty, of doubt and struggle. In *The Birth of Tragedy,* Dionysus is already "absolutely the first name"—just as Nietzsche felt that the name of Wagner, his earliest mask of Dionysus, was absolutely the first name in *Ecce homo.* In *Ecce homo* he writes of "Richard Wagner in Bayreuth": "Everything in this work foretells the future: the imminent return of the Greek spirit, the necessity of anti-Alexanders who will retie the Gordian knot of Greek culture after it had been loosened . . . and nowhere will one find a more magnificent expression for the event of *Zarathustra,* an act of immense purification and consecration of humanity, than one finds on pages 43 to 46."[127] But in *Ecce homo,* Dionysus is also the last name that occurs in the work, and the Dionysian dithyramb "Fame and Eternity" forms a conclusion that speaks in tongues, its highest ascent and deepest fall. And even the last pages for the last chapter of his unfinished masterpiece of prose (not song), *The Will to Power*—the chapter that was to have carried the name Dionysus—even they express once more, in a state of tremendous happiness, the vision of the New Man, the "imminent return of the Greek spirit,"[128] with the name of the god; in words that are at once ecstatic and clear, prophetic and perceptive, words of sacred sobriety,[129] which form perhaps the most beautiful words that the prose writer Nietzsche ever lent to the only singable secret of his prophecy:

> Only the very rarest and finest people attain to the highest and the most glorious human joys in which existence celebrates its own transfiguration: and those people only do so after they themselves and their ancestors have lived a long, preparatory life toward this goal, but without even knowing of this goal's existence. Then an overflowing abundance of the most diverse forces, and simultaneously the most nimble power of a "free will" and commanding authority, will find a harmonious home in a single person; then the mind will be just as comfortable and at home in the senses as the senses are at home and comfortable in the mind. . . . Such perfect and finely wrought people perceive in themselves a *kind of deification of the body.* . . . From that height of joy, where a person feels he is personally and thoroughly a deified form and self-justification of nature, all the way down to the joy of healthy peasants and half-human animals: the Greeks, not without the grateful shudder experienced when initiated into a secret, not without much caution and pious reticence, gave to this entire, long, enormous colorful spectrum of *happiness*—the divine name: *Dionysus.* What do all more modern people, the children of a fragile, disparate, ill and strange time *know* about the scope of Greek happiness, what could

they know about it! Where would the slaves of "modern ideas" even gain the right to Dionysian celebrations!

When the Greek body and the Greek soul "blossomed" . . . there arose that mysterious symbol of the highest world affirmation and transfiguration of existence which has been achieved on earth so far. Here a *standard* was established against which everything that has since grown up has been found to be too short, too poor, too narrow: one needs only to express the word Dionysus before the best modern names and things, before Goethe, for instance, or before Beethoven, or before Shakespeare, or before Rafael: and suddenly we feel that our best things and moments have been *condemned.* Dionysus is a judge. Have I been understood?—There is no doubt that the Greeks sought to interpret the ultimate secrets "about the fate of the soul," and everything that they knew about education and purification, about the unalterable hierarchical rank and inequality in the value of each person relative to others, in light of their Dionysian experiences: here, for everything Greek, there is the great profundity, the great silence—*one does not know the Greeks* as long as the hidden subterranean entrance here is still buried. Prying scholars' eyes will never see anything in these things . . . even the noble zeal of such friends of antiquity as Goethe and Winckelmann has here something unacceptable, almost immodest about it. Wait and prepare; wait for new sources to spring up; prepare in solitude for strange faces and voices; cleanse the soul of the carnival dust and noise of this time so that it becomes ever more pure; overcome everything Christian by means of something super-Christian . . . for the Christian doctrine was the counter-doctrine to the Dionysian one; rediscover the south in oneself . . . become *more Greek* . . . : whoever lives under such imperatives, who knows what can happen to him one day? Perhaps indeed—a *new day!*[130]

The prophet was to encounter it, this Greek new day. But this day was a bolt of lightning—it was the day on which he signed his last lines, in the powerful letters of a deadly ecstasy, with the name of his god, "Dionysus." The day on which he, like a prophet even here, descended into the long, premature night.

18

Socrates

. . . Almighty, you awaken
The pure souls of youths and teach
Wise ways to the elders; only the wicked
Become more so, would that they die sooner
When you, awesome one, seize them.[1]
Whoever has thought most profoundly loves what is most vital.[2]
—Hölderlin

. . . A layman must respect, however, what someone says who is so possessed by the daemon, and it must be seen as irrelevant whether he speaks out of feeling or knowledge, for the gods preside here and sow seeds for future comprehension. . . . To want to instruct him would be, even from someone of greater insight than me, sacrilege, because his own genius illuminates his path and often, as if it were lightning, gives him light where we sit in the dark and hardly fathom from which side the day will begin.
—Goethe on Beethoven (1810)[3]

If Nietzsche was a Christian—albeit in a secret, parodic, and paradoxical way—then he was a Christian, too, in that he loved his enemies. With a love, to be sure, in which Christian self-hatred and Hellenic competitive envy enter into a genuinely Nietzschean union. Nietzsche was never more grateful, he never devoted himself more, than to those whom he insulted and persecuted, a second Saul.[4] Thus Socrates, that most questionable figure of antiquity, as *The Birth of Tragedy* calls him, is thus so close to him—"just so as to admit it"—that he "was almost always waging a battle with him"[5] (in a surviving fragment from 1875 with the indicative title "The Struggle between Science and Wisdom"). How characteristic that is, this being "*so* close, that I am almost always waging a battle with him . . . !" There is a law expressed in such hostile proximity to that to which one is most intimately related, and one of the most important laws determining the course of Nietzsche's life in particular.

If one sets aside Richard Wagner, in whom the beloved enemy and hated beloved are intermingled for Nietzsche in an all-too-unique and singular fashion, and if one leaves the figure of Christ in the shadow of reserve and respect with which even the passionate Antichrist of the final years surrounds the founder of Christianity, whom he had persecuted with such a Saul-like vengeance ("Christ on the cross is the most sublime symbol—still,"[6] he writes even in the late Notebooks from the time of *The Antichrist*), then truly it is Socrates, as the passage in the Notebooks put it, who was the closest of the enemies with whom he thought it necessary and imperative to struggle throughout his life; Socrates was truly the one with whose disturbing proximity he was almost always waging a battle. He struggled with the haunting satyr shadow of Plato's great teacher more than he did with Paul, with Luther, with Pascal, with Schopenhauer. He struggled as if with the deadliest danger of his life and, like Jacob with the angel, for the blessing and meaning of his life. For in the furious: "I shall not let you go!" with which Nietzsche embraced the figure of Socrates all his life, there was always a combination of deadly hatred and a plea for his blessing. Only thus can the very particular tone be understood with which *The Birth of Tragedy*, in a phrase that could have almost come from Hebbel, calls Socrates "the one turning point and vortex of so-called world history."[7] For the history of his own world, of his individual cosmos, Plato's teacher was and remained the one turning point and "vortex of being." One can, if one wishes, see Nietzsche's intellectual development as circling around his relationship to Socrates, just as *The Birth of Tragedy* is no different in being composed around the murderer of tragedy, as *Twilight of the Idols* is built up around the kernel of hatred that he calls "the problem of Socrates."[8] Not only the enlightened *Human* sees "the roads of the most varied philosophical ways of living leading back to Socrates," that "simplest and least ephemeral of the wise middlemen."[9]

Nietzsche's love-hate relationship to Socrates combines self-hatred and self-transfiguration in a peculiar unity. Whom does he hate in Socrates? It is the man, the type he hated most—the man and type called Nietzsche: the theoretical man who is destined to put an end to myth and install knowledge of good and evil in place of the gods. He hated in Socrates the poisoner of true Greekdom, of the pre-Socratic Hellenism consisting of myth and Orphism[10] that was and remained for him the only genuine Hellenism. He hated the logician in him, the enlightener, the non-mystic, the optimist—the one who betrayed tragedy in favor of dialectics and whose applied sophism enticed away from myth toward knowledge of the human, all-too human. He hated him with all the hatred of Aristophanes—and almost with the means of his hatred.

He is seized by a "tremendous dubiety" whenever he is confronted by Socrates and it "prompts him again and again to understand the meaning and intention of this most questionable figure of antiquity. Who is he that, as a single individual, he may dare to negate the Greek character, which is certain of our astonished reverence as the deepest abyss and the highest height? What daemonic power is it that may be emboldened to pour this magic potion into the dust? What demi-god is it to whom the chorus of the noblest spirits of humanity must call out: 'Woe! Woe! You have destroyed it, the beautiful world / With your powerful fist; it is collapsing, it is crumbling!'"[11] (*The Birth of Tragedy*). "After the Hellenic spirit had exhausted its highest types, the Greeks disappeared with lightning speed. . . . A single, powerful eccentric like Socrates—and the rift was irreparable. The self-destruction of the Greeks takes place in him . . ."[12] "Older Hellenism revealed its powers in a series of philosophers. With Socrates this revelation ceases: he tries to engender himself and do away with all tradition.[13] . . . From Socrates onwards: the individual suddenly took himself too seriously"[14] ("The Struggle between Science and Wisdom," 1875). (Significantly, the incestuous character of pure individualism, which "attempts to engender itself," is self-critically emphasized, just as in *The Birth of Tragedy* "a wise magician" could be "created only through incest.")[15] Indeed, in the so Enlightenment-friendly *Human,* it was for Nietzsche "no idle question whether Plato, had he remained free of Socratic enchantment, would not have found an even higher type of philosophical man, who is lost to us forever."[16] And even in *Ecce homo,* he names as one of the two decisive innovations contained in *The Birth of Tragedy* the understanding of Socratism: "Socrates is recognized for the first time as an instrument of Greek disintegration, as a typical décadent."[17]

Socrates is for him "the type of an existential form that was previously unheard-of: the theoretical man"[18] (*The Birth of Tragedy*); his dialectic is a symptom of decadence—dialectic as the weapon of the weak—his glorification of *knowledge* as the basis of all ethics (knowledge of the good is synonymous with doing good, no person is knowingly and voluntarily evil) is the pernicious rationalism of an ugly and misbegotten man who has to uproot the powers of his passion in order to gain mastery over them instead of allowing them to thrive and flourish. Socrates is to him "a true monstrosity *per defectum.*"[19] And he sees in him the monstrous defect found in everyone who has a mystical tendency, "so that Socrates could be described as the specifically non-mystic in whom, through a super-fetation of the logical capacity, the logical nature is just as over-developed as instinctive wisdom is in a mystic"[20] (*The Birth of Tragedy*). Socrates a monster—this characterization of extreme hatred frequently recurs. In the Basel lecture on Socrates and tragedy, he explains: "Science and art are mutually exclusive: from this point of view it is significant that Socrates was the first great Hellene who was ugly, just as, in fact, everything about him is symbolic. He is the father of logic, which most strongly represents the character of science; he is the destroyer of musical drama, which had contained within it all of the strands of ancient art."[21] The "lack of respectfulness, that the great wise men are figures of decline," is something that Nietzsche "first realized in the case of Socrates: I recognized Socrates and Plato as symptoms of decay, as the instruments of the Greek dissolution, as pseudo-Greek, as anti-Greek. . . . Socrates belonged, in terms of his origin, to the lowest people: Socrates was rabble. ('The rabble achieved victory through dialectics.'[22] [*Will to Power*]) We know, we can still see, how ugly he was. But ugliness, in itself an objection, was among the Greeks almost a refutation. Was Socrates even a Greek?"[23] (*Twilight of the Idols*).

Not Greek—the most devastating judgment Nietzsche held in his quiver full of deadly arrows. A Scythian, the earliest "modern," a decadent—thus Nietzsche's hatred lashes Socrates, like Paul, to the stake of his psychology. He goes on to say in *Twilight of the Idols* that not only the admitted squalor and anarchy of his instincts pointed to decadence: the super-fetation of the logical pointed to that as well. . . . Everything about him is exaggerated, buffo,[24] a caricature; at the same time, everything is concealed, ulterior, subterranean ("Everything deep loves the mask"[25] he writes contrapuntally in *Beyond*). Indeed, Socrates "was the buffoon who made people take him seriously"[26] ("I don't want to be a saint, I'd much rather be a buffoon . . . perhaps I am a buffoon,"[27] comes the response out of the hidden corners of *Ecce homo*). Here Nietzsche reveals what he reveals so often: he hits himself with the vindictive arrows he shoots at the target bearing the satyr's countenance of his Socrates. He is thinking about Socrates and about Nietzsche as well when he says (in the Notebooks to *The Gay Science*): "If this person does not become a great virtuous man, he will become terrible, to himself and to others."[28] Nietzsche is alluding to the well-known Greek anecdote, which he also frequently told in his "French" manner, according to which a stranger walked up to Socrates at the marketplace in Athens and called his face a sanctuary of all evil desires—whereupon Socrates merely replied: "You know me, stranger." (Even Goethe confessed he possessed this dangerous, Socratic double possibility when he said two years before his death to Eckermann: "If I wanted to let myself go without restraint I would probably have it in me to destroy myself and my environment.")[29] What he writes about Socrates in the Notebooks to *Human* also applies to Nietzsche himself, who was burdened, Centaur-like, with qualities that had never been observed at once in a single person: "The Platonic Socrates is literally a caricature; for he is burdened with qualities that can never be together in *one* person."[30] *The Will to Power* finds a "morbid element" in Socrates: "There is a resistance to being preoccupied with morality when a mind is rich and independent. How is it that Socrates is a moral monomaniac? . . . When morality and religion are the principal interests, that is a sign of crisis."[31] But is that not also true above all of Nietzsche, the most passionate of our moralists? For the Antichrist, in whom "the religious instinct, that is, the instinct for *creating* gods, sometimes stirred at inconvenient times?"[32]

No doubt, in all of this Nietzsche uses the sharpest, indeed caricatured strokes of hate to draw the portrait of the enlightened rationalist, the logician out of decadence, whom he hates as himself. But through this portrait shimmers, like a palimpsest, the image of the *other* Socrates Nietzsche also felt himself to be; the image of a Socrates who overcame the logician within him and placed him in the service of a higher mission; the image, to use the expression from *The Birth,* of the music-making Socrates. This image, from the introduction of Plato's *Phaedo,* repeatedly returns in Nietzsche and, through its return, betrays a longing to equate Socrates's fate with his own. "That despotic logician occasionally had in the presence of art a feeling of a lack, an emptiness, of half of a reproach, a perhaps neglected obligation. Frequently, as he told his friends when he was in jail, one and the same apparition came to him in his dreams, which always said the same thing: 'Socrates, make music!' He consoled himself up until his final days with the notion that his philosophizing was the highest art of the muses, and he did not really believe that a divinity would remind him of that 'common, popular music.' Finally, in jail he reluctantly agrees to make the music of which he has such a low opinion. And in this frame of mind he composes a proem to Apollo. . . . That reference to the dream apparition is the only sign of hesitancy about the boundaries of logic: perhaps—he had to ask himself— . . . there is a realm of wisdom from which the logician is banned?"[33] (*The Birth of Tragedy*). The entirety of Nietzsche's first work is basically devoted to the single question it poses itself: "Will that reversal of insatiable optimistic knowledge into tragic resignation and desire for art lead to constantly renewed configurations of genius and of nothing other than a *music-making Socrates?*"[34] A fragment in the Notebooks to *The Birth* describes tragic man as none other than the music-making Socrates.[35] And if, in this first work, "the *dying Socrates* became the new, never-before-seen ideal of the young Greek nobility,"[36] then for Nietzsche it was probably also the final, secret music of this dying paragon that emanated the strongest magic.

What kind of music did Nietzsche project into his Socrates exit? It was the music of the girl flutist who accompanied Alcibiades to the symposium at Agathon's house, the music as Conrad Ferdinand Meyer interpreted it in his poem on the end of the symposium: " . . . Hush! The slumber flutes of death are sounding!"[37] "He went to his death," *The Birth of Tragedy* says, "with that calm which Plato describes when, having outlasted the other revelers, he left the symposium in the early dawn to begin a new day; while behind him, on the benches and on the floor, his sleepy table companions continued to dream about Socrates, the true eroticist."[38] It was the music whose name is Plato.

Nietzsche conscientiously allows this image of Socrates to rise before him and us only as an intimation and a shadow. But it is certain that his hatred for the inartistic logician Socrates would never have become so inextinguishable had the great artistic *teacher* Socrates not always been a secret, beloved image for him. In the same way, his hatred of Paul would never have arisen in him so powerfully, so almost fanatically, had not a subterranean Christianity of values (to use Nietzsche's phrase about Kant) lent the image of his great antagonist the fiery hues of fraternal hatred. It was the great teacher Socrates whom Nietzsche's distorting polemic wanted to purify of those traits that he had experienced and hated in himself as an objection to his own role as teacher. In relation to Socrates, Nietzsche's philosophy is truly what he calls it himself, namely an inverted Platonism: he stylizes Socrates, as Plato had done, but toward the negative, just as Plato had made his own doctrine, his own pedagogy, his own Platonism seductively shine through Socrates, in contrast to Socrates.

"The citizens of Basel will never have such a teacher again," Jakob Burckhardt decided as early as 1875 in conversation with a friend. That was true in a broader and deeper sense than even Burckhardt could have known. For, above all else, Nietzsche appears to us as a teacher and Socratic educator, with respect to both his constitution and his effect; and as the Socrates with whom he is almost always waging a battle. The hard or hardening fanatic of knowledge for its own sake, the incomparable, demonically vengeful psychologist, the Luciferian "free spirit," all initially stand, it is true, before the image of this Socratic Nietzsche. "That a psychologist who has no equal is speaking in my writings," he says in *Ecce homo,* "is perhaps the first realization that comes to a good reader—the kind of reader I deserve . . ."[39] But this incomparable psychologist in Nietzsche is as little able to conceal the educator for very long as the logician in Socrates could hide the one who could be Plato's teacher: his mastery of psychology, as self-aggrandizing, as self-sufficient as it occasionally appeared, particularly in the works of the middle period, enters into the service of the pedagogical ideal, just as the sophistic self-satisfaction of logic in Socrates enters into the service of a pedagogical "transformation through knowledge." And, once again, in *Ecce homo,* that most maliciously perceptive of Nietzsche's works, he also formulated that insight himself:

"With these works ('Schopenhauer as Educator,' 'Richard Wagner in Bayreuth'), I basically wanted to *do something completely different from psychology—a problem of education without equal,* a new notion of self-discipline, self-defense to the point of hardness, a path to greatness and world-historical tasks was its first expression."[40] It was not knowledge, which, in the final analysis, always remains a hybrid private enjoyment of the individual when it is pursued "for the sake of knowledge"; it was not knowledge—despite all the hypertrophy of his passion for knowledge in the years between the separation from Wagner and the first intimations of Zarathustra—that was the dominant passion of this life, which in the end was nevertheless sacrificed to dangerous knowledge and to deadly self-knowledge: but rather the education of the living for life, the intensification of the joy in existence into the will to create, the transformation of the merely egotistical individual into a shining image. Education, not knowledge; wisdom, not science; cultivation, not erudition—these are the guiding principles of the young pedagogue Nietzsche. "I am against deploying the egoistic desire for knowledge. What is needed above all: joy in the present, and it is the task of the teacher to help further that"[41] ("Introduction to the Study of Classical Philology," 1871). The essay "On the Use and Disadvantage of History for Life," as well as the last two *Untimely Meditations,* have their roots here, as does the youthful enthusiastic zeal of the lecture fragment "On the Future of our Educational Institutions," even though it is formally directed *against* the realistic decay of the old humanistic *Gymnasium,* with its principally descriptive education, against the proliferation of a school intended "to overcome the poverty of life"[42] within an organism designated as an "educational institution." In the midst of the most abstract philological problems, the most theoretical studies imaginable, the twenty-three-year-old student nevertheless envisions a Socratic life's mission as a truly practical teacher; he writes in the fall of 1867: "I have endeavored more to learn how one is a teacher than to learn what one otherwise learns at a university. . . . I envision as my goal to become a truly practical teacher and above all to awaken in young people the necessary circumspection and self-reflection that enables them to keep in view the Why? What? and How? of their studies. It won't escape you that there is a philosophical element in this position. A young man should first enter into the state of amazement that has been called the *φιλόσοφον πάθος κατ᾽ ἐξοχήν.*"[43] The newly appointed university professor repeats the same thing in a higher register, in a kind of Schopenhauerian Platonism. In the last letter from Leipzig, just before his departure for Basel, he writes to Gersdorff: "To impart to my students that Schopenhauerian seriousness which is stamped on the forehead of a thoughtful man—that is my desire, my bold hope: I would like to be something more than a breeder of competent philologists: the present generation of teachers, the care for the next brood to come, all of that stands before my soul."[44] The accents in which Nietzsche expresses his pedagogical ideal become more and more Platonic leading up to *Zarathustra.* In *Human* it becomes almost visionary: " . . . A more modern and fuller flourishing and expansion of the ideal of a teacher, in which the roles of clergyman, artist, physician, philosopher and wise man all merge, just as their individual virtues would appear as a general virtue in their teaching itself, in their lectures and their method—that is my vision, one that constantly comes back to me and which I firmly believe has lifted a corner of the veil of the future."[45] (That is entirely the ideal image of a romantic antiquity that Novalis had already celebrated in *Heinrich von Ofterdingen:* the ancient poets, we read there, were supposed to be prophets and priests, lawgivers and physicians simultaneously.) Education virtually becomes the name of his version of religion. "My religion, if I can still call anything that," he writes in the drafts to the essay "We Philologists" (1874/75), "lies in working for the creation of the genius; education is everything to be hoped for. . . . Education is love for our progeny, an excess of love that goes beyond self-love . . ."[46] And early on, lecturing before his students in Basel, Nietzsche touches on the secret of his own life and his own tragic fate with the almost Goethean words: "The deepest insights arise only out of love."[47]

Here we are already in the midst of the Socratic mythos of education. The deepest insights arise only out of love—that is a Greek sentence. The sentence around which the young Nietzsche thinks Plato's philosophy gravitates; the true "Open Sesame" that the enthusiastic teacher in Basel, who is so inwardly concerned about the future of German education, can use to unlock the entrance to the educational and pedagogical world of antiquity, that entrance buried under indescribable strangeness for the moderns: "Greek culture of the classical period is a culture of men. . . . Young people have probably never again been treated so carefully, so lovingly, in a way that was so thoroughly mindful of their best (virtus), as in the sixth and fifth century—that is, in Hölderlin's beautiful words, 'for a mortal, in loving, gives his best'"[48] (*Human*). In those words, a Socratic pedagogical idea is expressed that is frequently repeated during the German humanistic era (which comes to a magnificent conclusion in Nietzsche), during the century between 1770 and 1870, as part of a genuine legacy of antiquity. The letters of the Swiss historian Johannes von Müller formulate it in the effusive manner of the late rococo, but still full of lived knowledge of the law, perhaps most ancient of all: "Ideas are born in the arms of a wise friend,"[49] he writes in 1773, the year in which Goethe looked back on the transformative encounter with Herder, and six years later, sounding more like Klopstock: "It is impossible to have a beloved friend and not to wish eagerly for immortality."[50] But Eckermann heard the seventy-five-year-old Goethe say something that seems to hover eerily between Hölderlin's "A mortal, in loving, gives his best" and Nietzsche's "The deepest insights arise only out of love," namely: "We learn only from the one we love."[51]

In this Hölderlinian fashion, Nietzsche advanced his German Platonism beyond Socrates, indeed against Socrates; as Plato himself had once obeyed his pedagogical demon, which had been awakened and nurtured by Socrates, to go beyond Socrates, indeed against Socrates. What sets the Platonic Socrates apart from Xenophon's "real" Socrates, the turn away from the rational sphere toward the mystical, from the logical to the erotic—that is precisely what Nietzsche marshals against his all-too-real, mercilessly demythologized Socrates in favor of his own pedagogical Platonism. "The assumption that knowledge transforms one's nature is the common *error* of rationalism, with Socrates leading the way,"[52] he writes in 1870 to Deussen. Nietzsche goes further: even the transformation of knowledge without the transformation of one's nature becomes in his eyes a common rationalistic error. For, as Plato experienced through Socrates but did not learn from him, this transformation occurs only when one loves. Knowledge, when it is wisdom, not science, when it is to be productive and superindividual, is a phenomenon and product of love; Nietzsche offers variations of Goethe's "learns only when loving" throughout all of his phases. His own experience of exhilaration through Schopenhauer, his love of Wagner, finds ever new ways of expressing this *first* stage of the Great Education, whose second stage is the company of equally educated friends who have equal hopes, with the third represented by one's own edifying and exemplary mastery.

"We will certainly become indifferent to anyone who does not make us productive.[53] . . . In all human interaction there is only *one* thing that matters: pregnancy"[54] (Notebooks from the *Zarathustra* period). "A person is destined, one way or the other, to be either a father or mother"[55] (Notebooks to *Human*). "If you do not have a good father, then you should procure one"[56] (*Human*). "Schopenhauer as Educator," the most Socratic of the four *Untimely Meditations,* is entirely the expression of such lived wisdom. In this work, we also find the truly central sentence around which all of Nietzsche's early writings are grouped as if around a fiery core: "Only he who has hung his heart on some great man receives thereby the first consecration of culture."[57] The first great poet-educator from Bayreuth, the author of *Titan* and the Socratic teacher of the doctrine *Levana,* saw the law at the beginning of the century this way: "To be sure, every young boy and every great man who considers someone else great, considers him too great for that very reason. But in every noble heart there burns an eternal thirst for a more noble one, in a beautiful heart for one more beautiful . . . because the eminent man matures only in the presence of eminence. . . . A man we believe is great is, after all, our only foretaste of heaven."[58] Similarly, the young Goethe once perceived the mythos of Socrates, as he wrote in his letter from Frankfurt to Herder along with a copy of his *Götz von Berlichingen:* "Now I am studying the life and death of another hero. . . . It is still only a vague notion. It is Socrates, the philosophical heroic spirit . . . the divine calling to be the teacher of people. . . . I do not know if I can go from serving the idol that Plato portrays and gilds, and to which Xenophon pays homage, to serving the true religion, which is manifested not by a saint but by a great man, whom I can press to my breast with the enthusiasm of love and say: my friend and my brother! And to be able to say that with confidence to a great man!—If I were Alcibiades for a day and a night, I would then happily die!"[59] (End of 1771)—Goethe, who a few months before had written to Herder "in the throes of emotion": "My entire being is shattered. . . . Herder, Herder, never cease to be what you are to me. If I am destined to be your planet, then I want to be it, and be it gladly and truly. . . . Adieu, dear man. I shall not let you go! I shall not leave you! Jacob wrestled with the angel of the Lord.[60] And even if I shall become lame doing so! . . . I would pay with ___ to be with you now for an hour."[61] Nietzsche, too, experienced what Goethe expressed in these letters with the sacred audacity of his youth. Nietzsche, too, demonstrates the receptive enthusiasm of love, which incessantly urges the young man to "Become who you are!"[62] (Nietzsche's favorite quotation from Pindar). "For my part," he writes to Rohde in 1872, "for my part, to have a single spectator like Wagner, I would give up all the laurels that the world today has to offer; and the wish to satisfy him drives me more and higher than any other power. For that is *difficult*—and he says everything, whether he likes something or doesn't, and for me it is like a good conscience handing out punishments and rewards."[63] And for the young Nietzsche, the experience of Schopenhauer, like that of Wagner, was akin to Goethe's experience of Herder, even if it was Wagner who first fulfilled for him what the mute mouth, the remaining testament of Schopenhauer could no longer be. "I learn a great deal in Wagner's presence," Nietzsche writes to Rohde in 1869, "it is my practical course in Schopenhauerian philosophy."[64] How indescribably enthralled he still is in Leipzig to hear from Wagner's lips what he owes to Schopenhauer and how he is the only philosopher who had recognized the essence of music! Both, the philosopher and the musician, are to him the *same* experience, the *same* happiness. But it is Wagner who brings the true fulfillment of Schopenhauer, and just as Wagner is initially the living illustration of what Schopenhauer calls a genius, later, in "Schopenhauer as Educator," for example, Schopenhauer very often becomes merely a mask for Wagner, a mask that Nietzsche's "enthusiasm of love" for Wagner bashfully holds before his gratitude and rapturous devotion. For the young man does not want to be a reader, no matter how grateful he may be, but rather a son and pupil. He wants to be able to say: "I shall not leave you!" with all of the cosmic happiness in which the dawning Goethe orbited around Herder's star. "I sensed I had found in Schopenhauer the educator and philosopher I had sought for so long. But only as a book: that was a major shortcoming. I tried all the harder to see through the book and to imagine the living person whose great testament I had to read and who promised to make only those his heirs who wanted, and were able, to be more than merely his readers: namely, his sons and pupils"[65] ("Schopenhauer as Educator"). Thus it was a great man Nietzsche was seeking, not a great doctrine, a philosopher, not a philosophy, a living mouth, not a rigid testament. Not a dead man worthy of veneration, but an immortal living exemplar. "My estimation of a philosopher stands in direct proportion to the degree in which he is able to be a model"[66] ("Schopenhauer as Educator"). And again: "It is irrelevant what the propositions are, the nature of a man replaces a hundred systems. He may be wrong a hundred times as a teacher: but his character itself is right, that is what we should remember. There is something in a philosopher that can never be in a philosophy: namely, the cause of many philosophies, the great man"[67] (Notebooks to the third *Untimely*). But the essay on the educator Schopenhauer does not only come out of an experience of the Platonic enthusiasm of love, like *The Birth of Tragedy*, it already formulates the law of this experience itself, the Greek law of pedagogical love. "How can a person know himself? . . . To perform the most important interrogation, there is the following method. The young soul looks back on his life with the question: what have you truly loved until now, what attracted your soul, what dominated and simultaneously thrilled it? Imagine all of the things you cherish before you in a row, and through their nature and their order perhaps a law will become apparent to you, the basic law of your proper self . . . your true educators and cultivators will reveal to you what the true meaning and material of your being is. . . . Your educators can be nothing other than your liberators."[68] Which, ten years later, in the Notebooks to *Zarathustra*, reads in a masterfully concise formulation: "In which people did you once believe? Their sum reveals to you your belief in yourself."[69] Your educators can be nothing other than your liberators—or with the words of a letter to Deussen from the year 1870: "We will probably choose and love the philosophy that best explains our nature to ourselves"[70]—with that, Nietzsche already establishes the Socratic law (a law full of immanent tragedy) stating that all love is only a path to oneself—the law whose terrible relevance to himself would occur to him only later, but whose melancholy already threw a dismal shadow over the song of farewell, "Richard Wagner in Bayreuth."

And just as great philosophy was only a devious enticement that Eros used to tempt the young mind toward the great pedagogical man and finally beyond the educator toward his own completion, so too, for Nietzsche, even great art was merely a devious mask of Eros to seduce the young soul toward something that was more than art, namely—"The aesthetic drives and preferences of youth," he writes in the Notebooks to *The Gay Science,* "are the precursors of something that is more than aesthetic. Strange!"[71] But that is, in the form of marginal musings, the Platonic doctrine of procreative love, of beauty as the messenger that seduces toward the divine, as Socrates expresses this doctrine in mythological form in his great speech in the *Phaedrus.* The beautiful does not speak of the beautiful, but rather of something that is more than the beautiful—that is how Nietzsche early on understands the central Platonic doctrine. "The most beautiful body—merely a veil, In which something more beautiful—shrouds itself"[72] reads an almost Hebbel-sounding couplet in the "Speeches, Symbols and Images," which strangely conflates Christian and Ancient metaphysics of beauty. In its entirety, *The Birth of Tragedy* already seems to be a protest against impenetrable beauty, serene unto itself,[73] that beauty which is *only* beautiful. And "Richard Wagner in Bayreuth," while passionately rejecting any aesthetic interpretation of the Wagnerian musical cult, objects to the notion that the true pupils of Wagner could be concerned about art alone: "One could do us no greater disservice than to assume that we are concerned about art alone: as if it were to be regarded as medicine or as a narcotic that could be used to alleviate all other miserable conditions."[74] "Art alone"—in Schopenhauer, it is still a form of redemption, the highest uplift of the soul, indeed an immediate, blissful intuition of the world will: here it is almost contemptuously dismissed. What did the young Nietzsche affirm in art? Its transformative power. Its magical capacity to prepare and bring about new living communities, new forms of being. This shimmers through the letter he sent from Basel to Rohde after the great Wagner performance in Mannheim in 1871. "If I consider that only a few hundred people in the next generation will take from music what I have from it, then I expect a completely new culture!"[75] The heart of his belief in Wagner is the enthusiastic certainty that this transformative power to renew culture, indeed to create culture, was inherent in Wagner's music and personality. The notion of a "hundred transformed people," which was awakened in Nietzsche by Burckhardt's conception of the Renaissance and by an idealized Bayreuth, appears repeatedly in his first writings and early letters. "Assuming someone believed that no more than a hundred productive and active people raised in a new spirit would be needed to put an end to the kind of erudition that has recently become fashionable in Germany, how encouraged that person would be to see that the culture of the Renaissance rose up on the shoulders of just such a group of a hundred men"[76] ("On the Use and Disadvantage of History for Life"). Here, Nietzsche is still speaking, cautiously, hypothetically, indirectly, as someone raised by the great historical Perhaps. But in the same work, this same hope also sounds hortatory, confident, categorical. "Draw around yourselves the fence of a great and expansive hope. . . . Form an image within yourselves of what the future is supposed to be and forget the superstition that you are epigones. . . . Feast your souls on Plutarch and dare to believe in yourselves by believing in his heroes. With a hundred people raised in such an unmodern spirit, that is, who have become mature and accustomed to the heroic, the whole noisy, grotesque culture of our time could now be silenced."[77] Such notions of a Platonic academy of Knights Templar course through Nietzsche's early period in the most varied masks. Depending on the occasion and mood, he emphasizes at times more the serene Socratic element, at others the brooding Christian aspect of this new group of a hundred men. The idea of Knights Templar of truth, a monasticism of art, a freemasonry of those "baptized by art," an academy of believers in the Great Man, all fuse together, Centaur-like, in a way possible only with Nietzsche. Sometimes the preservation of the endangered old humanistic culture seems to be the essential task, sometimes the re-creation of a new Dionysian culture "out of the spirit of music." At one moment, the "academy" has an almost reactionary character, only to have an almost extravagantly futuristic, musical one at the next. But what remains constant is the basic notion of a community that would form the yeast of the coming culture. Characteristically, it first appears in an entirely pessimistic tone in 1870. In a mood that is strangely reminiscent of Flaubert's letters, he writes to Rohde immediately after the outbreak of the war: "Our entire threadbare culture is throwing itself on the breast of the most horrible daemon. What will we experience! . . . What are our goals? We might already be at the beginning of the end! What desolation! We will need monasteries again. And we will be the first fratres."[78] That this monastic reveling in extreme hopelessness was not merely the expression of a momentary cultural despair over the sudden glimpse of chaos is proven by similar statements during the subsequent period. The alliance of Wagner and Schopenhauer reveals to him (in the Notebooks to "Richard Wagner in Bayreuth") "that perhaps at some point soon, culture will continue to exist only in the form of monastically secluded sects that reject the surrounding world."[79] The letter to Rohde from December 15, 1870, contains a comprehensive plan of a half-Greek, half-monastic academy. From Basel he writes:

> Something truly revolutionary will never be able to emerge from university wisdom. We can become real *teachers* only by levering ourselves by all available means out of the atmosphere of this time. . . . In that way, we will eventually cast off this yoke, of that I am entirely convinced. And then we will form a new Greek academy. . . . Even

if we attract a few like-minded people, I still believe that we will reach a small island. . . . We will then be our mutual teachers, our books will be fishing hooks to garner recruits for our monastic-artistic brotherhood. . . . To show you how serious I am, I have already begun to limit my requirements in order to save a small portion of my fortune. . . . Shouldn't we be able to bring a new form of academy into the world "and should I, filled with mightiest yearning, Not bring to life the most exquisite figure?"[80] . . . Our philosophers' school is certainly no historical reminiscence or an arbitrary caprice—are we not driven to take this path by *necessity?*
Your loyal Frater Fridericus.[81]

Elsewhere he speaks of a kind of order of higher men, of a plan for a "Yearbook of Friends"—although "nothing is further from my mind than to compete with such pitiful rubbish as the *Bayreuther Blätter*" (1878).[82] "*Where* do we want to renew Epicurus's garden?"[83] he writes to Gast in 1879. The idea of a community of the chosen grows far beyond "Bayreuth" and into the Greek sphere as it slowly rises toward the Platonic vision of *Zarathustra.* As early as "in 'Richard Wagner in Bayreuth,' the 'idea of Bayreuth' had changed into something that will not be a puzzling notion to the readers of my *Zarathustra:* into that *great midday* where the most elect are consecrated for the greatest of all missions—who knows? The vision of a celebration that I will still experience . . ."[84] (*Ecce homo*). In the chapter of *Zarathustra* called "Of Endowing Virtue," one finds mention of this vision, Bayreuth's last embodiment, as a final word of farewell to the disciples: "I will then love all of you with another love. And one day you will have become my friends and the children of a single hope: then I will be with you for a third time, so that I will celebrate the great midday with you. And the great midday is when man stands at the midpoint of his path between animal and overman and celebrates his journey to the evening as his highest hope: for it is the journey to a new morning."[85]

The young Nietzsche enjoyed the happiness of discipleship—but the celebration of the High Midday with like-minded friends who were his peers ("perfect friendship exists only *inter pares*")[86] was not granted to him. The aftersong to *Beyond,* "From High Mountains," called out for the last time for these friends, for this Platonic "bliss *inter pares,*" for this celebration of the High Midday:

Oh, midday of life! Solemn time!
Oh, summer garden!
Restless happiness in standing and watching and waiting—
I await friends, ready night and day,
Where are you, friends? Come! It is time, it is time!

. . . In the highest, my table was set for you—
Who lives so close

To the stars, so close to the horrible distances of the abyss?
My realm—what realm has been more vast?
And my honey—who has tasted it?

. . . There you are, friends!—Woe, it is not I
Whom you sought?
. . . I became another? And strange to myself? . . .
You turn away?—Oh, heart, you have borne enough,
Your hopes remained strong:
Keep the door open to *new* friends!
. . . It drove them away that they became old:
Only he who changes remains akin to me.

Oh, midday of life! Second time of youth!
Oh, summer garden!
Restless happiness in standing and watching and waiting—
I await friends, ready night and day,
New friends? Come! It is time, it is time![87]

But "this song is over—the sweet song of yearning Died in my mouth"[88]—for his friend Zarathustra came, the "guest of the guests," with whom alone he now celebrates, transformed from One to Two, the feast of the High Midday, "the feast of feasts."[89] From then on there was for Nietzsche only the third stage of Socratic existence: the stage of his own mastery, the pedagogical glance cast downward, the joy of great responsibility. After he had been disciple and friend, he becomes the third and most difficult thing: teacher and master. Nietzsche was granted a descent in a great man. The phantom of a cultural community of friends, of those decisive hundred men on whom all great cultures were erected according to his philosophy of history (which was also Burckhardt's), that notion had helped him bear the years until *Zarathustra.* Now, at the pinnacle, he is only one thing: the great teacher, the genius of education, the Socratic master, whose image Nietzsche had attempted to draw prematurely in his lecture "On the Future of our Educational Institutions." The great responsibility of pedagogy has now become his conscious guiding ideal, as it had secretly been at the core of his nature from the time he was a child (we recall the many little "pedagogical" anecdotes that survive from Nietzsche's childhood and youth). The classical, truly Socratic relationship of the pupil to his master, of the master to his pupil, is a fundamental problem that preoccupies him in all of his writings. "Whoever is fundamentally a teacher takes all things seriously only with respect to his pupils—even himself"[90] (*Beyond*). "Whoever is a teacher, is usually incapable of doing something for his own good, he is always thinking of the good of his pupils, and everything he learns makes him happy only in so far as he can teach it"[91] (*Human*). "Part of the humanity of a master is to warn his pupils of himself"[92] (*Daybreak*). "The apprentice loves the master in one way, the master loves the master in another"[93] (*Human*). At the height of his enthusiasm for Schopenhauer, the student, in a letter, already passes judgment on the philosopher's "obtuse followers": "Pupils such as Frauenstädt are basically an insulting vulgarity toward the master."[94]

And, like the relationship between pupil and master, the relationship among the ideal pupils themselves preoccupies him continuously as well. He views it in a thoroughly Socratic, thoroughly Greek fashion: as the noble *agon,* the competition for the prize of most distinguished pupil. He sees the mark of true mastery in that it knows how to awaken the good *Eris,* the noble envy among those on whom she has an effect—thus, the youths of Athens thronged in dialectic rivalry around the derisively clever, provocatively questioning satyr's countenance that seemed to be constantly looking for the "best and most just" among their number. *Envious*—that is how Nietzsche saw the ideal pupil and the ideal Greek. Nietzsche mentions this fruitful Greek envy probably for the first time in the study "Homer's Competition" (1871/72) while referring to Hesiod's notion of Eris as *two* goddesses. Not only Aristotle, but all of Greek antiquity thought differently about envy than we do. "The Greek is *envious* and does not perceive this quality as a flaw, but rather as the effect of a *benevolent* divinity: what a chasm of ethical judgment between us and him! . . . The greater and more superior a Greek is, the brighter the ambitious flame shoots out of him, consuming everyone who travels on the same path with him. . . . Every great Hellene passes on the torch of competition; every great virtue ignites a new greatness."[95] In a way that is entirely consistent with his principal preoccupation, Nietzsche traces the pedagogical effect and use of this basic Hellenic drive. "Greek popular pedagogy stipulates that every talent has to unfold in struggle: whereas modern educators fear nothing so much as unleashing so-called ambition. . . . 'The artist, too, is resentful of the artist.' And modern man fears nothing so much in an artist as the personal impulse to fight, whereas the Greek knows the artist only as being in a personal battle. Where a modern man senses the weakness of a work of art, the Hellene seeks the source of his greatest power!! . . . Competition alone turns Plato into a poet, a sophist, an orator. What a problem is solved for us when we inquire into the relationship between competition and the conception of a work of art!"[96] In *Daybreak* there is still a warning based on the notion of competition as the most important pedagogical law: "The best way to ruin an adolescent is to teach him to respect someone who thinks the same way he does more highly than someone who thinks differently."[97] Competition—even with the master himself—that remains the Socratic ideal. Socrates's highest renown rested on his ability to educate a pupil like Plato beyond himself, just as Plato created a Socrates beyond Socrates. "One repays a teacher poorly if one always remains merely a pupil," *Zarathustra* cautions, "and why shouldn't you all want to pick at my wreath? You venerate me; but what if your veneration were to collapse one day? Take care that a statue does not crush you!"[98] (The metaphor is a reminiscence of the passage in Aristotle in which he says that to be crushed by a statue is an untragic death.)[99]

The pride and pleasure in responsibility felt by every born Great Teacher pour forth from these and all other statements by Zarathustra. Significantly, in the year of his estrangement from Wagner, the consciousness of the meaning of his own being as that of a new example and model asserted itself for the first time: "In the main, I have realized this much: the only thing that people of all kinds truly acknowledge and to which they defer, is the high-minded deed. Not for anything in the world even a nod toward accommodation! One can achieve great success only if one remains true to oneself. I see what influence I already have now, and I would harm or destroy not only myself, but also many people growing with me, if I wanted to become weaker and skeptical"[100] (1876 to Gersdorff). But he also knows the sudden *fear* of responsibility in the great teacher. A decade later, he is terrified by the thought that one day illegitimate and wholly unqualified readers will appeal to his authority. "But that is the anguish of every great teacher of humanity: he knows that he, under certain circumstances and accidents, *can* become as much a catastrophe for humanity as a blessing"[101] (1884). For the great teacher, just as he is the strongest transformative reality among people, is at the same time unavoidably a phantom as well, the most distant from reality among all of humanity's phantoms of love. Early on, Nietzsche knows that "the active person is a phantom, not a reality": "the significant man gradually learns that he is, insofar as he is active, a phantom in the minds of others, and he will possibly fall into the subtle mental torture of asking himself whether he ought not to uphold the phantom of himself for the good of his fellow human beings" (*Human*). Such mental torture, this notion of a duty toward a pedagogical lie, acquires a growing influence on Nietzsche's philosophical stance. It slowly becomes his real Socratic principle. What one keeps to oneself reveals to Nietzsche the master of education, as it had revealed to Schiller the master of style.[102] "It is the form of *my* humanity to live nicely silent about my ultimate intentions; and, in addition, it is a matter of prudence and self-preservation. Who wouldn't run away from me!—if people figured out what duties grow out of my way of thinking . . . I would break the one and ruin the other . . . it is very possible that one day I will fall silent out of love of humanity!"[103] (1884 to Malwida). That is the pedagogical love of Socrates, the lie as the human kindness of the knowing (as he writes in the Notebooks to *Zarathustra*),[104] the keeping of a last, destructive secret against all the temptations of the relief that a confession would bring, that ultimate silence that even the young Nietzsche attributes to none other than Socrates. The masked self-avowal in the aphorism "The Dying Socrates" in *The Gay Science* refers to that silence—perhaps the boldest, certainly the most Nietzschean exegesis of the image of the dying Socrates that so deeply unsettled Nietzsche. "I admire," we read there,

> the courage and wisdom of Socrates in all that he did, said—and did not say. This derisive and enamored fiend and pied-piper of Athens, who made the most spirited youths tremble and sob, was not only the wisest chatterbox there has ever been: he was just as great in being silent. I wish he would have also been silent in the last moment of his life—perhaps then he would count among an even higher order of spirits. Whether it was death itself or poison or piety or malice—at that moment something loosened his tongue and he said: "Oh Crito, I owe Asclepios a rooster." These ridiculous and terrible "last words" mean for the person who has ears: "'O Crito, life is a disease!" Is it possible! A man like him, who lived cheerfully and like a soldier before everyone's eyes—was a pessimist! He had merely put on a brave face toward life and all his life concealed his final judgment, his innermost feeling! Socrates, Socrates suffered from life! And he took his revenge for it—with those veiled, horrible, pious and blasphemous words! Did Socrates need to take revenge? Was a grain of generosity too much for his abundant virtue? Alas, friends! We have to overcome the Greeks as well![105]

And for the last time, *The Will to Power* mysteriously, discreetly, Socratically praises the notion of great mastery: "If one imagines a philosopher as a great educator, powerful enough to pull up long chains of generations up to his lonely heights: then one also has to grant him the enormous privileges of a great educator. An educator never says what he thinks himself: rather only what he thinks about a matter in relation to the usefulness it has for those he is educating. One may not suspect him of this pretence; it is part of his mastery that others believe in his honesty. . . . Such an educator is beyond good and evil; but no one is allowed to know that."[106]

Together with the previous aphorism from *The Gay Science,* this fragment from the field of rubble that is his last work offers something like a final Socratic self-portrait, like an eerie mirror phantom. The philosopher as great educator to whom one must grant the enormous privileges of a great educator; who cannot be found out in the mastery of his pretence, inwardly beyond good and evil, but unrecognized by those closest to him: that is, undoubtedly, the image of the dying Socrates as *The Gay Science* had portrayed him five years earlier—but of a Socrates in whom even the Greeks have been overcome, who, unlike Nietzsche's Socrates who "avenges himself on life" at the last moment, knows how to go over *silently* and thereby takes his place "in a higher order of spirits." At the same time, however, just as indubitably, it is the image of Zarathustra-Nietzsche, who alone believes himself to be, like Socrates, powerful enough to pull up long chains of generations up to his lonely heights. What does this encounter between Zarathustra and the dying Socrates in one and the same image mean? In the image of the one whose last act was to let his soul sing but let his word fall mute and magnanimously take a final secret with him? Is Nietzsche not offering a confession here, veiled three times in extreme reserve? Was he the more high-minded Socrates who did not share with any Crito those ridiculous and horrible "last words" that indicated that life was an illness? Did he, who had lived cheerfully and like a soldier before everyone's eyes, keep silent that he, too, was a pessimist, that he, too, had merely put on a brave face toward life and all his life had concealed his final judgment, his innermost feeling? Was it his silence, that enormous privilege of the great educator, who never says what he thinks himself but only what he thinks about a matter in relation to the usefulness it has for those he is educating? Was just this pretense, which no one was permitted to suspect, the mastery that fostered belief in his honesty? Was he beyond good and evil, that is: beyond life (in which he stood with one foot, as he admitted in *Ecce homo*)? Was his ultimate Dionysian panegyric to *life,* and only to life, the form of silence under the guise of which a great educator for life did not believe in life? And did he not indeed finally take his revenge with that veiled, horrible, pious and blasphemous gesture, *Ecce homo?* "But no one is allowed to know that."

Only one thing is certain: if Nietzsche, in and despite all of his proud and horrible solitude, truly was this Socratic philosopher in *The Will to Power,* the philosopher as a born great educator, then he occupied that role as an equally born tragic hero, for owing to his contradictory Nordic-Hellenic nature he was unable to find or to keep the personal pupils he so desperately sought all his life. And perhaps this impossibility is rooted in what *his* last words kept silent, what "no one could know." It has been said, as a way of explaining away the spectacle of this awful contradiction, that Nietzsche's extreme individualism fundamentally spurned the category of "disciple," just as, despite *Zarathustra,* he rejected the name of "prophet" or "religious leader" for himself. Unlike even the solitary Schopenhauer, so goes this claim, he studiously refused any kind of discipleship. As evidence for this view, people have pointed to passages in which the rigorous will to the absolute solitude of intellectual reclusion appears to have overcome all other inclinations and temptations; in which he speaks with contempt of any sort of discipleship. For instance, in the truly ghastly letter to his sister from Nice in March 1885: "Do you really believe that Stein's writings, which I would not have done even during the period of my worst Wagnerianism and Schopenhauer-mania, possess anything resembling the importance of the enormous task that rests on me? . . . Or do you think that it befits my dignity to beg for his friendship? I am much too proud ever to believe that a person could love *me.* For that would presuppose that he would know who I am. Nor do I believe that I will ever love anyone: this would presuppose that—miracle of miracles!—I would one day find a person of my rank. . . . I have never had a confidant and friend for what preoccupies, troubles, uplifts *me:* it is too bad that there is no God so that at least Someone would know."[107] Or, more quietly and less Byronically, in letters to friends: "It cannot be quiet and high and solitary enough around me for me to hear my innermost voices!"[108] (1883 to Gersdorff). "I have no one who knows about my work: no one, whom I would consider strong enough to help me. . . . I would destroy the one and ruin the other: just *leave* me in my solitude!!! . . . It was foolish of me recently to go 'among the people': I should have known beforehand what I would find there"[109] (1884 to Malwida). "I feel *condemned* to my solitude and fortress. There is no longer any choice. What still commands me to live, namely an unusual and difficult mission, also commands me to avoid people and to form no more human attachments. It may be because of the extreme scrupulousness which that very mission has forced on me that I can no longer stand 'people,' least of all 'young people,' who very often plague me (—oh, they are demanding and clumsy, like puppies!)"[110] (1887 to Malwida). A rebuff that appears, in stylized form, in Zarathustra's farewell at the conclusion of the first part and recurs at the end of the foreword to *Ecce homo:* "I am going now alone, my disciples! You, too, are now going away and alone! That is how I want it.

"Verily, I say unto you: go forth from me . . . perhaps Zarathustra has deceived you.

"You say you believe in Zarathustra? But what does Zarathustra matter? You are my believers; but what do all the believers matter? . . .

"Now I command you, lose me and find yourselves. And only when you have all forsaken me do I intend to return to you."[111]

That is certainly the most anti-Socratic attitude of an exemplary man one can imagine. But it is only one direction of his being, the solitary Nordic one determined by Protestant individualism. It is true that through his experience with Lou[112] in 1882 Nietzsche had been driven to an extreme mistrust of any overtures from potential disciples, which was contrary to his own discriminating pedagogical instinct. And, it is also true, that his personal closeness to Bayreuth had given him too deep an appreciation of the human and intellectual inadequacy of that type of discipleship that, while longing for the bliss of submission, tends to surround a powerful artistic personality for him to succumb to the temptation of being grateful for any disciple no matter what the cost, as for example Schopenhauer had done. But the fact nevertheless remains that Nietzsche could and did experience the strongest urge to form a community of pupils (what power of stylization, to the point of complete reconfiguration and regeneration, we find in the letters to the imaginary Lou or even to Gast!). It remains the case that Nietzsche, far from giving way to any experiential pessimism that he could have taken from beholding the discipleship in Bayreuth, instead viewed Wagner's power to form disciples and pupils with a deep and painful, *Greek* envy; he saw in him the only man who could and did take away from him the few people of his generation on whom it would have been worth having an immediate, personal effect. The letters to Gast document this Socratic envy of the Sophistic Wagner: "It disgusts me that *Zarathustra* has entered the world as a book of entertainment; who is serious enough for it! If I had the authority of the 'final Wagner,' things would be better. But now no one can save me from being thrown to the 'belletrists.'"[113] "With respect to the real Wagner, I still want to be in large measure his *heir*. . . . Last summer I felt that he had taken from me all the people in Germany on whom it made any sense to have an effect . . ."[114] (1883 to Gast). That is not how someone speaks who, in exalted self-sufficiency, consoles himself with posthumous mastery; only the Socratic man speaks thus, for whom life without a person-to-person effect in the present is a mistake. With almost Socratic words, Nietzsche expresses his Socratic destiny as early as the year of his decisive separation from his once revered master, exactly at the moment his own masterly maturity begins: he calls himself, as Socrates might have done, a man hunter. "I am always on the hunt for men, like a Corsair;[115] but not to sell these men into slavery, but to sell me with them into freedom"[116] (1876 to Seydlitz). "If a man has no sons, then he does not fully have the right to have a say concerning the needs of a single political body,"[117] he had already written in *Human*. "To have descendents—only then does a man become steady, consistent and capable of making sacrifices: it is the best education. . . . Only our works and pupils lend the ship of our life its compass and great direction,"[118] in the Notebooks to *The Gay Science*. But only after the moment that his former master closes his eyes does Nietzsche feel he is his legitimate heir and successor ("Wagner's death is a great relief to me"),[119] and precisely from that moment on, ever since the *Zarathustra* year, which is not entirely coincidentally the year of Wagner's death, there is also in Nietzsche's most personal utterances a proliferation of calls for pupils and heirs to his life, testimony of a consuming desire for an immediate human effect: "What I envy Epicurus are his *pupils* in his garden; indeed, *there* one can already forget noble Greece, and there one *might* forget ignoble Germany! And thus my fury ever since I understood, in the broadest sense, what pathetic means (disparaging my reputation, my character, my intentions) *suffice* to rob me of the confidence and thus the possibility of pupils. I trust that you will believe that I have not written one line 'for the sake of fame': but I thought my writings could be a good bait. For in the end: the urge to teach is *strong* in me. And *for that reason* I need even fame so that I will obtain pupils . . ."[120] (1883 to Gast). "Put briefly, I need disciples *while I am still alive:* and if my previous books do not act as fishing rods, then they have 'missed their calling.' The best and essential things can be communicated only from *person to person,* they cannot and should not be 'public'"[121] (1884 to Overbeck). "My desire for pupils and heirs occasionally makes me impatient and has, it seems, led me to some imbecilities in the last few years that were extremely dangerous"[122] (1885 to Overbeck). "It may be that I always secretly believed that at the point in my life *that I have reached* I would no longer be alone: that by then I would have received vows and oaths from many people, that I would have something to found and to organize, and similar thoughts with which I consoled myself over periods of terrible loneliness. In the interim, everything turned out differently. It is all still too early . . ."[123] (1884 to Overbeck). Even the unconditional surrender that, particularly with regard to Wagner's following, had so often appeared suspect to him, even that he no longer scorns, in fact, he would encourage it. If he had already written in *Human,* characteristically enough, but still impersonally, that the influence of a man and his work had never been great without blindly devoted pupils, if the young Nietzsche during the Tribschen period thinks that all cultivation begins with obedience, now this demand becomes deeply personally tinged: "By 'disciple,'" he writes to Malwida in 1884, "I would understand a person who would make an unconditional vow to me—and there would have to be a long trial period and difficult tests."[124] When, after *Zarathustra,* it seemed for a moment as if he had found this unconditionally devoted disciple during the visit in Engadin in the summer of 1884 by the young Wagner-enthusiast Heinrich von Stein, what a transport of happiness! What moving gratitude for the deceptive momentary image of a life's work and mission in the practical educative role of teaching and forming someone face-to-face! "The experience of the summer was the visit by Baron Stein," Nietzsche writes to Overbeck; "he is a splendid example of a human being and a man, and I understand and like him because of his fundamentally *heroic* temper. Finally, finally someone new who belongs to me and instinctively feels reverence for me! . . . In his presence I always keenly felt what kind of practical task would be part of my life's mission if only I had enough younger people of a very particular quality!—in the meantime, it is still impossible to speak of it, as indeed I have not spoken of it to anyone.

What a strange fate, to become 40 years old and still be carrying around all of one's most essential things, both theoretical and practical, as secrets!"[125] Certainly, Nietzsche longed for Zarathustra's disciples with all of the passionate fervor of the formative "genius of the heart," that Dionysian-Socratic genius of the heart as which he describes himself in a "curious piece of psychology" in *Beyond* and whose depiction he quotes verbatim, significantly, in *Ecce homo* "to give an idea of me as a psychologist."[126]

> The genius of the heart, which that great Cloaked One has, the tempter-god and born Pied Piper of consciences, whose voice knows how to descend into the underworld of every soul, who does not say a word, does not cast a glance, in which there is not some consideration and ulterior seduction, and whose mastery lies in his knowing how to seem—and not what he is, but what for those who follow him is a *further* compulsion to press closer and closer to him, to follow him more and more inwardly and completely. . . . The genius of the heart who makes everything loud and complacent fall silent and listen, that gives souls a taste of a new desire . . . the genius of the heart who uncovers the hidden and forgotten treasure, the drop of goodness and sweet spirituality under thick, clouded ice, and is a divining rod for every grain of gold . . . the genius of the heart whose touch leaves everyone richer, not blessed and surprised, not as if favored and oppressed by another's fortune, but rather richer in oneself, newer to oneself than before, opened up, thawed by a warming wind . . . less certain, perhaps, but full of hopes that do not yet have a name . . . [127]

"I forbid, by the way, any conjectures about whom I am describing in this passage,"[128] *Ecce homo* places as a significant *cave nomen* above this self-quotation, in which Nietzsche and Socrates, Zarathustra and Dionysus are transformed into each other, disguised by each other, discreet toward each other. It was the mask of his own Dionysian-Socratic mastery, the mask of the disciple-seeking god, whose mastery lies in knowing how to seem. But it was at the same time the coveted phantom of being a genius of the heart that lived in him only as a wish and painfully distant dream, not as an ability and divine presence. For, to be sure, these disciples, these Socratic pupils of his dreams, were forever denied to Nietzsche because they were necessarily denied to him, owing to an inner barrier that he was unable to transform into a threshold, owing to an ultimate individualism, that is, an ultimate indivisibility, an incommunicability of the individual, of which Nietzsche possessed a melancholy awareness. The personal mastery between two people was forever denied to him; for the same reasons, perhaps, for which his experience of his own discipleship to Wagner could not be completed: out of an innermost incapacity for fusion, a Protestant defiance of the individual, a Nordic pride, and a will to the seventh solitude of the ego.

A relationship like that to Heinrich von Stein demonstrates it: he did not keep his disciple because at the very bottom he did not *want* to keep him (his death only forestalled their separation); just as he did not keep his master, Wagner, his friend Rohde, because unconsciously, deep down, he had already determined not to keep them. "Richard Wagner in Bayreuth" and the congratulatory letter to his friend on 18 July 1876[129] are two tragic documents of this deep tendency, of the will to solitude.

But even the refuge of the seventh solitude was denied to the person whose Socratic passion nevertheless sent him out again and again to "hunt for men," pulled him out of "philosophy as he understood and experienced it, living voluntarily amidst ice and high mountains"[130] (*Ecce homo*), toward what "is more magnificent than storms and mountains and the sea"—namely, to the "son of man."[131] If even a Schopenhauer, the grandson of hard Dutch Calvinists, could not endure his freely chosen Rembrandt solitude until the end, instead pretending to hear responsive and encouraging voices out of the echo of his meager discipleship, how much more was Nietzsche drawn to the sounds and gratitude of people, he who thought he heard the voices of Platonic songs arising out of his old Lutheran musical inheritance, he, for whom wisdom began with two: "What I always needed most was the belief that I was not so completely alone . . . blindness with another"[132] (second preface of 1886 to the first volume of *Human*). And thus, we witness the dreadful secret, how this loneliest of men, whom no sound of love has reached for years, *invents* the friends, disciples, the love he needs; how he, similar to the Saul that Rembrandt painted at the end of his life, forcibly *seizes* the sound of love, the music of togetherness, for which he longs. This is symbolized by his extravagant stylization and exaggeration of the music of Peter Gast, his loyal Kurwenal,[133] into the quintessence of his envisioned music of the south: "One becomes old, one becomes wistful, even now, like King Saul, I already *need* music—Heaven has fortunately also given me a kind of David. . . . Actually, I also ought to have people around me who have the same composition as this music I love. . . . But not everyone who would like to find is able to seek . . ."[134] (1886 to Rohde). He creates the music that he will never hear; he creates the pupils he will never see; another Moses on Nebo, he creates for his eyes the land that his foot will never touch; and what he himself will never be, that Socratically transformative Great Educator, he creates as well—and *Zarathustra* is the result. *Zarathustra,* this most powerful pedagogical utopia that a Socratic will had erected since Plato; Zarathustra as the "ideal master," as the singing Socrates, whom Nietzsche dreams of as going beyond Socrates, as the mythos of the Dionysian educator, the educator and breeder toward the overman, as the kindest and the "most malicious of all the fishers of men: for it is *he* who I have been completely and from the beginning baiting, luring, reeling in, raising up, a cultivator, hatcher and breeder, who not for nothing once advised himself: 'Become who you are!'"[135] (*Zarathustra*). This is the highest pinnacle of Nietzsche's power to form myth, this vision of the "Midday Friend," but it tends in entirely the same direction in which it had expressed itself all along. "The drive to form myth goes out (henceforth) in search of the friend"[136] reads a significant passage in the Notebooks to *The Gay Science.* Wagner had already been such a mythos, whom Nietzsche had fashioned into the Alabanda[137] of an even more powerful Hyperion; his friends were such myths, Rohde above all; so were the sympathetic elders of Nietzsche's imagination, particularly Burckhardt, Keller, Taine (we recall that violent blindness with which his letters to Burckhardt try to maintain the phantom of a happiness *inter pares*); so, too, were Gast and Gast's music; so, too, Bizet's *Carmen.* Zarathustra is merely the most longingly powerful among them, heightened further through the extreme *will* to the power to form myth, just as he finds his expression in the explicitly pedagogical guiding phantom of the idea of the Eternal Recurrence of all things, of the ring of being, of the Great Yes to love and eternity. Powerful pedagogically, not as "truth"—Nietzsche makes this revelation that is so full of Socratic cunning ("it is a great idea for *breeding*"[138] . . ."the idea of Recurrence as a *selective* principle"[139] [*Will to Power*])—in the same way, Socrates employed his newly won dialectics as a seduction toward knowledge of the "good" and the knowledge of the "good" in turn as a seduction—to what? To new gods, in other words, to godlessness, as he was accused of doing? The answer and justification in the case of Socrates was called Plato. And the justifying answer in the case of Nietzsche? But Nietzsche's words were not heard, Nietzsche's new law was not obeyed by a Plato. The "ear of his love" listened into the void, just as Zarathustra's mouth, alone even with another, spoke into the void. "After such a call out of my innermost soul, as my *Zarathustra* was, to hear not a sound in response, nothing, nothing, only the silent, now thousand-fold solitude—that is something terrible beyond words, the strongest man could be broken by that—oh, and I am not the strongest!"[140] (1887 to Overbeck). But this terrible silence was the inevitable penance for Nietzsche's tragically innocent guilt, for the great tragic error of his life, an error that he did not commit, but that he *was:* that great error of thinking that through a structure of yearning such as *Zarathustra,* through an article of faith born of knowledge and will such as the Eternal Recurrence, he would be able to have the effect he dreamed of: a Socratic, that is to say transformative, one. In the end, he tragically failed to appreciate the eternal validity of Goethe's words that had circumscribed his own youth: "We learn only from the one we love"—and from love alone arise the deepest, that is, the most soul-transforming and world-renewing insights. Zarathustra, however, could only give—he was too proud, too magnificently egoistic, to receive; he grew too solitary and too high; he waited for love—and was struck by lightning.

Did he, in his final *Ecce homo* days, those autumn days in Turin full of ardent euphoria and closeness to death, perhaps have a presentiment of such a fate? Many passages in *Ecce homo,* certain intentionally secretive phrases in his last letters, point to some sort of inner Rubicon that he suspects he is about to cross; as if a final inner barrier were falling, as if a final recuperation were beginning, a recuperation like the one for which the dying Socrates's last words give thanks. Did something come to him in these days of elevated rapture that was comparable to the music of the dying Socrates, something to which he had failed to make a sacrifice his whole life long and which now, before the end, demanded this sacrifice? Did a final possibility over and above himself come close to him in these days, a possibility beyond Zarathustra? Something like an answer to the long question of his entire life, a new Why?

We do not know. We know only that it was not to be and that, whatever Nietzsche encountered in this golden fateful autumn, it would have been a form of his fate, of his predetermined end—as he himself sensed and attested to this *fatum* in all of his last encounters. His life *was supposed* to come to a close as the massive torso that it is, lying on the outermost edge of a bygone era, fatefully bound to time and timelessly pointing beyond itself. All youthful gratitude *was supposed* to come too late and everything *was supposed* to come too late that could have pleadingly implored him:

> There is no path that leads over the icy cliffs
> And aeries of dread birds—now it is time:
> To bind oneself to the circle that is closed by love . . . [141]

And thus the lament may fall silent that we can have no more of an idea of the "music of Socrates" before Nietzsche's end than we can of the music of Plato's perfected teacher, and Nietzsche's late lament may also fall silent: "It should have sung, this new soul—and not spoken!"[142]

It sang nonetheless, this soul. Just as Socrates, the "ugliest man," whose soul was inartistic yet secretly craved music, still sang his all, once in the face of death, and once more in the person of Plato—and sang so fervently that its melody reaches us and will reach all those in the future: so, too, Nietzsche's Greek-obsessed Nordic soul still secretly sang its own death to itself, inwardly certain of its own Platonic recuperation, its Platonic immortality; certain of its future power to clarify and form other souls ("some people are born posthumously . . ."[143] "it may happen that one day entire millennia will swear their highest oaths to my name . . .");[144]

and even he, the "most accursed man," was blissful in the Socratic certainty to which Goethe, close to his own death, gave expression in some of the last words he left us (spoken to Eckermann eleven days before he died)—the certainty that God will forever remain active in higher natures in order to lift up the lesser ones.[145]

19
Eleusis

Modesty befits a mortal . . .
If one day something true must
Appear between night and day,
Paraphrase it three times, yet,
Thou Innocent, it must also
Remain such as it is, unspoken.
—Hölderlin, "Germanien"[1]

The human mind, godlike, is
More destructive than fire and sword
When it cannot be silent and keep
its secret unrevealed.[2]
—Hölderlin, *Empedokles*

Zosimos, a historian from late antiquity who, though he lived in the fifth century, was not yet a Christian, transmits to us a peculiar Greek belief: the Greeks, he says, believed that their mysteries at Eleusis, that great pan-Hellenic cult, "held the human race together."[3] The human race—not, as one would expect, the Greek people alone in its proud exclusive entirety; because non-Greeks, "speechless barbarians" of every sort, were not permitted to be initiated into the Eleusian mysteries at all, which even the lowliest Greek slave was free to do. Nevertheless, Greek religious thought conceived of the sublimely extravagant idea of a cult on whose reverently preserved practice and continuation the cohesion, the unity of all humanity mysteriously depended: without this mystery, in which the largest part of humanity could not and should not have any share at all, without Eleusis the divine commonality of all those who lifted a human countenance up to the gods would be plunged into chaos. Visionary intuition, religious certainty about the innermost meaning of mystery as a secret that binds and preserves the world, has perhaps never been expressed in such magnificently muted fashion as in this simple record of the Greek Eleusian belief. There are echoes here of the wisdom of maternal Asia, perhaps of Babylonian and ancient Egyptian mystery traditions that, beyond all dogma, burdened their faithful with a secret that sealed their lips, namely that the mere existence of their mystery alone secured the structure of the world with iron clamps, that its preservation alone bound chaos into creation, just as being itself was always born anew from the maternal womb of Demeter. The strangely selfless pride of a cult that, through arduous centuries until the last stages of its disintegration, remained mindful that *it* alone carried the responsibility for the intellectual and spiritual cohesion of all humanity, even of all those who knew nothing about it and who would never be conceivable or desired as proselytes! How remote that is, how anti-Christian, how piously proud—how Greek! For it seems—reports such as those of Zosimos tell us as much—that this genuinely Hellenic feeling of intellectually soaring and divinely preordained *superiority* over the throng of barbarians, that it nevertheless simultaneously included an exceedingly unnationalistic and entirely unfanatical, indeed a genuine, religiously anchored consciousness of *responsibility* for all of non-Hellenic humankind. Possession of mysteries such as those at Eleusis entails obligations. If all of Hellas partook of that consecration of which Pindar sang: "Blessed is he who, after he has beheld it, goes under the earth: he knows the final meaning of life and the Zeus-given beginning"—then the feeling of exceptional responsibility slumbered in even the dullest participant in the mysteries. That the obligation of secrecy about what is "beheld"—an obligation, it is true, enforced by the penalty of death—with regard either to the content or the experience of the mystery, that it was never broken offers evidence of that feeling. The Eleusian mysteries were never destroyed through revelation, through sacrilegious "testimony"; even the Christian church fathers had to draw on impure and indirect sources to feed the hostility of their denunciations. Apparently, the feeling of responsibility was too powerful. One held back chaos with one's own hands. And never did the Greeks' innate dread of chaos, the inner measure with which they administered and formed their great and dangerous Asiatic heritage, never did it demonstrate greater self-discipline than before the Eleusian mysteries. Alcibiades, the chosen darling of Athens when it was at its height and already beginning to dissolve in skepticism, found that out, he who was seemingly permitted to do anything, who made everything seem permissible: the travesty of the mysteries that was said to have occurred in his house was too much for the city that was reflected in him.[4] The people who tolerated Aristophanes did not tolerate any mention of what was veiled by the word Eleusis.

To our knowledge, there was no such consecration lying over any of the other mysteries in antiquity: the fear of desecrating them corresponded to what they had to offer and seemed to promise to even the lowliest of the Greeks. The people instinctively felt that, corresponding to the binding and protective power that emanated from Eleusis, there was the slumbering violence of ultimate destruction and ruin if ever the unmentionable were mentioned. Thus the tremendous power over souls exerted by the Eleusian *reticence,* which, merely as the obligation of silence, was also owed and given to other ancient secret cults, but which is the only one we know of that includes the feeling of responsibility for the world. Nowhere else did the portal to all of humanity's futures hinge on a locally determined, locally practiced cult. Here a sacrament with unlimited demonic authority to bind and release was not enjoyed, but beheld, endured, and kept silent. And, entirely in accord with the Greek habit of thinking in visual images, this ecumenical responsibility was the expression of knowledge that one could render conceptually this way: the existence of what is most humanly valuable, the eternal effective agency of those forces that first form a human being into a human being, depends on the fact that somewhere in the world a mystery—that is, a spiritually procreative and soul-binding power—exists, is practiced and handed down. That somewhere in the world, again and again, a mystery-forming force brings together two or three souls in the name of god—that alone *preserves* the world. If, however, an unholy word should ever paralyze the active secret, the world would disintegrate back into its chaotic, original disorder.

Wherever the Greek experience spread, wherever the Greek essence was transmitted, there the Eleusian idea, Eleusian reticence, and responsibility also went. The ancient Christian church unwittingly and unwillingly adopted only a fraction of its legacy. Even outside of the church, Eleusis remained (or became again) more than just a symbol, such as the statue of Sais.[5] Its transmission always retained the power to become an element of intellectual history in times of crisis, whose convulsions reached down to the same unchanging sources of humanity. The rescue and preservation of mystery—not those of Eleusis as such, but rather of the idea of mystery in general—that remains a problem that has constantly arisen ever since the late days of vanishing antiquity: how do we save the mysteries in periods of dissolution, of individualization? For that is the undeniable calamity: for the individual, for the isolated ego, the ego of the intellect and of distinctions made to satisfy the voracious appetite for knowledge, for *this* individual, and be he intellectually of the highest rank, there *is* no mystery. It exists only within a community, only as community, and even if they are no more than two or three souls. That is the basic feeling in Nietzsche's profoundly cheerful letter (to Gast, 1881): "*One person* who is *alone* with his thoughts is considered a fool, and, often enough, he thinks so, too: but with two 'wisdom' begins . . ."[6] (Which is not just an echo of Novalis's community-minded mysticism: "Communal madness ceases to be madness and becomes magic.")[7] The wisdom of the individual *as* individual—and this is the sorrowful experience of so many thinkers throughout the centuries of late Christianity, particularly within Protestantism—is "godless," that is, "abandoned by God." Luther confessed that among the most terrible tribulations in the monastery was the cajolingly derisive voice: "Do you believe that you alone are wise?"[8] and Pascal, for whom the *idea* constitutes the greatness of a person, ends up at the *moi haïssable.*[9] "An isolated person never reaches his goal," Goethe writes to Willemer, in the year the first part of *Faust* appears in its complete form and thereby unconsciously concentrates the same experience of knowing despair that formed Faust's great monologue.[10] And Novalis, a few years earlier, wrote in *The Novices of Saïs:* "Understanding comes to no one who has torn himself away and become an island."[11] The contour of modern European intellectual history repeatedly raises the typical question: can we save the mystery? how do we transform what is unsalvageable? or how do we turn what is old and dying into something vital and new, yet still ancient? Moving, great, and hideous images of this pious and fearful spiritual toil proliferate particularly in the German development of the last two centuries, down to the secret societies of the eighteenth century, whose transfigured and stylized image Goethe gave us in the Tower Society in *Wilhelm Meister's Apprenticeship,* in the Pedagogical Province of *Wilhelm Meister's Travels,* but especially in the entirely Eleusian fragment, "Secrets";[12] up to Kant's *Critique of Pure Reason,* which after all wants to delimit and protect a *τέμενος,* a sacred grove, a prohibited zone, extending to the great, triadically structured systems of romantic thought, and finally to Novalis and Hölderlin, to Schopenhauer's musical metaphysics, to the Wagner of the *Tristan* heights. More: the intellectual history of the great demonstrates within itself and its development the tragically hopeless attempt to unify what cannot be unified, mystery and solitude, to achieve mystery on the ground of the *individual.* Nowhere more tragically than in the latest heir of all those mystery-forming German possibilities, the last heir to the throne of the cultural epoch stretching from Kant and Goethe to Wagner—in Nietzsche.

In no other visible figure does the mystery-destroying tendency of the solitary individual and of his entire intellectual remorselessness fight so clearly, in such a fatefully exemplary way, against every kind of sacred darkness with the warning reticence of a mystagogue who had remained to the end bound by religion than in the Voltairean who took himself up to Zarathustra and beyond. Zarathustra is the most powerful symbol, but not so much a triumphant symbol as a tragic one, of this already inwardly condemned will to the mystery of the individual. "Always one times one—in the long run that makes *two!*"[13] This Nietzsche confession solves the puzzle of Zarathustra's birth out of the self-division of the most terrible solitude, the birth of Zarathustra, the "Midday Friend": "It was at midday when One became Two . . . / And Zarathustra passed me by."[14] One of the earliest fragments in the Notebooks, from the year 1872, already reveals the self-dissection of the lonely intellect out of which *Zarathustra* emerges a decade later, the birth of a tragedy out of the spirit of isolation. The short fragment is called "Oedipus. Speeches of the Last Philosopher to Himself" and begins: "I call myself the last philosopher because I am the last man. No one speaks to me other than me, and my voice comes to me like that of a dying man! . . . Beloved voice . . . through you I deceive myself out of my solitude and lie my way into plurality and love, for my heart refuses to believe that love is dead, it cannot bear the horror of the loneliest solitude and forces me to speak *as if I were Two.*"[15] This voice, this phantom of love in the "last man" who can no longer bear the horror of the loneliest, most inescapable individuation—this specter of his own voice becomes *Zarathustra* ten years later. Out of the deepest "abandonment by god" in the Greek sense, from which Nietzsche suffered like almost no other, came the vision of this "guest of guests." For in Greek religious sentiment there is no Protestant "alone with his God"; that is a fundamentally *Nordic* form of religious experience. But Nietzsche, despite his deliberate, Protestant, and extreme individualism, yearned to feel, and believed he was, an "inner plurality," a member of an unreal community, a mystagogue. "What I always needed most was the belief that I was not so completely alone . . . blindness with another"[16]—"It always seems as if I were a plurality"[17]—"With Two wisdom begins."

> . . . A magician did it, the friend at the right time,
> The midday friend—no! ask not who he is—
> It was at midday when One became Two . . .
>
> Now we celebrate certain of joined victory,
> The feast of feasts:
> Friend Zarathustra came, the guest of guests!
> Now the whole world laughed, the horrid curtain tore,
> The wedding of light and darkness came . . . [18]

It was the clairvoyant fate of the enlightener and logician Nietzsche, the individualist addicted to knowledge, that he, while being obscurely driven by religious impulses, completely understood that and why the solitary individual *can* be and act only in a way that destroys mystery; that only when the individual belonged to some Eleusian community is it possible to partake of "contemplation," not mere knowledge, and act to form and preserve mystery.

"It is the ambition of the intellect to appear to be no longer individual,"[19] he writes in a revealing formulation in *Human, All Too Human.* It is also the curse of the intellect to know that this ambition can never be satisfied in reality, beyond appearance. For the intellect is what is eternally incapable of fusion, it is the individual in itself, the indivisible, the incommunicable. And every "communication" of the ego that is fed only by the intellect, that comes from ambition or the yearning delusion not to appear to be individual any longer, but rather a "plurality," bears the curse of being conceived in the incestuous marriage of the mind with itself: it does not reproduce, it does not change, it never becomes the wisdom that begins with Two. The great tragic example is Zarathustra's highest idea, the illusory revelation of the Eternal Recurrence, this idea that was supposed to rend the history of humanity into two parts through its transformative power, that was supposed to become the mystery of the higher men, supposed to call forth the overman out of the womb of man through its ability to breed and select—and which has never shaken, and will never transform, the soul of a single person. Because it never came out of the power of a soul, but rather out of a solitude of knowledge that had cried out for a new Why? "A Why? a *new* Why?—*that* is what humanity needs."[20] But a new Why is not born out of a knowledge of this need—but rather only out of the need itself, not out of the individual, but out of love. Nietzsche suspected, Nietzsche knew that; but his heart shuddered before solitude and he "lied his way into plurality,"[21] over into love. Nietzsche's tragedy, the magnificent but inwardly deeply hopeless magic of his *Zarathustra*, was the unwinnability, the deadly equilibrium of the two dominant opposing tendencies of his nature: the Socratically analytic, individualistic hunger for knowledge and the prophetically constructive, community-building will to mystery. The entire wretchedness of his century (Nietzsche once called it "the profound infertility of the nineteenth century")[22] is contained in this conflict. Like almost no other, Nietzsche's intellectual fate casts it in a glaring light. The burning cry for mystery, for a "new Why?" without which humanity withers, and the jeering laughter of intellectualism that thinks it is in irrefutable possession of all methods of revelation, of importunately prurient knowledge—they all come together to strike a hideously dissonant chord, nowhere more hideous than in *Ecce homo*. But this cacophony screeches through all his experiences and constructions: the relationship to Schopenhauer, Wagner, his friends; *Zarathustra*, the conception of the Recurrence, the Will to Power—every one a testament to an unbridled will, an intense fervor to create a life-sustaining, life-enhancing cult, a new mythos and a millennium given an Eleusian rejuvenation; and simultaneously a demystifying logic, a demonically secularizing skepticism, a delight in playing with the sacrilegious word, which if spoken ushers in chaos. A fantastic-tragic spectacle of fiendishly seductive allure: forces that form and destroy mystery in equal measure burst forth in mortal struggle as perhaps never before! The Goethe in the period of *Wilhelm Meister's Travels* versus Voltaire, Novalis versus Lichtenberg, Hölderlin versus Heine—the vessel holding the growing firestorm of these psychological antinomies had to break apart. The two final utterances of the autobiographical part of *Ecce homo* are the Voltairean phrase "Ecrasez l'infâme!"[23] and the mystery locution "Dionysus versus the Crucified One."

But just as in *Ecce homo* itself, these final prose words of the autobiography do not form the conclusion to the book, which is informed instead by the Dionysus Dithyramb "Fame and Eternity" that he added in the very last days before his collapse, so too Nietzsche's intellectual tragedy at the very moment of decline still seems to reveal to us the triumph of the Greek principle over the skeptical one, the victory of Eleusis over Ferney.[24] The last symbolic impression of this book's self-offering that escalates into horror is not that fateful dualism of the two final phrases; that responsibility, rather, is taken by the strophes of the Dionysian Dithyramb:

> Hush!
> About great things—I *see* great things!—
> One should remain silent
> Or speak greatly:
> Speak greatly, my enthralled wisdom!
>
> . . . Oh night, oh silence, o deathly quiet noise!
> I see a sign—
> From the most distant distances
> A constellation sinks slowly glittering toward me . . .
>
> Highest star of being!
> Canvas of eternal images!
> You are coming to me?
> What no one has seen,
> Your mute beauty—
> Can it be? it flees not before my glance? . . . [25]

The idea, the experience of "enthralled"—Dionysian—"wisdom," of its mute beauty and its deathly quiet noise, this Eleusian experience of great things about which one remains silent or speaks greatly—greatly, that is, in the transport and in the veiling cloak of the dithyramb—this Greek idea *triumphs* in Nietzsche only in the transformative moment of his intellectual disintegration, of his inner rupture and de-individualization. But we sense its presence and growth from the beginning of his intellectual existence: the Eleusian reticence, the Eleusian silence, which even in his positivistic period still draws a horizon of respect around his most audacious conclusions, these are the most genuine evidence of his innate Greek homesickness. He is still much closer to Hölderlin, his favorite during his years at the *Gymnasium,* closer to his humility before the gods and his Eleusian reserve than he would like to admit in later years—after all, as we know, all of *Zarathustra* rests on an Empedoclean foundation. The Nietzsche of *The Birth of Tragedy* and of *Beyond* and *Ecce homo* obeys, and even if it is in resisting, the deep guiding instinct of the late Hölderlin, who said that modesty befits a mortal and that something true must be paraphrased three times but remain unspoken.[26] A Pindaric feeling that it is sacrilege to express all of one's knowledge about the higher things keeps Nietzsche's secularizing will to knowledge bound by the silk reins of a Greek reticence:

> Let us stop! for it does not always avail, when
> Pure truth openly shows its countenance.
> More often, too,
> Silence is the wisest thing that the mind of man can devise. (Pindar)[27]

This consciousness of sacrilege is expressed early and vigorously in *The Birth of Tragedy,* in a perceptive prophecy of himself and his own fate:

"There is an ancient, especially Persian popular belief that a wise magus can be born only through incest. . . . Indeed, myth seems to want to whisper to us that wisdom, and particularly Dionysian wisdom, is an abomination contrary to nature, that whoever uses his knowledge to cast nature into the abyss of annihilation will also experience the dissolution of nature within himself. 'The tip of wisdom's spear turns against the wise man; wisdom is a crime against nature': myth shouts such sentences at us. . . . The best and highest things humanity can obtain are acquired through sacrilege."[28] This incestuous horror before ultimate knowledge, ultimate demystification, ultimate self-contemplation, and self-address. The final Nietzsche of *Ecce homo,* for whom the true measure of value increasingly became how much truth a spirit would risk and endure—that same person simultaneously expresses (in *Twilight of the Idols*) a decided rejection of knowledge: "Once and for all, I want *not* to know many things. Wisdom draws limits to knowledge, too."[29] That is an even higher, more reverential reluctance to unveil the cultic image of Saïs than even the young Nietzsche had shown in Basel when he writes to his friend Gersdorff in 1871: "The word is a dangerous thing. . . . How many things one is not permitted to say! And religious and philosophical convictions in particular count among the *pudendis.*[30] They are the roots of our thoughts and desires: for that reason they should not be brought to light."[31] These two documents frame Nietzsche's entire struggle with knowledge with a strange and moving hesitation arising from reticence and, as it were, a guilty conscience. Who can fully measure the depths of experience, in battling his conscience, that are at the bottom of words such as these: "Even the most courageous among us only rarely has the courage for what he actually *knows*"?[32]

(*Twilight of the Idols*). "The attraction of knowledge would be slight if there were not so much modesty to be overcome on the way to it"[33] (*Beyond*). Do we not hear in all of this the youth at Saïs, with youthful fervor, looking at what is not to be looked at? The traitor's conscience who, having seen the Eleusian consecration, says the unsayable—and who knows that death, some kind of death, is the price?

The objects, the intellectual justifications and expressions of Eleusian reticence change in Nietzsche according to his notion of the possibility of a new mystery at any given time; possibilities that, from Schopenhauer via Wagner up to Zarathustra, the Eternal Recurrence, and the Will to Power, are transformed but remain akin to each other. But common to all, even to the period of his greatest obsession with knowledge—namely after his turn away from Wagner—is that Nietzsche repeatedly perceives himself as fatefully curious, as a profaner of mysteries, who does not want, but is driven to, his role. A kind of Alcibiades-like exuberance is not entirely absent from his parodies of older forms of mystery; but confessions of a painful compulsion toward hyper-clarity predominate, as from the innocently guilty conscience of an *epopt*[34] who had to betray the unbetrayable thing he had beheld.

Initially, these pangs of conscience frequently still have a strongly Schopenhauerian coloration; where, in a world viewed entirely through Schopenhauer's eyes, does the drive for truth come from? "What does a man actually know about himself! . . . Doesn't nature keep most of it from him, even about his own body, in order to ban and lock him away off to one side in a proud fraudulent consciousness! It threw the key away: and woe to the fatefully curious person who looks through an opening in the chamber of consciousness and is able to see down below and now senses that humanity, complacent in its ignorance, rests on a pitiless, voracious, insatiable, murderous foundation, suspended in dreams, as it were, on the back of a tiger. Where, in this constellation, does the drive for truth come from!"[35] ("On Truth and Lie in the Extra-Moral Sense" [1873]). That is still a predominantly negative view, more fearful and respectful of life. But the question taken up again later in higher spirals: Where does the drive for truth come from? is already displaced in this early period by its mirror image: "Why is there the compulsion for concealment?"[36] *The Birth of Tragedy* as well as, in its particular sphere, the *Untimely Meditation* "On the Use and Disadvantage of History for Life" offer an answer.

"Without myth," *The Birth of Tragedy* says, "every culture loses its healthy, creative natural force; a cultural movement becomes unified only when it is enclosed by a horizon of myths."[37] This cloudy veil of myth and of its innermost and deepest effect, mystery, first *creates* the cultural sphere that it seems to delimit:

"Every kind of culture," a passage from the Notebooks of this time says, "begins when a substantial number of things are *veiled*."[38] The *Untimely Meditation* on history warns: "If only a couple of such modern biographers cause their readers to reflect on the birthplace of Christianity or the Lutheran Reformation; their sober pragmatic curiosity would have succeeded in making any spiritual *actio in distans* impossible. . . . Everything living needs to be surrounded by an atmosphere, a mysterious ambience. . . . But even every people, indeed every person who wants to become mature, needs such an enveloping delusion, such a protective and encompassing cloud."[39] A sentence from the Notebooks of 1872 puts it more pitilessly: "Humanity has in knowledge a beautiful instrument for its destruction."[40] And in *The Will to Power,* almost a shadow of Schiller's Cassandra words: "Comprehending is an end . . ."[41]

All of that is Greek, no doubt. And Nietzsche, whose initial stance was already a protest against the shameless historicism of his knowledge-lustful century, is here, too, a pupil of the Greeks, heir to the Greek historical sense, whose earliest master, Herodotus, significantly repeats no other formula as often as this naïvely mysterious utterance: "I am not permitted to say more; I do know the story about this or that, but I do not want to tell it."[42] Nietzsche already experienced Bayreuth in a Greek, Eleusian, way. "We, the disciples of resurrected art, will have the will to seriousness, deep, sacred seriousness! We must now perceive all the talk and noise . . . about art . . . as a shameless impertinence; everything obliges us to be silent, to maintain a five-year Pythagorean silence. . . . Who wouldn't need the purifying water, who wouldn't hear the voice that admonishes him: be silent and pure! silent and pure! Only as those who listen to this voice will we be given the great view . . . and only in this great view lies the *great future* of the event of Bayreuth"[43] ("Richard Wagner in Bayreuth"). To be silent and pure—and hanging the future on obedience to this Eleusian formula—certainly, that is Greek.

And it is also the Greeks who, for Nietzsche, most perfectly, instinctively understood the embeddedness of an entire culture in mystery, the life-preserving hesitancy to grasp, touch, behold denuded knowledge, and that they most consistently sustained it and kept it most sacred. They are for him the exemplary masters of modesty, the most profound worshippers of Olympian appearance. ("The feeling of true modesty was in no other people so native and innate as in the Greeks,"[44] says Nietzsche's romantic predecessor, Friedrich Schlegel.) They convert their pupils from the delusion of love of "truth at all costs." " . . . This will to truth, to 'truth at all costs,' this youthful madness in the love of truth has been spoiled for us: for that we are too experienced, too serious, too cheerful, too burned, to deep. . . . We no longer believe that truth still remains truth when one removes its veil; we have lived long enough to believe this . . . one should not see everything nude, not be present at everything, not want to understand and 'know' everything. . . . One should show more respect for the *modesty* with which nature hides behind puzzles and colorful uncertainties. . . . Oh, these Greeks! They understood how to *live:* for that it is necessary to stop bravely at the surface, the fold, the skin, to worship appearance, to believe in forms, sounds, words, in the entire Olympus of appearance! These Greeks were superficial—through profundity!"[45] (preface to *The Gay Science,* from the autumn of 1886).

Superficial through profundity—the wisdom of Greek modesty and the Hellenic instinct for life does not remain for Nietzsche on the level of Schopenhauerian pessimism, as *pudenda origo,* even less does it remain the mere projection of an overrefined *psychologie par ricochet*[46] on the background of Hellenistic intellectual history. This instinctive wisdom is incorporated into his psychological studies as a psychic, analyzable law, but it is entirely nourished by personal experience, personal sacrifices, opposed from the beginning and until the end to the Socratic covetousness and the passion for knowledge that enflames his psychological observations; it finds a place in his doctrine of biological values as the innate defensive instinct of every productive existence, it crosses over into his philosophy of revaluation as the doctrine of intellectual hierarchies (hierarchy of problems and of "truths"), and finally, in the graduated construction of his pedagogical will to power, his doctrine of the great educative, humanity-enhancing reverence, to take final shape in the untheoretical realm, to end up in untrodden, forbidden territory: in the entirely religious reverence for the mysteries in and outside of himself, in the idea of the great, unique responsibility. Like all of Nietzsche's "laws," this too is legitimated by his own experience and suffering. "How often," he writes in the autumn of 1882, "in all kinds of circumstances, have I had *this* very experience: Everything is clear, but everything is also at an end!"[47] Out of this experience—established early on in the theoretically negative sphere through Schopenhauer, undergirded positively through the experience of Tristan-Wagner and the image of the Eleusian Greeks and amplified into a law—the Socratic fanatic of wisdom and the radical logician in Nietzsche nevertheless becomes an equally passionate advocate of all self-preserving instincts in human nature against the deadly desire for nothing-but-the-truth; of that warning instinct that, in the words of *Beyond,* senses that one could come into the possession of truth *too early.* Even the man of knowledge himself "avoids self-knowledge and leaves his roots buried under ground"[48] (Notebooks from the *Zarathustra* period). More imperiously and unconditionally, as always, in *Ecce homo:* "That one becomes what one is presupposes that one does not have the slightest inkling *what* one is."[49] Those are entirely Goethean sentiments, comparable to the well-known words in a letter to Zelter (1812): "One never goes further than when one does not know where one is going"[50]—and the passage in the *Conversations with Eckermann* (1829): "I also do not know myself, and God forbid I ever will!"[51] In a dedication copy of *Daybreak,* the book that marks the pinnacle of Nietzsche's intellectualistic period of the "free spirit," he writes the verses:

> Whoever will have much to proclaim one day,
> Must long remain silent unto himself:
> Whoever intends to ignite lightning one day,
> Must long be—a cloud.[52]

To be a cloud—an annunciation that simultaneously gives birth to the Dionysian lightning and moment, and protects and enshrouds everything that wants to mature, the mysterious atmosphere and ambience of all living things—silent unto itself and waiting: in this favorite image lies his dual stance toward the secret on the one hand and the word, the true mortal danger to any secret, on the other. The strangest contradiction of this Janus-faced mind: only that which is incommunicable by words is, for this most intoxicated lover of the word the German language has ever known, what is truly communicable. Nietzsche the preacher, the servant to the word and the magus of the word, preaches that one learns nothing from the word: "One has no ear for that to which one cannot relate through experience."[53] Aristotle, just after beholding the Eleusian mysteries, the Epopty, says the same thing when he reports that this act of beholding is a *παθεῖν,* an "experiencing," not a *μαθεῖν,* a "learning." And it would have been Goethean, Nietzschean, to think that we know nothing about the Eleusian mysteries *because* the revelations beheld there (the *δρώμενα*)[54] refused to surrender to the word, could not be described, because their essence, their best element did not reveal itself through words (*λεγόμενα*)[55]. Nietzsche as Eleusian mystagogue, as a great educator of secrecy through secrets, embraces this Aristotelian *παθεῖν* as the highest form of all fruitful learning and "knowledge"; he embraces the primordial pedagogical words from Wilhelm Meister's certificate of apprenticeship: "The seeded fruits ought not to be milled. Words are good but they are not the best thing. The best thing is not revealed through words."[56] "The final meaningful words do not want to escape my breast; bound by the most curious natural necessity, I am unable to express them"[57]—thus Goethe to Schiller while he was working on *Wilhelm Meister,* which Schiller seems to answer as if in an echo in his distich on "language": " . . . If the soul *speaks,* then, alas, it is no longer the *soul* that speaks!"[58] "One must show respect for certain secrets," the *Travels* adds, "by concealing and keeping silent about them, even if they are evident."[59] Nietzsche feels exactly the same thing; and "the word" remains for him, as in the youthful letter, not only "a dangerous thing: how many things one is not permitted to say!"[60]—but it also becomes for him, the master and worshipper of the word, virtually a contemptible thing. As early as *Human* it significantly appears when he writes that the best author will be someone who is ashamed of becoming a writer. "As soon as we communicate our knowledge, we no longer love it enough,"[61] *Beyond* says, and in *Twilight of the Idols:* "We are inwardly already beyond what we have words for. In all speech there is a grain of *contempt.*"[62] "Sing, speak no more"[63]—thus Zarathustra's hymnic wisdom speaks to his own soul, and *The Will to Power* explains: "Compared to music, all communication through words is of a shameless variety: words dilute and stultify . . . words make the uncommon common . . ."[64] In the paralipomena to *Zarathustra* he writes, with sudden brusqueness: "We despise everything that can be explained,"[65] and: "He learned how to express himself, but since then no one believes him anymore. *Only the stutterer is believed.*"[66] Here Nietzsche is obviously drawing from his own experience, the legacy of his first great teacher and master of the word, Schopenhauer: "The actual life of an idea endures only until it reaches the limit of words. . . . As soon as your thought has found words, it is already no longer heartfelt, *no longer serious at the deepest level.* . . . As the poet also says: as soon as one speaks, one is already beginning to err."[67] And here he touches on the sphere of the writer who was in so many ways deeply related to him, namely Hebbel, who confided to his journal: "I cannot imagine a god who *speaks*"[68]—an utterance that is perhaps basically identical to Nietzsche's blasphemously pious: "I would believe only in a god who knew how to dance,"[69] that is, in a god who revealed himself Dionysically, not merely as "the word of god." But this constantly recurring *cave verbum* is expressed in a thoroughly Greek, thoroughly Eleusian manner in the strangely isolated passage in *Human* that seems entirely cast in secret phrases:

"It is best never to speak of two very high things: *measure* and *middle.* Very few know their power and omens in the paths of the mysteries of inner experiences and conversions: they revere in them something divine and shun the loud word."[70] The appearance of this ancient summons to silence in the middle of this secular, enlightened, and almost rationalistic book, *Human, All Too Human* (whose first edition was dedicated to Voltaire, "one of the greatest liberators of the spirit")[71] has something mysteriously paradoxical about it and proves the strength of the secret-forming forces in Nietzsche's being that at that moment were surging out of sight. The geological surface layer of his middle, positivistic period is rarely pierced so eruptively as in this passage, out of which, right through the middle of Voltaire, Herodotus suddenly speaks. The *cave verbum,* the reticence before the loud word, which is always impertinent, gradually becomes the sign of any reverence for the "last," that is to say "mystery-laden," things, which no one tried more audaciously, with more brooding vehemence, with more desperate curiosity to expose than Nietzsche himself. But his innermost being, the reverential force in him—speaking with Jakob Burckhardt—inclined from the beginning toward the late-Goethean maxim out of the Pedagogical Province: "There is one thing no one brings with him into the world, and yet is the thing on which everything depends for a human being to be a human being in all respects—reverence!"[72] A Goethean contempt for the irreverent person is expressed in a passage in a letter from his penultimate year: "One has to avoid the sort of person who lacks reverence";[73] or in sentences in *Beyond:* "A great deal has been achieved when the feeling has finally been bred into the masses that they are not permitted to touch everything; that there are sacred experiences before which they must remove their shoes and which they must not defile with their unclean hands—it is almost their highest escalation toward humanity."[74] Finally, adding detail and pungency, in the Notebooks of the last years: "I admire it more when someone, even as an historian, lets it be known when the ground under his feet becomes too hot or too holy. . . . The German scholars who invented the historical sense . . . betray without exception that they do not come from any ruling class; they are, as seekers of knowledge, intrusive and without shame."[75] Repeatedly, the warning: "All of you in the know: just take care that you are not lacking in modesty!"[76] "Spare what has such delicate skin! Why do you want to scrape Down from such things!"[77] "In the face of perfection, we have learned to forget to ask about becoming. Perfection is not supposed to have become."[78]

This reverential modesty, which forbids his own avidly questioning mind to question, also rests in Nietzsche on the foundation of a feeling of immense responsibility, of which he becomes increasingly conscious. So that "perfection" *can* become, "becoming" must remain untouched. And responsibility for the secret of the world, whose innermost essence is transformation—transformation understood in the most intensive sense, in the sense of a sacrament—lies also in his magisterially soaring reverence for himself, which culminates in the gigantic, seemingly hybrid expansions of himself in *Ecce homo.* For the more Nietzsche feels that mystery "out of the spirit of music," which he had previously, enthralled and disappointed, sought in others, and which he then, with horrified and devout modesty, sensed growing in himself, becoming to himself the bearer of possible mysteries of a future beheld in Eleusian silence, the deeper his reticence becomes to approach himself, to know himself, and discover any inner lack of horizon. "I am drawing circles around myself and sacred boundaries; I am building a mountain range out of ever more sacred mountains."[79] "You providence of my soul that I call fate! You In-me! Over-me! Keep and spare me for a great fate!"[80]

("Of Old and New Tablets"). "It is possible that I am a destiny for all people to come, *the* destiny—and it is therefore *very* possible that one day I will fall silent out of a love of humanity!"[81] (1884 to Malwida). "I only rarely have the courage for what I actually know"[82] (1887 to Brandes). Is it not symbolically suggestive that the person who likes to name the Genoese Columbus among the ancestors of his questing will for new oceans, that he, who "is fond of the sea and of everything related to the sea,"[83] whose exultant cry is: "The shore receded—now the last chain fell off of me—boundlessness rushes all about me . . ."[84]—that he nevertheless, in his penultimate spring, confesses to his friend Gast his apprehension before the malign and, as it seems to him, shameless unlimitedness of the open sea: "The ocean has, like all large things, something stupid and *indecent* about it"?[85] Thus even his inner Columbus eye shrinks from the vision of a horizonlessness to the future fate of his mind and from the too-distinct presentiment of the shores on which his "Genoese ship" may still be destined to land. *Ecce homo,* in its already deadly hyper-self-consciousness, turns, with complete pseudo-objectivity, even that into a law of his own life, into a "masterpiece in the art of self-preservation."[86] "One has to keep the entire surface of consciousness—consciousness *is* a surface—free from any of the great imperatives. Beware even any of the great words, any great attitude! They are all dangers that instinct will 'understand itself' prematurely— . . . The long, secret work and artistry of my instinct . . . its *higher care* proved to be so strong that at no moment did I even suspect what was growing in me—that one day all of my abilities suddenly sprang forth fully developed in their final perfection. . . . Even at this moment I look at my future—a *vast* future—as if at a calm sea: no desire ripples its surface."[87]

The feeling of being guided, of being ruled by trans-individual, secret-keeping forces that can be trusted unconditionally—that is the final form of Nietzsche's reverence for himself, the paramount form, according to Goethe. Even the extreme hubris in certain sections of *Ecce homo* and of the last letters is perhaps at its innermost core still a pious expression of the feeling of having achieved the highest, trans-individual, and even cosmically exalted moment that a human being is capable of experiencing as an individual; it is only a sort of hymnic grateful happiness that, in the words of the *Travels,* for the duration of this divine moment he was "permitted to consider himself the best thing that God and nature had brought forth, indeed that he can linger on these heights without being pulled back down into baseness through conceit or egoism."[88] It is a hubris out of the feeling of completion, of the beginning de-realization toward a new reality, of crossing over, a triumphant Gloria of "the perfect day where everything ripens,"[89] as the self-dedication to *Ecce homo* intones with a celebratory affirmative "And, behold, it was very good": "How should I not be grateful to my entire life?"[90]

A feeling that is at the deepest level not just related to but identical with the piously proud modesty before the gods felt at the end by Hölderlin as he was already crossing the divide: "All those who depart speak as if drunk and like to treat themselves festively"[91] (*Hyperion*):

> For it is all good. Thereupon he died. There would be many
> Lovely things to say. And his friends were the last to see,
> Him, Most Joyous, looking out victoriously.[92] ("Patmos")

It is the moment of a high euphoria, before the individual has to break through the boundary of individuality; and a sense of this moment was there from early on, slumbering ever more quietly, in Nietzsche's veiled prophetic feeling. He unwittingly expressed the law of his own Hölderlinian exit during his time in Basel, in his lecture on the history of Greek literature: "That is ancient Hellenic: the victorious individual is considered the incarnation of god, *retreats* into god."[93]

Was there something of this triumph of self-relinquishment, of this victorious retreat into god, in the euphoric ecstasy Nietzsche experienced in Turin? ("On September 30, a great victory; seventh day; idleness of a god along the Po. . . . I have never experienced such an autumn, nor did I ever think anything like it could be possible on earth . . . each day of the same unbridled perfection"[94] [*Ecce homo*]). And was perhaps the final wave of an extreme, almost maenadic lust for knowledge that once more floods Nietzsche's mind in the final, *Ecce homo* year, bursting through the middle of the opposite constraints of a magical reticence, but more ruthless, more vicious, more self-destructively brutal than had ever been the case in the over-illuminated, Enlightenment-friendly books of his middle period—was it perhaps *not* merely a periodic return of the cold intellectual current in Nietzsche's nature, but was it rather not already a form of secretly *desired* disintegration, was it the early annunciation, indeed the way of retreating into god? Does not Nietzsche himself seem to recognize this, during precisely that period of "transvaluation?" "Assuming that we are living owing to an error, what can the 'will to truth' be in that case? Should it not necessarily be a 'will to death?'"[95] Did he not know all too well that, as Hebbel said, man is the basilisk that dies when he sees himself? And did he not still force upon himself this deadly mirror image? "Zarathustra! You self-knower! You self-executioner!"[96] concludes the Dionysus dithyramb of 1888. For everyone there is some deadly knowledge, for every being an incantation before which it falls into dust—did he seek *his* ultimate knowledge in order to behold what is denied to the *individual* just as the mysteries are denied to the *word?* Does it not sometimes seem as if he wanted to cast off the reticence he proclaimed and demanded only in order to force the logician in him, the archenemy of all mystical knowledge, into silence, in order to eliminate him by means of logic itself: by hastening the disintegration of the individual through knowledge—for "knowledge is death," comprehension is an end, in every sense. Not only humanity as a whole, but also the individual human being has "in knowledge a beautiful instrument for its destruction."[97] Thus we imagine we see the final intellectualism of Nietzsche, which repeatedly breaks through the prophetic, Zarathustra layer until the very end, occasionally shimmering in the uncertain light of sacrifice, a self-sacrifice; and his hybrid blasphemies of what still remained most sacred to him—its symbol: the Wagner of *Tristan*—appear only as painful acts of self-destruction, the parody of mystery as the herald of self-renunciation, the violently impious revelation of a will to the great end. Consciously, like Empedocles, he throws himself into the crater of deadly knowledge, the murderously seductive perspicacity of logical ecstasy and analytical enthusiasm. An extreme Eleusian intoxication is in this festive descent into the untrodden, forbidden realm, in the solemnly drunken pride of knowledge: "Thus began Zarathustra's descent."[98] Mysteriously, the cloud of delusion, in which his intellectual death, a death of choice and sacrifice, overcomes him, takes him across the divide willingly and piously desirous of change, according to the strangely veiled words from a fragment that Hölderlin, already beclouded, already returned to his gods, copied out of Klopstock's mystical ode "The Future" for his consolation, "toward completion out of the veils of night into The land of knowledge."[99]

In the transitory yet eternal moment of such a passage, the struggle between knowledge and silence, between hubris and reverence, between sacrilege and piety is not fought to the end and decided, but rather dialectically resolved, compressed, and immortalized in magnificent exemplarity. The logical-Dionysian conflict that is irresolvable within the individual becomes a perceptible unity in the image of Nietzsche's life at the moment when he treads on the bridge of secrets, where he is both bridge and bridge builder, sacrificial victim and Pontifex in one. The powerful moment of the transformative sacrifice also transforms the entirety of his life that has been streaming toward it, secretly aimed at it, from a painfully divided imperfection into a dream play of mystery-like forcefulness, of exemplary, heroic, triumphal tragedy. The possibility of his own mystery, which had both darkly gladdened him and filled him with horrifically clear foreboding, becomes transpersonal reality; his life henceforth belongs among the great mystic images, whose reticence and secret, whose *symbol,* which disarms earthly death, holds humanity together. For the images of those great men who visibly represent the unbeholdable divine slowly grow—and this is the meaning and value of every biographical legend!—into new mysteries that demand reverence, new, entirely depersonalized timeless possibilities of "beholding with closed eyes," which is both the literal and deepest meaning of the word "mysticism."[100] Nietzsche's life and exit embody only one particular form of this ascendance into the mythical realm, he fulfills only superficially a tragic possibility of his century with his exemplary self-liberation. He himself gave conceptual expression to the form of his own mystery in a passage in the Notebooks to *Zarathustra:* "When skepticism and yearning are paired, mysticism is the result."[101] To be sure, it is not this fateful coupling in itself that constitutes Nietzsche's peculiarity and importance; Flaubert, too, was able to acknowledge his own psychological situation and that of his epoch by saying: "Je suis mystique et je ne crois à rien."[102] Nietzsche's active achievement and courageous self-sacrifice—the sacrifice of the pure logician in him, the most awe-inspiring *sacrificium* of the intellect since Pascal—is his determined overcoming of this very skeptical fanaticism through a great Empedoclean leap beyond the logical, the active self-liberation of a logical radicalism that, if followed to its conclusion, would have led only to the gruesome Don Quixoteism of Bouvard and Pécuchet,[103] where indeed the final communal-human ties are severed by words of utmost nihilistic irony. Once more, one last time, Nietzsche returns in a higher spiral to a birth of tragedy out of the spirit of mystery; once more his heroically taut, long will seeks a new, stronger bond for the human race, because his overfastidious intellectual conscience forbade him, unlike Pascal or Strindberg, a relaxing return to the *Ave crux spes unica.*[104] Was it a sublimely irrational and unfruitful private delusion, like the monomaniacal Recurrence of the Same, that pseudo-Dionysian mystery of the recluse, was it something else, a living, breathing guiding image, conveying the power to bring people, indeed all of humanity together, that appeared before him in that final winter solstice in Turin? Who can claim to know? *Was* it Dionysus who came to him, Dionysus himself, the "Twice-born One" as his sobriquet "dithyramb" says—the burning god who also causes his disciples to be born a second time, in the enraptured moment and in the beholding of his Eleusiacally veiled secret? Or was it, rather, that other Dionysus—for Dionysus also wears a dual countenance—whose suffering, dismemberment, and resurrection are endured as well by the viewers in the Eleusian mysteries, that Suffering God whose primordial passion means the creation and renewal of the world through pain, whose suffering gives consolation by offering the world its ultimate meaning and allows it to see death as overcome? That darkly glowing Godhead, which through his death and resurrection teaches that "the Godhead is great and the Sacrificed One was great," and the Godhead and the Sacrificed One are the *same?* "Nothing of the sort has ever been written, or felt, or suffered,"[105] says the enraptured self-renunciation of *Ecce homo* about Zarathustra's "Night Song," which ends: "And my soul, too, is the song of a lover"[106]—"nothing of the sort has ever been suffered: a God, a Dionysus suffers thus. . . . Even the deepest melancholy of such a Dionysus still turns into dithyramb. . . . The answer to such a dithyramb . . . would be Ariadne. . . . Who knows besides me what Ariadne is! No one had the solution to all such riddles before . . ."[107]

But the nonconceptual solution to such riddles is always the sole possession of someone already touched by an inner muteness, by a shudder of final silence. No matter what its name—the proud passage of this man, his deadly self-transport, the self-transport into the disintegration of madness, it was, like the end of all great men, that is, of all representative men who complete themselves in exemplary fashion, a mask of god. A sacrificial mask of the great Living Element that "yearns for death in flames,"[108] because it came from the flame; that in an ecstasy of fire victoriously "returns to the god" from which it came:

> Yes! I know from whence I came:
> Unquenched like the flame
> I burn and consume myself . . .
> Verily, I am a flame![109]

Notes

Translator's Introduction

1. Walter Watson, "Nietzsche: Philosopher, Psychologist, Antichrist," *Ethics. An International Journal of Social, Political and Legal Philosophy* 61 (1950), 231. Quoted from Hays Alan Steilberg, *Die amerikanische Nietzsche Rezeption von 1896 bis 1950* (Berlin: Walter de Gruyter, 1996), 282.

2. James Gutmann, "Nietzsche: Philosopher, Psychologist, Antichrist," *Journal of Philosophy* 48 (27 September 1951), 645. Cited from Steilberg, 282.

3. Steilberg, 281.

4. For a good overview of the entire phenomenon, compare Jennifer Ratner-Rosenhagen, "'Dionysian Enlightenment': Walter Kaufmann's *Nietzsche* in Historical Perspective," *Modern Intellectual History* 3 (2006), 239–69.

5. Walter Kaufmann, "Preface to the Fourth Edition (1974)," *Nietzsche: Philosopher, Psychologist, Antichrist* (Princeton, N.J.: Princeton University Press, 1974), iii.

6. *Nietzsche, Godfather of Fascism? On the Uses and Abuses of a Philosophy,* ed. Jacob Golomb and Robert S. Wistrich (Princeton, N.J.: Princeton University Press, 2002), 1.

7. Kaufmann, *Nietzsche,* 8.

8. Ibid.

9. Ibid., 11.

10. Ibid., 14.

11. Ibid.

12. Ibid., 12.

13. Ibid.

14. Ibid., 13.

15. Ibid., 12. Kaufmann was referring to the book by Ernst Bertram, *Von der Freiheit des Wortes* (Leipzig: Insel, 1936).

16. Kaufmann, *Nietzsche,* 237.

17. Ibid., 16.

18. An eighth, and final, edition appeared after the Second World War; Ernst Bertram, *Nietzsche: Versuch einer Mythologie,* with an afterward by Hartmut Buchner (Bonn: Bouvier, 1965). Its lack of resonance is indicated by a review published in French that begins: "The reedition of this work was not greeted by critics as the important event that

it ought to be." Compare Louis Leibrich, review of Ernst Bertram, *Nietzsche*, in *Études germaniques* 22 (1967), 128.

19. Hajo Jappe, *Ernst Bertram: Gelehrter, Lehrer und Dichter* (Bonn: Bouvier, 1969), 309. Bertram had completed his doctorate in 1907 with a published dissertation on the nineteenth-century Austrian writer Adalbert Stifter; Ernst Bertram, *Studien zu Adalbert Stifters Novellentechnik* (Dortmund: Ruhfus, 1907).

20. Jappe, 309.

21. Hermann Hesse, "Nietzsche. Von Ernst Bertram." *Vivos voco* 1 (1919/20), 78.

22. Ibid.

23. Reinhold Lindemann, "Die neue Nietzsche Literatur," *Der Gral* 19 (1924/25), 176.

24. Josef Hofmiller, "Neue Literatur," *Süddeutsche Monatshefte* (1919/20), 381.

25. Thomas Mann, "Vorspruch zu einer musikalischen Nietzsche-Feier," vol. 10, *Gesammelte Werke* (Frankfurt am Main: Fischer, 1960), 184.

26. Martin Heidegger, *Nietzsche,* vol. 1 (Pfullingen: Neske, 1961), 256. It is thus somewhat odd that in his "analysis" of the book, David Krell speculates that Heidegger "must have known Bertram's book, which dominated the discussion of Nietzsche throughout the 1920s and early 1930s." See Martin Heidegger, *Nietzsche,* vols. 3–4 (San Francisco: Harper & Row, 1987), 273.

27. Kaufmann, *Nietzsche,* 54. Kaufmann still let this judgment stand in the fourth edition of 1974.

28. Karl Jaspers, *Nietzsche. Einführung in das Verständnis seines Philosophierens* (Berlin: de Gruyter, 1936), 417. The other two books were by Ludwig Klages, *Die psychologischen Errungenschaften Nietzsches,* 2nd ed. (Leipzig: Ambrosius Barth, 1930) and Alfred Baeumler, *Nietzsche der Philosoph und Politiker* (Leipzig: Reclam, 1931). Jaspers's book is available in English translation as *Nietzsche: An Introduction to the Understanding of his Philosophical Activity,* trans. Charles F. Wallraff and Frederick J. Schmitz (Baltimore: Johns Hopkins University Press, 1997).

29. Gottfried Benn, "Nietzsche—Nach fünfzig Jahren," *Gesammelte Werke,* ed. Dieter Wellershof (Wiesbaden: Limes, 1967), vol. 4, p. 50.

30. For a detailed discussion of Bertram's relationship to George, see my *Secret Germany: Stefan George and His Circle* (Ithaca, N.Y.: Cornell University Press, 2002).

31. Saladin Schmitt, *Die so gegangen sind. Seine Gedichte und sein Verhältnis zu Stefan George,* ed. Robert Boehringer and Georg Peter Landmann (Düsseldorf and Munich: Helmut Küpper, 1964), 93.

32. See Heinz Raschel, *Das Nietzsche-Bild im George-Kreis. Ein Beitrag zur Geschichte der deutschen Mythologeme* (Berlin: de Gruyter, 1984). This account is corrected and amplified by Frank Weber, *Die Bedeutung Nietzsches für Stefan George und seinen Kreis* (Frankfurt am Main: Peter Lang, 1989).

33. See George S. Williamson, *The Longing for Myth in Germany: Religion and Aesthetic Culture from Romanticism to Nietzsche* (Chicago: University of Chicago Press, 2004).

34. Compare the useful overview of this development by Theodore Ziolkowski, "Der

Hunger nach dem Mythos. Zur seelischen Gastronomie der Deutschen in den Zwanziger Jahren," in *Die sogenannten Zwanziger Jahre,* eds. Reinhold Grimm and Jost Hermand (Bad Homburg: Gehlen, 1970), 169–201.

35. *The Birth of Tragedy,* 23; *Kritische Studienausgabe* (hereafter cited KSA) 1, 147.

36. Williamson, 236.

37. Notebooks, Fall 1885–Spring 1886 1[120]; KSA 12, 39.

38. Kaufmann, *Nietzsche,* 15.

39. Georg Lukács, *Die Zerstörung der Vernunft* (Berlin: Aufbau, 1954), 316.

40. Jaspers, *Nietzsche,* 154.

41. Wolfgang Müller-Lauter, *Nietzsche: His Philosophy of Contradictions and the Contradictions of his Philosophy,* trans. by David J. Parent, Foreword by Richard Schacht (Urbana: University of Illinois Press, 1999). It is thus a pity that Müller-Lauter apparently did not read Bertram's book with sufficient care or at all, deeming it in a footnote as simply "beyond discussion" (209n4).

42. Notebooks, Fall 1885–Fall 1886 2[155]; KSA 12, 142.

43. Kaufmann, *Nietzsche,* 13. In a footnote, Kaufmann produces part, but not all, of the original quotations, adding accusingly: "All this remained unchanged in the 7th rev. ed."

44. Bertram, *Nietzsche,* 12.

45. *The Gay Science,* fifth book, 356; KSA 3, 595.

46. Gary Shapiro, *Archaeologies of Vision: Foucault and Nietzsche on Seeing and Saying* (Chicago: University of Chicago Press, 2002), 399. It is also not quite right that Steven E. Aschheim, in his otherwise relatively balanced and well-informed account, asserts that "Bertram's *Nietzsche* also exemplified the frankly irrational epistemology which was to become a hallmark of the Weimar radical right." And it is simply wrong to align Bertram with "the völkisch worldview" and to suggest that he "exhorted heroic action." See *The Nietzsche Legacy in Germany, 1890–1990* (Berkeley: University of California Press, 1992), 152. See also footnote 72 in chapter 3, "The German Becoming," of this book.

47. Notebooks, Summer–Fall 1884 26[335]; KSA 11, 238.

48. *Goethes Gespräche. Gesamtausgabe,* ed. Flodoard Frhr. von Biedermann (Leipzig: Biedermann, 1910), 4, 236.

49. Josef Hofmiller, "Neue Literatur," *Süddeutsche Monatshefte* (1919/20), 382.

50. *Thomas Mann an Ernst Bertram. Briefe aus den Jahren 1910–1955,* ed. Inge Jens (Pfullingen: Neske, 1960), 77.

51. Raschel, 202.

52. Glöckner, 40.

53. See the letter from his friend, Ernst Glöckner, who urges him to write the book about Nietzsche when Bertram was still considering other subjects: "Don't object that the philos[ophical] part doesn't appeal to you: it doesn't occupy the space in this person, it is not so decisive for him as it would have to be the case with someone of lesser stature." Raschel, 184.

54. *Thomas Mann an Ernst Bertram,* 76–78. Mann was referring to the book by Friedrich

Gundolf, *Goethe* (Bondi: Berlin, 1916). Gundolf, one of Stefan George's closest and most able disciples, was one of the most influential scholars of German literature of the time.

55. Thomas Mann, "Lebensabriß," *Gesammelte Werke* (Frankfurt am Main: Fischer, 1960), 126–28.

56. *Thomas Mann an Ernst Bertram,* 178.

57. Ibid., 185.

58. Ibid. By "your poet," Mann meant, of course, Stefan George.

59. Ernst Bertram, "Deutscher Aufbruch," *Deutsche Zeitschrift* 46 (1933), 609–17.

60. *Thomas Mann an Ernst Bertram,* 277.

61. Letter by Max Planck to the De-nazification commission, 28 March 1947. Manuscript in Deutsches Literaturarchiv, Marbach am Neckar.

62. Rainer Gruenter, "Ernst Bertram zum Gedächtnis," *Euphorion* 51 (1957), 491.

63. Compare the letter Mann wrote to his son Klaus, on 19 March 1947, in which he reports: "Now he has been removed from his chair, is living with friends, ill and destitute, and complains that he had said things against the Nazis in his lectures that the students did not even want to write down." In *Thomas Mann und Alfred Baeumler: Eine Dokumentation,* ed. M. Baeumler, H. Brunträger, and H. Kurzke (Würzburg: Königshausen & Neumann, 1989), 191.

64. Thomas Mann to Walter A. Kaufmann, 6 July 1952; *Thomas Mann und Alfred Baeumler,* 216.

65. The link between Mann's fictional composer Adrian Leverkühn and Nietzsche is well known; less so is the degree to which Mann drew on Bertram's book for inspiration; compare Bernhard Böschenstein, "Ernst Bertrams *Nietzsche*—eine Quelle für Thomas Manns *Doktor Faustus,*" in *Euphorion* 72 (1978), 68–83.

66. *Thomas Mann und Alfred Baeumler: Eine Dokumentation,* 216.

67. *The Birth of Tragedy,* 5; KSA 1, 42.

68. *The Birth of Tragedy,* "Attempt at a Self-Criticism," 3; KSA 1, 14–15. Stefan George also used these words for the last two lines of his poem devoted to the philosopher; compare "Nietzsche," *Der Siebente Ring. Gesamt-Ausgabe* (Berlin: Bondi, 1931), 6/7: 13.

69. Ernst Bertram, *Nietzsche: Essai de mythologie,* traduit de l'Allemand par Robert Pitrou (Paris: Les Éditions Rieder, 1932), 7. Somewhat plaintively, he adds in a footnote: "We regret that, contrary to all the traditions of courtesy, the author believed it necessary to respond with silence to our requests for elucidation on certain points. Did he want to make us expiate the Treaty of Versailles?" I might add here that I found some of Monsieur Pitrou's ingenious unwindings of Bertram's knots very helpful in my own labors.

70. "On Truth and Lie in the Extra-Moral Sense," 1; KSA 1, 880.

71. The Nietzsche Channel can be found here: *http://www.geocities.com/thenietzschechannel/.*

72. To Hippolyte Taine, 8 December 1888; *Kritische Studienausgabe* (hereafter cited KSB) 8, 511.

73. To Georg Brandes, Beginning December 1888; KSB 8, 502.

Introduction

1. The sentence Bertram writes here—"Alles Gewesene ist nur ein Gleichnis"—is an allusion to the last lines of the second part of Goethe's *Faust,* "Alles Vergängliche / Ist nur ein Gleichnis." Verses 12104–5. Johann Wolfgang von Goethe, *Werke. Hamburger Ausgabe.* (Munich: Beck, 1981), vol. 3, p. 364. All further references to this edition will be designated as HA, followed by the volume and page number.

2. A reference to the nineteenth-century historian Leopold von Ranke (1795–1886), the pioneer of the modern historiographical method based on the rigorous exploitation of original sources. Ranke's famous dictum was that he sought to re-create history "wie es eigentlich gewesen." The full context reads: "You have reckoned that history ought to judge the past and to instruct the contemporary world as to the future. The present attempt does not yield to that high office. It will merely tell how it actually was." From the preface to *Geschichte der Romanischen und Germanischen Völker von 1492 bis 1535* (1824).

3. Goethe, Conversation with Eckermann, 15 (12) October 1825. In *Goethes Gespräche,* ed. Flodoard Frhr. von Biedermann (Leipzig: F. W. von Biedermann, 1910), vol. 3, p. 208. All further references to Goethe's conversations will be to this edition as *Gespräche,* followed by the volume and page number.

4. From chapter 7 of Theodor Fontane, *Frau Jenny Treibel* (Munich: Hanser, 1974), vol. 4, p. 360.

5. Nikolaus Franz Niembsch Edler von Strehlenau (1802–48), whose pen name was Nikolaus Lenau, published an extensive collection of "free verse" gathered under the title *Die Albigenser,* which refers to the members of a Catharist religious sect of southern France in the twelfth and thirteenth centuries, exterminated for heresy during the Inquisition. The word itself is medieval Latin, derived from plural of *Albigensis,* i.e. inhabitant of *Albiga,* or Albi, a town in southern France where the sect was dominant. *American Heritage Dictionary.*

6. Angelus Silesius (1624–77), religious poet of the German baroque.

7. Bertram is alluding to the etymology of "legend," which comes from medieval Latin "legenda," derived from Latin "legendus," gerundive of "legere," "to gather, select, read"; akin to Greek "legein," "to collect, gather, choose, speak," from which is derived "logos," or "word, reason, speech."

8. Jacob Burckhardt, *Griechische Kulturgeschichte.* Sections of this work are available in English as *The Greeks and Greek Civilization,* translated by Sheila Stern, edited and with an introduction by Oswyn Murray (New York: St. Martin's Press, 1998).

9. Notebooks, Fall 1885–Spring 1886 1[120]; KSA 12, 39.

10. *Beyond Good and Evil,* part 1, "Of the Prejudices of Philosophers," 2; KSA 5, 17.

11. Notebooks, June–July 1885 37[9]; KSA 11, 583.

12. Not found.

13. Possibly a reference to Notebooks, Spring 1888 14[119]; KSA 13, 299.

14. Notebooks, September 1876 18[47]; KSA 8, 327.

15. Greek (from the letter of James): "two-minded," "two-hearted," or "double-souled."

16. French: "One lends only to the rich."

17. Stefan George, "Jahrhundertspruch," in *Der Siebente Ring, Gesamt-Ausgabe* (Berlin: Georg Bondi, 1931), vol. 6/7, p. 208. All further references to George will be to this edition as GA, followed by the volume and page number.

Chapter 1: Ancestry

1. Friedrich Hölderlin, "Andenken," in *Sämtliche Werke,* ed. Friedrich Beiser (Stuttgart: W. Kohlhammer, 1955), vol. 2, p. 198. All further references to Hölderlin will be to this edition as SA, followed by the volume and page number.

2. Goethe, "Vermächtnis," HA 1, 370.

3. Catiline (ca. 108–62 B.C.E.), Roman aristocrat who became a demagogue and attempted to overthrow the Republic.

4. Latin: "No one may oppose a king except a king himself."

5. From the poem called "Ecce homo" in "Jest, Cunning and Vengeance. Prelude in German Rhymes." *The Gay Science;* KSA 3, 367.

6. Heidegger picks up on this phrase—without, however, mentioning its context—to dismiss Bertram's discussion. See Heidegger, *Nietzsche,* vol. 1, p. 256.

7. Goethe, "Zahme Xenien," 6, 1/3/361.

8. *Beyond Good and Evil,* "From High Mountains. Postlude"; KSA 5, 243.

9. *Thus Spoke Zarathustra,* part 3, "Of Old and New Tablets," 12; KSA 4, 255.

10. Notebooks, November 1887–March 1888 11[411]; KSA 13, 189.

11. Notebooks, 1875 10[13]; KSA 8, 187.

12. *The Gay Science,* fifth book, 356; KSA 3, 595.

13. To Georg Brandes, 20 November 1888; KSB 8, 482.

14. This quotation fuses two separate entries from the Notebooks, Summer 1876 17[22] and 17[26]; KSA 8, 300–301.

15. Goethe, "Reisetagebuch," 30 October 1775, *Sämtliche Werke. Propyläen-Ausgabe* (Munich: Georg Müller, 1909) 3, 157.

16. Schulpforta was a famous Protestant boarding school, or *Gymnasium,* founded in 1543 in a former Cistercian monastery in Saxony. Students have included Klopstock, Fichte, Ranke, and Nietzsche.

17. Notebooks, Spring 1871–Early 1872 14[25]; KSA 7, 385.

18. Not found.

19. *Twilight of the Idols,* "Skirmishes of an Untimely Man," 39; KSA 6, 141.

20. Ibid.

21. Ibid., 47; KSA 6, 149.

22. Notebooks, Spring–Summer 1883 7[90]; KSA 10, 273.

23. Notebooks, Fall 1887 9[49]; KSA 12, 359. Bertram neglected to include the ellipsis added here. The missing clause reads: "that is because at the time we were conceived our parents were usually not determined themselves."

24. To Elisabeth Förster, 7 February 1886; KSB 7, 147.

25. *Ecce homo,* "Why I am so Wise," 1; KSA 6, 264. Only the first clause before the colon comes from *Ecce homo;* the rest comes from the corrupted 1908 edition.

26. *Ecce homo,* "Why I am so Wise," 1; KSA 6, 264.

27. *Thus Spoke Zarathustra,* part 2, "Of the Tarantulas"; KSA 4, 129.

28. To Heinrich Köselitz, 23 April 1883; KSB 6, 366.

29. To Franz Overbeck, 14 September 1884; KSB 6, 530.

30. Paul Deussen, *Erinnerungen an Friedrich Nietzsche* (Leipzig: Brockhaus, 1901), 2.

31. From a forged letter by Elisabeth Förster-Nietzsche, 31 March 1888; GB 5/2, 770. There is a letter by Nietzsche to his sister from the same date but that is substantially different in content; compare KSB 8, 281–82.

32. To Bernhard Förster, 16 April 1885; KSB 7, 39.

33. To Carl von Gersdorff, 26 September 1875; KSB 5, 112.

34. Elisabeth Förster-Nietzsche, *Der junge Nietzsche* (Leipzig: Alfred Kröner, 1912), 49. There is an antiquated translation of this work by Anthony M. Ludovici, *The Young Nietzsche* (London: William Heinemann, 1912), 44–45.

35. Notebooks, Summer 1882 21[2]; KSA 9681–82.

36. Bertram is alluding to the novel, *Hyperion,* by Friedrich Hölderlin. Compare SA 3.

37. Not found. It is unclear to which biographer of Schopenhauer Bertram is referring.

38. From the bowdlerized edition of *Ecce homo,* still found in Schlechta 2, 1073.

39. To Georg Brandes, 10 April 1888; KSB 8, 288.

40. The previous biographical quotations appear to be corrupted excerpts from two letters Nietzsche wrote to C. A. Hugo Burckhardt, July 1887; KSB 8, 109 and to Heinrich Köselitz, 18 July 1887; KSB 8, 113.

41. Not found.

42. *Thus Spoke Zarathustra,* part 4, "Conversation with the Kings," KSA 4, 305.

43. Friedrich III (1831–88), king of Prussia and emperor of Germany for only ninety-nine days before dying of throat cancer on 15 June 1888.

44. *Ecce homo,* "Thus Spoke Zarathustra," 1; KSA 6, 337.

45. Not found.

46. *Human, All Too Human* I, 456; KSA 2, 295–96.

47. The *Gothaischer Genealogischer Hofkalender* was the standard reference book for the German nobility.

48. Notebooks, August–September 1885 41[3]; KSA 11, 678.

49. Notebooks, April–June 1885 34[24]; KSA 11, 428.

50. Notebooks, End of 1883 22[1]; KSA 10, 613.

51. *Thus Spoke Zarathustra,* part 4, "Of the Higher Man," 12; KSA 4, 363.

52. To Heinrich Köselitz, 21 July 1881; KSB 6, 108–9.

53. *Thus Spoke Zarathustra,* part 2, "Of the Priests," KSA 4, 119.

54. *The Gay Science,* fifth book, 354; KSA 3, 591.

55. Ibid.

56. *Twilight of the Idols,* "Skirmishes of an Untimely Man," 44; KSA 6, 145.

57. From the title of a section in *Thus Spoke Zarathustra,* "Of the Giving Virtue," part 1; KSA 4, 97; mentioned again in part 3, "Of the Three Evils," 2; KSA 4, 238.

58. *Twilight of the Idols,* "Skirmishes of an Untimely Man," 44; KSA 6, 145–46.

59. *The Case of Wagner,* epilogue; KSA 6, 52–53.

60. Notebooks, Spring 1888 14[208]; KSA 13, 388.

61. *Human, All Too Human* I, "From the Souls of Artists and Writers," 221; KSA 2, 181.

62. *Beyond Good and Evil,* part 6, "We Scholars," 208; KSA 5, 138.

63. To Reinhart von Seydlitz, 26 October 1886; KSB 7, 270.

64. Lectures of 1873–74 on pre-Socratics.

65. *The Gay Science,* first book, 9; KSA 3, 381.

66. *The Gay Science,* fifth book, 348; KSA 3, 583–84.

67. *The Gay Science,* fifth book, 349; KSA 3, 385.

68. Notebooks June–July 1885 37[13]; KSA 11, 588.

69. *The Gay Science,* first book, 9; KSA 3, 381–82.

70. Notebooks, July–August 1888 18[3]; KSA 13, 532.

71. Ibid.

72. *Twilight of the Idols,* "Skirmishes of an Untimely Man," 44; KSA 6, 145.

73. Ibid.

74. Plural of the Italian "papabile": someone considered qualified or capable of serving as Pope.

75. *Beyond Good and Evil,* part 6, "We Scholars," 213; KSA 5, 148.

76. Notebooks, Fall 1881 15[17]; KSA 9, 642.

77. Notebooks, Fall 1881 12[51]; KSA 9, 585.

78. Notebooks, Spring 1884 25[454]; KSA 11, 134.

79. *Beyond Good and Evil,* part 1, "On the Prejudices of Philosophers," 20; KSA 5, 34.

80. *Human, All Too Human* 1, part 4, 223; KSA 2, 186.

81. To Georg Brandes, 10 April 1888; KSB 8, 288.

82. KSB 8, 290.

83. Not found.

84. Nietzsche mentions that fact in a letter to Eduard Mushacke, 19 October 1865; KSB 2, 88.

85. Not found.

86. To Erwin Rohde, 9 December 1868; KSB 2, 351–52.

87. To Erwin Rohde, 30 April 1872; KSB 3, 313.

88. Compare the *Chronik* in KSA 15, 11.

89. Sung by Brünnhilde in Act 3, Scene 3 of *Siegfried;* the phrase, without attribution, is also found in Notebooks, Spring–Summer 1878 28[23]; KSA 8, 507.

90. *Ecce homo,* "Human, All Too Human," 5; KSA 6, 327.

91. To Heinrich Köselitz, 14 February 1883; KSB 6, 329–30.

92. To Heinrich Köselitz, 16 August 1883; KSB 6, 429.

93. Not found.

94. To Georg Brandes, 20 November 1888; KSB 8, 482.

95. *Ecce-homo,* "Thus Spoke Zarathustra," 4; KSA 6, 340.

96. Gobineau, Joseph-Arthur, comte de (1816–82), French diplomat, ethnologist, and social thinker whose works deeply influenced subsequent racial theories. His *Essay on the Inequality of the Human Races* (4 vols., 1853–55) was his most influential work.

97. From a forged letter by Elisabeth Förster-Nietzsche, End of October 1888, GB 5/2, 800. Not in KSB.

98. To Heinrich Köselitz, 20 April 1888; KSB 8, 300.

99. To Heinrich Köselitz, 24 February 1881; KSB 6, 66.

100. To Carl von Gersdorff, End of June 1883; KSB 6, 387.

101. Latin term for a beginning student.

102. To Heinrich Köselitz, 21 August 1885; KSB 7, 86.

103. To Heinrich Köselitz, 16 August 1886; KSB 7, 231.

104. *Human, All Too Human* 2, 338; KSA 2, 699.

105. *Ecce homo,* "Why I am so Clever," 10; KSA 6, 297.

106. *Ecce homo,* "Why I am so Clever," 4; KSA 6, 286.

107. Not found.

108. To Heinrich Köselitz, 1 July 1883; KSB 6, 388.

109. Goethe, *Faust,* lines 3781–82.

110. *On the Genealogy of Morals,* preface 3; KSA 5, 249.

111. To Heinrich Köselitz, 25 July 1882; KSB 6, 231.

112. Notebooks, Spring 1884 25[10]; KSA 11, 13.

113. Notebooks, Summer–Fall 1884 26[406]; KSA 258.

114. *Human, All Too Human* 2, preface 1; KSA 2, 369.

115. Goethe, "Urworte, Orphisch," HA 1, 359.

116. *Thus Spoke Zarathustra* part 3, "Of the Old and New Tablets," 3; KSA 4, 248.

117. KSA 4, 248–49.

118. *Untimely Meditations* 1, "On the Use and Disadvantage of History for Life," 6; KSA 1, 294.

119. KSA 1, 293–94.

120. Ibid., 294.

121. *The Gay Science,* first book, 34; KSA 3, 404.

122. Notebooks, Summer–Fall 1883 15[6]; KSA 10, 480.

123. Notebooks, November 1882–February 1883 4[17]; KSA 10, 113.

124. The word "Zauberberg" (magic mountain) first appears in Goethe's *Faust.* Nietzsche also uses the term, perhaps in conscious emulation of Goethe. The word then became the title of Thomas Mann's novel of 1924.

125. Not found.

126. John 3:30.

127. *Human, All Too Human* 2, "Assorted Thoughts and Sayings," 307; KSA 2, 504.

128. *Human, All Too Human* 2, "The Wander and His Shadow," 210; KSA 2, 644.

129. Notebooks, Beginning 1874–Spring 1874 32[58]; KSA 7, 774.

130. *Thus Spoke Zarathustra,* part 3, "Of the Old and New Tablets," 11; KSA 4, 254.

131. Ibid.

132. Ibid.

133. Ibid.

134. Ochlocracy: government by the mob; mob rule. From the Greek "ochlos," crowd or mob, and -"kratia" -cracy.

135. *The Gay Science,* fourth book, 337; KSA 3, 564–65.

136. *Thus Spoke Zarathustra,* part 3, "The Seven Seals," 1; KSA 4, 287.

137. This is an allusion to the lines by Hölderlin quoted in the epigraph to this chapter.

138. *Thus Spoke Zarathustra,* part 3, "Of the Old and New Tablets," 25; KSA 4, 265.

Chapter 2: Knight, Death, and Devil

1. Conrad Ferdinand Meyer (1825–98), Swiss realist poet and novelist.

2. To Georg Brandes, 27 March 1888; KSB 8, 279–80.

3. Not found.

4. Bertram probably means Hans Holbein the Younger (1497–1543), a prolific portrait painter.

5. Claude Lorrain (1600–82), French painter who worked mainly in Italy, known particularly for his landscapes. See also the chapter in this book by the same name.

6. To Franz Overbeck, 20 May 1883; KSB 6, 379.

7. *Human, All Too Human* 2, "Assorted Thoughts and Sayings," 177; KSA 2, 456.

8. Albrecht Dürer (1471–1528), the preeminent artist of the German Renaissance.

9. To Malwida von Meysenbug, just after 20 March 1875; KSB 5, 36.

10. Tribschen is a small town on Lake Lucerne, Switzerland, where Wagner lived and worked from 1866 to 1872.

11. See the letters sent on the same day to Franz Overbeck and his sister, 7 May 1885; KSA 7, 46–47.

12. To Erwin Rohde, 8 October 1868; KSB 2, 322.

13. To Richard Wagner, 22 May 1869; KSB 3, 9.

14. *The Birth of Tragedy,* 20; KSA 1, 131.

15. Notebooks, 1871 9[85]; KSA 7, 305.

16. Martin Luther, Sermon 1522 *Werke,* Weimarer Ausgabe, Schriften 10, vol. 3, p. 1b.

17. Notebooks, Spring 1888 14[226]; KSA 13, 398.

18. Bertram is of course referring to Goethe's *Faust,* based on the tale of a Renaissance humanist scholar who makes a pact with the devil.

19. Allusion to Luther's famous, though apocryphal, words at the Diet of Worms in April 1521. When asked whether he acknowledge his writings or whether he would recant, he is supposed to have said in defiance: "Here I stand. I can do no other."

20. Compare introduction to Martin Luther, Sermon 1522 *Werke,* Weimarer Ausgabe, Schriften 10, vol. 3, p. xlvii.

21. Notebooks, Fall 1884 28[11]; KSA 11, 303.

22. *On the Genealogy of Morals,* Third Section, "What do Ascetic Ideals Mean?" 5; KSA 5, 345.

23. *Human, All Too Human* 2, preface, 7; KSA 2, 376–77.

24. *Thus Spoke Zarathustra,* part 1, "War and Warriors;" KSA 4, 59.

25. *Thus Spoke Zarathustra,* part 3, "The Vision and Puzzle," 1; KSA 4, 199.

26. *Ecce homo,* "Why I am so Wise," 7; KSA 6, 274.

27. *Daybreak,* fifth book, 538; KSA 3, 307.

28. Notebooks, Winter 1880–81 8[1]; KSA 9, 384.

29. Notebooks, End 1880 7[159]; KSA 9, 349–50.

30. Johann Wolfgang von Goethe, *Maximen und Reflexionen. Zur Morphologie,* 304. HA 12, 407.

31. Notebooks, Fall 1887 9[123]; KSA 12, 407.

32. *Twilight of the Idols,* "Maxims and Arrows," 2; KSA 6, 59.

33. To Georg Brandes, 2 December 1887; KSB 8, 206.

34. To Franz Overbeck, 12 February 1887; KSB 8, 21.

35. *Ecce homo,* preface, 3; KSA 6, 259.

36. *Twilight of the Idols,* "Skirmishes of an Untimely Man," 17; KSA 6, 122.

37. Notebooks, Fall 1880 6[381]; KSA 9, 295.

38. Not found.

39. Cited from Conrad Ferdinand Meyer, *Huttens Letzte Tage,* "Erasmus," XXXIV.

40. Franz Overbeck, works.

41. Erwin Rohde, *Psyche.*

42. To Carl von Gersdorff, 7 November 1870; KSB 3, 155.

43. Notebooks, Summer 1875 10[14]; KSA 8, 187.

44. Not found.

45. *Ecce homo,* "Why I write such Good Books," 3; KSA 6, 303.

46. Notebooks, Fall 1887 10[103]; KSA 12, 513.

47. *Twilight of the Idols,* "Skirmishes of an Untimely Man," 38; KSA 6, 140.

48. *Daybreak,* third book, 207; KSA 3, 187.

49. Notebooks, Spring–Fall 1881 11[249]; KSA 9, 536.

50. To Carl Fuchs, 14 December 1887; KSB 8, 210.

51. "On the Future of our Educational Institutions," Lecture 2; KSA 1, 691.

52. *Beyond Good and Evil,* part 8, "Peoples and Fatherlands," 256; KSA 5, 203.

53. Frederick II of Hohenzollern, King of Prussia, also called Frederick the Great (1712–86).

54. *Beyond Good and Evil,* part 6, "We Scholars," 209; KSA 5, 141.

55. KSA, 141–42.

56. Another allusion to Goethe's *Faust:* Mephistopheles is the name of the devil in the play.

57. Frederick II of Hohenstaufen (1194–1250), Holy Roman Emperor.
58. Notebooks, April–June 1885 34[97]; KSA 11, 452–53.
59. Italian: "devil incarnate." Source not found.
60. This is one of the words that, in successive editions of the book, Bertram substituted with a less "foreign" equivalent. In the original, Bertram wrote "problem," but he subsequently replaced it with the more German "Rätsel," or "puzzle."
61. *Human, All Too Human* 1, "Of the First and Last Things," 26; KSA 2, 47.
62. Ibid.
63. Notebooks, April–June 1885 34[149]; KSA 11, 471.
64. *Beyond Good and Evil,* part 6, "We Scholars," 209; KSA 5, 141.
65. *The Antichrist,* 42; KSA 6, 216.
66. KSA, 215.
67. A favorite epithet of Nietzsche's. The Chandala: an Indian of low caste; outcast, untouchable; especially: the son of a Sudra by a Brahman woman.
68. *The Antichrist,* 45; KSA 6, 223.
69. Johann Wolfgang von Goethe, "Zahme Zenien" or "Sprüche," IX; HA 1, 335.
70. *The Antichrist,* 9; KSA 6, 175.
71. *Ecce homo,* "Why I am so Wise," 2; KSA 6, 266.
72. To Erwin Rohde, 28 February 1875; KSB 5, 27–28.
73. Notebooks, Fall 1885–Fall 1886 2[180]; KSA 12, 156.
74. The *Heliand* (from Old Saxon: savior) is an epic on the life of Christ in Old Saxon alliterative verse dating from about 830. It attempted to make the newly imposed Christian religion intelligible to the warlike Saxons. Christ was made a Germanic king who rewarded his retainers (the disciples) with arm rings; Herod's feast became a drinking bout; and Nazarethburg, Bethleemaburg, and Rumuburg had the homely familiarity of Saxon towns. *Encyclopedia Britannica,* 15th ed., vol. 5, p. 811.
75. Johann Wolfgang von Goethe, "Sprüche," IX; HA 1, 335.
76. *The Gay Science,* fifth book, 350; KSA 3, 586.
77. *Daybreak,* first book, 88; KSA 3, 82.
78. Heinrich Wölfflin, *Die Kunst Albrecht Dürers,* 2nd ed. (Munich: F. Bruckmann, 1908), 334.
79. Ibid., 222.
80. I Corinthians 15:55.
81. Wölfflin.
82. Ibid., 16.
83. *Thus Spoke Zarathustra,* part 4, "The Sign;" KSA 4, 408.
84. To Malwida von Meysenbug, just after 20 March 1875; KSB 5, 36.
85. To Heinrich Köselitz, 21 July 1881; KSB 6, 109.
86. To Erwin Rohde, 30 April 1870; KSB 3, 120.
87. Nietzsche uses this word—"unheimlich"—to describe the engraving in a letter to Franz Overbeck, 2 July 1885; KSB 7, 61.
88. To Franz Overbeck, 7 May 1885; KSB 7, 46.

89. *Human, All Too Human* 2, "The Wanderer and His Shadow," 149; KSA 2, 615.
90. To Heinrich Köselitz, 25 May 1888; KSB 8, 319.
91. Not found.
92. Notebooks, Spring 1884 25[162]; KSA 11, 56.
93. To Erwin Rohde, 22 February 1884; KSB 6, 479.
94. Notebooks, Spring 1884 25[173]; KSA 11, 60.
95. Notebooks, Spring 1884 25[172]; KSA 11, 60.
96. To Heinrich Köselitz, 20 June 1888; KSB 8, 338.
97. *The Birth of Tragedy,* 23; KSA 1, 146–47.
98. *Beyond Good and Evil,* part 8, "Peoples and Fatherlands," 252; KSA 5, 195.
99. *The Antichrist,* 61; KSA 6, 252.
100. *The Case of Wagner,* epilogue; KSA 6, 52.
101. Compare the numerous letters sent on 4 January 1889.
102. Notebooks, Winter 1869–70 to Spring 1870 3[62]; KSA 7, 77.
103. To Heinrich Köselitz, 9 December 1888; KSB 8, 515.
104. To Franz Overbeck, 7 May 1885; KSB 7, 46.
105. Franz Overbeck to Nietzsche, 1871.

Chapter 3: The German Becoming

1. From a poem by Friedrich Hebbel (1813–63), "An Seine Majestät, König Wilhelm I. von Preußen," in *Werke,* ed. Franz Zinkernagel (Leipzig: Bibliographisches Institut, 1914), vol. 1, p. 268.
2. Adalbert Stifter (1805–68), Austrian writer. Source not found.
3. Heraclitus, pre-Socratic Greek philosopher (ca. 435–475 B.C.E.), from Ephesus. He believed that the nature of reality was change itself and used the element of fire to exemplify his thought. He is most closely associated, however simplistically, with the phrase "panta rei" or "everything flows" or is "in flux."
4. *Beyond Good and Evil,* part 1, "On the Prejudices of Philosophers," 2; KSA 5, 17.
5. "Philosophy in the Tragic Age of the Greeks," 8; KSA 1, 835.
6. Ibid.
7. Notebooks, Summer 1872–Beginning 1873 19[62]; KSA 7, 439.
8. *Ecce homo,* "The Birth of Tragedy," 3; KSA 6, 312–13.
9. Notebooks, April–June 1885 34[73]; KSA 11, 442.
10. Notebooks, June–July 1885 36[27]; KSA 11, 562.
11. Notebooks, Fall 1881 15[48]; KSA 9, 651.
12. Notebooks, Spring–Fall 1881 11[293]; KSA 9, 554.
13. *On the Genealogy of Morals,* first treatise, "Good and Evil," "Good and Bad," 13; KSA 5, 279.
14. *Beyond Good and Evil,* "From High Mountains. Postlude"; KSA 5, 243.
15. "Philosophy in the Tragic Age of the Greeks," 8; KSA 1, 822.
16. KSA 1, 824.
17. *Ecce homo,* "The Birth of Tragedy," 3; KSA 6, 313.

18. *The Gay Science,* fifth book, 357; KSA 5, 599.

19. *Beyond Good and Evil,* part 8, "Peoples and Fatherlands," 244; KSA 5, 185.

20. Johann Gottlieb Fichte, *Reden an die deutsche Nation,* seventh speech.

21. Not found.

22. Novalis (Friedrich von Hardenberg), *Blütenstaub,* Sprüche, 49.

23. To Hetzler the Younger, 24 August 1770; Goethe, *Briefe* 1, 114.

24. Friedrich Hölderlin, *Fragment von Hyperion, Werke und Briefe,* ed. Friedrich Beißner und Jochen Schmidt (Frankfurt am Main: 1969), 1, 459.

25. Martin Luther, *Sämmtliche Schriften,* ed. Johann Georg Walch. New rev. Stereotypausgabe, bd. 1–23, (St. Louis: 1883–1910), 15, 1494–95.

26. Notebooks, Summer–Fall 1873 29[123]; KSA 7, 687.

27. *Twilight of the Idols,* "What the Germans Lack," 2; KSA 6, 104.

28. Bertram is exploiting a peculiarity of the German language here: the comparative form of the adjective "German"—"deutscher" (more German)—is the same as the word for a (male) German: "ein Deutscher." The same is not true of the adjectives in German for "French" and "English."

29. *Human, All Too Human* 2, "Assorted Thoughts and Sayings," 323; KSA 2, 511.

30. Notebooks, Summer–Fall 1884 26[395]; KSA 11, 255.

31. *Human, All Too Human* 2, "Assorted Thoughts and Sayings," 302; KSA 2, 502.

32. Part 2, chapter 9, "Aus Ottiliens Tagebuche, in Goethe, *Die Wahlverwandtschaften,* HA 6, 427.

33. Not found.

34. *Thus Spoke Zarathustra,* part 1, prologue, 3; KSA 4, 14.

35. Goethe, *Dichtung und Wahrheit,* book 12, HA 9, 546.

36. Goethe to Schiller, letter from 15 December 1795, in *Briefwechsel zwischen Schiller und Goethe* (Stuttgart: J. G. Cotta, 1881), vol. 1, p. 96.

37. Wölfflin, *Albrecht Dürer.*

38. *Ecce homo,* "The Birth of Tragedy," 4; KSA 6, 313.

39. Notebooks, April–June 1885 34[105]; KSA 11, 456.

40. Goethe to Eckermann, May 3, 1827, in *Gespräche* 3, 388.

41. Hölderlin, "An die Deutschen," SA 2, 10.

42. "On the Future of our Educational Institutions," lecture 2; KSA 1, 690.

43. *Beyond Good and Evil,* part 8, "Peoples and Fatherlands," 240; KSA 5, 180.

44. *The Case of Wagner,* 1; KSA 6, 357.

45. *Beyond Good and Evil,* "From High Mountains. Postlude"; KSA 5, 243.

46. To Heinrich Köselitz, 4 January 1889; KSB 8, 575.

47. Hebbel, source not found.

48. Wölfflin, *Albrecht Dürer.*

49. *Beyond Good and Evil,* part 8, "Peoples and Fatherlands," 255; KSA 5, 200.

50. Not found.

51. Not found.

52. Luther, *Tischreden,* 1532, 2, 98.

53. Hölderlin, "Gesang des Deutschen," SA 2, 3.

54. Friedrich Hebbel, *Diaries,* 4 January 1860; in *Tagebücher,* ed. Karl Pörnbacher (Munich: DTV, 1984), vol. 3, p. 269.

55. Not found.

56. Latin: "Hatred of the human race."

57. *Beyond Good and Evil,* part 8, "Peoples and Fatherlands," 244; KSA 5, 184.

58. Nietzsche is citing the famous phrase from Goethe's *Faust,* line 1112, HA 3, 41.

59. *Beyond Good and Evil,* part 8, "Peoples and Fatherlands," 244; KSA 5, 184.

60. Stendhal (Henri Beyle), Correspondence.

61. *Beyond Good and Evil,* part 8, "Peoples and Fatherlands," 244; KSA 5, 185.

62. *Ecce homo,* "Why I am so Clever," 9; KSA 6, 295.

63. Ibid.

64. *Beyond Good and Evil,* part 8, "Peoples and Fatherlands," 244; KSA 5, 185–86.

65. Goethe, *Dichtung und Wahrheit,* nineteenth book, middle.

66. "On Truth and Lie in the Extra-moral Sense," 1; KSA 1, 877.

67. Johann Paul Friedrich Richter (1763–1825), changed his name in honor of Jean-Jacques Rousseau. He was the author of sprawling novels characterized by psychological inwardness, eccentric characters, linguistic playfulness, a rather recherché wit, irony, and satire and, for some, interminable length.

68. Goethe, *Italienische Reise,* Venice, 9 October 1786; HA

69. Notebooks, Summer 1872–Beginning 1873 19[17]; KSA 7, 421.

70. Hölderlin, "Patmos," SA 2, 173.

71. Steven Aschheim, *The Nietzsche Legacy in Germany, 1890–1990* (Berkeley: University of California Press, 1992), 152, cites this passage as if Bertram were making reference to contemporary events, in particular the experience of World War I. As the entire context makes clear, this was not at all Bertram's intention.

72. *Ecce homo,* "The Birth of Tragedy," 4; KSA 6, 313.

73. Nietzsche spent every summer after 1881 until his mental collapse in the small southern Swiss village of Sils-Maria in the canton of Graubünden.

74. From a conversation in 1813 reported by the historian Heinrich Luden, *Rückblicke in mein Leben. Aus dem Nachlass,* (Jena: F. Luden, 1847), 119.

75. To Carl von Gersdorff, 21 June 1871; KSB 3, 203.

76. "On the Future of our Educational Institutions," lecture 3; KSA 1, 710.

77. *Untimely Meditations* 3, "Schopenhauer as Educator," 6; KSA 1, 391.

78. *Daybreak,* third book, 207; KSA 3, 185.

79. KSA 3, 187.

80. *Ecce homo,* "The Case of Wagner," 2; KSA 6, 359.

81. *The Case of Wagner,* postscript; KSA 6, 41.

82. *Ecce homo,* "The Case of Wagner," 2; KSA 6, 359.

83. *Nietzsche contra Wagner,* "We Antipodes"; KSA 6, 424.

84. Notebooks, Summer–Fall 1884 26[335]; KSA 11, 238.

85. *Human, All Too Human* 2, "Assorted Thoughts and Sayings," 302; KSA 2, 502.

86. Notebooks, Spring 1871–Beginning 1872 14[25]; KSA 7, 385.

87. Notebooks, Winter 1870–71 to Fall 1872 8[93]; KSA 7, 259.

88. "On the Future of our Educational Institutions," lecture 2; KSA 1, 691.

89. Ibid.

90. Ibid., lecture 3; KSA 1, 713.

91. Notebooks, Spring 1884 25[162]; KSA 11, 56.

92. *Thus Spoke Zarathustra,* part 4, "The Honey Sacrifice;" KSA 4, 297. The words in this quotation are a literal translation of the preceding Greek.

93. Angelus Silesius, *Fünfftes Buch Geistreicher Sinn- und Schluß-Reime,* Cherubnisher Wandersmann, No. 200.

94. "On the Future of our Educational Institutions," Lecture 2; KSA 1, 691.

95. Conflation of two quotations from Goethe, "Vorspiel auf dem Theater," *Faust* 1, HA, and *Gespräche mit Eckermann,* Insel 1981, 148.

96. "Homer und die klassische Philologie," Antrittsrede Basel 1869, paragraph 5.

97. *The Gay Science,* second book, 105; KSA 3, 463.

98. Not found.

99. *Human, All Too Human,* "Assorted Thoughts and Sayings," 219; KSA 2, 471–72.

100. "Philosophy in the Tragic Age of the Greeks," 1; KSA 1, 806.

101. Ibid.

102. *Untimely Meditations* 2, "On the Use and Disadvantage of History for Life," 10; KSA 1, 333.

103. The two Greek words mean, respectively, "wisdom" and "wise."

104. Lectures on history of Greek literature.

105. *The Birth of Tragedy,* preface, 7; KSA 1, 22.

Chapter 4: Justice

1. Goethe, *Maximen und Reflexionen,* "Allgemeines, Ethisches, Literarisches" HA 11, 738.

2. Source not found. Jacques-Bénigne Bossuet (1627–1704), French bishop and renowned theologian. Some have called him the most gifted religious orator in history.

3. Although this sentence is in quotation marks in the original, it is unclear if Bertram is citing Nietzsche's (or someone else's) words or simply formulating the question treated in this chapter.

4. Notebooks, August–September 1885 40[65]; KSA 11, 663; In his analysis of Heidegger's Nietzsche lectures, David Krell's comments on this chapter may be of interest. In the section, "Heidegger's discussion of Justice," Krell points out that the sixth chapter of Alfred Baeumler's *Nietzsche der Philosoph und Politiker* (Leipzig: Reclam, 1931) contains an extended analysis of "justice," as a fundamental component of Nietzsche's metaphysics. "Will to power," he [i.e. Baeumler] writes, "is merely another expression for supreme justice" (78). He now cites the first of the two notes cited by Heidegger (on justice as "*the supreme representative of life itself*") much in the way that Heidegger does. Yet this particular aspect of the Baeumlerian context is complicated by the fact that Ernst Bertram

here assumes special importance. However much Baeumler tries to contrapose his own account to that of Bertram, it is clear that Bertram's discussion of "justice" is by far the more original and decisive one. Bertram chooses *Gerechtigkeit* as the title of his fourth chapter (91–101 [here pp. 79–87]). He offers a sensitive, nuanced account of that notion in Nietzsche's writings from the early 1870s until the end—the "end" here meaning the doctrine of *amor fati* and the exaltation of justice as "supreme representative," with which aphorism Bertram's chapter in fact ends. The importance Bertram attaches to the notion of "justice" is indicated by the fact that not a single other rubric of Nietzsche's philosophy—neither will to power nor eternal return nor nihilism—appears in the book's table of contents. See Martin Heidegger, *Nietzsche,* trans. David Krell (San Francisco: Harper & Row, 1987), 2, 273.

5. *Untimely Meditations* 2, "On the Use and Disadvantage of History for Life," 6; KSA 1, 286.

6. KSA 1, 286.

7. Ibid.

8. Ibid., 287.

9. Ibid.

10. The reference is to *Human, All Too Human* 1, "Man alone with Himself," 636; KSA 2, 361.

11. *Untimely Meditations* 2, "On the Use and Disadvantage of History for Life," 6; KSA 1, 288.

12. Goethe, *Maximen und Reflexionen,* "Allgemeines, Ethisches, Literarisches," HA 6, 378.

13. *Untimely Meditations* 2, "On the Use and Disadvantage of History for Life," 6; KSA 1, 290.

14. *Thus Spoke Zarathustra,* part 1, "The Bite of the Asp;" KSA 4, 88.

15. Ibid., prologue, 3; KSA 4, 15–16.

16. Notebooks, Summer 1883 13[5]; KSA 10, 455.

17. *Untimely Meditations* 2, "On the Use and Disadvantage of History for Life," 6; KSA 1, 288–89.

18. *Untimely Meditations* 2, "On the Use and Disadvantage of History for Life," 6; KSA 1, 293–94.

19. KSA 1, 294.

20. *On the Genealogy of Morals,* second treatise, 11; KSA 5, 309.

21. KSA 5, 310–11.

22. *Human, All Too Human,* 8, "A Glance at the State," 451; KSA 2, 293.

23. *Untimely Meditations* 2, "On the Use and Disadvantage of History for Life," 3; KSA 1, 269.

24. Ibid.

25. *Human, All Too Human* 2, "On the History of Moral Sentiments," 92; KSA 2, 89–90.

26. *Human, All Too Human,* preface, 6; KSA 2, 20.

27. Notebooks, End 1880 7[25]; KSA 9, 322.
28. Notebooks, Fall 1880 6[416]; KSA 9, 304–5.
29. Notebooks, Summer–Fall 1882 3[1] 165; KSA 10, 72.
30. *Thus Spoke Zarathustra,* part 1, "The Bite of the Asp;" KSA 4, 88.
31. Ibid.
32. *Human, All Too Human* 1, "Of First and Last Things," 32; KSA 2, 52.
33. Notebooks, End 1876–Summer 1877 23 [133]; KSA 8, 451.
34. *The Gay Science,* third book, 140; KSA 3, 489.
35. *Human, All Too Human* 1, "Man Alone with Himself," 637; KSA 2, 362.
36. Notebooks, Fall 1881 13[5]; KSA 9, 619.
37. *Human, All Too Human* 2, "Assorted Thoughts and Sayings," 79; KSA 2, 409.
38. Notebooks, November 1882–February 1883 5[1] 241; KSA 10, 215.
39. Nietzsche is citing here from Goethe's poem, "Prometheus," HA.
40. *The Birth of Tragedy* 9; KSA 1, 67–71.
41. Notebooks, Fall 1869 1[107]; KSA 7, 42.
42. Notebooks, Summer 1871–Spring 1872 16[23]; KSA 7, 403.
43. "Philosophy in the Tragic Age of the Greeks," 5; KSA 1, 822.
44. KSA 1, 825–26.
45. Ibid., 826–27.
46. *Untimely Meditations* 4, "Richard Wagner in Bayreuth," 9; KSA 1, 493–94.
47. Notebooks, Spring 1884 25[484]; KSA 11, 141.

Chapter 5: Arion

1. Not found.
2. Schopenhauer, Über die Musik, third book, 52, 344.
3. The title of Brandes's first publication on Nietzsche was "An Essay on Aristocratic Radicalism" (1889); compare Georg Brandes, *Friedrich Nietzsche* (London: William Heinemann, 1914), 3–56. Nietzsche read this essay and told Brandes that "the expression 'aristocratic radicalism' that you use is very good. It is, if I may say so, the most intelligent thing I have yet read about myself." To Brandes, 2 December 1887; KSB 8, 206.
4. Heinrich Heine (1797–1856), one of the most important and influential German poets and journalists of the nineteenth century.
5. *The Birth of Tragedy* 21; KSA 1, 135.
6. To Heinrich Köselitz, 27 October 1887; KSB 8, 179.
7. Stefan George, "Nietzsche," *Der Siebente Ring,* GA 6/7, 13. George's poem is quoting Nietzsche's words in *The Birth of Tragedy,* "Attempt at a Self-Criticism," 3; KSA 1, 15.
8. Notebooks, August–September 1885 41[10]; KSA 11, 687.
9. Not found.
10. "Mein Leben," 1864.
11. To Heinrich Köselitz, 25 July 1882; KSB 6, 231.
12. Bertram is perhaps misquoting a passage in Deussen's memoirs where he mentions

that Nietzsche "knew how to improvise masterfully on the piano;" see Deussen, *Erinnerungen,* 8.

13. Förster-Nietzsche, *Der junge Nietzsche,* 122; compare Carl von Gersdorff, *Briefe an Friedrich Nietzsche,* ed. Karl Schlechta, 4 vols. (Weimar: Nietzsche-Archiv, 1934–37), 4, 56. The first sentence of the quotation appears to be a fabrication by Elisabeth Förster-Nietzsche.

14. Source of the anecdote not found.

15. To Carl von Gersdorff, 6 April 1867; KSB 2, 209.

16. To Sophie Ritschl, 2 July 1868; KSB 2, 298.

17. To Heinrich Köselitz, 2 April 1883; KSB 6, 353.

18. *Ecce homo,* "Thus Spoke Zarathustra," 1; KSA 6, 335.

19. To Heinrich Köselitz, 4 August 1882; KSB 6, 235.

20. To Heinrich Köselitz, 1 September 1882; KSB 6, 249.

21. To Malwida von Meysenbug, End March 1884; KSB 6, 490.

22. To Heinrich Köselitz, 25 February 1884; KSB 6, 480.

23. *The Birth of Tragedy,* "Attempt at a Self-Criticism," 3; KSA 1, 14–15.

24. KSA 1, 14.

25. *The Case of Wagner,* 1; KSA 6, 14.

26. To Carl Fuchs, 27 December 1888; KSB 8, 554.

27. *Ecce homo,* "Why I am so Clever," 6; KSA 6, 289.

28. To Erwin Rohde, 21 December 1871; KSB 3, 256.

29. *Ecce homo,* "Why I am so Clever," 6; KSA 6, 290.

30. *The Birth of Tragedy* 21; KSA 1, 135.

31. To Erwin Rohde, 21 December 1871; KSB 3, 256–57.

32. *The Birth of Tragedy* 7; KSA 1, 55–56.

33. Notebooks, Summer–End September 1875 12[29]; KSA 8, 267.

34. Notebooks, Spring–Summer 1888 16[10]; KSA 13, 486.

35. *Beyond Good and Evil* 8, "Peoples and Fatherlands," 253; KSA 5, 197.

36. Notebooks, August–September 1885 41[14]; KSA 11, 688.

37. Notebooks, Spring–Summer 1878 27[93]; KSA 8, 502.

38. Notebooks, November 1887–1888 11[315]; KSA 13, 133.

39. To Georg Brandes, 27 March 1888; KSB 8, 279.

40. Notebooks, Summer–Fall 1884 26[341]: KSA 11, 239–40.

41. Notebooks, Fall 1881 12[139]; KSA 9, 600. Clemens Brentano (1778–1842), a prominent German romantic poet.

42. *Beyond Good and Evil* 8, "Peoples and Fatherlands," 240; KSA 5, 179–80.

43. *Human, All Too Human* 2, "Assorted Thoughts and Sayings," 171; KSA 2, 450.

44. *Human, All Too Human* 1, "Of First and Last Things," 12; KSA 2, 32.

45. *Human, All Too Human* 2, "The Wanderer and His Shadow," 169; KSA 2, 622–23.

46. Palace in Florence, Italy, built between the mid-fifteenth to the mid-sixteenth centuries.

47. Notebooks, Spring 1888 14[61]; KSA 13, 247.
48. Notebooks, November 1887–March 1888 11[315]; KSA 13, 133.
49. Notebooks, Spring 1888 14[61]; KSA 13, 248.
50. *Human, All Too Human* 2, "Assorted Thoughts and Sayings," 171; KSA 2, 452.
51. *Human, All Too Human* 1, "From the Souls of Artists and Writers," 215; KSA 2, 175.
52. *Daybreak,* fourth book 239; KSA 3, 200.
53. *The Case of Wagner,* second postscript; KSA 6, 48–49.
54. *Human, All Too Human* 2, preface 3; KSA 2, 373.
55. Notebooks, Fall 1887 9[65]; KSA 12, 370.
56. Notebooks, Fall 1880 6[171]; KSA 9, 241.
57. Notebooks, Spring 1880–Spring 1881 10[D62]; KSA 9, 426.
58. Notebooks, Spring 1880 3[150]; KSA 9, 95.
59. *Beyond Good and Evil* 8, "Peoples and Fatherlands," 255; KSA 5, 201.
60. Ibid.
61. *Daybreak,* fifth book, 461; KSA 3, 277–78.
62. *The Gay Science,* second book, 104; KSA 3, 460.
63. Notebooks, Spring 1888 15[69] KSA 13, 451.
64. *The Gay Science,* second book, 103; KSA 3, 459–60.
65. Ibid., 460.
66. From the Greek meaning "song" or "melody."
67. *Human, All Too Human* 2, "The Wanderer and His Shadow," 168; KSA 2, 621–22.
68. Notebooks, Fall 1881 14[22]; KSA 9, 630.
69. The Scythians were considered in antiquity as the epitome of savagery and barbarism, hence the implication here that music understood solely as melody was the most primitive, or "Scythian," form imaginable.
70. Notebooks, Fall 1887 10[116]; KSA 9, 522.
71. Jakob Burckhardt, *Griechische Kulturgeschichte.*
72. Notebooks, Fall 1881 14[23]; KSA 9, 631.
73. To Gustav Krug, 10 March 1882; KSB 6, 176.
74. *The Gay Science,* second book, 104; KSA 3, 460.
75. To Heinrich Köselitz, 17 November 1880; KSB 6, 47–48.
76. *Ecce homo,* "The Case of Wagner," 1; KSA 6, 357.
77. Letter by Gast to Nietzsche 1887. Nietzsche refers to this episode in a letter to his sister, 11 November 1887; KSB 8, 193. The Italian read: "Magnificent! *That* is true Church music!"
78. Notebooks, Summer 1875 6[23]; KSA 8, 107.
79. In original: "Drittes Reich."
80. Not found.
81. *Ecce homo,* dedication; KSA 6, 263.
82. To Heinrich Köselitz, 5 March 1884; KSB 6, 483.

83. To Heinrich Köselitz, 15 January 1888; KSB 8, 231–32.
84. To Georg Brandes, 27 March 1888; KSB 8, 279–80.
85. To Heinrich Köselitz, 21 March 1888; KSB 8, 275.
86. *Ecce homo,* "The Case of Wagner," 1; KSA 6, 357.
87. Ibid.
88. To Heinrich Köselitz, 2 December 1888; KSB 8, 498–99.
89. *Ecce homo,* "Why I am so Clever," 7; KSA 6, 291.
90. *Thus Spoke Zarathustra,* part 3, "The Great Longing"; KSA 4, 280.
91. Ibid.
92. To Heinrich Köselitz, 4 January 1889; KSB 8, 575.
93. Notebooks, Summer–Fall 1884 26[395]; KSA 11, 255.
94. From the corrupted text of *Ecce homo.*
95. *The Case of Wagner,* second postscript; KSA 6, 49.
96. This story of Arion and the dolphin is told in book 1 of Herodotus's *History.*
97. Notebooks, Spring 1884 25[241]; KSA 11, 75.
98. Greek: "third middle," referring to harmonics.
99. To Heinrich Köselitz, 31 December 1888; KSB 8, 567.
100. To Heinrich Köselitz, 4 January 1889; KSB 8, 575.
101. *Thus Spoke Zarathustra,* part 3, "The Great Longing;" KSA 4, 280.

Chapter 6: Illness

1. Goethe, *Gedichte, Gott und Welt,* "Metamorphose der Tiere,"
2. *The Antichrist,* 61; KSA 6, 252.
3. Notebooks, May–July 1885 35[66]; KSA 11, 539.
4. To Heinrich Köselitz, 31 December 1888; KSB 8, 567.
5. Not found.
6. Notebooks, End 1880 7[187]; KSA 9, 355.
7. Notebooks, May–July 1885 35[66]; KSA 11, 539.
8. Notebooks, August–September 1885 39[16]; KSA 11, 626.
9. *Ecce homo,* "Thus Spoke Zarathustra," 4; KSA 6, 341.
10. Notebooks, May–June 1883 9[29]; KSA 10, 354.
11. Notebooks, May–June 1883 9[43]; KSA 10, 359.
12. Notebooks, Fall 1883 16[21]; KSA 10, 506.
13. *The Gay Science,* preface to the second edition, 3; KSA 3, 350.
14. Notebooks, Fall 1887 10[103]; KSA 12, 513.
15. Not found.
16. Blaise Pascal, "Le moi est haïssable," in *Pensées sur la religion et sur quelques autres sujets,* 597. (Edition du Luxembourg, Paris, 1951.)
17. *Thus Spoke Zarathustra,* part 3, "Of the Vision and Puzzle," 1; KSA 4, 199.
18. To Franz Overbeck, 31 December 1882; KSB 6, 314.
19. To Malwida von Meysenbug, 14 January 1880; KSB 6, 5.
20. To Malwida von Meysenbug, 1 January 1883; KSB 6, 314.

21. *On the Genealogy of Morals,* third treatise, "What do Ascetic Ideals Mean?" 13; KSA 5, 366.

22. KSA 5, 349.

23. To Franz Overbeck, 3 February 1888; KSB 8, 242.

24. *On the Genealogy of Morals,* third treatise, "What do Ascetic Ideals Mean?" 15; KSA 5, 374.

25. "What do Ascetic Ideals Mean?" 11; KSA 5, 367.

26. "What do Ascetic Ideals Mean?" 13; KSA 5, 366

27. "What do Ascetic Ideals Mean?" 27; KSA 5, 410. Nietzsche is quoting Cicero, *De Oratore* Liber II.

28. "What do Ascetic Ideals Mean?" 24; KSA 5, 399.

29. Notebooks, End 1880 7[187]; KSA 9, 355.

30. *The Antichrist,* 45; KSA 6, 223. Nietzsche cites 1 Corinthians, 1, 27–28.

31. Notebooks, Spring 1888 14[170]; KSA 13, 356.

32. *Ecce homo,* "Why I am so Clever," 6; KSA 6, 290.

33. Notebooks, Fall 1885–Fall 1886 2[110]; KSA 12, 115.

34. *Thus Spoke Zarathustra,* part 2, "The Famous Wisemen"; KSA 4, 134.

35. From the corrupted text of *Ecce homo;* see KSA 14, 473.

36. Not found.

37. Not found.

38. *Ecce homo,* "Why I am so Clever," 6; KSA 6, 290.

39. Novalis, pseudonym of Friedrich von Hardenberg (1772–1801), early romantic poet, whose major poetic work is the elegiac *Hymnen an die Nacht* (1800).

40. Novalis, *Enzyklopädie,* paragraph 391.

41. Not found.

42. Not found.

43. Hebbel, 1840s?

44. Hebbel, source not found.

45. Goethe, "Metamorphose der Tiere."

46. *The Gay Science,* fourth book, 316; KSA 3, 549.

47. Friedrich Gundolf, *Goethe* (Berlin: Georg Bondi, 1916).

48. In English in the original; source unknown.

49. *On the Genealogy of Morals,* first treatise, "Good and Evil," "Good and Bad," 7; KSA 5, 267.

50. *Human, All Too Human* 1, "Indications of Higher and Lower Culture," 224; KSA 2, 188.

51. *The Gay Science,* first book, 24; KSA 3, 399.

52. Notebooks, End 1886–Spring 1887 7[65]; KSA 12, 318–319.

53. *The Gay Science,* fourth book, 302; KSA 3, 541.

54. Ibid., first book, 45; KSA 3, 411.

55. *The Birth of Tragedy,* 3; KSA 1, 36.

56. *The Birth of Tragedy,* 4; KSA 1, 40.

57. *Human, All Too Human* 1, "From the Souls of Artists and Writers," 214; KSA 2, 174–75.

58. *Thus Spoke Zarathustra,* part 3, "The Convalescent," 2; KSA 4, 275.

59. Notebooks, Fall 1883; 16[85]; KSA 10, 529.

60. *Ecce homo,* "Why I am so Wise," 2; KSA 6, 266.

61. Not found.

62. Not found.

63. Not found.

64. *The Gay Science,* preface to the second edition, 1; KSA 3, 345.

65. *Human, All Too Human* 2, preface, 5; KSA 2, 374.

66. *Human, All Too Human* 1, preface, 4; KSA 2, 18.

67. *Ecce homo,* "Why I am so Wise," 2; KSA 6, 267.

68. *Ecce homo,* "Why I am so Wise," 1; KSA 6, 266.

69. *Untimely Meditations* 3, "Schopenhauer as Educator," 2; KSA 1, 348–49.

70. *Ecce homo,* "Thus Spoke Zarathustra," 2; KSA 6, 339. Nietzsche is repeating here verbatim a phrase he first wrote in *The Gay Science,* fifth book, 382; KSA 3, 636.

71. To Erwin Rohde, Beginning December 1882; KSB 6, 291.

72. To Hans von Bülow, Beginning December 1882; KSB 6, 290.

73. *The Gay Science,* preface to the second edition, 1; KSA 3, 349–50.

74. *The Gay Science,* third book, 120; KSA 3, 477.

75. Not found.

76. *Beyond Good and Evil,* first part, "On the Prejudices of Philosophers," 5; KSA 5, 19.

77. This is a reference to Luther's hymn "Aus tiefer Not schrei ich zu dir," "Out of the depths I cry to Thee," which J. S. Bach also set to music in a cantata by the same name (BWV 38).

78. Notebooks, Spring–Summer 1875 5[130]; KSA 8, 74.

79. Socrates's last words before he drank the hemlock were, "A cock for Asclepius." Compare Plato, *Phaedo.*

Chapter 7: Judas

1. It has been a mistake to read—or rather, because it is so often not actually read, to assume—that this chapter is about Wagner only. Rather, Bertram is interested in the deeper and broader problem of betrayal and especially of the nature and origin of evil in Nietzsche's life and thinking, of which his relationship to Wagner is only one, if the most significant and well-known, example. That Bertram's conception of Nietzsche's relationship to Wagner is not limited to the notion of betrayal is demonstrated by the following chapter, "Mask," which also focuses on Wagner in its exploration of theatricality and authenticity; see also James M. Robinson, *The Secrets of Judas: The Story of the Misunderstood Disciple and his Lost Gospel* (San Francisco: Harper, 2006).

2. Friedrich Gottlieb Klopstock (1724–1803), German poet; his major work was *Der Messias,* which was published in numerous versions beginning in 1748.

3. Compare Ernest Renan, *Vie de Jésus,* 9th ed. (Paris: 1864), 270–71.

4. These two unflattering references to Russians, typical of Stefan George's view of Russia and its literature, were removed in later editions. Interestingly, however, the later passage about "the Russian soul" below remained. Bernt von Heiseler mentioned George's aversion toward Russia, but pointed out: "It is worth mentioning that during all of his travels he never set foot in Russia, indeed avoided it as something 'foreign, dangerous, even terrible.'" Heiseler, *Gesammelte Essays zur alten und neuen Literatur* vol. 1 (Stuttgart: J. F. Steinkopf, 1966), p. 303.

5. In Norse mythology, a blind god, associated with night and darkness. Hod (or Hodur) was the son of the principal god, Odin, and his wife, Frigg. He was tricked by the evil fire god Loki into killing his brother Balder, who was the most beautiful and perfect of the gods. According to Norse mythology, after this deed the world was never again as good, loving, and just as it had been before Balder's death. *Encyclopedia Britannica.*

6. Matthew 26:24.

7. John 13:27.

8. John 19:30.

9. *Human, All Too Human* 3, "The Religious Life," 137; KSA 2, 131.

10. *Ecce homo,* "Why I am a Fate," 2; KSA 6, 366.

11. From the corrupted edition of *Ecce homo.* See "Why I am so Wise," 7; KSA 6, 275. In the corrected version, Nietzsche writes: "For me, to attack is a token of goodwill, possibly of gratitude."

12. To Erwin Rohde, 19 May 1887; KSB 8, 76–77. The edition Bertram used gives the date he indicates; compare *Gesammelte Briefe* 2, 580–81,

13. To Elisabeth Nietzsche, Middle March 1885; KSB 7, 24.

14. To Erwin Rohde, 11 November 1887; KSB 8, 194.

15. From a forged letter by Elisabeth Förster-Nietzsche, *Gesammelte Briefe,* 5/2, 805–7. Not in KSB.

16. Wagner to Nietzsche, 1873.

17. Source unclear.

18. Source unknown.

19. *The Case of Wagner,* foreword; KSA 6, 11.

20. Notebooks, Fall 1885–Fall 1886 2[34]; KSA 12, 80.

21. *Ecce homo,* "Why I am so Clever," 5; KSA 6, 288.

22. *Ecce homo,* "Why I am so Clever," 6; KSA 6, 289–90.

23. Notebooks, April–June 1885 34[254]; KSA 11, 506.

24. Notebooks, April–June 1885 34[205]; KSA 11, 491.

25. Not found.

26. *The Gay Science,* second book, 98; KSA 3, 452.

27. Ibid.

28. To Carl Fuchs, 27 December 1888; KSB 8, 554.

29. Notebooks, July–August 1882 1[70]; KSA 10, 28.

30. *Ecce homo,* "Why I am so Wise," 1; KSA 6, 266.

31. *Untimely Meditations* 2, "On the Use and Disadvantage of History for Life," foreword; KSA 1, 245. Bertram replaces "history" with "science (and knowledge)," but given what Nietzsche writes in the preceding sentences this seems a defensible substitution.

32. *Thus Spoke Zarathustra,* part 2, "The Famous Wisemen"; KSA 4, 134.

33. Source unknown.

34. Notebooks, Fall 1887 10[105]; KSA 12, 514.

35. Notebooks, November 1882–February 1883 5[1] 68; KSA 10, 195.

36. Compare Notebooks, July–August 1882 1[65]; KSA 10, 27.

37. *Thus Spoke Zarathustra,* part 1, "The Tree on the Mountain"; KSA 4, 51.

38. Nietzsche is quoting from Goethe's *Faust,* 3781–82, citing the words of the "Evil Spirit" speaking to Gretchen. HA 3, 120.

39. *On the Genealogy of Morals,* preface 3; KSA 5, 249.

40. Notebooks, Summer–Fall 1884 26[390]; KSA 11, 253.

41. *Ecce homo,* "Beyond Good and Evil," 2; KSA 6, 351.

42. *The Antichrist,* 29; KSA 6, 200.

43. Notebooks, Fall 1885–Spring 1886 1[205]; KSA 12, 57.

44. *The Antichrist,* 31; KSA 6, 201.

45. *The Case of Wagner,* epilogue; KSA 6, 50.

46. *Twilight of the Idols,* "Skirmishes of an Untimely Man," 45; KSA 6, 147.

47. On this notion, see Robert E. Norton, *The Beautiful Soul: Aesthetic Morality in the Eighteenth Century* (Ithaca, N.Y.: Cornell University Press, 1995).

48. *Human, All Too Human* 1, "From the Souls of Artists and Writers," 152; KSA 2, 145.

49. *The Gay Science,* book 2, 87; KSA 3, 445.

50. *Daybreak,* book 4, 216; KSA 3, 192–93.

51. *Thus Spoke Zarathustra,* part 3, "The Convalescent," 2; KSA 4, 274.

52. Notebooks, Summer–Fall 1884 27[46]; KSA 11, 287.

53. Jakob Burckhardt, *Weltgeschichtliche Betrachtungen* (Stuttgart: Kröner, 1935), 97.

54. Not found.

55. Notebooks, April–June 1885 34[149]; KSA 11, 471.

56. This is a good example of Bertram's habit of weaving the titles of Nietzsche's works into his narrative as a kind of lexical reinforcement of his biographical method.

57. *The Antichrist,* 61; KSA 6, 251.

58. *Thus Spoke Zarathustra,* part 4, "The Awakening," 2; KSA 4, 388–89.

59. *Thus Spoke Zarathustra,* part 2, "On the Happy Isles," 2; KSA 4, 110. Compare also Notebooks, June–July 1883 10[9]; KSA 10, 368, and Summer 1883 13[3]; KSA 10, 451.

60. Notebooks, Summer 1876 17[16]; KSA 8, 299.

61. Nimrod, son of Cush, is in the Bible described as a mighty man and hunter; compare Genesis 10:8–9.

62. *Dionysus-Dithyrambs,* "Between Birds of Prey"; KSA 6, 390.

63. *Twilight of the Idols,* "Skirmishes of an Untimely Man," 36; KSA 6, 135.

64. Notebooks, Summer 1886–Fall 1887 5[71] 11; KSA 12, 215.

65. Not found. Empedocles killed himself by throwing himself into the volcano of Mount Etna.

66. *Ecce homo,* "Why I am a Fate," 1; KSA 6, 365.

67. Not found.

68. *The Birth of Tragedy,* 9; KSA 1, 69.

69. French: "The gods are an insult to God. One day God will be an insult to the divine."

Chapter 8: Mask

1. Goethe, *Wilhelm Meister's Travels,* first book, chapter 3, Wilhelm to Natalie, HA 8, 32.

2. Goethe, "Parabolisch."

3. *The Gay Science,* fifth book, 361; KSA 3, 608.

4. Deussen, *Erinnerungen,* 10.

5. *The Gay Science,* fifth book, 368; KSA 3, 617.

6. Notebooks, April–June 1885 34[121]; KSA 11, 461.

7. In Homeric Greek, this word specifically refers to aristocrats. Socrates uses it to designate the "best, finest" ones.

8. Notebooks, Winter 1880–81, 878; KSA 9, 399.

9. Not found.

10. Greek: "on himself."

11. *The Birth of Tragedy,* 3; KSA 1, 15.

12. Ibid.

13. Ibid., 8; KSA 1, 61.

14. Ibid.

15. Ibid.

16. In ancient Athens, the Dionysia was a religious festival in honor of Dionysus, featuring the performance of tragedies and comedies. It was second in importance only to the Panathenaia.

17. "Greek Musical Drama"; KSA 1, 521–22.

18. "The Dionysian World View," 3; KSA 1, 570.

19. KSA 1, 567.

20. Notebooks, 1871 9[42]; KSA 7, 290.

21. To Reinhard von Seydlitz, 4 January 1878; KSB 5, 300.

22. To Paul Deussen, February 1870; KSB 3, 100.

23. *Untimely Meditations* 4, "Richard Wagner in Bayreuth," 7; KSA 1, 467–68.

24. Notebooks, Beginning 1874–Spring 1874 32[61]; KSA 7, 775.

25. Notebooks, Beginning 1874–Spring 1874 32[28]; KSA 7, 763.

26. Notebooks, Beginning 1874–Spring 1874 32[66]; KSA 7, 777.

27. Notebooks, Beginning 1874–Spring 1874 32[15]; KSA 7, 758–59.

28. Notebooks, Beginning 1874–Spring 1874 32[20]; KSA 7, 761.

29. Notebooks, Beginning 1874–Spring 1874 32[24]; KSA 7, 762.

30. Notebooks, Beginning 1874–Spring 1874 32[16]; KSA 7, 760.

31. Notebooks, Beginning 1874–Spring 1874 32[10]; KSA 7, 756.

32. *Untimely Meditations* 4, "Richard Wagner in Bayreuth," 3; KSA 1, 441.

33. Notebooks, End 1880 7[53]; KSA 9, 328.

34. *On the Genealogy of Morals,* third treatise, "What do Ascetic Ideals Mean?" 19; KSA 5, 386–87.

35. French: "an agreed-upon fairy tale or fable."

36. *The Case of Wagner,* postscript, "Note"; KSA 6, 41.

37. To Paul Rée, Last Week of December 1882; KSB 6, 309.

38. To Lou von Salomé, Middle December 1882; KSB 6, 299.

39. Notebooks, Summer–Fall 1882 3[1] 258; KSA 10, 84.

40. Notebooks, Fall 1884 28[12]; KSA 11, 303.

41. Notebooks, November 1887–March 1888 11[327]; KSA 13, 139–40.

42. *Beyond Good and Evil,* part 2, "The Free Spirit," 34; KSA 5, 54.

43. *Beyond Good and Evil,* part 4, "Sayings and Interludes," 97; KSA 5, 90.

44. Not found.

45. Notebooks, April–June 1885 34[3]; KSA 11, 424.

46. This clause—"I don't dare name even greater names, but I am thinking of them"—is an insertion from another (similar) passage in *Nietzsche contra Wagner,* "The Psychologist Speaks," 2; KSA 6, 434.

47. *Beyond Good and Evil,* part 9, "What is Noble?" 269; KSA 5, 224.

48. Latin: "actor," derived from the word for Etruscan.

49. *The Case of Wagner,* 8–9; KSA 6, 29–32.

50. *The Case of Wagner,* 11; KSA 6, 37.

51. *The Case of Wagner,* postscript; KSA 6, 40–44.

52. *The Case of Wagner,* 12; KSA 6, 39.

53. Count Alessandro di Cagliostro (1743–95), often held to be an imposter and charlatan, thought to be the pseudonym of one Giuseppe Balsamo, a poor and petty criminal.

54. Notebooks, April–June 1885 34[98]; KSA 11, 453.

55. Notebooks, Summer–Fall 1884 26[377]; KSA 11, 250.

56. Notebooks, October 1888 23[2]; KSA 13, 600–601.

57. Notebooks, August–September 1885 41[2] 9; KSA 11, 677.

58. *Thus Spoke Zarathustra,* part 4, "The Magician," 1; KSA 4, 313.

59. *Thus Spoke Zarathustra,* part 4, "The Magician," 2; KSA 4, 317.

60. KSA 4, 318.

61. Ibid.

62. KSA 4, 319.

63. Ibid.

64. *Thus Spoke Zarathustra,* part 1, prologue; KSA 4, 23.

65. *Thus Spoke Zarathustra,* part 1, "The Way of the Creative One"; KSA 4, 82.

66. François-Joseph Talma (1763–1826). French actor and theatrical company manager

whose reforms in acting styles, stage costuming, and scenery made him a leading precursor of nineteenth-century French romanticism and realism. Talma wrote "Réflexions sur Lekain et l'art théâtral" as a preface to the memoirs of the French actor Henri Louis Cain, known as Lekain.

67. *The Case of Wagner,* 8; KSA 6, 31.

68. Notebooks, September 1870–January 1871 5[91]; KSA 7, 117.

69. Notebooks, September 1870–January 1871 5[107]; KSA 7, 122.

70. *Human, All Too Human* 2, "The Wanderer and His Shadow," 175; KSA 2, 627.

71. *Human, All Too Human* 2, "Assorted Thoughts and Sayings," 232; KSA 2, 485.

72. *Human, All Too Human* 2, "Assorted Thoughts and Sayings," 338; KSA 2, 517.

73. *Human, All Too Human* 2, "Assorted Thoughts and Sayings," 330; KSA 2, 515.

74. *The Gay Science,* fifth book, 356; KSA 3, 596.

75. Notebooks, May–July 1885 35[76]; KSA 11, 543.

76. Notebooks, July–August 1882 1[20]; KSA 10, 13.

77. *Beyond Good and Evil,* part 2, "The Free Spirit," 40; KSA 5, 57–58.

78. *Beyond Good and Evil,* part 9, "What is Noble?" 270; KSA 5, 225.

79. KSA 5, 225–26.

80. *Daybreak,* fourth book, 421; KSA 3, 257.

81. *Human, All Too Human* 1, 9, "Man Alone with Himself," 504; KSA 2, 321.

82. To Heinrich Köselitz, 31 December 1888; KSB 8, 567.

83. *Ecce homo,* "The Birth of Tragedy," 4; KSA 6, 314–15.

84. "The Untimely Ones," 3; KSA 6, 319–20.

85. *Human, All Too Human* 2, "Assorted Thoughts and Sayings," 227; KSA 2, 482–83.

86. *Human, All Too Human* 2, "The Wanderer and His Shadow," 118; KSA 2, 602–3.

87. KSA 2, 602–3

88. KSA 2, 603.

89. To Carl von Gersdorff, 1 April 1874; KSB 4, 214.

90. French: "debased."

91. Notebooks, Spring 1884 25[138]; KSA 11, 50.

92. Notebooks, Spring 1884 25[34]: KSA 11, 20. The French reads: "'My two sole and immense desires, to be famous and to be loved.'"

93. Laurence Sterne (1713–68), British novelist and clergyman, best known for *The Life and Opinions of Tristram Shandy* (1759).

94. *Human, All Too Human* 2, "Assorted Thoughts and Sayings," 113; KSA 2, 424.

95. KSA 2, 424–25.

96. Novalis, *Die Enzyklopädie,* VI. Abteilung: Die philologischen Wissenschaften. 2. Poetik (1), 1424.

97. Notebooks, 1875 6[7]; KSA 8, 99.

98. Italian: "ironic."

99. Notebooks, April–June 1885 34[66]; KSA 11, 440.

100. Notebooks, Spring 1888 14[116]; KSA 13, 293.

101. *Beyond Good and Evil,* part 9, "What is Noble?" 278; KSA 5, 229.

102. Notebooks, April–June 1885 34[180]; KSA 11, 481.

103. Notebooks, Fall 1885–Fall 1886 2[33]; KSA 12, 79.

104. Greek: "two-minded," "double-souled."

105. *Human, All Too Human* 2, preface, 5; KSA 2, 374.

106. Not found.

107. Notebooks, Summer–Fall 1884 26[248]; KSA 11, 215.

108. Notebooks, June–July 1885 36[32]; KSA 11, 563–64.

109. *The Gay Science,* second book, 77; KSA 3, 433.

Chapter 9: Weimar

1. Goethe, 1782.

2. Goethe, "Das Märchen," *Unterhaltungen deutscher Ausgewanderten* (1795).

3. To Erwin Rohde, 26 August 1872; KSB 4, 48.

4. Literally the "Roman border," or the defensive wall that marked the boundary of the Roman Empire.

5. Cluster of seven hills—hence the name—southeast of Bonn, Germany. Rome, too, is surrounded by seven hills.

6. *Mulus,* Latin for "mule, donkey," nineteenth-century student slang for a beginning or dumb student.

7. To Franziska and Elisabeth Nietzsche, 8 October 1864; KSB 2, 7.

8. Wilhelm Heinrich Wackenroder (1773–98), one of the founders of German romanticism, together with his friend Ludwig Tieck (1773–1853) "rediscovered" medieval Germany, exemplified by Nuremberg.

9. Notebooks, March 1875 3[70]; KSA 8, 34.

10. Goethe's epistolary novel, *The Sorrows of Young Werther,* published in 1774 when he was only twenty-five, established his European fame with its highly sentimental depiction of unrequited love and the suicide of its protagonist.

11. "Storm and Stress": literary movement in Germany from roughly the late 1760s to the early 1780s.

12. Johann Peter Eckermann (1792–1854), a writer and admirer of Goethe. They met in 1823 and Eckermann became a close confidant of Goethe. After Goethe's death in 1832, Eckermann published his *Conversations with Goethe in the last Years of his Life* (1836).

13. To Heinrich Köselitz, 19 April 1887, KSB 8, 60–61.

14. Goethe to Eckermann, 18 January 1827.

15. *Human, All Too Human* 2, "The Wanderer and His Shadow," 109; KSA 2, 599.

16. *Untimely Meditations* 1, "On the Use and Disadvantage of History for Life," 8; KSA 1, 310

17. Notebooks, Summer–Fall 1873 29[119]; KSA 7, 686.

18. Goethe to Eckermann, 10 March 1830; *Goethes Gespräche* 4, 236.

19. To Carl von Gersdorff, 7 November 1870; KSB 3, 155–56.

20. To Carl von Gersdorff, 21 June 1871; KSB 3, 204.

21. Goethe to Eckermann, 1 April 1827, near end.

22. Goethe to Eckermann 31 January 1827, fourth paragraph.

23. Antrittsrede (inaugural address), "Homer and Classical Philology."

24. *Ecce homo,* "The Case of Wagner," 4; KSA 6, 363–64.

25. Goethe, *Faust,* part 2, Klassische Walpurgisnacht, "Am obern Peneios wie zuvor," line 7864, HA 3, 239.

26. Goethe to Herder from Rome.

27. *Human, All Too Human* 1, 4, "From the Souls of Artists and Writers," 221; KSA 2, 180–84.

28. Notebooks, Spring 1888 15[68]; KSA 13, 451.

29. *Human, All Too Human* 1, 4, "From the Souls of Artists and Writers," 221; KSA 2, 182.

30. KSA 2, 181.

31. Ibid., 183.

32. Ibid., 183–84.

33. Ibid., 184.

34. Notebooks, Summer–Fall 1873 29[117]; 7, 685.

35. Notebooks, End 1880 7[195]; KSA 9, 357.

36. Beethoven, who had long admired Goethe, met the poet in the spa town of Teplitz in 1812. Beethoven set a number of Goethe's works to music, most notably his play, *Egmont.*

37. Notebooks, Spring 1884 25[175]; KSA 11, 60.

38. Notebooks, Summer–Fall 1884 26[395]; KSA 11, 255.

39. *Human, All Too Human* 2, 1, "Assorted Thoughts and Sayings," 170; KSA 2, 448–49.

40. *Human, All Too Human* 2, 2, "The Wanderer and His Shadow," 107; KSA 2, 599.

41. Ibid., 125; KSA 2, 607.

42. *Beyond Good and Evil,* part 8, "Peoples and Fatherlands," 244; KSA 5, 184–85.

43. Notebooks, June–July 1885 36[38]; KSA 11, 567.

44. Notebooks, May–June 1885 35[66]; KSA 11, 539.

45. *Ecce homo,* "Why I am so Clever," 6: KSA 6, 289.

46. *Ecce Homo,* "The Case of Wagner," 4; KSA 6, 363.

47. *Twilight of the Idols,* "Skirmishes of an Untimely Man," 48; KSA 6, 150–51.

48. *The Case of Wagner,* 3; KSA 6, 19.

49. Goethe to Eckermann 2 April 1829, *Gespräche* 4, 81.

50. Notebooks, Fall 1887 10[181]; KSA 12, 565.

51. *The Case of Wagner,* epilogue; KSA 6, 52.

52. *Twilight of the Idols,* "Skirmishes of an Untimely Man," 51; KSA 6, 153.

53. Notebooks, Spring–Summer 1875 5[171]; 89–90.

54. Notebooks, Winter 1869–70 to Spring 1870 3[62]; KSA 7, 77.

55. *Thus Spoke Zarathustra,* part 1, "Of Reading and Writing"; KSA 4, 49.

56. Goethe, "Die Geheimnisse," HA 2, 278.

57. Ibid.
58. *Twilight of the Idols,* "What I owe the Ancients," 4; KSA 6, 159.
59. Notebooks, Beginning 1874–Spring 1874 32[67]; KSA 7, 778.
60. To Erwin Rohde, 22 February 1884; KSB 6, 479.
61. *Ecce homo,* "The Case of Wagner," 2; KSA 6, 359.
62. Notebooks, Summer 1878 29[1]; KSA 8, 513.
63. Notebooks, Summer 1872–Beginning 1873 19[280]; KSA 7, 507.
64. *Human, All Too Human* 2, 2, "The Wanderer and His Shadow," 124; KSA 2, 606.
65. Ibid.
66. Notebooks, September 1870–January 1871 5[49]; KSA 7, 105.
67. Ibid.
68. *Untimely Meditations* 4, "Richard Wagner in Bayreuth," 4; KSA 1, 453.
69. *Twilight of the Idols,* "Skirmishes of an Untimely Man," 49; KSA 6, 151.
70. Notebooks, Fall 1887 9[178]; KSA 12, 443.
71. Notebooks, June–July 1885 37[12]; KSA 11, 588.
72. *The Gay Science,* fifth book, 370; KSA 3, 622.
73. Ibid.
74. *Twilight of the Idols,* "Skirmishes of an Untimely Man," 49; KSA 6, 152.
75. *Twilight of the Idols,* "What I owe the Ancients," 4; KSA 6, 159.
76. *Ecce homo,* "Why I am so Clever," 4; KSA 6, 286.
77. Notebooks, Summer–Fall 1884 26[31]; KSA 11, 156.
78. Source unclear.
79. To Erwin Rohde, 22 February 1884; KSB 6, 479.
80. *The Birth of Tragedy,* 20; KSA 1, 131.
81. *Untimely Meditations* 4, "Richard Wagner in Bayreuth," 11; KSA 1, 510.

Chapter 10: Napoleon

1. Goethe conversation with Eckermann, 2 March 1831; 11 March 1828, *Gespräche,* 4, 338, and 3, 499. In the last part of the quote, concerning "the most productive men," Goethe is actually referring to Byron, not to Napoleon.
2. "Philosophy in the Tragic Age of the Greeks," 3; KSA 1, 815.
3. Ibid.
4. Hölderlin, "Der Archipelagus," SA 2, 109.
5. Hölderlin, *Empedokles,* 1, 4.
6. Hölderlin was born in 1770 in the southwestern region of Germany called Schwaben, or Swabia.
7. Hölderlin, "Der Archipelagos," SA 2, 108.
8. Notebooks, Summer 1883 13[1]; KSA 10, 432.
9. Ibid., 430.
10. Thomas Carlyle (1795–1881), Scottish essayist and historian; his *On Heroes and Hero Worship and The Heroic in History* was published in 1841.
11. Not found.

12. *Thus Spoke Zarathustra,* part 3, "Vision and Puzzle"; KSA 4, 199.
13. "Philosophy in the Tragic Age of the Greeks," 3; KSA 1, 815.
14. Ibid.
15. Greek: "authoritative, leading, or governing phantom image."
16. Notebooks, May–July 1885 35[65]; KSA 11, 539.
17. Not found.
18. *Beyond Good and Evil,* part 5, "On the Natural History of Morality," 199; KSA 5, 120.
19. Notebooks, Fall 1887 9[44]; KSA 12, 357.
20. This is a reference to the comments Goethe made in the epigraph to this chapter.
21. Hölderlin, "Buonaparte," SA 1, 239.
22. *On the Genealogy of Morals,* first treatise, "Good and Evil," "Good and Bad," 16; KSA 5, 287–88.
23. *Twilight of the Idols,* "Skirmishes of an Untimely Man," 48; KSA 6, 150.
24. Notebooks, Spring 1884 25[175]; KSA 11, 60.
25. Notebooks, Spring 1884 25[131]; KSA 11, 48.
26. Notebooks, Summer–Fall 1884 26[142]; KSA 11, 187.
27. Source not found.
28. *Daybreak,* book 4, 245; KSA 3, 203.
29. *Human, All Too Human* 1, 4, "From the Souls of Artists and Writers," 164; KSA 2, 155–56.
30. *The Birth of Tragedy,* 9; KSA 1, 69. Nietzsche also uses this phrase in "Socrates and Greek Tragedy"; KSA 1, 617.
31. *The Birth of Tragedy,* 19; KSA 1, 128.
32. Goethe to Riemer, 1807.
33. The reference is to Heraclitus.
34. Notebooks, Fall 1887 10[31]; KSA 12, 471. Bertram misquotes the last word of the citation: instead of "Entschuldigung," Nietzsche writes "Einschränkung," or "limitation."
35. Hegel to Niethammer, 13 October 1806. Original slightly different.
36. *The Gay Science,* fifth book, 363; KSA 3, 609–10.
37. Notebooks, Fall 1881 14[15]; KSA 9, 626.
38. *Human, All Too Human* 2, 2, "The Wanderer and His Shadow," 125; KSA 2, 607.
39. *Twilight of the Idols,* "Skirmishes of an Untimely Man," 50; KSA 6, 152.
40. *Ecce homo,* "The Case of Wagner," 2; KSA 6, 360.
41. *Untimely Meditations* 4, "Richard Wagner in Bayreuth," 4; KSA 1, 447.
42. Ibid.
43. The reference is to Diogenes, Greek philosopher (412–323 B.C.E.).
44. Ludwig II, King of Bavaria (1845–86), known for his eccentricity and profligacy, was also a strong supporter of Richard Wagner.
45. Goethe to Cotta, 1808.

46. *Beyond Good and Evil,* part 8, "Peoples and Fatherlands," 244; KSA 5, 185.

47. Ibid., part 6, "We Scholars."

48. *Twilight of the Idols,* "Skirmishes of an Untimely Man," 49; KSA 6, 151–52.

49. Notebooks, Summer–Fall 1884 26[304].

50. *Beyond Good and Evil,* part 7, "Our Virtues," 238; KSA 5, 175.

51. *Human, All Too Human* 1, 4, "Out of the Souls of Artists and Writers," 221; KSA 2, 182.

52. *Ecce homo,* "Why I am so Clever," 3; KSA 6, 285.

53. *Human, All Too Human* 1, 4, "Out of the Souls of Artists and Writers," 221; KSA 2, 182.

54. Not found.

55. Not found.

56. *On the Genealogy of Morals,* first treatise, "Good and Evil," "Good and Bad," 16; KSA 5, 288.

57. Not found.

58. "I closed again the anarchic abyss and organized the chaos. I ennobled the peoples."

59. Notebooks, Fall 1883 16[80]; KSA 10, 526.

60. *Nietzsche contra Wagner,* epilogue, 1; KSA 6, 436.

61. Not found.

62. Not found.

Chapter 11: Jest, Cunning, and Vengeance

1. Johannes Eckhart, also called Meister (Master) Eckhart von Hochheim (ca. 1260–1328), Dominican theologian and writer, who was the greatest German speculative mystic.

2. Heinrich Seuse or Suso (ca. 1295–1366), a pupil of Meister Eckhart, credited with the first autobiography in German.

3. Johann Tauler (1300–61), next to Meister Eckehart and Suso, was one of the chief Rhineland mystics. Tauler's sermons were valued highly by Martin Luther.

4. Hans Sachs (1494–1576), poet, "Meistersinger," and dramatist of the German Renaissance.

5. The *Knittelvers* (earlier also called "Knüttelvers") is a metric poetic form in which lines with four beats are rhymed in couplets. The *Knittelvers* was popular in German literature of the fifteenth and sixteenth centuries and is particularly associated with Hans Sachs.

6. Eighteenth-century opera in the German language, containing spoken dialogue and usually comic in tone. Its success was partly caused by a reaction by composers and audiences against the artificial conventions of the then-dominant Italian opera. The form reached its apogee in Mozart's *Die Entführung aus dem Serail* (1782; The Abduction from the Seraglio) and *Die Zauberflöte* (1791; The Magic Flute). From there the *Singspiel* ultimately gave rise both to German romantic opera of the nineteenth century and to popular Viennese operetta.

7. Goethe, "Zahme Xenien," VII. Not in HA.

8. Goethe, "Sprichwörtlich," Gedichte (Ausgabe letzter Hand. 1827) Zuerst im Druck veröffentlicht in Goethes Werke. Vollständige Ausgabe letzter Hand, Bd. 1–4: Gedichte, Stuttgart und Tübingen (Cotta) 1827.

9. *The Gay Science,* "Jest, Cunning and Vengeance," 35; KSA 3, 361.

10. *The Gay Science,* "Jest, Cunning and Vengeance," 9; KSA 3, 355.

11. Goethe, "Zahme Xenien," V; fourth from end.

12. *The Gay Science,* "Jest, Cunning and Vengeance," 1; KSA 3, 353.

13. *The Gay Science,* "Jest, Cunning and Vengeance," 4; KSA 3, 354.

14. *The Gay Science,* "Jest, Cunning and Vengeance," 62; KSA 3, 367.

15. Notebooks, Spring 1882 19[7]; KSA 9, 676.

16. *The Gay Science,* "Jest, Cunning and Vengeance," 26; KSA 3, 358.

17. Notebooks, Fall 1884 28[51]; KSA 11, 320.

18. Goethe, "Zahme Xenien," IX.

19. Notebooks, July–August 1882 1[107]; KSA 10, 36.

20. Notebooks, Fall 1884 28[42]; KSA 11, 316.

21. Notebooks, Fall 1884 28[43]; KSA 11, 317.

22. *The Gay Science,* "Jest, Cunning and Vengeance," 63; KSA 3, 367.

23. Nietzsche to August Bungert in Genoa, 14 March 1883 (written as a dedication in a copy of *Daybreak);* KSB 8, 597.

24. *The Gay Science,* "Songs of Prince Outlaw"; KSA 3, 649.

25. Notebooks, Fall 1884 28[57]; KSA 11, 322.

26. Notebooks, Summer–Fall 1882 3[2]; KSA 10, 107.

27. *The Gay Science,* "Jest, Cunning and Vengeance," 62; KSA 3, 367.

28. Goethe, *Westöstlicher Divan,* "Selige Sehnsucht," HA 2, 18.

29. Beckmesser is the name of the town clerk in Wagner's opera, *Die Meistersinger von Nürnberg.*

30. *The Gay Science,* "Songs of Prince Outlaw"; KSA 3, 639.

31. *The Gay Science,* "Jest, Cunning and Vengeance," 3; KSA 3, 353.

32. *The Gay Science,* "Jest, Cunning and Vengeance," 27; KSA 3, 359.

33. *The Gay Science,* "Jest, Cunning and Vengeance," 32; KSA 3, 360.

34. *The Gay Science,* "Jest, Cunning and Vengeance," 46; KSA 3, 363.

35. Notebooks, Fall 1883 17[58]; KSA 10, 556.

36. *The Gay Science,* "Jest, Cunning and Vengeance," 47; KSA 3, 363.

37. *The Gay Science,* "Jest, Cunning and Vengeance," 23; KSA 3, 357.

38. *The Gay Science,* "Jest, Cunning and Vengeance," 63; KSA 3, 367.

39. Notebooks, July–August 1882 1[105]; KSA 10, 35.

40. Nietzsche to August Bungert in Genoa, 14 March 1883 (written as a dedication in a copy of *Daybreak*); KSB 8, 597.

41. *The Gay Science,* "Songs of Prince Outlaw"; KSA 3, 649.

42. Notebooks, Fall 1884 28[66]; KSA 11, 331.

43. *The Gay Science,* "Jest, Cunning and Vengeance," 50; KSA 3, 364.

44. Notebooks, Spring 1882 19[9]; KSA 9, 677.
45. *The Gay Science,* "Jest, Cunning and Vengeance," 29; KSA 3, 359.
46. *The Gay Science,* "Jest, Cunning and Vengeance," 53; KSA 3, 365.
47. *The Gay Science,* "Jest, Cunning and Vengeance," 36; KSA 3, 361.
48. *Beyond Good and Evil,* part 7, "Our Virtues," 228; KSA 5, 165.
49. Notebooks, Fall 1884 28[52]; KSA 11, 320.
50. Notebooks, Fall 1884 28[49]; KSA 11, 319.
51. Notebooks, Fall 1884 28[45]; KSA 11, 317.
52. *The Gay Science,* "Jest, Cunning and Vengeance," 34; KSA 3, 360–61.
53. *The Gay Science,* "Songs of Prince Outlaw;" KSA 3, 648.
54. Notebooks, Spring 1882 19[13]; KSA 9, 679.
55. *The Birth of Tragedy,* "Attempt at a Self-Critique," 3; KSA 1, 15.
56. To Franziska and Elisabeth Nietzsche, 6 September 1863; KSB 1, 253.
57. In ancient Greek mythology, the Centaurs were a race that lived in the mountains of Thessaly and had bodies of horses and half-bestial natures. It was this duality that Nietzsche presumably meant.
58. Notebooks, Fall 1881 13[22]; KSA 9, 622.
59. Notebooks, Summer 1888 20[126]; KSA 13, 570.
60. Notebooks, Summer 1888 20[25]; KSA 13, 553.
61. Notebooks, Summer 1888 20[89]; KSA 13, 565.
62. Notebooks, June–July 1883 10[39]; KSA 10, 375.
63. Notebooks, Fall 1884 28[22]; KSA 11, 307. Bertram writes at the end of the first line "Wut"—"rage"—whereas Colli and Montinari read "Muth"—"courage."
64. Notebooks, Summer 1888 20[13]; KSA 13, 551.
65. Notebooks, Summer 1888 20[84]; KSA 13, 564.
66. Notebooks, Summer 1888 20[145]; KSA 13, 573.
67. Notebooks, Fall 1884 28[41]; KSA 11, 316.
68. Notebooks, Summer 1888 20[109]; KSA 13, 567.
69. Notebooks, Summer 1888 20[138]; KSA 13, 572. The third line cited by Bertram is not in the later edition.
70. Notebooks, Summer 1888 20[56]; KSA 13, 559.
71. Notebooks, Summer 1888 20[73]; KSA 13, 562.
72. Notebooks, Summer 1888 20[42]; KSA 13, 556.
73. Notebooks, Summer 1888 20[102]; KSA 13, 567.
74. Notebooks, Summer–Fall 1883 15[36]; KSA 10, 488.
75. Notebooks, Summer 1888 20[62]; KSA 13, 560.
76. Goethe, *Westöstlicher Divan,* "Moganni Nameh, Buch des Sängers," Hegire, HA 2, 8.
77. Notebooks, Fall 1884 28[34]; KSA 11, 314.
78. Notebooks, Summer 1888 20[1]; KSA 13, 549.
79. Notebooks, Fall 1884 28[9]; KSA 11, 301.
80. *Dionysus-Dithyrambs,* "The Sun Sets," 3; KSA 6, 396–97.

Chapter 12: Anecdote

1. Not found.

2. "Philosophy in the Tragic Age of the Greeks"; KSA 1, 803.

3. Theodor Fontane (1819–98), journalist and novelist famed for his ironic and urbane depictions of Prussian life and manners.

4. Novalis was known for his "fragments," or short, aphoristic, often cryptic pronouncements.

5. Grimm's *Wörterbuch* (German Dictionary) defines the "Streckvers" as a lyrical form invented by, and confined to, the poet Jean Paul.

6. Notebooks, Winter 1884–85 31[38]; KSA 11, 375.

7. *The Case of Wagner,* second postscript; KSA 6, 48.

8. To Sophie Ritschl, 2 July 1868; KSB 2, 299.

9. *The Case of Wagner,* 7; KSA 6, 28–29.

10. *Human, All Too Human* 2, "The Wanderer and His Shadow," 160; KSA 2, 619.

11. Not found.

12. See note 14.

13. *The Case of Wagner,* 7; KSA 6, 27.

14. Paul Bourget, *Essais de psychologie contemporaine,* "Théorie de la décadence."

15. *The Case of Wagner,* 7; KSA 6, 27.

16. Not found.

17. Not found.

18. *Ecce homo,* "Thus Spoke Zarathustra," 3; KSA 6, 340.

19. *The Case of Wagner,* 7; KSA 6, 27.

20. *Human, All Too Human* 1, 4, "From the Souls of Artists and Writers," 155; KSA 2, 146.

21. *Human, All Too Human* 2, 2, "The Wanderer and His Shadow," 152; KSA 2, 615–16.

22. *Human, All Too Human* 2, 2, "The Wanderer and His Shadow," 155; KSA 2, 617.

23. To Heinrich Köselitz, 2 April 1883; KSB 6, 353.

24. Notebooks, Fall 1884 28[59]; KSA 11, 324. The poem is actually titled "In the German November."

25. *Human, All Too Human* 2, 2, "The Wanderer and His Shadow," 152; KSA 2, 616.

26. "Philosophy in the Tragic Age of the Greeks"; KSA 1, 803.

27. *Ecce homo,* "Why I am so Wise," 2; KSA 6, 266.

28. Notebooks, Fall 1884 28[59]; KSA 11, 324.

29. *Twilight of the Idols,* "Skirmishes of an Untimely Man," 51; KSA 6, 153.

30. Notebooks, Summer–Fall 1882 3[1] 274; KSA 10, 86.

31. The German "Verweile doch!" is an allusion to Goethe's *Faust.* It refers to the wager Faust makes with Mephistopheles: if Faust ever utters this phrase—"Tarry awile, Thou art so fair!"—indicating that he has found satisfaction in a particular moment, situation, or experience, he will surrender his soul to the devil. *Faust,* line 1700, HA 3, 57.

32. *Thus Spoke Zarathustra,* part 3, "The Seven Seals," 1; KSA 4, 287.

33. Notebooks, End 1886–Spring 1887 7[38]; KSA 12, 307–8.

Chapter 13: Indian Summer

1. Hölderlin, "Mein Eigentum," SA 1, 303.

2. Conrad Ferdinand Meyer, "Fülle," *Werke,* ed. Heinz Schöffler (Berlin: Tempel-Verlag, 1967), vol. 1, p. 19.

3. Eduard Mörike (1804–75), German poet.

4. *Ecce homo,* "Why I am so Clever," 4; KSA 6, 286.

5. Reference to Adalbert Stifter's first work, *Studien* (1844).

6. Georg Christoph Lichtenberg (1742–99), physicist and philosopher, particularly known as an aphorist.

7. Johann Heinrich Jung, known as Jung-Stilling (1740–1817), ophthalmologist, economist, and writer, famous for his autobiography, which was a predecessor to the German "educational novel" or *Bildungsroman.*

8. The reference is to the series of novellas called *Die Leute von Seldwyla* ("The People of Seldwyla"). Seldwyla is a fictional Swiss town invented by the writer and poet Gottfried Keller (1819–90).

9. To this day, Stifter's *Nachsommer* has the unenviable (and undeserved) reputation of being one of the most boring works in German literature. It is true, however, that the work is very long (around seven hundred pages in most editions) and that it consists mainly of detailed descriptions of objects.

10. To Heinrich Köselitz, 11 December 1879; KSB 5, 469.

11. To Heinrich Köselitz, 19 April 1887; KSB 8, 61.

12. Bertram is referring to Stefan George, *Das Jahr der Seele* (1897), in particular the poems in the first section.

13. To Franziska and Elisabeth Nietzsche, 6 September 1863; KSB 1, 253.

14. To Erwin Rohde, 3 September 1869; KSB 3, 51.

15. KSB 3, 53.

16. To Erwin Rohde, 7 October, 1869; KSB 3, 61–62. At the end of the passage, Nietzsche is playing on the Greek etymology of "schola," which means "leisure, idleness devoted to learning."

17. *Ecce homo,* "Twilight of the Idols," 3; KSA 6, 356.

18. Ibid., 263.

19. To Franz Overbeck, 18 October 1888; KSB 8, 452–53.

20. Not found.

21. *Ecce homo,* "Twilight of the Idols," 3; KSA 6, 356.

22. Rolandseck is near Remagen on the Rhine.

23. "On the Future of our Educational Institutions," first lecture; KSA 1, 654.

24. *Thus Spoke Zarathustra,* part 2, "On the Happy Isles"; KSA 4, 109.

25. *Untimely Meditations* 4, "Richard Wagner in Bayreuth," 8; KSA 1, 484.

26. To Carl von Gersdorff, 18 November 1871; KSB 3, 244.

27. *Dionysus-Dithyrambs,* "The Sun Sets"; KSA 6, 395–97.

28. Jean Paul, *Hesperus,* 38. Hundposttag, "Die erhabene Vormitternacht," in second part of second book.

29. Ibid.

30. To Erwin Rohde, 26 August 1872; KSB 4, 48.

31. On this episode in Nietzche's life, see Robin Small, *Nietzsche and Rée: A Star Friendship* (Oxford: Oxford University Press, 2005).

32. Asperhof is the name of the estate owned by Freiherr von Risach in Stifter's novel. The Asperhof is also called the "Rosenhaus" by the novel's protagonist, Heinrich, because its facade is covered with roses.

33. Gottfried Keller's *Der grüne Heinrich* (1854; The Green Henry) is one of the canonical *Bildungsromane,* a genre that begins with Christoph Martin Wieland's *Agathon* (1776–77), includes Goethe's *Wilhelm Meister's Apprenticeship* (1795), Stifter's own novel, and arguably ends with Thomas Mann's *Der Zauberberg* (1924). Compare Martin Swales, *The German Bildungsroman from Wieland to Hesse* (Princeton, N.J.: Princeton University Press, 1978) and Todd Kontje, *The German Bildungsroman: History of a National Genre* (Columbia, S.C.: Camden House, 1993).

34. *Human, All Too Human* 2, 1, "Assorted Thoughts and Sayings," 99; KSA 2, 419–20.

35. Ibid., 420.

36. Gustav Heckenast was Stifter's publisher and supporter.

37. Not found.

38. Stifter, *Abdias* (1842).

39. According to legend, Ahasverus did not allow Jesus to rest at his door as he carried the cross to Golgotha. It is Ahasverus who becomes known as the "Wandering Jew."

40. "Hagestolz" means "bachelor" in German and is also the title of a story by Stifter (1845).

41. To Erwin Rohde, 18 July 1876; KSB 5, 177.

42. To Erwin Rohde, 22 February 1884; KSB 6, 480.

43. Stifter was considered an extremely progressive liberal and was a proponent of the revolutionary movement in the 1840s. He was thus disappointed by the failure to establish a parliamentary democracy in 1848.

44. Letter by Stifter from around 1848.

45. "Unwiederbringlich": this word has a particular resonance in German, especially in the nineteenth century. It is also the title of a novel by Thedor Fontane (1891).

46. Goethe to Zelter, 1825.

47. Not found.

48. *The Gay Science,* first book, 45; KSA 3, 411.

49. Genesis 1:31.

50. *Ecce homo;* KSA 6, 263.

51. To Emily Fynn, 11 August 1888; KSB 8, 387.

52. *The Case of Wagner,* 10; KSA 6, 37.

53. Notebooks, Spring–Summer 1888 16[66]; KSA 13, 507.

54. Hölderlin, "An die jungen Dichter," SA 1, 253.

55. The "Föhn" is a warm dry wind blowing down the side of a mountain, particularly in the Alps.

56. The "mistral" is a strong cold dry northerly wind in the Mediterranean provinces of France.

57. *Ecce homo;* KSA 6, 263.

58. *Ecce homo,* "Twilight of the Idols," 3; KSA 6, 356.

59. *Ecce homo,* "Why I am so Clever," 7; KSA 6, 290.

Chapter 14: Claude Lorrain

1. Not found.

2. Hölderlin, *Hyperion oder der Eremit aus Griechenland* (Fragmente).

3. Goethe to Eckermann, 9 October 1828, *Gespräche* 4, 30.

4. Not found.

5. Notebooks, Summer–Fall 1884 26[395]; KSA 11, 255.

6. *Ecce homo,* "Twilight of the Idols," 2; KSA 6, 355.

7. Notebooks, Spring 1884 25[162]; KSA 11, 56.

8. Notebooks, April–June 1885 34[97]; KSA 11, 453.

9. Goethe, "Römische Elegien," 15, HA 1, 167.

10. Notebooks, Fall 1881 12[181]; KSA 9, 607.

11. To Georg Brandes, 27 March 1888; KSB 8, 278–79.

12. *The Gay Science,* "Songs of Prince Outlaw," "In the South"; KSA 3, 641.

13. To Carl Fuchs, 14 April 1888; KSB 8, 294.

14. Notebooks, End 1880 7[236]; KSA 9, 366.

15. *Human, All Too Human* 2, 2, "The Wanderer and His Shadow," 338; KSA 2, 299.

16. Hebbel, *Tagebücher* (1837).

17. Goethe to Eckermann, 10 April 1829.

18. Not found.

19. Christoph Willibald Gluck (1714–87), German composer. His opera, *Armida,* was first performed in 1777.

20. To Franz Overbeck, 12 November 1887; KSB 8, 197.

21. Arthur Schopenhauer, *Die Welt als Wille und Vorstellung* (Zurich: 1977), 1, 331.

22. The adjective Bertram uses here—"lothringisch"—is derived from the German word "Lothringen," for the region we refer to by the French name, Lorraine.

23. Notebooks, July–August 1879 43[3]; KSA 8, 610.

24. Ibid.

25. *Ecce homo,* "Twilight of the Idols," 3; KSA 6, 356.

26. To Heinrich Köselitz, 20 October 1888; KSB 8, 461.

27. Bertram is being unusually autobiographical here. He held a deep aversion to Italy and Italians, which he expressed in quite drastic language. See Jappe, pp. 148–50.

28. To Malwida von Meysenbug, 7 November 1872; KSB 4, 80.

29. To Malwida von Meysenbug, 5 April 1873; KSB 4, 141.
30. Notebooks, End 1880 7[236]; KSA 9, 366.
31. To Malwida von Meysenbug, 26 March 1885; KSB 7, 31.
32. To Heinrich Köselitz, 14 February 1885; KSB 7, 10.
33. KSB 7, 11.
34. Not found.
35. *Ecce homo,* "Thus Spoke Zarathustra," 4; KSA 6, 340.
36. Notebooks, Spring 1884 25[162]; KSA 11, 56.
37. *Beyond Good and Evil,* part 8, "Peoples and Fatherlands," 254; KSA 5, 199–200.
38. Not found.
39. *The Case of Wagner,* 3; KSA 6, 16.
40. Not found.
41. Notebooks, Fall 1884 28[10]; KSA 11, 303.
42. *Beyond Good and Evil,* part 8, "Peoples and Fatherlands," 255; KSA 5, 200–201.
43. Goethe uses the word "divan" (a word derived from the Persian word for "account book") in the meaning of a collection of poems, particularly by a single author.
44. Goethe, *Westöstlicher Divan,* Hegire, HA 2, 7.
45. Notebooks, April–June 1885 34[149]; KSA 11, 471.
46. *The Gay Science,* fifth book, 350; KSA 3, 586.
47. "Inaugural Address."
48. Notebooks, August–September 1885 41[7]; KSA 11, 682.
49. Town and oasis in northeastern Algeria, on the northern edge of the Sahara.
50. To Heinrich Köselitz, 31 October 1886; KSB 7, 274–75.
51. To Reinhart von Seydlitz, 12 February 1888; KSB 8, 249.
52. To Heinrich Köselitz, 10 October 1886; KSB 7, 261.
53. To Franz Overbeck, 20 May 1883; KSB 6, 379.
54. In Norse mythology, Norn is a goddess presiding over personal destiny: a fate.
55. *Ecce homo,* "Twilight of the Idols," 3; KSA 6, 356.

Chapter 15: Venice

1. Goethe, *Italienische Reise,* HA 11, 85–86.
2. To Franz Overbeck, Second Half November 1880; KSB 6, 49.
3. To Jacob Burckhardt, 22 September 1886; KSB 7, 254.
4. To Jacob Burckhardt, 6 January 1889; KSB 8, 579.
5. To Marie Baumgartner, 30 August 1877; KSB 5, 282.
6. To Heinrich Köselitz, 7 April 1888; KSB 8, 285.
7. *The Gay Science,* fourth book, 291; KSA 3, 531–32.
8. Andrea Doria (1466–1560), Genoese statesman, *condottiere* (mercenary commander), and admiral who was the foremost naval leader of his time.
9. To Elisabeth Nietzsche, *Gesammelte Briefe,* 5/2, 469. Not included in KSB.
10. *Ecce homo,* "Twilight of the Idols," 3; KSA 6, 356.
11. To Heinrich Köselitz, 20 April 1888; KSB 8, 300.

12. To Heinrich Köselitz, 7 April 1888; KSB 8, 285.
13. Ibid.
14. The Po is the longest river in Italy. Flowing down from the Cottian Alps in the west, it passes through Turin and then turns east, finally emptying into the Adriatic Sea.
15. To Franz Overbeck, 24 March 1887; KSB 8, 47.
16. To Carl von Gersdorff, 9 April 1885; KSB 7, 38.
17. To Heinrich Köselitz, 5 March 1884; KSB 6, 484.
18. August von Platen (1796–1835), German poet who spent much of his life in Italy, especially Venice; he died in Syracuse.
19. Not found.
20. Not found.
21. Not found.
22. To Franz Overbeck, 30 April 1884, KSB 6, 498.
23. Not found.
24. Notebooks, Spring 1880 2[29]; KSA 9, 38.
25. *Ecce homo,* "Why I am so Clever," 7; KSA 6, 291.
26. *Human, All Too Human* 1, preface, 1; KSA 2, 14.
27. *Thus Spoke Zarathustra,* part 3; "The Convalescent," 2; KSA 4, 272.
28. *Ecce homo,* "The Case of Wagner," 1; KSA 6, 357.
29. To Carl Fuchs, 14 April 1888; KSB 8, 294.
30. *Untimely Meditations* 4, "Richard Wagner in Bayreuth," 8; KSA 1, 479.
31. Ibid.
32. Lord Byron lived in Venice from 1816 to 1820.
33. The first volume of Schopenhauer's *The World as Will and Representation* came out in 1818/19; the second volume did not appear until 1844.
34. *Ecce homo,* "Why I am so Clever," 4; KSA 6, 286.
35. Platen's *Sonette aus Venedig* appeared in 1825.
36. Conrad Ferdinand Meyer, "Auf dem Canal Grande," *Werke* 1, 100–101.
37. August von Platen, "Tristan," (1825).
38. Georg Simmel, "Venedig" (1907).
39. Ibid.
40. Not found.
41. *Untimely Meditations* 4, "Richard Wagner in Bayreuth," 8; KSA 1, 479.
42. *Ecce homo,* "Why I am so Clever," 6; KSA 6, 289.
43. *Ecce homo,* "Why I am so Clever," 7; KSA 6, 291.
44. *Ecce homo,* "The Case of Wagner," 1; KSA 6, 357.
45. To Heinrich Köselitz, 2 July 1885; KSB 7, 61.
46. Goethe, *Italienische Reise,* Venice, "Gesang der Schiffer," 6 October 1786; HA 11, 85.
47. Richard Wagner to Mathilde Wesendonk.
48. Goethe, *Italienische Reise.* The Italian reads: "It is strange how that song reverberates."

49. *The Birth of Tragedy,* "Attempt at a Self-Critique," 3; KSA 1, 15.
50. Notebooks, Summer 1888 20[1]; KSA 13, 549.
51. *Untimely Meditations* 4, "Richard Wagner in Bayreuth," 8; KSA 1, 479.
52. *Thus Spoke Zarathustra,* part 3, "The Convalescent," 2; KSA 4, 272.
53. *Ecce homo,* "Why I am so Clever," 7; KSA 6, 291.

Chapter 16: Portofino

1. Novalis, *Die Lehrlinge zu Sais.*
2. Not found.
3. *Ecce homo,* "Twilight of the Idols," 2; KSA 6, 355.
4. *Human, All Too Human* 2, 2, "The Wanderer and His Shadow," 338; KSA 2, 699.
5. Ibid.
6. To Carl Fuchs, 14 April 1888; KSB 8, 294
7. *Ecce homo,* "Thus Spoke Zarathustra," 1; KSA 6, 335.
8. Ibid., 337.
9. Ibid.
10. Bertram appears to be citing Hebbel, *Tagebücher* (1837); compare chapter 15, "Claude Lorrain."
11. Notebooks, Fall 1887 10[94]; KSA 12, 510.
12. *Thus Spoke Zarathustra,* part 3, "The Seven Seals," 1; KSA 4, 287.
13. *Thus Spoke Zarathustra,* part 3, "The Three Evils," 1; KSA 4, 235.
14. *The Gay Science,* first book, 54; KSA 3, 416–17.
15. Notebooks, Winter 1884–85 31[43]; KSA 11, 379.
16. *Ecce homo,* "Why I am so Wise," 1; KSA 6, 264.
17. *Human, All Too Human* 1, 4, "From the Souls of Artists and Writers," 223; KSA 2, 186.
18. Notebooks, Summer 1878 30[139]; KSA 8, 547.
19. *Nietzsche contra Wagner,* "A Music without a Future"; KSA 6, 423–24.
20. *The Gay Science,* fourth book, 281; KSA 3, 525.
21. Not found.
22. *Twilight of the Idols,* "Skirmishes of an Untimely Man," 51; KSA 6, 153.
23. *Thus Spoke Zarathustra,* part 1, "The Flies of the Marketplace"; KSA 4, 65.
24. *Thus Spoke Zarathustra,* part 1, "Reading and Writing"; KSA 4, 49.
25. *Beyond Good and Evil,* part 4, "Sayings and Interludes," 121; KSA 5, 94.
26. *Beyond Good and Evil,* part 4, 63; KSA 5, 85.
27. Notebooks, Spring–Summer 1878 27[24]; KSA 8, 491.
28. *The Gay Science,* fifth book, 382; KSA 3, 636.
29. *Ecce homo,* "Thus Spoke Zarathustra," 6; KSA 6, 343.
30. *Ecce homo,* "Why I write such Good Books," 4; KSA 6, 305.
31. KSA 6, 263.
32. *Thus Spoke Zarathustra,* part 3, "The Old and New Tablets," 20; KSA 4, 262.
33. *Thus Spoke Zarathustra,* part 3, "The Seven Seals"; KSA 4, 287.

34. *Daybreak,* fifth book, 575; KSA 3, 331.

35. Ibid.

Chapter 17: Prophecy

1. Hölderlin, "Der Rhein," SA 2, 152–53.

2. Novalis, *Vermischte Bemerkungen/Blütenstaub,* Nr. 21.

3. Reference is to Goethe's *Wilhelm Meister's Wanderjahre,* book 2, chapter 2.

4. Annette von Droste-Hülshoff (1797–1848), German poet and writer.

5. von Droste-Hülshoff, "Vorgeschichte."

6. Notebooks, Fall 1885–Spring 1886 1[177]; KSA 12, 50.

7. Not found.

8. Gaius Mucius Scaevola: legendary Roman hero who is said to have saved Rome (ca. 509 B.C.E.) from conquest by the Etruscan king Lars.

9. Erwin Rohde to Franz Overbeck, 1886.

10. Elisabeth Förster-Nietzsche, *Der junge Nietzsche,* 48.

11. Not found.

12. Elisabeth Förster-Nietzsche, *Der junge Nietzsche,* 48.

13. To Erwin Rohde, 3 September 1869; KSB 3, 51.

14. Not found.

15. "The Unknown God," 1864.

16. *Thus Spoke Zarathustra,* part 4, "The Magician," 1; KSA 4, 314–17.

17. To Franziska and Elisabeth Nietzsche, End February 1865; KSB 2, 46.

18. To the Franconia Society, 20 October 1865; KSB 2, 88–89.

19. Not found.

20. Friedrich Wilhelm Ritschl (1806–76). German classical scholar remembered for his work on Plautus and as the founder of the Bonn school of classical scholarship.

Ritschl resigned from Bonn (1865) after an academic quarrel with his colleague Otto Jahn and became professor at the University of Leipzig, where he remained until his death. *Encyclopedia Britannica.*

21. Socrates often referred to a *daemonion* or a mystical inner voice that always guided his actions.

22. Compare the long letter to Erwin Rohde, 9 November 1868; KSB 2, 335–42.

23. Hebbel, *Tagebücher* (as twenty-one-year-old).

24. To Carl von Gersdorff, 4 August 1869; KSB 3, 35–36.

25. To Paul Deussen, February 1870; KSB 3, 98.

26. To Erwin Rohde, 3 September 1869; KSB 3, 52.

27. To Erwin Rohde, 9 December 1868; KSB 2, 353.

28. *The Birth of Tragedy,* "Attempt at a Self-Criticism," 2; KSA 1, 14.

29. *The Birth of Tragedy,* "Attempt at a Self-Criticism," 13.

30. Ibid., 6; KSA 1, 19–20.

31. The word Nietzsche uses here, rendered by "censure," is "Fehm," which is rare in modern German (also spelled "Feme") and refers to a medieval special tribunal that passed

judgment on particularly serious crimes; from the twelfth to the sixteenth century it was a secret assembly that decided on the assassination of political opponents and traitors in its own ranks.

32. Jean Paul, *Levana oder Erziehlehre* (first ed. 1807, second ed. 1813), chapter 3 "Über den Geist der Zeit," paragraph 36.

33. *The Gay Science,* "Songs of Prince Outlaw"; KSA 3, 641.

34. Deussen, *Erinnerungen,* 85.

35. To Carl von Gersdorff, 1 April 1874; KSB 4, 214.

36. To Carl von Gersdorff, 18 January 1876; KSB 5, 133.

37. To Erwin Rohde, 7 October 1874; KSB 4, 262.

38. To Reinhart von Seydlitz, End February 1877; KSB 5, 224.

39. To Malwida von Meysenbug, 5 April 1873; KSB 4, 142.

40. *Daybreak,* first book, 14; KSA 3, 28.

41. To Erwin Rohde, 19 March 1871; KSB 3, 190.

42. Ibid.

43. To Erwin Rohde, 28 January 1872; KSB 3, 279.

44. *Untimely Meditations* 3, "Schopenhauer as Educator," 1; KSA 1, 340.

45. *Ecce homo,* "Why I am so Wise," 1; KSA 6, 264.

46. Notebooks, August–September 1885 40[65]; KSA 11, 664.

47. *The Gay Science,* fourth book, 307; KSA 3, 545.

48. To Marie Baumgartner, 2 August 1875; KSB 5, 95.

49. To Marie Baumgartner, 30 August 1877; KSB 5, 282.

50. *Human, All Too Human* 2, preface, 4; KSA 2, 373.

51. To Carl Fuchs, 14 December 1887; KSB 8, 210.

52. To Reinhard von Seydlitz, 18 November 1878; KSB 5, 364.

53. To Erwin Rohde, 24 March 1881; KSB 6, 75.

54. To Elisabeth Nietzsche, Middle July 1881; KSB 6, 108.

55. From a forged letter by Elisabeth Förster-Nietzsche, 29 November 1881; GB 5/2, 469. Not in KSB.

56. Not found.

57. Nietzsche writes: "Meine Stunde ist da." The biblical passage Bertram refers to in the standard Lutheran translation is "Meine Zeit ist nahe," (Matthew 26:18), which in the King James Version is "My time is at hand."

58. *Thus Spoke Zarathustra,* part 4, "The Sign"; KSA 4, 408.

59. *Ecce homo,* "Thus Spoke Zarathustra," 3; KSA 6, 339.

60. KSA 6, 339–40.

61. Johann Sebastian Bach, Mass in B Minor (1735).

62. Ludwig van Beethoven, *Missa Solemnis* (1822).

63. Stefan George, "Entrückung," *Der Siebente Ring* (1907).

64. To Karl Hillebrand, 24 May 1883; KSB 6, 380.

65. To Carl von Gersdorff, End June 1883; KSB 6, 386.

66. To Malwida von Meysenbug, First Week of June 1884; KSB 6, 509–10.

67. To Heinrich Köselitz, 20 September 1884; KSB 6, 535.

68. *The Gay Science,* fourth book, 316; KSA 3, 549.

69. "Philosophy in the Tragic Age of the Greeks," 8; KSA 1, 833–34.

70. Notebooks, Spring–Summer 1883 7[104]; KSA 10, 278.

71. From a forged letter by Elisabeth Förster-Nietzsche, December 1888; GB 5/2, 807. Not in KSB.

72. To Franz Overbeck, 5 August 1886; KSB 7, 223.

73. From a forged letter by Elisabeth Förster-Nietzsche, 17 September 1888; GB 5/2, 797. Not in KSB.

74. To Josef Paneth, Beginning May 1884; KSB 6, 503.

75. From a forged letter by Elisabeth Förster-Nietzsche, Middle June 1884; GB 5/2, 560. Not in KSB.

76. To Malwida von Meysenbug, 12 May 1887, KSB 8, 70.

77. To Elisabeth Nietzsche, 29 August 1883; KSB 6, 441.

78. To Franziska Nietzsche, 18 October 1887; KSB 8, 170

79. To Paul Deussen, 20 September 1886; KSB 7, 252.

80. Not found.

81. To Franz Overbeck, 14 April 1887; KSB 8, 57–58.

82. *Ecce homo,* "Why I am a Destiny," 1; KSA 6, 365–66.

83. *Nietzsche contra Wagner,* epilogue, 1; KSA 6, 436.

84. Notebooks, Summer–Fall 1884 26[442]; KSA 11, 268.

85. *Ecce homo,* "Why I am so Clever," 10; KSA 6, 297.

86. *The Gay Science,* epigraph; KSA 3, 343. The original is in Emerson's "History" in the *Essays: First Series.* See Ralph Waldo Emerson, *Essays and Lectures* (New York: Library of America, 1983), 242.

87. To Georg Brandes, 4 May 1888; KSB 8, 310.

88. Source unclear.

89. Title of an essay by Schopenhauer, "Transzendentale Spekulation über die anscheinende Absichtlichkeit im Schicksale des Einzelnen."

90. To Paul Deussen, 3 January 1888; KSB 8, 221. Greek: "against fate."

91. *Ecce homo,* "Why I am so Clever," 9; KSA 6, 294–95.

92. *Ecce homo,* preface, 3; KSA 6, 259.

93. Goethe, Zahme Xenien I, Gedichte, Ausgabe letzter Hand. 1827.

94. From lines 82 to 85, Canto XV of the *Inferno,* in which Dante addresses his teacher Brunetto Latini:

> Ché 'n la mente m'é fitta, e or m'accora,
> La cara e buona imagine paterna
> Di voi, quando nel mondo ad ora ad ora
> M'insegnavate come l'uom s'etterna. . . ."

"For in my mind is fixed, and now fills my heart, the dear, good, paternal image of you, when in the world hour by hour you taught me how man makes himself eternal." Translation by Charles Eliot Norton, Houghton Mifflin, 1919.

95. Compare Notebooks, Fall 1887 9[3]; KSA 12, 341. Nietzsche used the phrase again in Notebooks, November 1887–March 1888 11[21]; KSA 13, 14.

96. Notebooks, May–June 1888 17[4]; KSA 13, 525–26.

97. Goethe, *Maximen und Reflexionen.* Nr. 1348. Goethe is referring to the process of aging.

98. Not found.

99. Notebooks, Spring 1888 14[127]; KSA 13, 309.

100. To Carl Fuchs, 14 December 1887; KSB 8, 209.

101. *On the Genealogy of Morals,* preface, 2; KSA 5, 248.

102. Notebooks, End 1880 7[105]; KSA 9, 339.

103. To Heinrich Köselitz, 19 June 1882; KSB 6, 208.

104. To Heinrich Köselitz, 27 April 1883; KSB 6, 367.

105. "On the Future of our Educational Institutions," lecture 4; KSA 1, 713.

106. To Heinrich Köselitz, 27 October 1887; KSB 8, 178.

107. In French in the original: rancor, intense, malignant hatred or ill will.

108. *Ecce homo,* "Thus Spoke Zarathustra," 5; KSA 6, 342.

109. Notebooks, Summer 1880 4[137]; KSA 9, 136.

110. To Heinrich Köselitz, 14 August 1881; KSB 6, 112.

111. To Heinrich Köselitz, 13 July 1883; KSB 6, 397.

112. To Franz Overbeck, 6 February 1884; KSB 6, 475.

113. To Heinrich Köselitz, 16 December 1888; KSB 8, 528.

114. Novalis to Friedrich Schlegel, 20 August 1793; in Novalis, *Werke, Tagebücher und Briefe Friedrich von Hardenbergs,* ed. Hans-Joachim Mähl und Richard Samuel (Munich: Beck 1978), vol. I, p. 542.

115. *Untimely Meditations* 2, "On the Use and Disadvantage of History for Life," 9; KSA 1, 319.

116. Goethe, *Faust II,* "Am untern Peneios," spoken by Manto (end).

117. Notebooks, Summer 1875 11[18]; KSA 8, 204.

118. Notebooks, Summer–Fall 1882 2[6]; KSA 10, 45.

119. Hölderlin, *Der Tod des Empedokles,* Act 1, Scene 1, Panthea speaks.

120. Not found.

121. *The Gay Science,* fourth book, 342; KSA 3, 571.

122. *Thus Spoke Zarathustra,* prologue, 4; KSA 4, 16–18.

123. Nietzsche to August Bungert in Genoa, 14 March 1883 (written as a dedication in a copy of *Daybreak);* KSB 8, 597.

124. Notebooks, July–August 1882 1[102]; KSA 10, 34. Compare also KSA 10, 107.

125. *Thus Spoke Zarathustra,* prologue, 4; KSA 4, 18.

126. *Dionysus-Dithrambs,* "Ariadne's Lament"; KSA 6, 401.

127. *Ecce homo,* "The Birth of Tragedy," 4; KSA 6, 314–15.

128. KSA 6, 314.

129. The phrase Bertram uses here "sacredly sober"—"heilig nüchtern"—is an allusion to Hölderlin's poem, "Hälfte des Lebens," where Hölderlin coined the word and which,

uncannily, seems to foretell Hölderlin's own descent into madness. Stefan George also uses the phrase in *Der Stern des Bundes,* "Da zur begehung an des freundes arm," SW 8, 88, which is itself also a tribute to Hölderlin, whom George and his followers, particularly Norbert von Hellingrath, did so much to rescue from obscurity and neglect.

130. Notebooks, August–September 1885 41[6–7]; KSA 11, 680–82.

Chapter 18: Socrates

1. Hölderlin, "Der Zeitgeist," SA 1, 297.
2. Hölderlin, "Sokrates und Alkibiades," SA 1, 256.
3. Bettina von Arnim, Goethe's *Briefwechsel mit einem Kinde.*
4. The reference is to the biblical figure of Saul, who became Jesus's disciple Paul after he had renamed him on the road to Damascus.
5. Notebooks, Summer 1875 6[3]; KSA 8, 97.
6. Notebooks, Fall 1885–Fall 1886 2[96]; KSA 12, 108.
7. *The Birth of Tragedy,* 15; KSA 1, 100.
8. *Twilight of the Idols;* KSA 6, 66.
9. *Human, All Too Human* 2, 2, "The Wanderer and His Shadow," 86; KSA 2, 591–92.
10. The religion of the Orphic mysteries with its initiating rites, doctrines of original sin and salvation, and belief in the purification of the soul through a cycle of reincarnation. *Merriam-Webster.*
11. *The Birth of Tragedy,* 13; KSA 1, 90. In the last line, Nietzsche is quoting from Goethe's *Faust,* I, 1607–11; HA 3, 54.
12. Notebooks, Summer 1875 6[23]; KSA 8, 106–7.
13. Notebooks, Summer 1875 6[17]; KSA 8, 104.
14. Notebooks, Summer 1875 6 [13]; KSA 8, 102.
15. *The Birth of Tragedy,* 9; KSA 1, 66.
16. *Human, All Too Human* 1, 5, "Signs of Higher and Lower Culture," 261; KSA 2, 216.
17. *Ecce homo,* "The Birth of Tragedy," 1; KSA 6, 310.
18. *The Birth of Tragedy,* 15; KSA 1, 98.
19. *The Birth of Tragedy,* 13; KSA 1, 90.
20. Ibid.
21. "Socrates and Tragedy"; KSA 1, 545.
22. Not found.
23. *Twilight of the Idols,* "The Problem of Socrates," 2–3; KSA 6, 66–67.
24. Italian: "clownish, comical."
25. *Beyond Good and Evil,* part 2, "The Free Spirit," 40; KSA 5, 57.
26. *Twilight of the Idols,* "The Problem of Socrates," 5; KSA 6, 70.
27. *Ecce homo,* "Why I am a Destiny," 1; KSA 6, 365.
28. Notebooks, Fall 1881 12[108]; KSA 9, 595.
29. Goethe to Eckermann, 21 March 1830, *Gespräche* 4, 250.
30. Notebooks, September 1876 18[47]; KSA 8, 327.

31. Notebooks, Spring 1888 14[92]; KSA 13, 269–70.
32. Notebooks, May–June 1888 17[4] 5; KSA 13, 525–26.
33. *The Birth of Tragedy,* 14; KSA 1, 96.
34. *The Birth of Tragedy,* 15; KSA 1, 102.
35. Notebooks, End 1870 6[11]; KSA 7, 132.
36. *The Birth of Tragedy,* 13; KSA 1, 91.
37. Conrad Ferdinand Meyer, "Das Ende des Festes."
38. *The Birth of Tragedy,* 13; KSA 1, 91.
39. *Ecce homo,* "Why I write such Good Books," 5; KSA 6, 305.
40. *Ecce homo,* "The Untimely Ones," 3; KSA 6, 319.
41. Not found.
42. "On the Future of our Educational Institutions," lecture 4; KSA 1, 715.
43. Not found. The Greek means: "philosophical experience *par excellence.*"
44. To Carl von Gersdorff, 11 April 1869; KSB 2, 386.
45. *Human, All Too Human* 2, 1, "Assorted Thoughts and Sayings," 180; KSA 2, 458.
46. Notebooks, Spring–Summer 5[22]; KSA 8, 46.
47. Not found.
48. *Human, All Too Human* 1, 5, "Signs of Higher and Lower Culture," 259; KSA 2, 213. Nietzsche is citing Hölderlin, *Empedokles,* Act 2, Scene 4.
49. Not found.
50. Not found.
51. Goethe to Eckermann, 12 May 1825, *Gespräche* 3, 205.
52. To Paul Deussen, February 1870; KSB 3, 100.
53. Notebooks, Summer–Fall 1882 3[1] 13; KSA 10, 55. Nietzsche clearly liked this aphorism and repeated it often: compare KSA 10, 395, 463, 500.
54. Notebooks, July–August 1882 1[89]; KSA 10, 32.
55. Notebooks, September 1876 18[42]; KSA 8, 326.
56. *Human, All Too Human* 1, 7, "Woman and Child," 381; KSA 2, 266.
57. *Untimely Meditations* 3, "Schopenhauer as Educator," 6; KSA 1, 385.
58. Jean Paul, *Flegeljahre. Eine Biographie,* Vol. 4, Nro. 58, "Giftkuttel: Erinnerungen."
59. Goethe to Johann Gottfried Herder, Beginning 1772; *Briefe* 1, 130.
60. Genesis 32:24–26.
61. Goethe to Herder, ca. October 1771; *Briefe* 1, 128.
62. Pindar, *Pythian Odes* 2.73.
63. To Erwin Rohde, 25 October 1872; KSB 4, 72–73.
64. To Erwin Rohde, 16 June 1869; KSB 3, 17.
65. *Untimely Meditations* 3, "Schopenhauer as Educator," 2; KSA 1, 350.
66. Ibid.
67. Notebooks, Summer–End September 1875 12[7]; KSA 8, 248.
68. *Untimely Meditations* 3, "Schopenhauer as Educator," 1; KSA 1, 340–41.
69. Not found.

70. To Paul Deussen, February 1870; KSB 3, 100.

71. Notebooks, Fall 1881 12[188]; KSA 9, 608.

72. Notebooks, Fall 1884 28[41]; KSA 11, 316.

73. In the original, where Bertram writes that beauty is "selig in ihr selbst," he is alluding to the famous poem by Eduard Mörike, "Auf eine Lampe," whose concluding line is "Was aber schoen ist, selig scheint es in ihm selbst," "But what is beautiful appears serene unto itself."

74. *Untimely Meditations* 4, "Richard Wagner in Bayreuth," 4; KSA 1, 451.

75. To Erwin Rohde, 21 December 1871; KSB 3, 256–57.

76. *Untimely Meditations* 2, "On the Use and Disadvantage of History for Life," 2; KSA 1, 260–61.

77. *Untimely Meditations* 2, "On the Use and Disadvantage of History for Life," 6; KSA 1, 295.

78. To Erwin Rohde, 16 July 1870; KSB 3, 130–31.

79. Notebooks, Beginning 1874–Spring 1874 32[44]; KSA 7, 768.

80. Nietzsche is quoting here Goethe's *Faust* II, "Klassische Walpurgisnacht," "Am untern Peneios," 7438–39; HA 3, 227.

81. To Erwin Rohde, 15 December 1870; KSB 3, 166–67.

82. To Carl Fuchs, 20–27 July 1878; KSB 5, 340. The *Bayreuther Blätter* was the official journal founded in 1878 "in the spirit of Richard Wagner." The last issue was published in 1938.

83. To Heinrich Köselitz, 26 March 1879; KSB 5, 399.

84. *Ecce homo,* "The Birth of Tragedy," 4; KSA 6, 314.

85. *Thus Spoke Zarathustra,* part 1, "Of Endowing Virtue," 3; KSA 4, 102.

86. Not found.

87. *Beyond Good and Evil,* "From High Mountains"; KSA 5, 241–43.

88. Ibid., 243.

89. Ibid.

90. *Beyond Good and Evil,* part 4, "Maxims and Interludes," 63; KSA 5, 85.

91. *Human, All Too Human* 1, "From the Souls of Artists and Writers," 200; KSA 2, 168.

92. *Daybreak,* fifth book, 447; KSA 3, 271.

93. *Human, All Too Human* 2, "Assorted Thoughts and Sayings," 341; KSA 2, 518.

94. To Carl von Gersdorff, 8 August 1868; KSB 2, 310.

95. "Homer's Competition"; KSA 1, 787–88.

96. Ibid., 789–91.

97. *Daybreak,* fourth book, 297; KSA 3, 221.

98. *Thus Spoke Zarathustra,* part 1, "Of Endowing Virtue," 3; KSA 4, 101.

99. The passage is in Aristotle's *Poetics:* "Since the presentation is not only of a complete action but also of fearful and pitiable things, these things arise most of all when they happen beyond expectation, but through one another; for they will have the effect of wonder more in this way than if they arise spontaneously and by accident, since even

those things which arise by chance seem to be the most wonderful which appear to arise as though on purpose, e.g., as the *statue* of Mitys killed the man who caused the *death* of Mitys in Argos by falling on him. For such things appear not to happen at random; consequently, it is necessary for such plots to be finer." (1452a11)

100. To Carl von Gersdorff, 15 April 1876; KSB 5, 152.

101. To Malwida von Meysenbug, Beginning May 1876; KSB 6, 499. Bertram indicates this letter was to Nietzsche's sister because Elisabeth Förster-Nietzsche published it as being addressed to her, while leaving out the vehement statements Nietzsche made about her, in which he calls her, for example, a "vengeful anti-Semitic goose."

102. Bertram is alluding to the distich by Schiller, "Der Meister" ("The Master"):

> "Jeden anderen Meister erkennt man an dem, was er ausspricht;
> Was er weise verschweigt, zeigt mir den Meister des Styls."

> "One recognizes every other master by what he expresses;
> What he wisely keeps silent reveals to me the master of style."

103. To Malwida von Meysenbug, End March 1884; KSB 6, 489–90.

104. Bertram is referring to a passage in the Notebooks, Summer–Fall 1882 2[34]; KSA 10, 49.

105. *The Gay Science,* fourth book, 340; KSA 3, 569–70.

106. Notebooks, June–July 1885 37[7]; KSA 11, 580.

107. From a forged letter by Elisabeth Förster-Nietzsche, March 1885; GB 5/2, 596–97. Part of the original letter is found in KSB 7, 24.

108. To Carl von Gersdorff, End June 1883; KSB 6, 386.

109. From an apparently forged letter by Elisabeth Förster-Nietzsche to Malwida von Meysenbug, February 1884; GB 3, 610–11. Not in KSB.

110. To Malwida von Meysenbug, 12 May 1887; KSB 8, 69.

111. *Ecce homo,* foreword, 4; KSA 6, 260–61. Compare also *Thus Spoke Zarathustra,* part 1, "Of Endowing Virtue," 3; KSA 4, 101.

112. Lou Andreas-Salomé.

113. To Heinrich Köselitz, 6 April 1883; KSB 6, 359.

114. To Heinrich Köselitz, 19 February 1883; KSB 6, 333–34.

115. A Corsair was "a privateer of the coast of the Barbary States authorized by his government to prey upon the commerce and harry the shores of Christian nations." *Merriam-Webster Unabridged Dictionary,* 3rd edition.

116. To Reinhard von Seydlitz, 24 September 1876; KSB 5, 188.

117. *Human, All Too Human* 1, 8, "A Glance at the State," 455; KSA 2, 295.

118. Notebooks, December 1881–January 1882 16[19]; KSA 9, 663.

119. To Heinrich Köselitz, 16 March 1883; KSB 6, 344.

120. To Heinrich Köselitz, 26 August 1883; KSB 6, 436.

121. To Franz Overbeck, 6 November 1884; KSB 6, 554.

122. To Franz Overbeck, 31 March 1885; KSB 7, 34.

123. To Franz Overbeck, 12 July 1884; KSB 6, 512.

124. To Malwida von Meysenbug, Beginning June 1884; KSB 6, 510.

125. To Franz Overbeck, 14 September 1884; KSB 6, 531.

126. *Ecce homo,* "Why I write such Good Books," 6; KSA 6, 307.

127. *Beyond Good and Evil,* part 9, "What is Noble?" 295; KSA 5, 237.

128. *Ecce homo,* "Why I write such Good Books," 6; KSA 6, 307.

129. In a letter from 17 July 1876, Erwin Rohde informs Nietzsche of his engagement.

130. *Ecce homo,* foreword, 3; KSA 6, 258.

131. Notebooks, Summer 1883 13[1]; KSA 10, 430.

132. *Human, All Too Human* 1, preface, 1; KSA 2, 14.

133. Kurwenal is the name of Tristan's groom in Wagner's *Tristan und Isolde.*

134. To Erwin Rohde, 23 February 1886; KSB 7, 153.

135. *Thus Spoke Zarathustra,* part 4, "The Honey Sacrifice"; KSA 4, 297.

136. Notebooks, Fall 1881 14[10]; KSA 9, 625.

137. Alabanda is the companion of Hyperion in Hölderlin's novel of the same name.

138. Notebooks, Summer–Fall 1884 26[376]; KSA 11, 250.

139. Notebooks, Winter 1883–1884 24[7]; KSA 10, 646.

140. To Franz Overbeck, 17 June 1887; KSB 8, 93–94.

141. The verses are from Stefan George, "Nietzsche," in *Der Siebente Ring* (1907).

142. *The Birth of Tragedy,* "Attempt at a Self-Critique," 3; KSA 1, 15.

143. *The Antichrist,* foreword; KSA 6, 167. Nietzsche repeats this phrase in *Ecce homo,* "Why I write such Good Books," 1; KSA 6, 298.

144. To Franz Overbeck, 21 May 1884; KSB 6, 506.

145. Goethe to Eckermann, 11 March 1832.

Chapter 19: Eleusis

1. Hölderlin, "Germanien," SA 2, 160.

2. Hölderlin, *Empedokles,* Act 1, Scene 2, Hermokrates; SA.

3. Zosimos (ca. 450), obscure Roman historian.

4. Alcibiades (450–404 B.C.E.), brilliant but ruthless Athenian politician and military commander. He was accused of having profaned the Eleusian Mysteries in 420 and, after he fled to Syracuse, he was condemned to death in absentia. However, his reputation was later restored through several military successes, and he returned to Athens in 407. After more upheavals, he was finally murdered.

5. In his novel, *Die Lehrlinge zu Sais* ("The Apprentices at Sais"), Novalis allegorizes the subject of the novel, namely knowledge of nature, through a statue of the goddess Isis and its unveiling. A classical source seems to be Plutarch's *Peri Isidos,* chapter 9, where a statue of Athena is described at the base of which there was an inscription that read: "I am everything that has not yet been and is and will be, and no mortal has ever removed my robe."

6. To Heinrich Köselitz, 10 April 1881; KSB 6, 82.

7. Novalis, *Fragmente.*

8. Not found.

9. Blaise Pascal, *Pensées sur la religion et sur quelques autres sujets,* 597 (Edition du Luxembourg, Paris, 1951), "Le moi est haïssable."

10. The reference is to Faust's opening monologue, which begins:

"I've studied now Philosophy
And Jurisprudence, Medicine,
And even, alas! Theology
All through and through with ardour keen!
Here now I stand, poor fool, and see
I'm just as wise as formerly.
Am called a Master, even Doctor too,
And now I've nearly ten years through
Pulled my students by their noses to and fro
And up and down, across, about,
And see there's nothing we can know!"

11. Novalis, *Die Lehrlinge zu Saïs* (1788–89), section 2, "Die Natur."

12. "Die Geheimnisse. Ein Fragment" (1784–85) HA 2, 271–281; see also the commentary on pp. 705–11.

13. *Thus Spoke Zarathustra,* part 1, "The Friend"; KSA 4, 71.

14. *The Gay Science,* "Songs of Prince Outlaw"; KSA 3, 649.

15. Notebooks, Summer 1872–Beginning 1873 19[131]; KSA 7, 460–61.

16. *Human, All Too Human* 1, preface 1; KSA 2, 14.

17. Notebooks, End 1880 7[105]; KSA 9, 339.

18. *Beyond Good and Evil,* "Out of High Mountains"; KSA 5, 243.

19. *Human, All Too Human* 2, 1, "Assorted Thoughts and Sayings," 156; KSA 2, 443.

20. Notebooks, Fall 1887 10[17]; KSA 12, 463.

21. Notebooks, Summer 1872–Beginning 1873 19[131]; KSA 7, 461.

22. Notebooks, Fall 1883 16[5]; KSA 10, 497.

23. *Ecce homo,* "Why I am a Destiny," 8–9; KSA 6, 374. The French phrase was Voltaire's motto, meaning, more or less: "Do away with infamy!" with "infamy" meaning anything to do with the church, superstition, ignorance, or the "ancien regime."

24. The reference is to Voltaire, who in 1758 bought an estate in Ferney, located in France next to the Swiss border, allowing, as necessary, quick escape from the authorities on either side. It remained his home until his death in 1778.

25. *Dionysus Dithyrambs,* "Fame and Eternity," 3; KSA 6, 404–5.

26. The reference is to Hölderlin, "Germanien."

27. Pindar, NEMEAN 5 Pytheas of Aigina, boys' pankration, 483 (?) B.C.E., Stand I.

28. *The Birth of Tragedy,* 9; KSA 1, 66–69.

29. *Twilight of the Idols,* "Maxims and Arrows," 5; KSA 6, 59.

30. Latin: pudenda, neuter plural of pudendus, a gerundive of pudere, to be ashamed. Usually used to refer to human, especially female, genital organs.

31. To Carl von Gersdorff, 18 September 1871; KSB 3, 227.

32. *Twilight of the Idols,* "Maxims and Arrows," 5; KSA 6, 59.

33. *Beyond Good and Evil,* part 4, "Maxims and Interludes," 65; KSA 5, 85.

34. Greek: literally, overseer, watcher; from epopteuein: to watch, supervise; an initiate to the highest grade of the Eleusinian mysteries.

35. "On Truth and Lie in the Extra-Moral Sense," 1; KSA 1, 877.

36. This appears not to be a quotation, but, as in the opening paragraph of the *Judas* chapter, a rhetorical formulation of the issue to be treated subsequently.

37. *The Birth of Tragedy,* 23; KSA 1, 145.

38. Notebooks, Summer 1872–Beginning 1873 19[50]; KSA 7, 435.

39. *Untimely Meditations* 2, "On the Use and Disadvantage of History for Life," 7; KSA 1, 298.

40. Notebooks, Summer 1872–Beginning 1873 19[182]; KSA 7, 476.

41. Notebooks, Spring 1888 14[226]; KSA 13, 398.

42. Herodotus.

43. *Untimely Meditations* 4, "Richard Wagner in Bayreuth," 1; KSA 1, 434.

44. Not found.

45. *The Gay Science,* preface to second edition, 4; KSA 3, 352.

46. This seems to be a reference to a criticism made about Bertram's dissertation on Adalbert Stifter by Richard M. Meyer in *Deutsche Literaturzeitung* (21 March 1908), 736. There Meyer had expressed his "intense mistrust" in what he called Bertram's "psychologie par ricochet." Evidently the remark rankled Bertram.

47. Not found.

48. Notebooks, Summer–Fall 1882 3[1] 295; KSA 10, 88.

49. *Ecce homo,* "Why I am so Clever," 9; KSA 6, 293.

50. Not found.

51. Goethe to Eckermann, 10 April 1829.

52. Nietzsche to August Bungert in Genoa, 14 March 1883 (written as a dedication in a copy of *Daybreak*); KSB 8, 597.

53. *Ecce homo,* "Why I write such Good Books," 1; KSA 6, 300.

54. Greek: "things done."

55. Greek: "things said."

56. Goethe, *Wilhelm Meister,* book 7, chapter 9.

57. Goethe to Schiller, 9 July 1796.

58. Schiller, "Sprache" Tabulae Votivae Xenien, 1797.

59. Goethe, *Wilhelm Meister's Travels,* book 2, chapter 1 (fifth paragraph).

60. To Carl von Gersdorff, 18 September 1871; KSB 3, 227.

61. *Beyond Good and Evil,* part 4, "Maxims and Interludes," 160; KSA 5, 100.

62. *Twilight of the Idols,* "Skirmishes of an Untimely Man," 26; KSA 6, 128.

63. *Thus Spoke Zarathustra,* part 3, "The Seven Seals," 7; KSA 4, 291.

64. Notebooks, 1887 10[60]; KSA 12, 493.

65. Notebooks, Summer 1883 13[1]; KSA 10, 420.

66. Notebooks, Summer–Fall 1882 3[1] 136; KSA 10, 69.

67. Schopenhauer, "Über Schriftstellerei und Stil," paragraph 275. The "poet" Schopenhauer is citing is Goethe, Epigrammatisch, "Spruch, Widerspruch."

68. Not found.

69. *Thus Spoke Zarathustra,* "Reading and Writing"; KSA 4, 49.

70. *Human, All Too Human* 2, "Assorted Thoughts and Sayings," 230; KSA 2, 484.

71. *Human, All Too Human,* Nietzsche's note on the first edition, 1878; KSA 2, 10.

72. Goethe, *Wilhelm Meister's Travels,* book 2, chapter 1.

73. Not found.

74. *Beyond Good and Evil* 9, "What is Noble?" 263; KSA 5, 218.

75. Notebooks, June–July 1885 37[13]; KSA 11, 588.

76. Notebooks, Summer 1883 12[20]; KSA 10, 403.

77. Notebooks, Summer 1888 20[58]; KSA 13, 559.

78. *Human, All Too Human* 1, 4, "From the Souls of Artists and Writers," 145; KSA 2, 141.

79. *Thus Spoke Zarathustra,* part 3, "Of Old and New Tablets," 19; KSA 4, 260.

80. *Thus Spoke Zarathustra,* part 3, "Of Old and New Tablets," 30; KSA 4, 268–69.

81. To Malwida von Meysenbug, End March 1884; KSB 6, 490.

82. To Georg Brandes, 2 December 1887; KSB 8, 206.

83. *Thus Spoke Zarathustra,* part 3, "The Seven Seals," 5; KSA 4, 290.

84. Ibid.

85. To Heinrich Köselitz, 12 April 1887; KSB 8, 55.

86. *Ecce homo,* "Why I am so Clever," 9; KSA 6, 293.

87. KSA 6, 294–95.

88. Goethe, *Wilhelm Meister's Travels,* book 2, chapter 1 (end).

89. *Ecce homo,* dedication; KSA 6, 263.

90. Ibid.

91. Hölderin, *Hyperion.*

92. Hölderlin, "Patmos," SA 2, 176.

93. "Lecture on the History of Greek Literature."

94. *Ecce homo,* "Twilight of the Idols," 3; KSA 6, 356.

95. Notebooks, August–September 1885 40[39]; KSA 11, 649.

96. *Dionysus Dithyrambs,* "Between Birds of Prey"; KSA 6, 392.

97. Notebooks, Summer 1872–Beginning 1873 19[182]; KSA 7, 476.

98. *Thus Spoke Zarathustra,* part 1, prologue; KSA 4, 28.

99. Hölderlin, "Stammbuchblatt für einen Unbekannten," SA 2, 347.

100. The Greek *myein* means "to close," used specifically with reference to the eyes and lips.

101. Notebooks, Summer–Fall 1882 3[1] 274; KSA 10, 86.

102. "I am a mystic and I do not believe in anything."

103. Bertram is referring to the main characters of Flaubert's unfinished novel, *Bouvard et Pécuchet,* which chronicles the misadventures of two clerks who devote themselves to

researches into every conceivable subject—archaeology, history, literature, philosophy, religion, education, to name a few—but without ever achieving comprehension.

104. Latin: "Hail the Cross, our Only Hope."

105. *Ecce homo,* "Thus Spoke Zarathustra," 8; KSA 6, 348.

106. *Ecce homo,* "Thus Spoke Zarathustra," 7; KSA 6, 347.

107. *Ecce homo,* "Thus Spoke Zarathustra," 8; KSA 6, 348.

108. The reference is to Goethe's *Westöstlicher Divan,* "Moganni Nameh. Buch des Sängers," end: "Selige Sehnsucht," HA 2, 18.

109. *The Gay Science,* "Jest, Cunning and Vengeance," 62; KSA 3, 367.

Chronology

1844 15 October. Friedrich Wilhelm Nietzsche is born the son of a pastor in Röcken near Lützen in the province of Saxony.

1849 30 July. Nietzsche's father, Pastor Karl Ludwig Nietzsche, dies.

1850 Family moves to Naumburg.

1858 October through 7 September 1864. Pupil at the Schulpforta Gymnasium near Naumburg.

1864 October. Student of theology and classical philology at Bonn University. Pupil of Ritschl.

1865 October. At Leipzig University. First encounter with Schopenhauer's magnum opus.

1866 Beginning of friendship with Erwin Rohde.

1868 8 November. First personal encounter with Richard Wagner in Leipzig.

1869 February. Appointed to Basel University as associate professor of classical philology before receiving doctorate.
17 May. First visit of Wagner in Tribschen near Lucerne.
28 May. Inaugural address at Basel University on "Homer and Classical Philology."
Beginning of his relationship with Jakob Burckhardt.

1869–71 Writes *The Birth of Tragedy* (published January 1872).

1870 March. Named full professor.
August. Volunteers in the Franco-Prussian War as medical orderly; severe illness.
October. Return to Basel. Beginning of friendship with theologian Franz Overbeck.

1872 February–March. Basel lectures "On the Future of our Educational Institutions" (not printed until the Notebooks are published).
April. Wagner leaves Tribschen.
22 May. Laying of cornerstone for the Festspielhaus in Bayreuth. Wagner and Nietzsche in Bayreuth.

1873 The first *Untimely Meditation:* "David Strauss, the Confessor and the Writer."
The second *Untimely Meditation:* "On the Use and Disadvantage of History for Life" (appears 1874).

The fragment "Philosophy in the Tragic Age of the Greeks" (not printed until the Notebooks are published).

1874 The third *Untimely Meditation:* "Schopenhauer as Educator."

1875 October. First encounter with the musician Peter Gast (Heinrich Köselitz).

1875–76 The fourth *Untimely Meditation:* "Richard Wagner in Bayreuth."

1876 12 July. Wagner's last letter to Nietzsche.
August. The first Bayreuth Festspiele. Nietzsche in Bayreuth.
September. Beginning of friendly relations with the psychologist Paul Rée. Worsening health. October medical leave from Basel University. Winter in Sorrento with Rée and Malwida von Meysenbug.
October–November. Nietzsche together with Wagner for the last time in Sorrento.

1876–78 *Human, All Too Human.* First Part.

1878 3 January. Wagner's final communication with Nietzsche: he sends *Parsifal.*
May. Nietzsche's last letter to Wagner, along with *Human, All Too Human.*

1879 Severe illness. Resigns from chair at Basel University.
Human, All Too Human. Second Part.
"Assorted Thoughts and Sayings."

1880 "The Wanderer and His Shadow."
March through June. First sojourn in Venice.
November onward. First winter in Genoa.

1880–81 *Daybreak.*

1881 First summer in Sils-Maria.
27 November. Nietzsche hears Bizet's *Carmen* for the first time in Genoa.

1881–82 *The Gay Science.*

1882 March. Travels to Sicily.
April to November. Friendship with Lou Salomé.
November onward. Winter in Rapallo.

1882–88 Studies and sketches belonging to sphere of *The Will to Power. Attempt at a Transvaluation of all Values.*

1883 February. In Rapallo, writes the first part of *Thus Spoke Zarathustra* (published 1883).
13 February. Wagner's death.
June to July. In Sils-Maria, writes the second part of *Zarathustra* (published 1883).
December onward. First winter in Nice.

1884 January. In Nice, writes the third part of *Zarathustra* (published 1884).
August. Heinrich von Stein's visit to Sils-Maria.
November–February 1885. In Menton and Nice, writes the fourth part of *Zarathustra* (published privately 1885).

1884–85 *Beyond Good and Evil* (appears 1886).

1886 May to June. Together with Erwin Rohde for the last time in Leipzig.
First plan for *The Will to Power.*

1887 *Genealogy of Morals.*
February. First reads Dostoyevsky.
11 November. Last letter to Erwin Rohde.

1887–88 Works on *The Will to Power.*

1888 April. First sojourn in Turin. Danish scholar Georg Brandes holds lectures at Copenhagen University "on the German philosopher Friedrich Nietzsche" ("At which German universities today would lectures on my philosophy be possible . . ?" *Ecce homo,* October 1888).
May to August. *The Case of Wagner.* Finishes the "Dionysus Dithyrambs."
August to September. *Twilight of the Idols* (appears January 1889).
September. *The Antichrist. Attempt at a Critique of Christianity* (*Transvaluation of all Values* I).
October to November. *Ecce homo* (appeared 1908).
December. *Nietzsche contra Wagner. Documents of a Psychologist.* First published in the collected *Works.*

1889 In the first days of January, mental collapse in Turin.
Moves to his mother in Naumburg.

1897 Easter death of his mother Franziska née Oehler.
Moves with his sister to Weimar.

1900 25 August. Friedrich Nietzsche dies in Weimar.

Index

academy, Nietzsche's idea of, 274–75
actors: as Dionysian, 137; as phantoms, 145; problem of, 134, 139. *See also* disguises; theatricality
actuality, German concept of, 58, 59, 61, 65
Aeschylus, *Prometheus,* 84–85
aging, Goethe on, 354n97
Alcibiades, 359n4; travesty of mysteries, 290
amor fati, Nietzsche's, 82, 103, 182, 215, 241, 253–55, 325n4
ancestry: in *Beyond Good and Evil,* 19, 23; conflicting, 21–22; in *Ecce homo,* 17–18, 22, 27; in *The Gay Science,* 20, 24; in *Human, All Too Human,* 19; as intellectual category, 26; Napoleon's, 25; Nietzsche's reverence for, 11–36; of overman, 26; of philosophers, 25–26; responsibility toward, 19; of scholarly class, 23–24; in *Thus Spoke Zarathustra,* 17, 20; in *Twilight of the Idols,* 20–21; Wagner's obsession with, 34; in *Will to Power,* 19. *See also* atavism
Andreas-Salomé, Lou, 140–41, 254, 281
anecdotes: in literature, 193–95; musical, 199; Nietzsche's, 194–202, 265. *See also* aphorisms
Antichrist, The (Nietzsche): anecdotes of, 196; anti-Germanness in, xxiv, 71; "Cesare Borgia as Pope," 130; evil in, 129; Protestantism in, 53; St. Paul in, 48, 113–14
anti-Germanness: Luther on, 65; Nietzsche's, xxiv, 17, 63, 64–65, 70, 71–73, 75, 95, 178, 214, 215
aphorisms: Goethe's, 184; Hans Sachs's, 184, 190; Nietzsche's, 184, 185, 189–90, 192–93, 195, 279. *See also* anecdotes
Apollo: Dionysus and, 168; justice under, 85; Pythian, 257; Socrates' proem to, 266
architecture, German, 64
Ariadne, 307
Arion, myth of, 105–6, 329n96
aristocracy, embodiment of cultural heritage, 25
Aristophanes, 290
Aristotle: on Eleusinian mysteries, 300; on experiencing, 300; *Poetics,* 357n99; on poetry, 3
art: decline of, 233–34; figurative, 37–38; freemasonry of, 274; as mask of Eros, 273; transformative power of, 273. *See also* Landscape painting
art, German: Hellenic elements in, 107
artists: Greek idea of, 277; in *Human, All Too Human,* 27; necessity of illness for, 116; in Nietzsche's Notebooks, 149–50
asceticism, Nietzsche's, 111–13, 123
Aschheim, Steven E., 311n46, 323n71
Asia, mystery traditions of, 289
atavism: in *Beyond Good and Evil,* 26–27; Darwin's law of, 22, 26. *See also* ancestry
"Attempt at a Self-Critique" (Nietzsche), 114
authenticity, 331n1
autumn: Jean Paul on, 207; Nietzsche's love for, 203–12, 304
"Autumn" (Nietzsche), 200

Babylon, mystery traditions of, 289
Bach, Johann Sebastian: Mass in B Minor, 250; "Out of the Depths I Cry to Thee," 331n77; St. Matthew Passion, 51–52
Baeumler, Alfred, 310n28
Balder (Norse mythology), 332n5
Balzac, Honoré de, 150
barbarism: culture and, 158–59; Germanic, 62, 68; Hellenism's superiority over, 290; Nietzsche on, 160
Basel (Switzerland): bourgeoisie of, 224; humanism of, 223–24; Nietzsche at, 70, 90, 154, 223–24; Nietzsche's lectures at, 220, 243
beauty, Nietzsche on, 273
becoming: *versus* being, 56; Eternal, 56; in

German language, 62; in Germanness, 59–60, 62, 65–66, 69, 71; Hölderlin on, 63, 64; Nietzsche's concept of, 56–78, 302; violation of boundaries in, 84
Beethoven, Ludwig van: and Goethe, 98–99, 163, 262, 338n36; melodies of, 199–200; *Missa solemnis,* 200, 250; notebooks of, 199; Quartet in F Major, 254; songs of, 199
being: *versus* becoming, 56; German homesickness for, 68, 69; Heraclitus on, 58
Benn, Gottfried, xv
Bertram, Ernst: aversion to Italy, 347n27; death of, xxix; denazification of, xxix; dissertation on Stifter, 310n19, 361n46; following World War II, xxviii–xxix, 312n63; and George, xvi, xxv, 310n30; Germanness of, xxvii–xxviii, xxix, xxxi; influence of, xii, xiii, xv; Kaufmann's critique of, xii–xiii, xix, xx, xxi–xxii; literary talents of, xv–xvi, xxx–xxxi; love of music, xxii; Lutheran heritage of, xxii; Planck's support for, xxix; poetry of, xxix; relation to Nazism, xiii; under Third Reich, xxvii–xxviii; and völkisch worldview, xxviii, 311n46. *See also Nietzsche: Versuch einer Mythologie*
betrayal: in Nietzsche's works, 121–33, 331n1; pleasure of, 131; redemptive act of, 123–24
"Beyond Day" (Nietzsche), 228
Beyond Good and Evil (Nietzsche): ancestry in, 19, 23; anecdotes of, 196; atavism in, 26–27; disguise in, 145, 146, 152, 265; the French in, 219; "From High Mountains," 275–76; Germanness in, 60, 66, 93, 152; knowledge in, 297, 301; *Meistersinger* in, 150; music in, 98; mysteries in, 302; Napoleon in, 179, 181; philosophers in, 7; skepticism in, 21, 44–45; south in, 219–20; suffering in, 110, 120; theatricality in, 141; Wagner in, 94–95; "We Scholars," 25–26
Bible: German-language, 183, 213; Old Testament typology of, 27
Birth of Tragedy, The (Nietzsche), xviii; acting in, 135; anecdotes of, 195; Basel in, 224; beauty in, 273; Dionysus in, 176; enchantment in, 135, 136–37; ending of, 235; existence in, xxx; German music in, 63, 69; Goethe in, 170; Great Crime in, 79; hallucination in, 144–45; Hellenism in, 77; individualism in, 264; justice in, 84–85; *Knight, Death, and Devil* in, 38, 39–41; Luther in, 53; musicality of, 92, 104; myth in, 297–98; press notices of, 28; prophecy in, 245, 260; reception of, 247; sacrilege in, 133, 296; Schopenhauer in, 51; self-vision in, 72; Socrates in, 262, 263, 264, 266–67; suffering in, 117
Birth of Tragedy, The, Notebooks (Nietzsche): crucifixion in, 54; Greeks in, 165
Bismarck, Otto: *Kulturkampf* of, xxv; Nietzsche's distortion of, 72
Bizet, Georges: southern music of, 219. *See also Carmen* (Bizet)
Böcklin, Arnold, 224
Bondi, Georg, xvi
Bonn, Nietzsche at, 155, 243–44
book burning, during Third Reich, xxviii
Bossuet, Jacques-Bénigne, 79, 324n2
Bourget, Paul: *Baudelaire,* 197–98
Brandes, Georg, xxxiv, 27, 88; "An Essay on Aristocratic Radicalism," 326n3; Nietzsche's correspondence with, xxxiv–xxxv, 216, 254, 303
Brentano, Clemens, 94
Brockhaus encyclopedia, 315n47
Brutus, assassination of Caesar, 126
Bülow, Hans von: Nietzsche's correspondence with, 119
Burckhardt, Jakob, 302; in Basel, 223; concept of Renaissance, 273; on Greek music, 100; on historical sources, 5; on legends, 3; on Nietzsche as teacher, 267; Nietzsche's correspondence with, 224; philosophy of history, 117; on power of veneration, 172; on Schopenhauer, 43
Byron, Lord, 349n32; Manfred, 227

Caesar, Julius: assassination of, 126
Cagliostro, Alessandro di, 151, 335n53
Cain, Nietzsche's defense of, 130
Calvary, Nietzsche's vision of, 102, 328n77
Carlyle, Thomas, 172, 339n10
Carmen (Bizet), 286; African quality of, 219; final scene of, 234; Nietzsche's notes on, 104, 197, 234; *versus* Wagner's music, 126–27
Case of Wagner, The (Nietzsche): acting in, 144; *amor fati* in, 253–54; anecdote in, 197; anti-Germanness in, xxiv, 70, 71; aphorisms of, 195; Christianity in, 53; conflicting values in, 21; evil in, 129; Goethe in, 164; Luther in, 52–53; perfection in, 211; renunciation in, 124, 125
Catholicism, Nietzsche on, 220
Catiline, 34, 314n3; Nietzsche on, 11

Centaurs, 189, 343n57
chandalas (outcasts), 320n67; St. Paul as, 47, 114
chaos, Greek dread of, 290
Chopin, Frédéric, 17; Barcarole, 197
Christ, dual nature of, 5
"Christ Dancing" (Nietzsche), 165
Christianity: Eleusian mysteries and, 290, 291; Goethe on, 115, 164–65; and Hellenism, 117; illness in, 109, 113; Nietzsche's opposition to, 51, 110, 127; pessimism in, 167; Romantic, 114
Christianity, northern, 110; in *The Case of Wagner,* 53; Dürer's depiction of, 50; Goethe on, 49; Nietzsche's, 48–49, 53–54, 107–9, 262. *See also* Protestantism, German
church music, Protestant, 89
civilization: Great Men's role in, 177; hostility toward music, 93–94, 96; Napoleon's enmity to, 177; opposition to culture, 93
classicism: German, 168; Goethe's, 49, 158, 160–67; orgiastic, 168; Voltaire's, 161; Weimar, 159, 162, 165. *See also* Hellenism
Columbus, Christopher, 225, 249
community: Luther on, 291–92; madness in, 291; Pascal on, 292
competition, Nietzsche on, 277
conscience, Goethe on, 79
Copernicus, Nicolaus, 17
Cornelius, Peter, 50
correspondents, Nietzsche's: Brandes, 216, 254, 303; Burckhardt, 224; Deussen, 138, 245, 253, 272; Elisabeth Förster-Nietzsche, 16–17, 315n31; Fuchs, 249; Gast, 15, 20, 28, 29, 30, 53, 100, 104–5, 204, 218, 221, 225, 229, 275, 282, 303; Gersdorff, 16, 118, 206, 225, 244, 246, 268; Malwida von Meysenbug, 38, 112, 218, 278, 281, 283, 303; Overbeck, 15, 42, 111, 112, 120, 225, 253, 258, 283; Rohde, 28, 52, 92–93, 119, 125, 154, 170, 204, 207, 209–10, 246, 249, 271, 273, 274; von Bülow, 119; von Seydlitz, 246, 253; Wagner, 39; Wesendonk, 229
Corsairs, 282, 358n115
Corte (Corsica), 30
courage: in Germanness, 71; Nietzsche on, 41–44
creation, and destruction, 122–23
Creuzer, Friedrich: *Symbolik und Mythologie,* xvii
Crusoe, Robinson, 221
cults: in Greek religious thought, 289–90. *See also* mysteries
culture: aristocracy and, 25; and barbarism, 158–59; music as end of, 95–96; opposition of civilization to, 93
culture, French: Nietzsche's relationship to, 218–19

danger, Nietzsche on, 43
Dante, 353n94; depiction of Brutus, 126; depiction of Judas, 121; imagery of, 240; in *The Will to Power,* 255
Darwin, Charles: law of atavism, 22, 26
Darwinism, Nietzsche on, 24
Daybreak (Nietzsche): courage in, 41, 44; disguise in, 146; education in, 277; *esthloi* in, 134; the extreme in, 237; Germanness in, 71; Goethe in, 162–63; Luther in, 49; music in, 97; self-doubt in, 246–47; silence in, 300
Daybreak Notebooks (Nietzsche): acting in, 139; love/derision duality in, 131; music in, 97; nature in, 216
death: Nietzsche's desire for, 258; romanticism of, 40
Demeter, 290
depersonalization, Nietzsche on, 256–57
destruction, creation and, 122–23
Deussen, Paul, 15; memoirs, 326n12; Nietzsche's correspondence with, 138, 245, 253, 272
"Deutschland, Deutschland über alles": Nietzsche on, xxiii
development. *See* becoming
Diogenes, 340n43
Dionysia festival, 136, 334n16
Dionysus: and Apollo, 168; in *The Birth of Tragedy,* 176; duality of, 306; in Hellenism, 165–67; mysteries of, 166; Napoleon as, 180; Nietzsche as, 54, 78, 106, 108, 261; Nietzsche's ideal of, 165–66, 168; as Suffering God, 306–7; third realm of, 106, 110; transformative power of, 135–38; in *The Will to Power,* 166, 202, 260–61
"Dionysus Dithyrambs" (Nietzsche), 190, 192, 193, 242, 260, 295, 304, 307
disguises, 265; in Epicureanism, 146; Hellenic, 153; of mediocrity, 145; necessity of, 146; Nietzsche's, 147–48, 152–53. *See also* actors; theatricality
Doria, Andrea, 225, 348n8
Dostoyevsky, Fyodor, 129
drama, enchantment in, 135–36
dreaming: in *The Gay Science,* 233; in Nietzsche's works, 237; Novalis on, 231, 233

Droste-Hülshoff, Annette von, 240
duration: Nietzsche on, xxi, xxii, 13; of race, 25
Dürer, Albrecht, 318n8; depiction of St. Paul, 48, 50; masculine types of, 50; Melancholia, 38, 39; obstacles overcome by, 51; study of Italian art, 40; Wagner's appreciation for, 38–39. See also *Knight, Death, and Devil* (Dürer)

Earth Spirit, in German sensibility, 67
Ecce homo (Nietzsche): ancestry in, 17–18, 22, 27; anecdotes of, 196; anti-Germanness in, 64, 70; autobiography in, 294–95; autumn in, 205, 304; caricatures of, 173; consciousness in, 303; courage in, 41–42; creation and destruction in, 123; Dionysus in, 260; disguise in, 146; evil in, 128; the extreme in, 235; fatalism in, 16; feminism in, 43; Greek spirit in, 260; Heine in, 169; Heraclitus in, 56, 57; *hubris* on, 303; illness in, 114, 118, 120, 127; inspiration in, 198, 201; Lorrain in, 218; monarchy in, 18; music in, 90, 103–4; Nietzsche's mission in, 255; prophecy in, 260; rise and fall in, 233; self-condemnation in, 132; self-dedication to, 303; self-doubt in, 149; Socrates in, 264; style of, 254; superlativism of, 236; Thuringians in, 67; *Tristan* in, 114; Turin in, 225; Venice in, 226, 229, 230; Wagner in, 92
Eckermann, Johann Peter, 62, 337n12; *Conversations with Goethe,* 157, 158–60, 164, 181, 203, 217, 269–70, 300, 313n3
Eckhart, Johannes (Eckhart von Hochheim), 183, 341n1
education: German, 68, 269; Nietzsche on, 63, 268–71, 274, 276–79; Socratic mythos of, 269
Egypt, mystery traditions of, 289
Emerson, Ralph Waldo, 254
Empedocles, 56–57, 241; liminality of, 22; suicide of, 132, 182, 258, 334n65; and Zarathustra, 173
enchantment, Dionysian, 135–38
endings, Nietzsche on, 233–34
Engadin (Switzerland): Nietzsche's love for, 215, 216, 226, 283; in *Zarathustra,* 231
Enlightenment, skepticism of, xvii
Epicureanism, 210; disguise in, 146
Epicurus: pupils of, 282; suffering of, 116, 117
equality, Nietzsche on, 164
Erasmus, 43
Eris, 277
Eternal Return, doctrine of, xxvi, 12, 57, 173, 202; the extreme in, 235; genesis of, 231, 232, 251; Heidegger on, 314n6; as pedagogical lie, 151; as selective principle, 286; as self-martyrdom, 111; transformative power of, 294
evil: in Christian ethics, 127; meaning of, 121; Nietzsche's theology of, 121–33; origin of, 30, 128; Russian propensity for, 128; will as, 130
the extreme, in Nietzsche's work, 235–37

"Fame and Eternity" (Nietzsche), 260, 295
family types, Nietzsche on, 15
fatalism: in *Ecce homo,* 16; Napoleon's, 176, 182; Nietzsche's, 14, 31, 32, 248, 254, 255
Fehm (tribunal), 351n31
feminism, in *Ecce homo,* 43
Fichte, Johann Gottlieb, 59
figurative arts, Nietzsche and, 37–38
Flaubert, Gustave: *Bouvard et Pécuchet,* 306, 363n103
Föhn (wind), 212, 213, 347n55
Fontane, Theodor, 195, 201
Förster-Nietzsche, Elisabeth, 358n101; correspondence with Nietzsche, 16–17, 315n31; fabrications of, 327n13
Francis, Saint, 47
Frederick II (Holy Roman Emperor), 46, 47, 320n57; amoralism of, 130
Frederick the Great, 44; as Mephistopheles, 45
free speech, Nazi suppression of, xiii
Friedrich III (Emperor of Germany), 18, 315n43
Friedrich Wilhelm IV (King of Prussia), 18
friendship, Nietzsche on, 275–76, 286
Frigg (Norse mythology), 332n5
Fuchs, Carl: Nietzsche's correspondence with, 249
"The Future of our Educational Institutions" (Nietzsche), 44; music in, 93

Gast, Peter (Heinrich Köselitz), 228; music of, 99, 217, 219, 286; Nietzsche's correspondence with, 15, 20, 28, 29, 30, 53, 100, 104–5, 204, 218, 221, 225, 229, 275, 282, 303; on Nietzsche's musicianship, 90; playing of Nietzsche's music, 101–2; at Venice, 226
Gay Science, The (Nietzsche): acting in, 145; ancestry in, 20, 24; antiquity in, 153; aphorisms of, 279; dreaming in, 233; Epicurus in, 210; the extreme in, 235, 236; future hu-

manity in, 35–36; Genoa in, 224–25; Hegel in, 58; Hellenism in, 75–76; Heraclitean imagery in, 57; illness in, 118; "In Praise of Shakespeare," 126; justice in, 82; Middle Ages in, xxi–xxii; modesty in, 299; music in, 98, 100; Napoleon in, 177; north *versus* south in, 163; "On the Origin of Scholars," 23–24; Portofino in, 234; problem of the actor in, 134; reader opinion on, 256; recuperation in, 119; retroactive power in, 33; self-affirmation in, 248; Socrates in, 278; southern Catholicism in, 220; suffering in, 115, 116; verse prologue to, 184

Gay Science, The, Notebooks (Nietzsche): discipleship in, 282; friendship in, 286; music in, 99; youth in, 273

genius, Schopenhauer's doctrine of, 172

Genoa, Nietzsche at, 224–25, 228, 249

George, Stefan: Bertram and, xvi, xxv, 310n30; on Germanness, xxv; influence of, xii, xvi–xvii; Mann on, 312n58; poetry of, xvi, xvii; and Protestantism, xxv; view of Russia, 332n4. Works: *Das Jahr der Seele,* 345n12; "Nietzsche," 326n7; *Der Stern des Bundes,* 355n129

George-Kreis, xii, xvi; on scholarly apparatus, xxi

German empire, second, xvii, 70; Nietzsche's hatred of, 71–72, 73

Germania Association, 241

German language: becoming in, 62; Bible in, 183, 213; effect of Nazism on, xxxi; expressiveness of, 61–62; as literary medium, xxx–xxxi; Nietzsche on, 164; opera in, 341n6

German literature, mysticism in, 183

Germanness: audacity in, 45, 46; becoming in, 59–60, 62, 65–66, 69, 71; Bertram's, xxvii–xxviii, xxix, xxxi; courage in, 71; elimination of, 60–61; European dislike of, 65–67; foreignness in, 65, 76–77; George on, xxv; Goethe and, 67, 163–64, 215; and Hellenism, 63, 73–78, 92, 93, 95, 180; homesickness for being in, 68, 69; hostility toward, 65; individuality in, 67–68; Mann on, xxvii; of Mephistopheles, 45–46; music and, xxiv, 93–95; Nietzsche and, xxiii, xxiv–xxv, 17, 58, 77, 214; Nietzsche's attacks on, xxiv, 17, 46, 58, 63, 64–65, 70, 71–73, 75, 95, 178, 214, 215; northern Christian, 107–8; Other in, 69; pessimism in, 40, 41; Rome in, 213–14, 215; self-affirmation of, 59, 74–75; self-contradiction in, 67, 68; self-dissatisfaction in, 213–14; seriousness in, 39, 54; south in, 213–15, 219; suffering in, 64; in Switzerland, 223, 224; transformations in, 60, 68; Wagner's, 34–35, 44, 67

Germanness, super-: Hellas as, 98; Nietzsche's, 224

German poetry, meter of, 183, 184. *See also Knittelvers; Streckvers*

Germany, following World War I, xvii

Gersdorff, Carl, Freiherr von, 90; Nietzsche's correspondence with, 16, 118, 206, 225, 244, 246, 268

Glöckner, Ernst, 311n53

Gluck, Christoph Willibald, 347n19; *Armida,* 217

Gobineau, Joseph-Arthur, comte de, 29, 317n96

God: death of, xxvi; as father of evil, 128; Goethe on, 288; Nietzsche's experience of, 241, 293

Goethe, Johann Wolfgang von: on aging, 354n97; aphorisms of, 184; as Apollonian man, 168; and Beethoven, 98–99, 163, 262, 338n36; Bertram's fascination with, xxii; on *Bildung,* 62; classicism of, 49, 158, 160–67; conception of humanity, 167; on conscience, 79; as contemplative man, 167; defense of tradition, 161; errors of, 147–48; French influences on, 184; friendship with Herder, 271, 272; on German language, 62; and Germanness, 67, 163–64, 215; on German people, 70; on God, 288; as Great Man, 174; hostility to Christianity, 115, 164–65; on illness, 115–16; on immortality, 255; influence on Nietzsche, 156–70; isolation of, 163; on Italy, 68; late style of, 162; on legend formation, 3; on love, 286; love for south, 68, 215; on memory, 13; Mephistopheles of, 45, 46, 344n31; on music, 97; and Napoleon, 171, 176, 179–81; on Napoleonic Wars, xxiii; naturalism of, 158; Nietzsche on, 108, 147–48; Nietzsche's mythologizing of, 173; on northern Christianity, 49; pre-Weimar, 157; prose of, 184; reticence of, 240; on Romanticism, 164; in Rome, 213; on Socrates, 271; un-Dionysian constitution of, 166; on Venice, 229; verse forms of, 184; and Voltaire, 161, 294. Works: *The Elective Affinities,* 162; *Conversations with Eckermann,* 157, 158–60, 164, 181, 203, 217, 269–70, 300, 313n3; *Faust,* 52, 179, 213, 218n18, 292, 313n1, 344n31, 360n10; "Gany-

mede," 251; *Götz von Berlichingen,* 271; *Hans Sachs's Political Mission,* 183; *Italian Journey,* 223; "Journey through the Harz in Winter," 157; "Lion Novella," 157–58, 204; "Metamorphosis of Animals," 115; *Pandora,* 162; *Poetry and Truth,* 61, 67; *The Sorrows of Young Werther,* 337n10; "Step Verse," 184–85; *Tasso,* 148; *Westöstlicher Divan,* 8, 162, 184, 220; *Wilhelm Meister's Apprenticeship,* 292, 300, 346n33; *Wilhelm Meister's Travels,* 162, 165, 208, 240, 292, 300
Görres, Joseph von, xxviii
Great Crime, 79
Great Healthfulness, ideal of, 119
Great Men: contemporaries' perception of, 4; Hebbel on, 244; intellectual history of, 292; legends of, 3–5, 6, 8; Luther on, 114; Nietzsche's mythologizing of, 172–74, 237; rancor of, 257; role in civilization, 177; spiritual power of, 4; in *The Twilight of the Idols,* 25. *See also* overman
greatness, stages of, 11
Grimm, Jakob: *Deutsche Mythologie,* xviii
Gulf of Rapallo, 231–32
Gundolf, Friedrich, xxviii, 116, 311n54
Gustav Adolf Club, Nietzsche's speech for, 243
Gutmann, James, xi

harmony, *versus* melody, 99–101
Hebbel, Friedrich, 321n1; anecdotes of, 195; on Germanness, 65; on Great Men, 244; on heresy, 133; on illness, 115; on Judas, 121; on landscapes, 216–17; on music, 102, 105; on suffering, 64
Heckenast, Gustav, 209, 346n36
Hegel, Georg Wilhelm Friedrich: in *The Gay Science,* 58; Germanness of, 67; on Napoleon, 176–77; pyramid of, 33–34
Heidegger, Martin: on Eternal Return, 314n6; knowledge of Bertram, 310n26; Nietzsche lectures of, xv, 324n4
Heine, Heinrich, 88, 186, 326n4; on German romanticism, 169; *versus* Hölderlin, 294; Nietzsche's admiration for, 94
Heiseler, Bernt von, 332n4
Heliand (epic), 49, 320n74
Hellenism: in *The Birth of Tragedy,* 77; Christianity and, 117; degenerating, 49; the Dionysiac in, 165–67; in *The Gay Science,* 75–76; Germanness and, 63, 73–78, 92, 93, 95, 180; Goethe's understanding of, 166; Hölderlin's, 171, 174, 211; idea of divinity in, 171, 173; justice in, 84–86; modesty in, 298–99; Nietzsche's love for, 75–78, 108, 160, 171, 173, 211, 220, 263–64, 304; *versus* northern spirit, 48; pre-Socratic, 263; reawakening of, 73–74; Socrates' impact on, 263–64; suffering in, 116–17, 120; superiority over barbarianism, 290; in *The Will to Power,* 77. *See also* classicism; south
Hellingrath, Norbert von, 355n129
Heraclitus of Ephesus, 22; on being, 58; as Great Man, 174; metaphysics of, 85; Nietzsche's admiration for, 56–57, 85, 86, 251–52; and Zarathustra, 173
Herder, Johann Gottfried: Goethe's correspondence with, 160, 271; Goethe's friendship with, 271, 272; Hellenism of, 231; in *Human, All Too Human,* 148–49
heresy, 133
Hermes, 211
heroes, myths of, 6. *See also* Great Men
Hesse, Hermann, xv
history, unification with prophecy, 36
Hodur (Norse mythology), 121, 332n5
Hofmiller, Josef, xxiv
Holbein, Hans (the Younger), 37, 318n4
Hölderlin, Friedrich, 262, 339n6; on becoming, 63, 64; on death, 258; Dionysiac elements of, 168; and Empedocles, 22; German Greekness of, 73, 74; *versus* Heine, 294; Hellenism of, 171, 174, 211; hymns of, 190, 251; insanity of, 355n129; Nietzsche's love for, 165, 241, 296; students of, 241. Works: *Empedokles,* 258; "Hälfte des Lebens," 354n129; *Hyperion,* 304, 315n36, 359n137
Homer, suffering of, 116, 117
"Homer's Competition" (Nietzsche), 277
homesickness, Platonic, 201
Human, All Too Human (Nietzsche): ancestry in, 19; anti-Germanness in, 70; artists in, 27; back-dating in, 31; Chopin in, 197; communication in, 301; dedication of, 301; descendents in, 282; disguise in, 145; education in, 269, 277; evil in, 129; fatalism in, 248; *Faust* in, 166; Goethe in, 163; Herder in, 148–49; individuality in, 293; justice in, 79, 81, 82; memory in, 233; music in, 95–96, 97, 99; Napoleon in, 176; "On the Acquired Character of the Greeks," 76; past in, 34; prophecy in, 255; Schopenhauer in, 47; Socrates in, 263; Sterne in, 150–51; suffering in, 116, 117, 118; Wagner's copy of, 28; will to pessimism in, 41

Human, All Too Human Notebooks (Nietzsche), decline of art in, 233–34
Humanity: future, 35–36; Goethe's conception of, 167
Hutten, Ulrich von, 40, 43
"Hymn to Life" (Nietzsche), 16, 88, 91, 101; hubris in, 257

illness: Christian idea of, 109, 113; desirability of, 119; as First Nature, 119; Goethe on, 115–16; liberation through, 111; as magic, 115; necessity for artists, 116; Nietzsche's, 31, 109–10, 112, 114, 120, 127; Nietzsche's philosophy of, 107–20; Novalis on, 109, 114–15, 116; as philosophical act, 115; as suffering, 109; theodicy of, 117
immortality, Goethe on, 255
individualism: in *The Birth of Tragedy,* 264; effect on mysteries, 291, 293; in *Genealogy of Morals,* 256; in Germanness, 67–68; Nietzsche's, 284; Romantic, 194; Schopenhauerian, 230; Socratic, 202
"Industry and Genius" (Nietzsche), 192–93
inspiration: Mozart's, 200; Nietzsche's, 198, 199, 201, 249
"In the South" (Nietzsche), 216
intoxication, Hellenic valuation of, 110
Ischia, earthquake in, 29
Italy: Bertram's aversion to, 347n27; Goethe on, 68; Nietzsche's repugnance toward, 218. *See also* south

Jahn, Otto, 351n20
Jaspers, Karl: *Nietzsche,* xv
Jean Paul (Johann Paul Friedrich Richter), 67, 89, 210, 323n67; anecdotes of, 194, 195; on autumn, 207; on Herder, 231; *Streckvers* of, 344n4. Works: *Hesperus,* 207; *Levana,* 245
Jews: as scholars, 24; superiority of, 25
John, Gospel of: Judas in, 122
John the Baptist, 34
Judas: apologetic problem of, 121; in literature, 121; role in redemption, 122; suicide of, 122, 131
Jung-Stilling (Johann Heinrich Jung), 203, 345n7
justice: as active virtue, 81, 82; Aeschylus on, 84–85; Greek idea of, 84–86; and knowledge, 83; love and, 83; in Nietzsche's works, 79–87, 244, 324n4; originary character of, 82–83; Schopenhauer on, 79; socialistic, 81; transformations to, 83

Kant, Immanuel: and death of God, xxvi; scholasticism of, 167; on unity of perception, 7
Kaufmann, Walter: correspondence with Mann, xxix–xxx; critique of Bertram, xii–xiii, xix, xx, xxi–xxii; influence on Nietzsche studies, xi, 309n4; *Nietzsche: Philosopher, Psychologist, Antichrist,* xi–xii
Keller, Gottfried, 208, 345n8; *Der grüne Heinrich,* 346n33
"The Kingfisher" (Nietzsche), 186
Klages, Ludwig, 310n28
Kleist, Henrich von, 166
Klopstock, Friedrich Gottlieb, 269, 331n2; "The Future," 305; on Judas, 121
Knight, Death, and Devil (Dürer): in *The Birth of Tragedy,* 38, 39–41; Nietzsche's reactions to, 46, 50, 51, 52, 54; Overbeck on, 54–55
Knights Templar, Nietzsche's concept of, 274
Knittelvers (poetic form), 341n5; Goethe's use of, 185; Nietzsche's use of, 183, 184, 189, 190
knowledge: Aristotle on, 300; Nietzsche on, 268, 296–301, 305
Krause, Erdmuthe, 18
Krell, David, 310n26, 324n4

Lake Maggiore (Italy), Nietzsche at, 216
landscape painting: Lorrain's, 38, 217–22; Nietzsche on, 37, 38
landscapes: Hebbel on, 216–17; Nietzsche's affinity for, 216, 221–22
legends: accumulation of, 8; Bertram on, xviii–xix; changeability of, 7; etymology of, 313n7; fact and, 3; formation of, 2–3; of Great Men, 3–5, 6, 8; in historical tradition, 1; of personalities, 2. *See also* myths
Leibniz, Gottfried Wilhelm, 152; mask of Germanness, 153
Lenau, Nikolaus (Nikolaus Edler von Strehlenau): *The Albigenses,* 5, 313n5
Leonardo da Vinci, 220; enigmatic qualities of, 240
Lessing, Gotthold Ephraim: naturalism of, 161
Libra (astrology), Nietzsche's birth under, 7, 189
Lichtenberg, Georg Christoph, 7, 76; aphorisms of, 345n6; *versus* Novalis, 294
linguistic borders, national, 66
Loki (Norse mythology), 121, 332n5; Nietzsche's defense of, 130
"The Loneliest Man" (Nietzsche), 193
Lorrain, Claude, 150, 318n5; landscapes of, 38,

217–22; Nietzsche's regard for, 206, 217–18, 222
love: and derision, 131; Goethe on, 286; pedagogical, 272; procreative, 273
Luden, Heinrich, 323n74
Ludwig II (king of Bavaria), 340n44
Luther, Martin, 43; on anti-Germanness, 65; on becoming, 59; Bible of, 183, 213; in *The Birth of Tragedy,* 53; in *The Case of Wagner,* 52–53; cheerfulness of, 53; on communal wisdom, 291–92; in *Daybreak,* 49; at Diet of Worms, 318n19; as Dürer's knight, 40; free Christian man of, 54, 55; on Great Man, 114; influence on Zarathustra, 52; on music, 89; Nietzsche's hatred of, 46; in "Richard Wagner in Bayreuth," 53; in Rome, 213; on Tauler's sermons, 341n3. Works: "Out of the Depths I Cry to Thee," 331n77; *Table Talk,* 213–14

madness: communal, 291; Hölderlin's, 355n129; Nietzsche's, 63, 108, 295, 307
Mann, Thomas: on Bertram, xv, xxix, 312n63; on Bertram's *Nietzsche,* xxiv, xxvi–xxvii, xxx; burning of works, xxviii; correspondence with Kaufmann, xxix–xxx; exile of, xxvii; on George, 312n58; on Gundolf, 311n54. Works: *Death in Venice,* 227; *Doktor Faustus,* xxx; *The Magic Mountain,* 317n124, 346n33; "Of the German Republic," xxvii; *Reflections of an Unpolitical Man,* xxvii
martyrdom, wish for, 111
Matthew, Gospel of, 249
meaning, instability of, xix
mediocrity, mask of, 145
Die Meistersinger (Wagner), 150; Hans Sachs in, 186; opposition to civilization in, 93; overture of, 155
melody: *versus* harmony, 99–101; Scythian, 328n69
memory: Goethe on, 13; in *Human, All Too Human,* 233
Mephistopheles, 319n56; Germanness of, 45–46; Goethe's, 45, 46, 344n31; as Great Man, 174
Meyer, Conrad Ferdinand, 187, 217, 266, 318n1; "On the Grand Canal," 227
Meysenbug, Malwida von: Nietzsche's correspondence with, 38, 112, 218, 278, 281, 283, 303
Middle Ages, in *The Gay Science,* xxi–xxii
Mill, John Stuart, 175
mistral (wind), 212, 347n56
Mitys, statue of, 358n99
modesty: in Hellenism, 298–99; Nietzsche on, 298, 299, 302
Mörike, Eduard: "Auf eine Lampe," 357n73; Nietzsche's disdain for, 203
Mozart, Wolfgang Amadeus: German operas of, 341n6; inspirations of, 200
Müller, Johannes von, 269
Müller-Lauter, Wolfgang: *Nietzsche,* xix, 311n41
Muses' Monastery, Nietzsche's idea of, 207, 224, 241
Mushacke, Eduard, 316n84
music: anti-Christian, 102; as art of past, 102; Dionysian, 92; ecclesiastical, 89; as end of culture, 95–96; and Germanness, xxiv, 93–95; Goethe on, 97; Greek, 100; harmony in, 99–101; hostility toward civilization, 93–94, 96; instrumental *versus* vocal, 100; as last art, 234; liberating qualities of, 91; Luther on, 89; melody in, 99–101, 328n69; as metaphysical art, 217; mysticism in, 106; Nietzsche's compositions, 30, 31, 89–90, 91, 101–2, 206; Nietzsche's disavowal of, 95–97, 196; Nietzsche's love of, xxiv, xxvi, 37, 63, 88–106, 134, 196, 229, 285; northern and southern, 98–99, 101–2; operatic, 53, 341n6; Platonic, 200; Schopenhauer on, 105, 217; as suffering, 104; Venetian, 229–30
music, German: in *The Birth of Tragedy,* 63, 69; culmination of, 96; earnestness of, 100; effect of south on, 220; as Greek tragedy, 78; Nietzsche's prose as, 250–51; southern music and, 98–99; in *The Will to Power,* 94
"Music of the South" (Nietzsche), 219
"My Happiness" (Nietzsche), 188
mysteries: in antiquity, 289; of Dionysus, 166; effect of individualism on, 291, 293; epopts in, 297, 300, 361n34; longing for, 294; Nietzsche's experience of, 289–307; Nietzsche's parodies of, 297; Orphic, 355n10; Pindar on, 290; preservation of, 291
mysteries, Eleusinian, 289–91; Aristotle on, 300; Christianity and, 290, 291; epopts in, 300, 361n34; power of, 290–91; reticence concerning, 291, 297, 298
myths: creation by poetry, 3; formation of, 2; in German culture, xvii–xviii; of heroes, 6; Nietzsche's interest in, xviii; Norse, 332n5;

reality as, 5; rehabilitation of, xvii–xviii, 310n34; in Romanticism, xvii; self-assertion of, 3. See also legends

Napoleon: ancestry of, 25; antique character of, 174–76, 178; deceptions of, 240; as Dionysus, 180; effect on nationalism, 176; enmity to civilization, 177; as *ens realissimum,* 177, 179, 180; fatalism of, 176, 182; German behavior toward, 178; and Goethe, 171, 176, 179–81; *Mémorial de Sainte-Hélène,* 181; as nature, 175; Nietzsche's veneration of, 174–82; as overman, 175; on revolution, 13; theatricality of, 144; unity under, 177–78; and Zarathustra, 175, 177
Napoleonic Wars, Goethe on, xxiii
nationalism: Bertram on, xxiii; German, 72–73, 178; Napoleon's effect on, 176
naturalism: Goethe's, 158; Nietzsche on, 161
Naumburg *Gymnasium,* Nietzsche at, 241
Nazism: Bertram's relation to, xiii; effect on German language, xxxi; Nietzsche's dissociation from, xi–xii; subjective historiography of, xiii
Nice (France), Nietzsche in, 218, 221
Nietzsche, Franziska Oehler, 18
Nietzsche, Friedrich Wilhelm: admiration for Heraclitus, 56–57, 85, 86, 251–52; *amor fati* of, 82, 103, 182, 215, 241, 253–55, 325n4; anecdotes of, 194–202, 265; as Antichrist, 263, 266; anti-Christianity of, 51, 110, 127; anti-Germanness of, xxiv, 17, 46, 58, 63, 64–65, 70, 71–73, 75, 95, 178, 214, 215; anti-Romanticism of, 88, 126, 169; anti-theatricality of, 134–35; aphorisms of, 184, 185, 189–90, 192–93, 195, 279; asceticism of, 111–13, 123; astrological sign of, 7, 189; autobiography of, 15, 135, 294–95; back-dating by, 30, 31; at Basel, 70, 90, 154, 223–24; belief in demonic guidance, 254; Bertram's categories concerning, xxxi; betrayal in works of, 121–33, 331n1; at Bonn, 155, 243–44; childhood aspirations of, 154; childhood of, 240–43; Christianity of, 48–49, 53–54, 107–9, 262; coinages of, 234–35; concept of becoming, 56–78, 302; contradictions of, xix, xx; correspondence with sister, 14–15, 16–17; decadence of, 48, 132, 201; desire for death, 258; as devil's advocate, 128; as Dionysus, 54, 78, 106, 108, 261; disavowal of music, 95–97, 196; disguises of, 147–48, 152–53; disillusionment with Wagner, xviii, 72, 88, 96, 97, 101, 103, 124–27, 148, 156, 247, 254, 278; dislike of German empire, 71–72, 73; dislike of St. Paul, 49–50, 53, 110, 113–14, 263, 267; dissociation from Nazism, xi–xii; dualities of, 8, 11, 15, 131, 153, 160, 293, 295; effect of ancestral law on, 12; exemplification of century, 7; experience of God, 241, 293; experience of mysteries, 289–307; experience of south, 154–56, 214–22; fatalism of, 14, 31, 32, 254, 255; French influences on, 184, 218–19; at Genoa, 224–25, 228, 249; and German Protestantism, xviii, xx, xxiv–xxv, 134, 156, 293; German style of, 183; Goethe's influence on, 156–70; on his destiny, 248; on his productiveness, 246; illness of, 31, 109–10, 112, 114, 120, 127; immoralism of, 128; indeterminacy in works of, xix; insanity of, 63, 108, 295, 307; intellectual ancestors of, 26; isolation of, 252, 280–85, 292–93, 294; on justice, 79–87, 244, 324n4; Latinate influences on, 184, 187; leitmotifs of, 198–99; literary style of, xxxiv, 151, 184, 187, 188, 192, 234–35, 250; as logician, 304; longing for decline, 258; and Lou Andreas-Salomé, 140–41, 254, 281; love for autumn, 203–12, 304; love for Venice, 225–30; love for Wagner, xxv, 88, 92, 108, 126, 244–46, 270, 271, 273, 284; as man hunter, 282, 285–86; masculine style of, 50, 166; maternal ancestors of, 18; mission of, 248–50, 252–53, 255; musical compositions of, 30, 31, 89–90, 91, 101–2, 206; musicality of, xxiv, xxvi, 37, 63, 88–106, 134, 196, 229, 285; myth of, 6–7, 9; in Nice, 218, 221; nihilism of, 132, 325n4; personal documents of, 239; pessimism of, 280; as philologist, 5; philosophy of illness, 107–20; piano playing of, 30–31, 90, 99, 327n12; Platonism of, 267, 269, 270; as poet of knowledge, 89; at Portofino, 18, 221, 232; positivism of, 23, 256, 295, 301; pro-Hellenism of, 75–78, 108, 160, 171, 173, 211, 220, 263–64, 304; Promethean qualities of, 8; as prophet, 239–61; as proponent of legitimacy, 18; as psychologist, 267, 284; pulse rate of, 27; relationship of German people to, 69; relationship to Socrates, 75, 262–88; reticence of, 295–302, 304; reverence for ancestry, 11–36; reverence for tradition, 13–14; and Romanticism, 7, 33, 37,

88, 103, 126, 129, 132, 169; Schopenhauer's influence on, 28, 156, 157, 160, 271–72, 277, 301; at Schulpforta school, 13, 132, 204, 223, 241; Second Vision of, 247; self-certainty of, 252–54, 256; self-distancing by, 31; self-doubts of, 246–47; self-martyrdom of, 79, 241, 306; self-portrait of, 149; at Sils-Maria, 15, 70, 154, 167, 323n73; spiritual courage of, 41–42; spiritual election of, 239; student life of, 241–43; suffering of, 8, 109, 110, 111, 113, 152, 241, 299; super-Germanness of, 224; synthesizing will of, 199; as teacher, 267–71, 276–78, 280–86; on theatricality, 134–53; theology of evil, 121–33; transformations of, 11, 57–58, 169, 248; translations of, xxxiv–xxxv; at Tribschen, 38, 125, 207, 224, 244, 245, 246; in Turin, 29, 206, 222, 287, 304; ultramontanism of, 214; use of folk tradition, 184; veneration of Napoleon, 174–82; verse of, 183–93; view of disciples, xxv, 280–86; vision of Calvary, 102, 328n77; Voltaireanism of, 127; as wanderer, 214, 223, 251. *See also specific works*

Nietzsche, Karl Ludwig, 18; birth of, 27

Nietzsche: Versuch einer Mythologie (Bertram), xii, xvi–xxvi; "Ancestry," xxi, xxvi; "Arion," xxvi; biographical method of, 333n56; editions of, xiv, 309n18; "Eleusis," xxv, xxvi; "The German Becoming," xxii–xxiii, xxv, xxxiii; historical truth in, xviii; "Judas," xxvi; legend in, xviii–xix; literary style of, xxxi; Mann on, xxiv, xxvi–xxvii, xxx; metaphors of, xxxiii–xxxiv; mythological elements in, xxvi; neologisms in, xxxii–xxxiii; organization of, xvii, xix–xx, xxiii; "Prophecy," xxv; publication of, xxvi; quotations in, xx, xxi–xxii; repetition in, xxiii–xxiv; scholarly method of, xx–xxi, xxii; "Socrates," xxv; translation issues for, xxxi–xxxiv; "Weimar," xxiii

Nietzsche contra Wagner, 91; artistic creation in, 141

Nietzsche family: class consciousness of, 17; Polish descent of, 16, 17, 22

Nietzsche legend, German, xii

Nietzsche Prize, xv

Nietzsche scholarship, of interwar years, xii, xvi

Nimrod, 131, 333n61

nineteenth century: historicism of, 298; Nietzsche on, 294

Norns, 222, 348n54

Norton, Kurt, lxix

Notebooks, late: Germanness in, 215; justice in, 79; Napoleon in, 176, 182; Socrates in, 263; Wagner in, 141

Novalis (Friedrich von Hardenberg), 330n30; anecdotes of, 194, 195, 200; on becoming, 59; on dreaming, 231, 233; fragments of, 344n4; on illness, 109, 114–15, 116; versus Lichtenberg, 294; mysticism of, 291; romantic style of, 151; on suicide, 115; union of opposites in, 201. Works: *Heinrich von Ofterdingen,* 269; *Hymns to the Night,* 115, 251; *The Novices of Saïs,* 292, 359n15

ochlocracy, 35, 318n134

Odin (Norse mythology), 332n5

"Oedipus. Speeches of the Last Philosopher to Himself" (Nietzsche), 293

Old Testament, typology of, 27

"On the Future of our Educational Institutions" (Nietzsche), 70, 206, 243; Hellenism in, 73

On the Genealogy of Morals (Nietzsche), 23; asceticism in, 112; "Becoming in Morality," 57; evil in, 128; individuality in, 256; justice in, 81, 82; Napoleon in, 175, 181–82; Schopenhauer in, 41; suffering in, 116; Wagner in, 140

"On the Use and Disadvantage of History for Life" (Nietzsche), 13, 79–80, 158; education in, 268; the extreme in, 235; Germanness in, 59–60; Goethe in, 162; Hellenism in, 75; justice in, 79, 80; mystery in, 298; past and future in, 32–33; Renaissance in, 273; science in, 127

"On Truth and Lie in the Extra-Moral Sense" (Nietzsche), 297

opera, 53; German language, 341n6

Oratorium (Nietzsche), 30

Orpheus, Wagner as, 129

Other, Nietzsche's search for, 189

Overbeck, Franz, 39, 43; in Basel, 223; on *Knight, Death, and Devil,* 54–55; Nietzsche's correspondence with, 15, 42, 111, 112, 120, 225, 253, 258, 283

overman: ancestry of, 26; coinage of, 235; the extreme in, 235; Napoleon as, 175; Platonic form of, 174; third Reich of, 102; in Zarathustra, 35, 52, 61, 172–73, 174, 259. *See also* Great Men

south: German longing for, 68, 75; in Germanness, 213–15, 219; Goethe's love for, 68, 215; as lethal perfection, 215; in Nietzsche's imagination, 154–56, 214–22. *See also* Hellenism; Italy
"Speeches, Allegories and Images" (Nietzsche), 141, 190, 273
"The Sphinx" (Nietzsche), 190–91
Stein, Heinrich von, 251, 280–81, 283, 285
Stendhal, 66, 197
Sterne, Laurence, 150–51, 336n93
St. Gothard (Alps), 6
Stifter, Adalbert, 321n2; aesthetic writings of, 208; Bertram's dissertation on, 310n19, 361n46; correspondence with Heckenast, 209; Hellenism of, 211; liberalism of, 346n43; pedagogical works of, 208, 209. Works: *Bunte Steine,* 209; "Der Hagestolz," 209; *Indian Summer,* 11, 154, 203–12, 345n9
Streckvers (lyrical form), 195, 344n5
Stringberg, August, 306
"The Struggle between Science and Wisdom" (Nietzsche), 264
Sturm und Drang (literary movement), 157, 337n11
suffering: art of, 167; in Germanness, 64; Hellenistic idea of, 116–17, 120; illness as, 109; music as, 104; Nietzsche's, 8, 109, 110, 111, 113, 152, 240, 299; will to, 118
suicide: Empedocles', 132, 182, 258, 334n65; Judas's, 122, 131; Novalis on, 115
"Sun Sets, The" (Nietzsche), 193, 206–7
Suso, Heinrich (Heinrich Seuse), 183, 341n2
Switzerland, Germanness in, 223, 224

Taine, Hippolyte, xxxiv, 150; as historian, 124
Talma, François-Joseph, 144, 335n66
Tauler, Johann, 183, 341n3
theatricality: Napoleon's, 144; Nietzsche on, 134–53; Wagner's, 134, 138, 139–40, 142, 152, 331n1
Third Reich: Bertram under, xxvii–xxviii; book burning during, xxviii
"Thoughts on Richard Wagner" (Nietzsche), problem of the actor in, 139
Thucydides, 5; on justice, 82
Thuringians, 67
Thus Spoke Zarathustra (Nietzsche): ancestry in, 17, 20; anecdotes of, 196; autumn in, 206; courage in, 41; death in, 259; decline in, 258; Dionysian elements of, 163; discipleship in, 285; dream landscape of, 232; education in, 278; Empedoclean foundation of, 296; evil in, 129–31; the extreme in, 235–36; future in, 32, 36; genesis of, 231; glorification of body in, 108–9; illness in, 117; inspiration in, 199; intellectual ancestry of, 173; justice in, 81, 83; landscape of, 236; language of, 183; loneliness in, 222, 292–93; Luther's influence on, 52; mission of, 249; musical qualities of, 90; Nietzsche's confidence in, 251; Nietzsche's father in, 15; "Of Endowing Virtue," 275; origin in memory, 200; overman in, 35, 52, 61, 172–73, 174, 259; Pindar in, 74; power over past in, 35; prophecy in, 260; solitude in, 163, 286, 287; soothsaying spirit of, 236; as step beyond Goethe, 169–70; style of, 52; unity of speeches in, 199; verse in, 189; Wagner in, 143, 144; Zarathustra's farewell in, 281
Thus Spoke Zarathustra Notebooks (Nietzsche), 272; Caesar in, 182; evil in, 127; knowledge in, 299; mysticism in, 306; suffering in, 118
Tieck, Ludwig, 337n8
"To Goethe" (Nietzsche), 187
"To Hafis" (Nietzsche), 185–86
Tradition: Goethe's defense of, 161; Nietzsche's reverence for, 13–14
the tragic, will to, 41
Transfiguration Notebooks (Nietzsche), perfection in, 211
transformations: Dionysian, 135–38; in Germanness, 60, 68; Nietzsche's, 11, 57–58, 169, 248; theatrical, 135–36, 137. *See also* becoming
Transvaluation (Nietzsche), Leibniz in, 152–53
Transvaluation Notebooks (Nietzsche): ancestry in, 14; Dionysus in, 106; evil in, 129; German music in, 94; German scholars in, 24; Goethe in, 181; Nietzsche's mission in, 254; suffering in, 110; Wagner in, 125–26
Treaty of Versailles, 312n69
Tribschen (Switzerland), 318n10; Nietzsche at, 38, 125, 207, 224, 244, 245, 246
Tristan und Isolde (Wagner), 108, 229, 292; association with Venice, 226, 227, 230; in *Ecce Homo,* 114; sorrow in, 104
truth: instability of, xix; relativity of, xiii
Turin: Nietzsche in, 29, 206, 222, 287, 304; Nietzsche on, 225
Turner, J. M. W., 150
Twilight of the Idols, The (Nietzsche): ancestry in, 20–21; communication in, 301; courage

in, 42, 44; Germanness in, 60; Goethe in, 165, 167, 168, 180, 181; Great Men in, 25; Napoleon in, 175; rejection of knowledge in, 296–97; Socrates in, 263, 265; style of, 254

University of Leipzig, Nietzsche at, 28
"Unknown God, The" (Nietzsche), 241
Untimely Meditations, 69–70; Goethe in, 158; prophecy in, 245
Untimely Meditations, first, 71; barbarism in, 62
Untimely Meditations, second. *See* "On the Use and Disadvantage of History for Life"
Untimely Meditations, fourth. See "Richard Wagner in Bayreuth"

values, revaluation of, xxvi
Veil of Veronica, 50
veneration, power of, 172
Venice: duality of, 227–28; Goethe on, 229; music of, 229–30; Nietzsche's love for, 225–30; Rialto Bridge, 229; Wagner at, 226
"Venice" (Nietzsche), 230
Volk, Bertram and, xxviii, 311n46
Voltaire, 47, 181, 301; classicism of, 161; Ferney estate of, 295, 360n24; and Goethe, 161, 294; Mahomet, 161; motto of, 360n23

Wackenroder, Wilhelm Heinrich, 155, 337n8
Wagner, Cosima, 223
Wagner, Richard: appreciation for Dürer, 38–39; in *Beyond Good and Evil,* 94–95; as charlatan, 143–44; comedy in life of, 139–40; copy of *Human, All Too Human,* 28; death of, 28, 29, 282; as demagogue, 142; embodiment of Schopenhauer, 92; the extreme in, 235; Germanness of, 34–35, 44, 67; inspiration of, 198; lack of restraint, 139; leitmotifs of, 198; as Magician, 143; as miniaturist, 196–97; *My Life,* 140; Nietzsche's correspondence with, 39; Nietzsche's disillusionment with, xviii, 72, 88, 96, 97, 101, 103, 124–27, 148, 156, 247, 254, 278; Nietzsche's love for, xxv, 88, 92, 108, 126, 244–46, 270, 271, 273, 284; obsession with ancestry, 34; as Orpheus, 129; Schopenhauer's influence on, 271, 274; synthesizing will of, 199; theatricality of, 134, 138, 139–40; 142, 152, 331n1; at Venice, 226. *See also specific works*
Wandering Jew, legend of, 209, 212, 346n39
Watson, Walter, xi
Weimar: classicism of, 159, 162, 165; cultural sphere of, 156, 168; Goethe at, 154, 155; in Nietzsche's imagination, 155–56, 168–69; radical right of, 311n46; Schiller-Goethe circle in, 18
"We Philologists" (Nietzsche), 269
Wesendonk, Mathilde: Wagner's correspondence with, 229
Wieland, Christoph Martin: *Agathon,* 346n33
will: as evil, 130; to pessimism, 41; to power, 294, 325n4; primal, 130; to recurrence, 41; to salvation, 69; Schopenhauer on, 57, 130; to suffering, 118; world as, 57
Williamson, George S., xviii, xxv; *The Longing for Myth in Germany,* xvii
Will to Power, The (Nietzsche), 21; ancestry in, 19; aphorisms of, 195; civilization in, 93; communication in, 301; courage in, 42; Dante in, 255; devil in, 127; Dionysus in, 166, 202, 260–61; disguise in, 145; the divine in, 255–56; education in, 278; the extreme in, 232; free will in, 260; German music in, 94; Goethe in, 165, 167; Greek spirit in, 260; Hellenism in, 77; illness in, 114; inspiration in, 198; justice in, 86; leitmotifs in, 199; melody in, 99; music in, 96, 98; mystery in, 298; nihilism in, 132; prophecy in, 260; Recurrence in, 286; Socrates in, 265; suffering in, 111; theatricality in, 141; Turin in, 225
Winckelmann, Johann Joachim, 75, 166
Wölfflin, Heinrich, xv; on Dürer, 50, 51; on northern beauty, 62
"World, The" (Nietzsche), 185
World War I, Germany following, xvii
World War II, Bertram following, xxviii–xxix, 312n63

Xenophon, on Socrates, 151, 270

Zarathustra: Napoleon and, 175, 177; Nietzsche's vision of, 30, 32. See also *Thus Spoke Zarathstra*
Zelter, Carl Friedrich, Goethe's correspondence with, 210, 300
Zosimus, 289, 290

Ernst Bertram (1884–1957) was a scholar of German literature. In addition to *Nietzsche,* he published essays on Beethoven, Heinrich von Kleist, Friedrich Hölderlin, Georg Lichtenberg, Hugo von Hofmannsthal, and Stefan George. He also published several books of poetry.

Robert E. Norton is a professor of German at the University of Notre Dame. In 2003 his *Secret Germany* won the Jacques Barzun Prize in Cultural History from the American Philosophical Society.

INTERNATIONAL NIETZSCHE STUDIES

Schopenhauer and Nietzsche *Georg Simmel; translated by Helmut Loiskandl, Deena Weinstein, and Michael Weinstein*
Nietzsche's Revaluation of Values: A Study in Strategies *E. E. Sleinis*
Making Sense of Nietzsche: Reflections Timely and Untimely *Richard Schacht*
Nietzsche and the Problem of Sovereignty *Richard J. White*
Nietzsche: His Philosophy of Contradictions and the Contradictions of His Philosophy *Wolfgang Müller-Lauter; translated from the German by David J. Parent*
Nietzsche's Perspectivism *Steven D. Hales and Rex Welshon*
The Pre-Platonic Philosophers *Friedrich Nietzsche; translated from the German and edited by Greg Whitlock*
Nietzsche and the Transcendental Tradition *Michael Steven Green*
Reading Nietzsche *Mazzino Montinari; translated from the German and with an introduction by Greg Whitlock*
Basic Writings *Paul Rée; translated from the German and edited by Robin Small*
Nietzsche's Sister and the Will to Power: A Biography of Elisabeth Förster-Nietzsche *Carol Diethe*
Nietzsche on Language, Consciousness, and the Body *Christian J. Emden*
Nietzsche's Philosophical Context and Reading *Thomas Brobjer*
Nietzsche: Attempt at a Mythology *Ernst Bertram; translated and with an introduction by Robert E. Norton*

The University of Illinois Press
is a founding member of the
Association of American University Presses.

University of Illinois Press
1325 South Oak Street
Champaign, IL 61820-6903
www.press.uillinois.edu

painting, German: the inexpressible in, 64. *See also* landscape painting
Palazzo Pitti, 327n46
Panathenaia festival, 334n16
Paoli, Pasqualae, 29–30
Paris, Nietzsche's love for, 159, 218–19
parody, Nietzsche's use of, 186–87
Parsifal (Wagner): Nietzsche's anticipation of, 89; Nietzsche's objections to, 137, 164; Nietzsche's playing of, 30–31
Pascal, Blaise, 47, 306; on community, 292
Passion, Christian: cult of, 109
Paul, Saint: as chandala, 47, 114; conversion of, 109, 110; Dürer's, 48, 50; Hellenism of, 49; Nietzsche's dislike of, 49–50, 53, 110, 113–14, 263, 267; renaming of, 355n4
perfection, Nietzsche on, 211
pessimism: Christian, 167; Germanic, 40, 41; Nietzsche's, 280; Schopenhauer's, 49, 159, 235, 299; will to, 41
Pforta. *See* Schulpforta (boarding school)
Philoctetes, Nietzsche as, 251
philosophers: ancestry of, 25–26; as educators, 279
philosophers, German: Nietzsche's understanding of, 7
philosophers, Greek: One Principle of, 175
"Philosophy in the Tragic Age of the Greeks" (Nietzsche), 86, 171; anecdote in, 194; Heraclitus in, 56; justice in, 86; pre-Platonics in, 173
Pietism, influence on Nietzsche, 108
Pindar, 74, 190; on mysteries, 290; Nietzsche's love for, 271; on silence, 296
Pitrou, Robert, xxxi, 312n69
Planck, Max: support for Bertram, xxix
Platen, August von, 349n18; *Venetian Sonnets,* 227
Plato: dialogues of, 165; Ideas of, 200; on justice, 81; metaphysics of, 202; Socratic mask of, 147, 151, 153, 267, 270; as symptom of decay, 265. Works: *Phaedo,* 266; *Phaedrus,* 273; *Republic,* 81
Platonism: German, 59; Nietzsche's, 267, 269, 270
Plutarch, 274; *Peri Isidos,* 359n5
poetry, creation of myth, 3. *See also* German poetry
poetry, Nietzsche's, 183–93; caricature of Wagner in, 191; dithyrambic, 192, 193, 242, 260, 295, 304, 307; *Knittelvers* in, 183, 184, 189, 190; sound associations in, 188, 191; in *Thus Spoke Zarathustra,* 189
Po River, 225, 349n14
Portofino (Italy): in *The Gay Science,* 234; Nietzsche at, 18, 221, 232; in *Zarathustra,* 231, 232
positivism, Nietzsche's, 23, 256, 295, 301
power: Nietzsche's glorification of, 130; will to, 294, 325n4
prophecy: in Nietzsche's works, 239–61; transformative power of, 239; unification with history, 36
prophets, suffering of, 251
Protestantism, German: in *The Antichrist,* 53; becoming in, 66; George and, xxv; Germanness and, 107–8; isolation in, 40; Nietzsche and, xviii, xx, xxiv–xxv, 134, 156, 293. *See also* Christianity, northern
Prussian monarchy, Germany under, xvii
pudenda, female, 299, 360n30
Pythagoras, 56

race, duration of, 25
Ranke, Leopold von: historiography of, 313n2
Ratner-Rosenhagen, Jennifer, 309n4
reading, post-structuralist modes of, xix
reality: as myth, 5; reconstruction of, 1
recurrence, 286; will to, 41
Rée, Paul, 254
Reformation, courage during, 44
Renaissance, Burckhardt's concept of, 273
Renan, Ernest, 133; *Vie de Jésus,* 121
ressentiment, Nietzsche's idea of, xxvi
Revaluation Notebooks (Nietzsche): disguise in, 152; Goethe in, 164; Mephistopheles in, 45
revolution: ancestral past of, 11; Napoleon on, 13
Rhine River: in Nietzsche's imagination, 154; Nietzsche's trip along, 29; ties to Rome, 154, 155
"Richard Wagner in Bayreuth" (Nietzsche), 12, 34, 43, 54, 138, 147, 170; anecdotes of, 195; anti-Alexanders in, 179; autumn in, 206; death in, 258; disguise in, 146–47; German *versus* French principle in, 93; justice in, 86; love in, 272; Luther in, 53; self-vision in, 72; tragic sensibility in, 166–67; *Tristan* in, 228; Wagner in, 100, 138
Riemer, Friedrich Wilhelm, 115
Ritschl, Friedrich Wilhelm, 196, 244, 351n20

Rohde, Erwin, 43, 48, 244; engagement of, 359n129; Nietzsche's correspondence with, 28, 52, 92–93, 119, 125, 154, 170, 204, 207, 209–10, 246, 249, 271, 273, 274; Nietzsche's rejection of, 124; on Taine, 124
Rolandseck (Germany), 206, 345n22
romanticism: of death, 40; as decadence, 164; German, 94, 169, 236; individualism in, 194; myth in, xvii; Nietzsche and, 7, 33, 37, 88, 103, 126, 129, 132, 169; Novalis's, 151; *versus* skepticism, 194
Rome: in Germanness, 213–14, 215; Luther in, 213; Nietzsche in, 29; Nietzsche on, 219; ties to Rhine River, 154, 155
Rosenberg, Alfred: *Der Mythus des zwanzigsten Jahrhunderts,* xviii
Rothenburg (Germany), in Nietzsche's imagination, 155
Rousseau, Jean-Jacques, 175
Russia: George's view of, 332n4; propensity for evil in, 128
Russian literature, 121

Sachs, Hans, 185; aphorisms of, 184, 190; poetry of, 183, 341n5; Wagner's depiction of, 186
Sacrilege, in *The Birth of Tragedy,* 133, 296
saints, legends of, 2
Saïs, cult statue of, 291, 296, 297
salvation, will to, 69
Sanctus Januarius (Nietzsche), asceticism in, 112
Saul, King, 285
Scaevola, Gaius Mucius, 241, 351n8
Schelling, Friedrich: *Philosophie der Mythologie,* xviii
Schiller, Friedrich, 300
Schiller-Goethe circle, 18
Schlegel, Friedrich: anecdotes of, 194; on becoming, 59; on modesty, 298; *Rede über die Mythologie,* xvii; romantic circle of, 149–50
scholarly class, European: ancestry of, 23–24
scholars, German, 24, 302; as Christian knights, 45
scholars, Jewish, 24
Schopenhauer, Arthur: aesthetics of, 136; on ambiguity of life, 228; in *The Birth of Tragedy,* 51; as Christian intellectual, 47; cowardice of, 42–43; disciples of, 280, 282; doctrine of genius, 172; as Dürer's knight, 40–41; on evil, 130; free Christian man of, 54, 55; influence on Nietzsche, 28, 156, 157, 160, 271–72, 277, 301; influence on Wagner, 271, 274; on justice, 79; on materiality, 58; metaphysics of, 37, 117, 292; on music, 105, 217; Passion metaphysics of, 109; pessimism of, 49, 159, 235, 299; seriousness of, 39; solitude of, 285; un-Germanness of, 17; Wagner's embodiment of, 92; on will, 57, 130; *The World as Will and Representation,* 33, 54, 91–92, 158, 183, 244, 349n33
"Schopenhauer as Educator" (Nietzsche), 54, 147, 247, 270; anecdotes of, 195; Germanness in, 70–71
Schulpforta (boarding school), 314n16; Nietzsche at, 13, 132, 204, 223, 241
Schumann, Robert: Nietzsche's love of, 197, 203
sculpture, as anti-music, 102
Scythians, 99; melody of, 328n69
self-hatred, German, 64
seriousness, Germanic, 39, 54
Seydlitz, Reinhart von: Nietzsche's correspondence with, 246, 253
Shakespeare, William: enigmatic qualities of, 240; Nietzsche on, 181
Shapiro, Gary, xxiii
Siebengebirge (Germany), 337n5; Nietzsche at, 155
Silesius, Angelus, 47, 313n6
"Sils-Maria" (Nietzsche), 187
Sils-Maria (Switzerland): landscape of, 232; Nietzsche at, 15, 70, 154, 167, 32[illegible]n73
Simmel, Georg, 227
Singspiel, 341n6
skepticism: in *Beyond Good and Evil,* 21, 44–45; Enlightenment, xvii; *versus* romanticism, 194
Socrates, 47, 48, 102; anecdotes of, 201; *daemonion* of, 351n21; death of, 266, 279–80; decadence of, 264, 265, 266; as destroyer of Hellenism, 263–64; dialectic of, 264; Goethe on, 271; importance for Nietzsche, 75, 262–88; last words of, 120, 279, 287; as logician, 266, 267; on love, 273; music-making, 266–67, 285, 287; Nietzsche's lectures on, 264–65; in Plato, 147, 151, 153, 267, 270; proem to Apollo, 266; as teacher, 268, 269, 277; ugliness of, 265, 287; Xenophon on, 151, 270
song: as sorrow, 104; supremacy over instrumental music, 100. *See also* melody
Sophocles, 138
Sorrento (Italy), Nietzsche at, 207